THE ADVISOR'S GUIDE TO LIFE INSURANCE

HAROLD D. SKIPPER, Ph.D., CLU
WAYNE TONNING, FSA

SECTION OF REAL PROPERTY | TRUST & ESTATE LAW

Defending Liberty
Pursuing Justice

Printed in the United States of America by ABA Publishing.

Library of Congress Cataloging-in-Publication Data

Skipper, Harold D., 1947–
   The advisor's guide to life insurance / Harold D. Skipper, Wayne Tonning.
     p. cm.
   Includes bibliographical references and index.
   ISBN 978-1-61632-107-9 (alk. paper)
  1. Life insurance. I. Tonning, Wayne. II. Title.
   HG8781.S53   2010
   368.32—dc22

                                   2010049371

For Print Format:
ISBN: 978-1-61632-107-9

For PDF Format:
ISBN: 978-1-61632-108-6

12 11 10 5 4 3 2 1

Contents

About the Authors xix

Acknowledgments xxi

Introduction and Overview.................................. xxiii

Executive Summary xxvii

PART I
THE LIFE INSURANCE PURCHASE   1

CHAPTER 1
Introduction to Life Insurance   3

Psychological Aspects of Death and Planning..................... 4

    Anxiety 4

    Emotions... 5

Dealing With the Financial Consequences of Death 6

    Relatives 7

    Additional Savings/Investments 7

    Employer-Provided Death Benefits.......................... 8

    Individual Life Insurance 9

Life Insurance in Family, Estate, and Business Planning 10

    Determining Whether Life Insurance is Needed 11

    Determining the Appropriate Insurance Amount 12

    Determining the Most Suitable Policy 13

    Determining from Whom to Purchase the Policy 15

        Organizational Structures of Life Insurance Companies 15

        Importance of a Life Insurance Company's Target Market 18

Evaluation of Life Insurance as a Financial Instrument   22
    Advantages of Life Insurance.   22
    Disadvantages of Life Insurance   23
Conclusions   24

CHAPTER 2
Life Insurance Advice, Advisors, and Distribution

27

The Life Insurance Purchase Decision   27
Life Insurance Advisors.   29
    Insurance Agents   29
    Personal Financial Planners.   31
    Financial Institution Employees   31
    Attorneys and Accountants   32
Life Insurance Distribution Channels   33
    Captive Distribution   34
        Career Agents   34
        Multiple-Line Exclusive Agency.   35
    Independent Distribution   35
        Brokerage   35
        Producer Groups   36
        Independent Property/Casualty Agents.   37
Evaluating Life Insurance Agents.   37
    Tenants of Professionalism   37
        Fairness   37
        Competence   39
        Integrity   40
        Diligence.   41
    Sources of Information on Agents.   43
Conclusions   43

PART II
ASSESSING LIFE INSURANCE COMPANY FINANCIAL STRENGTH

45

CHAPTER 3
The Importance and Nature of Life Insurance Financial Strength

47

Why Assessing Life Insurer Financial Strength is Important.   47
    The Special Nature of Life Insurance   48
    Life Insurers in Financial Difficulty: Lessons from the Past   49
Insurer Management of Financial Strength.   51
    Incentives to Have Strong Financials   51
    Incentives to Avoid Holding Excess Capital   52

Overview of Life Insurers' Investments 53
   Bonds 55
   Mortgages and Real Estate................................. 56
   Stocks 57
   Policy Loans... 57
   Cash and Miscellaneous.................................. 57
Assessing Insurer Financial Strength 58
   Capital and Surplus Adequacy.............................. 59
   Leverage 60
   Quality and Diversification of Assets 60
   Liquidity 62
   Operational Performance.................................. 62
Conclusions 64

CHAPTER 4
Life Insurer Financial Regulation and Policyholder Protections   65

Nature and Purpose of Insurance Regulation 66
Areas of Insurance Regulation: Protecting Policyholders 66
   Organization and Licensing of Insurers 67
   Insurance Policy Forms and Rates 67
   Marketing Practices... 68
      Agent Licensing... 68
      Unfair Trade Practices 69
   Solvency 70
      Liability Valuation 70
      Asset Limitations and Valuation 71
      Accounting Standards 71
Solvency Surveillance Methods................................... 72
   Financial Statement Filings.................................. 72
   Ongoing Capital Requirements 73
   NAIC Automated Solvency Monitoring....................... 74
   Dividend Restrictions 75
   Cash Flow Testing 75
   On-site Financial Examinations 76
   Professional Oversight 76
Regulatory Responses to Financially Impaired Insurers 76
   Informal Actions 77
   Formal Actions... 77
   Rehabilitation.. 77
   Liquidation 78
   Role of Guaranty Associations............................... 78
Implications to Policyholders of Insurer Financial Difficulty 79

Implications to Policyholders of Regulatory Solvency Intervention 82
Conclusions 83

CHAPTER 5
Life Insurer Financial Strength Due Care   **85**

The Role of Rating Agencies. 85
    The Importance of Rating Agencies 86
    Four Major Rating Agencies. 86
        A.M. Best Company. 86
        Fitch Ratings 87
        Moody's Investor's Service 88
        Standard & Poor's 88
    An Example of an Agency's Rating Methodology 89
        Business Profile. 90
        Financial Profile. 91
        Other Considerations 92
    The Nature of Rating Agency Reports 92
        Rating Agency Reports. 92
        Rating Categories 93
    Using Rating Agency Reports and Ratings. 94
Other Sources of Insurer Information. 96
    The NAIC and State Insurance Departments. 96
        Financial Statement Information. 97
        Complaint Data 99
        Risk Based Capital Ratios 100
    Securities and Exchange Commission 101
    Insurance Companies 102
    Insurance Agents. 102
    Stock Analysts' Reports 103
    Publications 103
Conclusions 103

PART III
LIFE INSURANCE POLICY FUNDAMENTALS   **105**

CHAPTER 6
Life Insurance Basics   **107**

Generic Types of Life Insurance Policies 107
    Term Life Insurance. 107
    Cash Value Life Insurance 108

Life Insurance Pricing 111
    Mortality Charges 113
        Mortality Experience and Tables 113
        Influences on an Insurer's Mortality Experience 115
        Deciding on the Mortality Charges to Assess 116
        The Effect of Mortality Charges on Policy Values 122
    Interest Crediting Rate 123
        Investment Returns 124
        Influences on an Insurer's Investment Returns 124
        Deciding on the Interest Rate to Credit 125
        The Effect of Interest Crediting Rates on Policy Values 126
    Loading Charges 127
        Costs of Doing Business 127
        Influences on an Insurer's Costs of Doing Business 128
        Deciding on Loading Charges to Assess 129
        The Effect of Loading Charges on Policy Values 130
    Persistency 131
        The Importance of Persistency 132
        Influences on an Insurer's Persistency 133
        Deciding on Persistency Rates to Use 135
        The Effect of Persistency on Current Assumptions 135
Putting It All Together 135
Conclusions 137

CHAPTER 7
Common Life Insurance Policies   139

The Effects of Income Tax Law on Life Insurance Policy Design and
        Operation 139
    Tax Favored Status of Life Insurance 140
    IRC Definition of Life Insurance 140
    IRC Definition of Modified Endowment Contract 141
Term Life Insurance 142
    Types of Term Policies 142
    Key Features Unique to Term Policies 144
    Considerations 144
Universal Life Insurance 145
    Operational Details 145
    Considerations 149
Equity Indexed Universal Life 151
    Operational Details 151
    Considerations 152

Variable Life Insurance 154
   Operational Details 155
   Considerations... 156
No-Lapse Guarantee Universal Life 158
   Operational Details 158
   Considerations... 159
Whole Life Insurance.. 162
   Participating and Nonparticipating Life Insurance................. 163
   Types of Whole Life Policies 165
   Considerations... 166
Specialized Life Insurance 167
   Proprietary Life Insurance 167
   Private Placement Life Insurance 168
Life Insurance on Multiple Lives 168
   Second-to-Die Life Insurance 169
   First-to-Die Life Insurance 170
Conclusions 170

CHAPTER 8
Life Insurance Policy Attributes
171

Overview of Generic Policy Attributes........................... 171
Specific Life Insurance Policy Attributes 173
   Policy Overview... 174
   Death Benefits 176
      Nature and Duration of Guarantee 176
      Adjustability of Policy Duration 176
      Adjustability of Death Benefit Amount 178
      Choice of Level or Increasing Death Benefit Amount 178
   Cash Values 179
      Existence and Nature of Guarantees 179
      Location and Nature of Investments Backing Policy Reserves 181
      Likelihood of Lapse with Adverse Development of Current
         Assumptions 182
      Impact on Cash Values of Changes in Investments' Market Values .. 182
      Policyholder Control Over Fund Allocations 183
      Availability of Policy Loans 183
      Availability of Policy Withdrawals 184
      Relationship Between Cash Values and Death Benefits........... 184
      High Early Cash Values...................................... 185
      Protection Against Claims of an Insolvent Insurer's Creditors..... 185
   Premiums 185
      Premium Flexibility.. 185
      Ability to Mimic Any Other Type of Policy 187

Possibility of Skipping Premium Payments 187
Effect of Nonpayment of Premium 187
Resuming Premium Payments and Full Coverage After Premium
    Nonpayment 188
Mortality Charges 188
Guaranteed Maximum Mortality Charges 188
Actual Mortality Charges versus Those at Policy Issuance 190
Determination of Actual Mortality Charges. 190
Disclosure of Actual Mortality Charges 190
Volatility of Mortality Charges 190
Crediting Rates. 191
Guaranteed Minimum Crediting Rates. 191
Actual Crediting Rates versus Those at Policy Issuance. 191
Determination of Actual Crediting Rate. 193
Disclosure of Actual Crediting Rate 193
Volatility of Crediting Rate. 193
Inclusion of Dividend Income in Deriving the Crediting Rate. 194
Loading Charges 194
Guaranteed Maximum Loading Charges 194
Actual Loading Charges versus Those at Policy Issuance 196
Determination of Actual Loading Charges. 196
Disclosure of Actual Loading Charges 196
Volatility of Loading Charges. 196
Conclusions 196

CHAPTER 9
Life Insurance Policy Provisions and Features   197

Overview: Policy Content and Format 197
Life Insurance Policy Provisions 199
Provisions Protecting the Policyowner 199
    Entire Contract Clause 199
    Incontestable Clause. 200
    Premium Provision 200
    Grace Period Provision. 201
    Reinstatement Clause. 201
    Nonforfeiture Provision 202
    Participation/Policy Value Provision 202
    Misstatement of Age or Gender Provision. 203
Provisions Protecting the Insurance Company. 204
    Suicide Clause 204
    Delay Clause. 204
    Exclusion Clauses 204

Provisions Providing Policyowner Flexibility 205
   Right to Return Policy 205
   Death Benefit Provision 205
   The Beneficiary Clause. 206
   Settlement Options 208
   Nonforfeiture Options. 211
   Policy Loan Provision. 212
   Dividend Options 213
   Assignment/Ownership Provision 214
Common Life Insurance Policy Riders 215
   Riders Providing Life Insurance Coverage. 216
      Term Riders 216
      Family Riders 216
      Accidental Death Benefit Riders 217
      Guaranteed Insurability Option 217
   Living Benefit Riders. 218
      Terminal Illness Coverage 218
      Catastrophic Illness Coverage. 218
      Long Term Care Riders/Combination Plans 219
   Riders Protecting Against Policy Lapse 220
      Waiver of Premium/Charges Riders 220
      Overloan Protection Riders. 221
      No-Lapse Guarantee Riders 222
   Enhanced Cash Value Riders 222
Conclusions 222

PART IV
DETERMINING THE APPROPRIATE POLICY FOR EACH APPLICATION   223

CHAPTER 10
Life Insurance for Family Security   225

Introduction 226
U.S. Family Structures 227
Life Insurance Needs Analysis 230
   Identify Objectives 230
   Gather Information 231
      Assets 231
      Liabilities 232
      Income 232
   Analyze Information 233

Develop and Implement Plan: Matching Policies to Needs 235
   Financial Characteristics of the Client 236
   Nature of the Insurance Need 239
Conclusions 240

CHAPTER 11
Life Insurance in Estate Planning   241

Introduction 241
Overview of Federal Transfer Taxation 242
  Estate Taxation 242
   Calculating Estate Taxes 243
   Estate Taxation of Life Insurance 244
  Gift Taxation 244
   Calculating Gift Taxes 244
   Annual Gift Tax Exclusion 245
   Gift Taxation of Life Insurance 246
  Generation Skipping Transfer Taxation 247
Common Trusts Used with Life Insurance 247
  Marital Deduction and Credit Shelter Trusts 248
  Crummey Trusts 249
  Irrevocable Life Insurance Trusts 249
  Charitable Remainder Trusts 251
  Intentionally Defective Irrevocable Trusts 253
Life Insurance Analysis for Estate Planning 254
  Identify Objectives 255
  Gather Information 256
  Analyze Information 257
  Develop and Implement the Plan: Matching Policies to Goals 257
   Nature of Insurance Need Influencing Selection of Policy Types . . . 258
   Policy Options for Estate Liquidity with Families Composed of
    Husband and Wife 258
   Policy Options for Estate Liquidity with Other Family and
    Household Arrangements 260
   Policy Options for Other Estate Planning Goals 260
Conclusions 261

CHAPTER 12
Business Uses of Life Insurance   263

Introduction 263
Forms of Business Organizations 264
  Sole Proprietorships 264

Partnerships.   264
Corporations   265
   Problems Associated with the Death of a Majority Shareholder . . .   266
   Problems Associated with the Death of a Minority and 50/50
      Shareholder   267
Tax Considerations in Business Applications of Life Insurance   267
Business Applications of Life Insurance.   268
   Key Person Indemnification.   269
      Identify Objectives   269
      Gather and Analyze Information.   270
      Develop and Implement Plan.   270
   Business Continuation Arrangements   271
      Sole Proprietorships.   272
      Partnerships   273
      Corporations   275
   Nonqualified Executive Benefit Plans.   280
      Executive Bonus Plans   280
      Split Dollar Life Insurance   281
      Nonqualified Retirement Plans   284
   Group Term Carve Outs   285
Conclusions   286

PART V
LIFE INSURANCE ILLUSTRATIONS AND THE SUSTAINABILITY OF POLICY VALUES

287

CHAPTER 13
Life Insurance Policy Illustrations

289

Overview of a Policy Illustration   289
Uses of Policy Illustrations.   290
Non-Guaranteed Nature of Illustrations and Why Important   290
Content of Policy Illustrations   292
   Non-Variable Life Insurance Illustrations.   292
      Tabular Detail   292
      Narrative Summary.   296
      Numeric Summary   298
      Supplemental Illustrations.   299
   Variable Life Insurance Illustrations   301
   Interest Adjusted Indices   304
Conclusions   307

CHAPTER 14
Assessing the Sustainability of Illustrated Policy Values 309

Non-Guaranteed Assumptions Inherent in Life Insurance Illustrations . . 309
An Overview of Life Insurance Pricing 310
Influences on Illustrated and Actual Performance 310
    Crediting and Dividend Interest Rates 311
        Supported Primarily by Yields on Bonds and Mortgages 311
        Historical Interest Experience 311
        Crediting and Dividend Interest Rate Considerations 312
    Mortality Charges 312
        Supported by Mortality Experience 313
        Supported by Underwriting 314
        Historical Mortality Experience 314
        Mortality Charge Considerations 315
    Loading Charges 316
        Supported by Insurer Expenses 316
        Historical Expense Experience 317
        Loading Charge Considerations 317
The Sustainability of Illustrated Policy Values 318
    Complexity in Assessing the Sustainability of Illustrated Policy
        Values 318
    Illustration Assessment Process 319
        Review Crediting/Dividend Interest Rate 319
        Review Illustrated Performance 325
        Stress Testing 326
        Other Illustration Assessment Considerations 327
Conclusions 329

CHAPTER 15
Determining Appropriate Policy Funding Levels for
Flexible Premium Life Insurance 331

The Importance of Choosing an Appropriate Funding Level 331
Using Policy Illustrations to Determine an Appropriate Funding Level . . 332
    Setting Funding Targets 333
        Death Benefit Protection 333
        Cash Value Accumulation 333
    Death Benefit Protection Funding Targets 334
        Premium Length 334
        Target Cash Value 334

Illustration Stress Testing. 335
   Reduce Crediting Rate 335
   Increase Policy Charges 335
   Death Benefit Protection Stress Testing 336
   Cash Value Accumulation Stress Testing. 336
  Cost versus Risk Protection. 336
   Life Expectancy and Probability of Survival 337
   Death Benefit Protection: 10-Pay Examples. 337
   Death Benefit Protection: Pay-to-Age 120 Example 341
   Cash Value Accumulation: Minimum Non-MEC Death Benefit
     Example 343
Special Considerations for Specific Policies 344
  Variable Universal Life 344
  Equity Indexed Universal Life 345
  No-Lapse Guarantee Universal Life. 345
Conclusions 346

CHAPTER 16
Using Policy Illustrations for Competitive Comparison Purposes   349

Why Compare Illustrated Policy Values 349
Factors to Consider for Illustration Competitive Comparisons 350
  Non-Guaranteed Nature of Policy Illustrations 350
  Preparing Consistent Illustration Comparisons 351
   Rating Categories and Risk Classification Factors 351
   Premium Funding Levels, Death Benefits, and Cash Value
     Targets 353
   Illustrated Assumptions. 354
   Policy Options and Riders 354
  Other Considerations for Specific Policies 355
   Variable Universal Life 355
   Equity Index Universal Life 358
   No-Lapse Guarantee Universal Life. 360
Common Measures of Illustrated Policy Performance. 362
  Premium Measures 362
  Death Benefit Measures 363
   Death Benefit Internal Rate of Return 364
   Death Benefit Solve. 365
  Surrender Value Measures 365
   Surrender Value Amount 365
   Surrender Value to Premium Ratio. 366
   Surrender Value Internal Rate of Return 366
  Distribution Measure 367

Interest Adjusted Net Cost Indices 368
Example Illustrated Performance Comparison Summary 369
Considerations for Comparing Illustrated Performance between
      Different Policy Types 371
Comparing Whole Life to Universal Life. 371
Comparing Equity Indexed Universal Life to Generic Universal Life . . 374
Comparing No-Lapse Guarantee Universal Life to Generic Universal
      Life 375
Conclusions 376

PART VI
ONGOING POLICY MANAGEMENT   **379**

CHAPTER 17
Using Policy Reviews to Sustain Policy Viability and
Achieve Insurance Goals   **381**

The Importance of Policy Reviews 381
The Nature of Policy Reviews 382
Annual Reviews 382
    General Considerations 383
    Considerations Applicable to Particular Policies. 384
Detailed Reviews 388
Options to Achieve Insurance Goals. 391
When Policy Values are Insufficient 391
    Do Nothing. 392
    Make Additional Payments 393
    Reduce Future Death Benefits. 396
    Replace the Policy. 397
When Policy Values are Greater than Necessary 400
    Do Nothing. 401
    Reduce Future Payments 402
    Increase Future Death Benefits 404
    Take Policy Distributions. 404
Conclusions 407

CHAPTER 18
Securing Lifetime Values from Life Insurance   **409**

Introduction 409
An Overview of Income Taxation of Cash Values and Dividends 410
The Effect of Internal Revenue Code Definitions on Life Insurance
    Income Taxation 410

Income Tax Treatment of Cash Values 411
Income Tax Treatment of Dividends............................ 412
Policy Surrenders and Maturities 412
Income Tax Treatment of Surrenders and Maturities 413
Considerations in Policy Surrenders and Maturities 415
Policy Withdrawals, Partial Surrenders, and Loans 415
Income Tax Treatment of Withdrawals, Partial Surrenders,
    and Loans.. 416
Considerations in Withdrawals, Partial Surrenders, and Loans 418
Policy Replacements 418
Replacement Procedures 419
Income Tax Treatment of Replacements 420
Considerations in Replacements.............................. 421
Accelerated Death Benefits 424
Income Tax Treatment of Accelerated Death Benefits............. 425
Considerations in Taking Accelerated Death Benefits 425
Sale of the Policy in the Secondary Life Insurance Market 425
The Process and Economics of Life Settlements 426
Income Tax Treatment of Selling a Life Insurance Policy 427
Considerations in Selling a Life Insurance Policy.................. 428
Conclusions 429

APPENDICES   **431**

APPENDIX 1
Life Insurance Agent Questionnaire   **433**

APPENDIX 2
Descriptions of Four Rating Agencies' Rating Categories   **435**

A.M. Best Company 435
Fitch Ratings... 436
Moody's Investors Service 438
Standard & Poor's 439

APPENDIX 3
Attributes of Term and Cash Value Life Insurance Policies   **441**

APPENDIX 4
Example Term Life Insurance Tabular Detail   **447**

APPENDIX 5
Example Par Whole Life Insurance Tabular Detail   **451**

APPENDIX 6
Example No-Lapse Guarantee Universal Life Insurance
Tabular Detail   **455**

APPENDIX 7
Example Equity Index Universal Life Insurance Tabular Detail   **461**

Glossary 467
Index 499

About the Authors

Harold D. Skipper is *Professor Emeritus of Risk Management and Insurance* and former *Chairman* of the Department of Risk Management and Insurance in The Robinson College of Business at Georgia State University, from which he retired in 2005. His academic focus has been on life insurance and on insurance-related public policy issues. Besides several dozen articles, his publications include four books, the most recent being *Life and Health Insurance* (with Kenneth Black, Jr., 13th ed.) and *Risk Management and Insurance: Perspectives in a Global Economy* (with W. Jean Kwon), which received the outstanding book award from the American Risk and Insurance Association in 2009.

He has been a visiting professor at the University of Paris and at Nanyang Technological University in Singapore. In addition, he serves as a Research Fellow with the Chinese Center for Social Security and Insurance Research at Peking University and as a member of the Advisory Boards to the Center for Insurance Research at the Indian Institute of Management in Bangalore and to the Singapore College of Insurance.

His non-academic experience includes a three-year appointment, while on leave of absence from GSU, with the United Nations Conference on Trade and Development in Geneva. He has also worked with the Paris-based Organization for Economic Cooperation and Development (OECD), the World Bank, the Geneva Association, U.S. Department of Commerce, state and international insurance supervisors, the NAIC, as well as several major corporations and law firms.

He is past President of the American Risk and Insurance Association and past Vice President of the International Insurance Society. He was the moving force in 1996–97 in the creation of the Asia-Pacific Risk and Insurance Association for which its Board of Governors named its outstanding research award in his honor. His bachelor's degree is from Georgia State University and his masters and Ph.D. degrees are from the University of Pennsylvania where he was a Huebner Fellow in the Wharton School.

Wayne Tonning is Director of Product Management at M Financial Group and has more than two decades of experience with the company. In his current position with the M Product Management team, Wayne plays a lead role in M Financial's Due Care initiatives, conducting competition and product studies, managing M Financial's Due Care analysis, and participating in the development of new products. He also contributes to M Financial's in-force management activities, a critical component of the company's client advocacy strategy. Wayne is a primary author of M Due Care Bulletins and other related materials. Prior to joining M Financial's Product Management team, Wayne spent 12 years implementing and managing reinsurance arrangements for M Financial Re, M Financial's reinsurance company. Wayne is a Fellow of the Society of Actuaries, an educational, research, and professional organization dedicated to advancing actuarial knowledge.

Acknowledgments

Through long-time personal and professional relationships with members of the M community, I entered this project already having great respect for M Financial Group, its member firms, and its client advocacy approach. I consider this *Advisor's Guide to Life Insurance* to be yet another example of M Financial's commitment to the team approach that adds value to client relationships and understanding. I am honored to have been asked by so dedicated a group of professionals to lead the effort to produce this *Guide*.

As the primary author of this *Guide*, specifically Parts I–IV and VI, I have been privileged to work with the highly qualified team of professionals at M Financial. I wish to acknowledge, in particular, the critically important contributions of Wayne Tonning, Paul Yates, and Jacob Boston. Their expertise, perspective, and integrity during the process made this a positive experience for me, and their contributions—authoring Part V (Chapters 13–16), editing my work, and offering timely insight and sound critique—greatly enhanced the overall quality of the final product.

I would also like to acknowledge M Financial's Product Development Group, a committee comprised of five member firm representatives: Mac Nease (Chair), John Barry, Rick Chaffee, Jim Clary, and John Meisenbach. They have a passion for distinction and the relationships they maintain with clients and advisors. This passion was the driving force behind creation of this *Guide*. I want to thank them for their vision, focus, and appreciation of the fact that when producers and advisors work together, clients benefit.

My hope is that the reader of this *Guide*—whether a seasoned professional or one comparatively new to offering life insurance advice—will find information herein that enhances his or her ability to render sound client advice and, in the process, enhances the value of his or her practice. Even though several superb individuals contributed to making this volume the comprehensive treatise that we hope it to be, all errors and shortcomings remain those of the authors alone.

Harold D. Skipper, Ph.D., CLU
October 2010

Introduction and Overview

Have you ever felt overwhelmed by the complexities of life insurance or a bit insecure in advising a client about whether to purchase a particular life insurance policy? If you have, the *Advisor's Guide to Life Insurance* is for you.

Clients commonly seek the counsel of their professional advisors as to whether a life insurance policy recommended by an agent or broker offers good value and is from a financially sound company. To complicate matters for those advisors—whether they are attorneys, other agents, financial planners, or accountants—the client often seems to hold an inflated view of the depth of knowledge and insight that the advisor brings to the subject.

It's as if clients expect *their* advisors to know it all. It is not sufficient that you have mastered the particulars of estate and business planning as well as the many helpful applications of life insurance to such planning. If you understand those intricacies, surely you must be equally competent to analyze a life insurance policy illustration and to determine whether the life insurance company is financially sound and operationally efficient. Regrettably, being good at one aspect of life insurance does not translate to being good at all others.

This *Guide* is designed to assist advisors in making better informed life insurance recommendations to their clients. Secondarily, it also is intended as a training tool for advisors and their staffs.

The *Guide* provides information essential to the exercise of due care in the purchase and retention of life insurance policies. Its twin goals are to maximize the chances that (1) policies purchased and maintained by your clients offer good value for the premiums paid and (2) the insurance companies backing the policies are, and are likely to remain, financially sound. Advisors who master this material will be able to make more informed and superior life insurance recommendations, which translate into a significant benefit for their clients.

Decisions as to which insurers to select initially and to retain longer term lie at the heart of life insurance due care. Regrettably, conducting one's own assessment of an insurer's financial strength is exceptionally complex even for knowledgeable insurance advisors. Because of this complexity, advisors must place great reliance on the opinions and evaluations of rating agencies and others whose jobs are to conduct in-depth assessments.

The exercise of due care in decisions regarding life insurance policy selection and retention necessarily relies more on the advisor's examination of policy pricing, including understanding underlying assumptions and the sustainability of illustrated policy values. Learning to use and interpret policy illustrations—and knowing the questions to ask and issues to raise—are fundamental to life insurance due care.

We have structured the *Guide* to address the needs of both those with less life insurance knowledge who seek a focused, integrated approach to the entire subject area as well as those professionals who have need for the occasional refresher on a given subject. Stated differently, the *Guide* serves as both a primer and a reference source. Those readers taking the primer approach will find that the chapters build on each other, progressing logically from basic concepts and industry practices to more advanced topics.

At the same time, we limit the subject matter of each chapter to a specific area or topic that has proven useful and relevant to those who offer life insurance advice. This approach permits each chapter to be read independently of others. We purposely built in redundancy across the book, both to allow individual chapters to be read as reference works and to reinforce mastery of the material. For those with the time, we urge that the *Guide* be read in its entirety at least once. Because the world of life insurance is not static, we are confident that even the most knowledgeable advisor will learn something new and useful to his or her practice.

The *Guide* is careful to define the major life insurance terms used. In each case, the defined term appears in boldfaced font. Because terminology is not standardized within the life insurance industry, we also list other terms understood in the industry as having the same meaning. For quick reference, we also include a complete glossary of all defined terms, at the end of the *Guide*.

We make liberal use of cross references within each chapter to other chapters that cover material relevant to that chapter. Similarly, we make liberal use of information "boxes" throughout the *Guide* to offer insights on a specific topic and also of short examples, tables, and figures. Conversely, we limit our use of footnotes as we believe they can be a distraction, instead re-taining relevant information in the body of the text itself. The writing is closer to conversational than to traditional academe in style (while trying always to remember Strunk and White's rules of good grammar!).

The *Guide* is organized around six parts containing a total of 18 chapters. Each part explores a cohesive set of materials, with each chapter taking on a subset. Thus, Part I sets the stage for the *Guide* by examining "The Life Insurance Purchase," including an introduction to why and how life insurance is purchased as well as the role of advice and advisors in the process. Considerable life insurance industry terminology is introduced in this part.

Part II is our exploration of "Assessing Life Insurance Company Financial Strength." Within this part, we set out the characteristics and importance of an insurer's financial strength as well as the nature and role of the financial regulation of life insurers and accompanying policyholder protections. We then explain the role of rating agencies and other sources of information in carrying out an assessment of life insurance financial strength.

Part III, on "Life Insurance Policy Fundamentals," is a must-read part for those seeking to build their knowledge base. Yes, we delve a bit into the actuarial aspects of life insurance policies to ensure that the reader has a sound understanding for how life insurance companies price their products—but we avoid formulas, instead offering a common sense, intuitive approach. We include a chapter on the most commonly found types of individually issued life insurance policies, including descriptions of how they function. We follow that chapter with one that compares and contrasts these policies, using as reference the various attributes that the industry ascribes to policies. We believe that this chapter can be especially useful for advisors in offering sound client advice. We close this part with a summary of the contractual provisions included in life insurance policies and of various optional benefits common to them, taking the reader beyond the standard treatment of the life insurance policy as a contract.

Part IV is on "Determining the Appropriate Policy for Each Application." While the *Guide* is not intended to cover policy suitability issues, we do touch on suitability in order to illustrate the various family, estate, and business uses of life insurance.

The vitally important topic of "Life Insurance Illustrations and the Sustainability of Policy Values" is the subject of Part V of the *Guide*. We believe that the information in this part will be among the most eye-opening for many readers. Here we introduce how to understand and use life insurance policy illustrations, then how to dig more deeply to understand their underlying assumptions and assess their sustainability as well as insurers' intentions and practices in managing policy performance. These types of issues ensure that advisors can go the extra mile in the exercise of their responsibilities to clients. Determining the appropriate funding levels for various policies is yet another issue that warrants a full chapter.

Part VI closes out the *Guide* through an exploration of "Ongoing Policy Management." This topic has two components. First is the desirability and necessity for regular policy reviews to make certain that a policy remains viable and is on track to accomplish the client's financial goals. The second examines how to use an existing policy to provide values during an insured's lifetime, not just at death. This focus on lifetime policy values promises to expand the horizons for many readers, again for the ultimate benefit of their clients.

Some people say that life insurance is dull. Those of us involved with this project respectfully disagree; indeed, we find it (almost) exciting! But perhaps that perceived dullness explains why we find so few advisors who truly understand the subject and are able to offer sound, objective advice about it. Those who commit the time to the topic will significantly enhance their position to successfully serve their clients in today's competitive environment.

Executive Summary

As WE NOTE IN the Introduction and Overview, this *Guide* offers information essential to the exercise of due care in the purchase and retention of life insurance policies. Advisors who master this material will enhance their ability to make more informed, superior life insurance recommendations for the benefit of clients (and ultimately the advisor's practice).

Here we offer a summary of the *Guide*. We structure this Executive Summary identically to the structure of the *Guide*, around its six themes or parts, each of which presents a well defined, cohesive set of information.

Part I: The Life Insurance Purchase

Part I of this *Guide*, comprised of two chapters, provides an overview of the life insurance purchase decision. In this part, we briefly explore some of the psychological aspects that may affect the decision and discuss the options for dealing with the financial consequences that death can present for heirs and others. We also introduce a process for quantifying these financial consequences and offer factors to consider when contemplating life insurance as a solution.

This part also briefly discusses the various categories of professionals who are generally recognized as life insurance advisors, including attorneys, accountants, financial planners, and agents and brokers. As life insurance agents or brokers are usually involved in a life insurance sale, we provide an overview of the various classes of agents and brokers—often called producers—and the channels through which life insurance companies sell their products. In general, producers can be considered exclusive to one company or group of companies—sometimes called captive agents—or they work as independent distributors. As attorneys and accountants often need to evaluate not just the product recommendations of producers but also the producers themselves, we explore this important element of due care as well. In this process, we define several common industry terms and introduce the broad types of life insurance and life insurance companies.

Thus, we note that the decision whether to purchase life insurance rarely is a purely financial one. Rather, it is usually entangled with the psychological aspects of death and dying. Anxiety and emotions can be a hindrance to sound planning or can be used as the basis for motivating planning, depending on the client and on how sensitive and effective advisors treat these aspects. The setting of objectives with regard to the financial consequences of a client's death is a vital first step in the planning process. Quantification of these financial consequences logically follows, with individual life insurance commonly proving to be the most effective means of addressing these financial consequences.

Life insurance policies can be broadly classified as being either term life insurance or cash value life insurance. Within the cash value classification, universal life and whole life policies predominate. A seemingly endless variety of these policies is found in the market, regrettably abetting confusion.

Stock and mutual life insurance companies, the predominant forms worldwide, develop and sell these products. Stock insurers are owned by stockholders, and mutual insurers are owned by their policyholders. Stock insurers are far more prevalent today than in times past, thanks to demutualizations of many large mutual insurers. Both stock and mutual insurers decide on one or more target markets and then focus their resources on this. Several insurers (and agents and marketing organizations) target the high income/net worth market, having honed their expertise to provide meaningful added value for their clients. Independent advisors such as attorneys, accountants, and financial planners should, if asked, critically consider the target market of any insurer being recommended by a salesperson as well as the target market of the salesperson.

The advice given by agents selling life insurance can be enormously helpful to customers. Most agents undeniably offer sound advice, but not all are capable of doing so, especially for more complex situations. Even if an insurance policy offers good value and the insurer is financially sound, poorly conceived beneficiary designations, policyowner arrangements, policy funding levels, policy options, and a host of other elements can have an adverse impact on a client's financial plans. Conversely, the most logically conceived policy arrangements can fall apart if the policy proves to be unnecessarily costly or the insurer suffers financial reverses.

Agents should conduct their business with fairness, competence, integrity, and diligence. Those whose conduct comports with these attributes have a vital role to play in maximizing desirable client outcomes. Toward this end, we offer a short questionnaire intended to provide insight into an agent's professional competence, experience, and conduct.

Part II: Assessing Life Insurance Company Financial Strength

Part II, composed of three chapters, offers background information and concrete approaches to assessing life insurance company financial strength. This part is one of the *Guide's* most important. We observe that advisors should have a sound understanding as to why assessment of the financial strength of a life insurer is critical to the purchase decision and as to the competing incentives that insurance company managements have in maintaining financial strength. They also should know the components of financial strength. Even with this knowledge, an independent assessment of financial strength by an advisor remains a complex and daunting task for all but the most technically competent. We believe that advisors and insurance buyers must necessarily place the greatest weight on rating agencies' opinions and commentary as to a life insurer's financial strength. Rating agencies are not perfect, but their ratings continue to be good predictors of insurers' financial health.

The solvency record of the life insurance industry is impressive, especially in comparison to that of banks. The average policyholder is highly unlikely ever to be required to deal with the insolvency of a life insurer. But this very fact can lead to unwarranted complacency and lack of due care. Some, mostly small, life insurers do fail each year, and from time to time failures occur of insurers having household names. As we state, if a client's life insurer fails, it makes no difference to her whether failures are rare or whether the insurer is large or small or purple.

State insurance regulators are charged with protecting the insurance-buying public. While they avail themselves of multiple regulatory tools to (1) discourage excessive risk-taking behavior by life insurers, (2) identify such behavior if it exists, and (3) deal with its adverse effects if an insurer gets into financial difficulty, life insurance buyers and advisors should be vigilant in their initial selection and continuing use of insurers. Insolvencies cannot be wholly prevented nor can their financial consequences for policyholders be fully ameliorated by government actions, especially for those purchasing or owning more than moderate sized life insurance policies (e.g., in excess of $300,000).

Advisors should understand regulators' solvency-related responsibilities; the methods employed to prevent, detect, and respond to financial impairments; and their focus on protecting policyholders. More importantly, they should understand the implications to their policyholder clients from insurer financial difficulty and from regulatory solvency intervention, if they are to provide the full range of essential advice on the purchase of life insurance and on the wisdom of continuing with an existing life insurance carrier and program.

The analyses and opinions of rating agencies should necessarily factor greatly in the advisor's assessment of the financial strength of life insurers. The complexity and complications of trying to do otherwise are daunting. To utilize the rating agencies' information, advisors should have knowledge of those agencies whose analyses and opinions are respected, including particularly those that have been designated as *Nationally Recognized Statistical Rating Organizations*. Further, advisors should understand the key factors that drive insurer ratings and the rating categories used by the agencies. At the same time, advisors should be attuned to other sources of information, such as state insurance regulators and the *National Association of Insurance Commissioners*, the *Securities and Exchange Commission*, stock analyst commentaries, news from publications like *The Wall Street Journal*, and insurance companies and agents. These other sources can reinforce and supplement the reports and opinions of rating agencies.

Part III: Life Insurance Policy Fundamentals

Part III on life insurance policy fundamentals begins the *Guide's* shift in emphasis from insurance company financial strength to life insurance policies themselves. These four chapters provide background information on life insurance policies for those who may need a refresher on fundamentals or a crash course in the major types of life insurance policies and how they function and are priced. A full chapter is devoted to summarizing the important provisions and additional features that are required to be included or may be included optionally in policies. We continue the introduction of key industry terms and concepts throughout this part.

Thus, we note that life insurance pricing involves numerous factors and decisions by company actuaries, but these four pricing components are key:

1. Mortality charges;
2. Interest credits;
3. Loading charges to cover expenses, taxes, and contingencies; and
4. Persistency.

Although all life insurance policies rely on the same pricing elements, the details of how these elements are determined and function within a policy vary. Life insurance policies are considered to be either bundled or unbundled. Bundled policies are those under which the portions of premiums allocated to pay cost of insurance charges; to build cash values; to cover an insurer's operational expenses, taxes, and contingencies; and to support a scale of dividends are not disclosed to policyholders. The policyholder pays an indivisible premium, receiving a bundle of benefits. Other policies are unbundled in the sense that the policyholder knows where the portions of his or her premium are allocated. Whether a policy is bundled or unbundled is irrelevant to whether the above four pricing components are, in fact, used to develop policy pricing. They are.

As noted in Part I, all life insurance policies fall into one of two generic categories: term life insurance or cash value life insurance. Term life insurance pays the policy death benefit or face amount if the insured dies during the policy term, which is a specified number of years, such as 10 or 20 years, or to a specified age, such as age 65. If the insured lives to the set term, the policy expires, meaning that it terminates with no value. Term life insurance usually provides either a level or decreasing death benefit. Premiums either increase with age or remain level.

Cash value life insurance policies combine term insurance and internal savings—called cash values—within the same contract; that is, they accumulate funds that are available to the policyholder, much as with a savings account with a bank. Thousands of variations of cash value policies exist, consistent with insurers' product differentiation and target market strategies. However, virtually every cash value policy falls into one of three categories, even if the insurer does not label the policy as such: (1) universal life insurance, (2) whole life insurance, or (3) endowment insurance. Universal life policies come in several flavors, as do whole life policies. Very little endowment insurance is sold today.

Universal life (UL) insurance policies are unbundled, flexible-premium, adjustable death benefit contracts whose cash values and durations depend on the premiums paid into them. The policyholder pays as little or as much as he or she wishes into the policy, subject to insurer prescribed minimums and tax prescribed maximums. The higher the premium paid, the greater is the cash value, other things being equal. We cover these three types of UL policies:

- No-lapse guarantee (NLG) universal life policies guarantee that, if a specified minimum premium is paid as scheduled, the life insurance policy will not lapse for a specified period or for life, even if the account value goes to zero.

- ◆ Equity indexed universal life (EIUL) permits the policyholder to select an interest crediting rate based on the growth in an equity index, in part, and/or the life insurance company's regular crediting rate (primarily based on investment grade bonds and mortgages).
- ◆ Variable universal life policies are UL policies offering investment flexibility and the possibility of mutual fund-like returns and risk with no guaranteed minimum crediting rate as with UL.

Whole life (WL) insurance policies are bundled life products that pay the policy face amount whenever the insured dies and provide life insurance intended to remain in effect for the insured's entire lifetime. Unlike UL policies, premiums for WL policies (1) are directly related to the amount of insurance purchased, (2) must be paid when due or the policy will terminate, and (3) are calculated to ensure that the policy will remain in effect for the entire lifetime of the insured, which typically is age 120.

Life insurance policies are classified as being either participating (par) or nonparticipating (nonpar). Par policies are those for which the policyholder has a contractual right to share or participate in an insurer's favorable (and unfavorable) operational experience via dividends, which are declared by the insurer's board of directors. Nonpar policies are those for which the policyholder has no right to share in any distribution of surplus funds by the insurer. Most nonpar cash value policies contain non-guaranteed elements other than dividends that ensure that such policyholders can share in the favorable (and unfavorable) actual or reasonably anticipated operational experience of the insurer. Par policies are more closely associated with mutual life insurance companies, and nonpar policies are more closely associated with stock life insurance companies, although much nonpar UL is sold by stock subsidiaries of mutual insurers.

Each type of life insurance policy has its own attributes that will be appealing to some buyers but not others. Knowing each policy's attributes is an important part of due care. We emphasize that desirable attributes do not necessarily make for a desirable policy. By this we mean that a policy's performance characteristics should play a large part in both the decision whether to purchase a particular policy and to retain it. The insurer's financial strength obviously also plays an enormous role. We include several tables within this part that are intended to facilitate comparisons across policy types. The table below, which summarizes some of the key attributes of generic forms of life insurance, is one such table.

In our exploration of important life insurance policy features and riders, we point out that state insurance laws require life insurance companies to include so-called standard policy provisions within their life insurance contracts. Other provisions may be included at the option of the insurer. Applicants often wish benefits or options beyond those provided by these routine

Key Attributes of Generic Life Insurance Policies

Attribute	Term Life Insurance	Cash Value Life Insurance		
		Whole Life Insurance	Universal Life Insurance	Variable Life Insurance
✓ Income tax free death benefit?	Yes	Yes	Yes	Yes
✓ Accumulates cash values?	No	Yes	Yes	Yes
✓ Income tax free (or tax deferred) interest credited to cash value?	n.a.	Yes	Yes	Yes
✓ Can borrow against cash value?	n.a.	Yes	Yes	Yes
✓ Duration of coverage?	Fixed term	Lifetime	Lifetime, depending on premiums paid	Lifetime, depending on premiums paid
✓ Adjustable death benefit?	No	No	Yes	Yes
✓ Flexible premiums?	No	No	Yes	Yes
✓ Guaranteed policy elements?	Death benefit and premium	Death benefit, maximum premium, and minimum cash values	Death benefit, maximum charges, and minimum interest crediting rate	Maximum charges

provisions. These supplemental benefits or options are provided by what are called policy riders, which usually require additional premium payments. Riders can be grouped around those that provide additional life insurance coverage, offer living benefits, protect against policy lapse, and allow for enhanced cash values. Mastery by the advisor of these policy provisions and riders is a precondition for being able to provide sound advice to clients.

Part IV: Determining the Appropriate Policy for Each Application

While this *Guide* does not profess to offer advice about life insurance policy suitability broadly, Part IV necessarily delves a bit into the topic to illustrate how different applications call for different policies. In this part, we explore

(1) life insurance for family security, (2) life insurance use in estate planning, and (3) business uses of life insurance, devoting a chapter to each topic. We acknowledge throughout that this tripartite treatment is somewhat arbitrary as concern about the family often motivates the use of life insurance in all three situations. However, the underlying details warrant separate treatment. This part continues the practice of introducing and defining additional life insurance industry terminology.

Thus, in connection with purely family income and related needs, we note that the death of a family member can be both emotionally and financially devastating for the family. In the great majority of instances, only life insurance can be relied upon consistently to address a family's need for additional funds at death: the event that creates the financial problem simultaneously gives rise to the solution. The objective for family life insurance planning is to guide the customer/client toward a sound insurance outcome. In guiding the client, most advisors will follow more or less the same path: *identification* of the client's financial objectives if he or she were to die prematurely, *assembling and analyzing* relevant information, and *development and implementation* of a plan to accomplish the client's post-mortem life insurance objectives.

The nature of families and households in the U.S. has been changing for some time. Today's typical American lives longer, marries later, has fewer children, and divorces more readily than in past times. Having out-of-wedlock children carries less stigma than formerly, whether the mother lives with the child's father or not. Indeed, unwed mothers account for about two in every five births in the U.S. The proportion of nuclear families continues to decline in the U.S., while the proportion of single-parent families, blended families, and other non-traditional households rises. All of these and other demographic changes have contributed to an increasingly diverse profile for the American family, challenging advisors to be both sensitive to and knowledgeable about these diverse profiles.

Agents, brokers, and financial planners assist families by recommending the amount and type of life insurance to purchase. These recommendations flow from the objectives set by the client and from information gathered and analyzed. The recommendation will have been influenced by the nature of the insurance need as to amount, duration, and pattern as well as client characteristics in terms of financial ability and discipline to pay premiums and the risk tolerance. The agent, broker, or planner will then have used his or her knowledge of the attributes of different life insurance policies to select those that are compatible with the nature of the insurance need and client characteristics.

We then move to issues associated with death of wealthy persons. The most important usually are tax related. Much life insurance is sold to meet estate planning obligations and goals. The purchase of life insurance for estate liquidity purposes can permit the entirety of the client's wealth and investment program to be preserved for the family and/or other worthwhile purposes while avoiding having to hold a large chunk of liquid assets to pay government taxes. Life insurance is also used in other estate planning contexts.

In discussing the use of life insurance in estate planning, we do not assume that the advisor/reader necessarily has an estate planning focus. Consequently, we define many terms that will be well known to estate planning experts, and we offer short summaries of certain income and estate tax matters. In doing this, we avoid being very technical, with the understanding that the technically competent reader may from time to time cringe. For this we apologize and note that we welcome suggestions as to how to better bridge between the technical and facile.

Thus, we offer a short introduction to some of the common trusts wherein life insurance is found useful. This introduction necessarily involves trust-related definitions and background. For example, we define a trust as a legal arrangement whereby one party transfers property to someone else who holds the legal title and manages the trust property for the benefit of others. The person who establishes the trust is the grantor. The person who receives the legal title and manages the property is the trustee, and persons for whose benefit the property is held are the beneficiaries.

Many types of trusts exist, each designed to meet specific objectives. A trust created during life is referred to as a living trust. A trust created at death through a person's will is a testamentary trust. A living trust can be revocable or irrevocable. With a revocable trust, the grantor can terminate or alter the trust as he or she wishes and regain ownership of the property. With an irrevocable trust, he or she cannot terminate or alter the trust, permanently relinquishing ownership and control of donated property.

Some of the common applications of life insurance are with marital deduction and credit shelter trusts, Crummey trusts, irrevocable life insurance trusts, charitable remainder trusts, and intentionally defective irrevocable trusts. Of course, these and other planning instruments will have been identified in connection with the client's overall estate planning.

We then examine business uses of life insurance. Most people probably think about individually issued life insurance policies in the context of the family, including estate planning, but life insurance is also routinely used to foster business goals. The particular policy and arrangement followed will be influenced by whether the business is a sole proprietorship, partnership, or corporation and, for partnerships and corporations, its specific characteristics. Here we also introduce background information, including taxation, while avoiding technical detail.

A common business use of life insurance is in the form of key person insurance. Here the insurance is intended to hedge the business against financial loss occasioned by the death of individuals whose services are essential to its success. Life insurance is also routinely used to facilitate the smooth transition of closely held business ownership interests through buy/sell agreements while (1) sparing heirs the angst of deciding how to deal with that interest and (2) providing certainty to surviving owners. Life insurance also is often recommended to informally fund various nonqualified executive benefit programs, allowing the business to provide executives with tangible proof of their worth to the business. These and other business applications of life insurance seem likely to gain more prominence as both regulation and tax rates grow.

Part V: Life Insurance Illustrations and the Sustainability of Policy Values

Part V is the meat of the *Guide* in terms of understanding how to evaluate life insurance policies on behalf of clients. Composed of four interrelated chapters, it explores life insurance illustrations and their sustainability. We note that policy illustrations are almost always used in the sale of life insurance. In most cases, illustrations are required to be signed by the applicant and agent and included in the application package to the insurer. Illustrations are regulated by the states with the intention that they not be misleading and that they are understandable.

Illustrations show policy values as well as other valuable information such as a description of the policy being illustrated and available riders and options as well as definitions of key terms. Policy values are required to be shown using guaranteed policy pricing elements and are also typically shown using non-guaranteed policy elements as well. Non-guaranteed policy values may not be illustrated using non-guaranteed pricing elements or assumptions more favorable than those underpinning current non-guaranteed values. Policy illustrations are commonly used to compare possible future performance between competing policies and to show how the proposed insurance will fit into an overall financial plan.

We note that an insurer's mortality experience, investment earnings, expenses, and persistency are the primary drivers of life insurance policy performance. The historical trend in mortality rates has been downward, resulting in reduced cost of insurance charges, especially in new policies. Expectations are that mortality rates will continue to improve in the future but at a slower pace. Investment earnings are driven primarily by yields on the bonds and mortgages in an insurer's investment portfolio. Their historical trend also has been downward over the past couple of decades, resulting in lower interest crediting rates on policy cash values and lower dividend interest rates. Historically, expense efficiencies have been realized and passed on to policyholders through reduced policy loads, particularly on new policies. We expect expense efficiencies to continue through ever more effective applications of technology and to be priced into products.

Most policies sold today contain non-guaranteed policy values, and policy illustrations reflect this fact. The non-guaranteed policy elements or current assumptions that underpin these values will be in the form of excess interest credits, reduced mortality charges, and/or reduced loadings, with unbundled policies showing each element and par bundled policies usually combining all within its illustrated dividends. Illustrations are considered sustainable if these policy elements are based on current insurer experience. Determining whether they are so based is difficult, and consultation with a life insurance expert may be wise, although some insight can be gained into sustainability indirectly.

First, a review can be conducted of the crediting/dividend interest rate as we outline in this part. Second, a competitive comparison can be conducted to determine whether illustrated performance seems "too good to be true." Third, stress testing can be performed to gain an understanding of the effect of unfavorable changes in current assumptions on policy performance. More favorable consideration would ordinarily be accorded policies that hold up well when assumptions are changed for the worse. To complement this analysis, an understanding of the insurer's performance record, reputation, and policy management intentions is critical. We include a policy questionnaire that will elicit much of this information from an insurance company or knowledgeable insurance advisor.

Another vitally important issue with universal life insurance purchases and maintenance is an appropriate funding level. Figuring this out is not an exact science, unless the client wishes to purchase NLG UL or is willing to fully fund to maturity based solely on guaranteed policy values. Using NLG UL makes good financial sense in many situations, but it allows only minor cash value build up, which can be important if an objective is to utilize policy lifetime values. In addition, NLG UL does not offer the potential for better policy performance inherent in both par whole life and universal life. A UL policy fully funded based on guaranteed values also can make good sense in some situations, but doing so requires a comparatively high premium outlay.

For all other funding levels, a tradeoff between premium outlay and death protection coverage is required. Each policyholder is different with different risk/return profiles, and each policy will perform differently. Illustrations can be used to gauge the risk/return tradeoff. The programs that agents use to build illustrations can be instructed to solve for premium levels to achieve a specified cash value at a given age, with higher cash value targets providing more security, or to guarantee policy coverage for a specified number of years.

In this process, a baseline illustration is prepared using current assumptions, solving for the premium that achieves the specified target. Stress testing is then performed by varying the non-guaranteed elements of the illustration that impact product performance, including the interest crediting rate, mortality charges, and funding over different time periods. Premium outlays and the likelihood of not achieving a desired target objective are both revealed and used to estimate what appears to be the most appropriate funding level given the client's objectives and "feelings" about the implied risks. Results will vary significantly by policy type and funding level as well as changes in non-guaranteed policy elements. The certainty of variations in non-guaranteed policy elements in the future makes understanding the shortcomings and strengths of policy illustrations, the expertise of the life insurance advisor, and ongoing policy management critical to successful outcomes over the life of the policy.

We note that illustrated product performance should be an important factor in deciding which policy to purchase and later whether to retain it. To determine a policy's illustrated competitiveness, it must be compared to other policies. In doing so, the comparison parameters should be consistent across all policies. If complete consistency is unobtainable, any differences should be understood, noted, and reasonably accounted for, if possible. Complications can arise in trying to "level the playing field," particularly concerning the rate of return assumption for variable policies and the index crediting rate assumption for EIUL.

Several measures can be used to estimate future policy performance, with no one providing a complete picture, even ignoring the shortcomings attached to the unavoidable use of non-guaranteed values. For example, focusing purely on cash outflow (premiums paid) ignores the flexibility implicit in cash values, which, if the policy were surrendered, would be a cash inflow, offsetting the cash outflow. Likewise, focusing purely on the net of cash outflow and (possible) cash inflow ignores the value implicit in the death benefit, which, if the insured died during the policy term, would be a considerably greater cash inflow. As a minimum, measures of both possibilities are needed.

Part VI: Ongoing Policy Management

Part VI explores ongoing policy management, an essential, but too often overlooked component of life insurance due care. Within the two chapters of this part, we suggest why routine policy reviews are essential, how to conduct them, and what alternative actions may be considered to ensure that the policy continues to meet the client's financial goals. We also explore how to secure values during the insured's lifetime from life insurance policies.

Thus, we note that routine policy reviews are necessary because of the non-guaranteed nature of most policies' performances today. We have but to note the decades-long decline in insurers' investment returns and their negative impact on interest crediting rates on policy values to emphasize this point. When routine policy reviews are not conducted, policyholders over the past few years have said that they were surprised when they learned that values illustrated at the time of sale many years earlier failed to materialize, with the policy possibly in danger of lapse. Surprises of this type should not occur and will not occur with routine reviews.

Simple reviews should take place annually, relying on the annual policy statements that insurers provide to policyholders. These reviews consist of comparing current policy values with those of the last detailed review, which may have been at time of sale, to determine whether the policy is on target to meet the client's objectives.

In-depth reviews may take place less frequently, for example every three to five years, depending on changes in the client's circumstances, the magnitude of changes in non-guaranteed policy values, and any downgrades in insurer financial strength. These more detailed policy reviews rely on so-called in-force policy illustrations obtained from the insurer. They are used to determine whether some policyholder action is needed to maintain policy viability. Policyholder actions may include changing the level of funding or of death benefit coverage; of altering the premium allocation to different accounts; or of replacing the existing policy for a better performing one.

We close this part and the *Guide* with a discussion of how a life insurance policy can be an important source of value during the insured's lifetime. Life insurance is often sold and maintained for its dual roles: providing death protection and accumulating values for lifetime purposes. Its flexibility as a financial instrument combined with its favorable tax treatment can render life insurance a particularly valuable component of a financial plan.

Lifetime values can be accessed under life insurance policies in several ways, including via dividends, partial or complete cash surrenders, matured endowments, withdrawals, policy loans, and accelerated death benefits. Policies also can be sold in the secondary life insurance market. We cover all of these means. We also again define key terms and necessarily introduce important information about certain IRC definitions that influence tax treatment of lifetime values and also about generic income taxation associated with cash values and dividends.

We appreciate the opportunity to provide this information and welcome feedback on ways in which we can enhance usefulness of the *Guide* for future editions. Enjoy!

The Life Insurance Purchase

Introduction to Life Insurance | 1

WHAT SOME ECONOMISTS HAVE dubbed the Great Recession of 2008–09 painfully reminds us of the critical importance of making life insurance purchase decisions only after the most thoughtful deliberations. While life insurers fared far better than banks, most suffered material hits to their balance sheets and net incomes. Consequently, policy values have been negatively impacted either through reduced interest crediting rates or negative equity market earnings in variable contracts. Even so, the life insurance industry in general weathered the financial crisis quite well due to strong financial regulation, with most of the top life insurers still carrying high ratings.

An insurer's financial strength and product selection are more important to buyers than ever before. This *Guide*'s aim is to help advisors ensure that their clients make wise policy purchase (and termination) decisions whatever the economic environment.

This and the following chapter begin this process. This chapter introduces fundamental life insurance concepts and terminology.[1] As it explains, the purchase of life insurance can be a challenging experience because at times there is reluctance to

---

Authored by Harold D. Skipper.

[1]This chapter draws in part from Kenneth Black, Jr. and Harold D. Skipper, Jr., *Life and Health Insurance* (13th ed.; Upper Saddle River, NJ: Prentice-Hall, 2000), Chapters 14 and 17, and from Harold D. Skipper and W. Jean Kwon, *Risk Management and Insurance: Perspectives in a Global Economy* (Malden, MA: Blackwell Publishing, 2007), Chapter A6.

discuss death and dying and because the purchase decision is often complex. Chapters hereafter emphasize the importance and means of:

- Assessing advisor quality and life insurance company financial strength;
- Understanding life insurance policy fundamentals;
- Determining the appropriate policy for each application;
- Understanding policy illustrations and assessing their sustainability; and
- Conducting ongoing policy management.

We do not attempt to examine in detail the many ways that life insurance can be used to help solve family and business issues. Nor do we explore how policies should be structured for optimum efficiency and affect, including their structure, ownership, or beneficiary arrangement.

Psychological Aspects of Death and Planning

It can be helpful in the consultative process if the advisor understands some of the psychological aspects of death and planning. We offer a short introduction here.

The way a society and a family view death—whether it is celebrated, dreaded, or somewhere between the two extremes—influences how individuals plan for it. Death is intertwined with our culture, including religious beliefs and convictions. An intimate relationship between religious commitment and security can reinforce the view that we are not dealing solely with an economic problem.

Many individuals do not wish to discuss their own mortality. Often, there are psychological reasons for this reluctance, and understanding their source might help ameliorate reluctance.

Anxiety

Humans throughout history have exhibited a desire to reduce uncertainty. Uncertainty can cause anxiety. **Anxiety** is a collection of fears resulting in unpleasant uneasiness, stress, generalized pessimism, and risk averse attitudes. An individual's capacity to tolerate and manage anxiety is considered to be a measure of the degree to which the person is well adjusted. Also, the different roles (e.g., child, parent, etc.) and corresponding responsibilities that individuals assume throughout their lives can create anxiety.

Anxiety is not an absolute condition. It ranges from extreme neurotic anxiety with an overreaction to a perceived threat, to normal anxiety in which our reactions are proportionate to a perceived threat. Normal anxiety can be

TABLE 1-1
Rankings and Relative Degrees of Life Change in Selected Life Events

Rank	Life Event	LCU Score
1	Death of spouse	100
2	Divorce	73
4	Death of a close family member	63
6	Personal injury or illness	53
9	Retirement	45
11	Major change in health of a family member	44
16	Major change in financial state	38
17	Death of a close friend	37

Source: Richard H. Rahe, "Life Change and Subsequent Illness Reports," in *Life Stress and Illness*, E.K. Eric Gunderson and Richard H. Rahe, Eds. (Springfield, Ill.: Charles C. Thomas, 1974), pp. 60–61.

dealt with constructively at the level of conscious awareness, or it can be relieved by various risk management techniques.

Anxiety is often fostered through the financial planning process, especially when the discussion turns to death. In establishing objectives for the family, consideration is given to life changes that are among life's most stressful: death, loss of health and jobs, retirement, and divorce. This can be a reason why some clients wish to avoid or postpone needed financial planning.

A scale to measure the relative degrees of life change inherent in various life events has been developed. Table 1-1 lists several life changing events commonly associated with financial planning and shows their relative ranking and their so-called life change unit (LCU) value (with 100 being the greatest value). Life changes induce stress. Note that the death of a spouse is potentially the most stressful of life's events. Merely speaking about the possibility of death likewise can induce stress.

Financial advisors and life insurance salespersons often use the possibility of such life events and transitions to arouse anxiety within their clients in an effort to motivate them to reflect on the possible financial consequences of the occurrence of the events—and take action. Advisors can then paint a picture of freedom from anxiety that involves planning and products designed to reduce uncertainty.

Emotions

Emotions are a primary determinant of behavior. **Emotions** are learned reactions to a set of experiences or perceptions that have been either very favorable or very distressing. Contact with events or thoughts that recall these experiences can stimulate a desire to remove or satisfy the resulting emotions. For example, individuals who experienced severe financial difficulty as children because of the death or incapacity of a parent might be strongly motivated to avoid recurrence of that status for their families through the purchase of insurance.

Emotions can be learned from the experiences of others. Because emotions can be generalized from one set of circumstances to another, many advisors are successful in communicating to a client the emotional consequences of failing to make provision for adverse events, such as death. The purchase of insurance can provide individuals with an overt and constructive outlet for their emotional concerns.

External sources of additional money at the time of death, such as would be provided by individual life insurance, an employer, or the government, undoubtedly help dependents and loved ones from a financial point of view. Dependents and loved ones may infer something about the extent to which a deceased breadwinner cared about his or her family if the deceased person made thoughtful pre-death arrangements, including ensuring adequate funds for the surviving family. Indeed, one academic coined the term "the love theory" to explain the purchase of life insurance.[2]

Dealing With the Financial Consequences of Death

Death can create not only profound emotional distress but equally profound financial distress for families. If a family's economic livelihood depends on the wages of one person, that person's death could be financially devastating for the family. Having two breadwinners spreads the risk, but usually does not eliminate it. Even if a family is not financially dependent on one person's wages, his or her death could provoke substantial estate taxes, correspondingly reducing residual wealth passed to loved ones. The death of a breadwinner who also has a high net worth subjects the family to the potential of a double financial "whammy."

Businesses can be similarly devastated by the death of key employees, especially in smaller and closely held firms. Perhaps a key employee has special knowledge, skills, contacts, persuasiveness, or other attributes that would be difficult, if not impossible, to replace or could be replaced imperfectly and only at substantially higher costs.

Small and closely held businesses and families alike can fall victim to poor planning in connection with their owners' deaths. Heirs who have no interest in or skills relevant for the business may inherit stock that is illiquid, because no viable market exists for it. To add insult to (financial) injury, they may owe meaningful tax on the inheritance, yet not have the cash to pay it.

---

[2]Stuart Schwarzschild, "The Love Theory—New Rationale for the Purchase of Life Insurance," *Best's Review,* Life/Health ed., Vol. 73 (1972), pp. 46–48.

Surviving owners may seem to be the logical purchasers, but why should they, at this point, agree to purchase shares except at fire-sale prices. Fortunately for planning, business owners do not know which of them might die first, potentially leaving *their* heirs in such a disadvantageous situation, so all might have a motivation to avoid such an unpleasant situation.

In quantifying the financial consequences of death, as discussed later in this chapter, the advisor concludes either that the client's resources are sufficient to avoid adverse consequences or that they are not. If resources are insufficient, additional resources must be located. These resources can come from:

- Relatives,
- Additional savings/investments,
- Employer-provided death benefits, and
- Individual life insurance.

Relatives

Many individuals rely explicitly or implicitly on wealth transfer from either their relatives or in-laws to protect their families from a meaningful reduction in living standard, if not destitution, brought about because of the individual's death. Transfer may be via inheritance or gifting. In some circumstances, reliance on this strategy might be rational. In others, it can be foolhardy.

Most situations fall between these extremes. Even so, unless any such wealth transfer is a certainty as to amount and optimum timing, relying on it as a basis to fill death-related needs is likely unwise. In any event, reliance on this strategy places the financial well-being of the client's surviving family at risk to a greater or lesser degree. Obviously, each situation is different. Some persons seem to expect that their relatives will "save the day." The earlier discussion about the psychological aspects of death seems especially relevant in such situations.

Additional Savings/Investments

In financial planning, loss exposures can be retained or transferred. Meeting the death exposure via additional savings alone is tantamount to the exposure being retained until sufficient additional resources are accumulated. Retention ordinarily is not desirable. Hence, one of the other resource options typically is combined with this option during that interim period.

We can think of this approach as having near-term and longer-term components. In the near-term, inadequate time exists to accumulate sufficient savings to fill the financial gap. The longer term affords more alternatives. Presumably, sufficient time exists to implement an enhanced savings/investment program to fill the financial gap; in other words, retention becomes feasible.

In theory, the need for life insurance disappears when sufficient savings/ investments have been accumulated to cover the gap. This approach is consistent with the view of those who advocate the purchase of term life insurance over cash value insurance, with the idea of saving the excess of the cash value policy's premium over the term premium. In practice, however, few individuals have the diligence to fund the death need through savings.

Employer-Provided Death Benefits

One's employer can be a source of additional death benefits. Most employer-provided death benefits are from group term life insurance provided as an employee benefit. Such plans enjoy favorable income tax treatment for the first $50,000 of coverage. To minimize adverse selection, the amount of group life insurance for which an employee is eligible usually is determined by a system that limits the employee's ability to select the coverage amounts, which are themselves typically modest.

Supplemental life insurance sometimes is made available, subject to the employee meeting the insurer's underwriting requirements. The employee usually pays the entire premium. While available amounts may be larger than those provided under the tax-qualified group life insurance program, they ordinarily are not large.

Each of the above employer-provided death benefit plans can be important components for some individuals' financial plans—typically, those in the lower income category. Most group life insurance amounts are set by the terms of the employer's benefit plan and bear no necessary relationship to the individual's need. For individuals with families or other substantial financial obligations, additional insurance is almost always required.

Two other potential employer-provided death benefit programs are executive bonus plans and split dollar plans. Both of these plans are **nonqualified executive benefit arrangements**, meaning that they do not meet the requirements for preferential tax treatment and nondiscrimination among employees as set out under the Employee Retirement Income Security Act (ERISA) and the Internal Revenue Code (IRC). A detailed discussion of these plans is beyond the scope of this guide, but we offer an idea here of how they function, with slightly more detail offered in Chapter 12.

An **executive bonus plan** is a nonqualified executive benefit arrangement under which an employer pays for individually issued life insurance for selected executives. It is a simple arrangement. The employer agrees to pay the premiums for a policy that is owned by the executive. As a nonqualified benefit plan, the employer is free to discriminate among employees.

The premium payments by the business are compensation and, therefore, ordinarily tax-deductible, provided the death proceeds are not payable to the business. The executive must include the amount of the premium payment in his or her taxable income. Because the plan provides nonqualified life insurance, the executive cannot exclude any of the payment from taxable income. Some employers pay an additional bonus to executives to cover this income tax obligation.

As the owner of the policy, the executive may name the beneficiary and exercise all other policy rights. Of course, the death proceeds will be included in the executive's gross estate if he or she retains any ownership interest or if proceeds are payable to or for the benefit of the estate.

A **split dollar life insurance plan** is a nonqualified executive benefit arrangement under which the employer assists the employee in purchasing life insurance on the executive's life by sharing (splitting) the premium payments and policy benefits between the employer and employee. Under such arrangements, death benefits are split between the employer and executive's beneficiary, and living values are split between the employer and the executive. The employer's share of the death proceeds is intended as a reimbursement for the premiums that it paid and is equal to the sum of those premiums, with or without interest. The balance of the death proceeds is payable to the executive's designated beneficiary.

Split dollar insurance is a funding method, not a type of policy. It can provide executives with substantial amounts of life insurance protection at an outlay well below that which they would pay for the same policy. The employee can be allowed to purchase the policy from the employer at termination or retirement.

Individual Life Insurance

Perhaps the most widespread means of funding for the financial consequences of premature death is through the purchase of individual life insurance policies. Life insurance with a death benefit equal to the amount needed to fill any financial gap is a perfect hedge against the financial consequences of death. The event that gives rise to the need also gives rise to the solution. If purchased in adequate amounts, life insurance, in purely economic terms, replaces the deceased individual's future earnings, thereby protecting the family or business from suffering adverse financial consequences.

Issuance of individual policies is determined on a policy-by-policy basis. Insurance companies determine whether to issue the requested insurance policy based on an application submitted by the applicant—typically through an insurance agent—and, if the amount applied for is large, based also on results of one or more physical examinations, laboratory tests, and other information. The application contains questions of an administrative nature and those relating to insurability. Besides trying to determine the proposed insured's health status, the underwriter wants to be satisfied that the amount of insurance requested bears a reasonable relationship to the financial loss that the beneficiary would suffer upon the insured's death. The underwriter also wishes to know the purpose for the insurance and that the policyholder and beneficiary designations seem logical (i.e., insurable interest is present).

Life Insurance in Family, Estate, and Business Planning

Life insurance has an important role to play in most families' financial plans. This is evidenced by the fact that 78 percent of American families own life insurance.[3] It also plays an important and more specialized role in business continuation and estate conservation. In each of these circumstances, making a wise life insurance purchase decision involves five sequential determinations:

1. Whether life insurance is needed;
2. The appropriate amount;
3. The most suitable policy;
4. From whom to purchase the policy; and
5. How best to structure the policy to accomplish the goal.

In providing an overview of each of the five decision points, this section includes introductions to the generic types of insurance policies, to the types of insurance companies, and to how these companies position themselves in the market. This guide's focus, however, is on items 3 and 4 only—the policy and the insurer. Further, while logically these two decisions are separable, they usually are considered together. We begin this section by introducing some terminology that will ensure consistency of usage throughout this guide.

By **life insurance**, we mean a contract under which an insurer agrees to pay a specified sum of money, called the **face amount** (or **insurance amount**, **death benefit**, and a host of other terms by insurers), if the insured dies while the policy is in effect. The **insured** is the individual whose death triggers payment of the face amount. The person who applies for the policy, and usually will be the owner of the policy, is the **applicant**. In most instances, the proposed insured is also the applicant, but sometimes the applicant is someone else, especially when life insurance is being purchased for estate liquidity or business purposes.

The **policyholder** (or **policyowner**) is the person who owns the policy, exercises all contract rights, and with whom the insurer deals. The **beneficiary** is the person or entity designated by the applicant (policyholder) to receive the face amount on the insured's death. Of course, the policyholder must pay a stipulated consideration—called the **premium**—for the policy to become and remain in effect.

---

[3]*Life Insurers Fact Book* (Washington, D.C.: American Council of Life Insurers, 2008).

Determining Whether Life Insurance is Needed

The starting point of a life insurance needs analysis is an examination of the circumstances under which life insurance is needed. All insurance analyses have two dimensions: (1) the frequency of occurrence of loss-causing events and (2) the events' severity. Frequency of death is measured by **mortality tables** that display yearly probabilities of death by age and gender and sometimes other characteristics. **Life expectancy**, the average number of years of life remaining for individuals of a given age and gender and sometimes other characteristics, is derived from mortality tables.

For insurance planning purposes, probabilities of death or, equivalently, life expectancy, are relevant for large groups of insureds, as with employee benefit plans. They are of little relevance to a particular individual. A given person will either survive the year or not and is highly unlikely to live precisely to his or her life expectancy. Even so, many planners will use life expectancy to give the client some idea of the average remaining lifetime of similarly situated individuals or as an aid in determining the duration of coverage. Some marketing groups use life expectancy calculators derived from the mortality experience of their own clients, not those of the industry as a whole or even of a particular insurer.

Table 1-2 shows probabilities of death within the next year and prior to age 65 for selected ages, as well as life expectancies as of the ages shown, based on aggregate U.S. population data. The probability of death within one year for persons during their working years is small. The likelihood of death prior to age 65 is not. Indeed, approximately one in seven persons now aged 30 is expected to die before age 65. Also, for many persons, death after age 65 creates adverse financial consequences for families, and death probabilities after age 65 are high.

TABLE 1-2
Probabilities of Death

Age	Within One Year	Prior to Age 65	Life Expectancy
0	0.0068	0.1582	77.8
5	0.0002	0.1564	73.5
10	0.0001	0.1558	68.5
15	0.0005	0.1549	63.6
20	0.0009	0.1519	58.8
25	0.0010	0.1479	54.0
30	0.0010	0.1438	49.3
35	0.0013	0.1390	44.5
40	0.0019	0.1322	39.9
45	0.0030	0.1216	35.3
50	0.0044	0.1053	30.9
55	0.0063	0.0812	26.6
60	0.0095	0.0450	22.7

The key to planning for the death contingency is to focus on its financial consequences to the family or business, irrespective of its probability of occurring. One commonly accepted approach to beginning the process is to have the client answer a question akin to the following: *Will my death result in financial consequences that I find unacceptable for anyone?* If death would not create financial hardship on anyone—as is often the situation with children and single adults—there typically is no need for life insurance. Similarly, if death gives rise neither to estate taxes nor to business continuation issues, there likely is no need for life insurance for this purpose.

Note that the question's answer is from the perspective of what the *client* finds unacceptable. The client might, for example, find it perfectly acceptable *not* to provide financial support for one or more family members. If the client does not much care what happens to them, he or she is unlikely to buy life insurance for their benefit. We are reminded that we are not dealing with economic matters alone.

Determining the Appropriate Insurance Amount

Assuming a "yes" answer to the preceding question, the next question is: *How much life insurance is needed to address the financial consequences created by death?* The answer to this question gets to loss severity.

The possibility of a loss of earnings occasioned by the death of the family breadwinner is the major financial loss faced by most families. A business can suffer a parallel financial loss from the death of a key executive. As explained in Chapters 11 and 12, death can give rise to still other financial needs, including a desire to avoid having estate taxes diminish the estate corpus itself and to arrange for business buyouts. In each instance, advisors ordinarily derive a quantitative value of the need, which becomes the basis for making financial decisions about how most effectively to deal with it. To provide a feel for this process, here we sketch out how an advisor might go about estimating the financial impact on the family of a breadwinner's death. (Chapter 10 offers more detailed explanations for this use of life insurance.)

In such a situation, it would be necessary, first, to gather relevant quantitative and qualitative information to permit a sound identification of financial needs arising from the individual's death. This involves identification and valuation of the individual's assets and liabilities, and establishment of family objectives. For death planning purposes, this means that the family determines the income levels needed were either spouse to die. A commonly stated objective is to allow the family to maintain its current living standard. This might translate, for example, into a survivor income need of 70 percent of the pre-death family income, as the deceased spouse's self-maintenance expenses end. One ordinarily also establishes objectives regarding amounts to:

- ◆ Pay off liabilities;
- ◆ Cover funeral and other final expenses;
- ◆ Establish a family emergency fund;
- ◆ Establish a fund to finance children's education; and
- ◆ Give to charities or other organizations.

The advisor then determines the assets available to support the preceding objectives. These include existing personal and group life insurance, assets that could be liquidated on death, earnings on investments not to be liquidated, and future income from wages and Social Security survivor income benefits.

In analyzing future needs and resources, the advisor may make simple rough estimates for the value today of such future cash flows or may actually calculate present values at various interest and inflation rates. Such calculations require estimates for future investment returns and inflation rates, rendering them somewhat problematic. This fact is the reason that some advisors are satisfied with rough estimates.

In many instances, the need for the current year only is estimated. An attempt should be made to estimate future needs. This pattern can influence the type of insurance policy purchased. For example, if the future need were to pay off a mortgage loan, the amount of life insurance needed likely will decline with age—suggesting a decreasing term policy.

As for other circumstances, if the insurance need is to provide estate liquidity, a common means of determining the insurance amount is to base it on an estimate of future estate tax obligations. If the insurance need is to arrange for purchase at death of an owner's interest in a closely held business, a common means of determining the insurance amount is to base it on an estimate of the value of that business interest. Similarly, if the insurance need is to indemnify a business for the net income loss associated with the death of a key employee, a common means of determining the insurance amount is to base it on an estimate of that lost net income. These and other circumstances are explained in Chapters 11 and 12.

Numerous websites offer life insurance needs calculators. Additionally, one of the important value-added services of agents and financial planners is assistance in quantifying the need, especially in more complex situations.

Determining the Most Suitable Policy

After deciding on the amount of insurance, the client should decide on the most appropriate policy to buy. Several factors drive this decision, which we cover in detail in Chapter 10. In short, there will be personal and policy factors to consider. Here is a sampling of some of the personal factors to consider:

- The amount of money one is willing to spend on life insurance premiums;
- The likely pattern and duration of future life insurance needs;
- The likely pattern and accumulation of future policy cash values;
- The client's wealth transfer objectives;
- Financial discipline and risk tolerance; and
- Other saving options.

While Chapter 7 discusses in detail the common types of policies found in the market today, all fall into one of two generic categories: term life insurance or cash value life insurance. **Term life insurance** pays a death benefit if the insured dies within a set time period, such as 20 years, and pays nothing if the insured survives the period. **Cash value life insurance** combines term insurance and internal savings—called the **cash value**—within the same contract; that is, it accumulates funds that are available to the policyowner, much as with a bank savings account. Cash value life insurance is also sometimes referred to as **permanent life insurance**.

Virtually every cash value policy falls into one of three categories: (1) universal life insurance, (2) whole life insurance, or (3) endowment insurance. **Universal life insurance** policies are flexible-premium, adjustable death benefit contracts whose cash values and coverage period can be for the whole of life, depending on the premiums paid into them. **Whole life insurance** typically requires the payment of fixed premiums and promises to pay a death benefit whenever the insured dies and, therefore, is life insurance intended to remain in effect for the insured's entire lifetime. For both universal life and whole life policies, the policy values are credited with interest from underlying investments, typically investment grade fixed-income instruments, managed by the insurance company, and supported by a guaranteed minimum credited interest rate.

Endowment insurance makes two mutually exclusive promises: to pay a benefit if the insured dies during the policy term or if the insured survives the stated policy term. Very little endowment insurance is sold in the United States today, because its income tax treatment is no longer favorable. For this reason, we omit further treatment of it in this guide.

Cash value policies are also available as variable life insurance. With **variable life insurance**, the policyholder allocates the premium to investment options offered by the insurance company through what are called separate accounts with the policyholder carrying 100 percent of the investment risk, unlike non-variable policies. Thus, policy values fluctuate with changes in the market value of the investments backing the policy. The death benefit may vary with these changes in market value as well.

The issue of the type of insurance to purchase should not be divorced from the next issue—from whom to buy it. This is especially true for more complex insurance situations and where the need for cash value insurance is indicated. Chapters 6–18 focus on understanding, assessing, and managing life insurance products.

Determining from Whom to Purchase the Policy

The next decision is from whom to buy the insurance. This decision involves examination of the quality of the advisor and of the insurer. Chapter 2 explores the quality dimension of advisors. In this section, we introduce the two most common organizational structures of life insurers and also discuss the importance of their target markets. Chapters 3–5 explore how to assess the financial strength of life insurers.

Organizational Structures of Life Insurance Companies

The vast majority of life insurance purchased in the United States is sold by commercial life insurance companies organized as either stock or mutual insurers, and selling their products through agents.[4] Other sellers include fraternal benefit societies and certain agencies of the federal government with regard to veterans' insurance. Fraternal benefit societies operate under a lodge system and may sell insurance only to their lodge members and their families. Their share of the U.S. life insurance market has been in slow decline for some years, accounting for only 1.5 percent of all life insurance in force in 2008. Given their small market presence and limited target market, we omit them from further discussion or analysis. We omit government-provided insurance for veterans for the same reason.

At year end 2008, 976 life insurance companies were doing business in the U.S., the number having steadily declined from a 1988 peak of 2,343 companies. This drastic change has been due mostly to vigorous competition which, in turn, drove more mergers and consolidations, as many insurers realized that they were not sufficiently large to compete successfully against larger insurers. Besides consolidation, another recent trend is demutualization and the formation of mutual holding companies, in order to raise capital from the equity market to fund business growth or support business risk. In creating a mutual holding company, a mutual insurer either starts or acquires a stock company.

Many life insurance companies are stand-alone entities, with no insurer affiliate or subsidiary. Others are organized into groups or fleets of affiliates and subsidiaries. Table 1-3 lists the rankings of the 25 largest life insurance groups at year-end 2008 based on direct individual life insurance premiums writings, with stand-alone companies counted as a group of one. The table

---

[4]Information for this section is drawn from *Life Insurers Fact Book* (Washington, D.C.: American Council of Life Insurers, 2009).

TABLE 1-3
Largest 25 U.S. Life Insurance Companies by Form and Ownership
(Ranked by Individual Direct Life Insurance Premiums Written, 2008)

Ranking	Group Name	Premiums (000s)	Form	Ownership
1	American International Group	$24,201,968	Stock	USA
2	Northwestern Mutual	11,755,258	Mutual	USA
3	MetLife, Inc.	7,922,876	Stock*	USA
4	New York Life	7,388,752	Mutual	USA
5	Prudential Financial	6,507,556	Stock*	USA
6	Manulife Financial	5,686,086	Stock*	Canada
7	Lincoln Financial	4,577,432	Stock	USA
8	Massachusetts Mutual	4,449,165	Mutual	USA
9	AEGON USA, Inc.	3,956,284	Stock	Netherlands
10	State Farm	3,558,336	Mutual	USA
11	AXA Financial	3,534,597	Stock	France
12	Guardian	2,876,099	Mutual	USA
13	Pacific Life	2,450,678	Mutual	USA
14	ING North America	2,306,145	Stock	Netherlands
15	Allstate	2,197,648	Stock	USA
16	Protective Life	2,124,229	Stock	USA
17	Hartford Life, Inc.	1,859,794	Stock	USA
18	Genworth Financial	1,849,336	Stock	USA
19	Primerica	1,828,002	Stock	USA
20	Phoenix Life	1,638,628	Stock*	USA
21	AFLAC	1,600,341	Stock	USA
22	Principal Financial	1,493,701	Stock*	USA
23	Sun Life Assurance	1,441,657	Stock*	Canada
24	Thrivent Financial for Lutherans	1,370,988	Fraternal	USA
25	Torchmark	1,340,049	Stock	USA

*Demutualized to become a stock life insurer.
Source: ACLI 2009 *Life Insurance Fact Book*, as of December 31, 2008.

also shows whether the insurer is a stock or mutual company (and whether it has undergone demutualization) and its country of ownership.

Stocks and mutuals differ from each other based on the nature of their ownership. **Stock life insurance companies** are shareholder owned corporations authorized to sell life insurance products. Stock insurers have access to capital through the equity market to grow the business or to support business risk. They are owned and controlled by their stockholders, with net profits inuring to these stockholders. Stock insurers can be owned by other stock insurance companies, mutual life insurance companies, or companies outside the insurance industry. Stockholders elect the members of the company's board of directors. Policyholders are purely customers of the insurer and have no rights to exercise any control over the insurer.

By contrast, **mutual life insurance companies** are policyholder owned corporations authorized to sell life insurance products. Net profits inure to the benefit of policyholders. Only policyholders can own a mutual company. Mutual companies do not issue stock, which means they do not have direct access to the equity market to raise capital. Instead, to raise additional capital they must (1) grow it internally through accumulated surplus (profits), (2) form mutual holding companies thereby allowing indirect access to the equity market, or (3) issue state-approved surplus notes—which are hybrid promissory notes that regulators allow to be counted as surplus. The ability to raise capital through surplus notes is limited compared to equity capital funding. Policyholders elect the members of the company's board of directors. Policyholders are both customers and owners of the insurer.

Some 75 percent of life insurers are stock companies, 19 percent are mutuals, with the balance being mostly fraternals. Stock companies held 73 percent of life insurance in force and mutuals held 25 percent in 2008. Some 11 percent of all stock insurers are foreign-owned, with Canada, the Netherlands, France, the United Kingdom, and Switzerland accounting for 78 percent of all such companies.

In discussing essential differences between stocks and mutuals, issues of control and cost sometimes are raised, so we address each briefly here. Some proponents of the mutual form contend that it is superior to the stock form as mutuals are controlled by and operate for the benefit of policyholders, whereas the stock company is owned and controlled by its profit-seeking stockholders. While it is theoretically correct that policyholders have ownership and control rights in the mutual company, this is true in reality to a limited extent only.

In fact, very few policyholders in mutual insurers vote for the members of the companies' boards of directors, and when they do vote, they typically give their proxies to existing management. They do this because they (1) do not purchase insurance to be able to control the company, perceiving themselves more as customers than owners; (2) are numerous and widely scattered geographically, with little capacity or inclination for intercommunication necessary for effective control; (3) have comparatively small stakes in the insurer; and/or (4) do not understand or care about their rights to vote. As a practical matter, mutual companies typically are controlled more by their management group through proxy arrangements than by policyholders. This fact is not necessarily bad, provided management diligently works for the best interests of policyholders and does not abuse their capacity for self-perpetuation.

Some proponents of stock companies argue that stockholders take a greater interest in the control of the company, creating more incentive for management to maximize value (as compared to complacency that can occur with management of mutuals and their disinterested owners). As a practical matter, those stock companies with widespread and diverse ownership are also sometimes controlled more by their management groups through proxy arrangements.

Another issue in the stock versus mutual debate has been the question of relative product cost. Proponents of mutual companies have argued that, since profits flow to policyowners, their policies will be less costly than those sold by stock companies, as stockholders benefit from favored financial results. Conversely, proponents of stock insurers have argued that, being subject to the discipline of the market, their policies can be less costly by virtue of the company operating more efficiently.

Generalizations on the question of cost are not very helpful. Some mutual companies are more efficiently run than some stock companies and vice versa. Even if a given insurer is efficiently operated, there remains no guarantee that policyowners—whether in a mutual or stock company—will benefit from that fact. Stock companies may pay out substantial dividends to stockholders. Mutual companies may elect to restrict policyowner dividend payments in order to build surplus, as they have no direct access to the equity market. Whether a particular policy is low cost usually is not a function of the insurer's organizational form, but rather of its efficiency coupled with the extent to which the insurer passes efficiency gains to policyowners. This can be assessed by the company's history of passing on value to policyowners as measured by policy performance and the company's stated intention for passing on future experience gains. We explore this in Chapter 17.

Importance of a Life Insurance Company's Target Market

Life insurance companies, as with other commercial enterprises, do not try to be "all things to all people." Instead, they will have segmented large, heterogeneous markets into smaller, less diverse submarkets that have relatively similar product or marketing needs. From among these segments, most insurers (and agents) will have selected one or a few on which to focus their marketing efforts, called their **target markets**.

For example, some insurers' target market is the elderly who are not particularly wealthy, such as Colonial Penn Life Insurance Company, which targets the 50–85 age segment, offering modest amounts of cash value life insurance with no underwriting. At the opposite age spectrum, Gerber Life Insurance Company focuses on the juvenile market and sells relatively modest insurance policies directly to consumers, not through agents. Insurance groups that began as property/casualty insurers—such as Allstate, Farmers, and State Farm—typically sell life insurance through their agents as add-on coverage for those who already own homeowners and auto insurance with the group. Their target markets tend to be middle and upper-middle income families.

The selection of target markets strongly influences all marketing and related decisions taken by the insurer (and agent). It influences, if not dictates, what products it should develop, their pricing, and how they should be structured internally; the depth, quality, and quantity of needed actuarial, legal, investment, underwriting, and field support expertise; what reinsurance is needed; needed information systems support; the distribution methods to be adopted and compensation to be paid; and the nature of advertising and promotion—just to name a few.

Life insurers (and agents) select their target markets in a variety of ways. One way is to segment the market by (1) life stage, (2) financial status, (3) buying behavior, (4) affinity group, and (5) health. While shown here as distinct segments, in practice insurers usually combine subsets of each to develop their target markets.

Consider a target market keying off of, among other things, the household's financial status. Insurers could target their marketing efforts on one or more of these sub-segments:

◆ Households of modest financial means;
◆ Households of moderate financial means;
◆ Households of high financial means; and
◆ Affluent households.

A household's financial status is a function of its income and net worth. Obviously, different combinations of income and net worth exist. So target markets could be further segmented by these variables and others. For example, a further subdivision of the two highest financial categories could be:

◆ Professionals (perhaps further subdivided by profession; e.g., physicians),
◆ Non-professionals,
◆ Business owners (perhaps further subdivided by industry or size), and
◆ Individuals with inherited wealth.

Unsurprisingly, life insurers targeting the highest income and/or net worth market sell much larger policies on average than those targeting other income and/or net worth segments. Table 1-4 illustrates this point. As cash value policies are predominant in this market, and the need for life insurance typically is for long durations, the table is limited to insurers that sold at least 1,000 cash value policies during 2009 and whose average policy amount issued was at least $200,000, a comparatively modest amount. A minimum of 1,000 policies is used as a proxy for the insurer being a meaningful competitor and having sufficient sales to justify the high costs of providing the necessary personnel infrastructure to support their efforts in this market.

TABLE 1-4
Life Insurance Companies issuing at least 1,000 Cash Value Policies of $200,000 and greater during 2009

Rank	Insurance Company	Corporate Group	Number of Cash Value Policies Issued	Average Face Amount per Policy ($000)
1	Lincoln Life & Annuity Company of NY	Lincoln Financial Group	1,091	1,258
2	John Hancock Life Insurance Company USA	Manulife Financial	27,907	1,104
3	Sun Life Assurance Company of CA (US)	Sun Life Financial Group	1,743	1,085
4	John Hancock Life Insurance Company NY	Manulife Financial	3,321	972
5	Sun Life Assurance Co. of Canada USB	Sun Life Financial Group	4,773	954
6	Security Life of Denver Insurance Co.	ING USA Life Group	5,749	794
7	Penn Insurance and Annuity Company	Penn Mutual Group	2,059	787
8	Lincoln National Life Insurance Co.	Lincoln Financial Group	27,175	755
9	Allianz Life Insurance Co. of NA	Allianz Insurance Group	1,789	736
10	AXA Equitable Life Insurance Company	AXA Financial Group	14,197	730
11	PHL Variable Insurance Company	Phoenix Life Group	1,993	674
12	Minnesota Life Insurance Company	Securian Financial Group	8,630	604
13	MetLife Investors USA Insurance Company	Metropolitan Life and Affiliated Cos	22,244	580
14	Pacific Life Insurance Company	Pacific Life Group	13,122	491
15	Principal Life Insurance Company	Principal Life Group	11,155	478
16	Guardian Life Ins Co. of America	Guardian Life Group	25,845	440
17	Penn Mutual Life Insurance Company	Penn Mutual Group	6,517	434
18	Hartford Life Insurance Company	Hartford Life Group	1,577	416
19	RiverSource Life Insurance Company	Ameriprise Financial Group	11,668	401
20	Federated Life Insurance Company	Federated Life Insurance Company	2,304	400
21	Pruco Life Insurance Company	Prudential of America Group	21,561	387
22	Protective Life Insurance Company	Protective Life Corp	36,965	374
23	Aviva Life and Annuity Company of NY	Aviva USA Group	1,878	367
24	Acacia Life Insurance Company	UNIFI Companies	1,333	361
25	Nationwide Life Insurance Company	Nationwide Life Group	2,880	360
26	Massachusetts Mutual Life Insurance Co.	MassMutual Financial Group	40,968	360
27	MONY Life Insurance Company of America	AXA Financial Group	4,286	359
28	New York Life Insurance and Annuity Corp.	New York Life Group	26,240	359
29	West Coast Life Insurance Company	Protective Life Corp	4,094	352
30	Ameritas Life Insurance Corp.	UNIFI Companies	2,705	340
31	National Life Insurance Company	National Life Group	3,898	329

32	Hartford Life and Annuity Insurance Co.	Hartford Life Group	28,449	321
33	Ohio National Life Assurance Corporation	Ohio National Life Group	3,629	309
34	Aviva Life and Annuity Company	Aviva USA Group	26,404	301
35	National Western Life Insurance Company	National Western Life Insurance Company	8,213	292
36	Union Central Life Insurance Company	UNIFI Companies	4,465	282
37	North American Company for L & H Ins	Sammons Financial Group	6,015	253
38	Columbus Life Insurance Company	Western & Southern Financial Group	1,362	252
39	Western Reserve Life Assurance Co. of OH	AEGON USA Group	26,540	237
40	Ohio National Life Insurance Company	Ohio National Life Group	3,997	232
41	MTL Insurance Company	MTL Insurance Company	3,256	220
42	American General Life Insurance Company	AIG Life Group	10,916	215
43	Lafayette Life Insurance Company	Western & Southern Financial Group	4,805	213
44	Northwestern Mutual Life Ins Co.	Northwestern Mutual Group	144,188	210
45	Midland National Life Insurance Company	Sammons Financial Group	19,239	208

Source: A.M. Best Statement File.

It can be seen from Table 1-4 that, for several insurers, the average policy issue size was well above $200,000 and, for a few insurers, in excess of $1.0 million. Worth noting is the group affiliation of each insurer. In most instances, the group is composed of several other life insurers, each of which has its own target market, often focused on a geographical region, product type (e.g., variable), marketing method (e.g., brokerage), or other market segment.

It can be extremely important that each client's specific needs and circumstances match well with the target market of the insurer or insurers and agent being considered. Consider the client who requires complex estate planning and advice. Ordinarily, agents and insurers that do not specifically target this market would not be expected to bring much added value to the life insurance purchase, even if their products were priced competitively with those that did so specialize, which usually is not the case. Indeed, they could bring the very opposite if they were merely "order takers."

Evaluation of Life Insurance as a Financial Instrument

Life insurance is perhaps the most common financial instrument for dealing with death's adverse financial consequences. It offers several advantages not enjoyed by other instruments or techniques. It also carries some disadvantages.

Advantages of Life Insurance

Aside from the macro-advantages of life insurance to society, life insurance offers specific advantages to individuals. *First*, as noted earlier, life insurance can be the perfect hedge against the adverse financial consequences of death. The event that gives rise to the need also gives rise to the solution.

Second, life insurance enjoys tax treatment under the IRC not enjoyed by other comparable financial instruments. The tax that otherwise would be due on the interest earned on life insurance cash values is either deferred or avoided altogether, provided the policy qualifies as "life insurance" under the IRC (see Chapter 7). The tax is avoided altogether if the policy is retained until death. Because interest accrues on a tax-deferred basis, the cash value is greater than the after-tax value of equivalent taxable savings media for a term-plus-side-fund arrangement.

If the policy is terminated during the insured's lifetime, income tax will be due to the extent that the cash value and any other amounts received under the policy exceed the premiums paid, which is the cost basis. Even in this case, the tax will have been deferred for many years. Additionally, the IRC does not require a deduction from the tax basis for the economic value of the death benefit protection (i.e., the internal cost of insurance charges) provided over the years. This tax advantage can perhaps be seen more clearly by noting that the premiums paid for term life insurance under term-plus-side-fund arrangements cannot be counted as part of the arrangement's cost basis, thus resulting in a higher taxable gain of such an arrangement in comparison to that of an otherwise identical cash value policy.

Life insurance death proceeds are free of income tax to the beneficiary, irrespective of the length of time the policy had been in effect, provided certain minimum precautions are taken. Also, through reasonable planning, the death proceeds can be received free to estate taxes. Thus, every dollar of such a policy's death proceeds in the beneficiary's hands could be the equivalent of two dollars of assets retained in the taxable estate (assuming a combined 50 percent state and federal death tax rate).

Third, many life insurance policies today are exceptionally flexible in terms of being capable of adjusting to the client's changing financial and other circumstances. They are tax-favored repositories of easily accessible funds if the need arises. Yet the assets backing these funds are generally held in longer-term investments, thereby earning a higher return. Also, the policyholder usually can opt to deposit additional funds into the policy, thereby enhancing tax favored interest earnings and lowering the internal mortality charges while possibly extending the length of time that the policy will remain in effect. Likewise, with many policies sold today, the policyholder can change the amount of premium paid to accommodate changed circumstances, sometimes even paying nothing if sufficient policy value exists to sustain the policy.

If changed circumstances suggest a lesser amount of insurance is needed, the policy face amount easily can be reduced, with corresponding reductions in internal mortality charges or premiums. The opposite set of circumstances can be accommodated through an increase in the face amount, subject to satisfactory insurability.

Further, life insurance can prove invaluable for innumerable business and personal purposes. Executive bonus plans are but one example. So, too, is using life insurance to fund the purchase of a closely held business on the death of one of its owners. The owner's heirs receive cash for what might otherwise be an illiquid ownership interest. The surviving business owners enhance their ownership share and avoid the potential for conflict with the deceased owner's heirs.

Disadvantages of Life Insurance

Life insurance is not without its disadvantages. *First,* insurers necessarily incur operational expenses and taxes, and these must be paid for via loadings in the policy. Such loadings vary over time, ranging, for example, from 100 percent or more of the first year premium to 5–20 percent thereafter, depending on the type of policy and the insurer's target market.

Second, buyers of life insurance forego some current expenditure to pay policy premiums for this future hedge. Moreover, the person foregoing current expenditures to pay the policy premium is unlikely to realize the benefit of the hedge directly. Life insurance is purchased for the benefit of others and usually only indirectly for the benefit of the person whose life is insured.

Third, the life insurance purchase decision can be complex. Even the comparatively straightforward decision to purchase life insurance to cover one's family may not be simple. Is insurance needed and, if so, in what amount, what type, and from whom should it be purchased. The decision requires analysis at each stage, and the customer often is not well versed in life insurance.

Complexity can increase by orders of magnitude if the purchase is for estate liquidity or is to be used in business situations or complex family situations. The decision involves the same types of issues as with the family purchase, but others as well, such as: How best to structure the arrangement? How do we minimize income, gift, and estate taxes? How to maximize the possibility of all heirs feeling that they have been treated fairly? How do we go about ensuring that the insurance amount remains adequate over time and that the policy being considered offers needed flexibility for changing circumstances?

Conclusions

The decision whether to purchase life insurance can be entangled with the psychological aspects of death and dying. Anxiety and emotions can be a hindrance to sound planning or can be used as the basis for motivating planning, depending on the client and on how sensitive and effective advisors treat these aspects. The client's setting of objectives with regard to the financial consequences of his or her death is a vital first step in the planning process. Quantification of these financial consequences logically follows, with individual life insurance commonly proving to be the most effective means of addressing these financial consequences.

Life insurance policies can be broadly classified as being either term life insurance or cash value life insurance. Within the cash value classification, universal life and whole life policies predominate. A seemingly endless variety of these policies is found in the market, regrettably abetting confusion.

Stock and mutual life insurance companies are the predominant forms in life insurance markets worldwide. Stock insurers are owned by stockholders, and mutual insurers are owned by its policyholders. Stock insurers are far more prevalent today than in times past, thanks to the demutualization of many large mutual insurers. Both stock and mutual insurers decide on, and then focus their resources on, one or more target markets. Several insurers (and agents and marketing organizations) target the high income/net worth market, having honed their expertise to provide meaningful added value to clients. Independent advisors such as attorneys, accountants, and financial planners should, if asked, critically consider the target market of any insurer being recommended by a salesperson, as well as the target market of the salesperson.

Life Insurance Advice, Advisors, and Distribution | 2

THE PRECEDING CHAPTER INTRODUCED life insurance concepts and terminology and discussed why the purchase decision can be difficult and complex. This chapter continues the purchase theme by exploring additional elements of the purchase decision and by explaining why quality advice in connection with purchases is important. We also examine the groups of professionals who offer advice in connection with the purchase. Next, we focus attention on the various channels that insurers use to sell life insurance. We conclude with a discussion of how to evaluate the persons who represent insurers in the sales process.[1]

The Life Insurance Purchase Decision

Insurance purchasers want well-suited, low-cost insurance with favorable contractual terms, from a financially secure, well-managed insurer that will deal honorably with them over the years. Putting the pieces of this puzzle together is not simple. Purchasers need an advisor who will present the client's best interests and provide quality service on an ongoing basis.

Authored by Harold D. Skipper.
[1]This chapter draws in part from Kenneth Black, Jr. and Harold D. Skipper, Jr., *Life and Health Insurance* (13th ed.; Upper Saddle River, NJ: Prentice-Hall, 2000), Chapters 11 and 24.

Consider the differences between purchasing a common tangible good, say a TV, versus the purchase of a life insurance policy. All purchases involve balancing the benefits provided to us by the product against its price. For a TV, we know why we wish to buy it, and we know this without anyone having to convince us of a TV's benefits to us. We also have a good idea of the size TV that we would like and can easily learn, if we do not already know, the quality and reliability of its manufacturer. We can look it up in *Consumer Reports* or ask the salesperson who typically is paid by salary not commission. We can take the TV for a "test ride" by watching, listening to, and operating it before we purchase it, and many retailers provide an unconditional 30-day return policy.

The life insurance purchase experience offers none of these handy means of assessing benefits, quality, and reliability. The typical consumer needs someone (ordinarily, an agent) to point out the benefits to the family or business from the purchase and to convince the prospective buyer to make the purchase. The typical consumer also has little notion of the best "size" policy that should be purchased, again relying on the agent for advice.

Finally, the typical buyer hasn't a clue about the quality and reliability of the insurer's products or of the insurer itself. In the minds of consumers, the life insurance "product" is the policy contract on which thousands of words of insurance jargon are printed. But the policy form is not really the product. The product is intangible. It is the set of promises set out in the policy, the main ones being to (1) pay a benefit to the beneficiary on the insured's death, (2) credit interest on the cash value, and (3) pay the cash value if the policy-owner terminates the policy. These promises are only as good as the solidity of the company making them, which we explore in Chapters 3–5.

Moreover, on what basis does the consumer assess whether the premium being charged is reasonable in light of the package of promises? With the TV, we can easily compare prices for this commodity via the internet, by visiting local retailers, and by reference to *Consumer Reports*. With life insurance, none of these resources will be much help. A proper assessment requires someone who understands life insurance fundamentals and the life insurance market, as policy values and prices change over time, and the company that is competitive today might not be so in five years. Indeed, this aspect (insurer and product selection) of the life insurance purchase is the most difficult to assess. So, the consumer again relies on the advice of the agent trying to sell the policy. But how does the consumer assess whether the agent is both knowledgeable and unbiased?

A proper assessment of likely benefits versus premiums to be paid is prudent both at the time consideration is being given to policy purchase and after the purchase, on an ongoing basis. We must remember that most life insurance policies are intended to remain in force for decades. Even if the policy looked competitive at time of purchase, has it remained so?

Further, what may appear as small changes in policy charges or interest crediting rates can cause large differences in policy values over time. For example, if $10,000 of each yearly premium goes toward building cash value, that value would be about $5.8 million in 25 years at 6.0 percent interest. At a rate just 1.0 percent higher, the cash value would be $1.0 million greater. (And this simple analysis ignores the additional boost to cash values that would occur because the latter policy would incur lower internal cost of insurance charges—assuming a level death benefit.)

In summary, the life insurance purchase decision is complex, and the typical consumer is ill-equipped to deal with its many intangible elements. The consumer pays money today for a set of promises and options that he or she probably does not truly understand, which are themselves backed by a financial institution whose solidity the customer cannot easily assess. The purchase is based on trust that the agent and other advisors are giving informed, sound, unbiased advice and that the insurer will offer good product value and ultimately deliver on its promises, perhaps decades into the future.

Life Insurance Advisors

Many individuals offer life insurance advice—some for a fee and most for a commission. Competent, informed, trustworthy insurance advisors are a consumer's best assurance of making a wise purchase decision. The most common insurance advisors include:

- Insurance agents;
- Personal financial planners;
- Financial institution employees; and
- Accountants and attorneys.

Insurance Agents

Insurance agents are salespeople licensed by the state and under contract to sell an insurer's products, typically for a commission and on a face-to-face basis. Within the life insurance industry, they are commonly referred to as **producers**. For most individuals, the insurance agent is the source of both advice and the policy. Indeed, agents account for more than 90 percent of new individual life insurance sales and virtually all cases in which planning is complex, such as with estate and business planning. As such, we cover them in more detail in the sections below, explaining the various relationships between agents and insurers and offering guidance in how to evaluate them.

To become an agent, applicants must first secure an insurance license from the state in which they wish to sell insurance and contract with one or more insurers to sell their products. They qualify for a license by passing an examination and meeting character and residence requirements. Formal educational requirements, if any, are minimal. In total, these requirements are not onerous and are intended to ensure only a base level of competence. In many jurisdictions, agents must also meet certain minimum continuing education requirements annually to qualify to renew their licenses. They are required to understand and comply with relevant state insurance laws and regulations.

As explained later in this chapter, an agent may represent a single company or may place insurance with several companies. Agents who sell variable insurance products—that is, insurance products that offer policyholder directed asset allocations, including equity investments—must be registered with the Financial Industry Regulatory Authority (FINRA), formerly known as the National Association of Securities Dealers, and have a specialized state insurance license as well. To sell variable products, the individual must have qualified for what is commonly referred to as a series 6 license with FINRA. As part of the process, the individual must pass an examination. The exam covers a broad range of subjects on the markets, as well as the securities industry and its regulatory structure, ensuring a minimum level of understanding and expertise. Thereafter, the individual must meet certain continuing education requirements every three years.

Many life insurance agents hold professional designations. The oldest and most widely recognized designation oriented exclusively toward life insurance producers is the Chartered Life Underwriter (CLU) designation granted by The American College in Bryn Mawr, PA (http://www.theamerican college.edu/). To earn the CLU designation, the candidate must (1) pass eight examinations touching on life insurance fundamentals, planning, and uses; (2) have three years of qualified, fulltime experience; (3) meet an ethics requirement; and (4) agree to comply with the College's Code of Ethics. Individuals holding this designation can be presumed to be knowledgeable about life insurance and its applications, including a reasonable knowledge about more complex life insurance planning issues. As with all professional designations, however, the CLU is no guarantee of competency or unbiasedness.

Individuals holding the CLU designation often affiliate with the Society of Financial Service Professionals (SFSP), also in Bryn Mawr (http://www.financial pro.org/). Originally, only individuals holding the CLU designation could be members, but membership was considerably broadened several years ago to include a diversity of financial practitioners, from fee-only financial planners, estate planning attorneys and accountants, to asset managers, employee benefits specialists, and life insurance agents. The Society provides qualified continuing educational opportunities to its members, including those required for the CLU, CFP® (see below), the American Bar Association, and state accountancy boards. Further, members agree to be bound by the Society's Code of Professional Conduct.

Personal Financial Planners

Personal financial planners also offer advice on insurance. Most planners also sell insurance for a commission, which means that they must also be licensed insurance agents. They, therefore, must pass the state exam and meet other qualifications to obtain and retain their licenses and are charged with complying with state insurance laws and regulations. Thus, the discussions in later sections concerning agent distribution channels and agent evaluation should be understood to apply as well to financial planners who sell life insurance.

Some planners do not sell insurance, instead offering advice on a fee-only basis, on the theory that having no financial stake in the sale leads to better advice. In most states, anyone may hold him- or herself out as a personal financial planner. The term is largely unregulated, so no assurance of competency or being impartial necessarily attaches to the term.

Many planners hold the Certified Financial Planner™ (CFP®) designation. This designation signifies that the individual has (1) met minimum educational requirements (applicable course work or other professional designations plus a bachelor's degree), (2) passed 10 hours of comprehensive examinations, (3) at least three years of qualified fulltime experience, and (4) met standards of fitness and passed a background check. While the CFP® program includes the study of life insurance and its applications, it is much broader than life insurance alone (including income taxation, investments, retirement needs, and estate planning), and can allot only so much time and space to its mastery. Also, as with all professional designations, the CFP® is no guarantee of competency and fair-mindedness. It is, however, the most widely recognized professional designation in the field of personal financial planning and is well regarded.

The American College also offers the Chartered Financial Consultant® (ChFC®) professional designation. This designation requires candidates to pass nine examinations and meet the same requirements as applies to those seeking the CLU designation. Six of the ChFC exams qualify the individual to take the CFP® exams. In addition to insurance education, the ChFC® curriculum includes income taxation, retirement planning, investments, and estate planning.

Financial Institution Employees

Life insurance is sold by the employees of many financial institutions, including commercial banks, investment banks, thrifts, credit unions, and mutual fund organizations. Banks are important distribution channels in some markets, especially in Europe, but less so in North America. Banks' share of the overall U.S. life insurance market is less than 5 percent, although their share of new individual annuity sales exceeds 20 percent.

Of course, any employee of a financial institution who sells life insurance must also hold an agent's license from the relevant state, irrespective of whether the employee or the institution receives the commission from the sale. They, therefore, must pass the state exam and meet other qualifications to obtain and retain their licenses and are charged with complying with state insurance laws and regulations.

Deposit-taking institutions such as banks, credit unions, and thrifts tend to orient their insurance sales toward the middle income market, unless the institution owns a life insurance agency which specializes in higher income segments. Therefore, the institution, in either instance, is not much different from any other agent focusing on a particular target market. Banks hope to increase insurance sales by leveraging their existing customer base.

Securities firms hope also to leverage their existing, higher income customer base, in much the same way as do banks. These firms have focused more on variable products, although the recent recession has given pause to such sales, with more traditional products now being sold. Individuals selling such products must be registered with FINRA, as discussed above.

No professional designation exists that is oriented specifically toward stock brokers or employees of other noninsurance financial institutions giving life insurance advice. Given that any such employee must hold an agent's license to sell life insurance, the discussions in later sections concerning agent distribution channels and agent evaluation should be understood to apply to employees of financial institutions selling life insurance as well.

Attorneys and Accountants

Many accountants leverage their existing client base by offering insurance advice, most of them for a fee and some of them on a commission basis, which means that they are licensed insurance agents, in which case they must pass the state exam and meet other qualifications to obtain and retain their licenses and are charged with complying with state insurance laws and regulations. Attorneys often are involved in more complex insurance cases and offer their services for a fee as insurance advisors from a legal and tax viewpoint. Because accountants and attorneys are thought of by clients as fee-only advisors and not agents, those who are licensed agents and receive commissions in connection with the sale of policies to clients should disclose this fact to clients.

Accountants and attorneys will have met formal education requirements in their fields, but nothing in their ordinary courses of study would have provided extensive knowledge about life insurance or its application to estate, business, and family issues. Accountants and attorneys typically will have developed such expertise through experience in estate and/or business planning and by taking specialized professional development programs. Such programs are offered by the American Accounting Association and the American Bar Association as well as by other professional bodies, such as local chapters of the SFSP and of Estate Planning Councils (see http://www.naepc.org/). For complex matters involving insurance advice, it is desirable that the accountant or attorney have evidence of specialized insurance expertise (e.g., a CLU designation or other formal documentation of subject matter mastery) and/or recommendations from appropriate sources.

Life Insurance Distribution Channels

As noted above, the great majority of life insurance is purchased through agents, and they are the most important source of life insurance advice for consumers. As we know, anyone who sells life insurance is a life insurance agent, irrespective of what label may apply, including financial consultant, personal financial planner, insurance consultant, financial advisor, accountants, investment advisor, etc. Agents vary considerably in their expertise, independence, legal relationship with the insurer, and target market. It will prove instructive to provide an overview of the various **distribution channels**—also called **distribution systems** and **marketing channels**—through which life insurers market products to their customers.

Our focus here will be on those channels that rely on agents. We omit discussion of the 2 percent of life insurance sales—mostly smaller policies—that occur via the **direct response** distribution channel, in which the customer deals directly with the insurer, without any intervening intermediary or firm (think Ed McMahon). No face-to-face contact ordinarily is involved, with the customer responding to some type of solicitation directly from the insurer, such as through the mail, television, internet, or telephone.

We can divide producers into two broad classes, depending on whether the insurer is attempting to build its own captive agency sales force. Thus, many insurers rely on what is commonly called a **captive** or **agency building distribution** strategy under which they recruit, train, finance, house, and supervise their agents. Such insurers are heavily involved in recruiting individuals new to the insurance business.

Other insurers follow what is commonly called an **independent** or **nonagency building distribution** strategy under which they do not seek to build their own agency sales force, instead relying on established agents for their sales. Under this strategy, the insurer seeks experienced salespersons and avoids expenses associated with training, financing, and providing office facilities.

Of course, an insurer may use several distribution channels. The reason for multiple distribution strategies is to serve different target markets effectively. A market-driven strategy calls for an optimal market-product-distribution linkage.

Captive Distribution

Most students of the industry agree that life insurers utilizing the captive distribution strategy have been responsible for the widespread acceptance of life insurance. These insurers have provided the initial training essential to successful producers. Two major types of captive distribution channels exist:

- ◆ Career agency, and
- ◆ Multiple-line exclusive agency.

Career Agents

Career agents are commissioned life insurance producers who usually represent a single insurance company or group of affiliated companies. If they represent a single company or group only, they are commonly called **captive agents** or **exclusive agents** and may sell the products of the group only. They are probably the most commonly known life insurance agents. Well known life insurers using the career agency distribution channel include Northwestern Mutual, Metropolitan Life, Prudential Life, and New York Life.

Under the **career agency system**, agencies or offices—commonly called **field offices**—are established in various locations to recruit, train, finance, supervise, and house agents. Collectively, a company's agents are commonly referred to as the **field force**. Each field office is headed by a **general agent** or **branch manager**, depending on the details of the insurer's distribution system, who is primarily responsible for increasing sales and recruiting and developing career agents. The largest life insurers worldwide tend to use the career agency system. The general agent or branch manager is responsible for recruiting new agents within a given territory and training and helping and encouraging them in their work as solicitors.

The career agency system has both advantages and disadvantages in comparison to independent distribution (see below). If the insurance group is financially sound and its products of high quality, the fact that only the group's agents can sell their products can be a competitive advantage. Further, life insurers using the career agency system ordinarily have greater control over their agents, including their training, supervision, and marketing efforts. This fact can lead to greater consistency across agents and higher policy retention rates. A potential disadvantage is that agents typically have fewer options across insurers and products.

Multiple-Line Exclusive Agency

The second major agency-building life insurance distribution channel is multiple-line exclusive agency. **Multiple-line exclusive agents** (MLEAs) are commissioned captive agents who sell the life and health and property and liability insurance products of a single group of affiliated insurers. Well-known insurers using the MLEA distribution channel include State Farm, Allstate, and Farmers.

MLEAs' target market is mostly "middle America." They offer more or less the same advantages and disadvantages as do career agents except their life products ordinarily are not aimed at the high-end market.

Independent Distribution

Independent distribution is the other major life insurance marketing channel relying on agents. Three common independent distribution channels are:

◆ Brokerage,
◆ Producer groups, and
◆ Independent property/casualty agents.

Agents selling through these channels are always non-captive; i.e., they may sell for more than one insurer. Insurers that rely on independent distribution channels provide products and services to agents who are already engaged in life insurance selling. Thus, the key to this strategy is to gain access to the producer. The producer's loyalty is retained by quality service, good compensation, innovative products and pricing, and sound personal relationships.

Brokerage

Insurers relying on the brokerage system of distribution either rely on company employees or specialized general agencies to convince existing agents or brokers to contract with the insurer. Direct contracting in response to trade press advertising also is used.

The term **broker**, as used in life insurance distribution, refers to a commissioned salesperson who works independently of the insurer with whom insurance is placed and who has no minimum production requirements with that insurer. In property/casualty insurance, a broker usually is considered legally as representing the client rather than the insurer. In most U.S. jurisdictions, a life broker actually is an agent for the insurer but subject to less supervision and control than that found with career agents. He or she is an independent contractor.

The term *broker* is commonly used in another way within the life insurance business. Most captive agents *broker* business. Used as a verb in this way, it refers to the practice of full-time agents of one company occasionally selling the policies of other insurers. Captive agents may sell for other insurers if (1) their primary insurer does not offer the policy or coverage needed by the customer, (2) their primary insurer has declined or offered highly rated coverage, or (3) the customer wants quotes from more than one insurer.

A variation of brokerage is the **personal-producing general agent** (PPGA) who typically is an experienced, independent, commissioned agent who focuses on personal production but who is paid both direct and override commissions plus some type of expense allowance. (**Override commissions** are compensation based on an agent's production that is paid to an agent's supervisor.) For this, PPGAs supply their own office facilities and receive technical assistance in the form of computer services and advanced sales support. While PPGAs usually have contracts with more than one insurer, companies often try to be the PPGA's primary carrier. Some insurers appoint PPGAs to represent them within a given territory for the sale of a single product only, such as universal life or disability income insurance.

Companies seeking economic efficiencies through spreading their fixed costs have increasingly looked at supplementing their traditional channels of distribution with additional distribution outlets. Many insurers that traditionally have been exclusively captive agent "shops" now aggressively push their brokerage business.

Producer Groups

A second variation of the independent distribution strategy has been the development of **producer groups**, which are independent marketing organizations whose member agents specialize in the high-end market. The group is owned and governed by these agents, is self-supporting, and represents a handful of high-quality insurers that may have agreed to develop special proprietary products and provide dedicated services for the group.

Producer groups believe that their clients require more sophisticated support services than those ordinarily provided by insurers, given the target market. The group, in addition to the insurer, provides necessary sales and marketing support systems to their agents. Specialized software and other strong computer and research support are hallmarks of some producer groups, often affording their members a competitive advantage.

One producer group has created its own reinsurance company, to which its partner insurers cede portions of the underlying risk placed with those insurers. The group observes that favorable experience of its business is thus segregated, allowing insurers to develop and re-price in-force proprietary products based on this experience. Additionally, the group notes that access to underlying pricing assumptions means that it can more easily perform product due care analysis (e.g., review credibility of pricing). The prominent independent producer groups in the U.S. are M Financial Group (the oldest and largest), Partners Group, and First Financial Resources.

Independent Property/Casualty Agents

A third channel using the independent distribution approach is the independent property/casualty agent. **Independent property/casualty agents** are independent, commissioned agents whose primary business is the sale of property/casualty insurance for several insurers. Often, the property/casualty insurers that the agent represents will have life insurer affiliates, and they encourage the agent to take advantage of his or her customer relationships to sell life insurance for them. Additionally, unaffiliated life insurers often seek independent property/casualty agents as salespeople.

Evaluating Life Insurance Agents

Depending on a client's needs, it can be vitally important that he or she work with an agent whose business practices meet high standards of fairness, competence, integrity, and diligence—in other words, who conduct themselves according to professional precepts. An evaluation of producers against these tenets can minimize the chances of dealing with someone whose advice may be suspect or even wrong. We explore each of these tenets below and offer means of securing evaluative information.

Tenants of Professionalism

Each profession will have codes of conduct to which their members are expected to subscribe and follow. The discussion below builds on several organizations' codes but relies most heavily on the *Code of Professional Responsibility of the Society of Financial Service Professionals* (SFSP Code).

Fairness

The codes of conduct for innumerable professional organizations routinely cite fairness as a key tenet. It amounts to the Golden Rule. For example, the first canon of the SFSP Code states: "Fairness requires that a professional treat others as he/she would wish to be treated if in the other's position." It's a nice idea, but not always easy to implement in either professional or personal relationships.

The tenet has multiple dimensions. *First,* the agent should not misrepresent or conceal material information. Besides the obvious admonition of not purposefully misrepresenting or concealing relevant information, it means also that policy illustrations should be so constructed as to avoid unintentionally lending themselves to misleading or incorrect interpretations and should not omit information that might ordinarily be useful as an aid to understanding. Chapters 13–14 explore many elements of this mandate.

A *second* implication is that the advisor should disclose to the client all information material to the professional relationship, especially as relates to actual or potential conflicts of interest. Of course, agents have a financial stake in the sale of life insurance in the form of commissions and possibly other benefits. The SFSP Code here is insightful with regards to this potential conflict of interest. It states:

> A potential conflict of interest is inherent in the relationship between the client and the financial service professional when the professional is compensated by commissions on the sale of financial products. In such circumstances, if asked by the client or prospect, the professional should disclose, to the best of his/her knowledge, all forms of compensation, including commissions, expense allowances, bonuses, and any other relevant items.[2]

A *third* implication is that the agent should offer his or her best advice as to product suitability. Thus, the producer should take care to ensure that the recommendations as to insurance amount, policy funding, type of policy, and the way the policy is structured (e.g., ownership and beneficiary) are appropriate to the specific needs, circumstances, and goals of the client. Obviously, compliance with this tenet requires the agent to be competent to make an appropriate assessment. In turn, this requires that the advisor help the client to understand the available options to meeting his or her needs and goals. Chapters 10–12 explore this mandate.

Fourth, in offering advice and recommendations, the agent should maintain professional independence. This mandate constrains the advisor to offer best advice concerning policy illustrations and policy value, in the client's interest. Is the policy credibly illustrated and does it offer good value based on all available information? Obviously, compliance with this mandate also requires the advisor to be competent to make such an assessment. Chapters 15–16 explore this mandate.

While insurance agents are under no legal obligation to provide "best product" advice (unless they profess otherwise), this fourth mandate would hold them to a higher standard than that which exists in law. This can pose problems for captive agents as a given insurer is unlikely to have the "best" products in all categories and client circumstances. As noted in the SFSP Code:

---

[2]*Code of Professional Responsibility of the Society of Financial Service Professionals* [Code], at http://www.financialpro.org/About/CodeOfProfResp.cfm, A1.3a.

The requirement of professional independence . . . presents a special challenge for Society members who are contractually bound to sell the products of only one company, or a select group of companies. In such cases, the member must keep paramount his/her ethical duty to act in the best interest of the client, even if this means forgoing a sale.[3]

Fifth, the agent should take care to ensure that the recommended insurer is financially sound. Again, compliance with this mandate presumes competence to make such an assessment. Further, the same special circumstances faced by exclusive agents regarding "best product" advice applies here as well. Chapters 3–5 explore this mandate.

Competence

Like fairness, competence lies at the very core of professionalism. Competence is a synthesis of education and experience. It begins with mastery of a common body of knowledge required for the market served by the agent. The maintenance of competence requires a commitment to learning and professional improvement that must continue throughout one's professional life. Competence represents the attainment and maintenance of a level of understanding and knowledge that enables the agent to render services with facility and acumen.

Competence also has several dimensions.

First, an agent should have mastered the body of knowledge necessary to provide competent advice to clients within his or her target market. This mastery ideally would have its foundation in formal education, such as a bachelor's degree. One or more advanced degrees directly relevant to the agent's business (e.g., MBA, MS, JD, etc.) suggest a deeper commitment and understanding of the relevant body of knowledge. Of course, even individuals without college degrees could have achieved the necessary mastery of the body of knowledge required for his or her target market, but most such agents focus on lower-to-middle income market segments.

Evidence of mastery of the relevant body of knowledge for a life insurance agent often is demonstrated through holding appropriate professional certifications and membership and active participation in relevant professional societies. As noted earlier, common designations include the CLU, CFP®, and ChFC®.

Second, as a complement to the above mandate, an agent should refrain from giving advice in areas for which the agent does not have requisite training and competence, obviously including unauthorized areas. This mandate

---

[3]Code at A1.6a.

limits the scope of an agent's advice to that which is compatible with the body of knowledge mastered by the agent, which, most commonly, should comport with his or her target market. Most agents focus their sales efforts in simpler family situations. They usually lack the knowledge and training to be confident of offering sound advice in more complex estate, family, professional, and business circumstances. This mandate dictates that agents should refuse, seek consultation on, or refer to others those professional engagements that exceed the personal competence of the agent.

Third, the agent should have had a meaningful amount of business experience within his or her target market. Many observers recommend a minimum experience of five years. Of course, an agent with less experience may have support services or colleagues who can provide reasonable assurance that a lack of experience will not be detrimental to the client. Also, not every situation requires a highly trained agent.

Fourth, agents should enhance their knowledge in all relevant areas in which they are engaged through, among others, participating in continuing education activities. At a minimum, this tenet requires the agent to meet the continuing education standards set by the state and all professional societies and associations in which the agent is a member. For example, the SFSP requires 30 hours of qualified study every two years, as does the CFP Board of Standards. One would hope to find relevant activities beyond these minimal requirements.

Integrity

Integrity requires the agent to conduct him- or herself with candor, honesty, and trustworthiness. The agent is to observe the principles of objectivity and independence. This tenet also embeds several elements.

First, producers should respect the confidentiality of their clients' business, professional, and personal information and not disclose it except as business necessity or the law dictates. In the course of offering advice and helping clients qualify for needed life insurance, agents ordinarily learn information that can be quite sensitive. Agents and those who work for or with them should follow clearly established confidentiality safeguards and guidelines.

Second, an agent's business affairs should be conducted with the greatest emphasis on ethical behavior. Ethical responsibilities flow from society's unwritten standards of moral conduct and are not defined solely or entirely by either law and regulation or codes of professional conduct. One test of ethical behavior is whether the producer's peers would find his or her conduct above reproach if they were fully aware of all aspects of that conduct. As with confidentiality, agents and others with whom they work or are responsible should work under clearly established ethical guidelines.

Third, agent communication with existing and prospective clients and the general public should be objective, truthful, candid, and not have the tendency to mislead. The SFSP Code comments on this element as follows:

> Financial service professionals will not use words or make statements in brochures or advertising materials or in any client communication that create false impressions or have the potential to mislead. For example, products salespersons should not refer to themselves as financial/estate planners/consultants, if they do not provide these services. Words such as deposits or contributions should not be used to describe life insurance premiums. Life insurance policies should not be referred to as retirement plans. . . . Financial service professionals must avoid creating the impression that they represent a number of companies when they place business with only a few companies.[4]

Diligence

Diligence imposes the responsibility to conduct one's business affairs with thoughtfulness, patience, timeliness, thoroughness, and consistency. Several tangible aspects of diligence include the following:

First, recommendations to clients should be made only after acquiring a thorough understanding of the client's financial needs, goals, and circumstances, followed by appropriate research and documentation. This mandate lies at the heart of **due care,** which requires an agent to conduct his or her business affairs with diligence, prudence, and competence, including investigation of the quality, value, and suitability of recommended insurance. (As applied to variable products and other securities, the roughly equivalent term is **due diligence**—the process by which a broker/dealer ensures that an investment is as represented. The terms carry different legal connotations, with the latter carrying weightier legal consequences.)

An increasingly important aspect of an agent's responsibilities stems from common law standards of conduct. Generally, advisors must exercise at least that degree of care exhibited by a reasonably prudent person of their peer group. Thus, the conduct of an attorney expert in tax law will be judged against that of other tax attorneys. Similarly, a life insurance agent's conduct will be judged against that of other, reasonably prudent insurance agents.

The situation, however, can be complex. An agent professing no particular expertise other than that required of a licensed agent will not ordinarily be held to as high a standard of conduct as agents who hold themselves out as experts. The courts have been quite willing to judge agents' responsibilities and conduct on the degree of expertise that they themselves profess to have.

---

[4]Code at A4.4a.

Thus, in one case, an agent was found negligent in failing to arrange properly the ownership of a life insurance policy to fund a business continuation agreement, the consequence of which was unanticipated state and federal estate taxation.[5] In another case, a life insurance agent was held liable for selling a policy unsuitable to the insured's needs.[6]

Second, agents should cooperate fully with other relevant professionals in the client's interest. A track record of the agent having done so helps minimize concern by clients that their interests may fall victim to others' faulty communication or worse.

Third, agents should act with competency and consistency in promptly discharging their responsibilities to clients. Implicit in this mandate is a requirement to deliver superior service. One of the most important elements in this requirement is that the agent monitor and ensure that periodic information is provided to clients concerning their policies' performance and any material changes in insurer financial solidity and that clients understand the information. Of course, the necessary administrative arrangements must be in place to deliver superior service. Chapter 17 explores this mandate.

Fourth, and related to the third mandate, agents should be committed to and have a demonstrated record of effectively representing their clients' interests to insurers not only at time of sale but on an ongoing basis. This client-centric approach is facilitated by the agent having strong relationships with relevant insurers, which creates leverage for the agent when negotiating with insurers on the client's behalf. This leverage can come about in a variety of ways including from the agent having a history of placing quality business with the insurer, being recognized for his or her underwriting expertise (which facilitates negotiation with insurers on client risk), being recognized for his or her product expertise (which enhances initial and ongoing product due care), and being involved in important public policy issues the outcomes of which could negatively affect client planning and taxation.

A good proxy for overall client satisfaction with agents is the lapse rate on their business. A high first-year voluntary policy termination (lapse) rate by the agent's policyholders suggests that something is likely amiss. Maybe policyholders discovered that the policies sold by the agent did not offer good value, contrary to his or her assertions to the contrary, or that they were ill suited in light of the client's needs, goals, and circumstances. Either conclusion may not speak positively about the agent's diligence and general professionalism. Reasons external to the agent could explain high lapse rates,

---

[5] State Farm Life v. Fort Wayne National Bank, 474 N.E. 2d 524 (Ind. 1985).
[6] Knox v. Anderson, 159 F. Supp. 795, 162 F. Supp. 338 (D. Haw. 1958), 297 F.2d 702 (9th Cir. 1961) cert. denied, 370 U.S. 915 (1962).

such as the insurer suddenly changing the underlying pricing of newly issued policies (but why didn't the agent know of this possibility?) or the agent's target market experiencing economic turmoil (was such reasonably foreseeable?) or the agent's target market exhibiting high lapse rates, as with low income households (is the agent attempting to sell in other market segments for which he is not qualified?).

Sources of Information on Agents

The agent (him- or herself) often is the main source of information about the agent. Inevitably, the demeanor of the person will influence opinions as will the attitude and professionalism exhibited. Beyond these factors, the advisor who does not already know the agent may wish to use the short questionnaire that we include as Appendix 1. Its answers can provide greater insight into an agent's professional experience and conduct.

In addition, the advisor may wish to make inquiries about the agent with the state insurance regulatory authority. The insurance department can provide information about any complaints and the nature of the licensing of the individual.

For agents licensed to sell variable life policies, information can be sought from FINRA about the individual. FINRA's web site (www.finra.org) under "BrokerCheck Reports" provides a range of information about registered firms and brokers. It shows the person's credentials, current registrations, exams passed, and previous employment. It also shows information about client disputes with the individual as well as any regulatory actions taken against him or her. Registration agreeing to a list of terms and conditions for use is required, but it is free.

Conclusions

The advice given by the selling life insurance agent can be of enormous significance to customers. Most agents undeniably offer sound advice, but not all are capable of doing so, especially for more complex situations. Even if an insurance policy offers good value and the insurer is financially sound, poorly conceived beneficiary designations, policyowner arrangements, policy funding, policy options, and a host of other elements can wreck the client's financial plans. Conversely, the most logically conceived policy arrangements can fall apart if the policy proves to be unnecessarily costly or the insurer suffers financial reverses.

Producers should conduct their business with fairness, competence, integrity, and diligence. Producers whose conduct comports with these attributes have a vital role to play in minimizing undesirable client outcomes. Toward this end, the questionnaire at Appendix 1 might be useful in situations for which an advisor has been asked by a client to offer advice concerning a life insurance program proposed by an agent who may not be well known to the advisor. We hope that it might be useful as well for agents to apply it to themselves.

Assessing Life Insurance Company Financial Strength

The Importance and Nature of Life Insurance Financial Strength

3

THIS CHAPTER BEGINS PART II of the guide, a three-chapter analysis on assessing life insurance company financial strength.[1] Here we discuss the importance of making such an assessment on behalf of the client and explore the conflicting incentives that life insurer managers have to maintain financial strength while avoiding holding excess capital. We next offer an overview of insurers' investments and financial operations that determine financial strength. The two chapters that follow delve into state efforts to reinforce insurer financial solidity and how rating agencies and other information sources can be used in evaluating life insurer financial strength.

Why Assessing Life Insurer Financial Strength is Important

The life insurance industry is among the most heavily regulated industries doing business today. In an effort to protect policyholders, life insurance companies are subject to conservative

Authored by Harold D. Skipper.
[1] This chapter draws in part from Kenneth Black, Jr. and Harold D. Skipper, Jr., *Life and Health Insurance* (13th ed.; Upper Saddle River, NJ: Prentice-Hall, 2000), Chapter 11.

rules and requirements that involve, among other factors, how companies manage their finances and support the products they issue to customers. However, life insurance companies can and sometimes do fail. Because the failure of a life insurance company can have far graver consequences for its customers than can the failure of most other corporations (such as the failure of our TV manufacturer—see Chapter 2), greater scrutiny is warranted.

The Special Nature of Life Insurance

Embedded within life insurance policies are long term, intangible financial promises not found with other financial or consumer products. These promises differ from those of most other products in at least four important respects.

- *First*, the promises embedded within a life insurance policy usually are of considerably longer duration than those found with other financial instruments and consumer products. The insurer states, essentially, that it intends to fulfill all of its obligations under the insurance contract whenever it is called upon to do so, whether today or 60 or more years from now. No other financial product contains guarantees and options of such potentially long durations. Much can happen to the financial solidity of any firm over so long a period.
- *Second*, in insurance, the guarantee *is* the product. There is no inherent value in the pieces of paper called an insurance policy. Only the promises embedded in the policy have value, and they can be no more secure than the financial security of the entity that makes them.
- *Third*, as we note in Chapters 1 and 2, because of the great information gap that exists between life insurance buyers and sellers, buyers cannot easily assess the integrity of the insurer and, hence, cannot easily assess the value of its promises.
- *Finally,* combining the information gap issue with the fact that life insurance differs from most other financial and consumer products in that it touches on the sorts of psychological issues discussed in Chapter 1, the issue of insurer financial solidity should weigh even more heavily in the purchase equation. Life insurance is commonly purchased to provide financial security for those about whom the insured cares most deeply. The amounts involved often run into the millions, so the purchase should be undertaken with considerable thought and analysis.

For these four basic reasons, the financial strength and integrity of a life insurance company are more vital to its customers than is true of most other enterprises.

Life Insurers in Financial Difficulty: Lessons from the Past

While far fewer life insurance companies than banks got into financial difficulty in the recession that began in 2008, life insurers are not immune to financial difficulty, with some 616 having become financially impaired in some way since 1976.[2] We follow the A.M. Best definition of a **financially impaired insurer** as one for which its:

- ◆ Ability to conduct normal operations is impaired or,
- ◆ Capital and surplus have been determined to be insufficient to meet legal requirements or
- ◆ Financial condition has triggered regulatory concern.

Figure 3-1 shows the number of impairments per year since 1976. At first glance, the number of impairments may seem large, but it represents an average annual impairment rate of somewhat less than 19 companies per year, representing an annual average financial impairment frequency (FIF) of less than 0.9 percent. This amounts to less than one in 114 life insurers having become financially impaired annually over this study period.

FIGURE 3-1: Financially Impaired Life Insurers per Year (1976–2009)

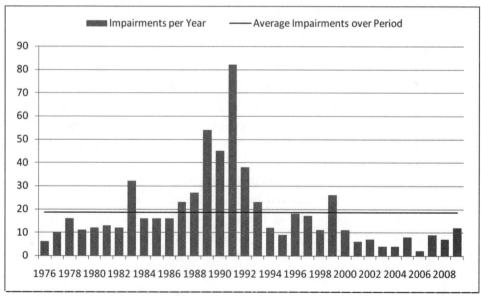

Source: A. M. Best Co.

---

[2]"L/H Insurers Grow More Vulnerable to Financial Impairment Due to Losses," *1976–2008 Impairment Study*. (A.M. Best; Oldwick, NJ, 2009), p. 12.

Fortunately, almost 92 percent of financially impaired insurers have been comparatively young and small, with capital and surplus of less than $20 million. The average annual FIF for these small insurers was 2.3 percent whereas the average for large insurers was only 0.03 percent. Additionally, most have gotten into difficulty because of adverse results from writing accident and health insurance.

Lest we leave an erroneous impression, we should also note that large, well-known life insurers have also become financially impaired. The list includes such well known firms as Confederation Life (1994), Executive Life (1991), Fidelity Bankers Life (1991), Fidelity Mutual Life (1992), First Capital Life (1991), General American Life (1999), Integrity Life (1999), Kentucky Central Life (1993), Mid-Continent Life (1997), Monarch Life (1991), and Mutual Benefit Life (1991), with the year of impairment shown in parenthesis. The year 1991 was an especially notable one in this regard, as shown in Figure 3-1. More than 80 life insurers became financially impaired that year. However, they accounted for less than 3 percent of total industry premiums written.

Unlike most other years, several large insurers are included in the 1991 total. The failures of 146-year-old Mutual Benefit Life and of Executive Life, California's largest domestic life insurer, were especially shocking. These two failures sent shock waves through both the insurance industry and the entire financial community. Only one year prior to their failures, both insurers were rated in the "secure" category by A.M. Best, a major insurance company rating agency (see Chapter 5).

The Executive Life failure holds especially important lessons for advisors. Its insurance products were routinely among the most competitive based on illustrated values, with interest crediting rates that were the envy of its competitors. It was able to support high interest crediting rates by investing heavily in high-yield ("junk") bonds. When the junk bond market collapsed, so too did Executive Life.

The rating agencies gave Executive Life among their most secure rating three years, then two years, then even one year before its failure. They acknowledged that they missed the mark (not unlike the situation with various derivative products in 2008). Even if the rating agencies "missed the mark" at that time, many within the insurance marketing community did not. A large number of agents, brokers, and marketing organizations refused to place business with Executive Life, because, having conducted their own due care evaluations, did not like what they found in its investment portfolio and the word on the street about Executive Life was negative. The moral: rely on rating agencies but be a bit skeptical, an approach we explore in Chapter 5.

We should note that rating agencies learn from their mistakes and have demonstrated an ability to tighten up their reviews and ratings in response to adverse events. Also note that regulations exist to protect policyholders of financially impaired insurers. A state insurance regulator works with the financially impaired insurer to facilitate either rehabilitation or liquidation of the company in whole or in part. The primary concern of state insurance regulators is ensuring that insurers honor their promises and have the ability to pay policyholder benefits. In addition, state guaranty associations support payment of policyholder benefits of financially impaired insurers. In recent insolvencies, 100 percent of death benefits and more than 90 percent of policyholder benefits have been covered in full, although with inevitable delays. Refer to Chapter 4 for an overview of regulations that protect policyholders.

A comment is in order regarding the world's most infamous financial impairment of an insurance group—AIG. AIG was well known for its many insurance companies worldwide, including a major presence within the U.S. life and nonlife insurance sectors. AIG's financial impairment was neither precipitated by nor related to its mainstream insurance operations.

Less well known was AIG's many financial activities outside of mainstream insurance. Its financial products division was heavily involved in selling **credit default swaps**—financial instruments bought by investors to insure against defaults on bonds. When the financial crisis hit in full force in 2008, innumerable bonds went into default, resulting in massive calls on AIG. Reserves were grossly insufficient to cover them. Because of concern that the failure of AIG could precipitate a domino-like failure of other major financial institutions, the federal government agreed to bail out AIG. AIG's mainstream insurance subsidiaries, including its life subsidiaries, were not directly affected by the impairment of the holding company. In fact, state insurance regulation protected the insurance assets.

Insurer Management of Financial Strength

The managements of life insurance companies, including their boards of directors, are responsible for knowing their companies' financial strength and determining the best course of action relative to it. Although it might seem that the natural inclination would be for them to aim to become and remain exceptionally strong financially, the incentives impinging on management are ambiguous. They have incentives both to have great financial strength and, simultaneously, to avoid holding too much capital and surplus.

Incentives to Have Strong Financials
Life insurance executives have natural motivations to ensure insurer financial strength and profitability. They and their employees have good jobs for which they are well compensated, and they would like to keep them. Executives and boards of directors also understand the importance of their companies being

sufficiently strong financially to garner decent ratings from the rating agencies and to avoid undue attention and criticism from state insurance regulators. Low ratings can be discouraging to the field force and can penalize sales. Unusual attention or criticism by regulators is always bad for any business, but can be especially damaging to businesses that rely on trust, as with life insurance.

To secure decent ratings, a life insurer must have sound financials, meaning that it operates profitably and has a strong balance sheet. A strong balance sheet is one in which assets exceed liabilities by a sufficient margin to enable the insurer to weather adverse operational and economic conditions with minimal disruption to operations and without provoking regulatory concern about the insurer's financial condition. The excess of assets over liabilities, commonly called a **net worth**, is referred to in insurance parlance as **capital and surplus** or sometimes simply as **surplus** and sometimes simply as **capital**. As we discuss later in this chapter, the nature and composition of the assets and liabilities are also key components for assessing financial strength, as are an insurer's liquidity, leverage, operational performance, and other characteristics.

Incentives to Avoid Holding Excess Capital

It is axiomatic, that, to the extent that an insurer's customers value financial soundness and are able to make reasoned assessments of that soundness, it is in the insurer's interest to strive to attain and then maintain financial soundness. Doing so is good for business. To the extent a company's board of directors subscribes to such a goal, it should ensure that the company's executives also are fully on board with the goal and put in place the necessary management incentives and controls to operationalize the goal successfully. However, how much security is enough? Can an insurer be too secure, meaning that it holds too much capital?

While policyholders want financially secure insurers (even if few know how to go about assessing financial security), they also want low-cost life insurance. This means that they want the insurer to credit high interest rates to policy values, to assess low loading and mortality charges, or to pay high dividends. Herein lies the dilemma for insurer management. The lower the interest rate credited and the higher the loading and mortality charges, the more financially secure the insurer likely will be. Doing so can build surplus. But doing so also makes for more expensive (i.e., less competitive) policies, at least for current policyholders.

We say "at least for current policyholders" because an insurer that accumulates excess surplus presently—called "hoarding surplus" and "surplus surplus" historically—can, in theory, offer lower-cost life insurance at some point in the future because of having retained excess surplus and thereby having more investments. Of course, the problem with this approach is that the current generation of policyholders would be paying more for their insurance in order to subsidize some future generations of policyholders. In private transactions, who among us wishes to provide financial subsidies for a future generation of strangers?

This scenario is a reason that existing policyholders who are not treated equitably may take their business elsewhere via policy exchanges. Moreover, poorly performing policies discourage new purchases by clients, with loss of associated profits. Management should administer policy performance equitably to sustain an ongoing profitable business. In addition, businesses have an underlying need to employ their funds effectively if they are to realize their target return on capital. Failure to do so penalizes overall financial performance.

Hoarding surplus not only can lead to issues of lower returns on capital and intergenerational equity, in the past it has led to insurer practices that state legislators have found offensive, such as excessive agent commissions and executive salaries and perquisites and overly lavish insurer buildings and offices. Some states have enacted laws limiting the amount of surplus that insurers may accumulate on behalf of participating policyholders because of these past abuses of consumer trust.

Thus, insurer management must strike a balance between maintaining a strong financial position and ensuring that policyholders receive good value through their policies. The first priority is the maintenance of a strong financial position, but we should recognize that this objective has limits.

Overview of Life Insurers' Investments

Insurance companies' financial solidity depends greatly on the nature and quality of their investments. As an aid to understanding, we present this short overview of the typical life insurer's investment portfolio.[3] Of course, the assets held by life insurers back the liabilities that arise from in force policies. Asset growth occurs when cash inflows are greater than cash outflows.

Life insurers' investments are required to be divided between two accounts that differ in the nature of the liabilities for which the assets are being held and invested. An insurer's **general account** supports guaranteed, interest crediting contractual obligations, such as those arising from traditional and many contemporary life insurance policies (including whole life and uni-

---

[3]This section draws from *Life Insurers Fact Book* (Washington, D.C.: American Council of Life Insurers, 2009).

versal life). An insurer's **separate accounts** support liabilities arising from pass-through products for which all investment risk is borne by the policy-holder, as with variable life insurance. State laws allow assets in separate accounts to be invested without regard to the many restrictions of general account investments due to their pass-through nature and because policyholders have control of asset allocations. Separate account investments usually are riskier than general account investments, as policyholders purchase variable products to access equity market returns.

Importantly, variable life policyholders must look mainly or solely to the values of the separate account were the insurer to fail. Other than the guaranteed benefits within the contract—a component that makes it important for variable policyholders to pay attention to financial strength—the insurer itself ordinarily has no obligation toward such policies. In addition, the separate account affords protection from general creditors of the life insurer were it to become insolvent.

In contrast, the insurer itself and all general account assets back policies whose liabilities are required to be held in the general account. The general account assets are not specifically earmarked for these liabilities, although policyholders have priority to these assets over general creditors. It is for this reason that we are primarily concerned here about the financial solidity of the insurer in relation to its general account obligations and attendant policies.

Figures 3-2a and 3-2b show the broad distribution of investments for life insurers for 2009 for their general accounts and their separate accounts. Total of investments held at year-end 2009 was $3.3 trillion in general accounts, unchanged from 2008, and $1.6 trillion in separate accounts, up 14 percent from the previous year.

FIGURE 3-2a: Life Insurer General Account Investments (2009)

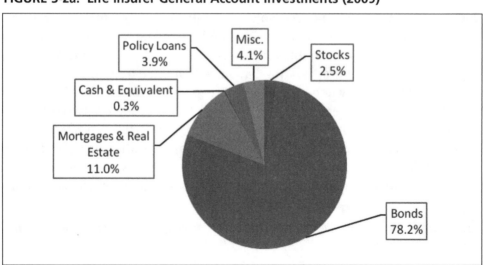

FIGURE 3-2b: Life Insurer Separate Account Investments (2009)

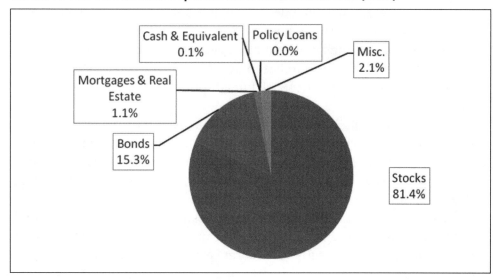

As can be seen, investments fall into these five main categories, each of which is summarized briefly below:

- Bonds,
- Mortgages and real estate,
- Stocks,
- Policy loans, and
- Cash and miscellaneous.

Bonds

Bonds, also referred to as **fixed income securities**, are publicly traded debt securities under which the borrower (seller of the bond) agrees to pay a fixed amount of interest periodically and repay a fixed principal at bond maturity. The issuer's obligation to make bond payments takes priority over the claims of the issuer's other lenders and of stockholders. Bonds fall into two generic categories: those issued by corporations and those issued by governments and government agencies. More than three-quarters of all bonds held by life insurers are corporate bonds.

Life insurers are significant investors in the corporate bond market, having been the largest such institutional holders since the 1930s. **Private placements**—where the financial institution negotiates directly with the corporation over the terms of the offering—account for a sizable share of life insurer investments in corporate bonds. Life insurers are the major lenders in the private placement market.

Bonds of the U.S. government include U.S. Treasury securities and others issued by federal agencies or sponsored by the federal government, such as the Federal National Mortgage Association and the Federal Home Loan Banks. Government bonds include guaranteed, special revenue, and other issues of the 50 states, the District of Columbia, Puerto Rico, and U.S. territories and possessions and their political subdivisions. The vast majority of long-term government securities purchased by life insurers are in U.S. government securities, as opposed to those of foreign governments and international agencies.

Bonds have limited lives and expire on a given date, called the issue's maturity date, ordinarily not greater than 30 years. Because of the long duration of life insurer's liabilities, the greatest proportion of bonds acquired by them have maturity dates of 20 years or greater. Relatively few bonds of maturity dates of less than five years are acquired.

As with all bond purchasers, insurers investigate the quality of the bonds that they consider acquiring. The higher the quality of the bond, the lower its risk, and the higher the degree of assurance that insurers will be paid their money back at maturity. Consequently, high-quality bonds are ideal for long-term capital accumulation. At the same time, the higher the quality, the lower the credited interest rate, other things being the same.

Included within this fixed-income security category are **mortgage backed securities** (MBSs), which are bonds backed by residential or commercial mortgages. While MBSs are included within the bond category, their risk profiles and values follow those of the real estate market. These securities comprise about 17 percent of insurers' total investments.

Because a life insurance company guarantees the payment of certain amounts to policyowners in the future, bonds, particularly those rated as investment grade, are their most popular investment medium with regard to general account products. Performance in this area can have a substantial impact on product performance. As seen in Figure 3-2b, bonds are much less prominent with regard to variable products supported by separate accounts, as policyholders direct their allocations primarily toward equities.

Mortgages and Real Estate

Mortgages are debt instruments by which the borrower gives the lender (i.e., the insurer in this case) a lien on property as security for the repayment of the loan. Mortgage loans have long been the second largest category of investments within insurers' general accounts. They are much less important within separate accounts. Together with real estate, they comprised about 11.0 percent of life insurer investments in 2009, as shown in Figure 3-2a. Some 93 percent of these mortgage loans are on commercial properties, the balance being on residential and farm properties. Historically, mortgages have been considered less risky than stocks and riskier than bonds. Life insurer investments in real estate are comparatively small. Most real estate is held to produce income, with much smaller proportions held for sale and for company use as home and regional offices.

The 11.0 percent figure is somewhat misleading. We must take account of the MBSs included within the bond category, thereby taking life insurer investments in mortgages and real estate to 28.0 percent of total investments. The recent financial crisis has taken and continues to take its toll on life insurers' mortgage and related investments. During 2008–09, insurers took financial hits from residential MBS defaults. Predictions are that they will take additional, perhaps quite large, financial hits from commercial MBSs and mortgages during the 2010–12 period.

Stocks

A **stock** is a financial instrument signifying ownership in a corporation represented by shares that are a claim on its assets and earnings. Historically, stocks have been a small percentage of the general account assets of life insurers because their price and earnings volatility did not match well with the guaranteed, fixed-dollar nature of insurers' general account liabilities. Stocks have an additional cost to insurers in the form of capital requirements being higher than fixed income investments. On the other hand, stocks figure prominently in separate account investments as policyholders tend to allocate their funds to equities. Figures 3-2a and 3-2b illustrate the great differences in investment allocations between the two accounts. Of course, stocks are generally riskier than bonds but carry a higher expected return over the long run.

Policy Loans

Life insurance policyholders have a contractual right to secure loans under their policies for an amount up to the policies' cash surrender values. Monies used to extend these policy loans would otherwise be invested to earn returns for the insurer, so the insurer naturally charges the policyholder interest for these loans to make good some of the lost investment earnings. Interest rates are modest and cannot exceed limits set in state insurance laws. Policy loans are secure investments as the loans may not exceed the policies' cash surrender values. When the policy is terminated by the policyholder or matures as a death claim, any policy loan is automatically deducted from policy proceeds.

Cash and Miscellaneous

Life insurers hold small amounts of cash or cash equivalent investments such as money market instruments, as shown in Figure 3-2. Cash is necessary to ensure that cash outflow demands can be readily met and occurs naturally because of insurers' cash flow characteristics. Additionally, insurers hold modest amounts of other investments that do not fall into the above categories.

Assessing Insurer Financial Strength

An assessment of an insurer's financial strength, as we have alluded to elsewhere, is essential but not simple. This section explores some of the financial elements of insurers that make up an assessment. Our purpose is not to arm the advisor with the full panoply of tools essential for such an analysis—although the ones discussed below would be included in such an analysis. Rather, we seek to provide background to enable the advisor to better interpret and appreciate the significance of financial information about insurers provided by rating agencies, state insurance regulators, insurers themselves, and others.

We should mention the sometimes debated issue of whether stock or mutual life insurers are the more secure financially. In fact, the debate is largely academic, because buyers purchase life insurance from a specific insurer, not from the universe of stock or mutual insurers, and a given mutual insurer may be sounder than a given stock insurer or vice versa. The basic issues underlying financial security are sound and efficient management and adequate supervision and control by government authorities, not the insurer's organizational form.

Publicly available financial data on life insurers are, for the most part, based on **statutory accounting principles**, the accounting conventions laid down by insurance regulators and required to be followed by life insurance companies, being based on the notion that an insurer is worth only that which it can use to meet its present obligations—and those obligations (policy liabilities) are themselves generally calculated conservatively. This approach may be contrasted with more widely used **generally accepted accounting principles** (GAAP) that are predicated on the concept of a business being a going concern. Stock analysts typically use GAAP data.

As SAP is more conservative and geared towards the ability to meet current financial obligations, analyses of life insurers' financial strength typically are built on SAP data. SAP data are gathered by rating agencies and others from the required annual financial statement submissions by insurers to the insurance regulators in each state in which they are licensed. Insurers are also required to submit abbreviated SAP financial information quarterly.

The traditional elements of financial analysis include (1) capital and surplus adequacy, (2) leverage, (3) asset quality and diversification, (4) liquidity, and (5) operational performance. We discuss ratio analysis exclusively. A problem with ratio analysis is that it fails to consider interrelationships among values, so it omits some potentially important information. Additionally, while this chapter's focus is on financial strength, indirect elements of an insurer's operations can have bearings on this strength, including market position and brand, distribution, product focus and diversification, and competence of management. These elements are included in the insurer reports prepared by the rating agencies, as discussed in Chapter 5.

This overview gives a flavor for why certain relationships can prove to be of vital importance. We make no attempt to suggest acceptable values for the ratios. Each ratio should be assessed against prevailing industry values at the time of any evaluation and further considered in light of the insurer's pattern of assets and liabilities, a task beyond the scope of our discussion.

Capital and Surplus Adequacy

The relative level of an insurer's capital and surplus (surplus) may be considered as the most important factor in assessing an insurer's financial condition. Insurers need surplus to absorb unanticipated fluctuations in asset and liability values and operational results, as the recent economic recession has reminded them. The greater an insurer's surplus relative to its obligations, the more secure it is, other things being the same.

In evaluating the adequacy of an insurer's surplus, it is necessary to make certain adjustments in the values shown on insurers' regulatory balance sheets. SAP requires the establishment of certain liabilities for the purpose of minimizing fluctuations in the value of insurer surplus. These are not true liabilities, as they do not represent amounts actually owed to anyone. As such, they should be excluded from all SAP liability values and added to SAP capital and surplus figures. All references to surplus in this chapter should be understood to have been so adjusted.

As an absolute figure, the amount of an insurer's capital and surplus has little meaning. Two surplus ratios, however, do offer insight into financial solidity. The first ratio is:

> *Surplus adequacy = Surplus / Liabilities*

The higher the ratio, the greater the indication of financial strength, although surplus and reserve levels can vary substantially, depending on an insurer's mix and age of business. The ratio ignores the degree of conservatism that may be inherent in one insurer's reserve calculation but not found in the calculation of another. For this reason, it is interpreted with care and ordinarily with similarly situated insurers.

A second useful measure of surplus adequacy is the rate of surplus formation:

> *Rate of surplus formation = Growth rate of surplus / Growth rate of liabilities*

Calculated over a reasonable time period, such as five years, this ratio ideally should be positive. A consistent, substantial increase in surplus relative to liabilities suggests that the insurer's financial security is increasing. The higher the ratio, the better, *ceteris paribus*. Other measures of surplus adequacy are sometimes used. Most are variations or refinements on the above two ratios.

Leverage

Leverage is a measure of how intensively a company uses its debt versus capital and surplus. Of course, debt is a liability and not part of equity capital. Leverage increases return on equity, but it also increases risk due to required interest and principle payments. In the context of insurance, three measures of leverage are commonly used. The first is the ratio of liabilities to surplus. The lower the ratio, the less the leverage. This ratio is the reciprocal of the surplus adequacy test discussed above, and, therefore, it is simply another way of viewing the same thing. Either ratio is used in financial evaluations.

The second ratio measures the intensity of surplus use in premium writings:

> *Net premiums written ratio = (Net premiums written + Deposits) / Surplus*

The ratio measures an insurer's exposure to pricing errors, a major cause of life insurer failures. The higher the ratio, the greater the exposure, *ceteris paribus*. Ideally, this ratio should be used to compare insurers of comparable product mixes.

The third ratio measures the ability of an insurer to cover its recurring interest and dividend obligations without stress.

> *Earnings coverage ratio = Net operating gain / (Interest expense and preferred dividends)*

Net operating gain or, equivalently, *net gain from operations* is the approximate SAP equivalent of earnings under GAAP. Because of the volatility of NGFO, this ratio ideally would be calculated as an average or a trend over a reasonable period of time, such as five years. The higher the ratio, the better able is the insurer to meet its ongoing obligations.

Quality and Diversification of Assets

The lower the quality of an insurer's assets, the greater the surplus needed to absorb adverse fluctuations, *ceteris paribus*. Indeed, an insurer can appear to be in a strong surplus position yet, because of the riskiness of its assets, may be vulnerable.

Assets back an insurer's liabilities. **Admitted assets** are those that may be included in determining an insurer's solvency under SAP (i.e., those counted in measuring the excess of assets over liabilities). **Non-admitted assets** are not recognized by regulatory authorities in assessing solvency and include items such as furniture, certain equipment, and agents' balances. By diversifying their investments, companies minimize the volatility of their portfolios.

Bonds of average or below average quality (so-called non-investment grade) can yield higher returns, but the principal and payment of interest may also be at risk. Some portion of an insurer's bond portfolio also can be in or near default, thus risking loss of both principal and interest. Investment prudence is the key. Limited investment in bonds of average or below average quality is not considered imprudent.

The ratio of non-investment grade bonds to surplus reveals the extent to which an insurer's surplus could cover those bonds in the event that a severe economic downturn affected their performance. Therefore, the first asset quality ratio is:

> *Investment in non-investment grade bonds ratio = Non-investment grade bonds / Surplus*

Non-investment grade bonds is taken here to mean the sum of an insurer's investments in below investment grade bonds and bonds in or near default. Obviously, the lower the investment in such bonds the better, *ceteris paribus*. Note that this ratio captures any below investment grade MBSs.

Next to bonds, mortgages are insurers' most prevalent general account investment. The trend in recent years has been toward commercial mortgages. In adverse economic times, insurers may experience adverse mortgage performance, as with the situation during the economic crisis that began in 2008. The ratio of mortgages in default to surplus indicates the extent to which an insurer's surplus can cover mortgage defaults. Thus:

> *Mortgage default ratio = Mortgages in default / Surplus*

Mortgages in default is taken here to be the sum of an insurer's mortgages on which interest is overdue by more than three months, mortgages in the process of foreclosure, and properties acquired in satisfaction of debt. The lower the mortgage default ratio, the better. Note that this ratio does not capture MBSs in default.

Another potentially important asset quality ratio is:

> *Investment in common stock ratio = Investment in common stock / Surplus*

Common stock value can fluctuate greatly from year to year. This ratio is an indication of the extent to which an insurer's surplus could be affected by these fluctuations.

Liquidity

Adequate liquidity should be maintained to meet an insurer's expected and unexpected cash needs. Otherwise, assets may have to be sold at disadvantageous prices. One useful measure of liquidity is:

> *Current liquidity ratio = Unaffiliated investments, excluding mortgages and real estate / Liabilities*

Unaffiliated investments refers to the assets of an insurer made up of investments other than bonds, stocks, and other investments held in affiliated enterprises, less property occupied by the insurer, typically its home office. The current liquidity ratio, therefore, measures the proportion of net liabilities covered by cash and unaffiliated investments other than mortgages and real estate. Mortgages and real estate are excluded as they are not always readily convertible into cash. The lower the ratio, the more vulnerable is the insurer to liquidity problems.

Three other useful liquidity ratios of importance are:

> *Affiliated investments ratio = Investments in affiliated companies / Surplus*

> *Investment in real estate ratio = Investment in real estate / Surplus*

> *Non-admitted assets ratio = Non-admitted assets / Surplus*

These three ratios measure the extent to which an insurer's investment portfolio may be illiquid. Also, these asset classes often produce no income, and excessive investment in them may result in financial difficulty. The lower these ratios, the better, *ceteris paribus*.

Operational Performance

Sound operational performance is essential for an enduring, strong insurer. It reflects the ability and competence of management. Insurers with comparable product mixes provide a more relevant basis for comparison. Results of insurers with substantially dissimilar life product mixes are subject to misinterpretation. For example, an insurer specializing in individual term life insurance would most likely show a higher expense ratio than one specializing in group term life insurance.

More than a single year should be examined to detect unusual trends and variations, as many factors may distort results. Five operational performance ratios are potentially important. The first is:

Return on equity = Net gain from operations / Surplus

This ratio reflects the return on an insurer's capital and surplus from insurance operations and investments. The higher an insurer's return on equity, the more effectively it uses owner funds. On the other hand, a high ratio can reflect excessive leverage or low capitalization.

An insurer's investment yield is a potentially important operational performance factor as well as an indicator of product performance. The ratio is:

Yield on investments = Net investment income / Invested assets

---

This ratio reflects how well investments are being managed. It does not include realized and unrealized capital gains (losses). The higher the yield, the better, other things being the same. Unfortunately, other things rarely are the same. A higher yield may reflect higher risk, as we noted above with regard to the failure of Executive Life. This is another reason why the asset quality evaluation is important.

Realized and unrealized capital gains and losses can be important components of insurers' investment performance. The following ratio includes such gains (losses):

Total return on investments = (Net investment income + Capital gains) / Invested assets

---

The rough insurer counterpart to return on sales is measured by the ratio of net operating gain to total income. That is:

Net operating gain ratio = Net gain from operations / Total operating income

---

Total operating income basically is the sum of premium and investment income. This ratio is a measure of the average profitability within each dollar of revenue. Clearly, the higher the ratio the better. Again, however, results should be interpreted with caution and only over time because of the use of SAP data.

Finally, we are interested in how much an insurer spends in commissions to procure and maintain business and on overall expenses, as a percentage of premium and deposit income. The ratio is:

Expense ratio = (Commissions and expenses) / (Net premiums written + Deposits)

Commissions and expenses include all commissions paid through the sales channels and all other insurance expenses, taxes, and fees. The lower this ratio the better, other things being the same—which is rarely the case for this ratio.

Conclusions

Advisors should have a sound understanding as to why assessment of the financial strength of a life insurer is of critical importance to the purchase decision, as to the competing incentives that insurance company managements have in maintaining financial strength, and as to the components of financial strength. Even with this knowledge, an independent assessment of financial strength by the advisor remains a complex and daunting task for all but the most technically competent.

As we discuss in Chapter 5, advisors and insurance buyers must necessarily place the greatest weight on rating agencies' opinions as to a life insurer's financial strength. As we highlighted above and will explore in Chapter 5, rating agencies are not perfect, but their ratings have been found to be good predictors of insurers' financial health.

Life Insurer Financial Regulation and Policyholder Protections 4

THIS CHAPTER CONTINUES THE theme of Part II on assessing life insurer financial strength. Here we examine the mechanisms that state insurance regulators have at their disposal for preventing life insurer financial difficulty, identifying insurers that are getting into or have gotten into difficulty, and helping to resolve the consequences of financial impairment.[1] The chapter that follows completes this part of the *Guide* by exploring how rating agencies and other information sources can be used effectively to evaluate the financial condition of life insurers.

We begin this chapter with a short explanation of the nature and purpose of insurance regulation. There follows an overview of the main areas of such regulation, a discussion of solvency surveillance methods, and regulatory responses to financially impaired insurers. The chapter closes with discussions of the implications for policyholders of insurer financial difficulty and regulatory solvency intervention.

Authored by Harold D. Skipper.
[1]This chapter draws in part from Kenneth Black, Jr. and Harold D. Skipper, Jr., *Life and Health Insurance* (13th ed.; Upper Saddle River, NJ: Prentice-Hall, 2000), Chapter 35, and from "Who's Watching your Back? An Assessment of Life Insurance Policyholder Protections in the Wake of the Financial Downturn," M Financial Group, June 2009.

Nature and Purpose of Insurance Regulation

In a nontechnical sense, insurance is purchased in good faith. Consumers implicitly rely on the integrity of the insurers with which they deal. However, the complex nature of this future-deliverable affords the easy potential for customer abuse. The mission of insurance is security. If the suppliers of security are themselves perceived as insecure, the insurance system could easily break down. Private insurance cannot flourish without public confidence that it will function as promised. The government's duty is to ensure that this confidence is neither misplaced nor undermined.

Viewed in its simplest form, insurance regulation seeks to ensure that *quality, fairly-priced* products are *available* from *reliable* insurers. In the U.S., we believe that competition should be capable largely of ensuring that the *quality, fairly-priced,* and *available* goals are attained, with selective oversight by insurance regulators. Government intervention is most evident and needed to ensure that insurers are *reliable.*

Thus, insurance regulation, like banking regulation, is focused chiefly on monitoring the financial condition of companies to be able to prevent insolvencies and, where prevention falters, to deal with the consequences in an orderly, reasonable manner. Unlike banking solvency monitoring that aims to prevent risks to the entire banking system, insurance solvency monitoring is aimed more at protecting policyholders from losses occasioned by insurer insolvencies.

Areas of Insurance Regulation: Protecting Policyholders

For historical reasons, insurance regulation in the U.S. is conducted at the individual state level rather than at the federal level. Each state has its own body of insurance laws and regulations, which are designed to protect policyholders, and its own executive officer—either elected or appointed by the governor—who is charged with enforcing these laws and regulations. Such officers are most commonly titled **insurance commissioner**.

Each state insurance regulator is a member of the **National Association of Insurance Commissioners (NAIC)** which is a trade organization composed exclusively of such regulators. The NAIC seeks to promote the public interest by, among other things, promoting regulatory uniformity among the states through the promulgation of model laws and regulations. These models have no legal weight, but the hope is that states will pattern their own laws and regulations after those endorsed by the NAIC, thereby promoting uniformity. The NAIC has been successful to varying degrees in this effort, with financial reporting requirements being one of the most successful areas.

Life insurance is one of the most highly regulated financial services industries. State insurance departments are primarily focused on protecting the public by providing greater certainty that life insurance companies will remain solvent in order to meet contractual obligations (paying death claims and surrender values). Regulations also extend to company and agent licensing, application and policy form language, and insurer marketing practices. We introduce these areas below.

Organization and Licensing of Insurers

Insurers already established in one state and wishing to conduct business within another state must apply and qualify for a license from that state. Thus, insurers wishing to conduct business in all 50 states must comply with 50 states' requirements and procure 50 separate licenses. Each state must be satisfied that the applicant insurer meets all of its requirements before it will issue a license.

To organize a new life insurer, state insurance codes require the drafting of a charter that describes the insurer's name and location, the lines of insurance it plans to write, the powers of the organization, and its officers. Frequently, the method of internal organization must be specified. A responsible state official investigates the character of the incorporators, its proposed plan of operation, and its marketing and financial projections. State minimum capital and surplus or, for mutual insurers, minimum surplus requirements must be met. These minimums vary by state from a few hundred thousand dollars to $2 million and more.

Insurance Policy Forms and Rates

In most states, policy forms are required to be filed with the insurance commissioner. In many states, formal approval is required before an insurer may sell that policy in the state, and sometimes also application forms must be approved. The insurance commissioner utilizes both general and specific legal standards as a guide to determine the appropriateness of forms in the public interest. As the application of general standards creates problems for both commissioners and the industry, the NAIC has developed specific standards designed to implement the general standard.

Most jurisdictions require life insurance contract forms to contain certain provisions as prescribed in the laws of the states. These statutory provisions include clauses related to the grace period, premium payment, incontestability, entire contract, misstatement of age, annual apportionment of dividends, surrender values and options, policy loans, settlement options, and reinstatement. We discuss these provisions in Chapter 9.

Rates for individual life insurance are regulated only in an indirect sense. Competition is believed to be an adequate regulator over any tendencies to rate excessiveness. As a practical matter, rate adequacy is sometimes a problem, and it is believed that minimum reserve requirements (see below) and expense limitations are sufficient safeguards against rate inadequacy. The states of New York and Wisconsin have complex laws limiting the amount of expenses that can be incurred in the production of new business and the maintenance of business in force.

Most states require that dividends under participating (dividend paying) policies be apportioned and paid annually. A few states limit the amount of aggregate surplus that may be accumulated by a mutual insurer. Although announced specific standards do not exist, some commissioners review dividend apportionment formulas from time to time.

Marketing Practices

Broadly interpreted, state regulation of marketing practices includes control over the licensing of agents and brokers and over unfair trade practices. While not discussed here, regulation extends as well to life insurer cost and benefit disclosure and advertisements.

Agent Licensing

The statutes of all jurisdictions contain provisions for the licensing of resident and nonresident agents and brokers. No person may act as agent or broker within the jurisdiction without first obtaining a license. No insurer may issue a contract through or remunerate any person (other than for deferred compensation where the agent has ceased to participate in new business development) unless the person holds a valid license.

The procedure that must be followed in obtaining a license is similar in all states. The applicant must first file an application for a license in which he or she gives information regarding his or her character, experience, and general competence. Each insurer for which the applicant is to be licensed must submit a notice of appointment (or intention of appointment), together with a certificate of trustworthiness and competence signed by an officer of the insurer. After these formalities, the applicant must then pass an examination covering the lines of insurance for which a license is sought.

Several states require new licensees to undertake a certain minimum number of hours (e.g., 40) of formal training in insurance before they can sit for the state examination. In addition to establishing a minimum standard of competency, these examinations are said to reduce turnover and to contribute to the general upgrading of insurance representatives.

The agent's license may be perpetual until it is revoked or it may be subject to renewal at stipulated intervals. Several states require agents and brokers annually to undertake specific continuing education in their fields in order to renew their licenses. The license may be refused, revoked, or suspended by the commissioner, after notice and hearing, on the any of the following grounds:

- ◆ Willful violation of the law in his or her capacity as an agent;
- ◆ Fraudulent or dishonest practices;
- ◆ Untrustworthiness or incompetence; and
- ◆ Material misrepresentation in the application for his or her license.

Unfair Trade Practices

All jurisdictions have *Unfair Trade Practices Acts* applicable to insurance. Usually, these acts give the commissioner the power to investigate and examine and, after notice and hearing, to issue cease and desist orders, with penalties for violations. The acts are designed to prevent numerous activities deemed to be unfair, including rebating, twisting, misappropriation, and commingling of funds, each of which is discussed here.

Rebating is the act of giving something of value to an applicant in return for purchasing life insurance, most commonly in the form of the agent giving the applicant a portion of his or her commission. Rebating remains illegal in most states. Anti-rebating statutes evolved decades ago in response to perceived marketplace abuses. Traditional arguments against rebating have focused on concerns about insurer solvency, unfair discrimination, and the unique nature of insurance. Critics of anti-rebating statutes claim that the prohibition unfairly prevents buyers from negotiating fully with sellers. The states of Florida and California allow rebating, although guidelines require no unfair discrimination in the granting of rebates.

Twisting is the practice by an agent of inducing a policyowner through misrepresentation to replace an existing life insurance policy with the purchase of a new one. In contrast to simple **replacement**—discontinuing one policy to purchase another—twisting is illegal. The purchase of any life insurance policy can be a complicated transaction, but the dual transaction of terminating one policy to purchase another is doubly complicated. The consumer can more easily make a mistake. In recognition of this fact, several states have promulgated versions of the *NAIC Model Replacement Regulation* that require the disclosure of certain information considered pertinent to the proposed replacement decision, as we discuss in Chapter 18.

Agents often handle large amounts of their policyowners' money. **Misappropriation** or misuse of these funds even on a temporary basis is illegal. Related to misappropriation is the practice of **commingling** of funds, which is the combining of monies belonging to policyowners with those belonging to the agent.

Solvency

State insurance regulators are charged with the protection of the public interest by ensuring a financially healthy insurance industry. This charge entails a careful balancing of the twin goals of having financially reliable insurers and of having available, affordable insurance products.

The objective is to establish the proper incentives for efficient as well as safe operation and to institute safeguards that keep insurer failures to an acceptable minimum. It is possible to design a regulatory system so restrictive that insolvencies would be virtually impossible, but coverage would be expensive or even unavailable for many consumers. Some insolvencies are inevitable within a competitive insurance market.

Regulators strive to detect financially troubled companies early, take corrective action to restore them to financial health when possible, and minimize the negative repercussions to policyholders of the financial failures that do occur. The various solvency surveillance methods used by state regulators are discussed later in this chapter. Here we provide needed background to that discussion by presenting various solvency-related regulatory constraints under which life insurers must operate.

These constraints require that insurance companies maintain at all times assets that are at least equal to their currently due and prospectively estimated liabilities plus the required minimum capital and surplus levels. While a large body of law and ample practice guidelines exist relating to these items, we can provide only a broad overview here.

Liability Valuation

The principal liabilities on life insurers' balance sheets are policy reserves. **Policy reserves** are balance sheet accounts established to reflect actual and potential liabilities under outstanding contracts—in other words, amounts to cover all present and future claims. Life insurers are required to establish reserves using methods and assumptions mandated in each state's laws or regulations. These methods and assumptions are purposefully conservative in the sense that they usually result in an overstatement of future expected claims costs.

For example, the mortality rates required to be used in reserve calculations are much greater than those actually experienced by insurers. This fact results in reserves being higher than they would be were realistic mortality assumptions used. In effect, this requirement means that insurers ordinarily have some surplus or cushion embedded within their liabilities. Conservative assumptions for expenses and interest earnings also provide for additional reserve cushioning.

Asset Limitations and Valuation

To ensure solidity and investment diversification, most state insurance codes establish quantitative and qualitative asset standards as well as techniques of asset valuation. Some refer to quantitative approaches as "pigeonhole" investment guidelines. A few states regulate under the prudent person standard, affording insurers greater investment latitude. Still other states rely on a blend of the two approaches. Whatever the approach, the intent is to prohibit or discourage insurers from undertaking what are considered imprudent investments.

The typical classes of investments permitted to back policyholder liabilities include government-backed securities, corporate bonds, mortgage and other loans, common and preferred stock, deposits, and real estate. Assets backing policyholder liabilities are routinely subject to more restrictive provisions than are assets backing capital or unassigned liabilities.

Most insurance codes state that the commissioner may specify the rules for determining the value of securities, subject (in some cases) to the limitation that these rules not be inconsistent with those established by the NAIC. Through its Securities Valuation Office, the NAIC values on a uniform basis the securities held in the portfolios of virtually every U.S. insurance company.

As mentioned in the capital requirements section below, insurers are required to hold additional capital for riskier assets, which provides a strong incentive for insurers to primarily hold investment grade assets. As of year-end 2008, approximately 94 percent of bonds held were investment grade and 98 percent of mortgages held were in good standing.

In the interest of conservatism, the states do not allow insurers to include or admit all types of assets in determining whether they meet required solvency standards. Such **non-admitted assets** are those deemed less reliable in being converted into cash and may not be counted in determining compliance with state solvency requirements, such as amounts owed the insurer by agents, furniture, certain equipment, and some other items.

Accounting Standards

If an assessment of an insurer's financial solidity is to be meaningful, insurers must follow similar procedures, for the terms "assets" and "liabilities" have meaning only in relation to some accounting convention. As we noted in Chapter 3, life insurers are required to follow the accounting conventions established by the states, called statutory accounting principles (SAP). Its emphasis is on insurer solvency and not on approximating the value of the firm as an ongoing enterprise, as with the accounting conventions followed by all other corporations—called generally accepted accounting principles (GAAP). SAP sets out what assets can be counted toward meeting the state's capital requirements and how they are valued. SAP also sets out how liabilities will be established and is the basis on which insurer's financial solidity is judged by state regulators.

Accounting standards extend not only to insurers' balance sheets (hence to assets and liability valuation) but also to insurers' income statements (summary of operations) and other financial statements. Important differences between SAP and GAAP arise in how expenses, income, and investment results are recorded, the effects of which generally are to render SAP financial statements more conservative than those prepared under GAAP.

Solvency Surveillance Methods

State insurance regulators employ several methods to monitor the financial solidity of insurers licensed in their jurisdictions. The overwhelming majority of each regulator's attention to solvency surveillance is directed toward insurers domiciled in the state. Tools relied on by regulators include the following, each of which is discussed below:

- ◆ Financial statement filings;
- ◆ Ongoing capital requirements;
- ◆ NAIC automated solvency monitoring;
- ◆ Dividend restrictions;
- ◆ Cash Flow testing;
- ◆ On-site examinations; and
- ◆ Professional oversight.

Financial Statement Filings

Each state requires that all licensed insurers file financial statements detailing their financial condition and operation. Detailed statements must be filed annually and others must be filed quarterly or more frequently if financial problems are suspected. These filings are to include supplements to the annual statement, including one on "Management's Discussion and Analysis." This supplement must include material events known to management that would cause the insurer's reported financial information not to be indicative of future operating results or of its future financial position.

The insurance commissioner reviews the statements to ensure appropriate disclosure and accounting treatment. The reviews also include financial analytics and commentaries. They help the state insurance commissioner determine if the insurance company is financially stable. If it is concluded that the insurance company is under financial distress, the commissioner takes actions to protect policyholders, as discussed later in this chapter. Reporting requirements are the core of insurer solvency surveillance.

Ongoing Capital Requirements

If one aspect of solvency regulation must be singled out as the most critical, it surely would be an insurer's relative net worth or capital position; i.e., the excess of assets over liabilities. Recall that we use the term *capital* synonymously with *surplus* and *capital and surplus*. In addition to conservative reserve valuation, life insurers are also required by state law and regulation to hold a capital cushion.

States now generally follow the NAIC's risk-based capital (RBC) model law to evaluate the adequacy of each insurer's capital and surplus. The intuition behind these models is that the riskier an insurer's operations, the larger the amount of capital that it should hold, other things being the same. Thus, an insurer that invests heavily in low grade bonds and thereby exposes itself to greater asset default risk is expected to hold more capital than an otherwise identical insurer that invests heavily in high grade bonds.

The classes of risks to which insurers are exposed have been dubbed **contingency risks** or **C risks** by actuaries and fall into four categories (cleverly called C-1, C-2, C-3, and C-4 risks by actuaries):

- ◆ Asset default risk—C-1 risks;
- ◆ Insurance (mortality) risk—C-2 risks;
- ◆ Interest rate risk (asset/liability interest disintermediation)—C-3 risks; and
- ◆ General business risk—C-4 risks.

A complex formula that involves the assignment of risk-based capital factors to many of the components of each insurer's C risks yields the amount of capital that each insurer theoretically should have to support its risks. This value is then compared to each insurer's actual capital with some adjustments via ratios of the actual adjusted capital to the formula-derived capital. If this RBC ratio is below certain thresholds, the insurance regulator is expected to undertake various, progressively more intrusive actions. Box 4-1 sketches how RBC requirements are determined and used.

The RBC requirements are intended to help regulators identify inadequately capitalized insurers and do not purport to provide a relative assessment of each insurer's financial strength. In fact, there is a poor relationship between insurers' RBC ratios and their financial strength as determined by the rating agencies. Because of concerns by regulators and many insurers about possible misuse of these RBC data, which are included in each insurer's publicly available annual statement filings, most states prohibit anyone engaged in the insurance business, including insurers and agents, from directly or indirectly disseminating RBC data.

BOX 4-1: Risk-based Capital (RBC) Requirements

The NAIC developed the RBC standards in an attempt to judge better the adequacy of each insurer's capital. The standards revolve around each insurer's risk-based capital ratio. To determine an insurer's **risk-based capital ratio**, an insurer's total adjusted capital is compared with its authorized control level RBC. The **total adjusted capital** (TAC) for an insurer equals its statutory capital and surplus adjusted for certain liabilities more properly classified as surplus. The **authorized control level** (ACL) **RBC** is a formula-derived capital and surplus figure based on the risks inherent in an insurer's assets, insurance, interest exposure, and business. The riskier the element, the larger the weighing factor and, hence, the larger the insurer's ACL RBC and the larger must be its expected TAC.

State laws ordinarily specify six levels for RBC ratios, with the name of each indicating the actions, if any, to be taken by the regulator. The levels are as follows:

RBC Ratios (% of ACL)	RBC Level	Regulatory Action
200 and above	"No action"	None
150–200	Company Action Level	RBC Plan required
100–150	Regulatory Action Level	RBC Plan and examination required plus corrective action order
70–100	Authorized Control Level	Insurer may be placed under regulatory control
Below 70	Mandatory Control Level	Insurer must be placed under regulatory control

Thus, if an insurer's ACL were $100 million and its TAC were $200 million or more, the insurer's RBC ratio would be greater than the company action level and, therefore, no special regulatory or company action ordinarily would be required. If the insurer's TAC were between $200 and $150 million, the company must file an RBC Plan with the commissioner of its domiciliary state. An **RBC Plan** describes the cause of the threat to the insurer's solvency, offers proposals to correct the situation, estimates five years of financial projections, and includes other relevant information. This is referred to as the *Company Action Level* as the company is required to take action.

If the insurer's TAC were between $150 and $100 million, an RBC plan would be required to be submitted and the regulator must perform appropriate analysis and examinations and may issue Corrective Orders—hence the name *Regulatory Action Level.* TAC between $100 and $70 million—the *Authorized Control Level*—would subject the insurer to possible regulatory seizure. TAC below $70 million—the *Mandatory Control Level*—requires regulatory seizure.

NAIC Automated Solvency Monitoring

The NAIC provides its member regulators with two types of automated solvency monitoring systems. Its *Financial Analysis Solvency Tools* (FAST) system screens selected companies for risk of insolvency. It does this by assigning different point values to 29 different ratios to develop a score for likelihood of insolvency. FAST system results are not generally disclosed. Researchers have found this system to be a better predictor of insolvency than RBC ratios.

Similarly but more broadly, the *Insurance Regulatory Information System* (IRIS) prioritizes insurance companies for further regulatory review. IRIS consists of two phases. The statistical phase employs 12 financial ratios to flag companies that show unusual results. This is followed by an analytical phase, in which a team of financial examiners analyzes the annual statements and ratio results of the flagged companies. Upon more detailed analysis, insurers may be prioritized for further regulatory review by their domiciliary states.

Dividend Restrictions

In the interest of protecting life insurer financial solidity, states impose restrictions on the ability of life insurers to transfer capital and surplus funds to their parent holding companies or other affiliated corporations. These regulations essentially create a wall between a life insurance subsidiary and its parent company and affiliates. Besides restricting capital and surplus fund transfers, the regulations require that all assets, reserves, and capital and surplus be maintained by the life insurance subsidiary separately from the group's other funds and obligations.

Any transfers that exceed certain limits must be approved by regulators. Before approving such transactions, regulators are required to confirm that the transaction would not impair the life insurance company's ability to pay policyholder benefits.

These policyholder protections were especially notable in the recent financial crisis with regards to AIG, one of the world's largest financial conglomerates. AIG's troubles stemmed from its financial products division and not from its insurance subsidiaries. This division's credit default swaps suffered huge losses due to the credit crisis. The assets within AIG's life subsidiaries remained isolated and protected for the benefit of these subsidiaries. Even had AIG the conglomerate been allowed to fail, its life insurers would have been largely insulated financially.

Cash Flow Testing

As part of their regulatory filings, life insurers are required to ensure that their assets and future cash flows are expected to provide sufficient liquidity to meet policyholder obligations, by modeling thousands of economic scenarios. Additional reserves will be required if the cash flow testing reveals liquidity risk above a stated threshold. Therefore, even if investment returns are adversely affected by a market downturn, there is comfort—via the modeling process—that insurers are required to demonstrate that sufficient liquidity exists to meet policyholder liabilities.

On-site Financial Examinations

On-site financial examinations of insurers are particularly useful regulatory tools. State laws typically require the insurance regulator to examine domestic insurers at least once every three to five years. These examinations involve a detailed review of all important aspects of operations. Investments are confirmed and their correct valuation checked. Liabilities are verified, as are income and expense items.

Targeted exams can be and are conducted more frequently, if circumstances dictate them. A targeted exam typically focuses only on certain aspects of an insurer's financial operations, such as reserves, investments, capital changes, and so on. The call for a targeted examination could be based on a CPA audit report, analysts' work papers, annual or quarterly statement filings, or RBC, FAST, or IRIS findings.

Professional Oversight

Greater reliance on the professions is an obvious, efficient, and effective means of discouraging inappropriate insurer behavior and of revealing it if it occurs. Insurance regulators routinely rely on the accounting and actuarial professions for additional solvency surveillance. Thus, actuarial opinions regarding the adequacy of an insurer's reserves are required, and insurers' financial statements are typically required to be audited annually by an independent accountant and results provided to regulators. With the development of more stringent corporate governance rules, insurers increasingly also conduct their own internal risk management assessments using audits and examinations, particularly at the prompting of the firm's board of directors.

Regulatory Responses to Financially Impaired Insurers

An objective of insurance regulation is to establish proper incentives for efficient and safe insurer operation and institute safeguards to keep the number of insurer insolvencies to an acceptable minimum. Within a competitive marketplace, some insurer financial impairments, including failures, are inevitable.

After identifying an insurer as financially impaired through surveillance mechanisms discussed in the preceding section, regulators elect one of four options: (1) informal actions, (2) formal actions, (3) rehabilitation, and (4) liquidation. In each case, regulators face this question: is the insurer's financial condition sufficiently grave as to justify my undertaking some action and, if so, which one? The regulator is aware that actions taken precipitously might needlessly harm insurers, assuring their demise because of adverse publicity. On the other hand, delayed action could lead to greater consumer (and possibly taxpayer) loss.

Informal Actions

A regulator's typical first responses to a financially impaired company are informal. The regulator may attempt to work with company management to identify and deal with the sources of difficulty. The success of such actions is dependent on the voluntary cooperation of the insurer, on its financial condition, and on the good will of other firms in the market or the coercive power of the regulator. Often, a friendly merger or acquisition results. Informal actions taken by regulators often are not public knowledge.

Formal Actions

States also take formal actions against financially impaired licensed insurers. Formal actions vary by state but ordinarily they consist of written directives—often called **corrective orders**—requiring an insurer to (1) obtain state approval before undertaking certain transactions, (2) limit or cease its new business writings, (3) infuse capital, or (4) cease certain business practices. Failure of an insurer to rectify the identified problem leads to more drastic action. The regulator also may revoke an insurer's license. All such actions are subject to court review.

Rehabilitation

Sometimes, despite the best efforts of regulators, insurers get into perilously troubling financial difficulty. In such circumstances, the state insurance regulator has the responsibility of assuming control over the entire company, in the case of domestic insurers, or over its assets, in cases for which the insurer is domiciled in another state. The action may require a court order, although in some states the regulator may assume control of an insurer without a prior order if the regulator has determined such action is urgent and necessary to preserve assets.

If the commissioner determines that reorganization, consolidation, conversion, reinsurance, merger, or other transformation is appropriate, a specific plan of rehabilitation may be prepared. Under an order of **rehabilitation**, the commissioner is granted title to the domestic insurance company's assets and is given the authority to carry on its business until the insurer is either returned to private management after the grounds for issuing the order have been removed or liquidated.

Among the statutory grounds under which the commissioner may apply for a rehabilitation order are (1) a finding that further transaction of business would be financially hazardous to policyowners, creditors, or the public; (2) a determination that the insurer's officers or directors are guilty of certain acts or omissions; and (3) when a substantial transfer of assets, merger, or consolidation is attempted without the prior written consent of the commissioner. Many state regulators place financially troubled insurers in rehabilitation to minimize adverse publicity and possibly massive policyowner withdrawals, then move the insurer to liquidation.

Liquidation

When it is found inadvisable to attempt rehabilitation or if rehabilitation becomes impracticable, the commissioner must petition the proper court for a liquidation order. Grounds for liquidation include those listed for rehabilitation and the additional ground that the insurer is insolvent. **Liquidation** is the winding up of the company's entire business operations, with the commissioner being given title to all assets of the insurer in his or her capacity as the receiver to make final settlement of the insurer's affairs.

A liquidator is appointed either by the insurance regulator or, more frequently, by a court. The liquidator musters the assets of the company and prepares for their distribution. Priorities for distribution are established, with the costs of administration, employee salaries, and policyowner claims receiving highest priorities. Ordinary creditors are next in line, with shareholders falling last.

In a technical sense, the statutes of several jurisdictions use the term **conservation order** to refer to the court order directing the commissioner to act as receiver for the conservation of assets of an insurance company within the jurisdiction. Grounds for the insurance commissioner's request are similar to those for liquidation and rehabilitation.

Role of Guaranty Associations

Each state, along with the District of Columbia and Puerto Rico, has a life and health insurance guaranty association to protect its residents if an insurance company is liquidated. All companies licensed to do business in the state are required to be members of the guaranty association. In other words, a company licensed to conduct business in 25 states would be a member of 25 guaranty associations.

When a company is liquidated, the state insurance guaranty associations in which the insurer is licensed are triggered to provide continuing coverage and benefits to the company's policyholders of that state. In most cases, policyholders who reside in states in which the insolvent insurer is not licensed are covered by the guaranty association of the company's domiciliary state.

If it is determined by the receiver that the company has insufficient funds to meet its obligations to policyholders, each state guaranty association assesses its member insurers a share of the amount required to meet the claims of resident policyholders. The proportion assessed each insurer is based on the share of premiums each company collects in that state for the kind of business for which benefits are required. In most states, maximum annual assessments range from 1 to 2 percent of net written premiums in the state.

State guaranty associations provide benefits only up to specified limits set out in each state's laws. While these laws vary somewhat from state to state, most states provide for payment of amounts up to these limits:

- ◆ $300,000 in life insurance death benefits;
- ◆ $100,000 in cash surrender or withdrawal value for life insurance;
- ◆ $100,000 in withdrawal and cash values for annuities; and
- ◆ $100,000 in health insurance policy benefits.

In some cases, it would be difficult for people who have lost coverage due to the failure of their insurance company to find comparable coverage elsewhere. To avoid this, guaranty associations provide continuing coverage, often by placing the policies of an insolvent insurer with a healthy insurer. In other cases, guaranty associations simply take on the policies and fulfill the terms themselves.

All 52 insurance guaranty associations are members of the *National Organization of Life and Health Insurance Guaranty Associations* (NOLHGA). Through NOLHGA, the associations work together to provide continued protection for policyholders affected by a multi-state insurance insolvency. NOLHGA establishes a task force of representative guaranty associations to work with the insurance commissioner to develop a plan to protect policyholders.

Implications to Policyholders of Insurer Financial Difficulty

Managers of insurance companies almost always know when their companies are trending towards financial difficulty—and usually before the regulator or the rating agencies know it. They are keen to reverse the trend if they can and ordinarily undertake voluntary actions to try to do so. These actions might be as direct as reducing operational expenses, changing the pricing factors for new policy sales, or changing pricing factors on existing policies (where they can do so). More drastic actions could involve seeking new infusions of capital; selling business units or blocks of business; purchasing surplus relief reinsurance; issuing surplus notes; exploring merger possibilities; trying to sell the company to another financially sound insurance group; and other actions.

Any of these actions can have an impact on existing policies. Obviously, unsuccessful actions could mean that the insurer becomes financially impaired and requires regulatory intervention. At this point, the dynamics can change dramatically, as we explore in the next section. Even successful voluntary actions are likely to have a cost, and these costs could be passed on to future or existing policyholders or both. The extent to which the costs are passed on will vary depending on whether we are discussing future policies or in force policies. For policies not yet issued, the insurer could, in theory, decide to undertake massive increases in the premium rates or the loadings and cost of insurance charges. Obviously, such a strategy is fraught with competitive difficulties.

With regard to existing policies, the insurer faces a more challenging situation when contemplating price increases to restore profitably. The most important point to remember here is that an existing life insurance policy is a contract. All policy contracts have some form of contractual guarantee(s) that must be respected. If the policyholder meets his or her obligations (i.e., pays the premiums on the policy), the insurance company must honor all contractual guarantees.

To explore these simple points more effectively, it will be helpful to define two terms. **Guaranteed policy elements** within a life insurance policy are those that cannot be changed unilaterally by the insurer. For universal life (UL) type policies, they include the maximum guaranteed loading and cost of insurance charges, the minimum guaranteed interest crediting rate (commonly referred to collectively as the **guaranteed assumptions**), and the policy face amount. For some forms, it also can include a maximum premium. For traditional whole life and term policies, guaranteed pricing elements include the policy face amount, cash values, and premiums.

Non-guaranteed policy elements within a life insurance policy are those that the insurer can change unilaterally. For UL type policies, they include the excess of the actual interest credited over the guaranteed crediting rate and the difference between the actual loading and cost of insurance charges and those guaranteed (commonly referred to as the current loads and charges and the current crediting rate or collectively as the **current assumptions**). Current assumptions are the actual loads and credits currently being assessed; however, these are subject to change based on emerging company experience. For some forms, it also can include the difference between the maximum guaranteed premium and the premium actually charged.

For traditional whole life and term policies, non-guaranteed policy elements include policy dividends. **Dividends** are intended to represent an equitable distribution under participating policies of the surplus that the insurer accumulated on behalf of the policies. **Participating (par) policies** are those for which the policyholder has a contractual right to share or *participate* in the insurer's favorable (and unfavorable) operational experience. Participating policies are most closely associated with mutual insurers.

Thus, an insurer may not unilaterally increase premiums or lower cash values for in force traditional life policies, although it can lower or even eliminate dividend payments under par policies. Even forms of life insurance that allow premiums to be increased unilaterally by the insurer contain ceilings beyond which the premiums may not be increased. And, of course, policy face amounts may not be decreased unilaterally. Additionally, all UL type policies, including variable UL, contain guarantees; neither current policy loadings nor cost of insurance charges can exceed guaranteed maximums specified in the contract, and the current interest rate credited on cash values can never fall below specified contractual guaranteed minimums for general account-backed policies.

Collectively, these guarantees in UL-type and traditional policies mean that the insurer can increase costs under existing policies to a limited extent only. For par policies for which it is paying dividends, the insurer can lower future dividend payments. For UL-type policies, the insurer can increase actual future loading and mortality charges provided it has been charging less than the guaranteed maximums and it can lower the future interest crediting rate provided it has been crediting a rate higher than the guaranteed minimum. For no-lapse guarantee UL, current assumptions may be changed by the insurer, but respecting policy guarantees, including the no-lapse guarantee premium (see Chapter 7).

In each instance, however, care must be exercised, as pricing increases can lead to increased policy terminations as insureds in good health replace their insurance with policies from more competitive insurers. The result can be that the original insurer is left with a group of insureds in overall poorer health and, thus, experience proportionately more death claims. Therefore, an in-force price increase can result in decreased profits for the insurance company, which is why rate increases should be given careful consideration. The current pricing on a particular product in relation to competitive market pricing is a major consideration influencing price changes.

Specifying precisely how an insurer will handle changes in non-guaranteed policy elements to accommodate financial stress is far from black and white. If losses are being generated from a given product line, the insurer is likely to reduce current performance via changes in non-guaranteed policy elements, paying due attention to guarantees. As an example, if the general account supporting the insurance liabilities is experiencing credit defaults (similar to the recent experience with residential mortgage-backed securities), the interest crediting rate could be reduced accordingly.

However, if a given product line is not experiencing losses, the insurance company has an incentive to maintain its current performance rather than increase profits to subsidize losses elsewhere. This is because an increase in policy charges or a decrease to the crediting rate or dividends results in reduced product performance and could cause healthy insureds to terminate their policies in favor of better performing ones elsewhere. The overall level of losses and product performance relative to the market will drive in-force pricing decisions.

Of those aspects of an insurer's operational experience (mortality, expenses, investment earnings, and lapse rates) that affect the values for non-guaranteed policy elements during the recent financial crisis only investment earnings have been negatively affected, with downward pressure on crediting rates. Mortality and expense experience continued to be good, suggesting current policy charges should be maintained. A concern remains that more policyholders may terminate or exchange policies due to a concern with insurer financial solvency, but this has not happened significantly. Policyholders appear to be recognizing that, while insurance companies are experiencing some financial stress, the companies are still strong. (In addition, and possibly as important, insurance policies have surrender penalties that discourage policyholders from terminating or exchanging their policies.)

Implications to Policyholders of Regulatory Solvency Intervention

As observed earlier, once the insurance regulator becomes involved with a financial impairment, the dynamics change dramatically. The regulator will be focused intensely on protecting policyholders. Through informal actions, he or she may seek a friendly merger with all of the attendant uncertainties for continuing policyholders about future coverage and pricing treatment. If blocks of life insurance are unprofitable, the regulator may allow or insist on changes to non-guaranteed pricing elements. The comments offered in the previous section apply here as well.

If the insurance company is placed in receivership, losses are far more significant, and there may be greater incentive to generate profits through a reduction in current performance. But, if the underlying product line is profitable, there is also an incentive for the insurance company to maintain the block.

Even guaranteed policy elements are not immune to change if the receiver believes changes are essential (and the relevant court agrees). Liens may be placed on policies, the guaranteed minimum interest rate cut, and other guaranteed elements altered. While a receiver would view changing guarantees as a last resort, it may make sense to enact a discounted guarantee rather than further impairing the company in a manner that ultimately prevents the company from paying any benefits. But what happens in the worst case when the insurer is not around to pay claims?

While the state-based guaranty association arrangement provides important protections to policyholders of failed companies, it does not offer the same types of assurances as those provided to bank customers via the *Federal Deposit Insurance Corporation* (FDIC). Guaranty associations are not backed by any government and do not necessarily have immediate access to needed funds, having to rely on a post assessment system. Further, the nature and degree of protection varies by the policyholder's state of residency.

Each relevant state guaranty association will pay claims in accordance with the limits established by that state's statute at the same time as attempts may be made to transfer policies to other insurers. To ensure coverage by the association, policyholders must continue to pay premiums on their policies, even if the insurer is insolvent—not a pleasant experience. Despite the existence of guaranty associations, policyholders of failed companies face uncertainty, delays, aggravation, and possible losses.

Further, as each state's guaranty association relies on post-event assessments of the state's licensed insurers, the association may face liquidity problems between the time claims are submitted and funds collected. Also, if the guaranty fund becomes depleted in a given year after having levied the statutorily mandated maximum assessment, it cannot levy another assessment until the following year. Claimants may have to wait until such funds become available. In past insolvencies, claims have taken six months or more to be paid.

Claims not paid by the guaranty association because they exceed the state limits become claims against the estate of the liquidated insurer. They are paid on a share basis along with all other claims on the estate. As noted previously, general creditors have no rights to assert a claim on the separate account assets held by insurers to cover liabilities from variable insurance contract.

Conclusions

The solvency record of the life insurance industry is impressive, especially in comparison to that of banks. The average policyholder is highly unlikely ever to be required to deal with the insolvency of a life insurer. But this very fact can lead to unwarranted complacency and lack of due care. Some, mostly small life insurers do fail each year, but from time to time failures occur of insurers with household names. If a client's life insurer fails, it makes no difference to her whether failures are as rare as hen's teeth or whether the insurer is large or small or purple.

State insurance regulators are charged with protecting the insurance-buying public. While they avail themselves of multiple regulatory tools to (1) discourage excessive risk-taking behavior by life insurers, (2) identify such behavior is it exists, and (3) deal with its adverse effects if an insurer gets into financial difficulty, life insurance buyers, nonetheless, should be vigilant in their initial selection and ongoing involvement with insurers. Insolvencies cannot be wholly prevented nor can their financial consequences for policyholders be fully ameliorated by government actions, especially for those purchasing or owning more than moderate sized life insurance policies (e.g., in excess of $300,000).

Advisors should understand regulators' solvency-related responsibilities; the methods employed to prevent, detect, and respond to financial impairments; and their focus on protecting policyholders. In circumstances for which large amounts of life insurance are needed, it can be wise to place needed insurance with multiple insurers. Advisors should understand the implications to their policyholder clients from insurer financial difficulty and from regulatory solvency intervention if they are to provide the full range of essential advice on the purchase of life insurance and on the wisdom of continuing with an existing life insurance carrier and program.

Life Insurer Financial Strength Due Care

5

THIS CHAPTER CONCLUDES THE theme of Part II on the exercise of due care by advisors in assessing life insurer financial strength. We first examine the role of rating agencies, ordinarily the most important source of financial strength information and guidance. We then explore other sources of information that can be helpful in assessing insurer financial strength.

The Role of Rating Agencies

In examining the role of rating agencies by the advisor, we first explain why rating agencies are so important to the evaluation of life insurer financial strength. We then provide an overview of four of the major life insurer rating agencies. We follow the overview with a short discussion of one rating agency's methodology. We then examine the nature of rating agency reports and rating systems and how to use these reports and ratings in the exercise of financial strength due care by the advisor.[1]

Authored by Harold D. Skipper.
[1]This chapter draws in part from Kenneth Black, Jr. and Harold D. Skipper, Jr., *Life and Health Insurance* (13th ed.; Upper Saddle River, NJ: Prentice-Hall, 2000), Chapter 35, and from "Who's Watching your Back? An Assessment of Life Insurance Policyholder Protections in the Wake of the Financial Downturn," M Financial Group, June 2009.

The Importance of Rating Agencies

As alluded to in the preceding two chapters, neither the typical life insurance advisor nor certainly the average life insurance buyer is technically capable of making a reasoned, independent assessment of an insurer's financial strength. Doing so requires mastery of specialized and sometimes confusing insurance terminology and, importantly, requires a high level of accounting, actuarial, and financial competence by those conducting the analysis.

Rather than try to undertake such an analysis, knowledgeable advisors assemble insightful information and data relating to an insurer's financial strength from numerous secondary sources to be able to counsel clients concerning financial strength. In the great majority of cases, the primary and most reliable sources are rating agencies. **Rating agencies** are businesses that provide commentary and opinions about the ability of firms to meet their obligations. Several rating agencies offer opinions about life insurers' financial strength and their ability to meet ongoing obligations to policyholders. The next section introduces four of the leading agencies.

These rating agencies assemble and analyze great quantities of financial and business-related information about the insurers that they rate. Their approaches are discussed below. In each instance, their goal is to develop an in-depth understanding of each insurer's ability to meet its obligations to policyholders on an ongoing basis. They express their opinions in the form of commentaries and ratings. Rating agencies employ analysts who are capable of conducting necessary in-depth analyses.

As the ratings of Executive Life and Mutual Benefit Life suggest (see Chapter 3), rating agencies are not infallible. But neither is anyone else in rendering never-erring opinions about insurer financial strength. Rating agencies have been found to be the most consistent and best predictors of insurers' financial condition. After all, this is their business, and their financial success and livelihood depend on their being right far more often than they are wrong.

Four Major Rating Agencies

Here we offer a short overview of four rating agencies that offer opinions about the financial strength of life insurance companies. While a few other rating agencies also offer such opinions, we limit our discussion to those agencies that have been designated by the *Securities and Exchange Commission* (SEC) as *Nationally Recognized Statistical Rating Organizations* (NRSROs). They are A.M. Best Company, Fitch Ratings, Moody's Investors Service, and Standard and Poor's. Contact information for each of these firms is shown in Box 5-1.

A.M. Best Company

A.M. Best has been publishing financial information about insurance companies for more than a century—longer than any other rating agency. It also

---

BOX 5-1: Contact Information for the Four NRSROs that Rate Insurers

A.M. Best
http://www.ambest.com/
(908) 439-2200

Fitch Ratings
http://www.fitchratings.com/
(800) 893-4824

Moody's Investors Service
http://www.moodys.com/
(212) 553-0377

Standard & Poor's
http://www.standardandpoors.com/ratings
(212) 438-2400

---

rates more life insurers than any other rating agency, numbering almost 1,000 in late 2009. Insurer ratings can be found at no charge on the A.M. Best website. Registration is required, but it is free.

The primary source of information contained in its reports is the financial statements filed with state insurance regulators. It supplements these data with information obtained from other publicly available sources, such as SEC filings and GAAP financial statements. It also seeks supplemental information directly from the insurers it rates, including via consultation with management, questionnaires, and internal reports prepared by or for the insurer.

Best states that its financial strength ratings are its "independent opinion of an insurer's financial strength and ability to meet its ongoing insurance policy and contract obligations." These ratings are said to be based on a comprehensive quantitative analysis of financial data provided by the insurer and of each insurer's balance sheet strength and operating performance, and a qualitative analysis of several aspects of its business profile, including spread of risk, composition of revenue, market position, and management.

If an insurer requesting a rating disagrees with Best's analysis, no rating is assigned. A previously assigned rating may be withdrawn on request, but Best announces that fact publicly and also what the rating would have been. Ratings are reviewed periodically, but not less frequently than annual and can be changed at any time. Insurers pay an annual fee to Best to be rated.

Fitch Ratings

Fitch had ratings for more than 300 life insurers as of late 2009. These ratings are available via its website at no charge. Registration is required but is free. Fitch's ratings are based on quantitative and qualitative information provided by insurers that seek ratings and on publicly available financial and other data. Fitch also provides ratings for some insurers that have not requested to be rated. In such instances, Fitch offers to meet with management and to receive data and information directly from the insurer. If the insurer chooses not to meet with Fitch, this fact is disclosed.

If an insurer requests a rating, Fitch will make the rating public even if the insurer disagrees with the rating. The insurer may, however, later request that the rating be withdrawn, in which case Fitch exercises its discretion whether to withdraw it. Also, insurers may request a tentative assessment based on less-than-complete information and may, thereafter, choose to abort the process, in which case Fitch makes no public announcement.

Fitch states that its ratings "provide an opinion on the relative ability of an entity to meet financial obligations. . . ." Ratings are reviewed frequently and can be changed at any time. Insurers pay an annual fee to Fitch to be rated.

Moody's Investor's Service

Moody's rated almost 200 life insurers as of late 2009. These ratings are available via the company's website at no charge, although registration (free) is required. Moody's ratings are based on each insurer's business and financial profile. See the following section on rating methodology. The business profile includes its market position, distribution systems, and product focus. The financial profile includes a range of financial ratios, most derived using financial data provided to state insurance regulators. In seeking a rating, insurers provide nonpublic information to and meet with Moody's analysts. Moody's rates only those insurers that have requested ratings.

Moody's ratings reflect its "opinions of [life insurers'] creditworthiness." Ratings are reviewed frequently and can be changed at any time. Insurers pay an annual fee to be rated.

Standard & Poor's

Almost 350 life insurers had requested and secured a rating from Standard & Poor's (S&P) as of late 2009. S&P relies on publicly and non-publicly available data and information and has its analysts meet with insurer management in formulating its ratings. A few dozen other life insurers that had not requested ratings are also rated based solely on publicly available information with the rating designated as such ("pi"). S&P ratings are available on its website at no charge, after (free) registration.

If an insurer requesting a rating disagrees with S&P's analysis, no rating is assigned. A previously assigned such rating may be withdrawn on request, but S&P announces that fact publicly and may assign a pi rating. S&P does not suppress the ratings of pi-rated insurers.

S&P's "insurer financial strength rating is a current opinion of the financial security characteristics of an insurance organization with respect to its ability to pay under its insurance policies and contracts in accordance with their terms." Ratings are reviewed periodically and can be changed at any time. Insurers requesting a rating are charged an annual fee.

An Example of an Agency's Rating Methodology

As is clear from the preceding short overviews, each rating agency relies on public and nonpublic data in preparing its reports and determining its financial strength ratings for life insurers. They also have their own methodology for utilizing these various data and information, with no two being identical. There is, however, similarity among the agencies in terms of the data and information examined as well as analysis applied. It is beyond the scope of this *Guide* to explore each rating agency's methodology, but it is instructive to an interpretation of their ratings to highlight the process in more detail. To do this, we have chosen to summarize the methodology followed by one of the four rating agencies—Moody's.[2] Please note that the summary offered below is necessarily abbreviated substantially from Moody's actual methodology description.

As noted above, Moody's ratings are predicated on each insurer's business and financial profiles. These profiles are mapped onto a *Rating Scorecard* that becomes a complement to detailed fundamental analysis of the insurer. In exploring the insurer's business profile, Moody's analysts review three sets of characteristics or factors. Its financial profile involves the review of five additional sets of factors. Each factor incorporates one or more quantitative and/or qualitative metrics derived from historical data. Rating levels from Aaa to Ba are mapped to numerical values of 1 through 12, with Aaa receiving a value of 1, Aa of 3, A of 6, Baa of 9, and Ba of 12. Each factor carries a weight, with all summing to 100 percent. The weighted sum of these factors' ratings is used as a rating predictor and as an input for the analyst-derived rating. Table 5-1 shows the eight factor categories and the weights ascribed to each factor.

TABLE 5-1
Moody's Business and Financial Profile Factors and Weights

Business Profile Factors	Weighting
Factor 1: Market Position and Brand	15%
Factor 2: Distribution	10%
Factor 3: Product Focus and Diversification	15%
Financial Profile Factors	
Factor 4: Asset Quality	5%
Factor 5: Capital Adequacy	10%
Factor 6: Profitability	15%
Factor 7: Liquidity and Asset-Liability Mgt.	10%
Factor 8: Financial Flexibility	20%

---

[2]This discussion is based on *Moody's Global Rating Methodology for Life Insurers,* Moody's Investors Services, September 2006 and *North American Life Insurance: 2008 Ratios for the Global Rating Methodology,* Moody's Investors Services, December 2009.

Business Profile

The business profile factors are intended to capture those characteristics that reflect the life insurer's presence in the market. These factors are more subjective than are the financial factors. Insurers that have sustainable competitive advantages in terms of market position and brand, distribution, and product focus and diversification can be expected to be able to maintain and enhance future profitability and financial strength.

- ◆ **Factor 1: Market Position and Brand.** Market position and brand represent an insurer's ability to develop and sustain competitive advantages in its chosen market. Market position considers market share in key lines of business; barriers to entry; scale advantages and their relation to expenses; control over pricing; and control over distribution. An insurer's brand encompasses its image, reputation, recognition, and perception by producers and customers, and their loyalty to the insurer. Insurers possessing these characteristics should be able to withstand prolonged difficult market conditions and capitalize on potentially new, profitable opportunities, suggesting higher ratings than insurers not so positioned. Relevant metrics here include absolute and relative market share as measured by premiums and deposits. The higher the better.

- ◆ **Factor 2: Distribution.** An insurer's access to distribution channels, its ability to control those channels, and its relationship with producers impacts its ability to increase revenues, retain business, align distribution to target markets, and control distribution costs. Diversity in distribution can mitigate sales disruption and allow for a better match between product and customer. The relevant metric here is the number of meaningful distribution channels used by the insurer and the degree of control over distribution. The greater the number and control, the higher the rating for this factor.

- ◆ **Factor 3: Product Focus and Diversification.** Different life insurance products have different risk profiles, which can mean either positive or negative effects on earnings and capital adequacy. Risks can be mitigated or exacerbated by an insurer's risk management practices and other elements of its business profile, including the extent of its product diversification. The relevant metric here is the insurer's relative share of low risk reserves (those backing policies with a high ability to share risk with policyholders) and the number of distinct lines of business comprising at least 10 percent of total premiums/deposits. The lower the reserve risk and the greater the lines of business, the higher the rating for this factor.

Financial Profile

An insurer's financial profile is of obvious relevance in measuring its financial strength. Moody's uses five factors to capture this profile. Together, these factors generally account for 60 percent of the overall rating, with the business profile representing the other 40 percent.

- ◆ **Factor 4: Asset Quality.** High-risk assets are those that carry increased risks of default, illiquidity, and price volatility. They include below-investment grade bonds, common stock, and real estate. Another asset of potentially uncertain value on some insurers' balance sheets is goodwill associated with acquisitions. The relevant metrics here are the percentage of these high-risk assets to total assets and of goodwill to capital and surplus. The lower the percentages, the higher the rating for this factor, although strongly capitalized insurers exhibit a higher tolerance for such assets.

- ◆ **Factor 5: Capital Adequacy.** The ability of an insurer to absorb economic and operational shocks is directly related to the relative level of its capital. Moody's uses the ratio of capital to total assets and also an insurer's relative risk-based capital ratio as metrics for capital adequacy. The higher the ratios, the higher the rating for this factor.

- ◆ **Factor 6: Profitability.** An insurer's earnings capacity is a critical component of its financial strength. It is a primary determinant of an insurer's ability to meet its obligations to policyholders and a source of internal capital generation. It also can mean more favorable terms when accessing the capital market. The relevant metrics are the five-year average return on equity (ROE) and a measure of net income growth to its volatility. The higher the ratios, the higher the rating for this factor, although an insurer's financial leverage should be considered. After all, management could increase its ROE by lowering "E," which would imply less financial cushion. For this reason, Moody's may also examine return on assets, which is less influenced by an insurer's financial leverage.

- ◆ **Factor 7: Liquidity and Asset-Liability Management (ALM).** Life insurer liabilities are sensitive to policyholder confidence in the insurer. Real or imagined financial problems for an insurer can lead to "run on the bank" behavior, with massive policy surrenders and attendant needs for liquidity and possible regulatory intervention. An insurer's ability to manage this asset-liability risk can be of critical importance, and its ALM process is one of the areas examined by Moody's analysts. The metric used for this factor is the ratio of liquid assets to policyholder reserves. The higher the ratio, the higher the rating for this factor, although the nature of the insurer's liabilities is also considered as is the effectiveness of its ALM processes.

- ◆ **Factor 8: Financial Flexibility.** Financial flexibility, a key determinant of financial strength, is reflected in an insurer's ability to finance business growth from internally generated capital, to maintain capital market confidence, and to meet its financial obligations without stress. Metrics of these characteristics include financial leverage (adjusted debt to adjusted debt and adjusted capital), earnings coverage (five-year average of adjusted earnings to interest expense and preferred dividends), and cash flow coverage (five-year average of dividend capacity from subsidiaries to interest expense and preferred dividends). The lower the financial leverage ratio and the higher the earnings and cash flow coverage ratios, the higher the rating for this factor.

Other Considerations

Moody's also examines subjective factors including management's credibility, experience, and reliability; depth of corporate governance; and risk management practices. Whether an insurer might be supported by a parent company or affiliate also is an important factor in developing its rating. If such support exists, the effect generally is to enhance what otherwise would be the insurer's standalone rating.

The Nature of Rating Agency Reports

Individual company ratings can be obtained at no charge for each rating service, as noted above. Full reports on insurers may be purchased from the rating agency, either via subscription to their services or on a case-by-case basis from their websites. Rating reports also should be readily available from insurance agents and insurance companies.

Rating Agency Reports

While the contents and formats of each rating agency's reports differ, they generally include similar types of information. They identify the insurer and provide its contact information. The agency's rating is provided along with an indication whether the rating outlook for the insurer is negative, neutral, or positive, although the terminology may differ. A rating outlook is important as it offers the agency's opinion about the likely trend in the insurer's rating. The agency's justification for its rating outlook is provided within the report, although perhaps not immediately after the rating.

There follows key financial data and ratios, discussions of the insurer's strength and weakness as perceived by the rating agency, and the rationale for its rating of the insurer. The order of these items is not the same with each agency nor are they labeled precisely in this way.

The agency's rationale for its rating may appear in summary fashion, followed by a detailed explanation of the components that have gone into the rating. These components typically include the same or similar categories of information and analysis discussed above with regard to Moody's methodology.

Thus, the insurer's current and likely future competitive position in its various target markets is often discussed. Management and corporate strategy usually is covered in some way, along with comments about its risk management capability. Quantitative and qualitative analysis and remarks are included about the insurer's investments, liquidity, capitalization, profitability, financial flexibility, and other related financial and operational elements. Various financial data and ratios are also provided.

Rating Categories

Each rating agency has its own rating categories. These categories and their descriptions are shown in the Appendix 2. In considering an insurer's rating, advisors should be certain to recognize the differences among categories and incompatibility of ratings. For example, an A+ rating from Best is its second highest rating, but it is Fitch's and S&P's fifth highest rating.

Table 5-2 lists each of the four rating agencies' categories along with a rank number that indicates where each rating ranks among those of each rating firm. Equivalent rank numbers *do not* mean equivalence of ratings, as the descriptions in the appendix show. Insurers receiving ratings shown in the

TABLE 5-2
Rating Rank Orders and Categories

Rank Number	Best	Fitch	Moody's	S&P
1	A++	AAA	Aaa	AAA
2	A+	AA+	Aa1	AA+
3	A	AA	Aa2	AA
4	A-	AA-	Aa3	AA-
5	B++	A+	A1	A+
6	B+	A	A2	A
7	B	A-	A3	A-
8	B-	BBB+	Baa1	BBB+
9	C++	BBB	Baa2	BBB
10	C+	BBB-	Baa3	BBB-
11	C	BB+	Ba1	BB+
12	C-	BB	Ba2	BB
13	D	BB-	Ba3	BB-
14	E	B+	B1	B+
15	F	B	B2	B
16		B-	B3	B-
17		CCC+	Caa1	CCC+
18		CCC	Caa2	CCC
19		CCC-	Caa3	CCC-
20		CC	Ca	CC
21		C	C	R

Shaded ratings are considered "vulnerable."

shaded area represent those falling into what the rating agency considers to be its "vulnerable" category. Insurers receiving ratings not appearing in the shaded area are considered "secure."

A possible annoyance with securing and using ratings from multiple agencies is their incompatible rating scales and possible confusion as to the meanings of the ratings themselves. Many advisors will secure the Comdex number for the insurers that they are reviewing. **Comdex** is a composite index of ratings, expressed as the average percentile of a company's rating; i.e., the proportion of rated insurers that are rated lower. While not itself a rating, it gives an insurer's standing, on a scale of 1 to 100, in relation to other rated insurers. Thus, a Comdex of 90 means that the composite of the insurer's ratings place it in the 90 percentile of rated companies; i.e., 10 percent are rated higher and 90 percent lower. See http://www.ebixlife.com/vitalsigns/.

Using Rating Agency Reports and Ratings

It is perhaps tempting for advisors simply to secure an insurer's ratings from one or more rating agencies and not procure and review the agencies' reports on the insurer. This practice is not advised if the objective is to conduct an appropriate degree of due care on behalf of clients. Agency reports provide context for their ratings. Reviewing reports from more than one agency can reveal subtle or perhaps not-so-subtle differences in their opinions, which might favor one insurer over another. The narrative and data will reveal the insurer's target markets, including whether the insurer specializes in products that the client is considering; e.g., high net worth customers. As discussed in Chapter 2, it can be important to match the client's need with the insurer's orientation. Reports also may identify whether the insurer's financial results in the lines of business most relevant to the client might be suffering adverse development and the reasons for such. Finally, reports often identify areas that may demand additional investigation.

In using rating agency reports and ratings, it is important to remember that they represent a summary of the agency's analysis of the insurer and its opinion of its financial soundness at the time the rating was assigned. Rating agency analyses and opinions often are similar, but sometimes they differ, especially based on how recently the rating was last reviewed. Circumstances change and so do ratings. For this reason, many experienced advisors follow the practice of first securing the most recent ratings from more than one rating agency. They then review the most recent commentaries about the ratings found on the agencies' websites. Thereafter, they review the latest full report on the insurer to gain a deeper understanding of both the agency's rating and the insurer itself.

Obviously, higher ratings are preferred to lower ones, other things being the same. Regrettably, other things are not always the same, and it is worth remembering that ratings are opinions and not guarantees or assurances of financial strength. A lower-rated insurer may offer better underwriting or more flexible or competitive products or superior advice and ongoing service. As the rating agencies themselves often point out, small differences in ratings, especially between adjacent categories, mean only slight perceived differences in financial strength. For example, in theory, an insurer that relied on more than five distribution channels and offered five or more distinct product lines, could be rated higher than an otherwise identical insurer that had fewer distribution channels and product lines.

Unless circumstances dictate otherwise, it is generally advisable to exercise great caution in dealing with life insurers whose ratings from one or more agencies fall within the vulnerable category or that have no rating from any of the major agencies. A vulnerable rating or no rating does not mean that the company necessarily is about to fail or that it is in financial difficulty. However, the failure rate of companies having vulnerable and no ratings has been considerably higher than those rated in the secure category. Insurers in financial difficulty often withdraw their ratings.

Rating agencies will commonly place a company's rating "under review." They do this for a variety of reasons that have the potential for meaningfully affecting some aspect of the insurer. For example, an acquisition by the insurer of another insurer or the pending sale of the company would be expected to cause a rating review. Likewise, either adverse or positive internal financial developments or senior management turnover often provokes a review.

Insurers whose ratings are under review are identified by the agency. Best adds the letter "u" to the rating. Fitch states "Rating Watch," Moody's "under review," and S&P "CreditWatch." The likely direction of the rating change is also indicated by terms such as "positive" or "negative" or the equivalent or "developing" or the equivalent where the direction of the likely change is uncertain. Advisors will want to follow such reviews carefully for their clients.

Many advisors are faced with the question whether to replace an existing life insurance policy with one from another insurer when a rating agency has downgraded the rating of the client's existing insurer. Replacements involve many considerations in addition to continued financial strength. We explore these in Chapter 18. As regards financial strength in isolation, most experienced advisors counsel caution. How severe is the downgrade and what is the agency's rationale for it? A downgrade from a very high rating to a merely high rating may not be significant (but could warrant close monitoring). Downgrades from secure to vulnerable ratings warrant careful analysis and possibly replacement, depending on all factors considered (including underwriting and product features and performance).

Related to the entirety of the company-specific information is the desirability for the advisor to understand the trends affecting the life insurance industry. We have but to consider the negative impact that the 2008–09 recession has had on life insurers' investment and operational results to realize the importance of external factors to insurers' financial strength and operation. Rating agencies publish research reports on matters that affect the entire life insurance industry, and clients are well served by advisors who keep current about such macro factors.

Other Sources of Insurer Information

While rating agencies are the most common sources of information on life insurer financial strength, advisors ordinarily will want to examine other sources as well. In this section, we introduce some of the more common non-rating agency sources, including the NAIC and state insurance departments, the Securities and Exchange Commission, insurance companies and agents, stock analysts' reports, and publications. These sources are by no means substitutes for rating agencies' analyses and opinions. Rather, some or all of them can be useful adjuncts to rating agency information, collectively providing the advisor with a more complete view of the companies that their clients are considering.

As noted earlier, neither the typical life insurance advisor nor certainly the average life insurance buyer is technically prepared to review financial statement information in order to assess an insurer's financial strength. Doing so requires mastery of specialized and sometimes confusing insurance terminology and, importantly, requires a high level of accounting, actuarial, and financial competence by those conducting the analysis. However, we are providing sources of insurer financial statements in this chapter for those who have an interest in reviewing such data. And as noted below, financial statements contain commentaries on company operations and risks, in addition to pure financial data, which can be insightful.

The NAIC and State Insurance Departments

State insurance regulators are charged with protecting and assisting insurance consumers and are, therefore, logical sources of information about insurers. Individual states are more or less effective in carrying out this mandate, so varying degrees of usefulness exist. To cite but one example, reports of the financial examinations of their domestic insurers are readily available on some insurance department web sites, but others do not make their reports so easily accessible.

Nonetheless, individual state insurance departments and the NAIC (*National Association of Insurance Commissioners*) house much potentially useful information about life insurers' financial condition, as well as information about other aspects of insurer operational performance (see Part V of this *Guide*). Recall that the NAIC is the trade association to which all state insurance regulators belong and that it helps to coordinate state insurance regulation (see Chapter 4). The information that it houses on life insurers is derived from each state's insurance regulatory official. Often, however, there is an advantage in securing needed information from the NAIC as opposed to the insurer's state of domicile as the NAIC often will make the information available electronically via its web site whereas not all states do so. Indeed, states often rely on the NAIC to perform this function for them.

In securing information about a specific life insurer from state insurance departments and the NAIC (and all other sources), the advisor should take care to ensure that he or she has the insurer's correct name and, ideally, state of domicile. Affiliated life insurers often have similar names. American General Life Insurance Company and American General Assurance Company are both AIG affiliates, although only the former is heavily involved in individual life insurance sales. Even unrelated life insurers have names that can be easily confused—American General Life Insurance Company and General American Life Insurance Company are unrelated.

Three types of information housed by state insurance departments and/or the NAIC can prove useful to advisors in conducting financial due care on behalf of their clients: financial statement information, complaint data, and risk based capital ratios, each of which is discussed briefly below. The relevant web addresses for such NAIC data are highlighted within the discussions. Web addresses and telephone numbers for state insurance departments are shown in Box 5-2.

Financial Statement Information

As discussed in Chapter 4, life insurers are required annually to file detailed financial information with state regulators, called the financial statement or statement blank. These financial statements are public record information, so they can be accessed at the insurance departments of the states in which the insurer is licensed. Unfortunately, they can run to hundreds of pages in length, going so far as to require the listing of every individual investment in an insurer's portfolio. Consequently, the majority of the information therein is of little interest to most advisors. And, as stated previously, the information is complex, and knowledge, experience, and great care should be taken when reviewing financial data for purposes of assessing company financial strength. On the other hand, some important nuggets reside therein.

BOX 5-2: State Insurance Department Contact Information

Alabama (334) 269-3550 www.aldoi.gov	**Illinois** (217) 782-4515 www.idfpr.com	**Montana** (406) 444-2040 www.sao.state.mt.us
Alaska (907) 465-2515 www.commerce.state.ak.us/insurance	**Indiana** (317) 232-2385 www.in.gov/idoi	**Nebraska** (402) 471-2201 www.doi.ne.gov
Arizona (602) 364-3100 www.id.state.az.us	**Iowa** (515) 281-5705 www.iid.state.ia.us	**Nevada** (775) 687-4270 www.doi.state.nv.us
Arkansas (501) 371-2600 http://insurance.arkansas.gov	**Kansas** (785) 296-3071 www.ksinsurance.org	**New Hampshire** (603) 271-2261 www.nh.gov/insurance
California (916) 492-3500 www.insurance.ca.gov	**Kentucky** (800) 595-6053 http://doi.ppr.ky.gov/kentucky	**New Jersey** (609) 292-7272 www.state.nj.us/dobi
Colorado (303) 894-7499 www.dora.state.co.us/insurance	**Louisiana** (225) 342-5900 www.ldi.state.la.us	**New Mexico** (505) 827-4601 www.nmprc.state.nm.us/id.htm
Connecticut (860) 297-3800 www.ct.gov/cid	**Maine** (207) 624-8475 www.maine.gov/pfr/insurance	**New York** (212) 480-6400 www.ins.state.ny.us
Delaware (302) 674-7300 www.delawareinsurance.gov	**Maryland** (410) 468-2000 www.mdinsurance.state.md.us	**North Carolina** (919) 807-6750 www.ncdoi.com
District of Columbia (202) 727-8000 www.disb.dc.gov	**Massachusetts** (617) 521-7794 www.state.ma.us/doi	**North Dakota** (701) 328-2440 www.nd.gov/ndins
Florida (850) 413-3140 www.floir.com	**Michigan** (517) 373-0220 www.michigan.gov/ofir	**Ohio** (614) 644-2658 www.ohioinsurance.gov
Georgia (404) 656-2070 www.gainsurance.org	**Minnesota** (651) 296-4026 www.state.mn.us	**Oklahoma** (405) 521-2828 www.ok.gov/oid
Hawaii (808) 586-2790 www.hawaii.gov/dcca/areas/ins	**Mississippi** (601) 359-3569 www.mid.state.ms.us	**Oregon** (503) 947-7980 www.cbs.state.or.us/ins
Idaho (208) 334-4250 www.doi.idaho.gov	**Missouri** (573) 751-4126 www.insurance.mo.gov	**Pennsylvania** (717) 783-0442 www.ins.state.pa.us
		Rhode Island (401) 462-9500 www.dbr.state.ri.us
		South Carolina (803) 737-6160 www.doi.sc.gov
		South Dakota (605) 773-3563 www.state.sd.us/drr2/reg/insurance
		Tennessee (615) 741-2241 www.state.tn.us/commerce
		Texas (512) 463-6169 www.tdi.state.tx.us
		Utah (801) 538-3800 www.insurance.utah.gov
		Vermont (802) 828-3301 www.bishca.state.vt.us
		Virginia (804) 371-9741 or 877-310-6560 www.scc.virginia.gov/division/boi
		Washington (360) 725-7000 www.insurance.wa.gov
		West Virginia (304) 558-3354 www.wvinsurance.gov
		Wisconsin (608) 266-3585 www.oci.wi.gov
		Wyoming (307) 777-7401 http://insurance.state.wy.us

For example, the financial data allows the calculation of the types of financial ratios discussed in Chapter 3. It also permits a double check of financial data provided by agents and others with a financial interest in the transaction, although a more efficient route typically is via rating agency information. One of the most interesting and potentially insightful elements of the annual statement filing is *Management's Discussion and Analysis* of the insurer. Here management is required to set out the company's background and organizational structure, discuss the likely effects of adverse economic events, and summarize its financial operations and liquidity and capital resources. The section wherein management explains the company's principal risks and uncertainties can be especially insightful, although the discussions can appear as laundry lists of everything that could go off its mark.

Few, if any, states make the statements available on their web sites, although they can be viewed at the state insurance department. Instead, the states rely on the NAIC to make them available to the public electronically. Selected financial information can be found at https://eapps.naic.org/cis/index.do. Advisors can learn from this same site the states in which the insurer is licensed. More detailed financial information, including annual statements, can be obtained from the NAIC Store at https://eapps.naic.org/insData/index.jsp. Registration is required but is free, as are the first five reports.

Finally, a few states make the reports compiled from on-site financial examinations of their domestic insurers available on their web sites. While these exam reports can be interesting and revealing, too often they are dated.

Complaint Data

Insurers that are tending toward financial difficulty often provoke higher levels of consumer complaints about poor quality service, claims handling, and marketing activities than they did formerly or more than their peer companies. Independent of whether high complaint frequency hints at financial difficulty, who wishes to deal with a life insurer for which its insureds and beneficiaries lodge an excessive number of complaints?

State insurance departments compile data on the nature and frequency of closed complaints lodged against licensed insurers. Such data typically are not available from the departments' web sites directly, but the NAIC compiles such data for the states that wish to participate in the NAIC system. State participation is voluntary, so the NAIC complaint data are not necessarily complete, although it appears sufficiently so to provide useful information.

The NAIC web site at https://eapps.naic.org/cis/index.do allows the user to compile various reports, including the following:

◆ *Closed complaint counts by state.* Displays the total number of closed complaints for the selected company in each state.

◆ *Closed Complaint Counts By Code.* Displays the total number of closed complaints by type of coverage, reason the complaint was filed, and disposition of the complaint.

◆ *Closed Complaint Ratio Report.* Displays the ratio of the company's U.S. market share of closed complaints compared to the company's U.S. market share of premiums for a specific policy type.

◆ *Closed Complaint Trend Report.* Displays total closed complaint counts by year with the percent change of counts between years.

The Closed Complaint Ratio Report and the Closed Complaint Trend Report ordinarily are the most informative. The Ratio Report normalizes the number of each company's complaints to its market share. Insurers with larger market shares can be expected logically to garner more complaints than insurers with smaller market shares, other things being the same. Complaint ratios of insurers with similar products and target markets should be compared. A national median complaint ratio is also provided, allowing for a comparison of the specific insurer's complaint ratio to the national median. The Trend Report highlights whether claims are increasing meaningfully, but this should be considered in relation to market share or increases in business.

Risk Based Capital Ratios

As discussed in Chapter 4, insurers are required to calculate and provide their risk based capital (RBC) ratios to state insurance regulators. The RBC system was created to provide a standard for insurer capital adequacy intended to reflect each insurer's unique risks. The higher are a life insurer's asset, insurance, interest, and business risks—as measured by a complicated formula—the greater its required capital level, other things being the same. This required capital level is measured by taking the ratio of an insurer's adjusted capital to its total control level RBC. The higher the ratio, the better able the insurer should be able to weather adverse developments. Also note that there are disincentives to holding excess capital, such as poorer performing policies, and therefore a balance is required regarding capital positions. See Chapter 3 for a discussion of this topic.

As noted in Chapter 4, individuals and companies within the insurance business are prohibited from disclosing insurers' RBC ratios. Presumably, individuals and businesses *not* engaged in the business of insurance are not. It is for this reason that one of the few public sources of life insurers' RBC ratios is a former insurance-academic-turned journalist, Joseph M. Belth. His publication, *The Insurance Forum,* offers these ratios each year, although his calculations differ somewhat from those prescribed by the NAIC—which he explains. See www.theinsuranceforum.com/.

Thus, the advisor who is not engaged in the business of insurance can secure these ratios and utilize them to inform him- or herself and clients about insurers' relative risk. Care, however, should be taken in doing so, as we discuss in Chapter 4. Further, rating agencies provide to the public their own risk adjusted capital ratios, which is a factor in their overall insurer financial strength ratings.

Securities and Exchange Commission

Public companies above a certain minimum size must annually file with the *Securities and Exchange Commission* (SEC) an annual report of the company's performance on **Form 10-K**. This annual report is far more detailed than the similarly named glossy annual report provided to shareholders. The 10-K includes detailed information related to the company's history, nature of its business, organizational structure, risk factors, equity, subsidiaries, and audited financial statements, among other information. Stock life insurers are required to file these reports.

Relevant accounting data in these reports are based on GAAP, not statutory accounting principles. Recall that GAAP measures an insurer on a going concern basis, while SAP is a conservative measure of the insurer's ability to meet its obligations to policyholders. See Chapter 3 for a discussion of both accounting conventions.

Every annual report must be composed of four *Parts*, each of which is divided into *Items*. These reports can run into hundreds of pages in length, with resulting information overload akin to that which can occur with the financial statements filed with state insurance regulators. Typically, the most relevant items within a 10-K for a life insurance company are:

◆ *Item 1—Business.* This item describes the nature of the company's business, the subsidiaries that it owns, and the markets in which it operates. It will also include discussions of effects that are significant to particular industries, as with competition and regulation in an insurance context.

◆ *Item 1A—Risk Factors.* In this item, the company is required to state the risks that it faces; i.e., anything that could go wrong. This includes likely external effects, possible future failures to meet obligations, and other risks sufficient to ensure that current and potential investors are adequately warned. This item is especially relevant for life insurance companies, with a litany of possible negative effects typically discussed and, to some degree, analyzed.

◆ *Item 7—Management's Discussion and Analysis.* Within this item, management is required to discuss the operations of the company in detail and usually compares the current period to prior periods. It provides an overview of the company and a summary discussion of the key issues that it faces; the company's outlook; and results from operations. A related item here is a discussion of market risk. These comparisons provide the advisor with an overview of the operational issues and the causes of increases and decreases in business. This discussion can be especially insightful.

In addition to the 10-K, which is filed annually, a company is also required to file abbreviated quarterly reports on Form 10-Q. If significant material events occur, such as a change in CEO or bankruptcy, between filings of the 10-K and 10-Q, companies are required to report them on Form 8-K. Form 10-K, as well as other SEC filings, should be searched at the EDGAR database on the SECs website at http://www.sec.gov/edgar/searchedgar/companysearch.html.

Insurance Companies

Insurers being considered by clients are logical sources of information about their financial health. They can provide copies of their annual reports that contain summary financial data and, importantly, commentary about their strategic directions, plans, and operations. Such information is also commonly available on the insurers' web sites. They will have available as well brochures and/or other materials used for promotional purposes with their customers and agents. While such materials can be expected to be self-serving, they can provide a useful perspective as to how the company views itself and its relationship with its customers.

If potentially adverse financial information is revealed about an insurer that is being seriously considered by the client, through rating agencies and/or other sources, the insurer can be invited to respond to the negative information. In some instances, the information may be of minor consequence, but the onus should be on the insurer (or its agent) to make such a case. Again, we note the obvious admonition to be skeptical of self-serving commentary.

Insurers can also be a source of useful information about their competitors. Insurers are understandably reluctant to criticize competitors directly—in part because doing so can run afoul of state insurance regulation. But they often will have conducted their own financial analyses of competitors and will make it available to their agents and customers. Care should be taken in interpreting these analyses, especially when they are supported by simple comparisons of various financial ratios, as such ratios cannot provide the in-depth insight that rating agency evaluations entail.

Insurance Agents

Life insurance agents whose target markets are consistent with the needs of an advisor's client often maintain or have access to resources of the type mentioned here. They can be helpful resources. Additionally, experienced, successful agents ordinarily have an "ear to the ground" that enables them to pick up the latest "chatter" about insurers against which they compete regularly. As noted earlier, many agents were at the vanguard of suspicions concerning the financial strength of Executive Life Insurance Company before its collapse.

Of course, the advisor will be mindful that some agents will have a tendency to emphasize the positive aspects of the companies that they represent and do the opposite regarding those that they do not represent. Captive agents who do not represent insurers rated within the secure range can be in an especially awkward situation in this regard.

Stock Analysts' Reports

Reports on the valuation of individual insurer stocks prepared by major investment houses can provide additional insight into an insurer's financial position. Regrettably, only a few such companies (notably Citigroup and Credit Suisse) conduct extensive analyses of stock insurance companies.

These reports are naturally geared toward stockholders, not policyholders, with their emphasis on profitability and return on equity, not necessarily financial strength. For example, a strengthening of an insurer's reserves may be appealing to policyholders but not for stockholders. Doing so will reduce earnings and may depress the stock price, yet this result provides additional protection for policyholder benefits. Even with these types of reservations, these reports can add another dimension of the insurer's operational performance and, importantly, its near term financial outlook.

Publications

Of course, major business publications such as *The Wall Street Journal, Fortune, Business Week, The Financial Times,* and others will carry news about life insurers, just as they do about other major corporations. Monitoring news and archival research can reveal information that may be helpful.

Publications whose focus is insurance in general and life insurance in particular generally are more relevant. *The Insurance Forum* was mentioned earlier. Others include *Best's Review* and *The National Underwriter,* among others.

Conclusions

The analyses and opinions of rating agencies should necessarily factor greatly in the advisor's assessment of the financial strength of life insurers. The complexity and complications of doing otherwise would be daunting. To utilize the rating agencies' information, advisors should have knowledge of those agencies whose analyses and opinions are respected, including particularly those that have been designated as NRSROs. Further, advisors should understand the key factors that drive insurer ratings and the rating categories used by the agencies. At the same time, advisors should be attuned to other sources of information, such as state regulators and the NAIC, the SEC, stock analyst commentaries, news from publications like *The Wall Street Journal*, and insurance companies and agents. These other sources can reinforce and supplement the reports and opinions of rating agencies.

Life Insurance
Policy Fundamentals

Life Insurance Basics

6

$\mathbf{T}$HIS CHAPTER BEGINS PART III of the *Guide*, which explores life insurance fundamentals.[1] Here we introduce the basics of life insurance pricing. Chapter 7 discusses the more common life insurance policies that advisors are likely to encounter. Chapter 8 offers comparisons of these policies, including templates intended to allow advisors quickly to compare different product characteristics. Chapter 9 closes this part of the *Guide* with an examination of the typical features and provisions of life insurance contracts and the optional riders available with them.

Generic Types of Life Insurance Policies

As discussed in Chapter 1, all life insurance policies fall into one of two generic categories: term life insurance or cash value life insurance. We explore them in somewhat more detail here to ensure context for our introduction of life insurance pricing.

Term Life Insurance

Recall that **term life insurance** pays the policy face amount if the insured dies during the policy term, which is a specified number of years, such as 10 or 20 years, or to a specified age, such as age

---

Authored by Harold D. Skipper.
[1]This chapter draws in part from Kenneth Black, Jr. and Harold D. Skipper, Jr., *Life and Health Insurance* (13th ed.; Upper Saddle River, NJ: Prentice-Hall, 2000), Chapters 25–27 and 30.

65. If the insured lives beyond the set term, the policy **expires**, meaning that it terminates with no value.

Term life insurance usually provides either a level or decreasing death benefit. Premiums either increase with age or remain level. Term policies with level death benefits and increasing premiums are commonly referred to as being renewable, a term synonymous with increasing premiums, for the policyholder merely pays the next billed premium to "renew" the policy. Thus, **yearly renewable term** (YRT)—also called **annual renewable term**—provides term insurance whose premiums increase yearly. These policies expire at age 65 or a higher age.

Figure 6-1 illustrates a YRT policy that expires at age 65. Under this YRT life policy, the insurer will pay $1.0 million to the beneficiary only if the insured dies by age 65 and required premiums have been paid. Nothing is paid if the insured lives beyond age 65. Although not shown, premiums increase each year.

FIGURE 6-1: Illustration of a Term-to-Age 65 Life Insurance Policy

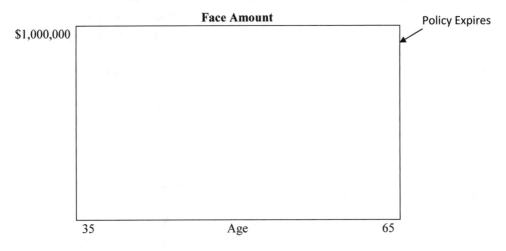

Cash Value Life Insurance

As we know from Chapter 1, **cash value life insurance** policies combine term insurance and internal savings—called the **cash value**—within the same contract; that is, they accumulate funds that are available to the policyowner, much as with a savings account with a bank. A policy's full cash value is not available on some policies if they are terminated within the first few policy years. Rather, a type of "penalty for early withdrawal" is applied in the form of a **surrender charge**, also called a **back-end load** or **loading**, that is subtracted from the policy's cash value to yield what is often called the policy's **cash surrender value** or simply **surrender value**.

Terminology here is not standardized, so it is important that the advisor determine precisely what the agent or insurer means by the terms used. For example, some agents and insurers—especially those selling unbundled products—use the term cash value to mean its surrender value; i.e., net of back-end loading. When used in this way, what we define as a policy's cash value may be called its **account value**, **policy value**, or **accumulated value**, especially with universal life policies. Unless stated otherwise, we will use these three terms as synonyms for a policy's cash value as defined above; i.e., before deducting surrender charges.

All cash value policies can be considered as a combination of YRT insurance and a savings account, such that the combination always precisely equals the policy's contractually stated death benefit, often called the **face amount**. Thus, for policies with level face amounts, the amount of term insurance purchased each year changes by precisely the same amount but in the opposite direction as the cash values change. The difference between the policy death benefit and the cash value is called the **net amount at risk** (NAR). (Some policies have a level NAR rather than a level death benefit, as discussed in Chapter 7.) This concept is illustrated in Figure 6-2 which shows a cash value policy with a $1.0 million level death benefit and level annual premiums whose cash values increase each year and, therefore, whose NAR decreases each year by precisely the same amount as the cash value increases.

FIGURE 6-2: Illustration of a Level-Premium Cash Value Policy Funded to Age 121

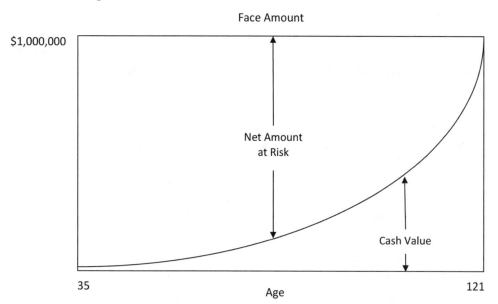

Thousands of variations of cash value policies exist, consistent with insurers' product differentiation and target market strategies. However, as noted earlier, virtually every cash value policy falls into one of three categories, even if the insurer does not label the policy as such: (1) universal life insurance, (2) whole life insurance, or (3) endowment insurance.

Universal life (UL) insurance policies are flexible-premium, adjustable death benefit contracts whose cash values and coverage periods depend on the premiums paid into them and can range to the whole of life to shorter periods. UL policies are usually nonparticipating (i.e., they are not eligible for policy dividends), but they routinely share in the insurer's operational results via non-guaranteed policy elements other than dividends. Recall from Chapter 4 that **non-guaranteed policy elements**, also called **current assumptions**, are those that are not guaranteed and that the insurer may change (more or less favorably), subject to contractual guarantees. They commonly include mortality and loading charges and interest credits.

Whole life (WL) insurance typically requires the payment of fixed premiums and promises to pay a death benefit whenever the insured dies and, therefore, is life insurance intended to remain in effect for the insured's entire lifetime. WL policies often are participating, but nonpar policies also are found. Most nonpar WL policies contain non-guaranteed elements akin to those found in UL policies. For some nonpar policies, all policy elements are guaranteed and fixed (i.e., the policies have guaranteed policy elements only), with no means of policy values being changed because of changing insurer operational results.

Endowment insurance makes two mutually exclusive promises: to pay a stated benefit if the insured dies during the policy term or if the insured survives the stated policy term. Historically, this benefit equaled the policy face amount and, if paid on survival, the policy was said to **endow** or **mature**. Thus, an endowment at age 65 policy paid the face amount if the insured died before age 65 or paid the same amount if the insured survived to age 65. Very little true endowment insurance is sold today because of adverse tax treatment. However, WL and UL policies can endow if the policy remains in force until the end of the mortality table used to calculate policy reserves, which is age 100 for older policies and age 121 for newer policies (see below). Most newer policies do not actually mature at age 121, even if the cash value equals the death benefit, instead continuing in force with no required premium payments or mortality or other charges, until the insured dies.

We know from Chapter 1 that cash value policies are also available as variable life insurance. With **variable life insurance**, the policyholder allocates the premium to investment options offered by the insurance company through what are called separate accounts, and the policyholder carries 100 percent of the investment risk, unlike for non-variable policies. Thus, policy values fluctuate with changes in the market value of the investments backing the policy's liabilities. The death benefit may vary with these changes in market value as well.

Life Insurance Pricing

Life insurance pricing involves numerous factors and decisions by company actuaries, but these four pricing components are key:

1. Mortality charges;
2. Interest credits;
3. Loading charges to cover expenses, taxes, and contingencies; and
4. Persistency.

These policy pricing components will vary in the importance in particular policies. For example, the interest component may be of little relevance for term policies, whereas the mortality component will be highly relevant. Further, we find hundreds of variations for each of these components in the market. Mortality charges, for example, can vary by age, gender, health, weight, smoking status, occupation, and many other characteristics, the effects of which can mean that 50 or more different mortality "cells" (mortality rates determined by considering many variables) can be applicable to 55-year-old insurance applicants, *within the same company*. Multiply these different cells by the number of life insurance companies—almost 1,000—and we sense the magnitude of the different possibilities that can exist in the market for life insurance policies.

The many variations of these components are mixed by insurance actuaries in innumerable ways to develop different versions of the same generic policy types mentioned above as well as products with special attributes, thereby rendering them more relevant to certain target markets and uses. Each variation carries different opportunities for gain (and loss) by the insurer and the policyholder.

Although all life insurance policies rely on the same pricing elements, the details of how these elements function within a policy vary. Traditionally, life insurance policies have been characterized as being **bundled** in the sense that the policyholder did not know the portion of the premium allocated to cover the insurer's operational expenses, taxes, and contingencies; to pay for the NAR part; to build cash values; or to support the scale of dividends for par policies.

All term and many whole life policies continue to function in this way or some variation of it. The policyholder pays an indivisible premium, receiving a bundle of benefits for it:

- A promise to pay a stated death benefit if the insured dies during the policy term;
- A promise to pay a stated cash surrender value on policy surrender, for permanent policies;
- Entitlement to receive (non-guaranteed) dividends declared by the insurer, for par policies; and
- Advice and administrative services of an agent and the insurer.

Universal life and many whole life policies are **unbundled** in the sense that the policyholder knows the portion of his or her premium that is allocated to pay for the YRT part; to build cash values; and to cover the insurer's expenses, taxes, and contingencies. These internal policy allocations do not necessarily track the insurer's actual mortality, investment, and expense experience. Nonetheless, the policyholder is able to see how the premium is allocated among these policy elements.

Whether a policy is bundled or unbundled is irrelevant to whether the above four pricing components are, in fact, used to develop policy pricing. They are. With bundled policies, while no allocation of the premium among policy elements is ordinarily provided to the policyholder, and no disclosure typically is made of the current assumptions as to mortality, interest, and expenses underlying policy dividends, the components are there. With unbundled policies, the components are more evident. Neither bundled nor unbundled policies disclose how persistency influences policy pricing and values, for reasons explained below.

Each pricing component and its variations are based on actual experience, usually from the insurer itself but sometimes from actuarial consulting firms, public sources, industry-wide data, or reinsurers. The actual results experienced by an insurer as to mortality, investment returns, expenses and taxes, and persistency are collectively called **experience factors** by actuaries and insurance regulators. From these experience factors, actuaries derive actual mortality charges to be levied against policies, interest rates to be credited to their cash values, and loading charges to be levied, irrespective of whether they are stated this way or are disclosed.

The gross premiums for many bundled par whole life policies are calculated using the maximum mortality and loading charges and minimum guaranteed interest rates, resulting in comparatively high, conservatively set premiums. Because of conservative pricing, the policies as a group are expected to experience (1) lower mortality rates, (2) higher investment earnings, and (3) lower expenses than those built into the policy's premiums and values. The excess amounts from these expected favorable deviations of actual experience from that assumed in pricing can be returned to policyholders in the form of dividends.

Nonparticipating (nonpar) policies originally differed from par policies in that they (1) did not pay dividends and (2) all policy elements (premiums, cash values and death benefits) were fixed at issuance and never changed. Today, nonpar policies commonly provide some means of allowing policy elements to change in accordance with the insurer's actual or anticipated operating results—in much the same way that par policies allow participation in the insurer's actual operating results. Almost all UL and many WL policies are nonpar and operate in this way.

Participating life insurance historically has been associated closely with mutual (i.e., policyholder-owned) insurance companies and nonpar has been associated more closely with stock (i.e., stockholder-owned) insurers. In fact, most par insurance is still sold by mutuals and most nonpar by stocks, although each may sell the other form as well.

Mortality Charges

That mortality is a component of life insurance pricing is self evident. It is the job of actuaries to estimate the likelihood of paying death claims under policies each year and devise an equitable means of assessing each policy for its proportionate share of these claims. Annual mortality charges are assessed on each policy's net amount at risk, irrespective of whether they are identified as such to the policyholder; i.e., whether the policy is bundled or unbundled. The total yearly (or monthly) charge is the product of that year's (or month's) NAR in thousands and the mortality charge per $1,000 for the insured's attained age, gender, and other rating and classification factors. We can think of this charge as paying for the policy's internal YRT insurance.

All UL and WL unbundled policies—both variable and not—contain a set of explicitly stated, guaranteed maximum mortality charges that may not be exceeded. Bundled policies do not contain a set of explicitly stated, guaranteed maximum mortality charges, but they can be constrained to assess charges no higher than those used to derive guaranteed cash values, depending on some technical operational details of the policy. Most insurers assess mortality charges at less than the maximum permitted, with the current charge explicitly stated with unbundled products and not so stated with bundled products. To explain this process, we start with a short discussion of mortality experience and tables.

Mortality Experience and Tables

Obviously, the likelihood of paying a death claim each year under a given policy is the likelihood of the insured dying in each policy year. In turn, this likelihood is measured by mortality tables that display yearly probabilities of death by age and gender and sometimes other characteristics. They show a hypothetical group of individuals beginning with a certain age and tracing the history of the entire group year by year until all have died. Mortality tables are classified in many ways. Those relevant to our purposes are:

◆ **Population versus Insured Mortality.** The two main sources of mortality statistics are (1) census enumerations and death returns filed with registration offices and (2) deaths under life insurance policies. Both census enumerations and death registration records are frequently inaccurate or incomplete. On the other hand, the mortality statistics of insured lives tend to be quite accurate. The nature of the insurance process leads to a careful recording of the date of birth, issue date, gender, date of death, and other characteristics of insured individuals. This facilitates derivation of accurate death rates for the various mortality cells used by insurers. Importantly, mortality experience among insured lives is significantly better than that of the general population, because most insured lives have been subjected to an insurer's underwriting process. Virtually all mortality tables used today by life insurers are based on the experience of insured lives.

◆ **Valuation versus Basic Tables.** A **basic mortality table** reflects the actual experience of the insured populations from which it was drawn. These tables are more or less unadulterated, containing no margins. They are used by some insurers in the calculation of the gross premiums to be charged, to develop the current mortality charges for UL and similar policies, and to develop dividend scales and payments on participating policies. The most recent basic table is the *2001 Valuation Basic Table (2001 VBT)*, constructed from mortality data of several insurers from 1990 to 1995 and projected to the year 2001 using recent mortality improvement trends.

A **valuation mortality table** is used as the basis for calculating minimum reserves and cash values. Margins (additional deaths) are added to such tables to render them conservative. The use of such tables is prescribed by state law. Valuation tables are also used by some insurers to calculate gross premiums on par policies. The most recent valuation table is the *2001 Commissioners Standard Ordinary (2001 CSO) Table*, which is based on the *2001 VBT*, with margins added. In replacing the *1980 CSO* table for regulatory purposes, the *2001 CSO* table provided for lower mortality and extended the terminal age to 121 from age 100.

◆ **Smoker versus Nonsmoker Tables**. Because smoking and other tobacco usage has such profound negative effects on mortality rates, separate basic and valuation mortality tables have been developed for tobacco users and non-users, commonly titled simply smokers and nonsmokers. Except for the very old and young, the death rates of smokers is about twice that of nonsmokers, resulting, according to one study of population data, in a 10-year shorter life expectancy for smokers than for nonsmokers. Most insurers today use this smoker/nonsmoker differentiation, either in charging higher premiums or levying higher internal mortality charges for smokers than for nonsmokers.

Influences on an Insurer's Mortality Experience

Large insurers develop mortality charges for their life insurance products from a study of their own recent mortality experience. This experience will have been determined by the characteristics of the cohort of insureds from which the experience was drawn. A host of factors influences mortality, including age, gender, health, body mass, occupation, avocations, lifestyle, smoking status, and drug and alcohol usage, as explained in more detail below. Ideally, the study will have categorized mortality across these and other characteristics, permitting their use to form both rating categories and underwriting classifications (see below). In making these categorizations, two interrelated factors must be considered: (1) the market from which the experience was gathered and (2) the nature and degree of underwriting applicable to the experience group.

First, as we have noted, insurers develop products to be relevant and appeal to certain target markets. These markets can vary enormously from each other in their composition and so too can their mortality experience. For example, we know that individuals with low incomes and wealth do not live as long on average as those of moderate incomes or wealth, and that individuals of still higher incomes and wealth live longer still. It is, therefore, important that the target market from which mortality experience underlying a product's mortality charges was drawn be similar to the target market for the new product or that appropriate adjustments be made.

Second, the degree and rigor of underwriting applied to the experience group has a strong influence of the mortality experienced. For example, the mortality experience under guaranteed issue ("take all comers") life insurance, which involves no underwriting, and under simplified issue ("accept or reject") life insurance, which involves minimal underwriting, reveals comparatively high mortality rates. Mortality experience under life insurance policies issued on a nonmedical basis—meaning without a physical exam but with health questions and the reports of the proposed insured's health care professionals—would be better but still not superior. Policies issued with rigorous underwriting tend to result, unsurprisingly, in superior mortality experience. And, in general, the larger the policy face amount, the more rigorous is the underwriting.

These two factors are interrelated and can be mutually reinforcing. For example, high income individuals purchase larger policies (and undergo greater underwriting scrutiny) than do low income individuals, other things being equal. Simplified issue policies of modest amount appeal more to low- and middle-income individuals than do regular underwritten policies purchased most frequently by higher-income individuals.

Deciding on the Mortality Charges to Assess

After determining the most relevant mortality experience, actuaries use this information as the basis for setting the charges to be assessed different insureds. These charges can be viewed as falling into two categories. First, sets of standardized mortality charges will be established for each age and gender combination and usually subdivided further into smoking status. Second, sets of optional mortality charges will be established to be added to the standardized charges for those proposed insureds whose characteristics suggest a shorter life expectancy than that implicit within the standardized charges.

Developing Standardized Morality Charges. If the product being developed and priced is to be targeted to insureds possessing, as a group, more or less the same characteristics as those of the historical group, then its expected mortality can be expected to track experience mortality. Actual mortality charges to be assessed within this new product can logically be derived directly from the historical mortality.

Targeting less risky prospects (e.g., slim, physically active, rich, non-smokers, with no current or historical health issues and with long-lived family members) would be expected to result in superior future mortality experience relative to the historical group as a whole. Mortality charges could be adjusted downward accordingly. Conversely, developing a guaranteed issue or simplified issue life insurance product would be expected to result in proportionately more deaths, so mortality charges should be higher.

In developing standardized mortality charges, underlying mortality experience will be sorted (if possible) according to the various rating categories intended for use. Typical rating categories include age, gender, and smoking status, at a minimum (see below). Next, either implicitly with bundled products or explicitly with unbundled products, **mortality margins** are added to the underlying mortality rates to develop the actual mortality charges to be assessed within the policy. These margins can be comparatively high or low, commonly called wide or thin respectively. Here is the procedure:

Procedure for Setting Actual Mortality Charges

        Estimate relevant historical mortality experience rates
    + Mortality margin
    = Mortality charges

Mortality (and other) margins are a part of an insurer's overall pricing structure and are not necessarily intended to represent mortality and its risk only. They provide a cushion against adverse developments and can be a source of insurer profits, surplus accumulations, and/or expense recovery.

For bundled products, the set of internal current mortality charges typically is not revealed to prospective applicants. For unbundled products, the set of current mortality charges either is explicitly stated in the policy illustration or can be obtained on request, with the guaranteed maximum rates stated in the contract itself. Mortality charges for unbundled products typically are called **cost of insurance** (**COI**) rates. Whether bundled or unbundled, all life insurance policies are assessed mortality charges to pay for the policy's pure (YRT) insurance component or, stated equivalently, each policy's fair share of yearly death claim benefits paid.

Hence, a specific set of premium or COI rates is developed for each age-gender-smoking status combination. Agents commonly estimate premiums for clients based on these factors, either directly with bundled products or indirectly within unbundled products (COI rates implicit in the premium selected). The information is easily obtained. Increasingly, insurers also provide even lower premium and COI rates for proposed insureds who exhibit "preferred" characteristics (e.g., low weight in relation to height, no family deaths from cancer or heart disease before age 60, no adverse personal health history).

Of course, the older the proposed insured, the higher the mortality charge, other things being the same, as the likelihood of death increases with increasing age. Males are charged higher rates than similarly situated females, as females live about eight years longer than males on average. Smokers are charged more than nonsmokers for the same reason. Individuals having preferred characteristics live longer than do those who do not, all else equal. To illustrate these differences, here are the annual COI rates per $1,000 of NAR for an insurer with four rating categories:

Life Insurer with Four Rating Categories							
Age [55]							
Females				Males			
Nonsmoking		Smoking		Nonsmoking		Smoking	
Preferred [$1.18]	Standard [$1.75]	Preferred [$5.10]	Standard [$5.10]	Preferred [$1.38]	Standard [$2.00]	Preferred [$5.56]	Standard [$6.17]

Unsurprisingly, the chart shows that the lowest annual rates, $1.18 and $1.38 per $1,000, are for nonsmoking, preferred-class females and males respectively. For comparison, the rates 10 years later are $3.86 and $4.31, about three times higher. They are higher for two reasons: (1) the insured would be 10 years older and (2) the benefits of underwriting on mortality are diminishing. Note the substantial rate differences for nonsmokers and smokers, reflecting higher probabilities of death for smokers than for nonsmokers and probably other pricing considerations as well.

Determining Mortality Charges for a Proposed Insured. Except for guaranteed issue life insurance involving no underwriting, policies sold to individuals are underwritten by life insurance companies. **Underwriting** is the process by which an insurer decides whether to issue requested insurance and, if so, on what terms. Underwriters are a life insurer's "gatekeepers" in the sense that they are responsible for ensuring that individuals to whom they agree to issue insurance pay a premium that bears a reasonable relationship to the risk of death being insured.

For bundled life insurance policies, the most important of the terms is usually the gross premium to be charged, which contains an implicit COI charge. For unbundled life insurance, the most important of the terms usually are the COI rates to be applied, which are explicitly embedded in the resulting premium. In making their decision whether to issue a requested policy and on what terms, the insurer's underwriters consider carefully those characteristics of the proposed insured that have been associated with either an increased or decreased likelihood of death of similarly situated individuals. Two types of information are obtained and used: rating and classification.

Rating categories—age, gender, smoking status, and possibly preferred status—are typically used by agents to inform applicants of the premium or COI charges for the policies being requested. Unless the applicant misstates his or her age, gender, smoking status, or preferred status (admittedly, a trickier exercise), the agent will know the relevant premium or COI rate, *provided* no adverse underwriting information is developed. If no adverse information is developed, the standardized premium or COI rates apply.

But such is not the case for many applicants, and, in general, the older the proposed insured, the more likely some health or other issues exist. It is the underwriter's job both to (1) verify the accuracy of the rating information, correcting any found to be inaccurate, and (2) ferret out any characteristics that would be reasonably expected to lead to a shortened life expectancy in comparison to that implicit in the standardized rates. The underwriter's greatest skills come into play in performing the latter task, in his or her evaluation of the risk classification factors. **Risk classification factors** are used by underwriters to determine whether the proposed insured's health and other characteristics dictate the assessment of charges beyond those dictated by the rating factors (age, gender, smoker, etc.). Thus, besides verification of rating information, the underwriter will secure and review the following types of information:

◆ **Health**. The proposed insured's current and past health condition is of obvious importance in the underwriting process. Underwriters use detailed data on the relationships between various health conditions and shortened life expectancy. To secure needed health information, a physical exam, along with urine and blood samples, are usually required and, depending on the amount of insurance applied for and the age of the proposed insured, a more involved medical workup may be required. Additionally, a health history will be required and any hospital records and attending physician statements obtained.

◆ **Family History.** A history of family members living to old age without serious health impairments suggests an increased likelihood of the proposed insured doing likewise, other things be the same. The reverse is of concern to underwriters.

◆ **Alcohol and Drug Usage.** Excessive alcohol use and especially abuse is associated with higher mortality, as is drug abuse. Abuse of either can lead to a refusal to issue any life insurance.

◆ **Occupation.** Less important than in past times, some occupational hazards persist that warrant additional charges. Underwriters secure information on the proposed insured's job and whether any unusual hazards exist.

◆ **Sports and Avocations.** Not ordinarily a basis for additional mortality charges, some sports and avocations are, nonetheless, associated with higher than normal mortality. These can include skydiving, scuba diving, hang gliding, competitive racing, and the like.

◆ **Aviation and Military Service.** Being a private pilot and sometimes a commercial pilot can lead to additional charges, but passengers are not subject to any such charges. Those serving in the military are almost never charged extra, although, if an ongoing military conflict is sufficiently extensive, the risk of death from military action may be excluded from coverage in the policy. See Chapter 9. We are unaware of any insurers including such exclusions today.

◆ **Financial Status and Circumstances.** Underwriters are keenly interested in the purpose for which the insurance is being purchased, particularly for policies running into the millions of dollars. They wish to satisfy themselves that the amount of insurance being requested bears a reasonable relationship to the financial consequences that would result from the proposed insured's death. For example, if the insurance is being requested to cover estate obligations, underwriters will follow their guidelines that are intended to ensure that the insurance amount is not excessive in relation to estate taxes due on the insured's estate.

Underwriters will also need to satisfy themselves that the beneficiary designation and the policy ownership arrangement are logical and contain no hints of "speculation," which is the purchase of insurance by others in hopes of profiting from the insured's early death. Underwriters do not want an insured "worth more dead than alive," meaning that the life insurance amount should be a type of indemnification for heirs and others for their financial loss and not encourage anyone to have a financial motivation to hasten the insured event! If speculation concerns or other inconsistencies exist in the financial underwriting phase, the underwriter will seek to resolve the inconsistency or concern. If it cannot be resolved, the application will be declined.

As the underwriter is reviewing the above information, he or she is also determining whether one or more elements require additional charges because of an anticipated probability of death higher than that implicit in the premium or COI rates derived from the rating factors. The actual premiums or mortality charges assessed a given policyholder are a function of the extent to which the underwriter assesses the insured's characteristics as deviating negatively (or positively) from the mortality embedded in those premiums or COI rates charged.

Underwriters commonly make this assessment via assignment of numerical ratings to proposed insureds. This rating is the underwriter's estimate of the expected mortality of the group of persons whose characteristics match those of the proposed insured or, stated equivalently, the life expectancy of the cohort of persons into which the proposed insured falls. Obviously, the underwriter is *not* asserting that the proposed insured's life span will necessarily be that life expectancy.

A numerical rating of 100 is considered a normal or standard risk, one whose classification factors are all positive. Numerical ratings range from 75 or less to a high of 500 or more. For most insurers, ratings of 115 or less are considered standard or preferred. Ratings above 500 (or 1,000 with some insurers)—meaning expected mortality of 500 percent of average—are considered to be uninsurable. The expected mortality is simply too high for the insurer. A scale of numerical ratings for a company might be as follows:

Preferred /	Standard /	Substandard . . . /	Uninsurable
75 85	100 115	125 150 175 . . .	500 600

Insurers and reinsurers have accumulated considerable statistics on health impairments and other characteristics associated with higher-than-standard mortality rates. From these statistics, actuaries have developed **substandard ratings** that are intended to quantity the additional anticipated mortality beyond that inherent in the standard rate. By far the most common substandard rating method is the **multiple table extra**, also called **table rating**, under which so-called substandard risks are divided into broad groups according to their additional expected mortality as measured by their numerical ratings. Premium rates or mortality charges are based on mortality experience corresponding to the average numerical ratings in each cell. An example of a numerical scale of substandard classifications is shown in Table 6-1. Some insurers use alphabetic rather than numerical scales; i.e., Table A, B, etc., but the result is the same.

TABLE 6-1
Illustrative Scale of Substandard Mortality Classifications

Table	Mortality (%)	Numerical Rating
1	125	120–135
2	150	140–160
3	175	165–185
4	200	190–210
5	225	215–235
6	250	240–260
7	275	265–285
8	300	290–325
10	350	330–380
12	400	385–450
16	500	455–550
Uninsurable	—	Over 550

A special mortality table—hence the term, *table* rating—is, in effect, developed for each substandard classification, reflecting the experience of each, from which implicit (bundled) or explicit (unbundled) additional mortality charges are assessed for each class. Table 6-2 shows illustrative COI rates at standard and various substandard classifications for a 55-year-old male. These rates are applied to an unbundled policy's NAR, which means that their impact on premiums and policy values diminishes for a level face amount as these premiums and values increase and vice versa. Bundled policies accomplish the same thing via averaging the additional mortality charge over time and adding it to the standard premium, but the underlying actuarial principles should be the same; i.e., a table rating applied to the NAR. For both bundled and unbundled policies, the table rating method results in additional mortality charges that effectively increase with increasing age.

Some life insurers offer what are termed **table shaving programs** under which proposed insureds normally issued at Table 3 or 4 ratings or less can be offered life insurance at their standard rates. Certain impairments disqualify the client, such as alcohol abuse, from such programs, and amounts and types of insurance are limited. In many instances, such carriers' standard rates are higher than those found with carriers not offering such programs.

TABLE 6-2
Illustrative COI Rates—Standard and Substandard, Male, Age 55

		Table 1	Table 2	Table 3	Table 4
	Rates for NS	125%	150%	175%	200%
Classification	**Standard Risks**	(120–135%)	(140–160%)	(165–185%)	(180–210%)
COI Rate per $1,000 Net Amount at Risk	2.00	2.50	3.00	3.50	4.00

Another substandard rating method is the **flat extra**, under which a level additional charge unrelated to the insured's age is added to the standard premium. This method results in additional mortality charges that remain constant with age, such as commonly found with substandard ratings for hazardous occupations, sports, aviation, and avocations.

The Effect of Mortality Charges on Policy Values

A permanent policy's cash or account value is simply the amount remaining from the premiums paid each year after deducting mortality and loading charges and adding interest. Obviously, the lower the mortality and loading charges and the higher the interest crediting rate, the higher will be the resulting account value, but just how important are the mortality charges to this process? The answer is "it depends."

It depends on the interaction of the policy's net amount at risk and the COI rates. The higher the NAR, such as results from lower funding, the higher must be the total mortality charges assessed against the policy and the lower the policy value, other things being equal. Similarly, the higher the COI rates, the higher must be the total mortality charges assessed against the policy and the lower the cash value, other things being equal.

Of course, COI rates increase with increasing age. If a policy's NAR also increases with increasing age, which implies likely underfunding of the policy, the effect of each year's total mortality charges on policy value—being the product of the two figures—can be profound. This is especially true because mortality rates are exponential; i.e., they increase at an increasing rate with age. In general, the older an insured, the greater the impact, depending on the precise funding level.

Consider two UL policies, identical in every way except that 10 years of funding for Policy A is illustrated at time of purchase as causing the policy cash value to equal the policy face amount of $1.0 million at age 121, and 10 years of funding for Policy B is illustrated at purchase as taking it to age 121 with a cash value of but $1.00. Taking into consideration a 5 percent time value of money (i.e., discounting future values), all COI charges as a percentage of premiums for Policy B are almost 25 percent higher than those for Policy A over the life of both policies. This stark difference occurs because the NAR of Policy A declines throughout the entire policy period whereas Policy B's NAR increases in later years, imposing considerably higher COI charges.

Another factor to be considered by advisors is the orientation intended for a given policy by the insurer. Some policies are designed with comparatively low COI rates with the intention of having a stronger appeal to those customers with a greater interest in the policy death benefit. Such clients usually are interested in minimal funding levels. Other policies—intended to appeal to those with a strong interest in the cash accumulation element of the

FIGURE 6-3: Effect of Table 4 Rating (100 percent Increase in COI Rates) on Universal Life Premiums, Male, Age 55, Preferred

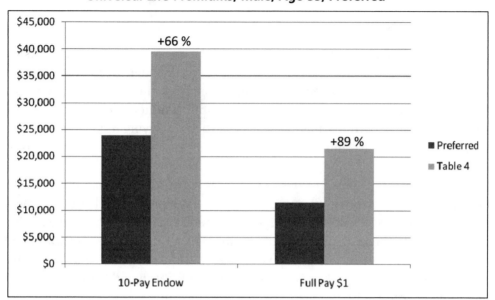

policy—may be designed with comparatively high COI rates. Such clients usually are interested in higher funding levels, with the idea of having the NAR decrease rapidly. Of course, the higher the funding level, the more rapidly the NAR decreases, other things being the same.

Finally, consider the effect of substandard ratings on policy funding levels. Figure 6-3 shows a preferred-rated UL policy that, based on current assumptions, can be funded with 10 premium payments to cause the cash value to equal the $1.0 million face amount at the terminal age of the mortality table, age 121, or can be funded with level premiums for the entire time period to cause the cash value to equal $1.00 at age 121, commonly referred to as **full pay**. To cause the policy cash value to equal the death benefit at age 121 with a Table 4 rather than a preferred rating, each of the first 10 premiums must be increased by 66 percent. For full pay maturity, on the other hand, all premiums must be increased by 89 percent, a higher relative figure by virtue of the full pay funding having higher NARs. Of course, these results are not necessarily representative of that which would be found with other policies or funding levels.

Interest Crediting Rate

The interest rate credited to policy cash values is the second policy element in life insurance pricing. The ultimate cost of life insurance products is highly dependent on the insurer's investment returns, which, in turn, drive the interest crediting rate. Insurers that earn above-average returns can price products more favorably than those that do not. Insurers that earn below-average returns may not be able to retain customers in a competitive market.

Investment Returns

As we know from Chapter 3, the investments backing the liabilities arising from variable insurance products are managed through accounts separate from an insurer's general account assets that back the liabilities of its non-variable products. The cash values of variable products are determined by and linked directly to the market values of the underlying investments in the separate account. No minimum interest rate is guaranteed to be credited to their cash values.

By contrast, the cash values of non-variable products do not change with the market performance of any underlying investments, and the contracts guarantee to credit a specified minimum interest rate; e.g., 2.5 percent. The cash values of these UL and WL policies are neither determined by nor linked directly to the market values of investments in the insurer's general account. The interest credited to these cash values is significantly *influenced* by but not directly *determined* by the insurer's investment returns.

Influences on an Insurer's Investment Returns

As we also know from Chapter 3, the liabilities arising from individual life insurance are of long duration, with the contracts remaining in force for decades. Insurers seek to match the duration and nature of its investments with those of the liabilities; i.e., investments of long duration and fixed nature for general account products. For this reason, life insurers invest heavily in long-term, high quality bonds and mortgages. In fact, their investment returns are highly influenced by their bond yields.

As with other investors, life insurers prefer higher returns to minimize the cost of their insurance products and to maximize profitability. However, greater risk is associated with higher expected returns, so life insurers establish investment guidelines in an effort to limit the risks to acceptable levels. In addition, insurers are required to hold more capital for riskier assets, which provides a strong incentive for insurers to limit investments in below investment grade instruments.

Insurers' investment guidelines address not only asset quality but also the duration or maturity of investments. We know that longer maturing investments generally carry higher returns than shorter maturing investments, so insurers have incentives, as we saw in Chapter 3, to invest longer. However, life insurers also must be mindful of the duration or average maturity of their liabilities. In general, they strive to match the duration of their assets to that of their liabilities, thereby minimizing risks associated with a mismatch causing losses. Thus, other things being the same, insurers with longer duration liabilities can more safely invest in longer duration assets. And the longer that policies remain in force, the longer will be the duration of the liabilities associated with those policies, other things being the same. Thus, insurers with higher persistency rates—meaning that fewer policies lapse or are surrendered—can have longer duration liabilities.

Deciding on the Interest Rate to Credit

Unlike the situation with mortality charges that are insured-specific, the interest rate credited to a policyholder's cash value ordinarily is unrelated to any characteristic or behavior of the policyholder. All policies within a given block are credited with the same interest rate. (An exception to this statement can occur in policies that have policy loans outstanding and that link the interest rate credited on the cash value or the dividend to the policy loan interest rate.)

Insurers' current crediting rates are commonly greater than the guaranteed minimum crediting rates. The current crediting rate will be a function, first, of the insurer's investment returns. The difference between the insurer's actual investment return and its interest crediting rate is called variously the **interest margin**, the **investment margin**, or the **spread**, as shown here.

Procedure for Setting Current Interest Crediting Rate

      Current investment return
  − <u>Interest margin</u>
  = Interest crediting rate

Spreads typically range from 50 to 200 basis points. Insurers' target spreads are influenced by numerous factors. The product's target market can affect the margin. Thus, if the product is aimed toward customers who wish to accumulate higher cash values, the insurer may seek to build in a comparatively thin spread, especially if the target market is highly competitive. Also, the larger the average policy size, the lower can be the spread, because of size economies.

Obviously, insurers with high profit objectives for a product line may well expect correspondingly wider spreads. Also, the higher the risk perceived from a product line, the greater might be interest margin. For example, products containing comparatively high guaranteed minimum crediting rates may be expected to produce higher interest margins. Some insurers expect the interest margin to contribute toward expense recover.

Some insurers vary the current crediting rate by the length of time policies have been in force, in recognition that investments accumulated on behalf of different generations of policies will earn different yields. A variation of this approach occurs when insurers artificially segment their investment portfolios, allocating the segments to different blocks of policies. In each instance, investment returns can vary across different generations and segments.

Other insurers base their currently credited interest rate on the average investment return of their entire investment portfolio, called the **portfolio average method**. This method does not segregate policies into generations or segments; instead, it uses the same interest rate for all policies. This method produces a more stable interest crediting rate than the approaches discussed earlier.

The Effect of Interest Crediting Rates on Policy Values

Customarily, changes in the interest crediting rate have a more profound effect on policy values than do changes in any of the other policy pricing elements. And the greater the cash value in relation to the death benefit, the greater is that effect. Further, insurers change interest rates more frequently than they change COI rates and policy loadings (see below).

Figure 6-4 illustrates the effect on policy funding levels of a reduction in the crediting rate. Again we show a preferred risk UL policy funded for the first 10 years to cause the cash value to equal the face amount at age 121 and also full pay funded. We show next to each policy the higher premium required to ensure that the cash value equaled the death benefit at age 121 and full pay were the interest crediting rate to fall by 100 basis points and, next to that result, the total premium required for each funding option were the crediting rate to fall to the guaranteed rate.

FIGURE 6-4: Effect of Decrease in Interest Crediting Rate by 100 BP and to Guaranteed Interest Rate, Universal Life Premiums, Male, Age 55, Preferred

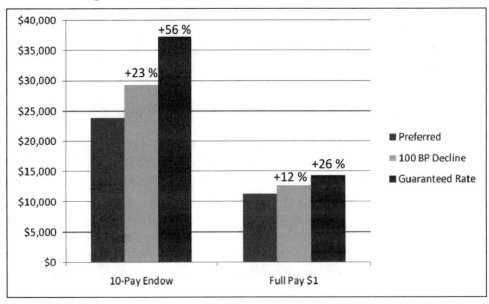

These results are interesting. Note that the decrease in crediting rates has a more profound effect on the first policy than the full pay arrangement. This is the opposite relative effect as that seen with increases in the COI rates. The reasons are, in a sense, the same. Whereas the COI rate increase was relatively more profound with the policy whose NAR was higher, the crediting rate decrease has a relatively more profound effect with the policy whose cash values are higher. Of course, these results are not necessarily representative of that which would be found with other policies or funding levels.

Loading Charges

Insurers obviously incur expenses in the marketing, underwriting, and various other processes necessary for the successful prosecution of their business. They also must pay taxes to the federal government as well as to the states in which they conduct business. Finally, they wish to make profits or accumulate surplus and to allow for unforeseen contingencies. These elements are appropriately charged against the policies to which they relate. In deciding the means to charge policies for these elements, actuaries make estimates of future expenses, taxes, profits (or surplus accumulations), and contingencies to develop a set of charges—called variously **loading charges, expense charges, fees,** and **policy loads**—intended to compensate the insurer for some or all of these elements.

Unbundled policies contain a set of guaranteed maximum loading charges that the insurer may assess. Insurers typically charge less than the maximum permitted. Bundled policies contain no stated guaranteed maximum charges but are constrained as to how much they can assess policies by virtue of having guaranteed gross premiums.

Costs of Doing Business

Insurer expenses may be classified in many ways. Generally, they fall into two broad categories: investment expenses and operating expenses. **Investment expenses** are the costs of making, processing, and protecting the insurer's investments. As they are related directly to the production of investment income, they are usually deducted from the gross investment income. They are, thus, taken into account in determining the interest crediting rate or calculation of a bundled policy's gross premium and dividends and are not ordinarily considered explicitly in connection with policy loads.

Operating expenses are the costs incurred in normal business operations. Insurers usually record such expenses as falling into one of four categories:

1. **Acquisition expenses**, sometimes called **first-year expenses**, are those costs relating to the procurement and issuing of new business, including underwriting.

2. **Development expenses** are those costs incurred in developing a new product line.
3. **Maintenance expenses**, also called **renewal expenses**, are those costs incurred to maintain and service policies after they are in force.
4. **Overhead expenses**, also called **administrative expenses**, are those costs incurred that are not directly related to a specific product, such as executive salaries, rent, utilities, etc.

Insurers also separate operating expenses as to whether they are direct or indirect. **Direct expenses** are those directly attributable to a specific product (e.g., agent's commission). Most acquisition expenses are direct. Identifying direct expenses and allocating them to a particular product line is relatively straightforward. All product pricing systems include direct expenses in a product's pricing structure.

In contrast, **indirect expenses** are those that cannot be attributed to one specific product line only. Expenses such as senior management compensation, accounting expenses, utilities, and information systems exist and continue whether the insurer offers a particular product. Development, maintenance, and overhead expenses are mostly indirect. Identifying and allocating indirect expenses to a product line during the pricing process is complex and often arbitrary.

For purposes of determining a proper amount of loading, operating expenses may be assigned to three major groups:

1. Expenses that vary with the amount of premiums—for example, agents' commissions and premium taxes.
2. Expenses that vary with the amount of insurance—for example, underwriting costs tend to vary with policy size.
3. Expenses that vary with the number of policies—for example, the cost of preparing policies for issue, establishing the necessary accounting records, and sending of premium notices.

Each of these three allocations results in a cost per some measured unit and are called **unit costs**. In view of the arbitrary and difficult nature of allocating indirect expenses, some companies allocate only direct expenses to a specific product, called **marginal costing**. In contrast, traditional **full costing** allocates both direct and indirect expenses to each product. In the case of marginal costing, indirect expenses may be allocated to each overall product line rather than to particular products.

Influences on an Insurer's Costs of Doing Business

For 2008, the average life insurer spent about 11.5 percent of its total income (premium plus investment) to cover operational expenses and 0.7 percent for taxes and fees. Less than one-half of total operating expenses were paid as agent commissions, the balance going to cover home and field office expenses. These averages mask wide variations in insurers' costs of doing business. An insurer selling many small policies will have proportionately higher expenses than one selling many large policies, and those selling exceptionally large policies should enjoy even larger efficiencies. Insurer operational costs also vary by insurer size, distribution channels utilized, product offerings, geographical location, and a host of other factors.

Taxes and fees are omnipresent. Federal income taxes apply across the board, based on insurer profitability, so their impact on insurers varies with profitability. As with all other employers, insurers must pay Social Security taxes on behalf of their employees, representing a surprisingly large outflow because of the labor intense nature of the business. Another surprisingly high effective tax for life insurers is the tax on premiums that each insurer must pay to each state in which it has insurance in effect. This tax averages about 2 percent of all life insurance premiums received by insurers. State premium taxes are often passed on directly to the policyholder.

Deciding on Loading Charges to Assess

The foregoing suggests that loadings ideally would consist partly of a percentage of premium charge, partly of a charge for each $1,000 of insurance, and partly of a charge per policy. In fact, the loadings of many unbundled products are structured in this tripartite manner. Many unbundled products omit one or more of the three elements in their loads, with a few having no identifiable charges. In the latter situation, of course, the insurer's expenses must be met from mortality and interest margins.

After conducting studies as to past operational expenses and taxes and making adjustments for reasonably anticipated future changes including inflation, actuaries develop unit costs based on expense categories, as alluded to above. The determination of unit costs involves both the amount of expense incurred, as shown by cost evaluations, and the time of its occurrence. From these unit costs, final loading charges and fees to be assessed policies are derived by adding expense margins, as shown here:

Procedure for Setting Current Loading Charges

      Estimate historical expenses and patterns
   <u>+ Expense margin</u>
   = Loading charges

The **expense margin**, also called **safety margin**, is intended to provide for contingencies, for profits or surplus accumulation, and/or to cover losses associated with early policy lapses (see section below on *Persistency*). Of course, mortality margins and interest margins can cover the same elements, although we tend to associate each particular margin with its policy element.

Once all unit costs are developed and appropriate expense margins added to these costs, actuaries typically combine them to yield explicit loading patterns for unbundled policies of a (1) flat annual (or monthly) amount per-policy or as a percentage of the account value (commonly called an **administrative charge**), (2) a percentage of the first-year premium and a lower percentage of renewal premiums (called **front-end loads**), and, sometimes, (3) a charge per $1,000 of face amount. Additionally, some policies assess back-end loads against cash values withdrawn in early policy years, as discussed earlier in this chapter. Policies usually do not have both front- and back-end loads.

Bundled policies accomplish their loading goal through a difference process. One common means is to solve for the gross premium necessary to equal the present value of all durational benefits, unit costs assigned in various ways (see above), and taxes and adding a percent of premium and per unit margins for profit, desired permanent surplus contributions, contingencies and, where applicable, dividends. In all instances, such tentative premiums are tested under various scenarios.

For most unbundled products, the identifiable loading charges assessed against a particular policy typically will be determined by the magnitude of the premiums paid and sometimes the account value and death benefit amount. For bundled products, loading will be embedded as an indivisible component within the premium (and usually cash value) but will likely have been derived as a percentage of first-year and renewal premiums as well as flat policy charges and possibly an assessment based on the face amount. Unlike mortality charges, individual insured characteristics have no effect on loading charges, although loads may be banded by policy size.

Loading charges for variable life insurance are typically configured somewhat differently. As variable products are subject to the rules and regulations applicable to other securities, all charges and fees must be disclosed. Most meaningful charges are expressed as a percentage of the account value, such as investment management fees and mortality and expense (M&E) charges. M&E charges typically are not intended to cover routine death claims (mortality) but to provide mortality and expense margins akin to and for the same reason as those applicable to general account policies.

The Effect of Loading Charges on Policy Values

As loadings embedded into bundled products are an indivisible component of the policy's premium (and usually cash values), we cannot illustrate their effect on policy values. As we discuss in Chapter 16, however, we can infer the importance of policy loadings for bundled as well as unbundled products through internal rate of return and other cost comparison methods.

Figure 6-5 offers an illustration of the impact on premiums of an increase in front-end loads from $200 to $400 per month for the same preferred risk UL

FIGURE 6-5: Effect of an Increase in Loading Charges from $200 to $400 per Month on Universal Life Premiums, Male, Age 55, Preferred

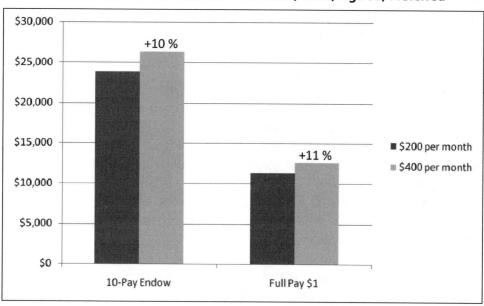

policy and funding arrangements as discussed in earlier figures. Again, one funding arrangement is calculated to ensure that the policy cash value equals the death benefit at age 121 with 10 annual premium payments, with values derived from current assumptions, whereas the other assumes a full pay arrangement. As can be seen, a doubling of the front-end load does not have a profound effect on either required funding level, although the fee has a somewhat greater relative effect on the less heavily funded arrangement. This fact is not surprising given its lower annual premium. The reason for the relatively light effect of a change in loading charges is that the charges are constant over time and do not increase exponentially with age as with the COI charges and do not decrease with increases in the cash value. Of course, these results are not necessarily representative of that which would be found with other policies or funding levels.

Persistency

Persistency is the percentage of life insurance policies not terminated by lapse, typically within one year. A **lapse** occurs whenever a premium necessary to maintain the policy in full effect is not paid. The premium not paid may have been that required on a scheduled basis, as with bundled contracts, or it may have been one that was needed to ensure an adequate account value to maintain a universal life policy in force. Also, a lapse occurs whenever a policyowner terminates a policy for its surrender value or ceases to pay premiums and allows some insurance to remain in partial effect under one of the so-called nonforfeiture options (see Chapter 9).

Persistency is the measure of a company's retention of its insurance business. In general, the greater a company's persistency for a group of policies, the greater are the surplus funds arising from that business. These surplus funds can be used to enhance policyholder benefits or insurer profits or both.

The Importance of Persistency

Persistency is not a policy element as are mortality charges, interest credits, and loading charges. Rather, it enters actuaries' policy pricing indirectly, ordinarily as it influences policy loadings. It can be factored into mortality or interest margins, as well. Persistency is directly relevant to life insurance policy pricing, because the assets that insurers accumulate from having sold a block of policies rarely precisely equal the liabilities that arise from those policies. When the accumulated assets arising from a group of policies are allocated proportionately among those policies, we get each policy's share of assets or what is called its **asset share**.

If a policy is surrendered and its asset share is less than its cash surrender value, then the surrender imposes a cost on the insurer. Conversely, if the asset share is greater than the surrender value, the surrender results in a gain for the insurer. For example, assume that a policy was issued precisely one year ago, and an annual premium of $1,000 was paid at that time. Assume further that the insurer paid $1,200 for the policy's share of death benefits and acquisition expenses of selling, underwriting, administering, and issuing the policy last year. (Expenses after the first year are substantially lower.)

Thus, the insurer had a cash inflow of $1,000 and an outflow of $1,200 (ignoring interest), resulting in a $200 drain on the insurer's assets during the first policy year. Stated differently, the policy's first year share of assets or asset share is –$200. Assume now that the policyholder surrenders the policy, one year later, for its $300 surrender value. This $300 must be paid from the insurer's assets. Thus, this policy has imposed a cost of $500 ($200 + $300) on the insurer or, more accurately, on the persisting policyholders of the group. The higher the first-year termination rate for this block of policies, the greater the costs imposed on the remaining policyholders, because the asset share ends up being less than the cash value by $500.

Our simple example reflects reality more closely than the reader may suspect. It is routine that policies' first-year asset shares are less than their first-year surrender values, and common for the asset share not to equal the surrender value for three or more years. All policies that are expected to lapse or be surrendered during these times impose costs on persisting policyholders as reflected in the underlying product pricing. Actual surrenders or lapses in excess of those assumed in pricing may result in additional costs to persisting policyholders through less favorable non-guaranteed assumption changes.

Another way of thinking about the impact of persistency in pricing is that policies are typically designed to lose money in the first year (i.e., first-year issue expenses exceed premiums collected), followed by profits in succeeding years. Good persistency is needed for renewal profits to repay early-year losses. These early losses are often called **surplus strain**, which is the drain on an insurer's surplus that results from having negative cash flows during policies' early years. A common profit target is stated as some internal rate of return on the underlying negative and positive cash flows. The number of years to break-even is another common profit measurement. **Break-even** is the year in which accumulated profits cover prior years' losses, with the lower the break-even year the better for the insurer.

A reverse example could be concocted easily wherein the asset share exceeded the cash value at some future time. In these instances, each policy that lapses or is surrendered results in an immediate gain to the insurer by the amount of the difference between the two figures. First impressions can be that life insurers, therefore, would like all policies to lapse or be surrendered during the time periods wherein the asset share was greater than the cash surrender value. Ordinarily, this is not true, as the insurer would be foregoing even larger future gains if the policies remain in force.

In some instances, however, this supposition is accurate. Some insurers have engaged in so-called **lapse-supported pricing,** which is the practice of pricing some products such that later gains from lapses and surrenders are allocated to subsidize early policy cash flows. State regulations limit this practice.

Thus, in developing the pricing for a particular policy, insurance actuaries must estimate future lapse and surrender rates. They must do this to account properly for the gains and losses associated with terminations of these policies. Other things being the same, losses (asset share less than value on surrender) diminish policy value (e.g., could lead to higher premiums or charges to make good the losses), and gains enhance policy value (e.g., could lead to lower premiums or charges). It is for these reasons that a life insurer's policy termination rates are an important component of life insurance policy due diligence (see Chapters 3 and 14).

Influences on an Insurer's Persistency

Actual persistency rates experienced by an insurer are a function of many factors, including the following:

- ◆ **Target market.** Each of an insurer's policies ordinarily is aimed at a particular market segment. In general, we know that the higher the income or wealth of person in a particular market, the higher is the persistency, other things being equal (but see below). Thus, policies aimed at individuals of low or modest means tend to experience the highest lapse rates and, therefore, incur higher loadings for this fact.

Markets can be segmented by factors other than income or wealth. For example, policies targeted to certain professions or affinity groups often experience better persistency than otherwise would be found for that group's income or wealth characteristics.

- **Policy suitability.** Individuals who purchase life insurance policies that are unsuitable are more likely to terminate their policies. Policies may be unsuitable because the premium is too high in relation to family income, the face amount too small or too large given the insurance need, or the policy type does not fit with the long term need.

- **Nature of policy sale or service.** Related to but slightly different from policy suitability issues is the situation in which a policy is inappropriately sold or serviced. A policy can be sold inappropriately for many reasons, some of which are that the customer did not truly understand what he or she was purchasing, the recommended premium to be paid was either too small or too large in relation to the goal for the policy, the beneficiary and/or policyowner arrangement was defective or not fully reflective of the customer's wishes, and so on. Poor customer service falls into the same category. When customers believe that they have not been advised or otherwise dealt with fairly or appropriately, the tendency is to terminate the relationship.

- **Policy cost.** A not uncommon situation arises when an individual purchased a policy only to discover that it does not offer good value in relation to its premiums. Issues of policy cost can arise many years after policy purchase. A policy may have been reasonably priced at time of purchase, but the insurer could not or did not continue such favorable pricing over time. Expensive policies tend to experience higher lapse rates than less costly policies.

- **The economy.** Policy lapse rates vary with the performance of the economy. In economic downturns, lapse rates tend to rise. In good times, they tend to be lower.

- **Surrender charges.** Policies that provide for higher penalties—surrender charges—for early termination often experience better persistency than those providing smaller or no such penalties.

- **Commission charge-backs.** If a policy is terminated by the policyholder during the first year, many life insurers require the agent to repay some or all of the commission paid. This practice gives the agent a greater financial incentive to ensure that the policy was sold and serviced appropriately.

As should be clear, several of these factors are within the control of the insurer, the agent, or both. Life insurers that market their policies through agents who exhibit the traits of fairness, competence, integrity, and diligence (see Chapter 2) should experience lower policy termination rates than others.

Deciding on Persistency Rates to Use

Actuaries will have conducted studies of the persistency experience of the various policies that the insurer has sold over time. In developing a new product, they will use these experience studies to inform them as to the most likely persistency rates to use in new product development, assuming that the product characteristics and target market are similar to past experience. If they differ, appropriate adjustments would be made in the data. Additionally, the actual rates used in pricing are influenced by the insurer's pricing goals and projected cash flows associated with the block of policies.

The Effect of Persistency on Current Assumptions

As an example of the effect of a higher than expected lapse rate, consider a policy originally priced with a 3 percent lapse assumption but results in a 10 percent lapse rate. If the insurer is to restore its original profit objective for these policies, it will have to increase COI or loading charges or decrease the interest crediting rate or some combination thereof. For example, a decision to restore the profit target via a decrease in the crediting rate would require a 30 basis point reduction.

Putting It All Together

The preceding discussion makes clear that life insurance pricing components can be and are mixed in different ways by insurers to accomplish different marketing and profit objectives. The precise mix will be driven by the competing interests of policy performance and profitability, coupled with the insurer's underlying mortality, investment, expense, and persistency experience. Strong results in each category can lead to good policy performance and sound profitability for the insurer. In each instance, the advisor will wish to know the extent to which illustrated policy performance matches with such underlying experience, as we analyze in Chapter 14.

Profitability is, of course, essential for insurer long-term viability. Precisely how expected profitability is embedded into product pricing will be a function of product and market factors. Profits will be built into some or all of the preceding four key pricing components, depending on the product target market and competition within that market. Just as the pricing elements can be mixed in different ways, so too can expected profits be allocated in innumerable ways among these components.

Besides the vital role that profitability plays in product design, reserves that life insurers are required to maintain can be an important factor in product pricing. In general, the higher the reserves required to be maintained, the greater is the cost to an insurer in terms of having to earmark assets to back the reserves and having a correspondingly lower capital and surplus. Thus, policies designed to appeal to buyers who want large amounts of life insurance at comparatively low premium outlays may require insurers to establish correspondingly large reserves. If such policies' premiums are very low, the insurer may be required to establish additional reserves in recognition that future policy funding will be lower than that associated with higher-premium contracts yet the death benefit promise may be the same. These sorts of opportunity cost issues must be accommodated in product design and pricing.

In deciding on this mix and the premiums needed to fund the insurance package, considerations such as adequacy, equity, legal limitations, competition, and specific insurer objectives all enter into the process. Adequacy clearly is the most important requirement, because insurer solvency can be jeopardized by inadequate charges. Equity in premiums and charges is primarily for the benefit of policyowners, although there is a practical limit to the degree of equity that can be attained. At some point, the marginal cost of efforts to improve equity becomes greater than the value of the improvement, due to expense considerations.

Also, charges must not be in conflict with any law. Competition will, obviously, affect an insurer's premium rates and charges. In setting growth and profit goals, other objectives, such as markets selected, products emphasized, or compensation philosophy, can all affect the pricing structure finally adopted.

Of course, contingencies can cause adverse deviations from underlying assumptions, as discussed above. They can arise from adverse mortality, investment, lapse, and/or expense deviations. The expense, morality, and interest margins—collectively called **product margins**—help ensure that the insurer will be able to meet its contractual obligations even under adverse circumstances. Of course, these product margins also are intended to be sources of profits or surplus accumulation. For participating insurance, it is customary to insert a specific allowance in the margins for the purpose of creating additional surplus from which dividends can be paid.

Margins within life products are commonly described as being thin or wide; thin meaning relatively small margins and wide being relatively large margins. Whether product margins are thin or wide for a given life insurance policy is influenced by a policy's risk characteristics. Table 6-3 shows the general relationship between various characteristics and the magnitude of product margins.

TABLE 6-3
Likely Effect of Selected Risk Characteristics on Product Margins

Policy Characteristic	Assessment	Degree of Product Margin
Mortality and expense charge guarantees	Weak	Thin
	Strong	Wide
Guaranteed minimum interest rate	Low	Thin
	High	Wide
Magnitude of surrender charges	Low	Thin
	High	Wide
Who bears investment risk?	Policyholder	Thin
	Insurer	Wide
Non-guaranteed policy elements present?	Yes	Thin
	No	Wide
Level of early anticipated lapse rates	Low	Thin
	High	Wide
Market competitiveness	High	Thin
	Low	Wide
Insurer profit objective	Low	Thin
	High	Wide

The table is largely self-explanatory, if highly simplified. The lower the insurer's perceived risks, the lower can be the product margins and vice versa. Obviously, that margins *can* be thin is no guarantee that they *will* be thin.

Conclusions

Advisors who master a basic understanding of life insurance pricing will be of far greater benefit to their clients in the exercise of policy due care than those whose knowledge is superficial. As we examine in Chapter 14, it is possible to gain insight into such fundamental issues as the likelihood of a given life insurance policy performing as illustrated and whether the insurer is pricing its products in a fair, reasonable manner. Basic pricing knowledge also helps the advisor to determine an appropriate funding level (as covered in Chapter 15) and in dealing with in-force performance deviations (as covered throughout Part VI).

Common Life Insurance Policies

7

WITH MASTERY OF THE life insurance basics provided in Chapter 6, this chapter continues the Part III theme on life insurance fundamentals. Here we discuss the more common types of term and especially cash value policies that the advisor is likely to encounter in his or her practice.[1] While we do not purport to cover all types of policies, policies encountered by the advisor that we do not cover will probably prove to be close variations of those analyzed herein. If not, the advisor might consider discussing the policy with respected, knowledgeable life insurance agents.

The Effects of Income Tax Law on Life Insurance Policy Design and Operation

Before providing an overview of the more common life insurance policies, it will prove useful to provide a brief discussion of how federal income tax law influences life insurance policy design and operation. We begin by a short discussion of the tax favored status of life insurance then discuss the importance and nature of the Internal Revenue Code (IRC) definitions of life insurance and of modified endowment contract.

Authored by Harold D. Skipper.
[1]This chapter draws in part from Kenneth Black, Jr. and Harold D. Skipper, Jr., *Life and Health Insurance* (13th ed.; Upper Saddle River, NJ: Prentice-Hall, 2000), Chapters 4–6.

⌐x Favored Status of Life Insurance

As discussed more fully in Chapter 18, a life insurance policy ordinarily enjoys favorable income tax treatment in two respects if the policy meets the definition of life insurance and is not a modified endowment contract (see below). First, death proceeds are received free of income tax, unless the policy is payable to the employer or policy ownership has been transferred (sold) for a valuation consideration. Even here, exceptions exist to both exceptions (see Chapter 12 for employer-owned life insurance), rendering most death proceeds income tax free.

Second, income tax otherwise due on the interest credited to policy cash values is either deferred until a policy is surrendered or matures (endows) or is excused altogether if the insured dies. If a policy is surrendered or matures as an endowment, the general rule is that the excess of a policy's gross proceeds over its cost basis is taxable as ordinary income. **Gross proceeds** are the amounts paid by an insurer on surrender or maturity, including the cash value of any paid up additions. The **cost basis** of a life insurance contract, also called **investment in the contract**, normally is the sum of the premiums paid less any untaxed distributions. Untaxed distributions include any withdrawals, the sum of any dividends received as distributions, and policy loans.

IRC Definition of Life Insurance

The IRC provides the above tax favored treatment only if cash value policies issued after December 31, 1984 meet the code's **definition of a life insurance** by satisfying one of two actuarial tests: (1) a cash value accumulation test or (2) a guideline premium and cash value corridor test. If at any time the contract fails to meet its relevant test, it loses its tax favored treatment. The IRC was amended to include this definition because of what were perceived as abuses of policies' favorable income taxation, by policyholders who were funding their policies beyond reasonable levels in order to shelter income from taxation. The tests, in effect, mandate that a qualified policy's cash value or funding may not exceed specified levels deemed reasonable.

The **cash value accumulation test** requires that a policy's cash value may not at any time exceed the *net* single premium that would be required to fund future insurance benefits (defined to be mainly death and maturity benefits) provided under the contract, net of loadings, at the insured's attained age and based on certain required assumptions. For example, consider a $1 million whole life policy with a cash surrender value of $250,000. Under the test, the single premium for $1 million of whole life insurance based on the required assumptions and net of loadings must not be less than $250,000. If it is less, the policy fails the test, is considered overfunded, and loses its tax preference status. Insurers will ordinarily not let this happen, automatically increasing a policy's death benefit if necessary to ensure compliance.

The **guideline premium and corridor test**, intended for unbundled policies, is a two-part test that is met at all times if the total of the gross premiums paid under a contract do not exceed the guideline premium limitation and meets a cash value corridor requirement. The **guideline premium limitation** is met if the gross premiums paid do not exceed the greater of a guideline single premium or a guideline level premium. These tests limit the amount of premium that can be paid into a contract for a specified amount of coverage.

The **guideline single premium (GSP)** is the *gross* single premium that would be required to fund future insurance benefits (defined to be mainly death and maturity benefits) provided under the contract at the insured's attained age and based on certain required assumptions. The **guideline level premium (GLP)** is the level annual amount payable over a period ending not before the insured's age 95 for the contract benefits, based on the same assumptions as the GSP except at a lower interest rate. Thus, the actual cumulative gross premiums paid into the contract may not exceed the greater of the cumulative GLP or the GSP. The cumulative GLP equals the simple sum of GLPs to each policy year.

For example, assume a policy GSP is determined to be $420,000 and that its GLP is $36,000. Assume further that cumulative gross premiums paid through policy year 10 total $400,000. The guideline premium test would be met as it permits gross premiums of the greater of $420,000 or $360,000 to have been paid into the contract through policy year 10.

The **cash value corridor test** is met if the policy's benefits at all times are at least equal to certain percentage multiples of its cash value. These percentages range from 250 percent for insureds of attained ages up to 40, grading to 100 percent for attained age 95. Thus, if a 35-year-old owns a policy whose cash value is $100,000, the policy death benefit must be at least $250,000 ($100,000 x 250 percent) for the policy to meet the corridor requirement. If it is less than $250,000, the policy fails the corridor test, is considered overfunded, and loses its tax preference status. As with the cash value accumulation test, insurers ordinarily will not allow this to happen by automatically increasing a policy's death benefit if necessary to ensure compliance with the test.

Under the corridor test, a policy's death benefit can equal its cash value only at age 95 or greater. If a policy's cash value equals its death benefit before age 95, it loses its tax preferred status. As mentioned earlier, this is one of the reasons that little endowment insurance is sold today.

IRC Definition of Modified Endowment Contract

Another important IRC definition that determines the income tax treatment of life insurance policies is that of a **modified endowment contract** (MEC), which is any policy entered into after June 20, 1988 that meets the IRC definition of life insurance, but that fails to meet the so called seven-pay test. A life insurance policy fails to satisfy the **seven-pay test** if the cumulative amount paid under the contract at any time during the first seven contract years exceeds the cumulative amount that would have been paid had the policy's annual premium equaled the net level premium for a seven-pay contract of the same type, using certain required assumptions.

The seven level premiums are determined at policy issuance, and the policy death benefit is taken to be that of the first contract year, irrespective of any scheduled benefit decreases. Thus, if the net level premium for a seven-pay WL contract is $50,000, premiums actually paid into the contract may not exceed $50,000 in policy year one, $100,000 in policy year two, etc., and $350,000 for policy year seven. Thereafter, barring a material change in benefits, premiums may be of any level and not run afoul of MEC requirements.

A MEC is subject to income tax rules during the insured's lifetime that differ from those applicable to non-MEC policies. The IRC was amended to include this differential tax treatment because of the practice of many insurers selling single premium whole life policies more as tax preferred savings instruments than as policies providing protection against the financial consequences of premature death. The tax treatment of death benefits is unaffected by whether a policy is a MEC. Insurers' and marketing organizations' information systems test policy illustrations and in force policies for compliance.

For non-MEC policies, distributions in the form of dividends, loans, and withdrawals are not taxed as income, up to the cost basis of the policy, which usually equals the cumulative premiums paid. Only after distributions exceed the cost basis are they taxed. Distributions under MECs, however, are considered first a withdrawal of any untaxed gain in the policy, and only after all gain is taxed are distributions considered as coming from the cost basis. In addition, a 10 percent penalty tax is applied to all distributions under MEC policies that occur before age $59^1/_2$.

Term Life Insurance

As we already know, **term life insurance** pays the policy death benefit (face amount) if the insured dies during the stated policy term but pays nothing if the insured survives the term. The policy term may be stated as a set number of years, such as 10 or 20, or to a specified age, such as age 65. Recall that a term policy is said to **expire** if the insured lives to the set policy term.

Types of Term Policies

Term life insurance policies are bundled contracts typically providing either level or decreasing death benefits, with some increasing death benefit coverage sold. The great majority of term life insurance provides level death benefits. Decreasing term life is sold primarily to cover an insured's debts, particularly home mortgage loans, and to provide income protection.

Some life insurance policies or riders attached to policies (i.e., supplemental policy benefits) promise to pay the face amount and to "return the premiums paid" if the insured dies within a certain period, such as 20 years. Of course, the insurer does not actually return the premiums paid. Rather, this feature is increasing term insurance whose death benefit is set each year to equal the sum of the premiums paid to that point, in addition to the policy face amount. Other policies provide that the death benefit will increase each year with increases in inflation. Usually, this increasing term feature is paid by the policyholder, as he or she is billed each year for the increased insurance amount.

Term premiums either increase with age or remain level. Term policies with increasing premiums are said to be **renewable**, a term synonymous with increasing premiums. Thus, we find term policies whose premiums increase yearly—called **yearly renewable term (YRT)**, **annual renewable term (ART)**, or simply **increasing premium term**. Other term policies have premiums that increase every three, five, or ten years—called **three-year renewable term**, **five-year renewable term**, and **ten-year renewable term**. Whatever the renewal period, premiums increase at each renewal, more or less tracking the increase in mortality rates for the insured's attained age or an average of future such rates over the next term period.

Other term policies have the same premiums each year. Such term contracts may be written for a set number of years or to cover the typical working lifetime. Contracts of the first type include **10-year** and **20-year term** policies that sometimes can be renewed for another term, or they become YRT thereafter. Contracts of the second type provide essentially the same protection but are not renewable include **life-expectancy term** and **term-to-age 65** (or to other ages), although very few of these policies are sold today.

Premiums for most term policies are fixed and guaranteed at policy issuance. Some term policies pay dividends but most do not. Additionally, some term policies provide that the insurer can unilaterally change premiums from time to time, based on changing insurer operational experience, subject always to guaranteed maximum premiums set out in the contract.

Traditionally, term policies expired not later than age 65, and this is the requirement still in some states. Increasingly, however, we find term policies that extend coverage beyond this traditional cutoff age, such as to age 85 and even higher. For example, one well-known insurer's term to age 90 policy provides coverage to age 90, with level premiums for the first 10 years and YRT thereafter.

A recent and quite popular introduction to the term market is the **return of premium (ROP) term policy**. Unlike the return of premium death benefit discussed above, this policy promises to return the premiums paid for the policy if the insured survives the policy term, which may be from 10 to 30 years, depending on the insured's age and insurer's requirements. Of course, the insurer does not actually return the premiums. Rather, the policy provides for the payment of an endowment at the end of the policy term whose amount is set precisely equal to the sum of the premiums paid to that point.

Unsurprisingly, premiums for the policy are considerably higher than those for a regular term policy of the same amount and duration. For example, one insurer's regular 20-year term policy for $1.0 million carries an annual premium of $1,165. Its $1.0 million ROP policy issued on the same basis carries an annual premium of $4,450. The annual premium difference of $3,285 pays for the ROP/endowment of $89,000 ($4,450 x 20) payable in 20 years, if the insured survives to that point.

Key Features Unique to Term Policies

Term insurance policies often include a **conversion** feature that allows the policyowner to exchange the term policy for a cash value policy without having to prove insurability, for an amount up to that of the term policy. Conversion rights typically must be exercised by a certain number of years shorter than the policy term or age, such as by age 55, 60, or 65, then expire. The premiums for the new cash value policy typically will be based on the insured's attained age and original rating class. The conversion feature can be an important component of term policies, as original needs that called for temporary protection sometimes change.

Some term policies include a **reentry provision** that affords the policyowner the possibility of paying a lower premium than otherwise if the insured can demonstrate periodically that he or she meets continuing insurability criteria. For example, one company's policy provides that every five years insureds who can demonstrate continued insurability can enjoy much lower premiums than those who do not. The reentry feature, in effect, encourages insureds to self-declare their expected mortality status, thus making for a more refined risk classification.

Considerations

Initial premium rates per unit of coverage are lower for term life insurance than for other life products issued on the same basis. Premiums, however, can escalate rapidly with policy duration, depending on age. Term product prices are more easily compared than are prices of other life products, as term policies are usually structurally simpler than cash value policies, even though they are considered bundled products. Term products usually have no cash values. They also often pay no dividends, thus permitting policy price comparisons on the basis of premiums alone.

Some proponents of term insurance argue for its use to the virtual exclusion of cash value insurance, with others advocating the opposite viewpoint. Term insurance can be useful for persons with modest incomes and high insurance needs (a situation that occurs often with early family obligations). Also, term life insurance is well suited for ensuring that mortgage and other loans are paid off on the debtor/insured's death and as a vehicle for ensuring that education or other desired funds will be available if death were to cut short the period needed for the provider/insured to save the needed funds. Term insurance is also a natural for all situations that call for temporary income protection needs. Finally, the inclusion of term insurance within cash value policies can prove cost effective. See Box 7-4 below.

Universal Life Insurance

As we know from discussions in earlier chapters, **universal life (UL) insurance** policies are unbundled (transparent charges/loads and credits), flexible-premium, adjustable death benefit contracts whose cash values and durations of coverage depend on the premiums paid into them. After deciding on the policy death benefit and pattern (see below), the applicant must pay premium of at least a certain minimum amount to get the policy started. Thereafter, the policyowner pays as little or as much as he or she wishes into the policy, subject to insurer prescribed minimums and tax prescribed maximums. The higher the premium paid, the greater is the cash value, other things being equal. The policy remains in force as long as the cash value is positive, and the policy terminates (lapses) when the cash value goes to zero.

Operational Details
Figure 7-1 illustrates the operation of a typical UL policy. It shows the cash or account values at the end of each of the first three months and at any month n in the future and the reconciliation of each month's cash flow. Thus, at policy purchase, the owner pays the decided-upon premium to put the policy in effect. Thereafter, the owner may pay whatever premium he or she wishes, subject to tax-prescribed maximums and company-prescribed minimums. Perhaps most policyholders choose to pay a fixed amount monthly or annually. From any premiums paid is subtracted a premium or front-end load typically expressed as a percentage of the premium paid, for example 10 percent. A load of 10 percent results in 90 percent of the premium flowing into the account value.

FIGURE 7-1: Universal Life Funds Flow Illustration

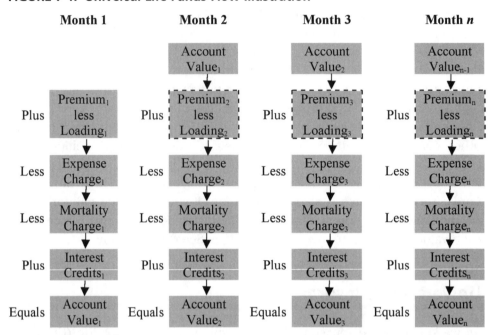

Expense charges, also called administrative fees, are assessed monthly against the policy value. These fees are stated as a flat dollar amount such as $10, a charge per $1,000 of death benefit such as $0.10, and/or sometimes a number of basis points of the account value. Thus, at $0.10 per $1,000, a $1 million policy would be assessed $100 per month plus perhaps a flat $10.

The mortality or cost of insurance (COI) charge is also assessed monthly, based on the policy's net amount at risk (NAR). Recall that the NAR equals the total death benefit less the account value. Thus, if the COI charge is $0.35 per $1,000 of NAR for the month, a $1 million policy whose account value was $400,000 would be assessed $210 [($1,000,000 − $400,000) x $0.35/$1,000] for the policy's share of that month's death claims.

The monthly interest credit is the interest crediting rate applied to the account value on a daily basis, after other charges have been deducted. If the interest crediting rate is 5.0 percent per year, it would translate into a monthly rate of 0.407 percent. Thus, our $1 million UL policy whose end-of-month account value is $399,680 ($400,000 − $10 − $100 − $210) would receive an interest credit for the month of $1,627 ($399,680 x 0.00407), for an end-of-month cash (account) value of $401,307 ($399,680 + $1,627).

This process is repeated on a monthly basis using current assumptions, respecting the guarantees in each instance. The same process applies to all UL policies and to current assumption whole life (CAWL), except that with CAWL, the payment of premiums is required. If, at any time during the policy's existence, the cash value is insufficient to cover monthly mortality and expense charges, the policy lapses unless additional funding is provided within a specified grace period, which typically is 31 or 61 days.

Typically, two death benefit options are available. Under Option A (or 1), the death benefit remains level. The NAR decreases as the account value increases (and vice versa). Under Option B (or 2), the death benefit equals what is commonly called the face amount in UL parlance (which is the same as death benefit in Option A) plus an additional death benefit equal to the account value, resulting in a level NAR. Some policies also offer an Option C (or 3) in which the death benefit equals the face amount plus an additional amount equal to the sum of premiums paid. With Option C, the NAR is the difference (1) the two death benefits combined and (2) the account value. The NAR will increase in years when the premiums paid are greater than that year's increase in account value and will decrease when the opposite result obtains. Other things being the same, COI charges will be higher under Options B and C than under Option A, which is logical as Options B and C are purchasing more insurance. Figure 7-2 illustrates the first two patterns.

Usually, the policyholder may change the death benefit option after policy issuance. If the change would result in an increase in future NARs, as for example would occur in moving from Option A to Option B, the insurance company usually will require satisfactory evidence of insurability.

FIGURE 7-2: The Two Generic Universal Life Death Benefit Patterns

Option A: Level Death Benefit

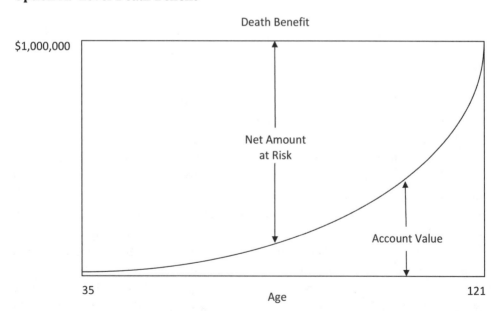

FIGURE 7-2: The Two Generic Universal Life Death Benefit Patterns

Option B: Level Net Amount at Risk

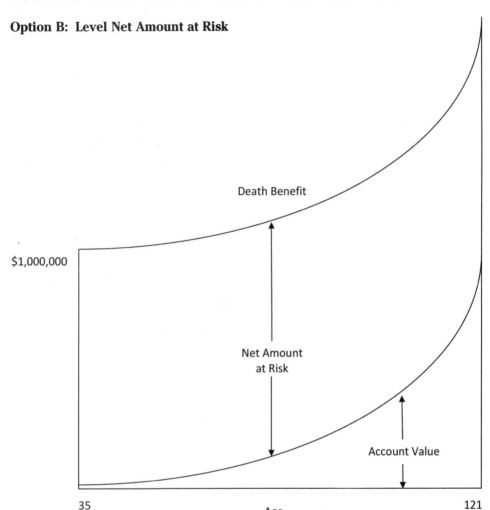

As already emphasized, a UL policy's death benefit is adjustable—the policyholder may request that it be reduced or increased at any time. Underwriting is required for unscheduled face amount increases. Some insurers offer a guaranteed purchase rider (see Chapter 9) that provides an option for limited increases and other policies provide for automatic, scheduled face amount increases, both without evidence of insurability. Unscheduled face amount decreases are always allowed but are constrained by the IRC definition of life insurance and may be restricted by policy minimums.

As we know, UL contracts contain guaranteed maximum COI and loading charges, but insurers commonly charge less than the maximums permitted. For UL policies issued in recent years, COI rates may not exceed those derived from the *2001 CSO Mortality Table* (see Chapter 6). Minimum guaranteed interest crediting rates are also set out in the UL contract, but insurers routinely credit higher rates. Typical minimums today are in the 2 to 4 percent range, with older policies sometimes having higher minimums. UL policies are said to be **transparent**, meaning that their internal operation, interest rates, and charges for COI and loadings are disclosed each year to the policyowner. In any event, resulting cash surrender values must be at least as high as those mandated by state nonforfeiture laws.

Typically, as we know from Chapter 6, loading charges in the early policy years are insufficient to cover the insurer's actual expenses, taxes, and desired profits. Insurers take one or both of two design approaches to recover these early net cash outflows not explicitly included in the loadings. *First*, UL policies often carry **back-end loads**, also called **surrender charges**, which ordinarily are a decreasing graded penalty applied against the cash value if the policy is surrendered within a few years (such as ten years) of issue. *Second*, insurers usually build margins into the COI charges and interest credits that provide renewal year profits in order to recoup the early-year losses.

As with all cash value policies, UL policies may be surrendered for their cash surrender values, which equals their account value less any surrender charges. The value received on surrender would be further reduced by any policy loans outstanding, for they must be repaid on policy termination whether by surrender or death, thus yielding a policy's net cash surrender value. As explained more fully in Chapter 9, the right to borrow funds from the insurance company for an amount up to and on the security of a policy's cash value is a feature of all cash value policies.

In addition to accessing policy value via loans, UL policyholders also may make withdrawals from the account value at any time. Withdrawals reduce the account value, and thereby interest credits, as well as the policy face amount dollar for dollar. The NAR remains unchanged. The insurer may limit the number of withdrawals per year, such as to four, and may assess a modest fee for each withdrawal, such as $25.

More recently, specialized versions of UL have emerged. **Death benefit UL**, also called **protection UL,** products emphasize policies' death benefits and allow very competitive premiums per $1,000 of face amount but typically also offer low cash value accumulation and/or have heavy surrender charges. **Accumulation UL** products emphasize efficient cash value accumulation but require higher premiums per $1,000 of face amount.

Considerations

In thinking about how UL can fit into a financial plan, it is often more insightful to think of UL not as a generic type of life insurance but as a flexible platform or shell that allows it to become whatever generic type of life insurance the customer wishes. As the policyholder, not the insurer, determines the magnitude of premium payments, the policyholder thereby determines the magnitude and rate of the cash value buildup in the policy and its generic type. In fact, a UL policy *will* turn out to provide term life insurance, whole life insurance, or endowment insurance, depending on the premiums paid and other policy factors. The policyholder's actions determine the type prospectively, but this, too, can change with time. Because of this premium flexibility, policyholders can effectively design their own policies to reflect their own needs and changing financial circumstances.

For example, perhaps the initial premium paid is just sufficient with interest to meet all policy loads and COI charges for the balance of the year, so no further premiums need be paid during the year. The cash value at year's end would be zero, based on current assumptions. The following year, a second premium is paid, again just sufficient to carry the policy through that year with no residual cash value at year's end, and so on each year thereafter. In this instance, the UL policy would be mimicking YRT insurance (admittedly not usually a wise means of purchasing YRT insurance, but a possibility). It is building no cash value—except for minor amounts during each policy year— and each year's premium payment must increase to cover each year's higher COI (YRT) rates.

Similarly, an agent could solve for the level premium that, if paid for 20 years, would cause the UL policy to lapse with no value at the end of the 20-year period, in which case the UL policy would be providing 20-year level-premium term insurance. Theoretically, term insurance coverage for any duration and any premium payment pattern can be arranged.

Consider the other extreme: a very large premium is paid at policy inception, such that future guaranteed interest credits alone would be sufficient to meet future internal policy charges (based on guaranteed assumptions) and allow the policy cash value to equal its death benefit at the end of the mortality table; i.e., insured's age 121. This is the definition of a single-premium whole life insurance. A still higher initial premium payment would cause the policy to endow at age 97, so the policy would be providing single-premium endowment insurance to age 97.

Theoretically, any endowment period and any premium funding pattern could be created, although practically, endowments before age 95 are not desired as they lose their favorable income tax treatment. Subject to tax and insurer constraints, a UL policy can replicate any term, whole life, or endowment insurance benefit and premium payment configuration. In doing so, it provides great flexibility in planning both for its financing and for the adverse consequences of death. The ability to access its value via loans, withdrawals, and/or policy surrender provides another dimension of flexibility.

Equity Indexed Universal Life

Equity indexed universal life (EIUL), also called **indexed UL**, is a comparatively recent UL variation with the same operational characteristics and platform as the generic UL products but with an interest crediting rate determined by reference to one or more equity indexes, such as the S&P 500 index.[2] While the rate is determined by reference to an index, the policyholder does not participate directly in that index's market. EIUL differs from generic UL (as well as variable UL—see below) in this interest crediting mechanism.

Operational Details

As with other non-variable life products, the EIUL account value is backed by the insurer's general account assets, but it is divided into two or more accounts: a fixed account and one or more index accounts. The policyholder decides on the funds to be allocated to each account. The fixed account crediting rate is typically the same as that found with the insurer's other UL policies, being influenced by the investment returns in its general account, as described in Chapter 6. The **index account** is that portion of the EIUL cash (account) value for which the crediting rate is determined by changes in an equity index, subject to a guaranteed minimum crediting rate, called the **growth floor**, and a maximum crediting rate, called the **growth cap**. The growth floor limits the downside potential and the growth cap limits the upside potential.

The change in the index's market value is its **index performance rate**. Importantly, dividend income ordinarily is *not* included in deriving this rate. Each transfer of funds into the index account creates a new **segment** of a specified duration, called the **segment term**. The index performance rate is measured over this term. Common segment terms are one and five years.

The relevant index performance rate is then multiplied by each segment's **participation rate**, which is the proportion of the index performance rate that can be counted in deriving the actual crediting rate, to yield the **growth rate**. A participation rate of 100 percent means that the entire growth rate is considered and a rate of 80 percent means that 80 percent of the growth rate is considered. Other things being the same, a higher participation rate is preferred to a lower one. The crediting rate to be applied to the index account, called the **index crediting rate**, is the growth rate adjusted to take account of the segment growth floor and growth cap.

---

[2]This section draws from "Equity Index UL Primer," *Due Care Bulletin* (October 2008), M Financial Group and from "Indexed Universal Life Insurance" presentation (no date), Barry, Evans, Josephs and Snipes.

The following example of three segment terms will clarify the interaction among these terms and factors. Note that both upside and downside returns are truncated by the growth cap and floor.

(1)	(2)	(3) [(1) x (2)]	(4)
Index	**Participation Rate**	**Growth Cap**	**Index Crediting Rate**
Performance Rate (% change in index)	(% of growth rate used in calculation)	**Growth Rate** *subject to . . .* **Growth Floor**	(applied to account value at segment maturity)
22.00%	90%	Subject to 12% cap	12.00%
9.00%	90%	Within cap/floor range	8.10%
−19.00%	90%	Subject to 0% floor	0.00%

Upon maturity of each segment, the index crediting rate calculation is restarted. The effect of this reset is to carry forward gains and avoid carrying forward losses, as the 0 percent floor insulates the account value.

Index strategies are different from product to product, and some index products offer more than one index strategy. Differences occur in the growth cap rate, the floor rate, the participation rate, and the index itself. Other differences may include how the performance rate is calculated, including:

- **Point to point**—the index is the percentage change in the ending index value over its beginning value for the segment term.
- **Point to average**—the index is the percentage change in the simple average of the end of segment term monthly index values over the beginning value for the segment term. The simple average typically applies to the last twelve months of the segment term.
- **Monthly cap**—the index is the sum of monthly point to point changes in value for the segment term with a cap applied to the monthly increase and a floor applied to the ending sum of rates.
- **Multi-index**—the index is the weighted sum of several indexes, such as point to point returns for the S&P 500, NASDAQ, and Dow Jones, with a 50 percent weighting for the best return, 30 percent for the second best return, and 20 percent for the worst return.

Considerations

In addition to understanding the broad mechanics for deriving the interest crediting rate for the index account, the following should be considered by the advisor when reviewing EIUL products, as they can impact product performance:

- **Index returns omit dividends.** Dividends historically have accounted for an additional annual return of 1 to 3 percent.

- **Mid-term segment surrenders exclude interest credit.** Surrender value within a segment term equals its value at the beginning of the term, less policy charges, plus any interim interest credited (see below) during the term. Index interest credit will be provided only for end-of-term segment surrenders. This is an issue more relevant for segment terms of greater than one year. For example, if the segment term is five years, and one year remains in the term at time of surrender, four years of index credit would be lost.

- **Is interim interest credited?** For example, if the segment term is five years, is interest credited during the five years or only at segment maturity? Typically, EIUL products credit interim interest equal to the growth floor. Thus, if the floor is 1 percent, then 1 percent is credited during the segment term. At the end of the term, the index crediting rate is determined, and a retroactive credit, net of the interim credit, is applied.

- **Is partial index interest credited?** For example, if $10,000 in charges was deducted in the 11th month of a one-year segment term and if the product allows partial index interest, the index account value would receive index credit on the $10,000 charge for the 11 months that the funds were in the account, otherwise the $10,000 will be ignored for purposes of calculating interest.

- **For how long is the minimum growth floor guaranteed?** Typically, the growth floor is guaranteed for life. If not, the floor is guaranteed for the current segment term only and can be changed for future segments, a less favorable approach.

- **For how long is the minimum growth cap guaranteed?** Typically, the growth cap is guaranteed for the current segment term only and can be changed for future segments. A guaranteed minimum growth cap establishes a minimum rate for the life of the policy.

- **For how long is the minimum participation rate guaranteed?** Unless stated explicitly, the current participation rate is guaranteed for the current segment term only. A guaranteed minimum participation rate establishes a minimum rate for the life of the policy.

While the basic mechanics of an EIUL policy can be considered as being relatively straightforward, the proverbial "devil is in the details." These policies can be misunderstood by clients if not explained thoroughly, they require careful monitoring and service, and the details affecting the interest crediting rate might seem bewildering to some clients. Nonetheless, EIUL policies occupy an important place between traditional UL policies and variable UL policies. They can be considered as providing much of the downside protection of a traditional UL policy with some of the upside potential of a variable UL policy.

Variable Life Insurance

Variable life insurance policies, as we know, permit their owners to control their policies' investment allocations and, thereby, determine the levels of risk that they are willing to assume. They may select from a menu of available funds in which to have their funds invested within the insurer's separate account offerings. They also may change funds as they wish, altering the risk/return profile of their policies, subject to insurer administrative requirements. The policies' separate account investment risks are borne totally by the policyholder, a characteristic not found in generic universal and whole life insurance where the insurance company provides a minimum guaranteed interest crediting rate. Figure 7-3 offers an illustration of the differences in the risk and return profiles of variable UL, EIUL, and generic UL.

All variable products, their separate accounts, and related sales are subject to regulation by the *Securities and Exchange Commission* (SEC), in addition to state insurance regulators. Variable products are securities and, as such, potential purchasers must be provided with a prospectus. This lengthy booklet includes the identity and nature of the insurer's business, the use to which the insurer will put the premiums, financial information on the insurer, the fees and expenses to be charged, and policyowner rights.

FIGURE 7-3: Risk/Return Profiles of Three Universal Life Policies

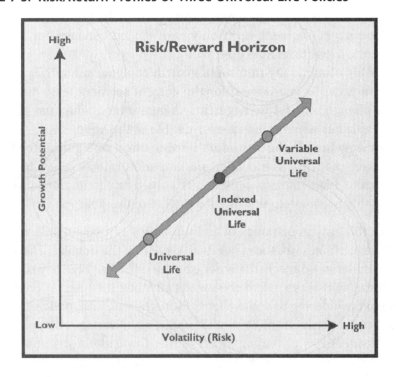

Under laws administered by the SEC, the entity that distributes variable life insurance—the insurer—usually must register as a broker-dealer. Also, agents and home office personnel involved with variable products must pass an examination on the securities business. Additionally, specific requirements apply to advertising, annual reports to shareholders, shareholder proxies, and financial reporting.

Operational Details

Most variable policies sold today are based on the UL platform. Thus, while **variable universal life** (VUL) policies exhibit the same traits as generic UL policies as to transparency, premium flexibility, death benefit adjustability, account value mechanism, death benefit options, and use of current assumptions as to mortality and loading charges, they differ in their investment flexibility and risk/return opportunity. The separate accounts backing the cash values are mutual funds (and must be registered as investment companies with the SEC) in which policyholders are permitted to invest in various bond, stock, balanced, international, and other qualified funds. Separate accounts are not subject to the restrictions applicable to an insurer's general account investments, with most focused on equity investments.

Thus, the VUL policy cash value is linked directly to and determined by the investment results of the separate account in which the policyholder has chosen to invest. If the account earns 15 percent, the VUL policy is credited with 15 percent, less applicable charges. If the account loses 15 percent, the policyholder suffers a corresponding loss. Most VUL policies contain no guarantees as to minimum interest crediting rates. They also typically contain no guaranteed minimum death benefit, unless they contain a no-lapse guarantee feature (see below) and required minimum premiums have been paid.

The VUL policyowner may hold investments in numerous accounts simultaneously in an effort to diversify his or her exposure. Increasingly, insurers allow policyowners to direct investment into funds not controlled by the insurer, such as those controlled by third party mutual fund companies.

The policyowner has the right of periodically transferring funds from one account to another. Most insurers allow up to four transfers per year at no charge. Additional transfers often incur a $25 charge. Many insurers allow policyowners to establish automatic monthly transfers at no fee, usually from a money market (separate) account to one or several of the equity accounts, utilizing a dollar cost averaging approach to investment. As all transfers are within a life insurance policy, no taxable gain (or loss) is realizable because of the transaction—a distinct advantage over taxable mutual fund transfers.

The earliest variable life policies were in the form of whole life insurance. **Variable whole life** differs from VUL in that (1) premiums are fixed, (2) the policy is guaranteed to remain in effect for the whole of the insured's life (assuming required premiums are paid when due), even if the separate account investment returns are not as high as those used to calculate premiums, and (3) not only the cash value, but the face amount varies with the performance of the underlying assets.

Considerations

VUL policies require the same type of discipline as does UL. The prospective purchaser should commit to ensuring that the policy always has sufficient funds to be self-sustaining, ideally with investment income sufficient to cover all policy charges with some residual to ensure cash value growth. VUL policies are potentially useful for those persons who desire to treat their life insurance policy cash values more as an investment than a savings account. Thus, the policy is more suitable to those with greater investment savvy and who understand the volatility and long term nature of equity markets while hoping to reduce their COI charges by earning higher returns.

The owner assumes the investment risk. The danger is that, if separate account investment results are not favorable, the policy's cash value could be reduced substantially and the policy could require substantial additional premium payments. This risk should be considered most carefully. One of the strengths of the life insurance industry historically has been its investment guarantees. With variable products, consumers are largely forgoing these guarantees.

On the other hand, as the assets backing the reserves of variable policies are held in separate accounts, they are not subject to the claims of the creditors of an insolvent insurer, unlike the situation with policies whose reserves are backed by the insurer's general account assets. This protection does not extend to the purely insurance elements of variable life, which are backed by an insurer's general account. Hence, the portion of any death benefit that becomes payable from the insurer's general account—a policy's NAR—is not shielded from creditors' claims.

Prospects may wish to consider VUL policies that contain an option for a no-lapse guarantee. As with the NLG products discussed below, a minimum premium must be paid. These premiums typically are higher than those for non-variable NLG products, as the insurer's risks are higher, and there may be restrictions on fund allocations.

The usual withdrawal and loan privileges applicable to all cash value policies are available with variable policies as well. An important difference is that the insurer typically will permit loans for only 75 to 90 percent of the then cash value. Also, the portion of the cash value that stands as security for the loan is removed from its separate account and is credited with interest at a rate no higher than the loan rate and often a somewhat lesser rate.

Finally, while most variable life policyholders elect to invest in equities, other separate account investment options exist, including investing in the insurer's general account. Doing so gains the policyholder the normal general account crediting rate, but looses creditor protections. Some insurers provide for an enhanced general account yield if the policyholder commits to longer duration investing, but fund transfers from such arrangements are restricted, typically to no more than 10 percent per year.

Box 7-1 offers a comparison among UL, EIUL, and VUL relative to various characteristics of their approaches to crediting rates.

BOX 7-1: Comparisons for Three Major Universal Life Policies

Characteristic	Universal Life	Equity Indexed Universal Life	Variable Universal Life
Funds held in general account or separate account?	General account. Funds not protected from creditors upon insurer insolvency.	General account. Funds not protected from creditors upon insurer insolvency.	Separate account. Funds protected from creditors upon insurer insolvency.
Allocation of policyholder funds?	By insurer largely to fixed investments, called fixed account.	Policyholder determines allocation between indexed account and fixed account.	Policyholder determines allocation among available separate account investment options.
Main investments?	Investment grade bonds and mortgages.	Investment grade bonds and mortgages and equity index call options.	Equity and bond mutual funds.
Basis for valuing investments?	Book value, which provides more stable reported earnings than market value.	Market value for indexed account. Same as UL for fixed account.	Market value for separate account. Same as UL for fixed account (general account).
Degree of investment risk transferred to policyholder?	Marginal, only for crediting rates in excess of the guaranteed rate.	Partial, for indexed account between the floor and cap. Same as UL for fixed account.	100 percent of fund risk, including negative returns for the separate account. Same as UL for fixed account.
How is crediting rate determined?	Book value investment return of entire investment portfolio or segments thereof less spread, subject to guarantee.	Percentage change in index for indexed account, subject to participation rate, floors, caps. Same as UL for fixed account.	Percentage change in market value of funds for the separate account. Same as UL for fixed account.
Does the crediting rate include dividend income?	Indirectly, via book value investment return.	No, for indexed account. Same as UL for fixed account.	Yes for separate account. Same as UL for fixed account.

No-Lapse Guarantee Universal Life

No-lapse guarantee (NLG) universal life policies guarantee a minimum death benefit to a certain age or for life, even if the account value becomes depleted before that time, provided a specified premium is timely paid.[3] Not all NLG policies are so labeled, but, if a UL policy provides an option, whether at an additional premium or not, to pay a stipulated premium and have the insurer guarantee that it will remain in force to a certain age, even if the cash value falls to zero, the policy is a NLG contract.

The great advantage of these policies is that lifetime guaranteed insurance coverage can be purchased with a low premium outlay in comparison to that required for other lifetime guarantee policies such as WL. The great risk of these policies resides in the possibility that, because of their complexity and perhaps because of client naivety or ignorance, the client (and possibly agent) fails to understand fully the purpose, nature, and risks—in other words, that the product is unsuitable for the client.

NLG products are usually configured as UL policies, which means that premiums are flexible, but this very flexibility can put coverage at risk if inadequate premiums are paid. The required NLG premium results in slow and ultimately only modest cash (account) value development. Indeed, cash values typically taper to zero at about the insured's life expectancy based on current assumptions and guaranteed lifetime funding. And typically NLG policies have heavy surrender charges for the first ten to twenty policy years. Because of having modest or nonexistent cash values, many advisors urge clients to consider NLG products as providing term insurance.

Operational Details

As NLG products typically operate via a UL chassis, the observations about UL operation in general apply here as well, although practical limitations exist, as explored below. The main operational element within NLG products that differs from generic UL is the internal policy mechanism for determining whether the NLG promise remains in effect. Policies use one of two mechanisms: a specified premium test or a shadow account.

The **specified premium test**, the original NLG mechanism, provides that coverage remains guaranteed as long as a certain minimum premium is paid in which actual premiums paid equal or exceed a cumulative premium requirement to date. Some policies set a minimum annual premium. NLG premiums must be paid on time if the policyholder is to avoid loss of the NLG feature or a reduction in guarantee benefits (duration or amount).

---

[3]This section draws from "An Assessment of No-Lapse Guarantee Products and Alternatives," (no date), M Financial Group.

Some specified premium products offer a **catch-up provision** that permits payment of additional premiums to restore the guarantee if the premium requirement was not met. Some products also include a **reset** feature that permits the guaranteed duration or the amount of guaranteed coverage to be reset based on adjusted future specified premiums.

Most NLG products offered today promise that the NLG remains in effect if either the policy's regular UL account value or what is called its shadow account value remains positive. A **shadow account** functions much like the regular UL account value except that its value is determined by use of a set of guaranteed charges and credits that differ from those applicable to the regular account value. If neither the regular account nor the shadow account has a positive value, the policy lapses.

The shadow account approach offers lower premiums and generally provides greater flexibility as regards premium payments and the duration and amount of the guarantee in comparison to the specified premium approach. For example, assume that actual premiums paid were less than the original premiums required to ensure a positive shadow account value for life (i.e., to age 121) and that these lower premiums result in a projected shadow account balance of zero at age 95. The duration of the NLG would then be reset to age 95. Alternatively, sufficient catch-up premiums (with interest) could be paid or the death benefit sufficiently lowered to re-establish the NLG for life. The shadow account determines the guarantee coverage only and is not available for cash withdrawals or policy loans.

Considerations

Much has been written about NLG products, both positively and negatively. Below, we provide an overview of its strengths and explain its risks to clients. NLG strengths are said to include the following:

- **Easily understood.** The insurer's promise actually is simple: if the policyholder pays the requisite premium on time, the insurer guarantees the death benefit for life (or to a certain age).
- **Guarantees.** The NLG means that the policyholder need not be exposed to or particularly concerned about the downside risks of decreased crediting rates or increased loads or COI charges that attaches to other current assumption products (although cash values will be negatively affected by less favorable changes). Interest crediting rates in particular have been declining for more than 20 years, with additional premiums having been required to keep many UL policies on track.
- **Lower cost lifetime guarantee of coverage.** NLG policies generally provide a lower-cost lifetime *guarantee* of coverage in comparison with other guaranteed lifetime policies (such as WL).

- **Flexible guarantee.** The shadow account approach provides flexibility as relates to
  - Amount and timing of premium payments, as with other UL policies,
  - Duration of the NLG, which can be for life or less,
  - Guarantee amount, which can be reduced or increased, subject to satisfactory evidence of insurability,
  - Catch-up premiums, and
  - Reset, permitted after policy issuance to change the guarantee premium, NLG duration, and/or guarantee insurance amount.
- **Insurer services for keeping the intended guarantee on track.** Many insurers offer the following services to help keep the intended guarantee on track:
  - **Early premium notices.** Premium notices provided one month before the premium is due to help minimize late payment.
  - **Automated premium monitor system.** A notification is sent to the agent of record and the policyowner when the intended guarantee is in jeopardy (which can result from late or missed premium payments or from withdrawals or loans). Typically the system will also provide information on any required additional premium to re-establish the original guarantee.
  - **Late payment provision.** Late premium payments are automatically backdated to the prior monthly anniversary date, typically available for premiums up to 30 days late.
  - **1035 exchange provision.** Funds received up to six months after a 1035 policy exchange (see Chapter 18) are automatically backdated to the issue date of the new policy.

NLG products have raised concerns in the planning community about the risks run by its purchasers, some of which are as follows:

- **Little or no cash surrender value.** Low account and surrender values relative to other current assumption products affords little flexibility if policyholder needs change in the future (e.g., limited or no opportunity to use cash values for retirement income, collateral, short term cash, and tax-free policy exchanges). A NLG contract's use is largely limited to serving the purpose for which it was originally purchased.
- **Adverse liquidity consequences.** In addition to having little or no surrender value, the consequences of accessing cash in a NLG product can be more negative than accessing cash in other current assumption products. Within a NLG product, cash value withdrawals and loans decrease the strength of the guarantee, which defeats its original purpose.
- **Limited upside performance potential.** NLG products have limited ability to participate in favorable future experience such as higher interest earnings or mortality improvements. As these products provide

protection from unfavorable deviations, insurers are not keen to share benefits arising from favorable deviations with policyholders. Other current assumption products offer greater potential for improved policy performance, as favorable experience is more likely to be passed through.

◆ **Requirement of timely premium payments.** If the required premium is not paid on time, guarantee coverage may be terminated or reduced in duration or amount. Where catch-up premiums are an option, the amount needed includes lost interest earnings.

◆ **Potential for shadow account confusion.** The operation and function of the shadow account can be confusing to policyholders, especially with the passage of time. It could be misunderstood to be the cash value. Its complexity could make it difficult for policyholders to make informed decisions. For example, a policyholder who considers funding a NLG policy to guarantee coverage to age 100 may make the assumption that, if he or she lives past 100, the additional funding needed to extend the guarantee would be similar to the annual premium required before age 100. However, for most policies, the catch-up premium required to cover the post-age 100 shadow account mortality charges would be considerably larger.

◆ **Strings attached to the guarantee.** A clear, ongoing understanding of how to maintain the contract in a guarantee status is critical. Included among those critical items are:

  ◆ The policy's NLG mechanism, specified premium or shadow account;
  ◆ The grace period for premium payments and policy exchanges; and
  ◆ Existence of catch-up provisions and/or reset features.

◆ **Need for ongoing monitoring.** Ongoing monitoring of the policy and policyholder's circumstances is highly desirable to ensure that required premiums are paid on time or, if a payment is missed or late, to get the NLG back on track. Agent compensation for NLG products is typically low and may include no commissions after policy years 10 or 15, which may reduce the incentive for some agents to properly service the product.

◆ **Insurer insolvency risk.** Concern exists in the market that insurer reserves to support their NLG products may be inadequate and that lapse supported pricing is utilized (i.e., pricing subsidies are included from anticipated later year lapses when projected asset shares are greater than surrender values—see Chapter 6). If lapse rates prove lower than anticipated, the subsidies will not materialize, leading to insurer losses. To date, insurer financial strength ratings have not been materially affected by NLG business. Many advisors, nonetheless, recommend purchasing NLG products only from highly rated carriers and/or from multiple carriers in order to spread the insolvency risk.

Box 7-2 provides a comparison of key characteristics of NLG universal life and of generic UL policies.

BOX 7-2: No-Lapse Universal Life versus Traditional Universal Life

Characteristic	No-Lapse Guarantee UL	Generic UL
Provides a lifetime guaranteed death benefit at a guaranteed cost?	**YES** Death benefit is guaranteed for life if the required guaranteed premium is paid on time.	**NO** At funding levels similar to NLG premiums, coverage is typically guaranteed up to life expectancy based on guaranteed policy element.
Future performance can be better than illustrated at issue?	**NOT LIKELY** NLG premiums are likely locked in and will not decrease based on improved emerging experience. Minimal upside cash value potential.	**YES** Better emerging experience can permit lower ongoing premium payments or higher cash values and death benefits.
Future performance can be worse than illustrated at issue?	**NO** Guaranteed premiums cannot be higher nor death benefit lower than originally illustrated if guaranteed premiums are paid on time; cash value performance can be worse.	**YES** Cash values can be lower and additional premium payments required to maintain policy in force if emerging experience is worse than originally illustrated.
Provides cash surrender values?	**MINIMAL** Little or no surrender values in early years due to heavy surrender charges, with cash values going to zero in age 80s. Some versions offer higher cash values but with higher premiums.	**YES** Particularly if well funded and minimal surrender charges. Actual values dependent on premiums paid.
Low premium outlay for death protection?	**YES** Among the lowest outlays for lifetime protection; most competitive at ages 65 and higher.	**YES** Current outlays may compare favorably with NLG, particularly at ages 65 and below; ultimate nets costs and outlays dependent on emerging experience.

As the preceding discussion makes clear, advisors should ensure that a NLG product is suitable for the client and that the client fully understands both its strengths and risks. The advisor will particularly want to know by whom and how ongoing monitoring will take place. NLG products are appropriate for many clients, especially older ones who have a demonstrated need for guaranteed cost, lifetime protection. Any discussion, however, should extend well beyond price and guaranteed death benefits.

Whole Life Insurance

As we know from earlier discussions, **whole life (WL) insurance** policies are bundled life products that pay the policy face amount whenever the insured dies and, therefore, provide life insurance intended to remain in effect for the insured's entire lifetime. Unlike universal life policies, premiums for whole life insurance policies (1) are directly related to the amount of insurance purchased, (2) must be paid when due or the policy will terminate, and (3) are calculated to ensure that the policy will remain in effect for the entire lifetime of the insured, which with recently issued WL policies is to age 121.

Participating and Nonparticipating Life Insurance

As we also know, life insurance policies can be participating (par) or nonparticipating (nonpar). Recall that par policies are more closely associated with mutual life insurance companies and nonpar policies are more closely associated with stock life insurance companies, although much nonpar UL is sold by stock subsidiaries of mutual insurers. **Participating** policies are entitled to share via non-guaranteed policy elements called **dividends** in any distribution of the insurer's surplus funds that it decides to make to those policies.

Insurers selling par policies typically price them conservatively. This conservative pricing means that the policies as a group are highly likely to generate profits—called surplus. Following each year's operations, the insurer's board of directors decides how much of these surplus funds—called **divisible surplus**—may be passed on to par policies in the form of dividends.

Actuaries then seek to divide this divisible surplus among the par policies in an equitable manner, commonly following what is called the **contribution principle,** which holds that divisible surplus should be distributed to policies in the same proportions as the policies are considered to have contributed to the surplus. In operationalizing this principle, actuaries usually follow an approach that recognizes that surplus derives from three sources, often called factors:

1. **Gains from investment earnings:** actual investment earnings being higher than the guaranteed rate;
2. **Gains from Mortality:** actual mortality experience being less than that implicit in policy pricing, meaning that death claims payments were less than priced into policies; and
3. **Gains from loadings:** actual expenses being lower than that implicit in policy pricing.

The sum of these three factors yields a policy's dividend. The actual gains from each factor historically have not been disclosed to policyholders; only the total. Some insurers, however, now disclose some or all components. For example, one insurer illustrated how its dividend was derived for a 20-year-old whole life policy as follows:

Guaranteed cash value (BOY)	$ 65,217
+ Gross annual premium	+ 1,593
− Mortality & expense charge	− 191
= Balance	$ 66,619
+ Interest credit	+ 4,097
= Policy value	= 70,716
− Guaranteed cash value (EOY)	− 68,235
= Dividend	= $2,481

We do not know the actual gains from the mortality, loading, and interest components for the above policy, only the amounts assessed and credited to this policy. But we can see how the insurer made its calculation. Another insurer showed the actual gains by component. Below we show how its 20-year dividend per $1,000 of face amount was derived for a policy:

Interest credit	$ 9.21
+ Mortality gain	+ 5.33
+ Loading gain	+ (3.11)
= Dividend	= $ 11.43

Both insurers also disclose the rate used to calculate the interest credit, but no other underlying factors are disclosed. Also, note that the second insurer's gain from loading is negative, meaning that the allowance for expenses, taxes, and profits built into its original premium was insufficient to cover these charges by $3.11 per $1,000 in the year of this calculation. This deficit was made good from the gains from the other two factors.

Insurers selling par policies provide prospective purchasers with a **dividend illustration** that shows the dividends that would be paid under the policy if the mortality, expense, and interest experience implicit in the current scale of illustrated dividends were to remain unchanged in the future. Obviously, this result is unlikely. The dividend illustration is usually based on the recent past mortality, expense, and interest experience of the company.

Dividends actually paid, the schedule of which is a **dividend history**, are, as its name implies, amounts actually paid as dividends in the past. Dividends actually paid usually exceed those originally illustrated when investment returns are increasing. The opposite also applies.

Dividends are payable on a par policy's anniversary date. As par premiums are set in anticipation of paying dividends, the Internal Revenue Service considers dividends to be a return of premium and not taxable income, unless the sum of dividends received exceeds the sum of premiums paid.

Dividends may be taken in one or more of several options, the most common being:

- ◆ Purchase chunks of paid up (i.e., single premium) whole life insurance, commonly called **paid up additions (PUAs);**
- ◆ Netted against the premium due, called **reduce premium;**
- ◆ Cash;
- ◆ Accumulate at interest; and
- ◆ Purchase one-year term insurance either for whatever amount the dividend will support or for an amount equal to the policy cash value.

Nonparticipating policies are not entitled to share in any distribution of surplus funds by the insurer, but most nonpar cash value policies contain non-guaranteed elements other than dividends that ensure that such policyholders can share in the favorable (and unfavorable) actual or reasonably anticipated operational experience of the insurer. Other nonpar cash value policies—typically those of more modest face amounts—do not contain any non-guaranteed elements, which means that they cannot share in the operational experience of the insurer. All policy elements are guaranteed and fixed at policy issue. The market share of such nonpar life insurance is small, which is understandable as companies are unwilling to offer liberal pricing guaranteed for decades into the future.

Types of Whole Life Policies

With some WL policies—called variously **ordinary life, whole life,** or **level-premium whole life**—uniform premiums are assumed to be paid over the insured's lifetime. The policy illustrated in Figure 6-2 from the previous chapter could be such a policy. If the underlying policy pricing elements were identical, the required premium for a traditional ordinary life policy would be the same as that required to cause a UL policy's cash value to equal its death benefit at the end of the terminal age of the mortality table (i.e., age 100 or 121).

Other WL policies—called **limited-payment whole life**—provide that premiums will be paid over some period shorter than the insured's entire lifetime. Thus, **paid-up-at-65 whole life** is WL insurance with premiums payable to age 65; **10-pay whole life** is WL insurance with premiums paid for the first 10 policy years; and **single-premium whole life** is WL insurance paid for with one (large) premium. Of course, a limited pay policy remains in effect after all premiums have been paid, with the insurer guaranteeing by contract that no further premiums are due; the policy is said to be **paid up**.

Obviously, the shorter the premium payment period for a WL policy, the higher must be the premiums paid and will be its cash values, other things being equal. Thus, the WL policy with the lowest premium (and the lowest cash values) is ordinary life. The WL policy with the highest premium (and the highest cash values) is single-premium WL insurance, with other limited pay policies lining up between these two extremes.

The necessary annual premium to fund these policies equals the level amount that would have to be paid into a UL policy over the relevant premium paying period to cause its cash value to equal the face amount at the end of the policy's mortality table, assuming policy pricing elements for the WL and UL policies were the same. The more compressed the premium paying period, the higher must be its premiums and the higher will be its cash values. In turn, the lower will be the policy's internal mortality charges.

Another WL policy, called **modified whole life** or some variation thereof, provides WL insurance under which premiums are redistributed so that they are lower than an otherwise identical ordinary life policy during the first three to five years and higher thereafter. Thus, one company's "modified 5" policy carries a premium during the first five years that is one-half of the premiums thereafter.

Several mutual companies offer a participating WL policy that uses dividends to provide some form of level coverage at a lower than usual premium. The details, including the name given the plan, vary from company to company. Under these policies, dividends are earmarked. Under one approach, the face amount of a special ordinary life policy is reduced after a few years. However, dividends are used to purchase deferred paid up whole life additions, such that at the time the policy face amount is to be reduced, the paid up additions fill the gap, with the result that the total death benefit is (intended to be) at least equal to the original face amount (based on illustrated dividends).

Under another approach, the actual policy face amount may be 60 to 80 percent of the initial death benefit, with the difference made up by the purchase of paid up additions and term insurance in such proportions that the total death benefit is intended to be no less than the initial death benefit. It is hoped that paid up additions eventually are sufficient to require no further purchase of term insurance.

Several insurers offer nonpar WL policies with non-guaranteed elements. These unbundled WL policies are commonly called **current assumption whole life, interest sensitive whole life,** or **fixed-premium universal life** policies. Many operate identically to universal life policies except that premiums are set by the insurer and must be paid to maintain the policy in force. Others provide that favorable changes in current assumptions can result in lower premium payments, rather than higher policy values.

Considerations

Whole life cash values are available to the policyowner at any time by surrender of the policy. Also, under par policies with dividends having purchased paid up additions, the additions may be surrendered for their then value, with no impact on the policy proper. Also, policyowners of both par and nonpar policies may obtain a policy loan from the insurer for amounts up to that of the policy's net cash surrender value. Of course, interest is charged for this loan, and the loan is deducted from the cash surrender value if the policy is surrendered or from the face amount if a death claim is payable. Policy loans may, but need not, be repaid at any time and are a source of policy flexibility.

Contemporary WL policies offer greater flexibility and value than did earlier versions. For persons whose life insurance need is expected to extend for 15 or more years and who are interested in accumulating savings via life insurance, WL can be an attractive option, as can UL. By leveling premium payments, WL outlays can be relatively modest. Interest credited on cash values enjoys the same favorable income tax treatment as other qualified cash value policies, rendering the policy a potentially attractive means of accumulating savings.

Most WL policies prove costly for those who terminate their policies within the first 10 to 15 years and whose life insurance need is less than 15 or so years, as the typically heavy front-end expenses penalize short- and medium-term values. For some persons, WL policies can serve as a quasi-forced savings plan due to the required high funding levels.

For many persons whose careers are just beginning, the premium payment required for an adequate amount of ordinary life insurance may be too great, given other priorities. Rather than reduce the insurance amount to that with an affordable premium level, good risk management principles argue for placing primary emphasis on the insurance needed to cover the potential loss, with secondary emphasis on product type. The only effective choice may be to purchase term insurance.

Specialized Life Insurance

Highly specialized life insurance products exist in the form of proprietary and private placement life insurance products. Both types of products are targeted to individuals of high net worth, but the similarity mostly ends there.

Proprietary Life Insurance

A **proprietary life insurance** product is any life insurance policy that is targeted and priced for a specific market and available to be sold exclusively by a cohesive group of agents. For example, one marketing organization offers proprietary products specifically targeted and priced for the ultra-affluent market and sold exclusively by its agents who sell primarily to high net worth clients. By targeting a specific market, the product can be priced to reflect more closely the actual and reasonably anticipated mortality, lapse, and other experience of that market. Thus, because the ultra-affluent individuals live longer on average than the insured population in general, proprietary products designed for that market can be priced with lower mortality charges than otherwise. Most proprietary life products are built on a UL chassis. These products may be distinguished from those intended to appeal to a broader or less favorable target market and sold via multiple distribution systems.

Captive life insurance agents who have the exclusive right to sell the products of their insurers can be considered as selling proprietary life insurance products if pricing reflects the characteristics of a specific market. Thus, if such an insurer offers a class of policies with high minimum issue requirements (e.g., $1.0 million) and if these policies' mortality, persistency, and face amount experience is favorable and constitutes a separate experience class for purposes of pricing, they would be considered as proprietary products.

Private Placement Life Insurance

Private placement life insurance (PPLI) products are individually tailored variable life insurance policies not subject to SEC regulation, which are designed specifically for and available only to certain qualifying investors. To purchase PPLI, individuals must qualify as accredited investors or qualified purchasers. An **accredited investor** is a wealthy investor who meets SEC requirements as to minimum net worth (in excess of $1.0 million) or annual income (in excess of $200,000). A **qualified purchaser** is any individual or family organization with net investments of $5.0 million or more.

PPLI is similar to retail variable life insurance in that it must meet the IRC's definition of life insurance to retain favorable tax treatment, the underwriting process is the same, rating classifications are the same, the proposed insured must demonstrate a financial need for the requested insurance, and the mechanics of the PPLI policy itself are the same. PPLI differs from retail life insurance in that commissions and policy loads may be negotiated and are sometimes lower; neither the PPLI policy nor the non-registered separate accounts are subject to SEC oversight; no sales material or advertising is permitted; investment options are considerably broader, including private equity and hedge funds; the insurer need not be domestic; and the client can invest only after reading a private placement memorandum akin to a prospectus.

PPLI products may require a minimum investment of as low as $1.0 million, but $5.0 to $10.0 million and even more seem more common, often with payments spread over some years. Buyers of PPLI are said to be less interested in the actual insurance component than in the tax and investment diversification benefits, although exceptions exist.

Life Insurance on Multiple Lives

Life insurance most commonly insures the life of one person. It is theoretically possible to write life insurance on any number of lives and to construct it to pay on the death of the first, second, third, etc., or last of the group to die. In practice, two important plans have evolved: (1) the second-to-die life policy and (2) the first-to-die life policy.

Second-to-Die Life Insurance

Second-to-die life insurance, also called **survivorship life insurance** and **last-to-die life insurance**, insures two (or sometimes more) lives and pays the death proceeds only on the death of the second (or last) insured to die. These policies can be in the form of WL, UL, VUL, or term insurance. NLG features are also found with these policies.

As the policy promises to pay only on the death of the second of two insureds, the policy's premiums are quite low relative to those that would be charged for a separate policy on each insured. If this year's probability of death is, say, 1 per thousand for one insured and 2 per thousand for the other insured, the probability of both insureds dying and, therefore, the policy face amount having to be paid is only 2 per million (i.e., 0.001 times 0.002). Premiums are based on such joint probabilities and are correspondingly low. The underlying mechanics and risk sharing (mortality, investment income, expenses) for single life and survivorship policies are identical, whether whole life or universal life, with only the mortality charge rate being lower for survivorship. The policy options and riders available for single life policies typically are also available for survivorship policies.

A so-called split option is available in many policies. The **split option** allows the survivorship policy to be split into two individual policies, one on each insured. Some insurers levy a separate charge for this option. The option can be elected only under certain conditions, such as on divorce. Also, some policies provide that a dramatic change in estate tax laws can trigger the option, as the usual reason for having purchased the policy may have disappeared.

Under U.S. estate tax law, assets bequeathed in a qualifying manner to a surviving spouse escape all federal estate taxation on the death of the first spouse. At the death of the surviving spouse (and assuming no remarriage), any remaining assets are subject to estate taxation at potentially high rates. The second-to-die policy is well situated to meet the need for cash to cover these estate taxes and related expenses on the second death.

These policies are also commonly used to provide financial security for a disabled child or dependent relative in situations where one death would not necessarily result in financial disaster for survivors, but the deaths of both husband and wife (or other breadwinners) would. Many companies offer more flexible underwriting with survivorship life than with single life policies, such as when one of the individuals is uninsurable or highly rated.

First-to-Die Life Insurance

In contrast to the survivorship life insurance, **first-to-die life insurance**, also called **joint life insurance**, promises to pay the face amount of the policy on the first death of one of two (or more) insureds covered by the contract. The policy is often used to insure both a husband and wife, with each being the beneficiary for the other, and in business buy-out situations involving multiple partners or major stockholders. The policy pays only on the death of the first to die and is terminated at that time.

Contracts usually provide, however, that the survivor has the right to purchase a cash value policy on his or her life without providing evidence of insurability. Some contracts continue insurance temporarily, and most provide that if both insureds die in a common disaster, the insurer will pay the face amount on each death.

The premium for a given face amount would be smaller than the total premiums that would be paid for two individual ordinary life policies covering each individual. Joint life coverage is also available under term and UL plans and NLG. Joint life insurance is less popular today than in past times and is typically sold in comparatively modest amounts.

Conclusions

It should be evident from the above discussion that the advisor has a wealth of policy-related information to digest and retain if he or she is to be able to provide first-rate service to clients. We hasten to add that the preceding discussion has but introduced what we believe to be the most salient features of the products. The advisor should expect to be required to delve more deeply into the subject from time to time, relying not only on professional research but also on knowledgeable agents whose opinions he or she respects.

Life Insurance Policy Attributes | 8

THIS CHAPTER EXAMINES THE fundamental attributes of the policies presented in Chapters 6 and 7 and how they differ from one another. Our goal is to provide an easy, quick means of facilitating policy comparisons. This chapter is not a substitute for the preceding chapters' in-depth discussions, instead building from and in some instances supplementing those discussions.

Overview of Generic Policy Attributes

We know that all life insurance policies can be classified as falling into the term insurance or cash value (permanent) insurance category. Many variations of term and cash value policies exist, each differing from the other to a greater or lesser degree. Table 8-1 reminds us of the key attributes of what we refer to as generic term life insurance and of the three most common generic cash value policies: whole life (WL), universal life (UL), and variable universal life (VUL).

Thus, life insurance death benefit payments ordinarily are received income-tax free, irrespective of the type of policy. An exception to this treatment occurs if the policy is owned by an employer (see Chapter 18) or is transferred for a valuable considera-

---

Authored by Harold D. Skipper.

TABLE 8-1
Key Attributes of Generic Life Insurance Policies

Attribute	Term Life Insurance	Cash Value Life Insurance		
		Whole Life Insurance	Universal Life Insurance	Variable Life Insurance
✓ Income tax free death benefit?	Yes	Yes	Yes	Yes
✓ Accumulates cash values?	No	Yes	Yes	Yes
✓ Income tax free (or tax deferred) interest credited to cash value?	n.a.	Yes	Yes	Yes
✓ Can borrow against cash value?	n.a.	Yes	Yes	Yes
✓ Duration of coverage?	Fixed term	Lifetime	Flexible, up to lifetime	Flexible, up to lifetime
✓ Adjustable death benefit?	No	No	Yes	Yes
✓ Flexible premiums?	No	No	Yes	Yes
✓ Guaranteed policy elements?	Death benefit and premium	Death benefit, maximum premium, and minimum cash values	Death benefit, maximum charges, and minimum interest crediting rate	Maximum charges

tion, called a **transfer for value**. With both exceptions, the excess of the gross death proceeds over the policy's cost basis would be taxable to the beneficiary. The Internal Revenue Code (IRC) exempts some employer owned life insurance and some transfers from these exceptions, making their death proceeds income-tax free.

The interest credited each year on tax-qualified policies' cash values—often called the **inside interest buildup**—is not included in the policyholder's taxable income for that year. If the policy is ultimately surrendered, some of this previously untaxed interest will be taxed in the year of surrender if a gain is realized on surrender, as discussed in Chapter 18. If the policy matures as a death claim, none of this previously untaxed interest ordinarily will be subject to income taxation, as the cash value (including the untaxed interest) becomes an indistinguishable part of the death proceeds. Tax-qualified policies are those whose funding in relation to their death benefits does not exceed limits laid out in the IRC, as described in Chapter 7. (The great majority of life insurance meets these limits.)

Other attributes of these generic policy forms are self explanatory, following from materials presented in Chapters 6 and 7. Thus, all cash value policies permit policy loans. UL policies' durations are a function of the premiums paid into them: too little and they lapse; enough and they can endow for the face amount, thus mimicking whole life policies. UL has flexible premiums, and the death benefit can be adjusted.

Specific Life Insurance Policy Attributes

We now explore in detail the attributes that may distinguish one type of policy from another. Whether and the extent to which particular attributes are valued by a client should naturally inform the buying decision. Our approach here is not to color that decision but, rather, to provide a comprehensive overview based on the elements that collectively constitute a life insurance policy. We make no effort to address issues of policy suitability here, offering some limited coverage of the topic in Chapters 10–12, or policy performance, leaving that for Part V of this *Guide*. Our focus is purely on the policies themselves.

We start with a short overview of each policy. We then examine each policy element in turn, starting with the death benefit then moving onto cash values, premiums, mortality charges, interest crediting rates, and policy loading charges.

The discussion at each major heading begins with a table showing each attribute that we examine within that heading. This table also indicates how that attribute applies to term life insurance and to each of seven types of cash value insurance. There follows an elaboration of each table intended to expand on its points, sometimes introducing additional information to round out a point. As most term life policies sold today contain no non-guaranteed policy elements, our analysis assumes this position. Some participating (par) term policies are sold, but they tend to pay either no or low dividends.

We omit survivorship life and joint life policies in our discussion. These policy forms are generally available as any of the eight policies examined herein. They differ from the single-life policies discussed here only in a need for these contracts to deal with two deaths. This attribute is the only substantive difference between the two classes of policies and does not seem to warrant explicit treatment here.

The seven types of cash value insurance policies examined comprise three types of WL and four types of UL policies. The three types of WL are (1) nonparticipating (nonpar) fixed WL, (2) nonpar current assumption WL (CAWL), and (3) par WL. We label as nonpar fixed WL, policies for which all policy elements are fixed and guaranteed and cannot be changed. Nonpar CAWL includes policies that might be called interest sensitive WL or fixed premium UL. The four types of UL are (1) what we call generic UL, (2) no-lapse guarantee (NLG) UL, (3) equity indexed UL (EIUL), and (4) variable universal life (VUL). We believe that these seven types of cash value policies encompass the great majority of permanent life insurance sold today. For easy reference, Appendix 3 contains a table that includes all of the individual tables found in each of the sections of this chapter.

Policy Overview

Table 8-2 lists each of the eight policies that we will examine and summarizes each policy's likely primary appeal to buyers. Thus, we know that the appeal of term life insurance is that large amounts can be purchased for comparatively low premiums because of its temporary nature and/or because there is little or no policy prefunding. Little or no prefunding means that each year's premium payment more or less covers that year's mortality and loading charges.

Each WL policy offers a guarantee of lifetime coverage provided required premiums are paid. The nonpar fixed policy would appeal to WL buyers who place a high value on guarantees and who are quite risk averse. The nonpar current assumption policy would appeal to WL prospects who value transparency within life policies and who also value savings that are conservatively based. The par policy would appeal to similar WL prospects who are less interested in policy mechanics.

Each UL policy offers premium flexibility and death benefit adjustability within a transparent framework. The generic UL policy would appeal as well to the conservative saver, whereas the EIUL prospect presumably would be drawn to its possibility of providing equity-like returns but with floors on losses and caps on gains. VUL should appeal to prospects content with even greater investment risk/opportunity. The NLG UL policy would appeal to those who desire assured lifetime coverage, provided specified premiums were paid, and who value low guaranteed premium outlays.

The table reminds readers how each policy is configured, whether bundled or unbundled. Some commentators contend that whether a policy is transparent in its operations is largely irrelevant to the decision whether to purchase or retain a policy, as what is important is how the policy performs overall, not how each component has performed. Others argue that, because unbundled policies are transparent, their owners can gain an understanding of the details of policy performance, thereby offering a superior means of ongoing policy monitoring (see Chapter 17).

Finally, the table indicates whether each policy contains any non-guaranteed policy elements and, if so, the form that they take. We know that the non-guaranteed policy elements in par policies take the form of dividends. For other policies, non-guaranteed policy elements take the form of current mortality and loading charges, excess interest credits, and/or changes in either equity indexes or market values.

TABLE 8-2
Overview of Term and Cash Value Life Insurance Policies

Attribute	Term Life Insurance	Cash Value Life Insurance							
		Whole Life Insurance			Universal Life Insurance				
		Nonpar Fixed	Nonpar Current Assumption	Par	Generic	No-Lapse Guarantee	Equity Indexed	Variable
Overview								
✓ Primary Policy Appeal?	Guaranteed coverage for specific period and low premium outlay	Guaranteed lifetime coverage with all policy elements fixed	Guaranteed lifetime coverage, transparency, backed by conservative investments	Guaranteed lifetime coverage, backed by conservative investments	Flexibility, transparency, backed by conservative investments	Guaranteed lifetime coverage at low premium outlay	Flexibility, transparency, with limited equity-like returns and a guaranteed floor	Flexibility, transparency, with mutual fund returns
✓ Bundled or unbundled?	Bundled	Bundled	Unbundled	Bundled	Unbundled	Unbundled	Unbundled	Unbundled
✓ Contains non-guaranteed policy elements?	No, typically	No	Yes, via current interest credits and charges	Yes, via dividends	Yes, via current interest credits and charges	Yes, via current interest credits and charges for cash values; no for guaranteed coverage	Yes, via equity index changes and current charges	Yes, via market value changes and current charges

Death Benefits

Attributes associated with each of the eight policies' death benefits are shown in Table 8-3. For each attribute, we indicate whether it applies to each policy and, if necessary, how.

Nature and Duration of Guarantee

Each of the policies, other than VUL, guarantees a minimum policy face amount assuming, of course, that premiums are paid as scheduled and the insurer remains solvent. The fact that the death benefit is guaranteed does not mean that it will not fluctuate, as with Option B for UL policies for which the total death benefit varies directly with changes in account values.

The death benefit is guaranteed for the duration of each policy. With term and WL, the contract duration is known. If required premiums are paid, the policy will remain in effect for that stated duration and death benefit. With all UL policies, durations are dependent on the premiums paid. If sufficient premiums are paid, these policies will remain in force for life.

Adjustability of Policy Duration

This attribute addresses the extent to which the durations of life insurance policies may be adjusted and on a continuing basis; e.g., periodically shortening, then lengthening, then shortening, etc. The durations of term policies are fixed by contract. Obviously, their durations can be shortened by not paying premiums, but doing so will cause the policies to lapse. (See premium attribute section below for consequences of not paying premiums.) A term policy's duration cannot be lengthened beyond the term period. If the policy contains a conversion option allowing the exchange of the term policy for a cash value policy without evidence of insurability, this can accomplish the goal of lengthening coverage but at a higher premium outlay.

The duration of life insurance coverage can be reduced under all forms of WL by electing to have the cash value applied as a net single premium under the policy's nonforfeiture option to purchase paid up term insurance, called the extended term nonforfeiture option. Two major problems present themselves with this approach. First, the duration of coverage is determined by the cash value and the insured's age and gender and not the policyholder's wishes. Second, this option may be impossible to unwind, as doing so requires having to prove insurability and paying all back premiums with interest.

While the duration of par WL policies can be reduced to a desired age through artful manipulation of paid up additions (PUAs) and policy nonforfeiture options (see premium section below), doing so usually is neither simple nor easy. The duration of CAWL policies also can be reduced by allowing policies to go into runoff, coupled perhaps with withdrawals. Once done, however, it may be impossible to unwind either policy if the policyholder's circumstances change, for the same reasons mentioned in the preceding paragraph.

TABLE 8-3
Death Benefit Attributes of Term and Cash Value Life Insurance Policies

Attribute	Term Life Insurance	Cash Value Life Insurance							
		Whole Life Insurance			Universal Life Insurance				
		Nonpar Fixed	Nonpar Current Assumption	Par	Generic	No-Lapse Guarantee	Equity Indexed	Variable	
Death Benefits									
✓ Guaranteed?	Yes	Yes	Yes	Yes	Yes	Yes	Yes	No	
✓ Duration?	Fixed term	Life	Life	Life	Flexible, including life	Flexible, including life	Flexible, including life	Flexible, including life	
✓ Adjustability of duration?	No	Not easily	Not easily	Not easily	Yes	Yes	Yes	Yes	
✓ Death benefit adjustable?	No	No	Yes	Not easily	Yes	Yes	Yes	Yes	
✓ Choice of level or increasing?	No, typically	No	Yes	Yes, via riders or dividends	Yes	Yes	Yes	Yes	

The duration of UL policies, in contrast, can be set to whatever fits the client's desires by selecting appropriate funding. Thus, a client wishing to have insurance to age 100, not 121, on the theory that he or she is highly unlikely to live that long, can arrange such. If, at age 99, it appears the insured will make it past age 100, additional premium payments can be made to ensure continued coverage beyond age 100. Care must be exercised with NLG UL policies in altering anticipated policy duration via withdrawals or premium payment cessation, as the NLG period is shortened.

Adjustability of Death Benefit Amount

This adjustability attribute addresses the ease with which a policy's death benefit can be adjusted upward and downward over time. The death benefit for all CAWL and UL policies can be adjusted downward on request (subject to meeting minimums defined in the IRC) or upward, subject to providing evidence of insurability satisfactory to the insurer (including financial justification). Mortality charges are adjusted accordingly thereafter.

The death benefits of term and nonpar fixed and par WL policies are fixed, but often can be lowered by requesting the insurer to cancel portions of the policy. For these WL policies, doing so typically is accomplished by what are called partial surrenders and usually done extracontractually. Thus, if the policyowner wishes to reduce a WL policy's face amount to $500,000 from $1.0 million, one-half of the policy would be surrendered. If the policy's surrender value were $200,000, the change in face amount would result in a $100,000 surrender payment. Premiums thereafter typically would be a bit more than one-half the original premium. Another means of reducing a par WL policy's death benefit can be through surrendering portions of any paid up additions accumulated under the policy.

Raising the death benefit for term and WL policies is less easily accomplished. Commonly, this is not permitted with term policies. Instead, the purchase of a new policy to supplement or replace the existing one is required. An increase can be accomplished with a par WL policy via a change in the dividend option, say, from paying in cash to purchasing paid-up additions or, if available, one-year term insurance. In both instances, the additional insurance amount is determined by the magnitude of the dividend and age and gender of the insured, not the magnitude of the need creating the demand for additional insurance. Also, evidence of insurability would be required to change to the term option if the insurer offers it and may be required for the PUA option.

Choice of Level or Increasing Death Benefit Amount

Neither term nor nonpar fixed WL policies generally permit a choice of level or increasing death benefits, except for some companies via return of premium or cost of living riders. Such riders are available as well for many par policies. Additionally, some par WL policies can effectively allow a choice of level or increasing death benefits if dividends can be used to purchase one-year term insurance. The option might be available in one or both of two forms. One form applies the dividend as a net annual premium to purchase as much one year term insurance protection as it will buy or perhaps in an amount up to some multiple, such as twice, the policy face amount. The other form purchases one-year term insurance in an amount equal to the policy's cash value, with the excess dividend portion applied under one of the other dividend options. The latter form can mimic the UL Option B death benefit pattern.

Another dividend option offered by some insurers is the **add-to-cash-value option**, which is similar to the paid-up additions option in that it permits dividends to accumulate as additional cash value but, unlike the additions option, adds no net amount at risk under the policy. The option generates exactly a unit of additional death benefit for each unit of additional cash value.

UL and many CAWL policies permit the applicant to select among three death benefit patterns: level, increasing (decreasing) as account value increases (decreases), and increases in amount equal to sum of premiums paid. The policyholder may change options over time, although moving from the level option to one of the other options usually requires evidence of satisfactory insurability.

Cash Values

Cash value attributes of our eight policies are listed and commented upon in Table 8-4. Although seemingly stark differences appear, most relate more to differences in policy mechanics and not necessarily to differences in results, except for VUL.

Existence and Nature of Guarantees

Term life policies do not commonly have cash values, and cash value policies, well, have cash values. A difference between WL and UL policies occurs in the nature of cash value guarantees. WL contracts contain a schedule of guaranteed future cash values, derived using conservative mortality, interest, and loading assumptions. If premiums are paid, the future guaranteed cash values will be precisely as shown.

For CAWL and par WL policies, favorable deviations from underlying conservative pricing assumptions can be provided to the policyholder in the form of excess interest and perhaps lower mortality and/or loading charges for the

TABLE 8-4
Cash Value Attributes of Term and Cash Value Life Insurance Policies

Attribute	Term Life Insurance	Cash Value Life Insurance						
		Whole Life Insurance			Universal Life Insurance			
		Nonpar Fixed	Nonpar Current Assumption	Par	Generic	No-Lapse Guarantee	Equity Indexed	Variable
Cash Values								
✓ Builds cash values?	No	Yes	Yes	Yes	Yes	Yes	Yes	Yes
✓ Guaranteed?	n.a.	Yes	Yes, if not relying on non-guaranteed premium	Yes, except for illustrated cash values attributable to dividends	Yes, if funded to guarantees	Yes, if funded to guarantees	Yes, if funded to guarantees	No
✓ Location and nature of underlying investments?	General account; bonds and mortgages	General account; bonds and mortgages	General account; bonds and mortgages	General account; bonds and mortgages	General account; bonds and mortgages	General account; bonds and mortgages	General account; bonds and mortgages and equity index call options	Separate account; fixed income and equity mutual funds
✓ Increased likelihood of lapse with adverse development in current assumptions?	No	No	No, unless relying on non-guaranteed premium	No, unless relying on dividends to fund	Yes, but can be managed with additional premiums	No	Yes, but can be managed with additional premiums	Yes, but can be managed with additional premiums
✓ Impact of changes in market value on cash value?	n.a.	None	Indirect and muted	Indirect and muted	Indirect and muted	Indirect and muted	Indirect and moderate	Direct
✓ Policyholder control of fund allocations?	n.a.	None	None	None	None	None	Allocations to index account	Total
✓ Policy loans available?	No	Yes	Yes	Yes	Yes	Yes, but will impact NLG	Yes	Yes
✓ Withdrawals available?	No	No	No	Yes, indirectly via surrender of PUAs	Yes	Yes, but will impact NLG	Yes	Yes
✓ Fixed relationship to death benefit?	n.a.	Yes	Yes	Yes	No	No	No	No
✓ High early cash values?	n.a.	No	Yes	No, typically	Yes, often	No	Yes, often	Yes, often
✓ Protected from claims of insolvent insurer's creditors?	n.a.	No	No	No	No	No	No	Yes

nonpar policy and dividends under the par policy—which are themselves derived from favorable investment, expense, and mortality experience. Some CAWL policies contain only one or two non-guaranteed policy elements, such as excess interest only, with all other elements guaranteed. Interest-sensitive WL was commonly configured in this way. Non-guaranteed policy elements can result in an augmentation to these policies' cash values, but this augmentation is separate from the guaranteed cash values.

UL policies do not guarantee a schedule of cash values, because such a schedule could be derived only if the insurer knew what premiums were to be paid, which it does not. Rather, UL policies provide guarantees relative to those policy elements from which cash values are derived. Thus, if the applicant or policyholder tells the insurer or agent what premiums he or she will pay in the future, the insurer or agent can tell the policyholder what the guaranteed minimum policy cash values will be in the future. Conversely, if the policyholder or applicant wishes to have guaranteed cash values at a certain level in the future, the insurer (agent) can tell the individual what premium payments would be required, at guaranteed policy assumptions, to produce those cash values.

Location and Nature of Investments Backing Policy Reserves

Investments backing reserves for all policies except VUL are held in the insurer's general account, the same account that houses the reserve liabilities. Such investments are unallocated, meaning that they back all of the insurer's liabilities and are not earmarked for any particular policy's reserves. Investments backing VUL policy reserves, on the other hand, are specifically allocated to these reserves.

As discussed in Chapter 3, the majority of life insurance companies' general account investments are composed of investment-grade bonds and mortgages. Each insurer has its own investment philosophy and guidelines. It is difficult for the advisor to discern whether the par WL policies of insurer A are backed by investments that differ in a meaningful way from those backing the par WL policies of insurer B, or whether either insurer A's or B's investments differ meaningfully from those backing the UL policies of insurer C. We are not discouraging the advisor from attempting this exercise; quite the contrary. But the likely result will be that, for highly-rated insurers, their investment portfolios are sound and similar and can be relied upon to provide the necessary conservative financial underpinning to their policies.

For variable policies, whose reserves are backed mostly by the equity funds in which policyholders have chosen to place their funds, each client situation is unique. The extent to which policies enjoy sound financial underpinning is dependent on the nature of the investments within the separate account chosen by the policyholder.

Likelihood of Lapse with Adverse Development of Current Assumptions

Deterioration in an insurer's investment, mortality, and/or expense experience should, in itself, have no effect on the likelihood of lapse under term and non-par fixed WL policies. Similarly, we ordinarily expect little or no effect on CAWL and par WL policies given their fixed premium structure, with two caveats. First, some CAWL policies offer to adjust premiums instead of cash values with changes in current assumptions. To the extent that doing so raises the premium, the likelihood of lapse increases somewhat. Second, if a par WL policy's dividends are earmarked to cover a portion or all current and future premiums, less favorable dividends will cause a need for higher cash payments by the policyholder, which can lead to an increased likelihood of lapse.

With UL policies, an adverse development in current assumptions relative to those illustrated at issue could lead to an increased likelihood of lapse if not managed. Thus, if a policyholder had been paying planned or target premiums, to be paid to policy maturity, and based on originally illustrated assumptions, continuing to pay such premiums would result in lower account values than originally planned and perhaps an inadvertent lapse. In other situations, a policyholder may be paying whatever premium he or she wishes or none at all, with the same result. In still other situations, the policyholder may have aimed at policy issue and based on assumptions prevailing at that time to pay a few premiums (such as ten annual premiums) large enough to build an account value such that the policy's illustrated future interest credits would be sufficient to cover all future policy charges, thus requiring no additional premium payments. Adverse developments in such current assumptions could necessitate the payment of unanticipated additional premiums if the policy is to remain on track, and therefore may increase the likelihood of lapse. Worth noting is that payment of sufficiently high premiums, such as those derived from guaranteed policy elements and being akin to those under par WL policies, would have avoided the issue altogether.

Impact on Cash Values of Changes in Investments' Market Values

Changes in the market value of investments held in an insurer's general account have no short-term effects and typically only minor long-term effects on the cash values of general-account-backed policies, for three reasons. First, no direct link exists between the market values of an insurer's investments and such policies' cash values. Second, neither realized nor unrealized capital gains and losses ordinarily enters into an insurer's calculation of its investment yield for purposes of determining its interest crediting rate, so market value changes do not affect the crediting rate. Third, the use of book value accounting allows insurers to avoid changing the reported values of certain assets, especially bonds and mortgages, in response to changes in their market values. The theory for this treatment is that the assets are not available for sale and are held to maturity, so their maturity values are the most relevant metrics in financial statement reporting. It is for these reasons that we have Table 8-4 indicating that their effects on CAWL, par WL, and generic UL are indirect and muted.

As for EIUL policies, we know that the indexed account will have interest crediting rates that vary over time with the policy's relevant equity index growth rate, subject to policy floors and caps. While the variation in the market value of the index is not linked directly to and does not cause a corresponding change in the index account value, it does impact the cash values via changes in the crediting rate. For VUL policies, we know that the effect of changes in the market values of investments held in separate accounts are linked directly to and cause proportionate changes in policy cash values.

Policyholder Control Over Fund Allocations

Owners of the types of WL policies shown above and of generic UL and NLG UL have no voice in how or where the insurer invests its funds, including attendant premiums. Owners of EIUL determine whether attendant policy funds are allocated to the insurer's general (fixed) account or its indexed account(s), thereby exercising limited control over fund allocations. Of course, owners of VUL policies have complete control over fund allocations, subject to the fund choices that insurers make available.

Availability of Policy Loans

Cash value insurance contracts routinely provide that their owners may borrow from the insurer an amount up to that of the net cash surrender value, sometimes reduced further by policy charges (UL policies) and unpaid loan interest to the next policy anniversary. **Net cash surrender value** is the current account value less surrender charges, policy loans, and any withdrawals. VUL policies may have a further deduction against account values in recognition of the volatility in policy values.

The contract specifies a fixed interest rate to be paid or an indexed method by which the rate is set as discussed in Chapter 9. Some insurance contracts link the current crediting rate applicable to the account (cash) value backing any loan to the policy loan rate in what is called **direct recognition**. The portion of the cash value backing a policy loan is sometimes called the **loaned cash** (or **account**) **value**, although the cash value itself is not actually loaned. Thus, if a policy contains this feature and the loan rate were 5 percent, the interest rate credited on the policy's loaned cash values or used for dividend computation purposes on such loaned values might be, for some insurers, the same 5 percent rate or the rate reduced by a stated percentage, such as 1 percent, for other insurers. Having a crediting rate equal to the loan rate is called a **wash rate**, a desirable feature.

The effect of direct recognition usually is to have two policy crediting rates; the one declared by the insurer (or determined via indexes or the separate account) applicable to the "unloaned" cash values and another determined by the loan rate applicable to the "loaned" cash value. Thus, while all cash value policies offer policy loans, it can be important for the advisor to examine both the policy loan rate and any direct recognition feature. Loans shorten the guarantee duration for NLG UL.

Availability of Policy Withdrawals

Neither term policies (no cash values) nor nonpar fixed WL policies permit withdrawals from cash values. Technically, withdrawals cannot be made from par WL policies either, although approximately the same result can be obtained via surrender of some or all of a policy's PUAs, if it has any. All UL and CAWL policies permit cash value withdrawals, although doing so lowers the cash value and face amount dollar for dollar and would shorten the guarantee duration of a NLG UL policy.

Relationship Between Cash Values and Death Benefits

A fixed relationship exists between the cash values of a WL policy and its face amount. Indeed, one way of thinking about any WL policy's pricing is that its premiums are determined by, first, calculating the (present) value today of the policy's share of all future death claims (mortality charges) over the entire duration of the policy's underlying mortality table. This lump sum present value is then spread evenly over whatever premium payment period for which the policy is being designed; say, over a single year for single-premium WL, over 20 years for a 20-pay WL, or over lifetime for an ordinary life policy.

The shorter the premium payment period, the greater is the prepayment or prefunding of the policy's share of all future mortality charges. State insurance laws prohibit these prefunded amounts from being forfeited if a policy terminates. The measure of the extent to which the policyholder is entitled to be paid these prefunded mortality charges on policy surrender or lapse *is* a WL policy's cash surrender value. (This is the reason for a policy's cash surrender value and other options on policy lapse being called "nonforfeiture" options.)

Thus, we can see that there exists a fixed relationship among all of a WL policy's pricing elements, as required funding is intended to keep the policy in force for life. This fixed relationship is both the source of strength and durability of WL policies and the source of their rigidity. While UL policy cash surrender values can also be viewed as prefunding for future mortality charges, no fixed relationship exists among its policy elements, thereby permitting greater premium flexibility but also potentially carrying greater risk of policy underfunding. Note that UL policies are subject to state nonforfeiture requirements as well.

High Early Cash Values

Most WL and many UL policies have comparatively high early surrender charges, the effects of which are to penalize early cash values but also to discourage early policy lapse. The surrender charges on many UL policies are not as high as with WL policies, resulting in comparatively higher early cash values. Of course, NLG UL is known for its especially high surrender charges.

Protection Against Claims of an Insolvent Insurer's Creditors

While insolvency is infrequent among life insurers, it can and does occur, as we explore in Chapter 3. As with any insolvency, creditors line up to protect their interests. Fortunately, state laws provide that the claims of all unsecured creditors of an insolvent life insurer fall in order behind policyholder claims. Nonetheless, battles are known to ensue among creditors and policyholders over residual assets.

VUL policies are the only ones whose cash values are immune from such creditor claims, as the separate account is just that: separate from the (general account) assets whose titles are held by the insurer. Death claims payable under VUL policies are not so immune, with their net amounts at risk being payable from the insurer's general account. VUL policies typically also offer general account options, which are subject to creditor claims.

Premiums

The attributes of premiums for the eight policies along with our comments about the extent to which and how they apply to each policy are shown in Table 8-5.

Premium Flexibility

The attribute of premium flexibility refers to the ease with which different premiums can be paid over time. As we know, UL is characterized by flexibility in premium payment, although planned premiums are paid with most UL policies. The policyholder decides the amount of premium to be paid each period. The higher the premium payment, the greater will be the cash value, other things being the same. A caveat here is that owners of NLG products must take care to manage the NLG if premiums are not paid as illustrated. Prefunding can reduce future outlays and underfunding will require higher future outlays to maintain the intended guarantee.

Neither WL nor term policies offer such flexibility. Dividends under par WL can allow some premium accommodation but not much in the early policy years. Also, an automatic premium loan provision within a WL policy can provide additional flexibility. An **automatic premium loan (APL)** provision is an option offered by insurers whereby premiums not paid within the grace period (typically 30 to 61 days following its due date) are paid automatically via

TABLE 8-5
Premium Attributes of Term and Cash Value Life Insurance Policies

Attribute	Term Life Insurance	Cash Value Life Insurance						
		Whole Life Insurance			Universal Life Insurance			
		Nonpar Fixed	Nonpar Current Assumption	Par	Generic	No-Lapse Guarantee	Equity Indexed	Variable
Premiums								
✓ Flexible?	No	No	No	No	Yes	Yes, but need to manage NLG	Yes	Yes
✓ Ability to mimic any other policy type?	No	No	No	No	Yes	Yes	Yes	Yes
✓ Skipping premium payment possible?	No	Not easily	Not easily	Not easily	Yes	Yes, but will reduce NLG duration	Yes	Yes
✓ Effect if premium not paid?	Lapse	Paid via policy loan if APL elected, o/w lapse to NFB*	Paid via policy loan if APL elected, o/w lapse to NFB*	Paid via policy loan if APL elected, o/w lapse to NFB*	Nothing, smaller policy value	Nothing, but will reduce NLG duration and policy value	Nothing, smaller policy value	Nothing, smaller policy value
✓ How to resume premium payments and full coverage after premium non-payment?	Pay past due premiums and re-qualify for insurance	If under NFB, pay past due premiums and re-qualify for insurance	If under NFB, pay past due premiums and re-qualify for insurance	If under NFB, pay past due premiums and re-qualify for insurance	Payments optional; full coverage remains if sufficient value	Payments optional; full coverage remains if sufficient value	Payments optional; full coverage remains if sufficient value	Payments optional; full coverage remains if sufficient value

* APL = **automatic premium loan**, an option offered by insurers whereby premium not paid within the grace period (typically 30–61 days following its due date) is paid automatically via a loan established against the policy cash value. NFB = **nonforfeiture benefits**, triggered when a premium is not paid within the grace period whereby the cash value is used to purchase either (1) **extended term insurance**, which is single premium term insurance in an amount equal to the policy face amount for whatever duration the cash value will fund or (2) **reduced paid up insurance**, which is single premium whole life insurance for whatever amount the cash value will fund. The automatic NFB ordinarily is extended term insurance. Reduced paid up insurance can be elected.

a loan established against the policy cash value. A danger of the APL provision is that resulting loans can grow rapidly, resulting in zero net cash surrender value and policy lapse. Worth recalling is that WL policy premiums are usually considerably higher than UL charges, so WL APLs typically reduce net policy values more rapidly than would the charges assessed against a UL policy's cash values were no premium paid under the UL policy.

Ability to Mimic Any Other Type of Policy

As we noted in the preceding chapter, UL can be thought of as being more of a life insurance chassis or platform than a generic form of life insurance. The policyholder designs his or her own policy based on premiums paid, death benefit option elected or adjusted, and any policy withdrawals and loans. In mimicking other policy types, the policyholder decides the policy death benefit amount over time, the premiums to be paid (or not), the policy duration, and the policy endowment amount, if any. Neither WL nor term policies can mimic other insurance arrangements in this way.

Possibility of Skipping Premium Payments

Premium payments with all UL policies may be skipped, although an obvious risk in doing so is the danger of underfunding and possible lapse. Premiums for term policies must be paid, or the policy terminates by lapse. Premiums for WL policies similarly must be paid, by APL or otherwise, or they, too, lapse.

Effect of Nonpayment of Premium

If a term policy premium is not paid when due, the policy terminates with no value. If a WL policy premium is not paid when due, one of two results ensues automatically in the absence of any policyholder action. If the APL feature is included in the policy, the past due premium will be paid via a loan against the policy cash value, if sufficient. The number of premiums that may be paid in this manner usually is limited.

If the APL feature is not included in the policy or the cash value is insufficient to support another APL or the allowable number of APLs has been reached, one of two nonforfeiture options will kick in automatically to ensure that the policy cash value is not forfeited: extended term insurance or reduced paid up insurance. **Extended term insurance (ETI)** is single premium term life insurance purchased with the policy's net surrender value in an amount equal to the policy death benefit less policy loans for whatever duration that value will sustain the coverage. **Reduced paid up insurance** is single premium whole life insurance purchased with the policy's net cash surrender value for whatever amount that value will purchase. ETI is the usual automatic option, although the policyholder can change this.

The effect on UL policies of premium nonpayment is that the account value will be smaller than it would be had a premium been paid. If the account value is sufficient to cover policy charges in the absence of a premium payment, the policy remains in force in all respects. Of course, nonpayment of the premium for a NLG product will reduce the duration of the NLG, although the original duration may be restored by payment of additional premiums that include charges and interest.

Resuming Premium Payments and Full Coverage After Premium Nonpayment

This attribute covers situations in which a premium is not paid, and the policyowner wishes to resume premium payments and full coverage. In such circumstances, both term and WL policies require payment of all past due premiums at interest and formal requests for policy reinstatement, even if some coverage remains in effect under one of the WL policy's nonforfeiture options. The reinstatement application will be reviewed by an underwriter to determine whether to reinstate the policy. If adverse health or other characteristics are present, offer of a substandard rating or denial is likely. The reinstatement request may involve simplified underwriting if the time elapsed between nonpayment and the reinstatement request is short, say a few weeks, or if the ETI has many years to run (because of a high net cash value relative to face amount and/or low age)—the insurer would just as soon be collecting premiums if it will be "on the risk" anyway for many years.

With UL policies, the policyholder has but to resume premium payments, assuming the policy did not lapse because the account value was insufficient to cover charges. In this latter situation, payment is required in an amount equal to the unpaid charges for the coverage provided during the grace period (typically 61 days with UL policies) plus monies sufficient to meet the next two or three months' internal charges. Additionally, a reinstatement request like that discussed immediately above is necessary.

Mortality Charges

We now change our exploration of policy attributes from the traditional ones of policy death benefits, cash values, and premiums to policy pricing elements that underlie those attributes in more traditional insurance and that are applied directly in UL and related policies. We begin with mortality charges that are embedded implicitly in term and nonpar fixed and par WL policies and explicitly embedded in UL and CAWL policies. Table 8-6 list several attributes of mortality charges for our eight policies along with our comments about the extent to which and how they apply to each policy.

Guaranteed Maximum Mortality Charges

Guaranteed maximum mortality charges are features of all policies in our grid, with one small possible exception. Par WL dividends, as discussed in Chapter 7, are based on gains from three factors: (1) investment returns being greater

TABLE 8-6
Mortality Charge Attributes of Term and Cash Value Life Insurance Policies

Attribute	Term Life Insurance	Cash Value Life Insurance						
		Whole Life Insurance			Universal Life Insurance			
		Nonpar Fixed	Nonpar Current Assumption	Par	Generic	No-Lapse Guarantee	Equity Indexed	Variable
Mortality Charges								
✓ Guaranteed maximum mortality charges?	Yes	Yes	Yes	Yes, if mortality gains cannot be negative	Yes	Yes	Yes	Yes
✓ Can actual charges differ from those at policy issuance?	No, typically	No	Yes	Yes	Yes	Yes for cash value; no for NLG	Yes	Yes
✓ Who determines mortality charges?	Insurer	Insurer	Insurer	Insurer	Insurer	Insurer	Insurer	Insurer
✓ Actual mortality charges disclosed to policyholder?	No, but premium may be near actual	No	Yes	No	Yes	Yes	Yes	Yes
✓ Volatility of mortality charges?	None, typically	None	Low	Low	Low	Low for cash value; none for NLG	Low	Low

than those used in policy pricing, (2) actual expenses, taxes, and contingency charges being less than loading charges used in policy pricing, and (3) mortality experience being more favorable than that used in policy pricing. Add the three, and we have that year's dividend.

We cannot rule out the possibility that an insurer would allow mortality "gains" to be negative, which implies effective mortality charges higher than those derived from the contract's mortality table. If investment and/or expense gains can subsidize a mortality loss, akin to what we saw in Chapter 7 with a subsidy of expense losses, the policy still has an implicit maximum for mortality charges, which is the totality of investment and expense gains. Dividends can be zero, which can occur if negative factors equal positive factors, but they cannot be negative. As a practical matter, however, the likelihood of this occurring seems remote, even assuming that such would be considered, given the typically conservative mortality pricing and long-term downward trend in insured mortality rates.

Actual Mortality Charges versus Those at Policy Issuance

Mortality charges shown or implicit in policy illustrations at the time of policy issuance can be changed for all in force UL, CAWL, and par WL policies, assuming that the original illustration was not based on guaranteed mortality charges. Mortality charges for most term and all nonpar fixed WL policies will not differ from those implicit in the original policy illustration.

Determination of Actual Mortality Charges

The insurance company unilaterally determines the level of current mortality charges with all eight policies, although, of course, it cannot change them for in-force term or nonpar fixed WL policies, and it must respect all guarantee maximums.

Disclosure of Actual Mortality Charges

The level of current mortality charges assessed policies is disclosed annually to owners of CAWL and UL policies. The actual mortality charges are not disclosed under term, nonpar fixed WL, and par WL policies.

Volatility of Mortality Charges

Of course, most term and all nonpar fixed WL, having guaranteed mortality charges only, experience no volatility of mortality charges on in-force business. Even for the policies with non-guaranteed mortality charges, which includes CAWL and par WL and all four UL policies, insurers generally have not made major changes in their schedules of current charges for in-force policies. As mortality rates for insured lives have been falling at an average of about 1–2 percent per year for some years, there has been no need for insurers generally to increase mortality charges on in-force business. In fact, some commentators express concern that some insurers have *not* lowered mortality charges at all or as much as they could have. See Chapters 6 and 14 for a further discussion of mortality.

Given no or low mortality risk volatility, the risks borne by owners of WL and UL policies are correspondingly low, especially for NLG products as the mortality component for the NLG is guaranteed. This low risk assessment could change, as it has in the past with major flu epidemics.

Crediting Rates

We continue the analysis of policy pricing elements that underlie all life insurance policies with an examination of several attributes related to policies' crediting rates. Recall that, for most cash value policies, the crediting rate often is the most important driver of policy performance. Table 8-7 lists several attributes of interest crediting rates for our eight policies along with our comments about the extent to which and how they apply to each policy.

Guaranteed Minimum Crediting Rates

Each of the three WL policies contains guaranteed minimum crediting rates, although we cannot totally rule out the possibility that an insurer could allow gains from investments within their dividend formulas to be negative, which implies an effective interest rate lower than that stated in the contract. If mortality and/or expense gains can subsidize an investment loss, the policy still has an implicit minimum crediting rate, which is the totality of mortality and expense gains; i.e., dividends cannot be less than zero. As a practical matter, however, the likelihood of this occurring seems remote, even assuming that such would be considered, because guaranteed rates are usually quite low and most insurers selling par policies use a dividend interest rate based on their portfolio rates of return, which is highly stable.

All UL policies, except VUL, contain minimum interest guarantees as well. VUL policies do not guarantee to credit a minimum rate on the cash value, with the policyholder bearing the full investment risk (including losses).

Actual Crediting Rates versus Those at Policy Issuance

Crediting rates shown or implicit in policy illustrations at the time of policy issuance can be changed for all in-force UL, CAWL, and par WL policies, assuming that the original illustration was not predicated on guaranteed rates. Rates for all nonpar fixed WL policies will not differ from those implicit in the original policy illustration. VUL policy illustrations show purely hypothetical investment returns, so actual earned rates will certainly differ from those illustrated. Crediting rates for other policies with non-guaranteed elements are also highly likely to differ over time from those illustrated at issue.

TABLE 8-7
Crediting Rate Attributes of Term and Cash Value Life Insurance Policies

Attribute	Term Life Insurance	Cash Value Life Insurance						
		Whole Life Insurance			Universal Life Insurance			
		Nonpar Fixed	Nonpar Current Assumption	Par	Generic	No-Lapse Guarantee	Equity Indexed	Variable
Crediting Rates								
✓ Guaranteed minimum crediting rate?	n.a.	Yes	Yes	Yes, if investment gains cannot be negative	Yes	Yes	Yes	No
✓ Can actual crediting rates differ from those illustrated at issue?	n.a.	No	Yes	Yes	Yes	Yes for cash value; no for NLG	Yes	Yes
✓ Who determines crediting rate?	Insurer	Insurer	Insurer	Insurer	Insurer	Insurer	Insurer and index	Actual investment return
✓ Actual rate disclosed to policyholder?	n.a.	n.a.	Yes	No, except for some insurers	Yes	Yes	Yes	Yes
✓ Volatility of crediting rate?	None	None	Low to moderate depending on allocation method	Low to moderate depending on allocation method	Low to moderate depending on allocation method	Low to moderate for cash value; none for NLG	Low to high depending on allocation	Low to very high depending on fund choice
✓ Crediting rate includes dividend income?	n.a.	n.a.	Yes, but modest	Yes, but modest	Yes, but modest	Yes, but modest	No	Yes

Determination of Actual Crediting Rate

The insurance company unilaterally sets the crediting rate in all policies except EIUL and VUL. Some CAWL and UL policies link the crediting rate to one or more external indexes, such as money market indexes. With EIUL policies, the crediting rate for funds allocated to the fixed account is set by the insurer. The crediting rate for funds allocated to the index account is determined by reference to an external equity index, subject to participation rates and floors and caps. With VUL, the implicit earned rate is determined by the changes in the market value of investments held in the policies' separate accounts. Of course, with all but VUL policies, the guaranteed minimum interest rate floor must be respected.

Disclosure of Actual Crediting Rate

The non-guaranteed crediting rate applied to policy cash values is disclosed to the policyholder at least annually with CAWL and all UL policies. Some issuers of par WL also disclose the dividend interest rate annually.

Volatility of Crediting Rate

Policyholders bear no crediting rate risk with term and nonpar fixed WL. Also, for NLG UL products, the policyholder incurs no crediting rate risk as regards the NLG itself. All other WL and UL policies expose their policyholders to varying degrees of crediting rate volatility, including the cash value component for NLG UL.

The crediting rate volatility for EIUL policies will be a function of the extent to which the policyholder allocates funds to its indexed account versus the fixed account. Heavier allocations to the indexed account result in greater expected volatility, although the extremes are removed by floors and caps. With VUL policies, the extent of such volatility is determined by the market risk inherent in the policyholder's choice of funds. Thus, the risk could range from low for the fixed account, to high for some equity account choices, to quite high with some sector-specific equity funds.

Crediting rate risk for other WL and UL policies ordinarily will be influenced by the method that the insurer uses to allocate investment income. Thus, crediting rate risk is comparatively low if the insurer follows a **portfolio average method (PAM)**, which bases the crediting rate on the average return for the insurer's entire general account investment portfolio. Portfolio rates of return change slowly, given the long durations of most investments coupled with the use of book value accounting that smoothes changes in some asset values. Some insurers follow the **investment generation method (IGM)**, which bases the crediting rate on the average return on assets acquired over some period (*generation*) more or less approximating the lifetime of one or more blocks of policies. Crediting rates founded in the IGM will change more often than will rates founded in the PAM, although the IGM relies on book value accounting also which dampens fluctuations.

The dividend crediting rates for par WL policies are more likely to be based on the PAM than are the crediting rates for CAWL and non-variable UL policies. Crediting rates for CAWL, generic UL, and the fixed account with EIUL and VUL policies are commonly based on the investment income of a dedicated segment of the insurer's investments and/or some variation of new money rates akin to the IGM. This is the reason that crediting rates for these policies tend to adjust more quickly than do crediting rates under par policies and, thus, are more volatile even though book value accounting dampens swings here as well.

Inclusion of Dividend Income in Deriving the Crediting Rate

Equity investment returns are influenced by whether they include dividend income. Dividend income is included in VUL policies' values. It is specifically excluded from the derivation of the equity index with EIUL policies, thus penalizing yields by about 1 to 3 percent. Dividend income is included in the calculation of the overall rate of return for an insurer's general account assets. However, recall that equity investments constitute but a small proportion of most insurer's general account investments, so the impact of dividends is muted. Thus, the current crediting rates within current assumption and par WL policies as well as generic UL and the fixed account within EIUL and VUL policies will have been derived from a rate of return containing a minor dividend income component.

Loading Charges

We now examine several attributes related to policies' loading charges. Recall that all policies are loaded to cover the insurer's costs of doing business. Commonly, actuaries will have included specific policy loading charges to cover some or all of these costs. These charges may be explicit as with UL and CAWL policies or implicit as with term and other WL policies. Also, explicit policy loading charges often are set at low levels for marketing purposes and are known to be insufficient to cover the insurer's actual costs of doing business. In such situations, mortality and/or interest margins may be widened to provide additional funds to cover expenses, as discussed in Chapter 6. Table 8-8 lists several attributes of loading charges for our eight policies along with our comments about the extent to which and how they apply to each policy.

Guaranteed Maximum Loading Charges

All of the policies examined here guarantee maximum loading charges in some fashion. Of course, such charges embedded within term and nonpar fixed WL policies are locked in. All UL and CAWL policies have set maximum charges but usually charge somewhat less than the maximums permitted. Par WL policies that do not allow gains from expenses to be negative also are implicitly guaranteeing their loading charges. If mortality and/or investment gains can subsi-

TABLE 8-8
Loading Charge Attributes of Term and Cash Value Life Insurance Policies

Attribute	Term Life Insurance	Cash Value Life Insurance						
		Whole Life Insurance			Universal Life Insurance			
		Nonpar Fixed	Nonpar Current Assumption	Par	Generic	No-Lapse Guarantee	Equity Indexed	Variable
Loading Charges								
✓ Guaranteed maximum loading charges?	Yes	Yes	Yes	Yes, if expense gains cannot be negative	Yes	Yes	Yes	Yes
✓ Can actual charges differ from those illustrated at issue?	No	No	Yes	Yes	Yes	Yes for cash value; no for NLG	Yes	Yes
✓ Who determines loading charges?	Insurer	Insurer	Insurer	Insurer	Insurer	Insurer	Insurer	Insurer
✓ Actual loading charges disclosed to policyholder?	No	No	Yes	No	Yes	Yes	Yes	Yes
✓ Volatility of loading charges?	None	None	Low	Low	Low	Low for cash value; none for NLG	Low	Low

dize expense gains, as we saw with one of the par policies in Chapter 7, the policy still has an implicit maximum for its loading charges, which is the totality of mortality and investment gains; i.e., the lowest value for dividends is zero.

Actual Loading Charges versus Those at Policy Issuance

Future loading charges under most term and all nonpar fixed WL will be identical to those implicit at policy issuance as they are fixed and locked for the policy duration. Loading charges for NGL UL as regards the NLG may not be changed. Actual future loading charges for all other WL and UL policies (including the cash value component for NLG UL) may be changed, subject to the guaranteed maximums specified in the contract.

Determination of Actual Loading Charges

The insurance company unilaterally determines the actual loading charges to be assessed after policy issuance, subject to the contract maximums.

Disclosure of Actual Loading Charges

Actual assessed loading charges are disclosed at least annually to owners of all UL and CAWL policies. No disclosure is made ordinarily of such charges for term or the other two WL policies.

Volatility of Loading Charges

Insurers tend to change loading charges infrequently. Additionally, the margin between the guaranteed maximum charges and actual charges usually is not great. Thus, the risks borne by policyholders are generally low.

Conclusions

Each type of life insurance policy has its own attributes that will be appealing to some buyers but not others. Knowing each policy's attributes is an important part of due care. Worth emphasizing, however, is that desirable attributes do not necessarily make for a desirable policy. By this we mean that a policy's performance characteristics should play a large part in both the decision whether to purchase a particular policy and to retain it. The insurer's financial strength obviously also plays an enormous role.

We have attempted to set out in summary fashion a comparison of the key attributes of the major life insurance policies sold today. Appendix 3 offers a compilation of all individual tables for easy reference. We believe the commentary accompanying each individual table to be important and encourage the reader to digest the entirety of this chapter, not just its summary tables.

Life Insurance Policy Provisions and Features 9

THIS CHAPTER CONCLUDES PART III on life insurance policy fundamentals. Here we explore the life insurance policy as a contract.[1]
We first provide an overview of the physical format and content
of life insurance policies, along with an explanation of the role of
the states in this process. We next examine the major provisions
commonly found in life insurance policies. These collectively define the insurer's promise to the policyholder. Thereafter, we explore common riders or features that may be optionally included
in policies, typically for an additional premium charge. As this
Guide is not intended as a legal treatise, we delve but lightly into
legal interpretations and implications of these provisions and riders and only where necessary to add context.

Overview: Policy Content and Format

State insurance laws require life insurance companies to include
so-called standard policy provisions within their policies. The
laws do not mandate actual wording for these provisions. Rather,
they provide that policies must contain provisions whose language is at least as favorable to the policyholder as that of the

---

Authored by Harold D. Skipper.
[1]This chapter draws in part from Kenneth Black, Jr. and Harold D. Skipper,
Jr., *Life and Health Insurance* (13th ed.; Upper Saddle River, NJ: Prentice-Hall,
2000), Chapters 8, 9, and 10.

statute. Certain other provisions may be included in life insurance contracts at the option of the insurer. We cover both types of provisions in the following section, noting whether each is required or optional. Note that some provisions are called clauses.

Policy forms proposed for use by insurers are required to be submitted to and often formally approved by the insurance department of each state in which the insurer wishes to sell the policy. In addition to including the standard policy provisions, forms may not contain certain prohibited or restricted provisions, and the policy language must meet certain minimum readability standards. Forms also must comply with specific administrative guidelines established by each state.

In general, life insurance policies may be physically arranged in whatever format the insurer chooses, with the exception of a few aspects of the first page of the policy and provided the format is not misleading. This page ordinarily identifies the life insurer by its full name and address, may show the name of the insured and the policy number, and gives the insurer's promise to pay the amounts due, subject to compliance with policy conditions. Facsimile signatures of the insurer's president or CEO and secretary also appear.

States require that the first page include a summary description of the policy. Summary descriptions might be as follows:

FLEXIBLE PREMIUM UNIVERSAL LIFE INSURANCE POLICY

or

WHOLE LIFE INSURANCE POLICY

Immediately under these descriptions typically are short statements relative to the policy death proceeds (e.g., "Sum Insured Payable at Death"), the length of the premium payment period (e.g., "Premiums Payable for a Stated Period"), and whether the policy is participating or nonparticipating.

Also required to appear on the first page is a statement typically headed by:

RIGHT TO RETURN POLICY

This provision advises that the policy may be unconditionally returned to the insurer within 10 days of receipt, explains how to return it, and states that any premiums paid will be refunded promptly.

Immediately following, typically, will be a table of contents for the policy and policy specifications. The policy specifications will list relevant information specific to the policy, including the insured's name, age, gender, and underwriting classification; the policy type, number, face amount, premium (planned or otherwise) and payment period, and issue date; policy date, policyowner, and beneficiary (sometimes); and death benefit and dividend options, if applicable. Additional details about the policy often are also included. One or more pages of definitions of terms used in the policy might follow the specifications page, with some insurers including tables of relevant policy values at this point.

The balance of the policy's physical arrangement will follow no standard format but will contain the standard policy and optional provisions, presented and worded as the insurer wishes. Copies of Parts I and II of the application (see Chapter 6) along with any supplemental application forms (e.g., aviation questionnaire) will be included within this area, often near the end of the policy. Also commonly included at or near the end of the contract will be any policy amendments and optional riders.

Life Insurance Policy Provisions

Certain policy provisions can be considered mainly as protecting the policyowner in terms of making payment of policy benefits more secure. Other provisions can be considered mainly as protecting the insurance company from risks that it has not priced for in the policy. Still other provisions provide policyholders with additional flexibility or options. Our discussion of policy provisions is structured around these three classifications. Our terminology and provision titles will not necessarily follow that of any one insurer.

Provisions Protecting the Policyowner

All of the provisions discussed in this section are required to be contained in all life insurance policies sold in the United States. Each is intended to provide greater assurance of the policy benefit being paid by addressing circumstances that might otherwise lead to nonpayment.

Entire Contract Clause

The **entire contract clause** provides that the policy itself and the application, if a copy is attached to the policy, constitute the entire contract between the parties. A required provision, the clause protects the policyowner in that the company cannot, merely by reference, include within the policy its procedural rules or any oral or other statements made by the applicant or proposed insured except for those contained in the application, provided a copy of the application is physically attached to the policy. If the insurer believes that it has been materially misled in the application process, ordinarily it must look solely to the application attached to the policy to justify its attempt to reform or rescind the policy.

This clause also protects the company in that the application, if made part of the contract (which it ordinarily is), becomes part of the consideration for the contract. Any material misrepresentation made by the applicant or proposed insured in the application can be used by the company in seeking reformation or rescission of the contract (but see the following section on the incontestable clause). A **material misrepresentation** is an inaccurate statement by a proposed insured or applicant that causes an insurer to issue a policy on terms or at a price more favorable than it would, had the statement been accurate.

Incontestable Clause

The **incontestable clause** provides that the validity of an insurance contract may not be contested after it has been in force for two years. A typical incontestable clause reads as follows:

> Except for accidental death and disability premium payment benefits, we cannot contest this policy after it has been in force for two years while the insured is alive.

The clause has been given a broad interpretation. It prevents a life insurance company from voiding a life insurance contract after the passage of the specified time on grounds of material misrepresentation and, generally, even fraud. The rationale for this broad interpretation is the protection of beneficiaries. It removes the fear of lawsuits at a time—the insured's death—when it may be difficult for the beneficiary successfully to combat an insurer's charge of misrepresentation by a person who is no longer alive to present his or her side of the case. The company agrees not to resist claim payment if premiums have been paid, if no violation of the contract has come to light during the stipulated time limit, and if, during the time, the company has taken no action to rescind the contract.

Even though the clauses have been accorded broad interpretation, some challenges to contract validity after expiration of the period of contestability have been successful. Certain fraudulent actions have been found to be so outrageous as to permit the insurer to rescind the policy. In other cases, the incontestable clause was held not to bar policy rescission wherein the applicant was found to lack an insurable interest in the insured's life at policy inception or for which another person substituted for the insured in a required physical examination.

Premium Provision

Life insurance policies are required to contain a **premium provision** that explains the nature of premiums due or otherwise payable under the policy. For bundled policies, this can mean a statement as simple as premiums are due and payable in advance. For unbundled policies, the premium provision may explain that premiums may be paid at any time, subject to insurer minimums and tax-constrained maximums. If loads are assessed against premiums paid, this too may be referenced in this provision.

The provision may advise the owner that premiums can be paid monthly, quarterly, semi-annually, or annually by check, automatic draft, or electronic funds transfer. The provision itself ordinarily does not state the actual premiums due or premium loads. That information usually appears on the policy specifications page.

Grace Period Provision

The **grace period provision** requires the insurer to accept premium payments for a certain period after the premium due date or if the policy has insufficient account value to permit it to continue in force. State laws require a minimum grace period of 30 or 31 days. Universal life (UL) polices typically offer 61-day grace periods, with at least one state requiring this length. During this period, the insurer (1) is required to accept payment even though it is technically late (i.e., past the due date) and (2) may not require evidence of insurability as a condition of premium acceptance.

If the insured dies during the grace period, the company must pay the claim but is permitted to deduct any overdue premium or charges plus interest from the death benefit payment. The provision's purpose is to protect the policyowner from unintentional lapse.

Reinstatement Clause

Another required provision, the **reinstatement clause**, gives the policyholder the right to reinstate a lapsed policy under certain conditions. The two most important conditions are furnishing evidence of insurability and paying past due premiums or charges.

The insured is required to furnish evidence of insurability that is satisfactory to the company. Otherwise, those in poor health would routinely apply for reinstatement, as experience has shown. Most lapses are unintentional and are followed within a couple of weeks by a reinstatement application. Insurers usually take a liberal position in such cases, even though they have the contractual right to require a medical examination and other detailed evidence of insurability. The longer the time period since lapse, the more closely reinstatement requirements resemble those for new applications.

The term *evidence of insurability* is broader than the term *good health*. Insurability connotes meeting standards with regard to occupation, other insurance, and financial condition, as well as the physical characteristics and health status of the insured. The term *satisfactory to the company* has generally been held to allow the insurer to require evidence that would be satisfactory to a reasonable insurer.

The second condition for reinstatement is the payment of past due premiums or charges. With whole life (WL) and term policies, the usual terms require payment of the overdue amounts, less any dividends that would have been paid, usually with interest at 6 or 8 percent. For universal life (UL) policies, a different approach is followed. The policyholder usually is not required to pay all back charges; only those applicable for the grace period during which coverage was provided plus enough to keep the policy in force for the next two or three months. Any outstanding policy loans under both WL and UL must be either repaid or reinstated through payment of past due interest.

Reinstatement ordinarily is not permitted if the policy has been (1) surrendered, (2) continued as extended term insurance and the period of coverage has expired, or (3) lapsed five (sometimes three) or more years. If the extended term period has not expired and has several years to run, insurers often will reinstate the policy with little or even no evidence of insurability.

Nonforfeiture Provision

In the early days, insurance policies had no cash surrender values. If a policy lapsed, the policyowner "forfeited" all contributions in excess of those necessary to cover current and past mortality charges and expenses. The states' *Standard Nonforfeiture Laws* prohibit such forfeitures today for non-variable policies.

These laws set out the circumstances under which policies must have nonforfeiture values and stipulate the minimum required values. These laws are not applicable to variable policies. In effect, the laws require cash values under all life insurance policies that involve a substantial prefunding of future mortality charges. These laws also require that cash value life policies include **nonforfeiture provisions** that state the mortality table, rate of interest, and method used in calculating the policy's nonforfeiture values and the options available if the policy is terminated or lapses. These options provide policy flexibility so are covered in that section below.

Participation/Policy Value Provision

Policies are required to state whether they are participating (par) or nonparticipating (nonpar). Par policies are required to contain what may be called a **participation** or **distributable surplus provision,** which states that the policy will participate in any surplus that the insurer decides to distribute to policyholders. Nonpar policies will have a **nonparticipating provision** or equivalent that states simply that the policy does not share in any insurer surplus or perhaps does not pay dividends.

Nonpar policies containing non-guaranteed policy elements that permit excess interest credits and/or lower-than-guaranteed charges will contain a **policy value** or **account value provision** or equivalent that explains the nature of the non-guaranteed elements and how they are determined and applied within the policy. Cost of insurance (COI) charges, loading charges, and crediting rates will be explained, with guaranteed maximum charges and, if applicable, the minimum crediting rate indicated.

The provisions ordinarily stipulate that the insurer's board of directors will annually determine the dividend or other non-guaranteed policy elements, except for the crediting rates under variable policies. Subject to a few states' laws limiting surplus accumulation by mutual life insurers and to any regulatory (e.g., requirement for equitable treatment of policies) and policy (e.g., guarantees) constraints, the insurer's board of directors ordinarily has sole discretion to determine how these elements will be derived and applied to nonvariable policies. Chapters 6 and 7 discussed how these non-guaranteed elements are derived for both bundled and unbundled policies. As dividend options are a source of policy flexibility, we cover them in that section below.

Misstatement of Age or Gender Provision

States require that life insurance policies include a **misstatement of age provision** stipulating that if, on the insured's death, his or her age is found to have been misstated, the amount of insurance will be adjusted to be that which would have been purchased by the premium or the then COI charges had the correct age been used at policy issue. Although not a standard provision, insurers commonly also include misstatement of gender within the same provision, whereby the amount payable is similarly adjusted if the application contains a misstatement of gender. (Misstatements of gender are not common and usually occur because of a transcribing error, not because the proposed insured was unsure of his or her gender!)

If the error in age or gender is discovered while the insured is alive, the procedure followed for bundled policies depends upon the actuarial effect of the misstatement. If the age has been understated or the insured's gender incorrectly recorded as female, the owner of a bundled policy usually is given the option of paying the difference in premiums with interest or of having the policy reissued for a reduced amount. With an overstatement of age or an incorrect recording of the insured as a male, a refund is usually made by paying the difference in reserves for bundled policies. For unbundled policies, the account value is debited for age understatements (or incorrectly showing the insured as a female) or credited for age overstatements (or incorrectly showing the insured as a male) by an amount equal to the sum of the differences in the COI charges.

Without this provision, some misstatements of age or gender could be interpreted as material misrepresentations. With this provision, they cannot. Also, as the incontestable clause does not apply to age or gender misstatements, adjustments may be made in policy benefits after the period of contestability has expired.

Provisions Protecting the Insurance Company

Several life insurance contract provisions primarily protect the life insurance company. These include the suicide clause, the delay clause, and certain exclusion clauses.

Suicide Clause

Death by suicide is included in the mortality tables used by insurers for pricing their products. As such, this cause of death is logically covered under life insurance contracts, as with all other causes of death. An exception occurs when insurance is purchased in contemplation of suicide. It is for this reason that insurers may, at their option, include a **suicide clause** in their contracts that excludes payment of claims if the cause of death is suicide occurring within the first two policy years. Probably all insurers include this clause where permitted, although some limit the exclusion period to one year.

A typical suicide clause reads as follows:

> For the first two full years from the original application date, we will not pay if the insured commits suicide (while sane or insane). We will terminate the policy and give back the premiums paid to us less any loan.

Delay Clause

Life insurance policies must contain a so-called **delay clause** that grants the company the right to defer cash surrender value payments, withdrawals, or the making of a policy loan (except for purposes of paying premiums) for up to six months after its request. This provision, which does not apply to the payment of death claims, is intended to protect the company against "runs" that could cause the failure of an otherwise financially sound company. The clause has only rarely been invoked.

Exclusion Clauses

The great majority of life insurance policies contain but a single exclusion—for suicide—and even here, the exclusion is time-limited. States permit a few other, optional exclusions that can be applied on a case-by-case basis, the two most important of which are as follows:

- ◆ **Aviation Exclusion.** Occasionally, an underwriter will add an **aviation exclusion** that excludes coverage if the insured dies in an aviation accident. It is included in life insurance contracts today only under exceptional circumstances, such as with insureds who are military pilots or fly experimental aircraft. Virtually all coverage restrictions can be eliminated if the policyowner is willing to pay an extra premium.

All companies cover fare paying passengers on regularly scheduled airlines. Similarly, anticipated flights on unscheduled airlines usually do not result in any policy restrictions or an increased rate. Even private pilots and the pilots and crews of commercial airlines are insured with standard or with only slight extra rates.

- ◆ **War Exclusion. War exclusion clauses** provide that the insurer need not pay a claim if the insured's death occurs under certain military conditions. The insurer returns all premiums paid with interest or refunds the policy's reserve. Companies have inserted war clauses in their contracts during periods of impending or actual war, particularly for policies issued to persons of draft age. Relatively few, if any, insurers presently include such clauses; rather, they carefully screen military applicants at underwriting. War clauses are canceled at the end of the war period.

  There are two types of war clauses: (1) the status clause and (2) the results clause. Under the **status clause**, the insurer need not pay the policy face amount if death results while the insured is in the military service, regardless of the cause of death. Under the **results clause**, the insurer is excused from paying the face amount only if the death is a direct *result* of war.

Provisions Providing Policyowner Flexibility

We now examine provisions in life insurance policies that provide policyowners with greater flexibility. In effect, these provisions provide owners with a package of options, thus enhancing the value of the contract.

Right to Return Policy

As noted earlier, insurers are required to include a **right of return policy provision** within their contracts, which gives policyowners an unconditional right to return a policy to the insurer within 10 days of its receipt. Some insurers extend the required period to 20 or more days. A full refund of premiums paid must be made on policy return.

Death Benefit Provision

UL policies contain what are sometimes called **death benefit provisions** or the equivalent in which the contract sets out the various death benefit options (see Chapter 7) and explains the method of determining the policy death benefit. The policyholder's rights to change the death benefit amount and option are set out, along with the operational details and procedures for effectuating any change. Thus, the policy advises that any change in the amount or option that can have the effect of increasing the policy net amount at risk will or may require evidence of insurability. Decreases require but a written request.

The Beneficiary Clause

The beneficiary designation ordinarily is the most important element of a life insurance policy and warrants great care in selection and wording. For this reason, we devote considerable space to its discussion.

The **beneficiary clause** in a life insurance contract typically states that the policyowner may have policy death proceeds paid to whomever and in whatever form desired, subject to contract terms. The policyowner can prepare a plan of distribution in advance that accomplishes his or her personal objectives by allowing appropriately for future contingencies.

Nature of Designations

Primary and Contingent Designations. The person named as the first to receive policy death proceeds is called the **primary beneficiary**. More than one person may be designated as primary beneficiary. The person named to receive death proceeds if no primary beneficiary is alive at the time of the insured's death is called the **contingent** or **secondary beneficiary.** If no named beneficiaries are alive at the insured's death, death proceeds are paid to the insured's estate—a potentially undesirable outcome as proceeds will be included in the insured's gross estate for estate tax purposes and will incur probate costs.

Any contingent or later (called **tertiary beneficiary**) designation typically is made at the same time as the primary beneficiary is designated. A beneficiary designation with both primary and contingent beneficiaries might read as follows:

> Proceeds to be paid to Christine B. Butterworth, wife of the insured, if living; otherwise to Bart B. Simpson, nephew of the insured.

The importance of exercising care in the beneficiary designation cannot be overemphasized. If the policyowner's intentions are to be carried out effectively, the language must be precise and unambiguous. "To my children" is a designation that invites misunderstanding and possibly litigation. So, too, are designations that include the terms "dependents," "relatives," and "heirs."

Beneficiary designations should always carry the full given names of natural persons as well as their relationships to the insured so as to remove the possibility of any misidentification. They also should provide for the possibility that one or more beneficiaries may predecease the insured through use of contingent and, if needed, tertiary designations. If multiple beneficiaries are named at one level, the designation should indicate whether the share of any deceased beneficiary is to be shared among surviving beneficiaries (*per capita*) or among the deceased beneficiary's heirs, if any (*per stirpes*).

Revocable and Irrevocable Designations. The partition of rights between the policyowner and the beneficiary depends upon whether the beneficiary designation is revocable. A **revocable designation** is one that may be changed by the policyowner without the beneficiary's consent. An **irrevocable designation** is one that can be changed only with the beneficiary's express consent.

Irrevocable designations are not commonly used except in situations in which a policyowner may not retain the right to change beneficiaries, such as with a divorce decree. Irrevocably named beneficiaries have a vested right in the policy that is so complete that neither the policyowner nor his or her creditors can impair it without the beneficiary's consent, including surrendering the policy or taking policy loans.

Changing the Beneficiary

Policies typically contain a provision stating that the policyowner has the power to change the beneficiary designation while the policy is in force. When this right is reserved, the named beneficiary obtains no vested rights in the policy or in its proceeds while the insured is alive. The beneficiary possesses a "mere expectancy until after the maturity of the contract."

In the absence of contractual constraints, the policyowner may change the designation whenever and to whomever he or she wishes. The contract ordinarily states the method for accomplishing the change. In the majority of cases, a beneficiary change is a routine matter. Some policyowners have attempted a beneficiary change through their wills. In general, courts will not recognize a change via one's will if the policy sets forth an exclusive procedure for effecting a change.

Simultaneous Death of Insured and Beneficiary

The beneficiary's right to receive life insurance policy proceeds is usually conditioned on his or her surviving the insured. If the insured and the beneficiary die in the same accident and no evidence shows who died first, the question arises as to whom to pay the proceeds. Most states have enacted the *Uniform Simultaneous Death Act* that provides that "where the insured and beneficiary in a policy of life or accident insurance have died and there is not sufficient evidence that they have died otherwise than simultaneously, the proceeds of the policy shall be distributed as if the insured had survived the beneficiary."

This resolves the question of survival, but it fails to solve the main problems facing policyowners. Specifically, if the proceeds are payable in a lump sum and no contingent beneficiary is named, no matter who is determined to have survived, the proceeds will be paid into the estate—of either the insured or the beneficiary—commonly an undesirable outcome. Related to this issue is the short term survivorship situation in which the beneficiary survives the insured by a short period of time.

Many companies allow use of a **survivorship clause** (also called a **time clause**), which provides that the beneficiary must survive the insured by a fixed period after the insured's death to be entitled to the proceeds. This clause, in conjunction with the naming of contingent beneficiaries, can prevent the proceeds from falling into the probate estate of either an owner/insured or the original beneficiary.

Settlement Options

The majority of death proceeds are paid to beneficiaries as a single sum of money shortly after the insured's death. Beneficiaries may be ill-prepared emotionally and otherwise to make decisions concerning the disposition of what may be large sums. Poor investment and purchase decisions are too easily made during periods of great stress. Use of a trust as beneficiary or settlement options may be desirable. **Settlement options** grant policyowners (and beneficiaries) options as to how death proceeds will be paid. Most insurers also permit cash surrender values to be paid under settlement options. These can be particularly valuable options at retirement.

Settlement options are set out in the policy, and most contracts provide a choice from among the options discussed below. The policyowner may give the beneficiary as much or as little flexibility in designating the settlement option as he or she desires. Thus, a policyowner could fix absolutely the manner in which proceeds are to be paid, with the beneficiary having no right to alter the arrangement at the insured's death. Alternatively, the policyowner could design a settlement agreement that gave the beneficiary total freedom to alter its terms.

Cash

Most death proceeds are paid as a **lump sum** of cash (check or bank draft). In a strict sense, this is not an option, because life insurance contracts usually stipulate a cash settlement in the absence of any other direction by the policyowner or beneficiary.

In an effort to provide better service to beneficiaries and to retain more of the policy proceeds within the insurer corporate family, many insurers provide beneficiaries with the option of having proceeds paid into an insurer sponsored **retained asset account,** which is an interest bearing account on which drafts may be written. The beneficiary is free to leave proceeds in this account or to write checks to withdraw any portion or all of the proceeds.

This option meets the objective of providing the beneficiary with time to decide about the disposition to be made of the funds, while permitting the beneficiary immediate access to the full proceeds if desired.

Interest Option

Under the **interest option**, the proceeds remain with the company and only the earned interest is paid to the beneficiary. A minimum interest rate is guaranteed in the contract, although companies routinely credit higher rates. In most companies, interest may not be left to accumulate and compound. As legal limits restrict the length of time a principal sum may be kept intact, companies frequently limit the time that they will hold funds under this option to the lifetime of the primary beneficiary or 30 years, whichever is longer.

The interest option's main advantage is that, like the flexible spending account, it assures the beneficiary freedom from immediate investment worries while guaranteeing both principal and a minimum rate of return. The rights of withdrawal and to change to another option provide flexibility.

Fixed Period Option

The **fixed period option**, as its name indicates, provides for the payment of proceeds systematically over a defined period of months or years, usually not longer than 25 or 30 years. It is one of two options based on the concept of liquidating principal and interest over a period of years, without reference to life contingencies. The other is the fixed amount option (discussed below).

If the primary beneficiary dies during the fixed period, the remaining installments (or their commuted value) are paid to a contingent beneficiary. The amount of proceeds, the period of time, the guaranteed minimum rate of interest, and the frequency of payments determine the amount of each installment. Any interest in excess of the guaranteed rate is usually paid at the end of each year. The fixed period option is valuable when the most important consideration is providing income for a definite period, as in the case of a readjustment period following the insured's death or while children are in school.

Fixed Amount Option

The **fixed amount option** also systematically liquidates the death proceeds but with the income amount, rather than the time period, fixed. A specified amount of income is designated, such as $10,000 per month, and payments continue until the principal and interest thereon are exhausted.

Fixed amount options can be more advantageous than fixed period options, because they are more flexible. Most companies permit policyowners to specify varying amounts of income at different times, and beneficiaries may be given full rights of withdrawal or the right to withdraw up to a certain sum in any one year on a cumulative or non-cumulative basis. With both fixed period and fixed amount options, the commencement of installments can be deferred to a future time by holding the proceeds under the interest option until that time.

Single Life Income Option

The several forms of single life income options represent the other broad class of settlement options—those that liquidate principal and interest *with* reference to life contingencies, that is, whether the insured is alive. The amount of each installment depends on the type of life income selected, the amount of the proceeds, the rate of interest being credited, and the age and gender (where permitted) of the beneficiary when the income commences. The most common forms of life income options (life annuities) are (1) pure life income option, (2) refund life income option, and (3) life income option with period certain.

With the **pure life income option**, installments are payable only for as long as the primary beneficiary (the income recipient) lives. No further payments are due to anyone when the primary beneficiary dies. The pure life income option provides the largest life income per $1,000 of proceeds. Most persons hesitate to risk forfeiting a large part of the principal on early death, particularly if there are others to whom they wish to leave funds.

The refund life income option may take the form of a **cash refund annuity** or an **installment refund annuity**. Both annuities guarantee the return of an amount equal to the principal sum less total payments already made. The difference in the two forms is that, under the cash refund option, a lump sum settlement is made following the primary beneficiary's death instead of installment payments being continued.

Under the **life income option with period certain**, the most widely used life income option, installments are payable for as long as the primary beneficiary lives, but should this beneficiary die before a predetermined number of years, installments continue to a second beneficiary until the end of the designated period. The usual contract contains two or three alternative periods, the most popular ones being 10 and 20 years, but others may be obtained on request.

Joint and Survivorship Life Income Option

Under the **joint and survivorship life income option**, life income payments continue for as long as at least one of two beneficiaries (annuitants) is alive. It may continue payments of the same income to the surviving beneficiary or reduce the installments and continue payment of this reduced amount for the surviving beneficiary's lifetime.

Other Settlement Arrangements

In many instances, policyowners find that they can best provide for beneficiaries by selecting combinations of settlement options. Virtually any desired income pattern may be obtained by using the options either singly or in combination.

Notwithstanding the variety of settlement plans offered, situations arise when the standard options do not fit well. Upon submission of the facts, companies usually are willing to develop special settlement plans, within reasonable limits. Where an individual desires still greater flexibility, consideration should be given to use of a trust. This is particularly to be considered if discretionary powers are indicated. Life insurance companies ordinarily will not accept any arrangement whereby they must exercise discretion in carrying out the terms of the agreement.

Nonforfeiture Options

As noted earlier, traditional cash value policies are required to contain **nonforfeiture options** that are activated automatically on policy lapse or can be elected by their owners if they choose to terminate their policies. The three options ordinarily provided are:

- ◆ **Cash.** The policy may be terminated and its net surrender value paid in cash to the owner. Of course, protection ceases and the insurer has no further obligations under the policy. A policy's **net cash surrender value** is the gross account value decreased by any withdrawals and surrender charges and the amount of any policy loans outstanding and increased by the cash value of any paid up additions, any dividends accumulated at interest, and any prepaid premiums.

  Cash can, of course, be secured from cash value policies in ways other than policy surrender, including policy loans, cash value withdrawals under UL policies, and partial surrenders under some traditional WL policies. Traditional par WL policies provide that any paid up additions may be surrendered, in whole or in part. Furthermore, as a matter of practice (usually not by contract), many insurers permit a partial surrender of traditional cash value policies.

- ◆ **Reduced Paid Up Insurance.** The **reduced paid up insurance** nonforfeiture option permits the policyowner to use the net surrender value as a net single premium to purchase a reduced amount of paid up insurance of the same type as the basic policy. All riders and supplementary benefits, such as premium waiver and accidental death, are terminated, and no further premiums are payable. The exchange is made at net rates, so it is based on mortality and interest only.

◆ **Extended Term Insurance.** The **extended term insurance (ETI)** non-forfeiture option gives the policyowner the right to use the net surrender value as a net single premium to purchase paid up term insurance for the policy face amount less policy loans, for whatever duration that value will carry the policy. Policy loans reduce both the net surrender value and the face amount. Paid up additions increase both.

If the policyowner fails to pay a required policy premium within the grace period and the premium is not paid via the automatic premium loan feature (see below), the policy's net surrender value will be applied automatically under either the reduced paid up or ETI option to continue coverage. Ordinarily, ETI is the automatic option.

UL policies typically do not offer nonforfeiture options as such, as they are not needed. The termination of a UL policy for its net surrender value (cash) is always an option. The reduced paid up nonforfeiture option can be duplicated under a UL policy by ceasing to pay any premiums and reducing the face amount to that which the account value will support to the end of the applicable policy mortality table, calculated based on the guaranteed crediting rate and COI and loading charges. The ETI option can be duplicated under a UL policy by ceasing to pay any premiums and allowing the account value along with future interest credits to sustain the policy for as long as it can by covering internal charges.

Policy Loan Provision

All states require inclusion of a **policy loan provision** in cash value policies under which insurers must make requested loans to policyowners, subject to certain limitations. The provision usually contains these key elements:

1. the insurer will lend to the policyowner an amount not to exceed the net policy cash surrender value less interest to the next policy anniversary (and, for variable policies, a further reduction typically of 10 percent) and, with UL policies, a deduction for charges for the balance of the policy year;
2. loan interest is payable annually at a rate or by a method specified in the policy;
3. any due and unpaid interest will be paid automatically by a further loan;
4. if total indebtedness equals or exceeds the cash surrender value, the policy will terminate, subject to the grace period;
5. the policyowner may repay the loan in whole or in part at any time; and
6. if the policy terminates by surrender or death, the indebtedness will be deducted from policy proceeds.

Policy loans can be a source of flexibility. No one need approve the loan, and it is confidential. The loan interest rate is favorable and contractually set (see below). The loan's automatic continuation is one of its unique features.

Policy Loan Interest Rate

The policy loan interest rate or the procedure for determining it is stated in the policy. In the past, state laws required insurers to use a stated, fixed loan rate of 5, 6, or 8 percent. Under the NAIC's *Model Policy Loan Interest Rate Bill*, adopted by the majority of states, insurers now may use a fixed rate of not greater than 8 percent or use a variable rate approach that allows them to change the policy loan interest rate up to four times each year provided the rate does not exceed the greater of Moody's Composite Yield on seasoned corporate bonds two months prior to the determination date or the interest rate credited on cash values plus 1 percent. Companies are required to evaluate the need for a loan rate change at least once each year.

When market interest rates decline, the law requires the company to reduce the loan interest rate whenever the ceiling rate has declined to at least one half of 1 percent below the rate currently being charged on policy loans. This requirement generally assures that the loan interest rate will decline as market rates decline.

Automatic Premium Loans

Although not usually required, many companies include an **automatic premium loan (APL)** provision within their policies, which provides that, if a premium is unpaid at the end of the grace period, and if the policy has a sufficient net surrender value, the amount of the premium due will be advanced automatically as a loan against the policy. UL policies, by their nature, do not have APL provisions.

In some jurisdictions, the policyowner must specifically elect to make the provision operative. The purpose of the APL provision is to protect against unintentional lapse, as when a premium payment is overlooked. A disadvantage of the APL is that it may encourage laxity in payment of premiums and can result in indebtedness exceeding the cash value.

Dividend Options

Except for requiring policies to permit policyowners to take their dividends in cash, state laws ordinarily do not mandate the options under which dividends may be applied under par WL policies. Insurers, however, have long included options within these policies. The policyowner elects the desired option at the time the policy is purchased, but it can be changed at any time under most policies, although evidence of insurability may be required if the effect of the change would be to increase the policy's future net amount at risk. Here we restate and expand a bit on the options introduced in Chapter 7. These options can be potentially important sources of flexibility. The five most common dividend options are:

- ◆ **Cash.** The insurer mails a check for the dividend to the policyowner each year.
- ◆ **Apply Toward Premium Payment.** Reduces the policyowner's current outlay.
- ◆ **Purchase Paid-Up Additions.** The dividend is applied as a net single premium at the insured's attained age to purchase as much paid-up WL insurance as it will provide. Paid-up additions themselves may be par or nonpar. If they are par, annual dividends on the paid-up additions further enhance the policy's total cash value and death benefit.

  Some individuals do not wish to purchase single premium WL insurance, even if small in amount. Some consider it wiser to use dividends to reduce current premiums to permit the purchase of additional insurance. Even so, purchasing paid-up additions can be a worthwhile approach to increasing insurance protection and offering flexibility because of their cash value.
- ◆ **Accumulate at Interest.** Dividends may be allowed to accumulate at interest under the contract. The insurer guarantees a minimum crediting rate, although companies typically credit higher rates. Accumulations can be withdrawn at will. On the insured's death, the policy's face amount plus dividend accumulations are paid, and, in the event of surrender, the cash surrender value plus dividend accumulations are paid.
- ◆ **Purchase One Year Term.** Some companies make available an option to apply the dividend to purchase one year term insurance. The option takes one of two forms. One form applies the dividend as a net annual premium to purchase as much one year term insurance protection as it will buy. The other form purchases one year term insurance in an amount equal to the policy's cash value, with the excess dividend portion applied under one of the other dividend options.

Companies often permit dividends to be used in other ways. One is the **add-to-cash-value option**. Another follows essentially the same approach but does not augment the death benefit, instead causing a more rapid decrease in the policy's net amount at risk, thereby hastening the time when the policy can be self-sustaining with no further premium payments required.

Assignment/Ownership Provision

Ownership rights in life insurance policies, like other types of property, can be transferred by the current owner to another person. Policies usually contain **ownership provisions** that state that the policyowner may exercise all rights under the policy without the consent of anyone else, unless a beneficiary is named irrevocably. Although the ownership of most policies can be changed in the absence of a permissive policy provision, the ownership provision might also state that the owner has the unilateral and sole right to change policy ownership, subject to any irrevocable beneficiary. Some policies show the change of ownership statement in a separate **assignment** provision. Although much variation exists in the wording, one company's provision reads:

> You can assign this policy. We will not be responsible for the validity of an assignment. We will not be liable for any payments we make or actions we take before notice to us of an assignment.

Assignment/ownership provisions do not prohibit an assignment/ownership change without the insurer's consent, but provide that the insurer need not recognize it until it has received written notice of it and that it assumes no responsibility as to its validity. Assignments are of two types: **absolute** and **collateral**.

- **Absolute Assignments.** An **absolute assignment** is the complete transfer by the existing policyowner of all rights in the policy to another person or entity. It is a change of ownership. In the case of a gift, the assignment is a voluntary property transfer involving no monetary consideration.

  From time to time, a life insurance policy is sold for a valuable consideration. As with a gift, these transactions are accomplished through an absolute assignment of policy rights, typically by using an absolute assignment/change of ownership form furnished by the insurer. A common situation calling for use of an absolute assignment is with life settlements whereby a policy, often no longer needed, is sold to someone. See Chapter 18.
- **Collateral Assignments.** A **collateral assignment** is a temporary transfer of only some policy ownership rights to another. Collateral assignments are commonly used to assign life policies as collateral for loans from banks and other lending institutions. Such assignments are partial in that only some (not all as with an absolute assignment) policy rights are transferred. They are temporary in that the transferred partial rights revert to the policyowner upon debt repayment.

Common Life Insurance Policy Riders

The foregoing features of life insurance policies are either required to be included or optional with the insurer or policyholder. In each instance, their inclusion adds nothing to policy premiums or charges. Applicants often wish benefits or options beyond those provided by these routine provisions. These supplemental benefits or options are provided by what are called policy **riders** that usually require additional premium payments. Our discussion here is of the most commonly found such riders. A given insurer may offer a greater or lesser variety of riders, with the details of operation and terminology differing from those explained below.

Riders Providing Life Insurance Coverage

Several types of riders are available that provide life insurance coverage beyond that provided by the basic policy to which they are appended. We discuss four generic types below.

Term Riders

Insurers have for decades permitted policyowners to attach term riders to basic policies to enhance the total death benefit. More recently, a modified application of this practice, known as term blending, has emerged. Term blending can be accomplished using term riders but blending is not available with every cash value policy or from every insurer. Term blending is also not without some risks.

Depending on the situation, limited term blending may lead to better overall performance. However, if current assumptions are prospectively less favorable, term blending may adversely impact policy performance and increase lapse risk (compared to a policy with no term blending). In addition, guaranteed assumptions may be less favorable with term blending, or the term face amount may terminate early (such as age 100). Therefore, the policyowner's specific circumstances, objectives, and expectations play a critical role in the ultimate effectiveness of term riders.

Family Riders

Many companies offer riders that provide insurance on the lives of one or more members of the family of the person who is the insured under the base policy to which the rider is attached. These riders are referred to by various names depending on the nature of the coverage, including **family rider**, **spouse rider**, **children's rider**, and **additional insured rider**, among others. A rider might provide coverage on the spouse and children, the spouse only, or the children only.

Coverage on the spouse usually is term life insurance to age 65 or so, either for a stated amount, such as $100,000, or varying in amount with age. The insurance is typically convertible without evidence of insurability to a permanent policy. Insurance on the children is ordinarily term to some age between 18 and 25 and for a modest fixed amount, such as $10,000. All children living with the family are covered, even if they were adopted or born after the policy is issued. Coverage usually is convertible without evidence of insurability, often for a multiple of the fixed amount, such as five times.

Accidental Death Benefit Riders

An **accidental death benefit** (sometimes called **double indemnity**) rider provides that double (or other multiple) of the face amount is payable if the insured dies as a result of an accident. From a financial planning standpoint, there is seldom a reason why double or triple the policy face amount is needed because death was caused by an accident, as compared with death from other causes, but this rider is popular, perhaps because the premium is comparatively modest (reflecting a low probability of this type of death) and maybe because many people believe that they are most likely to die in an accident (which statistically is not accurate).

A typical clause includes the following definition of accidental death:

Death resulting from bodily injury effected solely through external, violent, and accidental means independently and exclusively of all other causes, with death occurring within 90 days after such injury.

The numerous exclusions in the accidental death benefit clause speak to the practical difficulties inherent in this form of coverage. Death typically must occur within 90 or 120 days of an accident. The purpose of this restriction is to ensure that the accident is the sole cause of death. Coverage usually expires at age 65 or 70. Most insurers grade premium charges by age at issue.

Guaranteed Insurability Option

The **guaranteed insurability option (GIO)**, also known as the **additional** or **guaranteed purchase option**, permits an insured to purchase additional insurance without providing evidence of insurability. It was developed to permit younger individuals to be certain that they would be able to purchase additional insurance as their circumstances changed, regardless of their insurability. The usual rider gives the insured the option of purchasing additional insurance at periodic, set intervals (commonly three years), provided the insured has not attained a specified age, such as age 40, at which age the rider expires. Option dates may be advanced for life events such as birth or adoption of a child and marriage.

In most cases, the amount of the additional insurance is limited to a multiple of the basic policy face amount or an amount stipulated in the rider, whichever is smaller. Insurers offer up to $100,000 or more per option date. The option requires an extra premium that is based on the company's estimate of the extra mortality that will be experienced on policies issued without evidence of insurability. The premium is payable to the last option date.

Living Benefit Riders

Living benefit riders (or provisions), also called **accelerated benefit** riders, promise to pay some or all of a policy's face amount prior to the insured's death if the insured suffers some specified adverse health condition. Under each, the policyowner must request that living benefit payments be made and the amount, and proof must be provided that the insured's condition qualifies for the payments. Such coverage typically takes one of three forms, as follows:

Terminal Illness Coverage

Many insurers offer some type of **terminal illness coverage**, also called **accelerated death benefits**, that provides that a specified maximum percentage of from 25 to 100 percent of the policy's face amount can be paid if the insured is diagnosed as having a terminal illness, usually subject to a specified overall maximum payment, such as $250,000. Most provisions require that the insured have a maximum of one year to live, unless state law mandates otherwise. The insurer requires satisfactory evidence that the insured suffers a terminal illness, including (1) certification by a physician, (2) hospital or nursing home records, and, possibly, (3) a medical examination (paid for by the insurer). Some companies make no explicit charge for the coverage while others assess an administrative expense charge (e.g., $200) for processing the request and may reduce the amount payable to reflect lost interest. The benefit may be included in any type of policy.

Catastrophic Illness Coverage

Catastrophic illness coverage provides benefit payments on approximately the same terms and conditions as terminal illness coverage, except that the insured must have been diagnosed as having one of several listed catastrophic illnesses. Also referred to as **dread disease coverage**, the rider or provision typically covers stroke, heart attack, cancer, coronary artery surgery, renal failure, and similar diseases.

Both terminal illness and catastrophic illness coverages provide that policy death benefits are reduced on a one-for-one payout basis. Cash values are reduced on either a one-for-one basis or in proportion to the death benefit reduction. According to the NAIC *Accelerated Benefits Guideline for Life Insurance,* prospective buyers of these coverages must be given numerical illustrations that reflect the effects of an accelerated payout on the policy's death benefit, cash values, premiums, and policy loans. Additionally, consumers must receive a brief description of the accelerated benefits and definitions of the conditions or occurrences triggering payment. Any separate, identifiable premium charge must be disclosed.

Long Term Care Riders/Combination Plans

A third type of living benefit—**long term care (LTC) insurance riders**—provides that monthly benefits can be paid if the insured suffers a chronic health condition. Historically, LTC insurance was most commonly purchased as a stand-alone policy, but many observers believe that most LTC insurance will be purchased as riders to life insurance and annuity contracts in the future. This belief is fostered by changes in the federal tax law effective in 2010 that are favorable to what are called combination plans. **Combination plans** are life insurance or annuity contracts combined with LTC insurance riders. Insurers have sold versions of such plans for perhaps 15–20 years, but with different tax treatment and often different operational details.

LTC riders originally paid benefits to the insured in the form of accelerating a life policy's death benefit, as with terminal illness and catastrophic illness coverages. Both the cash value and death benefit were reduced dollar for dollar. Perhaps most riders continue this approach. Thus, a monthly benefit of up to 2 percent of the policy's face amount and subject to a further maximum monthly benefit amount might be provided for a qualified health condition. Some insurers offered a LTC rider that was itself purely LTC insurance, like a standalone LTC policy, with benefit payments having no effect on the underlying life insurance policy.

Insurers specializing in this market began to combine the two approaches, offering various combinations. For example, a base life policy with an LTC acceleration rider might offer a 24- or 36-month payout period over which the policy's full death benefit could be paid out. Upon exhaustion of the policy death benefit, a further rider, called a **continuation rider** or **extension of benefits rider,** provides pure LTC insurance that picks up payments for whatever additional period (e.g., three to five years or more) was selected at policy issuance. Benefits might be inflation adjusted, and return of premium features might be included.

The base plan may be any type of insurance, but most often is WL, UL, or variable UL. Single premium plans are popular, especially with older, wealthy clients, but continuous premium plans are also available, often appealing more to younger and less wealthy clients.

LTC benefits paid under qualified LTC insurance and from accelerating life insurance death benefits continue to be received income tax free. Prior to 2010, charges against a policy's cash value to pay for an LTC rider were treated as distributions under the policy. To the extent that the policy had undistributed gains, these charges were taxable income to the policyowner. As of 2010, these charges are still treated as distributions, but they are not considered taxable income, even if the policy has undistributed gains. Distributions still lower the policy's tax basis, but never below zero. Thus, a policy surrender or sale results in higher taxable gains, a potentially important implication for tax planning. This lowered tax basis is moot if the policy's full death benefits are accelerated or the policy terminates by payment of a death claim.

Riders Protecting Against Policy Lapse

Insurers have incentives beyond the APL provision to help policyowners minimize the chances that their policies will lapse. We here discuss two such riders, each aimed at addressing a different issue that can arise but with the common goal of minimizing lapse.

Waiver of Premium/Charges Riders

Insurers offer disability riders, called **wavier of premium (WP)** or simply **premium waiver (PW)** riders, that will pay or "waive" premiums otherwise due under fixed premium products if the insured becomes disabled. Parallel riders are available with UL policies that will pay or "waive" a specified premium amount—called **wavier of a specified premium** or the equivalent—or waive the monthly COI and expense charges—called **wavier of monthly charges** or the equivalent—if the insured becomes disabled. A supplemental premium ordinarily is levied for all of these riders, although a few companies levy no separately identifiable premium for the coverage, including its cost in the policy gross premium.

The waiver benefit is an earmarked disability income payment in an amount set precisely equal to the referenced premium or charges. The benefit does not truly *waive* or *excuse* premium payments but provides a benefit that makes the payment on behalf of the insured upon his or her disability. Thus, dividends continue to be paid on par policies, cash values continue to increase, and loans may be secured. Such riders typically expire at age 60 or 65.

The question arises as to the meaning of *disabled*. Most policies state that the insured must be *totally disabled* or *totally and permanently disabled* to qualify for the benefit, often before age 60. **Total disability** commonly is defined in the policy as inability of the insured, because of illness or injury, to perform either (1) the duties of his or her own occupation or (2) the duties of any occupation for which he or she is reasonably suited by reason of education, training, or experience. Insurers will use either definition or combine them to provide that the first, more liberal definition, applies for the first few years (e.g., two) of disability, with the second definition applying thereafter.

The word *permanent* appearing in the definition is not as daunting as might seem. Any total disability lasting longer than the waiting period specified in the policy—typically six, but sometimes as little as three, months—is deemed to be permanent, even though technically it might not be.

How the WP rider interacts with the conversion feature in a term policy can be important. Assume that term premiums are being waived because of a qualifying disability, and the policyowner wishes to convert the term policy. Will its premiums then be waived? It depends on the type of WP feature in the term policy. Three different term WP provisions are found in the market. *First,* and most conservatively, the policy provides that premiums on any newly converted cash value policy will not be waived. *Second,* and most liberally, premiums on the new policy will be waived. *Third,* and middle of the road, some policies provide that premiums on the new policy will be waived, but only if the conversion is delayed until the end of the period during which conversion is allowed.

Overloan Protection Riders

Several companies offer **overloan protection riders (OPRs)** whose purposes are to guarantee that a policy will not lapse if policy loans equal or exceed the policy account value. If loans equal or exceed the policy value and the policy lapses, a significant income tax event may be created for its owner. This rider is intended to avoid this situation. Box 9-1 offers additional insight into this issue.

The OPR permits the policyowner to elect to pay a one-time fee after a certain age (typically 75) and, subject to various conditions (e.g., the policy has been in force for at least 15 years; loan balance in excess of 95 percent of account value), all policy charges cease and the policy becomes paid up or frozen. It continues in this state until the insured's death or, unwisely, policy surrender. On death, the death benefit is received by the beneficiary income-tax free.

BOX 9-1: When Overloan Protection Riders make Good Sense

Here is an example of the issue intended to be addressed by these riders. Assume that a UL policy was issued 15 years ago to Alain. He is now 55 years old. He paid a total of $1.0 million in premiums during the first ten policy years. Based on current assumptions, at age 65 Alain can institute a systematic program of annual withdrawals of $100,000 for 10 years followed by 10 annual policy loans of the same amount to provide retirement income. By age 75, when withdrawals ceased, they would have totaled $1.0 million. As withdrawals reduce a policy's cost basis, his cost basis at that time would be reduced to zero. By age 85, policy loans of $1.0 million also had been taken.

Assume that the policy's account value at age 85 would be just slightly more than the loan totals. With no further premium payments, the policy would lapse before the end of the coming policy year, as the loan balance plus interest due would exceed the account value. If this were to occur, roughly $1,000,000 (in the form of the loan payoff) would be taxable to him as ordinary income. If the policy did not lapse because of an overloan protection rider and continued until Alain's death, no income taxable event would have occurred. (See the short discussions in Chapters 7 and 18 on income taxation of policy proceeds.)

No-Lapse Guarantee Riders

No-lapse guarantee (NLG) riders guarantee that the policy to which they are attached will not lapse for a specified period or for life, even if the account value goes to zero, if a specified minimum premium is paid. When riders guarantee coverage for less than the whole of life, they are sometimes called **guaranteed minimum death benefit riders.** The details of NLG policies were discussed in Chapter 7 and apply equally to policies containing NLG riders.

Enhanced Cash Value Riders

An **enhanced cash value rider**, offered by several insurers, eliminates or reduces surrender charges applicable to qualified policies during the first few policy years. The insurer may assess a one-time upfront charge for the rider, and/or the policy may provide for somewhat lower cash values at later durations. This feature can be important in situations for which premiums are financed via external loans and collateral is required. The greater a financed policy's cash surrender value relative to premiums paid, the less external collateral that the policyholder need tie up.

The feature also can be important for corporate owned life insurance. The usual accounting treatment for such insurance is that the difference between the yearly premium paid and yearly change in the cash surrender value (CSV) is recorded as an expense if the difference is negative (i.e., premium greater than change in CSV) and as income if the difference is positive. The higher the CSV increases each year, the less likely the corporation is to realize an expense charge. The rider ensures a higher CSV increase.

Conclusions

Life insurance policies are among the most secure types of insurance contracts and the simplest on which to collect. The policyowner and beneficiary can be assured that the insurance company will pay the agreed-upon amount of money on the death of the insured occurring at least two years after the policy issue date if but two simple conditions are met: (1) premiums sufficient to keep the policy in force have been paid and (2) the simple process of filing proof of death is completed. If death occurs within the first two policy years, we add but two further conditions: (3) death was not caused by suicide and (4) the application questions were answered accurately. That's it (except for the insurer not having become insolvent, which is rare. See Chapters 3–5).

Although the conditions for collection are simple, the contract itself and, importantly, how it is structured and used, can be complex. This chapter has introduced the life insurance policy as a contract, including supplemental benefits that can be included in it. Mastery of this fundamental policy information is a precondition for the advisor being able to provide sound advice to clients.

Determining the Appropriate Policy for Each Application

Part V

Life Insurance for Family Security

10

THIS CHAPTER BEGINS PART IV of the *Guide*, on determining the appropriate life insurance policy for each application. Part IV is composed of three chapters, with each focused on one of the common classes of applications or uses of life insurance.[1] This chapter explores life insurance in connection with family security. Chapter 11 explores uses of life insurance in estate planning, and Chapter 12 examines uses in the context of business planning. A client may have other motivations for the purchase of life insurance, such as cash value accumulation, charitable objectives, or maximizing inheritance. In this *Guide*, we highlight a needs-based approach and focus primarily on three key areas that represent the substantial majority of life insurance purchases.

Of course, life insurance for estate planning *is* life insurance for family planning, and the same can be said of the great majority of business applications as well. We explore each use separately as we want to highlight the different considerations that underpin each application and, therefore, that underpin the policy chosen for each application.

In this chapter, we explain the characteristics of the life insurance need and of the life insurance purchaser that influence

---

Authored by Harold D. Skipper.
[1]This chapter draws in part from Kenneth Black, Jr. and Harold D. Skipper, Jr., *Life and Health Insurance* (13th ed.; Upper Saddle River, NJ: Prentice-Hall, 2000), Chapter 14.

225

policy choice. To provide background and context for these explanations, it is necessary to provide an overview for how life insurance agents, brokers, and financial planners determine the nature and magnitude of the need for which life insurance is purchased. Doing so requires us, in turn, to explore briefly some aspects of policy suitability. We emphasize, however, that neither this *Guide* nor this chapter is intended to provide an analysis of policy suitability.

Introduction

The death of a family member can be both emotionally and financially devastating for the family. Chapter 1 introduced the potential means available to families to deal with these financial consequences, including (generous and sharing) relatives, additional savings/investments, employer-provided death benefits, government/social programs, and life insurance. As the chapter made clear, in the great majority of instances, only life insurance can be relied upon consistently to address this need, with each of the other options having drawbacks.

Chapter 1 also introduced a process by which one can make decisions concerning life insurance purchases. Recall that this process involved these four sequential determinations:

1. Is any life insurance needed? if so;
2. The appropriate amount;
3. The most suitable policy; and
4. From whom to purchase the policy.

This process was intended to offer an intuitive way of thinking about life insurance purchase decisions. Those advising and recommending the purchase of life insurance to individuals and families typically engage in each of these steps along the way, although they may not think of it precisely in this way. The objective in all instances, however, is the same: to guide the customer/client toward a sound life insurance outcome. In guiding the customer, most advisors will follow more or less the same path. That path involves the *identification* of the client's financial objectives if he or she were to die prematurely, *assembling and analyzing* relevant information, and *development and implementation* of a plan to accomplish the client's post-mortem life insurance objectives. This path goes by several names, all meaning the same thing, including **life insurance programming**, **life insurance needs analysis**, **personal financial planning**, **personal risk management**, and several others. We will call it life insurance needs analysis.

U.S. Family Structures

As the focus of this chapter is family economic security, it will prove useful to provide a short introduction to the many structures of families in the U.S., how they have changed over the past decades, and the possible life insurance needs implicit within each structure. As will be seen, the myriad structures suggest substantial continuing needs for life insurance benefits.

Today's typical American lives longer, marries later, has fewer children, and divorces more readily than in the past. Indeed, many people never marry, electing to remain single, and, if they marry, may choose to have no children. Many couples who in former times would have married, choose simply to live together. They may or may not elect to have children.

Having out-of-wedlock children carries much less stigma than formerly, whether the mother lives with the child's father or not. Indeed, unwed mothers account for about two in every five births in the U.S.

The proportion of nuclear families continues to decline in the U.S. while the proportion of single-parent families, blended families, and other non-traditional families rises. It is not unusual to find adult children with financial or other difficulties returning home to live with their parents and to find grandparents who hoped for a calm retirement raising grandchildren. Many people find it necessary to have an elderly parent or other relative move in with them for adequate care.

All of these and other demographic changes have contributed to an increasingly diverse profile for the American family. Figure 10-1 shows the distribution as of 2009. Below we briefly define and explore the likely characteristics of the main family structures.

- **Nuclear families** consist of a married couple and their children under age 18 sharing living facilities together. Such families account for a bit more than one in five U.S. households, down from roughly 40 percent in 1970. Nuclear families tend to rely less on other relatives for economic support than do some of the other family structures, especially the extended family. In more than 60 percent of such families, both parents are employed outside the home. In only 27 percent of such families is the father the sole breadwinner, the so-called **traditional family**. As dependent children live in the household, the death of either parent can and usually does result in financial problems for the surviving parent, particularly if the deceased is the sole family breadwinner.

- **Husband-wife families** are married couples living in one household with no children under the age of 18 present. They make up 30 percent

FIGURE 10-1: Distribution of Households in the United States, 2009

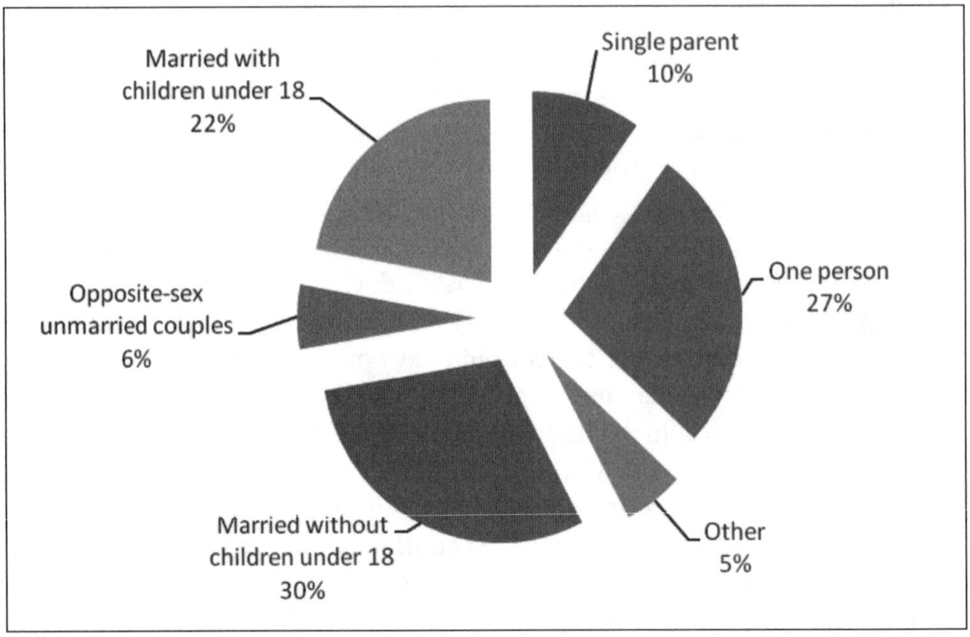

Source: U.S. Census Bureau.

of U.S. households. Husband-wife families in which both are in the labor force, often called **dual income, no kids (DINKs)**, constitute about 43 percent of such families. Another 27 percent are not in the labor force, often because they are retired, with the remaining 30 percent being composed of either the husband or the wife, but not both, being in the labor force. DINKs are often affluent, although many are not. Except for husband-wife families with a single wage earner, the death of either partner often will have less financial impact on the survivor than is true for many of the other living arrangements.

◆ **Single-parent families** are composed of a single parent plus dependent children. They have become more common than in past times, thanks to high divorce rates, willingness to have children out of wedlock, and, to a lesser extent, spousal death. They account for about 10 percent of all U.S. households, up from 5 percent in 1970. More than 80 percent of such families are headed by the mother. The death of the parent can have devastating financial implications for the children.

◆ **One-person households** are comprised of individuals living alone and constitute 27 percent of all U.S. households. Many such people are elderly, relying primarily on themselves for their care. Even if not elderly, these persons often have little need for life insurance except as others depend on them financially or they have estate tax obligations that they wish to address.

◆ **Extended families** are composed of one or more nuclear families living together along with other relatives, such as aunts, uncles, and/or grandparents. Extended families often are also multigenerational families (see below). Less common today than in times past, extended families were and remain important sources of economic security in many instances. To the extent that family members are financially or physically dependent on one or more other members of the family, the death of such a member could result in financial hardship.

◆ **Blended families**, also called **reconstituted families** and **step families**, are the families created when one or both members of the couple have children by a previous marriage. The traditional definition applied only to married couples, but many now apply the term as well to unwed couples living together. It is sometimes said in counseling situations that blended families are born out of loss. Such families, included in the Figure 10-1 married couple statistics, have become more common in recent times because of increasing numbers of divorces. Because divorce is commonly associated with such families, financial responsibilities, including in death, often extend outside the marriage to a blended family of the former spouse.

◆ **Opposite-sex unmarried couples** living together represent almost 6 percent of U.S. households. In about two-thirds of these households, both people are in the labor force. In about 40 percent of such households, at least one biological child under the age of 18 is present. In many such households, couples view themselves as committed to each other, and life insurance often is considered positively. If children are present, the need is even greater.

◆ **Same-sex couples** (or **partners**) are defined by the Census Bureau as those who share living quarters and have a close personal relationship. Gay and lesbian couples officially constitute less than 1 percent of U.S. households, although underreporting is believed to be substantial. Children under the age of 18 are found in about one in five households. The economic profile of same-sex couples is similar to that of married couples, although children have access to fewer public resources. When children are present or if one partner is financially dependent on the other, the need for life insurance can be great.

◆ A **multigenerational family** is one in which three or more generations of people related by blood or marriage live together. About 4 percent of all U.S. households are multigenerational families, with most composed of one or more parents, children, and grandparents. Extended families can be multigenerational but need not be. These families often involve the care of elderly parents by children, more particularly the daughter or daughter-in-law. Indeed, the average American mother spends about 17 years raising children and 18 years helping aged parents. The financial consequences of her premature death can be significant to the family. Some 35 percent of family businesses rely on multiple generations.

Life Insurance Needs Analysis

A given life insurance agent or broker or financial planner will have gathered and analyzed information and helped to identify post-mortem objectives on the customer/client to be able to recommend the type and amount of life insurance to be purchased. Ideally, this preliminary process involved careful probing and a sound suitability analysis, but some advisors may take shortcuts: "buy a term policy equal to 10 times your annual salary" or "buy as much cash value life insurance as you can afford."

However the advisor came to his or her recommendations, they will involve a suggested policy type and policy amount. Then the recommendation must be implemented if it is to have meaning, which is accomplished by completing the purchase of the policy. We structure this overview of life insurance needs analysis around the steps that advisors take, either implicitly or explicitly, to devise their policy recommendations.

1. Identify objectives;
2. Gather information;
3. Analyze information; and
4. Develop and implement plan.

Within the third area, we structure our examination of the types of life insurance that seem most relevant to each generic family structure. The fourth, more detailed, area explores how the nature of the identified and quantified life insurance need and specific client characteristics commonly influence the choice of policy type to meet the client's objectives.

Identify Objectives

The advisor typically asks questions that guide the client through an objective setting exercise, even if the client does not recognize it as such. Easy, friendly conversation can accomplish this task. Objectives may be changed or adjusted as the costs of their implementation become clearer. A common overarching family objective is to allow the family to maintain its current living standard on an individual's death. Specific operational objectives typically are cash and income based.

Cash objectives (or needs) require a single sum cash amount to fulfill. They are the easiest to estimate. Cash objectives commonly fall into these categories:

- Liabilities to be paid off on death;
- Amounts necessary to cover final expenses;
- Amounts (if any) to establish a family emergency fund;
- Amounts (if any) to establish a fund to finance children's education; and
- Bequests (if any) to friends and relatives and to charitable or other institutions.

The *income objective* might translate into a survivor needing from 60 to 75 percent of the pre-death family income. The amount is less than the current total family income, as the deceased person's self maintenance expenses cease.

The income objective may involve providing amounts that are not predicated on the client's current income. For example, if the individual enjoys exceptionally high earnings, a rational decision might be to replace only that amount necessary to ensure the family a comfortable but not an elaborate lifestyle. Conversely, an income earner early in his or her career but with promising prospects for much higher income later may set an income objective higher than current earnings. Also, the income objective may relate to someone other than the immediate family members, as when a former spouse provides alimony and/or child support payments.

Gather Information

After setting objectives, relevant quantitative and qualitative information must be gathered. This step involves identification and valuation of the individual's assets and liabilities, as well as information on the person's income and expenditures. The information is often gathered through a fact finding questionnaire.

Assets

Assets usually are either liquid or illiquid. **Liquid assets** are those assets available to be liquidated on the client's death with reasonable price certainty. These would be available to meet income or cash needs. They normally include stocks, bonds, money market and savings accounts, mutual funds, amounts available in pension, profit sharing, and individual retirement accounts.

The death benefit of any life insurance on the client's life and payable to or for the benefit of the family will be included as a liquid asset. The cash values of any life insurance on the client's life are not normally shown as separate assets for death planning purposes as they are subsumed in life insurance death proceeds.

Illiquid assets are those assets not available to meet income or other monetary needs because they cannot or will not be liquidated on death. They commonly include the family's home, automobiles, personal effects such as clothing and jewelry, and household goods. These assets are usually passed to heirs intact. In addition, other real estate and any interest in a closely held business ordinarily are considered to be illiquid as they cannot be liquidated with reasonable price certainty, unless advance arrangements have been made for their sale. These special situations are covered in Chapters 11 and 12, respectively.

Liabilities

A review of the individual's liabilities will show those to be paid at death and those to be transferred to heirs. Most liabilities must be paid at death. Some liabilities may be assumable by others (e.g., some mortgage loans), or they may be in more than one person's name.

Typical liabilities to be paid on death include outstanding balances on credit and charge cards, tax obligations, personal loans and notes, and auto loans. If the home mortgage loan is to be paid, its outstanding balance is included. If it is not to be paid off at death, mortgage loan payments are included as an income need (see below).

Income

The current and likely future income of the individual or family is an important driver in agents' and planners' estimates of future resources and needs. Information on income will have been developed in the information gathering process. The importance and security of future income typically varies depending on the individual's employment status and family structure.

- ◆ **Nuclear family.** If both parents are in the labor force, income information on both will have been gathered and each situation analyzed separately (see below). If neither parent is employed, no wage income would be included. If they are dependent on relatives or others for income, the security of that income source would be examined. The nuclear family in which only one parent earns an income often is similar to the single-parent family in terms of vulnerability to income loss because of death of the wage earner (see below). Often overlooked is that the family may also suffer financially on the death of the non-wage earner parent. This spouse usually provides valuable household services and, increasingly, assists in various ways where a family owned business is involved. No monetary wage may be paid for either class of service but a need may exist for increased income to meet additional family expenses.

♦ **Husband-wife family.** As with the nuclear family, one, both, or neither spouse may be in the labor force, and income information would have been gathered accordingly.

♦ **Single-parent family.** For a single parent family, income usually is derived primarily or solely from the parent's salary. A single parent family unit is more likely than a nuclear family to have income from outside the unit. A divorced individual may be receiving alimony or child support payments. A divorced person sometimes receives financial support from parents or grandparents, and a widowed spouse may be receiving income from the deceased spouse's investments, employer, insurance, or government sources. Each income source should have been recorded with the notation that the family's income would be disrupted by the death of the former spouse who provides child support or the voluntary financial assistance of a parent or relative.

♦ **One-person household.** Whether and the extent to which others rely on the individual for financial support is the relevant income information gathered here.

♦ **Extended family.** Family income may be from several sources each of which should have been recorded and analyzed by the agent or planner for its loss impact on the family.

♦ **Blended family.** The blended family, as a variation of the nuclear family, would have been treated similarly. A difference between it and other nuclear families is that it is more likely to receive alimony or other external income payments.

♦ **Opposite-sex unmarried couple.** Depending on the nature of the relationship and whether children live in the household, such a couple may have been approached in the same way as the nuclear family. On the other hand, recognition may have been given to the possibility that the living arrangement will not prove lasting.

♦ **Same-sex couple.** Similar considerations and information gathering applies here as with heterosexual unmarried couples and, if the same-sex couple is married, as with married couples.

♦ **Multigenerational family.** These families are more likely to have multiple income sources than are other households, except for extended families (which can be a type of multigenerational family). All sources should have been identified and quantified.

Analyze Information

The third step in the process is to analyze the relevant information in light of the individual's stated objectives. This step involves an attempt by the agent or planner to measure the financial consequences to the family from the death of those on whom the family relies for financial and possibly other support. It provides the basis for the recommended amount of life insurance to purchase.

The analysis is not always simple and almost never precise as it necessarily involves assumptions concerning the future, and actual results will invariably differ from those assumed. It can provide an idea of the possible range of the family's financial loss as well as the extent of disruption to present plans that could occur.

Several approaches are followed in measuring the financial consequences to a family of the death of one of its members. In all cases, however, the basic approach will have been the same. The family (or others) will have certain resources from which to meet its objectives (in whole or in part). To the extent that existing resources do not meet the objectives fully the client will have been identified as needing additional life insurance. The financial objectives usually fall into the cash or income categories, as mentioned earlier.

Quantifying cash objectives is ordinarily straightforward. It involves a simple calculation of the amount needed today to meet the cash needs were death to occur today. Thus, if an objective was to pay off the mortgage on the family home, the amount needed today is the outstanding loan amount.

The income objective also will have been quantified in the same way. Advisors often will have converted the gross income objective to a net figure by deducting from this gross amount the income that was identified as likely to continue to the family after the death of the client. Thus, all continuing wages, such as those of the surviving spouse; any Social Security survivor or children's benefits; earnings on investments not to be liquidated; and any other expected income to the family from other sources would have been deducted.

This process is simple in concept, but its application can be complex. Two common methods used to analyze death-related income needs are (1) the capital liquidation and (2) the capital retention approaches. The **capital liquidation approach** assumes that both principal (capital) and interest are liquidated over the relevant time period to provide the desired income. The **capital retention approach** assumes that the desired income is provided from investment earnings on the principal and that no part of the desired income is from capital. In other words, the capital is retained undiminished, even after death, ordinarily to be passed on to future generations.

Each method has advantages and drawbacks. The liquidation approach requires a smaller capital sum to provide a given income level than does the retention approach. The retention approach permits a capital sum to be passed on to the family's next generation (or to whoever is designated). It is considered more conservative, as in an emergency capital could be invaded.

The interest rate selected for discounting future values can greatly influence results, especially when sums are discounted over many years. The interest rate chosen affects both needs and resources. The interest rate ordinarily is that which can be earned after taxes in the present economic environment on secure, fairly liquid investments. To simplify tax considerations, the selected interest rate often is an after tax rate. The effects of inflation on anticipated future income needs and resources are sometimes factored into an analysis. Many people will use the real interest rate—the prevailing interest rates less the inflation rate—to discount any calculations, thereby allowing for inflation in a simple way.

The final element of the analysis is to net the resources available against the cash and income objectives to derive a figure for the shortfall (or overage) of resources to meet objectives. This figure represents a measure of the net financial consequences of death to the family, based on the objectives identified earlier and underlying assumptions. Some agents and planners use programs that convert the traditional approach of "what are the financial consequences to my family if I die today" to a dynamic approach that provides a projection of future insurance needs.

Develop and Implement Plan: Matching Policies to Needs

The next step in a life insurance needs analysis is the development and implementation of a plan to accomplish the objectives. We here assume that the agent or planner has identified a need for additional life insurance and made recommendations as to the amount and type needed. In this section, we set out the types of personal characteristics and insurance need characteristics that ordinarily influence an agent's or planner's recommendation as to the most suitable policy. While we treat each of these areas as separate considerations below, in fact, they cannot be separated easily in terms of deciding on the most suitable policy, as will become evident.

We emphasize again that neither this *Guide* in general nor this chapter in particular is intended as a treatise on policy suitability. Rather, we offer this brief overview on policy suitability tactics to suggest how agents and planners often determine the policies that they believe to be most suitable to the client's situation. Our hope is that advisors might find this overview useful in better understanding the fundamentals of the policies discussed in the *Guide*, and perhaps it will also spur thinking about the critically important issues surrounding policy suitability.

Suitability, in any event, is about much more than selecting the best generic type of policy for the client's financial and insurance need situation. It extends as well to issues such as how best to pay premiums, how quickly to fund the policy, and what riders should be included. It also includes contract issues such as having accurate and complete beneficiary designations and the most efficient policy ownership arrangements. Ideally, decisions about policy suitability will not have evolved in isolation from other personal financial planning objectives, such as establishment or revision of wills and trusts.

We necessarily must be quite general in our treatment of agent and planner recommendations. In each instance, those recommendations flow also from the nature of the policies themselves, as we discussed in Chapter 8 and earlier. They are not repeated here, but the reader may wish to refer back to them before proceeding further.

Financial Characteristics of the Client

Certain of the client's financial characteristics will have an enormous influence on deciding the best policy for the client. These characteristics include the monies available now and in the future to pay life insurance premiums, the client's risk tolerance or appetite, and his or her financial discipline.

Ability to Pay Premiums

A family's ability to pay premiums is of paramount importance. It usually is a function of the family's income and wealth in relation to its expenditures. Premiums are typically paid from a family's discretionary income, unless assets are to be liquidated or loans taken to pay them. **Discretionary income** is what's left after paying taxes, covering family necessities, and meeting financial commitments. The higher the discretionary income, the greater is the ability to pay premiums. Some families spend all discretionary income and may believe that they are unable to allocate any money for premiums to purchase new life insurance. This is an issue of family priorities and values.

For purposes of discussion, we can think in terms of families having limited, moderate, or substantial ability to pay premiums, although these terms are relative. A wealthy family may have what it considers only a moderate or even limited ability to pay additional premiums while, in truth, compared to a middle-income family, the wealthy family could perhaps pay virtually whatever premiums it wanted to.

Families and individuals with only a limited ability to pay premiums often have no choice but to purchase low-premium term life insurance if they are to meet their objectives. If the amount needed is modest and the duration of the need is long, universal life (UL) policies may prove feasible. If they need substantial amounts of life insurance for long durations, they may face a dilemma, as long-duration term policies can become expensive in later life. Most knowledgeable observers urge families in such situations to give priority to the short term death exposure.

Families and individuals with a moderate ability to pay premiums have more options. The policy decision will commonly have been determined by other need and family characteristics, such as the amount, duration, and pattern of the likely future insurance need and the client's risk tolerance and financial discipline. The policy recommended for families and individuals having substantial premium paying ability similarly will have been influenced by the other client characteristics, as we explore in more detail below.

Risk Tolerance

Individuals' tolerances or "appetites" for risk vary widely. Risk tolerance is required to be considered carefully in connection with any financial decision, with life insurance being no exception. While indirect means of assessing one's risk tolerance exist, such as that offered on Vanguard's web site, making a good assessment remains a challenge for agents, planners, and other advisors. Nonetheless, individuals, especially those with experience with investments or who own their own businesses, usually have a good idea of their own risk appetite. For purposes of discussion, we can think in terms of individuals having low, medium, or high risk tolerance.

In taking client risk tolerance into consideration in making policy recommendations, agents and planners likely will have examined the risk profiles of different policies and policy funding levels. As to policies themselves, ignoring funding levels, we know from earlier chapters that variable life products can carry the greatest financial risk (and opportunity) of all life policies, other things being the same. Thus, recommendations for a client with a high risk tolerance could be variable universal life (VUL), assuming all other personal and insurance characteristics are consistent with that choice. (Recall that VUL can be structured to be less risky, as well.)

Equity indexed UL (EIUL) could be the recommendation for clients of medium risk appetites as they fall someplace after VUL in terms of riskiness. (Recall that EIUL's riskiness depends on allocations to the indexed account.) Generic UL, nonparticipating (nonpar) current assumption WL (CAWL), and par WL policies that rely on an investment generation allocation method typically fall behind EIUL in terms of cash value riskiness, so they may have been recommended for clients of low to medium risk tolerance. Policies whose interest crediting rates rely on the portfolio average method of investment income allocation (as described in Chapter 8), such as many par WL policies and perhaps some UL policies as well, should have less fluctuation in interest crediting rates than other cash value policies, so they may have been recommended for clients with still less risk tolerance. NLG UL (assuming required premiums are paid) and term life could be recommended for clients with low risk tolerance. Nonpar fixed WL policies may have been recommended to clients with very low risk tolerance. *With each policy mentioned in this paragraph, we are making the critically important assumption that all other client and insurance attributes are consistent with the policy choice.*

The other aspect of a policy risk profile relates to funding level. Ordinarily, the lower the level at which a policy is funded, the greater the risk of its failing to meet client objectives. Thus, for clients whose risk tolerance is low and whose other characteristics suggest the need for cash value insurance, a recommendation might be funding at a higher level, which then provides a cushion for downside policy performance (or perhaps missed premium payments). Such funding could be accomplished through endowment targets, which are automatic with WL, or assuming less favorable assumptions for a given policy funding objective, such as using a crediting rate of 50 basis points below the current crediting rate. See Chapter 15 for a discussion of funding levels.

Financial Discipline

The payment of life insurance premiums ordinarily does not give the policyholder that marvelous feeling we often receive from buying that new car or set of golf clubs or skis. Indeed, it is not uncommon for policyholders to view their life insurance premium payment as being somewhat akin to paying taxes: "I know that I should do it, but I'd prefer—if I could—to use the money in other ways." It is perhaps for these types of reasons, coupled with the too frequent problem of simple forgetfulness, that some individuals are less disciplined than others when it comes to making timely premium payments, irrespective of their discretionary income level. For many people, the most suitable policy will be the one that is most likely to remain in force, and several policy attributes may come into play in matching policy to person. Part of policy suitability assessment ideally would have been gaining insight into the individual's financial discipline as relates to premium payments. We will characterize such discipline as being weak, moderate, or strong.

With regard to clients whose financial discipline could be characterized as weak, we would reasonably expect the agent or planner, first, to have suggested a policy structured to have premiums paid automatically from the client's (or some other willing payor's) bank account. Second, for "weak" clients of moderate or substantial premium paying ability and whose other characteristics suggest a need for cash value insurance, many agents and planners believe that premiums are more likely to be paid on traditional WL policies with their required payment structure than with the flexible premium structure of generic UL policies. Third, for these "weak" clients whose other characteristics suggest a need for cash value insurance, a further recommendation may be to accelerate policy funding, subject to tax limitations, such as with a 10-pay approach.

Recommendations for clients with strong discipline might be to pay premiums annually for life and, depending on the other characteristics, to purchase a NLG UL policy (although even NLG UL has premium flexibility as regards the guarantee). Recommendations for clients with moderate discipline could be the same as or fall somewhere between those for the "weak" and "strong."

Nature of the Insurance Need

The nature of the need for life insurance is determined by its amount, length or duration, and its pattern over time. The absolute amount of needed coverage is relevant as the larger the amount, the higher will be the premium, other things being the same. This aspect of the insurance need is addressed above in the ability of pay discussion. We examine the duration and pattern elements below.

Duration of the Need

An analysis may have determined that the single-parent client with two teenage children has a need for life insurance on her life only until both children have completed their collegiate education and have had sufficient time to be well out of the "nest" (although, with greater numbers of adult children returning home to live with parents, selecting what would be "sufficient time" could prove challenging). The duration of the need in this instance may be ten years or less, suggesting some type of term life insurance. Conversely, an analysis for the dual-income married couple with the young child whose health problems make it highly unlikely that he will ever be able to join the labor force may have revealed an expected need that is reasonably expected to last for the entirety of both parents' lifetimes, suggesting some type of cash value life insurance.

Pattern of the Need over Time

Agents and planners ideally will have some idea of not just the duration of the client's need for insurance but also its likely pattern. Admittedly, discerning the likely pattern will often involve a little voodoo or the equivalent, but the pattern can have an important influence on policy type. Consider the needs analysis just completed by Enrique Lagana, CLU, for a single-income blended family composed of her three teenage children, of his two college-age children, and of their two young children. It shows a likely future pattern of their need for insurance on the life of the income earner that varies significantly over time, with a large decrease when his two children have completed their collegiate education, then another decrease after her three children have done likewise. Perhaps a further decrease is projected 15–20 years beyond that for their two children, underpinning all of which is a continuing permanent need for sufficient insurance to ensure that the non-wage earner would have income for life. In this situation a combination of term policies and a cash value policy may be recommended or possibly just one cash value policy with a decreasing death benefit schedule, as can be found with UL.

In general, forecasted future patterns could be characterized as being decreasing, level, increasing, some combination of the preceding, or too uncertain to make an informed estimate. If the forecasted need pattern as devised by the agent or broker is not level, it is not unusual to find recommendations focused on some type of UL policy, as they provide for adjustability of face amount, depending on other factors.

Plan Implementation

Once the recommended policy type has been determined along with needed riders, a competitive analysis may be performed among different insurers in terms of carrier financial strength (see Part II) and appropriate funding levels (see Chapter 15) and competitiveness (Chapter 16). The selected policy(ies) then must be secured. The necessary insurance applications must be completed and submitted to the insurance companies, the policies underwritten, and funds set aside to pay the first premiums. If changes are needed in existing policies or if policies are to be replaced, the necessary forms must be secured, completed, and furnished to the appropriate insurers. The insurance dimensions of the plan are not fully implemented until needed policies are issued on an acceptable basis and structured in line with earlier established goals.

Conclusions

This chapter has offered an exploration of how agents, brokers, and financial planners go about deciding on the amount and type of life insurance to recommend to their customer/clients. These recommendations flowed from the objectives set by the client and from information gathered and analyzed by the agent, broker, or planner. The recommendation will have been influenced by the nature of the insurance need as to cost, duration, and pattern as well as client characteristics in terms of financial ability and discipline to pay premiums and the risk tolerance. The agent, broker, or planner will then have used his or her knowledge of the attributes of different life insurance policies to select those that are compatible with the nature of the insurance need and client characteristics.

Life insurance for estate and business planning purposes should not, in most family situations, be separated from what we call life insurance for family security. We emphasize again that we do so in this part of the *Guide* for ease of presentation.

Life Insurance in Estate Planning

11

THIS CHAPTER CONTINUES PART IV of the *Guide*, on determining the appropriate life insurance policy for each application. This chapter explores uses of life insurance in estate planning, with Chapter 12 examining uses in the context of business planning.[1]

As observed in Chapter 10, life insurance for estate planning *is* life insurance for family planning. We explore it separately as use of life insurance in estate planning involves special considerations, with the amount of insurance needed determined by the specific application to which the death proceeds will be put. Likewise, the nature of these applications greatly influences the types of policies commonly considered to be most suitable to cover them.

Introduction

The death of a wealthy person can trigger transfer tax obligations. The most common application of life insurance in estate planning is the use of death proceeds to cover that obligation. The event that creates the obligation simultaneously creates the resources to meet it for an annual premium payment of perhaps

---

Authored by Harold D. Skipper.
[1]This chapter draws in part from Kenneth Black, Jr. and Harold D. Skipper, Jr., *Life and Health Insurance* (13th ed.; Upper Saddle River, NJ: Prentice-Hall, 2000), Chapters 13 and 15.

1 to 3 percent of the benefit received, depending on the policy type and the insured's rating characteristics. The entirety of the client's wealth and investment program is preserved for the family and/or for other worthwhile purposes while avoiding having to hold a large chunk of liquid assets to pay government taxes. Life insurance is also used in other estate planning contexts, as discussed in this chapter.

To provide background and context, we first provide an overview of federal transfer taxation, as the recommendations of agents, brokers, and financial planners regarding the amount of insurance and policy type will have been grounded in paying or minimizing these taxes. We emphasize that neither this *Guide* nor this chapter is intended to provide an analysis of policy suitability in the context of estate (or any other) planning. Rather, our purpose in this superficial dip into suitability is to illustrate the applications of the various types of policies in commonly incurred circumstances.

Overview of Federal Transfer Taxation

The federal government levies a tax on the right of a person to transfer property both at death and during life. Estate planning in general and the use of life insurance in estate planning in particular are inextricably linked to these taxes, so a basic understanding of them is essential. Here we provide overviews of federal estate, gift, and generation skipping transfer taxation.

Estate Taxation

As life insurance purchased for estate planning purposes is most frequently used to pay estate taxes or relates to these taxes in some other way, it is essential to have a basic understanding of how that system is structured. This overview is based on the system's structure as created by the *Economic Growth and Tax Relief Reconciliation Act of 2001* (EGTRRA), which set in motion decade-long automatic changes in the estate tax rates and in the amounts that are exempt from estate taxation. The exempted amounts began at $675,000 and increased to $3.5 million for deaths occurring in 2009. The federal estate tax rates are graduated, starting at 18 percent and building to a maximum marginal rate of 45 percent for deaths occurring in 2009.

EGTRRA provides that the estate tax is repealed altogether for the year 2010 but reinstated in 2011, with the same tax rates and exemption amount as existed in 2001. The exemption amount would revert to $1.0 million and the maximum marginal tax rate would be 55 percent for deaths occurring in 2011 and thereafter if the U.S. Congress makes no changes in the law. Further, an additional estate tax of 5 percent would be levied on estates valued between

$10,000,000 and $17,184,000, thus eliminating the effect of the marginal estate tax rates, effectively creating a flat 55 percent estate tax rate for estates valued at $17,184,000 or greater.

Regrettably, as this *Guide* was going to press, we did not know the details for a possibly revised estate tax system, although many observers expect the 2010 and 2011 provisions to be modified, perhaps retroactively. Much discussion centered on a $3.5 million exempted amount and a maximum marginal tax rate of 45 percent.

Calculating Estate Taxes

The first step in calculating the federal estate tax due is to measure the value of the decedent's gross estate. The **gross estate** is, roughly, the value of all property or interests in property owned or controlled by the deceased person. Next, allowable deductions are subtracted from the gross estate, resulting in the **taxable estate**. **Allowable deductions** include funeral and administration expenses, debts of the decedent, as well as bequests to charities and the surviving spouse. Bequests to the surviving spouse, called the **marital deduction**, may be of any portion or all of the qualifying gross estate, the effect of which can be to greatly reduce or even eliminate estate taxes due on the death of the first spouse.

Adjusted taxable gifts are added to the taxable estate to yield the **tentative tax base**. **Adjusted taxable gifts** are gifts made after 1976 and for which a gift tax return was required to be filed. The reason for this addition is that the estate tax law is part of a so-called unified transfer tax law that applies to transfers made at death and during life. It is necessary to add the value of lifetime taxable transfers (gifts) back to the tax base to derive the appropriate marginal tax bracket.

The appropriate tax rate is then applied to the tentative tax base to derive the **tentative federal estate tax**. Certain credits for gift and other taxes paid and the unified credit are subtracted from the tentative tax. The **unified credit** is the transfer tax credit that everyone has available to offset estate taxes. (A separate credit applies to gift taxes, as discussed below.) Advisors typically think in terms of the value of property that the unified credit permits to be passed free of tax (the exemption amount, as discussed above) rather than the value of the credit itself. After applying all applicable credits against the tentative federal estate tax, we have the amount of **federal estate taxes owed**.

Federal estate tax returns are required to be filed and taxes paid within nine months of the death of any U.S. citizen or resident whose gross estate exceeds the year's exempted amount. Up to a 10-year extension for payment of the taxes may be granted for reasonable cause, which includes ownership interests in certain closely held businesses.

Estate Taxation of Life Insurance

It is highly desirable that life insurance death proceeds used for estate planning purposes not be included in the decedent's gross estate, otherwise much of the reason for buying the life insurance in the first place is thwarted. Death proceeds payable under a life insurance policy are included in a decedent's gross estate if (1) the proceeds are payable to or for the benefit on the insured's estate or (2) the insured possessed any incidents of ownership in the policy at death.

Thus, a beneficiary designation of "Estate of Insured" means that the death proceeds are included in the insured's gross estate even if the insured did not own the policy. Similarly, if some or all death proceeds were earmarked in a formal way (e.g., via collateral assignment or will) to pay a liability of the insured, that earmarked portion of proceeds would be included in the insured's gross estate even if the insured did not own the policy and the estate was not beneficiary.

If the deceased insured possessed no incidents of ownership in the policy and if proceeds are not payable to or for the benefit of the estate, proceeds generally escape inclusion in the gross estate under the IRC code. Incidents of ownership include the right to change the beneficiary, the right to surrender or otherwise terminate a policy, the right to assign a policy, the right to obtain a policy loan, and, in general, the ability to exercise any important right of a policy. Complete policy ownership certainly will cause death proceeds to be included in the estate, but possession of only one important policy right can cause the entire proceeds to be included in the gross estate.

A policy owned by the insured can be removed from the gross estate if it is given or sold to someone else via a transfer of ownership (also called an absolute assignment). If the ownership transfer is via gift and occurs within three years of the date of death, however, the policy proceeds will be included in the gross estate.

Gift Taxation

As with the federal estate tax, the federal gift tax is imposed on the right to transfer property to another person. The estate tax reaches those transfers that take place when a property owner dies, whereas the gift tax reaches those transfers that take place during the property owner's lifetime. Gifting offers tax and other advantages and is common in estate planning, including with regard to life insurance. For this reason, we here offer an overview of gift taxation generally and of gift taxation in the context of life insurance specifically.

Calculating Gift Taxes

A **gift** is the voluntary transfer of property ownership for less than adequate consideration. The difference between the property's fair market value and its sales price defines a gift and its value. A lifetime gift to an individual incurs a federal gift tax generally at the same rate as the federal estate tax. As in the estate tax calculation, a credit or, equivalently, an exemption amount is applied directly to reduce the tentative gift tax. Unlike the estate tax, gift taxation is not repealed for 2010. It has carried its own $1.0 million exemption amount since 2004, slated to continue at that amount for 2011 and later if not changed by Congress. The top gift tax rate is 35 percent for 2010 and will equal the highest individual marginal income tax rate effective 2011 and later.

The general rule is that any gift is subject to the tax. Gifts not subject to gift taxation include:

- Gifts of present interest not greater than the annual exclusion (see below),
- Tuition or medical expenses paid directly to a medical or educational institution for someone,
- Gifts to one's spouse (as with the federal estate tax marital deduction, the **gift tax marital deduction** permits tax free transfers between spouses in a heterosexual marriage if both are U.S. citizens),
- Gifts to a political organization for its use, and
- Gifts to qualifying charities.

The amount of gift tax payable in a specific taxable period is determined by a three-step process:

1. Add the current and all previous lifetime taxable gifts (not all gifts are taxable).
2. Apply the unified rate schedule to the total taxable gifts to derive the tentative tax.
3. Subtract any previous gift taxes paid and any available gift tax credit to yield the gift tax payable for the current period.

Annual Gift Tax Exclusion

Excluded from the reach of the federal gift tax is the value of any gift of a present interest (see below) that is no more than the **annual gift tax exclusion**, which for 2010 is $13,000. This exclusion applies annually to each donee (person receiving the gift) and not to each donor (person making the gift), irrespective of the number of recipients. The exclusion amount is indexed for inflation, rounded to the next lowest multiple of $1,000.

The annual exclusion is available for gifts of a present interest only. A **present interest** is one wherein the donee must have possession and enjoyment of the property immediately rather than at some future date. The exclusion is not available for gifts of **future interest** in property; that is, any interest in property that does not pass into the donee's possession or enjoyment until some future date.

When a married individual makes a gift to someone other than a spouse, it may be regarded as made one-half by each spouse. This gift-splitting privilege is extended only to property given away by a married couple within a heterosexual marriage. The taxpayer is given the advantage of doubling the annual exclusion. Therefore, married individuals can make gifts of $26,000 (indexed) per year to each beneficiary without incurring any gift tax liability if the spouse consents to splitting the gift.

The gift tax exemption amount of $1.0 million is available to be applied against gifts in excess of the annual exclusion amount and those that fail to qualify as present interest gifts. Using this exemption amount during life is, in effect, using the equivalent amount of the estate tax exemption available at death, as taxable gifts over the annual exclusion amounts are added back to the taxable estate at death. You don't get both exemption amounts (but the value of gifts equal to or less than the annual exclusion amounts is not added back).

Gift Taxation of Life Insurance

Gifts of life insurance are common. They can include gifts of the contract itself, gifts of premium payments, and gifts of policy proceeds. Thus, if an insured irrevocably assigns all of his or her rights in an existing insurance contract for less than an adequate consideration, he or she has made a gift of the contract and gift taxes may be due. The gift may not be subject to gift taxation if it falls into any of the excluded categories mentioned above, and the annual exclusion and/or lifetime exemption may be available to reduce the value of any taxable gift. The value of the policy for gift purposes is its fair market value, which is generally its replacement cost. For cash value life insurance, the fair market value is roughly the policy's cash value, net of loans, as of the date of the gift, plus the value of unearned premiums and accumulated dividends.

Establishing the fair market value for newer forms of life insurance, such as some term policies and no-lapse guarantee (NLG) universal life, can be more complex than simply relying on some measure of the cash value. Insurers are inconsistent in how they calculate value for these types of policies because federal tax guidelines were drafted before many of these policy forms existed. Insurers commonly derive the transfer value based on some measure of the policy's reserve, which is higher than the policy's cash value. As insurers may calculate reserves in different ways, they similarly, may provide a different transfer value for the same policy type. The advisor will want to secure a completed IRS Form 712 from the insurer as this form is filed by the insurer with the IRS.

Making premium payments on a life insurance policy not owned by the payer is a gift to the policyowner, and gift taxes may be due. Thus, premiums paid by an insured who is not the owner of the policy are gifts to the owner.

Again, the gift may not be subject to gift taxation if it falls into any of the excluded categories, and the annual exclusion may be available to reduce its taxable value.

Under ordinary circumstances, life insurance death proceeds are not gifts. In some extraordinary instances, however, they may be taxed as gifts. When one person owns a policy, a second is the insured, and a third is the beneficiary, the IRS may take the position that a gift has been made from the policyowner to the beneficiary at the insured's death. The amount of the gift equals the full amount of the insurance death proceeds.

Generation Skipping Transfer Taxation

The IRC provides for a **generation skipping transfer** (GST) **tax** to be levied when a property interest is transferred to persons who are two or more generations younger than the transferor, with some exceptions. The **transferor** for property subject to the federal estate tax is the decedent and, for property subject to the gift tax, the donor. The GST tax is intended to ensure that transfer taxes are paid by wealthy persons who might otherwise avoid a generation of transfer taxes by passing their property to heirs (so called **skip persons**) beyond those of the immediately following generation. For example, in the absence of the GST tax, a gift from a grandparent to a grandchild could avoid all transfer taxes that otherwise might have been incurred.

The GST tax is repealed for 2010 along with the federal estate tax and is to resume in 2011 at its 2001 lifetime exemption amount ($1.0 million indexed for inflation) and the 55 percent flat rate. In other words, the value of any transferred property in excess of the exemption would be subject to 2001's maximum prevailing transfer tax rate of 55 percent.

Life insurance death proceeds, irrespective of the manner in which they are paid, can attract the GST tax if they are paid to a skip person. This unpleasant result can be avoided by excluding the death proceeds from the insured's estate and through appropriate use of trusts. Generally, funds or policies transferred to a skip person or to a trust under which a skip person is a beneficiary are considered a GST. The annual gift tax exclusion and the lifetime GST exemption may be available to reduce or eliminate any GST tax.

Common Trusts Used with Life Insurance

Trusts are effective estate planning tools. They often supply elements that are impossible to obtain through a direct gift, provide needed flexibility, and can save on income, estate, and gift taxes. A **trust** is a legal arrangement whereby one party transfers property to someone else who holds the legal title and manages the trust property for the benefit of others. The person who establishes the trust is the **grantor** (also called the **creator** or **settlor**). The person who receives the legal title and manages the property is the **trustee**, and persons for whose benefit the property is held are the **beneficiaries**.

Many types of trusts exist, each designed to meet specific objectives. A trust created during life is referred to as an **inter vivos** or **living trust**. A trust created at death through a person's will is a **testamentary trust**. A living trust can be revocable or irrevocable. With a **revocable trust**, the grantor can terminate or alter the trust as he or she wishes and regain ownership of the property. With an **irrevocable trust**, he or she permanently relinquishes ownership and control of the donated property.

A revocable trust might be desirable as a device for transferring assets directly to beneficiaries outside of the probate estate, avoiding related costs, and allowing the trust's business to be done on an uninterrupted, confidential basis. A revocable trust, however, provides no income, estate, or gift tax savings, as the grantor retains effective ownership of the trust corpus. When property or funds are given to an irrevocable trust, generally a complete gift has been made that may have gift tax consequences. Of course, income and estate tax savings applicable to any gift may result.

Marital Deduction and Credit Shelter Trusts

The marital deduction can be vitally important in estate planning. It is possible to leave everything to the surviving spouse and incur no federal estate tax, but doing so usually is inadvisable as it fails to take advantage of the exemption amount and the possibility of having that amount bypass inclusion at the death of the surviving spouse. Testamentary trusts are established to permit the surviving spouse to have substantial enjoyment of all of the deceased's property and to qualify an optimal amount of the assets for the estate tax marital deduction.

First, a **marital trust** is established to receive property that qualifies for the marital deduction when the first spouse dies. The trust ordinarily receives property equal in value to the taxable estate less the exemption amount. When the surviving spouse dies, any amounts not consumed or given to others will be taxed in his or her estate. Although the establishment of a trust for the marital deduction property is not essential, it often proves convenient for investment management and administration purposes.

Second, property equal in value to the exemption amount is placed in a second trust known as a **credit shelter trust** (also called a **bypass trust**, a **B trust**, a **non-marital trust**, and a **residuary trust**). The surviving spouse often has the right to the income for life from the credit shelter trust property but does not control the trust. The income from the trust could supplement the income provided by the marital trust and the principal could also be made available, if needed, for health, education, and support reasons. On the death of the surviving spouse, all right to income from the residuary trust is terminated, and the trust property would not be taxed in his or her estate. This gives the surviving spouse the effective use of all the decedent's property during his or her lifetime, without having the bypass trust assets included in that spouse's estate for federal estate tax purposes.

If the surviving spouse is unlikely to need the income from the credit shelter trust, it often is sound estate planning to fund this trust with appreciating assets and the marital deduction trust with more conservative assets. In this way, the bypass trust beneficiaries benefit from the trust's asset appreciation free to estate taxes. In these situations, it is not uncommon to have the trust purchase, own, and be beneficiary of insurance on the life of the surviving spouse to leverage the assets passed estate-tax free to the beneficiaries. Trust income pays the premiums on the life insurance, so no consideration need be given to possible gift taxation.

Crummey Trusts

In spite of its name (which is that of a successful litigant), the Crummey trust is a useful device. With a **Crummey trust**, also referred to as a **Crummey provision** or a **Crummey power** (within an irrevocable trust), gifts to the trust qualify as present interest gifts and thus the annual exclusion, provided the trust beneficiaries have a reasonable opportunity to demand distribution of amounts contributed to the trust. Otherwise, if trust beneficiaries do not have the right of their immediate enjoyment, they are gifts of future interest and do not qualify for the annual exclusion.

A Crummey provision ordinarily works as follows. The grantor makes a gift to an irrevocable, living trust. The trust beneficiaries often are the grantor's children, grandchildren, or both. The beneficiaries are notified by the trustee that they have the power for a defined period (e.g., 15 to 60 days) to withdraw some portion of recently gifted property. The simultaneous acts of the grantor transferring property to the trust and the beneficiaries being permitted to withdraw the same property from the trust is tantamount to the grantor giving the property to the beneficiaries outright, thus qualifying for the $13,000 annual exclusion.

Of course, it is not anticipated that the beneficiaries will withdraw any property from the trust during the defined period. By not executing their powers, the beneficiaries permit their powers to lapse, which has gift tax implications, but examining them is beyond the scope of this short discussion.

Irrevocable Life Insurance Trusts

Irrevocable life insurance trusts (ILITs) are popular and efficient means of having life insurance death proceeds avoid inclusion in an insured's gross estate and are often an important element in having these proceeds provide liquidity to the estate to cover taxes or for other estate planning purposes. The ILIT either purchases a life insurance policy or the trust grantor gifts a policy to the trust. The ILIT owns and is beneficiary of the policy. If the grantor owns a life insurance policy that would otherwise be included in his or her estate, gifting of such a policy can be smart. The full face amount is removed from the estate yet it is valued at its much lower replacement cost for gift tax purposes. If the grantor lives more than three years from the date the trust is established, death proceeds should not be a part of his or her taxable estate. If the policy is applied for and owned by the trustee from its inception, policy death proceeds should be excluded from the gross estate even if death occurs within the first three years, provided the purchase of the insurance was at the discretion of the trustee.

The trustee pays policy premiums from either trust corpus or from annual gifts to the trust from the grantor. The latter is the more common approach, although the gifts are not designated as premium payments. The trustee will have been given the authority (at his or her discretion) but not required to purchase insurance and, if desired, to use trust funds—including those gifted annually by the grantor—to pay premiums.

Figure 11-1 illustrates the functioning of an ILIT. We assume that the estate tax law has been changed to allow an exemption amount of $3.5 million

FIGURE 11-1: Illustration of Irrevocable Life Insurance Trust

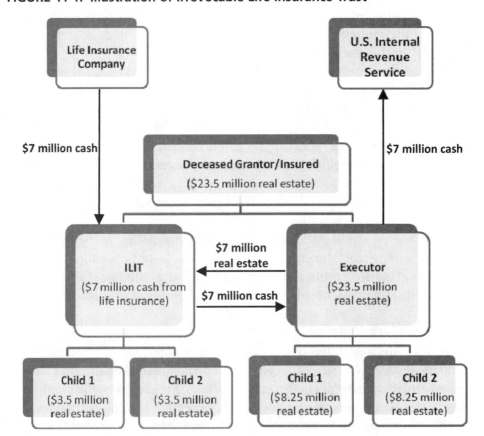

and a tax rate of 35 percent. After paying debts, covering administrative expenses of settling the estate, and meeting her charitable bequests, the widow's remaining estate is composed almost exclusively of timberland valued at $23.5 million, which has been in the family for decades and neither she nor her two children wish to sell it. After taking the $3.5 million exemption from this amount, the taxable estate is $20 million. At a flat 35 percent tax rate, estate taxes of $7 million are due to the government.

The widow's will provides that her two children are to share equally in her estate. She had wisely and accurately estimated her estate taxes at $7 million and had created an ILIT whose trustee had elected to purchase a $7 million policy insuring her life. On her death, the life insurance company paid the $7 million death proceeds to the trust.

The trust agreement authorized the trustee to purchase property from the estate, which the trustee elected to do, thus acquiring family land valued at $7 million and simultaneously providing the executor with cash to pay estate taxes. The trustee distributed the land valued at $7 million to the two children in equal proportions. After paying the IRS, the executor distributed the remaining $16.5 million of family land equally to the children. We can see that the life insurance, which was not included in the gross estate thanks to sound estate planning, has enabled the family to retain ownership of the land and to meet estate settlement obligations.

Charitable Remainder Trusts

A **charitable remainder trust** (CRT) is a living, irrevocable, tax-exempt trust in which the donor contributes property to the trust, reserving to him- or herself (or someone else) an income stream from the trust, with the residual trust corpus, called the **remainder interest**, ultimately passing to a charity. The CRT can be an effective means of helping a charity and of saving on transfer taxes. Many estate planners consider the CRT to be one of the best, simplest, and most underutilized estate planning tools.

A typical CRT arrangement is as follows. First, an individual with highly appreciated assets, such as stock, real estate, or interests in a closely held business, transfers the property to the trust. Often, the property has provided a low income in relation to its value. The trustee promises to make a stream of income payments to the trust beneficiary (often the grantor), which is called a **retained interest** in the trust, either over the beneficiary's lifetime (and possibly that of the spouse also) or for a term not to exceed 20 years. This income usually is subject to income taxation.

The trustee often will sell a part or all of the donated property, investing the proceeds to provide some or all of the needed income to the beneficiary. Because the trust is tax exempt, any sale is free from capital gains taxation. Thus, considerably more money is available than if the grantor had sold the property and paid taxes. Because a charity is entitled to the remainder interest, the grantor is entitled to an income tax deduction immediately in an amount equal to that interest. The amount of the deduction is determined actuarially in accordance with IRS procedures. In general, the more distant the remainder interest and the higher the retained interest, the less the deduction, and vice versa.

Figure 11-2 illustrates the CRT process, assuming highly appreciated property valued at $2 million and with a tax basis of $200,000 is donated to the charity via a trust. Here, Scott is the grantor and is to receive a lifetime income of 5 percent of the initial trust value or $100,000 per year. The remainder interest is valued at $700,000 by IRS procedures and is deductible immediately as a charitable contribution.

FIGURE 11-2: Illustrative Functioning of a Charitable Remainder Trust

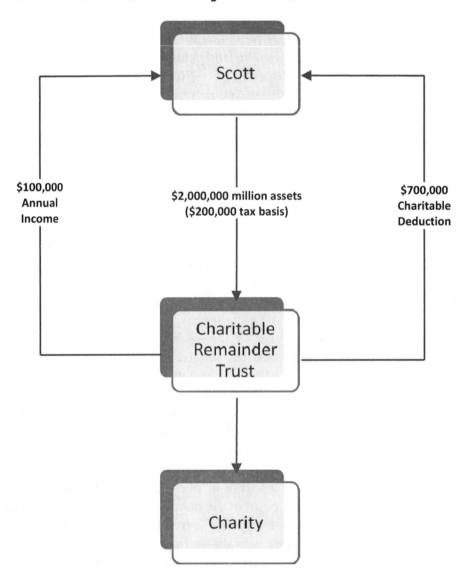

Of course, the grantor loses ownership and control of the property transferred to the CRT. The CRT, thus, saves estate taxes but the transfer deprives heirs of the value of the property, a dissatisfying result for many individuals. To overcome this problem, many donors establish **wealth replacement trusts**, which are ILITs containing insurance whose death benefit roughly equals the value of the property transferred to the CRT. The life insurance premium might range from 1 to 3 percent of the policy face amount, almost certainly well below the income from the CRT. Of course, such trusts can prove attractive in other circumstances, as when property is given for non-charitable purposes. Death proceeds should not be included in the grantor's gross estate.

Thus, for example, Scott might create a wealth replacement trust with his children as trust beneficiaries. The trust would purchase a $2 million life insurance policy on Scott's life, and he would make annual gifts to the trust in the amount of the policy premium, funded from the CRT income stream.

Intentionally Defective Irrevocable Trusts

An **intentionally defective irrevocable trust** (IDIT), also called an **intentionally defective grantor trust**, is a deferred sale arrangement between a grantor and an irrevocable trust that allows the grantor to make transfers of appreciated income producing property to junior generations free of gift tax. The individual sells assets to the IDIT in exchange for an installment note, freezing the current value of appreciating and income producing property and removing future appreciation from his or her estate.

Traditionally, individuals creating irrevocable trusts wished to avoid running afoul of the so-called grantor trust rules, as doing so made the grantor the effective owner of trust assets for income tax purposes. An IDIT purposely runs afoul of these rules. The grantor, therefore, is personally liable for all income (ordinary income and capital gains) attributable to trust assets and must take it into his or her taxable income. By paying all income taxes incurred by the IDIT, its assets grow unreduced by such taxes, thereby increasing the value of assets available to trust beneficiaries. In effect, the payment of income taxes by the grantor is a gift to trust beneficiaries that is not subject to gift taxation, and they reduce the grantor's gross estate. Even though the grantor is considered owning trust assets for income tax purposes, he or she should not be treated as owner for estate tax purposes, as separate tax rules govern each determination.

Implementation involves the following steps:

◆ The grantor establishes an IDIT.
◆ The grantor sells income producing and highly appreciating assets to the IDIT in exchange for an installment note payable over time bearing an interest rate equal to the appropriate applicable federal rate. As the

grantor is treated as the owner of trust assets, the sale should produce no income or capital gain taxes.

- Prior to the execution of the sale, the grantor seeds the IDIT with at least 10–15 percent of the value of the installment note to adequately fund the IDIT and avoid the entire transaction being challenged by the IRS as being a transfer to a trust with a retained interest. This should be the only gift to the trust that is taxable.

- The IDIT uses income generated from the trust assets to make payments on the note to the grantor. Any income remaining in the IDIT after payment may be used by the IDIT trustee to pay premiums on a life insurance policy insuring the life of the grantor. This allows the grantor to fund a life insurance policy outside the estate without the imposition of gift taxes on the premium payments.

- At the end of the installment note period or on the grantor's death, all property held in the IDIT, including life insurance death benefit proceeds, should pass to the IDIT beneficiaries free of estate taxes. If the grantor dies during the term of the installment note, only the balance of the note would be included in the grantor's estate.

IDITs also should appeal to individuals wishing to pass wealth to their grandchildren and great-grandchildren without incurring the GST tax, as the GST tax is a tax on gifts, not sales. Only amounts used to seed the trust should be considered to be a GST.

Life Insurance Analysis for Estate Planning

The previous chapter pointed out that the objective in life insurance planning is to guide the client toward a sound insurance outcome. In guiding the customer, agents, brokers, planners, and other advisors in the estate planning arena will cover the same generic elements as discussed in that chapter; i.e., the *identification* of the client's post-mortem financial objectives, *assembling and analyzing* relevant information, and *development and implementation* of a plan to accomplish the client's objectives. As with the previous chapter's structure, we here structure our discussion of life insurance analysis in the context of estate planning around these elements.

The depth to which an advisor goes in each step will be a function of the precision that the client or situation demands. For example, going through the steps to determine the amount and type of life insurance needed to fund a wealth replacement trust is comparatively simple: the amount likely is the market value of the gift, and the policy ordinarily will be one that remains in effect for the whole of life. Similarly, some advisors will estimate their client's estate taxes in a back-of-the-envelope manner by taking some percentage of the person's net worth (50 percent is common at press time) in excess of the exemption amount (or if the marital deduction will be used, twice that amount) as being a reasonable approximation. Others will more or less follow the steps laid out in the IRC to derive an estimate. Whether a straightforward replace-the-wealth approach, a detailed analysis, back-of-the-envelope approach, or any other is taken, its purpose is the same: to provide key information to the advisor that informs his or her recommendations as to the suggested policy type and amount.

Identify Objectives

Obviously, the client will have made the decision—set the objective—that he or she wishes to explore the use of life insurance for estate planning purposes. This decision and ensuring analysis is often combined with a family needs analysis akin to that discussed in Chapter 10. It also may be combined with an analysis of possible business uses of life insurance as discussed in Chapter 12.

Life insurance can be used in several estate planning situations, the most common of which is estate conservation. **Estate conservation**, also called providing **estate liquidity**, involves using death proceeds from life insurance on the decedent's life to cover some or all of the estate taxes due on his or her death. Unlike the typical family situation discussed in Chapter 10, the client will not necessarily have decided in the early stages of discussions the amount or proportion of estate taxes to be covered by life insurance death proceeds. This decision often occurs only after determining the potential current and future estate tax liability and considering the options available to use life insurance to cover the obligation. The client must also consider the magnitude of the premium payments and any gift tax implications of such payments.

Life insurance is useful in other estate planning situations as well. For example, life insurance may be used for charitable purposes (e.g., via a CRT or an outright gift of a policy to a charity). With an outright gift, the policyowner donates a policy on the insured's life to a charity or authorizes the purchase of a policy on his or her life. The charity becomes the policyowner and beneficiary. The market value of the policy is a measure of the value of the gift and would be deductible for income tax purposes as a charitable donation. Future premium payments on the policy would also be tax deductible donations. In addition, some clients use life insurance to replace the value of wealth given to others or donated to non-profit organizations, which otherwise would have been left to heirs.

Life insurance also can be useful in estate planning to help the client achieve a more equitable distribution of wealth on his or her death. For example, if grandfather Joe wants to leave his deceased wife's $5 million necklace to Susie and only $3 million in other assets is available to be left to his other grandchild, Ralph, he could purchase a $2 million policy payable to Ralph to equalize the value of assets left to each grandchild. This type of use can arise whenever it is desired not to liquidate high value assets, and the assets are by nature or preference indivisible, as with a family business in which only one of three children is interested and capable of running.

Whatever the intended estate planning objective for life insurance, there likely will be a need to create or amend legal documents, such as trusts, to ensure full implementation of those objectives. Intertwined with the many details associated with ensuring appropriate legal documents are life insurance issues such as who should own the policy, who will pay premiums and how, who should be beneficiary, and many others, some of which we touch on below.

Gather Information

In general, the same types of asset, liability, and income information discussed in Chapter 10 will be needed here as well, along with certain other information. Thus, the advisor will have gathered data about the nature and value of the assets owned by the client but also as to other property that he or she controls (yielding the gross estate) and the nature and value of the client's liabilities plus anticipated charitable and spousal bequests (yielding the deductions). If a spousal bequest is anticipated, information gathering and planning ordinarily would be conducted for both spouses. If the client possesses *any* incidents of control of a life insurance policy on his or her life, including the right to change the beneficiary, assign the policy, borrow under it, surrender it, or any other rights, some or all of the death proceeds will be included in his or her gross estate.

Assets generally are valued at their fair market value at time of death or six months thereafter. The executor may choose which date to use. It is beyond our reach here to discuss what constitutes fair market value of various asset classes, but we note that establishing a value that the IRS might accept for some assets can be a challenge. The value placed on real estate, especially large tracks of land, is notoriously contentious. Agreeing on the fair market value of a closely held business also can be challenging.

If the estate planning use to which life insurance may be put is other than estate liquidity, necessary information will have been gathered to permit an analysis to be conducted. For example, for wealth replacement, the advisor will have determined not just the magnitude of the desired replacement but also information about the person or persons to whom the life insurance would be paid and whether a trust seems desirable.

Finally, the advisor ideally will have learned important financial characteristics about the client that will help guide the advisor toward the policies most suitable for the client, along the lines discussed in Chapter 10. These characteristics include the client's ability or, more commonly, willingness to pay premiums along with his or her financial discipline and risk tolerance.

Analyze Information

For estate settlement purposes, an estimate is made of the client's and, if applicable, his or her spouse's likely federal estate taxes owed were either to die this year. Other scenarios are also examined, such as simultaneous death and projections of values should death(s) occur at certain ages. Admittedly, such projections are speculative, not just because of changing values of assets and liabilities but also because of the possibility of changes in the federal estate tax law. Nonetheless, such projections are often desirable both because they can be informative to the client and because they can be useful to the agent in convincing life insurer underwriters as to the reasonableness of the amount of requested insurance. Other estate planning purposes typically involve less analysis, as the goal is, by definition, often quantitative.

Whatever the estate planning purpose, existing liquid assets and cash coming into the estate as a result of prearranged asset sales, such as with interests in a closely held business (see Chapter 12), may be netted against the goals to derive a residual amount to be covered by insurance. Analyzing estate planning related information serves two purposes:

1. To determine figures for the amounts of taxes due or to fund other estate goals; and
2. To select the policy type that will most closely track the goal over time.

Develop and Implement the Plan: Matching Policies to Goals

The next step is to develop and implement a plan to accomplish the stated objectives. This step commonly involves the amendment or creation of trusts and related estate planning legal documents. A discussion of the details of such documents is beyond the scope of this *Guide*, but we note that they usually evolve along with the details of the insurance purchase.

We now know, from the preceding step, the details of the nature of the insurance need. We know the amounts of life insurance needed to meet the objectives, the duration of the need, and have some idea of its possible future pattern, taking existing resources into consideration. The advisor will also have some understanding of the client's financial characteristics. Thus, the advisor will have some idea about the client's ability or willingness to pay premiums and his or her financial discipline and risk tolerance. The advisor will also have knowledge of the client's attitudes toward having to pay estate and gift taxes. These factors will influence the choice of policy or policies recommended.

The agent or planner will have been considering throughout the analysis and plan development processes which policy types seem most appropriate and can be expected to offer the best value. This consideration extends to whether existing life insurance is appropriate in terms of amount, type, arrangement, and competitiveness. We take up issues related to understanding and analyzing new and existing policy illustrations in Chapters 13–17.

Nature of Insurance Need Influencing Selection of Policy Types

Selecting among the various types of life insurance policies for purposes of achieving estate planning goals often is simpler than doing so for family income and related purposes of the type discussed in Chapter 10. This is because of the nature of the insurance need for estate planning purposes is oriented toward accomplishment of but a single or a very few specific, quantifiable goals. (Note that the nature of the *need* is simpler, not associated planning and implementation.) These are the characteristics of the typical estate planning need for life insurance that drive most policy choices.

- ◆ **Coverage needed for the entirety of life.** The life insurance coverage is purchased to meet a need or goal that does not ordinarily diminish with age, remaining for the individual's entire life. For this reason, the selected policy ordinarily will be a cash value variety that will remain in force for the entirety of life, either whole life (WL) or universal life (UL).
- ◆ **Death benefit oriented.** The life insurance policy purchased for estate planning purposes ordinarily is intended to be a source of funds on the insured's death and not to provide or make available funds for the insured or others during his or her lifetime. For this reason, cash value development may be of less or even no importance in the policy selection process, so WL or UL or no-lapse guarantee UL are often the policies of choice. Even so, advisors often recommend that consideration be given to cash value accumulation as it provides flexibility for changing circumstances for which cash may be needed (emergencies, retirement, or value applied for a policy replacement).
- ◆ **Motivated to minimize premium outlay.** As cash value development is of less importance and as the payment of premiums often involves gift tax considerations, the insured's motivation is to pay premiums at the lowest feasible level that will still meet his or her estate planning goals. For this reason, recommended policies typically will carry comparatively low premiums per $1,000 of face amount.

Policy Options for Estate Liquidity with Families Composed of Husband and Wife

For nuclear and other families composed of a husband and wife, the marital deduction coupled with the unified credit may eliminate or greatly reduce estate taxes at the death of the first spouse, focusing the need for liquidity to meet estate taxes on the second spouse's death. Several types of policies can provide the desired cash, each approach being a matter of personal preference, which include the following:

- Purchase individual policies on the life of each spouse in a total amount sufficient to meet the projected need with each policy held in a separate ILIT. On the death of the first spouse, the death proceeds would be paid to the ILIT, with investment income thereon used to augment the surviving spouse's income or accumulate providing additional estate tax-free wealth to trust beneficiaries on the surviving spouse's death. Suitable policies commonly are NLG UL or some form of par WL or UL. This approach usually requires higher premium outlays than other options and, for this reason, is not the approach of choice for most clients.
- Purchase a low-premium joint life permanent policy that provides for payment of the face amount at the first death. As with the two-policy approach, proceeds from the first death can be used to augment the survivor's income or to pass additional wealth to heirs. Special care should be taken in designating ownership of joint policies. If the surviving spouse/insured is owner of the policy, the proceeds will be included in the estate of the second to die. This approach usually requires a somewhat lower premium outlay than the two-policy approach.
- Purchase an appropriate WL or UL policy on the life of one spouse only. If the insured is the first to die, the proceeds would be retained as above for ultimate liquidity needs. This may be the only feasible solution if one spouse is uninsurable, and it is a reasonable one even if both are insurable. Proceeds would be invested, augmenting the surviving spouse's income.
- Purchase a second-to-die policy that pays the face amount when the second insured dies. Assuming both spouses are insurable at reasonable rates, this approach should involve the smallest premium outlay, other things being the same. This approach may also be an option in the event one spouse is uninsurable, as some carriers will issue a survivorship policy with only one insurable life.

In large estates and with large amounts of insurance, the insurance is ordinarily owned by someone other than the insured or spouse. An ILIT may be the most common alternative. A child can be another. Use of an ILIT as owner can be especially wise if the insurance is not to be used at the first death, but instead retained for meeting estate liquidity needs on the second death and only one policy or a joint life policy is to be purchased.

Policy Options for Estate Liquidity with Other Family and Household Arrangements

Family and household arrangements not composed of a husband and wife cannot benefit from the unlimited marital deduction. Rather, they must rely on the other estate planning tools and the unified credit only to minimize estate settlement costs.

The nature of the insurance need as discussed above ordinarily would not be affected by the family structure, so emphasis usually will be on lifetime coverage with minimal premium outlay and less emphasis on cash values, suggesting the same low cost death benefit oriented products as with husband/wife households. Certainly, second-to-die policies would find less relevance here.

Policy Options for Other Estate Planning Goals

Situations arise for which estate planning calls for additional life insurance for wealth replacement, charitable purposes, or to meet other goals in addition to estate liquidity. The most suitable types of policies ordinarily will track those used for estate liquidity but being owned by and payable to separate trusts or follow other separate arrangements.

While most estate planning situations place a low priority on cash value accumulations and their availability, not all do so. Some family situations may suggest a desire to allow the non-insured spouse to be able to access future cash values for family emergencies or other purposes. This goal can be accomplished through a spousal access lifetime trust, as discussed in Box 11-1.

BOX 11-1: Making Cash Values Available using a Spousal Lifetime Access Trust

Some married couples with likely estate tax obligations wish to retain the option of accessing a policy's cash value for possible future needs, such as unforeseen adverse financial developments or children's educational costs. Of course, they wish to keep policy death proceeds out of the gross estate, so an ILIT may be the approach of choice, except that ILITs ordinarily may not provide either spouse access to policy cash values without endangering the favorable estate tax status of the death proceeds.

A **spousal lifetime access trust** (SLAT), a special type of ILIT, can preserve the favorable estate tax treatment of the death proceeds while allowing indirect access to the policy cash values. As with an ordinary ILIT, the SLAT trustee is permitted, but not required, to purchase a life insurance policy on the life of one of the spouses, with premiums commonly paid via grantor gifts to the trust. The terms of the SLAT provide that the trustee may, at its discretion, make policy loans and withdrawals, which should be free of income tax to the SLAT, subject to IRS rules. If the SLAT has no taxable income, the trustee may, at its discretion, then make distributions to the non-insured spouse that are free of income and gift tax.

Several other issues remain to be addressed in this stage. Who should own the policy? How should the beneficiary designation be structured? How should the insurance be structured to have the funds available for the person who must pay estate obligations or to meet other estate planning goals? These issues will have been addressed as a byproduct of the overall estate planning.

Conclusions

Life insurance is one of the most flexible and efficient means of providing funds to meet estate planning goals, including estate liquidity. The event that creates the financial problem simultaneously gives rise to the solution. Policy choices for estate planning purposes ordinarily are simpler than those for pure family purposes, as the nature of the insurance need is simpler, although the planning itself commonly is far more complex.

Business Uses of Life Insurance

12

THIS CHAPTER CONCLUDES PART IV of the *Guide*, on determining the appropriate life insurance policy for each application. Here we examine the most common business-related applications of life insurance.[1] As emphasized in the preceding two chapters, overlap commonly exists between purely family income and related needs, as covered in Chapter 10; estate planning needs, as discussed in Chapter 11; and business uses of life insurance. We intend this three-part categorization to allow us more easily to focus on the underlying objectives for which life insurance is purchased.

We again emphasize that this *Guide* is not intended to cover policy suitability issues related to these applications. Rather, we present minimal background information touching on suitability solely to provide context for the discussion about determining the need for life insurance and possible applications of different policy types to these needs.

Introduction

While we most often think about individually issued life insurance policies in the context of the family, they are also routinely

---

Authored by Harold D. Skipper.
[1]This chapter draws in part from Kenneth Black, Jr. and Harold D. Skipper, Jr., *Life and Health Insurance* (13th ed.; Upper Saddle River, NJ: Prentice-Hall, 2000), Chapters 16 and 17.

used to foster business goals. Even within a business context, many life insurance purchases ultimately are intended to facilitate family financial goals. As we will discover, their beneficial uses extend over a range of special business applications.

As background to discussion of these applications, we first introduce the major forms that business enterprises may take in the U.S. and some tax considerations applicable to business uses of life insurance. The introduction to these forms of businesses includes short analyses of potential issues of each form in terms of business continuity.

Forms of Business Organizations

Businesses in the U.S. operate as sole proprietorships, partnerships, and corporations. Variations exist of the latter two forms, but a discussion of these variations is outside the scope of this *Guide*.

Sole Proprietorships

A **sole proprietorship** is an unincorporated business owned by an individual who usually also manages it. No legal distinction exists between the proprietor's personal and business assets and liabilities. In the absence of work in professions or trades that themselves require licensing or other documentation, the sole proprietor may establish himself or herself in business by the mere declaration that he or she is in business.

More than 22 million sole proprietorships exist in the U.S., accounting for about 4 percent of total U.S. business revenue. The great majority of sole proprietorships are small, having fewer than ten employees.

A sole proprietorship is a fragile business enterprise because of its dependence on a single individual. Upon the death of the proprietor, his or her personal representative generally is obligated to liquidate the business, thus possibly losing its value as a going concern.

Partnerships

A **partnership** is a voluntary association of two or more individuals for the purpose of conducting a business for profit as co-owners. Business assets and liabilities are owned by the partnership. Almost 3 million partnerships exist in the U.S., accounting for about 13 percent of all U.S. business receipts. Most engage in commercial activities, in contrast with professional activities such as law or medicine.

Partnerships are of two basic types. A **general partnership** is one in which partners are actively involved in the management of the firm and fully liable for partnership obligations. A **limited partnership** is one having at least one general partner and one or more limited partners who are not actively engaged in partnership management and who are liable for partnership obligations only to the extent of their investment in the partnership.

The partnership form of business has several advantages, but it is subject to the general rule that any change in the membership of the partnership causes its dissolution. On the death of a general partner, the partnership is dissolved and, in the absence of arrangements to the contrary, the surviving partners become liquidating trustees. They are charged with the responsibility of winding up the business and paying to the estate of the deceased a fair share of the liquidated value of the business. From the viewpoint of remaining partners and the deceased partners' heirs, liquidation not only produces losses to them by shrinkage in asset values but, more important, may destroy their source of income.

The seriousness of the consequences often leads surviving partners to attempt to continue the business by buying out the interest of the deceased partner and reorganizing the partnership. This procedure may not be practicable for two reasons. First, it may be impossible to quickly raise the necessary cash. Second, even if the surviving partners can raise the cash, they must prove that the price paid for the interest is fair—a tough call given their fiduciary status. The record of litigation indicates that, in the absence of advance agreement among the partners, attempts to continue the business are fraught with legal and practical complications.

Corporations

A **corporation** is a business legally separate and distinct from its owners and possesses these characteristics:

- ◆ Owners' liability for corporate obligations is limited to their investments in the corporation;
- ◆ Easy transfer of owners' interests in the corporation by sale of their shares of stock; and
- ◆ Owners' deaths have no effect legally on the corporation's continued existence.

Some 5.8 million corporations exist in the U.S., accounting for 83 percent of all U.S. business receipts. Most corporations are **closely held corporations**, also referred to as **close corporations** and **closed corporations**, meaning that they typically are owned and managed by a small number of investors, often family members, with their shares of stock not listed on any organized exchange.

Although a shareholder's death legally has no effect on a corporation's continued existence, the nature of a closely held corporation can lead to practical problems. The practical difficulties encountered in attempting to continue operation of such a business following a shareholder's death stem from the very characteristics of a closely held corporation.

Problems Associated with the Death of a Majority Shareholder

Consider the situation of typical majority shareholders of close corporations. They likely run the business as its chief executive, being paid a handsome income that their families enjoy. On their death and in the absence of a legally binding arrangement to dispose of their interest at death, the family inherits that interest, but all income ceases as closely held corporations typically do not pay dividends. Of course, as majority owners (and voters), the family has options; it can:

1. Insist that another family member already employed in the firm, or that the firm will hire, be paid a sufficiently high income;
2. Insist that the corporation begin paying dividends of sufficient amount to enable the family to continue their former lifestyle;
3. Sell their stock to persons with no existing ownership interest in the firm; or
4. Sell their stock to persons with an existing ownership interest in the firm.

The viability of these options will vary depending on circumstances. With the first option, a family member with no previous meaningful involvement in the business normally would be unable to contribute much to the business and might be a source of disruption and even conflict. Existing owner/managers may conclude that their best interests are served by leaving, perhaps beginning their own competing business. All parties could lose economic value were this to happen.

The second option likely would be unpalatable to the other owners. They would, in effect, be taxed twice on dividend income that they would prefer not to have in the first place, at least not in that form. If they were expected to take over the former responsibilities of the deceased CEO/owner in addition to paying high dividends, resentment could be expected, perhaps leading to resignations. Of course, if the minority owners could somehow block the efforts of heirs to have the company pay high dividends, dissatisfaction by the heirs could lead to other challenges.

The third option, selling to outside interests, could be feasible in appropriate circumstances but also could be viewed by potential purchasers as a "fire sale" opportunity. This is particularly true as outsiders are likely to recognize that the principal value of the business is in the remaining employees, who could resign. Further, associates in a close corporation, as in a partnership, typically join forces because they work well together and each makes a certain contribution that, taken together, produces a vigorous, profitable combination. Outsiders may not fit well in this corporate family, leading to disruption of the business or, in extreme cases, even to liquidation. Perhaps of greater importance to the minority shareholders, they would know that compensation and dividend policy would be in the hands of the new majority shareholders. Again, they may find leaving the firm the best option, allowing the new folks to fend for themselves.

The final option is likely the most efficacious, provided agreement can be reached as to a fair price and the minority owners are able to raise the necessary cash. The heirs may perceive themselves to be in the superior bargaining position and insist on a high price or simply refuse to sell their interests.

Problems Associated with the Death of a Minority and 50/50 Shareholder

The minority and 50/50 shareholder situations likely pose even more formidable problems. The minority shareholder's heirs, while they may not be able to exercise control, nonetheless may be able to render life miserable for the majority shareholder/managers. All shareholders have rights, such as being entitled to a proportionate share of dividends, to examine the corporate records (with legitimate reason), and generally to participate in all shareholder activities. Lawsuits by disgruntled minority shareholders are not uncommon.

A majority shareholder's beneficiaries can enforce their wills on the surviving shareholders; a minority shareholder's beneficiaries generally cannot. The minority shareholder's heirs are potentially in a most unenviable position. They own stock that was possibly subject to substantial federal estate taxes yet the stock may have little or no marketability. Few would rationally purchase a minority interest in a closely held corporation. Additionally, they receive no income from their investment, as closely held corporations rarely pay dividends.

Similar circumstances apply to the death of a shareholder who owns precisely 50 percent of the business. In fact, such circumstances often are worse for all concerned, as deadlocks are possible in which no business decisions can be made.

Tax Considerations in Business Applications of Life Insurance

As we explore below, in many corporate applications of life insurance, the policy is owned by and payable to the corporation. The tax treatment of the insurance can be of enormous importance, so we offer an overview here of such taxation.

The general rule is that life insurance death benefits received under insurance payable to the employer—called **employer owned life insurance**

(EOLI) under the IRC—are subject to income taxes to the extent that the benefits exceed the employer's cost basis in the policy. Fortunately, the law also provides that death benefits payable under EOLI policies meeting either one of two exceptions and for which certain notice and consent requirements are met will not be treated as taxable income. The two exceptions are:

1. Insureds are present or former directors or highly compensated employees. A highly compensated employee is one who, at the time of policy issuance, meets one of the following conditions:
   a. Owned 5 percent or more of the corporation's shares at any time during the preceding year,
   b. Earned compensation of $110,000 (indexed) during the preceding year,
   c. Was among the five highest paid officers, or
   d. Was among the highest paid 35 percent of all employees.
2. Life insurance death proceeds are paid to the insured's heirs (or a trust for the heirs) or used by the employer to redeem stock owned by the insured in the employer.

In addition to meeting one of the two preceding exceptions, the insured must have been given notice prior to the insurance purchase that such insurance was to be purchased and consented to its purchase. The notice must state that the employer intends to be the owner and beneficiary of a life insurance policy on the executive's life and that the employer may choose to continue the coverage beyond the executive's employment. The notice must also state the maximum amount of life insurance that could be placed on the executive's life.

Finally, employers must annually report any such life insurance arrangements to the IRS. The report must include the number of employees insured by the employer and the number of employees for whom valid consent was obtained. It is exceedingly important that all requirements be met if the policyholder is to avoid having death proceeds subject to income taxation.

Business Applications of Life Insurance

The previous two chapters pointed out that the objective in life insurance planning is to guide the client toward a sound insurance outcome. As with estate planning, advisors in the business applications of life insurance will cover the same generic elements of *identification* of the client's business-related objectives for which life insurance can be a solution, *assembling and analyzing* relevant information, and *developing and implementing* a plan to accomplish the client's objectives. While each of these elements is covered in this chapter for each application, the organization of the material differs in some areas from that of the previous two chapters. We cover three applications here:

- ◆ Key person indemnification;
- ◆ Business continuation arrangements; and
- ◆ Nonqualified executive benefit plans.

Key Person Indemnification

Many businesses have been built around a single individual whose capital, energy, technical knowledge, experience, or power to plan and execute makes him or her a particularly valuable asset of the organization and a necessity to its successful operation, at least in the early stages of the organization's existence. Where would Microsoft have been without Bill Gates, Apple without Steve Jobs, or Berkshire Hathaway without Warren Buffet? And how many thousands of firms today, particularly small- to medium-size firms, are similarly dependent on one or two key employees for their continued success or even viability? In each instance, the death of the key employee could have profoundly adverse financial effects on the firm.

As with insurance that indemnifies the firm for property and liability losses, so too can life insurance indemnify the firm for losses caused by the death of key individuals. **Key person insurance**, also called **key employee** (and **key man**) **insurance**, is purchased to indemnify a business for the decrease in earnings brought about by the death of one or more key persons. This generic term encompasses individuals who are employees as well as those who might not technically be employees but whose death could adversely affect a business, such as the author who received a multi-million dollar advance, the award-winning actor the studio landed to make a movie, and so on.

Identify Objectives

The first step is to identify whether anyone's death, commonly that of an employee, might lead to a material deterioration in the firm's financial situation, precisely paralleling the effort undertaken with families. What is material to one firm will not necessarily be so with other firms. A firm's financial position could deteriorate in several ways. Gross revenues may deteriorate meaningfully on the death of the firm's star saleswoman, innovative biologist, brilliant CFO, best-selling author, world-class soccer player, and so on. Compounding any of these declines in gross revenue could be meaningfully higher expenses because of a need to replace the key person.

One area sometimes overlooked in thinking about the financial effects on the firm of the death of key persons is the loss of a firm's high credit rating. Insurance on their lives could assure banks and other lending institutions as well as suppliers that the business will have a financial cushion if one or more of them were to die. Similarly, if prospective lenders or other creditors are assured of the firm's continuation as a going concern in the event of the death of key owner/manager(s), the firm usually will be able to obtain a larger line of credit and on better terms. These types of assurances can be especially important to small- and medium-size firms.

Gather and Analyze Information

Businesses purchase all types of insurance to stabilize their financial position. Usually, we think of stabilization in terms of protecting the value of the firm. One widely recognized measure of the value of a business is the present value of current and future net cash flows. The market establishes this value for businesses whose stock is publicly traded. The market will penalize the stock price if it perceives that any major operational, property, liability, or personnel loss negatively affects cash flows. Property, liability, business interruption, key person, and other insurance can be thought of as the business hedging this possibility, such that any loss will be indemnified, thus shoring up share prices. Publicly traded firms might establish the risk management objective that no insurable loss to the firm—whether a property, liability, business interruption, or personnel loss—should cause the share price to fall by more than a certain percentage.

Establishing value for businesses whose stock is not publicly traded on an organized exchange poses more challenges. While the value of such a business is the present value of current and future net cash flows, this value is not established by a market and must be estimated. Some advisors estimate this figure by taking some multiple of the business's net worth as shown on its balance sheet or by estimating the present value of future profits. Thus, a closely held business might want to ensure that no loss to the firm would cause the net worth or future profits to fall by a more than a certain percentage.

As applied to key person insurance, consideration must be given to questions such as how do we estimate the actual impact on the firm's finances of a key person's death, whether the loss would be temporary or permanent, and the appropriate discount rate to use. The degree of accuracy inherent in these and other factors used to estimate the value of the economic loss produced by the death of a key person varies according to the type of business, particular function of the key person, and other circumstances.

Develop and Implement Plan

After deciding that the death of one or more key individuals could have unacceptable financial repercussions for the firm and quantifying those repercussions, a plan for dealing with them must follow. Succession planning comes into play here, but it takes time and there is no guarantee of success. Life insurance is a common financial response.

For insurance on key executives, the business provides written notice to the key executive that it intends to buy life insurance on his or her life. The notice must state (1) that the employer will be the beneficiary of the policy and may remain so even after the executive is no longer employed by the business and (2) the maximum amount of the insurance to be purchased on his or her life. Written consent to proceed with the purchase must be obtained. Other requirements for EOLI as discussed earlier also must be met.

The business then applies for the policy for which it will be the owner and beneficiary. It also pays the premiums. Key person insurance is not a type of policy but a special application of the usual types of insurance. Thus, the policy type should be selected based on the expected nature of the insurance need including its magnitude, duration, and pattern as well as the financial characteristics of the firm, including its ability and willingness to pay premiums and its risk tolerance and discipline. The latter two items are more relevant to small than to large firms.

Another consideration is whether it is desirable to have cash values available for other purposes (e.g., as loan collateral or to informally fund a deferred compensation arrangement—see below). If a cash value form of life insurance is used, the firm's liquidity is enhanced through the accumulation of cash values. Cash values are balance sheet assets.

Whole life (WL) and universal life (UL) policies are most often recommended for key employee indemnification. Term life insurance is commonly recommended to cover short term needs, such as arise with individuals under performance contracts or if funds can be put to better use outside the life insurance policy.

Business Continuation Arrangements

Businesses whose ownership interests have no ready market are referred to as **closely held businesses**, of which closely held corporations are an important component. The problems of business continuation are particularly acute for such firms. These problems stem from the typical characteristics of such businesses, as alluded to earlier:

- *Unity of ownership and management.* The owners typically manage the firm, receiving a salary. Indeed, of families having any business interests in 2007, 92 percent reported having an active role in the business.
- *Small number of owners.* The great majority of closely held businesses are owned by fewer than ten individuals.
- *Ownership interest not readily marketable.* Because ownership interests in closely held businesses are not traded on organized exchanges, there typically is no ready market for that interest. The only persons ordinarily interested in purchasing such an interest are the other owners and possibly competitors.

Closely held businesses are a major source of U.S. economic activity and employment. Almost 20 percent of nonfinancial assets held by U.S. households in 2007 (latest year) is composed of privately held business interests, a larger proportion than that which households held in shares of public corporations. Nine of every 10 businesses are family run.

Problems of business succession are, by definition, particularly acute for privately held firms, yet owner/managers more often than not fail to address them. In one survey, only 45 percent of family business owners who planned to retire within the next five years had identified a successor.[2] Apparently, no question was asked in the survey about having identified a successor in case of death, but the percentage almost certainly would have been even lower.

Moreover, even business owners who plan for succession often overlook critically important issues. Survivors often find themselves facing creditors who doubt their business abilities and, therefore, reduce credit lines and call loans. Many customers try to take advantage of successors, as do many employees. Every ownership transfer involves some difficulty, with the U.S. Small Business Administration reporting only 30 percent of family businesses succeeding into the second generation and only 15 percent into the third. The greater the care and thought exercised in business continuation planning, the greater the likelihood of business survival for the benefit of all stakeholders. Yet, surprisingly, in the majority of situations, those who built and control the business do no planning.

The problems of business stability and continuation following the death of one or more of the owners of a closely held business are critically important to both the family of the deceased owner and the surviving owners and employees. While the essential issue is the same irrespective of business organizational form, the details for addressing the issue will vary based on form, so our discussion below is structured around each of the three major forms.

Sole Proprietorships

As noted earlier, sole proprietorships are fragile, usually quite small operations. In seeking to preserve any going concern value of the firm following the death of the proprietor, either a family member steps in or purchasers must be identified. Of course, the time for planning for either eventuality is well before death, for, if a sale is contemplated, heirs are not likely to be in a strong bargaining position.

If a sale is desirable, the owner ideally would have both identified the purchaser and made pre-death arrangements to effectuate a buyout on his or her death via a one-way buy/sell agreement. A **one-way buy/sell agreement** obligates the estate of a sole owner of a business (including a corporation) to sell and another party to purchase that owner's interest.

---

[2]http://www.massmutual.com/mmfg/pdf/MM_Success_Plan.pdf

Prospective buyers might include a friendly competitor. A binding buy/sell agreement between the proprietor and a friendly competitor could be negotiated. The agreement can be funded by insurance purchased on the proprietor's life by the competitor and under which the competitor is owner and beneficiary or by a trust. Premiums would be paid by the competitor.

Alternatively, one or more key employees, dependent perhaps on the business for their livelihood, might find the prospects of acquiring the business to be attractive. A buy/sell agreement funded by insurance on the proprietor's life could guarantee their eventual ownership while acting as an inducement for these key employee(s) to remain with the business. The policy could be owned by and payable to the employee or owned by and payable to a trust that collects the proceeds and supervises execution of the agreement.

Premiums for such insurance are not tax deductible, but policy proceeds should be received free of income tax and not taxable in the proprietor's estate. If the key employee(s) have insufficient funds to pay the required premiums, the proprietor could assist the employee(s) financially, for example through a split dollar arrangement (see later in this chapter). The nature of the insurance need commonly suggests the purchase of some form of WL or UL insurance, with the precise details being influenced by cash flow issues.

Partnerships

To avoid the difficulties noted earlier when one partner dies, members of a partnership commonly enter into a buy/sell agreement. This agreement binds the surviving partners or the partnership to purchase the partnership interest of the first partner to die at a prearranged price set by the agreement and obligates the deceased partner's estate to sell this interest to the other partners. The value of the partnership interest is determined at the time the agreement is entered into and periodically revalued or a formula for value determination is included in the agreement.

Types of Business Continuation Arrangements

Most buy/sell agreements are of one of two types: entity and cross purchase. Under an **entity buy/sell agreement**, the business entity itself is obligated to buy the ownership interest of any deceased partner, with each partner having bound his or her estate to sell if he or she were to be the first to die. Under a **cross purchase buy/sell agreement**, each owner binds his or her estate to sell his or her business interest to the surviving owners, and each surviving owner binds himself or herself to buy the interest of the deceased owner. The agreement is among the business owners themselves, not between the business enterprise and its owners.

Other forms of buy/sell agreements exist, but are found less frequently. For example, an **option buy/sell agreement** affords a party the option of buying a business interest but does not require it.

The business continuation arrangement of a professional partnership (e.g., for attorneys or physicians) usually differs from that discussed above. Provision usually is made for a continuation of income to the deceased partner's estate or heirs for a specified time period, with the income amount possibly based on a profit sharing agreement. A separate agreement might provide for the purchase and sale of the deceased partner's tangible business assets.

Use of Life Insurance

Life insurance commonly is used to fund such agreements. Under the entity approach, the partnership itself applies for, owns, and is beneficiary of a life insurance policy on each partner's life. The face amount of each policy usually equals the value of the insured partner's ownership interest. Under the cross purchase approach, each partner applies for, owns, and is beneficiary of a life insurance policy on each of the other partners' lives. The face amount of each policy usually equals the agreed upon value of the interest that the surviving partner/policyowner would purchase from the deceased partner's estate.

Agents and planners commonly recommend cash value life insurance for partnership buy/sell agreements because of the nature of the insurance need. Participating (par) WL, UL, and no-lapse guarantee (NLG) UL policies can each fit the need, depending on other circumstances. Joint life and multiple life policies are also sometimes suggested, each possibly requiring careful consideration for necessary arrangements after the death of the first partner.

Figures 12-1 and 12-2, shown below in the discussion on corporate buy/sell arrangements, applies also to partnerships. As illustrated in the two figures, upon the first death among the partners, the operation of the plan is straightforward. The life insurance proceeds are used by the partnership or surviving partners, as the case may be, to purchase the interest of the deceased from his or her estate. The partnership is reorganized by the surviving partners and continues in operation, and the heirs of the deceased receive in cash the going concern value of the involved partnership interest. All parties benefit by the arrangement, and the problems of liquidation obviated. The surviving partners can enter into a new buy/sell agreement or amend the original agreement to account for changes in the value of their respective interests.

The Tax Aspects of Life Insurance in Partnership Buy/Sell Agreements

The income tax treatment of life insurance purchased to fund a cross purchase agreement is the same as that for personal insurance. Premiums are not deductible whether paid by the partnership or a partner. Death proceeds normally would be received free of income tax. The cost basis of each surviving partner's interest is increased by the amount paid for the deceased partner's interest under a cross purchase plan. The tax treatment of life insurance purchased to fund an entity plan ordinarily will be the same as that for a cross purchase plan provided the EOLI exceptions and requirements are met.

Life insurance death proceeds are excluded from the gross estate of the insured unless the insured possessed any incidents of ownership or the proceeds are payable to or for the benefit of the insureds estate. Any death proceeds payable to the partnership normally would increase the value of the partnership for estate tax purposes.

Corporations

Numerous complexities and uncertainties can accompany managing and/or selling the ownership interest in a closely held corporation after the death of an owner. These issues can be avoided by having made advance arrangement for the orderly continuation of the business via buy/sell agreements. The agreement generally requires the estate of the deceased shareholder to sell and either the corporation or other shareholders to buy the decedent's interest in the business at an agreed upon price. Additionally, the plan can allow for continuity in business management, provide income for the deceased owner's family, and offer direction for future ownership of the business.

Establishing a fair value for the business is of enormous importance not only to the buyers and sellers but also for estate tax valuation purposes. Many advisors counsel their clients to engage a business valuation specialist to assist in establishing the value, ideally following methods acceptable to the IRS. Accountants often assist their clients in identifying such specialists. Also specialists can be found at the National Association of Certified Valuation Analysts (www.nacva.com) and Institute of Business Appraisers (www.go-iba.org).

Business continuation plans usually are structured in one of three ways: entity (more commonly called a **stock redemption**), cross purchase, or wait-and-see buy/sell. The essential difference among the three structures is the process for determining who will purchase the shares. In a stock redemption, the business will purchase the shares. In a cross purchase, individuals, usually other shareholders, will purchase the shares. A **wait-and-see buy/sell agreement** allows the shareholders and the business to postpone the decision between a cross purchase and stock redemption agreement until the death of a stockholder. The corporation has the right of first refusal to purchase stock under the agreement, with individual stockholders obligated to purchase the stock if the corporation refuses. Box 12-1 lists some of the factors that can influence the choice of buy/sell arrangement.

In some instances a buy/sell arrangement is undesirable, perhaps because the principal shareholder wishes to pass his or her interest to family members or because no willing buyer can be located. A not mutually exclusive but alternative means of selling some of the stock and securing cash for

---

BOX 12-1: Factors Influencing the Choice of Buy/Sell Agreement

Many factors will influence the decision involving which of the three business continuation approaches seems most appropriate, among them are the following:

Taxation. If the corporation is in a lower tax bracket than the shareholders, a redemption plan may be preferred and vice versa. This is because premium payments would take a smaller share of the corporation's after tax income than it would of the shareholders' after tax income and vice versa.

Ease of Administration. Administration of a cross-purchase plan becomes complex quickly as the number of shareholders involved increases. Under a stock redemption plan, the corporation purchases but one policy per shareholder. Under a cross purchase plan, the total number of policies needed is $n(n-1)$, where n is the number of shareholders. Thus, with five shareholders, 20 policies would be needed. Trustee cross purchase agreements can mitigate this issue.

Effect on Cost Basis. With a stock redemption plan, the purchased stock becomes treasury stock. The other shareholders retain their original stock with no increase in cost basis. Upon subsequent sale, their taxable gain could be substantial. With a cross purchase plan, the purchased stock acquires an increase in basis equal to the purchase price of the new shares. Upon any subsequent sale, this higher basis reduces the amount of any realized taxable gain. (If shareholders are likely to retain their stock until death, the cost basis issue may be moot, as the stock will obtain a stepped up basis equal to its fair market value at time of death, *assuming changes in the estate tax law follow the historical pattern.*)

Accumulated Earnings Problem. The IRC imposes a penalty tax on corporations that accumulate earnings and profits beyond that needed for legitimate business purposes to prevent the amounts from being taxed to shareholders. The tax is tied to the tax rate applicable to dividends, currently 15 percent but proposed to go higher. It is in addition to the corporation's regular tax liability. A cross purchase plan avoids this concern altogether.

Corporate Creditors. Under a stock redemption plan, any policy cash values and death proceeds are subject to attachment by the creditors of the corporation, as the policy is a general corporate asset. This issue is not encountered under a cross purchase plan.

State Law Restrictions. The laws of most states provide that corporate redemptions can be made only from available corporate surplus; hence, insufficient surplus, no redemption. Insurance proceeds and contributions to capital can help alleviate this problem under a stock redemption plan. The problem does not occur under cross purchase buyouts.

Loan Limitations. Many closely-held corporations operate on credit. The loan agreements used by most banks contain restrictions on the payment of dividends or redemption of stock without the bank's consent. A stock redemption agreement could fail unless fully funded and any indebtedness satisfied, so that creditors would not object to a redemption. This issue does not arise with a cross purchase agreement.

Attribution Rules. A complete redemption of a shareholder's stock by a corporation ordinarily results in capital gains treatment. Redemption of only a portion of a shareholder's stock generally invokes dividend treatment. Hence, most stock redemption plans involve a complete redemption. A problem can arise, however, in certain family owned and other corporations because of the IRC's **attribution rules**, the effect of which is to attribute the stock owned by family members or estate beneficiaries to a decedent. Fortunately, the family attribution rules can be waived under certain circumstances.

Cash Flow. Shareholders often prefer a stock redemption approach because they prefer to spend the corporation's funds on life insurance premiums rather than their own, even if doing so might be inferior to using other metrics.

the estate is a **Section 303 stock redemption** through which an income tax free redemption is permitted for qualifying estates in an amount to cover federal and state death taxes, funeral expenses, and estate administration expenses. To qualify, the value of the stock must be included in the decedent's gross estate and must represent more than 35 percent of the decedent's adjusted gross estate. The redemption must be made within four years of the filing of the estate tax return.

Use of Life Insurance

These agreements are commonly funded by life insurance. For buy/sell agreements, each shareholder is insured for the value of his or her stock interest owned, the insurance being owned by either the corporation or the other shareholders. Upon the first death among the shareholders, the life insurance death proceeds are used by the corporation or surviving shareholders, as the case may be, to purchase the stock of the deceased person from his or her estate. The business future of the survivors is assured, and the estate beneficiaries receive cash instead of what could prove to be a speculative interest.

Wait-and-see agreements funded by life insurance follow the cross purchase approach with each shareholder owning policies on the lives of the other shareholders. If the corporation elects to purchase the stock on an owner's death, surviving shareholders contribute the necessary cash to the corporation from the insurance proceeds, as either capital contributions or interest bearing loans.

Life insurance is also used to fund Section 303 redemptions. The corporation applies for, owns, and is the beneficiary of a policy whose face amount is sufficient to provide the corporate funds needed to affect the redemption.

Figures 12-1 illustrates the workings of an insurance funded stock redemption plan and Figure 12-2 illustrates the operation of an insurance funded cross purchase plan. The wait-and-see approach will function as one of these two plans.

FIGURE 12-1: Entity Buy/Sell Agreement

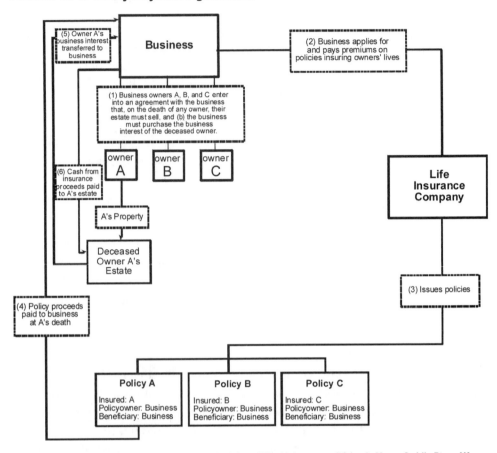

Source: Kenneth Black, Jr. and Harold D. Skipper, Jr., *Life and Health Insurance* (13th ed.; Upper Saddle River, NJ: Prentice-Hall, 2000), p. 420.

As the purpose of the life insurance is to provide funding for the buyout of a deceased business owner's interest, irrespective of when death occurs, some form of cash value insurance is most commonly recommended by agents and planners, mostly commonly par WL or generic UL. If a succession plan involving a lifetime buyout is in place and is to take place within the next few years, term life insurance might be recommended.

The Tax Aspects of Life Insurance in Corporate Business Continuation Agreements

Premiums paid for life insurance to fund corporate buy/sell agreements and Section 303 redemptions are not tax deductible. Death proceeds in excess of the policy's income tax basis—ordinarily, premiums paid—will be subject to income taxation as EOLI unless an exemption and notice and consent requirements are met, as discussed earlier in this chapter. Ordinarily, these con-

FIGURE 12-2: Cross Purchase Buy/Sell Agreement

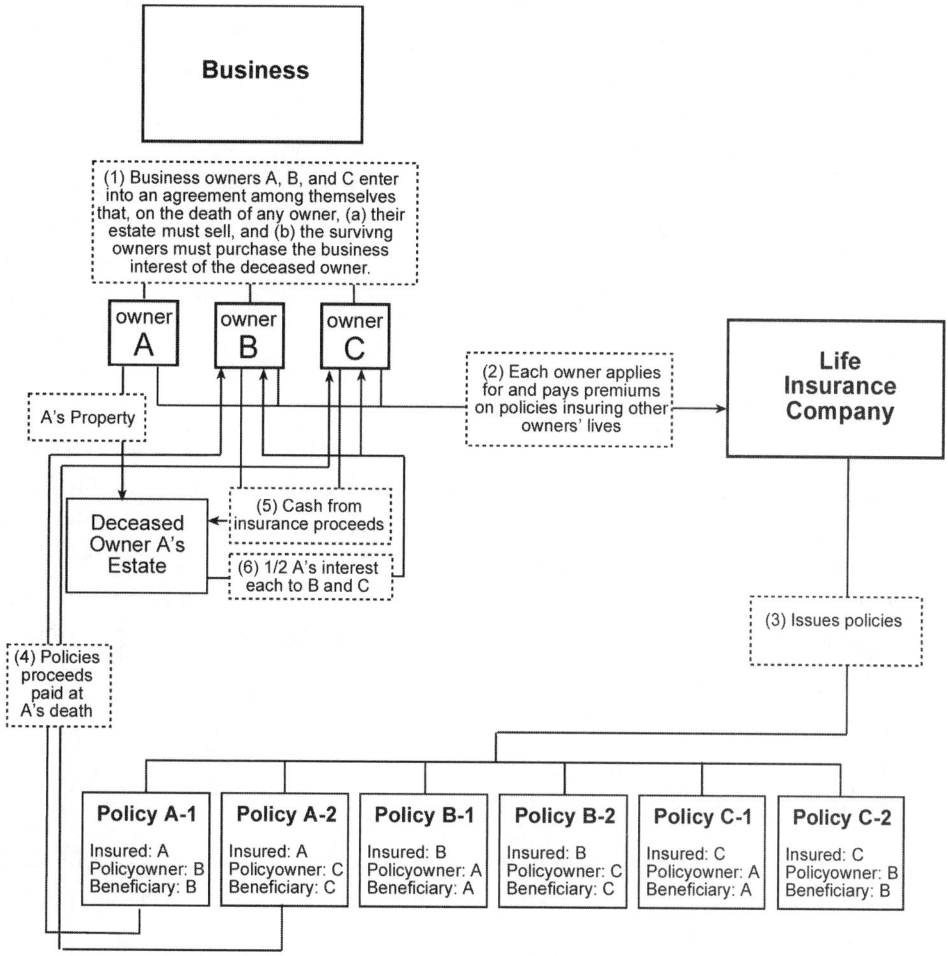

Source: Kenneth Black, Jr. and Harold D. Skipper, Jr., *Life and Health Insurance* (13th ed.; Upper Saddle River, NJ: Prentice-Hall, 2000), p. 420.

ditions will have been met, and death proceeds will be received by the beneficiary free of income tax. Interest credited to policy cash values similarly will not usually generate taxable income.

Life insurance death proceeds paid under cross purchase arrangements will not ordinarily be included in a deceased shareholder's gross estate. Proceeds payable under stock redemption plans could cause an increase in the value of the business, thus causing an increase in the value of the deceased shareholder's stock within the estate.

Another consideration in using life insurance to fund general stock or Section 303 redemptions agreements is whether cash value increases or policy death proceeds would invoke the alternative minimum tax (AMT) applicable to C-corporations. This tax may be imposed on tax preference items. The AMT could apply when (1) a policy's yearly cash value increase exceeds that year's premium or (2) death proceeds paid exceed the policy's cash value. Small corporations, generally those with gross receipts not in excess of $7.5 million, are exempt from the AMT.

If corporate ownership of a life insurance policy would trigger the AMT, consideration would be given to the cross purchase approach. Note also that the AMT could be triggered by key person life insurance as well as other instances involving corporate owned life insurance (see below). For the majority of corporations, however, cash value increases are unlikely to cause an AMT problem.

Nonqualified Executive Benefit Plans

Nonqualified executive benefit plans can be structured to provide virtually any package of benefits and can provide them to whomever the business wishes. Indeed, the very purpose of nonqualified benefit plans is to discriminate in favor of a few select employees. These plans are "nonqualified" in the sense that they do not meet the IRC and ERISA requirements of qualified plans, especially as to nondiscrimination. Here, we explore three types of nonqualified benefit plans:

- ◆ Executive bonus plans,
- ◆ Split dollar life insurance, and
- ◆ Nonqualified retirement plans.

Life insurance policies often are used to fund these plans. The insured employees typically are those whose skills, talents, and experience make them particularly valuable to the business.

Executive Bonus Plans

An **executive bonus plan**, also called a **Section 162 plan**, is an arrangement under which the employer pays the premiums on life insurance policies for selected executives who own the policies. Par WL, generic UL, and variable UL policies are often recommended by agents and planners. The employer is free to discriminate among employees benefitted by this plan. The premium payments by the business are compensation and, therefore, ordinarily tax deductible. To claim this deduction, the death proceeds cannot be payable to the business.

The executive must include the amount of the premium payment in his or her taxable income. Because the plan provides nonqualified life insurance, no portion of the premium paid by the employer may be excluded for the executive's taxable income. Some employers pay an additional bonus to cover this income tax obligation.

As the owner of the policy, the executive may name the beneficiary and exercise all other policy rights. Death proceeds will be included in the executive's gross estate if he or she retains any ownership interest or if proceeds are payable to or for the benefit of the estate, which typically is not the case.

Split Dollar Life Insurance

Split dollar life insurance is a funding arrangement that helps an individual, commonly an employee, obtain life insurance at a lower outlay than otherwise would be possible, by sharing (splitting) the premium payments and policy benefits between two parties. It is a funding method, not a type of policy. The objective of split dollar plans is to join together the needs of one person with the premium paying ability of another. Specifically, the parties purchase an insurance policy on the life of the employee and agree, in writing, to split the premium payments as well as the policy's death proceeds and cash value. The concept works with any cash value policy, including WL, UL, and second-to-die policies.

Choice of Split Dollar Plans

Split dollar plans commonly take one of two forms: endorsement or collateral assignment. Under the **endorsement approach,** insurance on the employee's life is applied for and owned by the employer that is primarily responsible for premium payments. The employer is beneficiary for that portion of the proceeds equal to its premium payments. The policy is endorsed to provide that the employee designates the beneficiary to receive the remainder of the death proceeds. The employer is considered by the IRS as providing a taxable "economic benefit" to the employee equal to the value of those death proceeds plus the cash value (if any) to which he or she has access that was not taken into income in prior years. Any portion of premiums paid by the employee is netted against these taxable amounts.

If the plan is terminated prior to the death of the insured employee, the employer recovers its premium outlay directly from the cash value that it controls as owner of the policy. This may be accomplished by surrendering the policy or giving the insured employee the option to purchase it for an amount equal to its cash surrender value.

Under the **collateral assignment approach**, the insured employee applies for and owns the policy and is primarily responsible for premium payments. The employee designates his or her own personal beneficiary. In a separate agreement, the employer obligates itself to lend the employee the agreed upon amount of each premium. This loan may be interest free, but income taxes will be due on the loan interest foregone, based on the applicable federal interest rate. The employee is responsible for additional premiums, if any. The employee collaterally assigns the policy to the employer as security for the loan. At the insured employee's death, the employer recovers the amount of its loan from the death proceeds, not as a beneficiary of the policy, but as a collateral assignee.

The approach recommended by the agent or planner will be influenced by several factors. A fundamental issue is whether the employer or employee controls the policy. If the employer wants the cash value available for use in its business, the endorsement approach is preferable. If the employee is not an officer or shareholder, the endorsement method may be preferable to the employer as a means of retaining key employees. Also, the endorsement approach is ordinarily recommended if the parties intend the policy to fund a nonqualified retirement arrangement (see below).

Tax Consequences of Split Dollar Plans

Split dollar life insurance plans are subject to complex tax rules, the totality of which is well beyond the scope of this short overview. As noted above, the typical split dollar plan results in a taxable economic benefit to the employee. This benefit is determined by reference to a set of IRS-prescribed rates, called the Table 2001 rates or, if lower, the insurer's rates for term policies that it sells. Premiums paid by an employer on insurance covering the life of an employee and for which the employer is directly or indirectly a beneficiary under the policy are not tax deductible. Death proceeds ordinarily are received income tax free provided EOLI exceptions and requirements are met with respect to endorsement split dollar.

Insurance death proceeds are included in the gross estate of a decedent/insured if he or she possessed any incidents of policy ownership or if proceeds are payable to or for the benefit of the insured's estate. Under the usual endorsement system, the employer is the sole owner of the life insurance policy. To protect the insured employee's rights under the agreement, the ownership rights of the employer are modified by an endorsement that provides that the insured employee's personal beneficiary cannot be changed without the insured employee's consent. This is an incident of ownership. This ownership right might be avoided if the agreement provides that the beneficiary cannot be changed without the consent of the beneficiary, rather than of the insured. Even if the death proceeds are included in the insured's gross estate, they should qualify for the unlimited marital deduction if they are paid to the surviving spouse.

Under the collateral assignment system, the insured employee often is the policyowner, so full policy death proceeds less amounts owed to the employer via the collateral assignment would be included in his or her gross estate. If the employee wishes to avoid inclusion of the proceeds in his or her gross estate, the beneficiary for the insured/employee's share of the proceeds commonly applies for and owns the life insurance policy. The owner/beneficiary may be a trust, the insured's spouse, or any other third party.

Any split dollar plan between a corporation and a majority shareholder/ employee/insured can be expected to result in death proceeds payable to a beneficiary other than the corporation being included in the gross estate of the insured. This result is based on an estate tax regulation that imputes the incidents of ownership possessed by a corporation in an insurance policy on the life of a majority shareholder to the shareholder to the extent that the proceeds are not payable to or for the benefit of the corporation. There are ways to avoid this result, but their examination is beyond the scope of this short discussion. Proceeds payable to the corporation are not included in the shareholder's estate but are considered in establishing the value of the decedent's stock.

Split Dollar Plan Variations

Agents and planners will craft their recommended split dollar life insurance plans to fit each set of facts. Several different arrangements are found, with varying premium splits. Additionally, split dollar plans are commonly recommended in situations other than as a nonqualified benefit for important employees. Some other split dollar uses are shown in Box 12-2.

BOX 12-2: Split Dollar Life Insurance Variations

In addition to the traditional use of split dollar life insurance as a nonqualified executive benefit, it also has been found effective in the following situations:

Sole Proprietor Buyout. A sole proprietor may not have any family members to whom he or she wants to leave the business at death and no outsider is interested in purchasing it. In such a situation, the business owner may offer to sell the business to an interested employee at the business owner's death. To solve the problem of the employee having insufficient funds, the employer may enter into a split dollar plan with the employee, with insurance on the life of the employer.

Split Dollar in a Cross Purchase Buy/Sell Agreement. One drawback to the use of a cross purchase buy/sell agreement is that the shareholders are personally responsible for the payment of premiums on insurance used to fund the plan. One solution is to have the corporation help finance the purchase of needed insurance through a split dollar plan. The arrangement proceeds as usual, with the exception that each shareholder collaterally assigns the policies that he or she owns on other shareholder's lives to the corporation as security for the corporation's loans.

Split Dollar in a Nonqualified Retirement Plan. A split dollar arrangement can provide the mechanism for informally funding a nonqualified retirement plan (see below). Policy values provide the means from which payments ultimately are made or the employer reimbursed.

Family Split Dollar. Parents or grandparents wishing to assist a family member in the purchase of life insurance and not wishing to reduce the share of their estates to be passed on to others may find a split dollar approach appealing. As this is not an employer/employee arrangement, there should be no taxable income.

Nonqualified Retirement Plans

Agents and planners often will recommend the use of life insurance in informal funding for nonqualified retirement plans. These plans offer employers advantages and disadvantages relative to qualified plans. Advantages include being able to select the key employees who will participate in the plans without fear of running afoul of ERISA nondiscrimination requirements. Additionally, administrative expenses of nonqualified plans should be less than those of qualified plans. The main disadvantage from the employer's perspective is not being able to take immediate tax deductions for plan funding. Two common such plans are:

- Nonqualified deferred compensation plans, and
- Supplemental executive retirement plans.

Nonqualified Deferred Compensation Plans

A **nonqualified deferred compensation plan** is a contractual arrangement under which compensation for services rendered is postponed, usually until retirement. The employee will not pay tax on these deferred amounts until they are received (e.g., at retirement), when the individual may be in a lower marginal income tax bracket. The employer does not obtain an income tax deduction for these payments until such time as payments actually are made.

The plan may be either employer or employee initiated. In both instances, the idea is to postpone some portion of present compensation or raises or bonuses, in return for which the employer agrees to pay an income in the future, often at a rate augmented by interest. If the plan is employee initiated, the employer and employee agree to postpone compensation to which the employee otherwise is entitled to avoid present income taxation to the employee and to save for retirement. Employer-initiated plans often are intended as a supplemental benefit to encourage retention of highly valued employees. They function in the same way as employee-initiated plans.

Funding for the payment of the deferred compensation is not directly linked to the obligation for tax reasons. Agents and planners often recommend the use of life insurance as the informal funding device. The employer applies for, owns, and is beneficiary of the policy. The employee or employer will have selected a specific amount or percentage of the executive's compensation to be deferred. The employer may view premiums on the policy as deriving from these deferred sums. Policy cash values accumulate at competitive interest rates on a tax deferred basis.

At retirement, the employer makes withdrawals, initiates policy loans, and/or surrenders portions or the entirety of the policy to fund its retirement income obligation to the employee. If the employee dies while employed, life insurance death proceeds would be received by the employer income tax free provided EOLI exceptions and requirements as discussed earlier were met and could be used to fund any death-related obligations under the plan, to reimburse the employer for premiums paid, or to fund retirement benefits for other executives.

A deferred compensation plan variation—a **death benefit only** (DBO) **plan**—promises to pay an income benefit to the employee's survivor on the employee's death. No retirement benefit is promised, often because the employee will have an adequate retirement income from a qualified plan. DBO plans are less costly than other forms of deferred compensation plans and usually are intended to help retain employees. Life insurance again is a natural funding medium.

Supplemental Executive Retirement Plans

A **supplemental executive retirement plan** (SERP) is a nonqualified retirement plan that provides retirement benefits to selected employees only. Some SERPs provide a flat amount per year to participating employees. Other SERPs—called **excess SERPs**—provide a benefit amount equal to the difference between (1) the full amount under its qualified retirement benefit formula that would be paid to the executive but ignoring any ERISA-imposed limits and (2) the actual retirement benefits payable to the executive under the qualified retirement plan and Social Security. Another popular SERP—called a **target SERP**—is intended to replace retirement benefits lost by ERISA-imposed limits *and* counteract the bias in Social Security retirement benefits in favor of low income workers.

Life insurance is often the recommended informal SERP funding device. As with nonqualified deferred compensation plans, the employer applies for, owns, and is beneficiary of the policy. The policy death benefit and premiums are determined by the retirement benefit promised to the executive. Otherwise, the policy payout options on death and in life are the same as with deferred comp plans, with taxation also being the same.

Group Term Carve Outs

Group term life insurance is a popular if largely ignored tax qualified employee benefit. Premiums are deductible to the employer, and the employee is not taxed on the first $50,000 of coverage. The value of amounts in excess of $50,000 is taxable income to employees. The value is determined by applying the IRS's Table 1 rates to these excess amounts.

Table 1 rates increase with increasing age, which means that older employees face ever-increasing taxable income from their employer-provided group term life insurance. The amount of group insurance for which an employee is eligible often is some multiple of his or her salary, such as three times. Executives, who tend to be both older and more highly compensated than other employees, may be required to take substantial amounts into their taxable income from this employee benefit. Further, as rates are pooled for group life insurance, the cost to the employer of including even a small number of older, highly-paid employees can have a significant effect on overall plan costs.

These factors led to the development of the **group term carve out** (GTCO) concept in which older, higher-paid employees are "carved out" of the group plan and are instead provided with cash value life insurance. The process is simple. The amount of group term coverage on highly paid executives is reduced to $50,000. At a minimum, what the employer would have paid for the group term coverage in excess of $50,000 is applied toward the premiums for a permanent policy owned by the employee, not the employer. The payment is still deductible to the business and now taxable to the employee as direct compensation, instead of Table 1 "compensation."

Advantages of this approach include the fact that the increasing amounts that executives must take into taxable income now go toward premiums to purchase insurance that builds cash values. Alternatively, the employer can set a level premium payment, thus insulating the group term program from the high cost of providing large amounts of life insurance on highly paid employees. For owner/employees, the insurance becomes a source of both death protection and cash value buildup that can be important for retirement and other living purposes.

Conclusions

Individually issued life insurance policies have been used creatively and effectively in businesses for decades. They are used to hedge the business against financial loss occasioned by the death of individuals whose services are essential to its success. Life insurance is routinely used to facilitate the smooth transition of closely held business ownership interests through buy/sell agreements while (1) sparing heirs the angst of deciding how to deal with that interest and (2) providing certainty to surviving owners. Life insurance also is often recommended to informally fund various nonqualified executive benefit programs, allowing the business to provide executives with tangible proof of their perceived worth to the business. These and other business applications of life insurance seem likely, not only to continue, but perhaps to gain even more prominence as both regulation and tax rates grow.

Life Insurance Illustrations and the Sustainability of Policy Values

Part

V

Life Insurance Policy Illustrations* | 13

THIS CHAPTER BEGINS THE *Guide's* Part V, a four-chapter analysis describing and assessing life insurance policy illustrations. We first provide a general description of life insurance policy illustrations, followed by uses of illustrations, and then the importance of the non-guaranteed nature of illustrations. The core of the chapter reviews the content of policy illustrations, including examples. The remaining chapters in this section explore the assumptions behind illustrations, the sustainability of illustrated policy values, considerations for illustration design, and methods for comparing illustrated policy performance.

Overview of a Policy Illustration

A life insurance policy illustration is typically thought of as the illustrated policy values of planned premium, account value, surrender value, and death benefit, collectively referred to as the tabular detail. Table 13-1 is a sample abbreviated tabular detail for a universal life (UL) policy. In addition, transactions such as partial surrenders, withdrawals, and loans would also be included in the tabular detail if applicable.

In addition to the tabular detail, policy illustrations also contain other valuable information such as a description of the policy (including policy mechanics and assumptions), descriptions

---

*Authored by Wayne Tonning.

TABLE 13-1
Sample Abbreviated Universal Life Tabular Detail

Yr	Age	Premium Outlay	Guaranteed Values (EOY) @ 3.00%			Non-Guaranteed Values (EOY) @ 5.45%		
			Account Value	Surrender Value	Death Benefit	Account Value	Surrender Value	Death Benefit
1	70	50,551	10,238	0	1,000,000	39,469	19,079	1,000,000
2	71	50,551	17,850	0	1,000,000	79,085	60,961	1,000,000
3	72	50,551	23,459	7,600	1,000,000	119,775	103,917	1,000,000
4	73	50,551	26,786	13,193	1,000,000	161,512	147,919	1,000,000
5	74	50,551	27,673	16,346	1,000,000	204,552	193,225	1,000,000
6	75	50,551	11,373	2,311	1,000,000	249,807	240,745	1,000,000
7	76	50,551	0	0	0	296,874	290,078	1,000,000
8	77	50,551	0	0	0	346,150	341,619	1,000,000
9	78	50,551	0	0	0	397,945	395,679	1,000,000
10	79	50,551	0	0	0	452,427	452,427	1,000,000

of available riders and policy options, tax information, and definitions of key terms. Supplemental and concept reports may also be provided by the illustration software and are reviewed later in this chapter.

Uses of Policy Illustrations

Life insurance illustrations generally have five primary uses:

1. To show the buyer the mechanics of the policy (see Chapter 7).
2. To review funding and coverage levels, uses of riders and policy options, and risk tolerance by varying the non-guaranteed elements and assessing resulting illustrated policy values (see Chapter 15).
3. To compare the cost or illustrated performance of different policies (see Chapter 16).
4. To provide a baseline for ongoing policy management in order to keep the policy on track (see Chapter 17).
5. To show how the policy fits into the policyholder's financial plan (see Chapters 10–12).

Non-Guaranteed Nature of Illustrations and Why Important

Illustrated policy values (i.e., account value, surrender value, death benefit, policy loans, etc.) are dependent upon assumptions for policy charges and credits (such as interest). Illustrations may not represent what actual policy performance will be over time if the assumptions for loads and credits applied to the policy are subject to change by the insurer. Illustrations also must provide illustrated policy values based on guaranteed elements. However, more attention is usually paid to non-guaranteed or current illustrated values as those are typically expected to be more representative of actual policy performance than illustrated values based on guaranteed elements.

Recall that guaranteed policy elements are the contractually guaranteed maximum charges and minimum credits and may not be changed unilaterally by the insurer. Actual loads and credits applied to the policy may not be less favorable than the guaranteed elements.

Non-guaranteed policy elements, also called current assumptions and non-guaranteed assumptions, are the actual charges and credits currently being applied to the policy as of the policy illustration date. Current assumptions are not guaranteed (but are constrained by the guaranteed elements). Current assumptions are based on current company experience for mortality, investment earnings, expenses, and lapses. Current assumptions may change as emerging company experience changes (for better or worse). As an example, if emerging investment earnings are 20 basis points (bps) lower than what is currently reflected in the crediting rate, the insurer may lower the current crediting rate by 20 bps. Or if mortality experience improves, the insurer may decide to lower the cost of insurance (COI) charges. Chapter 14 covers illustration assumptions in more detail.

Non-guaranteed policy elements may not be illustrated as more favorable than the current assumptions or less favorable than the guaranteed elements. For UL illustrations, typically the charge (also referred to as load) assumptions are specified as either current or guaranteed. However, the interest crediting rate for UL and the dividend interest rate for whole life (WL) can be specified to be any rate ranging from the guaranteed minimum rate to the current rate.

Also, policyholder actions can affect policy values. If actual premiums are paid later or earlier than originally illustrated, if a premium is missed, or if a payment amount differs from the original illustration, resulting policy values will be different. Changes to or the exercise of policy options and riders, such as policy loans and face amount changes and turning on an overloan protection rider can also impact policy values.

As noted in Chapter 7, illustrations for participating whole life (WL) policies will include the current dividend scale in effect as of the preparation date of the illustration. As with the current assumptions for UL, the current dividend scale for WL can also be changed by the insurer based on emerging insurer experience. This illustrated scale may not be more favorable than dividends actually being paid under such policies. All other elements of par WL policies are guaranteed.

The non-guaranteed nature of illustrations is critically important to the potential policyowner as:

1. Illustrated values are not guaranteed and are subject to change (for better or worse) based on emerging experience (see Chapter 14);

2. Illustrated values may not be sustainable because current assumptions are not sustainable based on current experience, thereby subjecting the policy to an increased likelihood of less favorable policy performance (see Chapter 14);

3. The illustration design should consider providing cushion for the potential of less favorable current assumption changes (see Chapter 15); and

4. Ongoing policy management after policy issue is needed in order to deal with changing current assumptions or policyholder actions (see Chapter 17).

Content of Policy Illustrations

Life insurance illustrations used in the sale of a life insurance policy must satisfy the applicable requirements of illustration regulations. Illustration regulations provide rules for life insurance policy illustrations that protect consumers and foster consumer education. The goals of these regulations are to ensure that illustrations do not mislead purchasers of life insurance and to make illustrations more understandable. Illustrations used in the sale of a life insurance policy must be signed by the applicant and agent and included in the application package sent to the insurer. Separate regulations apply to non-variable and variable life insurance illustrations.

Non-Variable Life Insurance Illustrations

Non-variable life insurance illustrations must comply with the *Life Insurance Illustrations Model Regulation*, as adopted by the *National Association of Insurance Commissioners* (NAIC) and by state insurance commissioners. (Recall from Chapter 4 that insurance is regulated by the individual states.) As provided by the illustration model regulation, non-variable life insurance illustrations must contain a tabular detail, a narrative summary, and a numeric summary. Supplemental reports may also be provided, samples of which are provided later in the chapter.

Tabular Detail

When advisors and agents think about life insurance illustrations, most mainly consider or review the tabular detail (also referred to as "ledger pages"). The **tabular detail** must show the planned (in the case of UL) or contract (in the case of WL) policy premiums along with the guaranteed death benefits and surrender values for at least each policy year from one to ten and every fifth policy year thereafter for the possible policy duration; policy values based on current assumptions may also be included (and they almost always are so included). The illustrated non-guaranteed values are to be based on current assumptions or on assumptions less favorable than the current assumptions but no worse than the guaranteed elements. For example, if the current crediting rate is 5 percent and the guaranteed minimum crediting rate is 3 percent, a non-guaranteed illustrated crediting rate assumption from 5 percent to 3 percent must be used. Assumptions more favorable than current assumptions are not allowed.

Reviewing the tabular detail is important as it shows illustrated policy values (typically for all policy years), which can be used for policy performance comparisons and to show how insurance will fit into an estate or business plan. The tabular detail is also critical in determining appropriate policy design and showing downside risk potential via less favorable assumption changes.

Table 13-2 provides a sample tabular detail illustration for a UL policy (see Chapter 7) from a prominent life insurance carrier. After the table, notes are provided that describe each numbered item in the tabular detail. Sample tabular detail illustrations for other policy types (term, whole life, no-lapse guarantee universal life, and equity index universal life) are provided in appendices 4, 5, 6, and 7.

TABLE 13-2
Example Universal Life—Tabular Detail

(1) ABC Life Insurance Company			(2) UL 123—Life Insurance Illustration
			(3) Flexible Premium Adjustable Life Insurance Policy
			(4) Form # EFG—For Presentation in CA
(5) Insured Name	(8) Death Benefit Option = A		(11) Producer Name & Address
(6) Male, Age 70	(9) Total Face Amount = $1,000,000		
(7) Nonsmoker	(10) Premium Frequency = Annual		(12) Run: 10/01/2010

Basic Illustration Tabular Detail

			Guaranteed Values (EOY) @ 3.00%			Non-Guaranteed Values (EOY) @ 5.45%		
			(16)			(17)		
Yr	BOY Age	Premium Outlay	Account Value	Surrender Value	Death Benefit	Account Value	Surrender Value	Death Benefit
(13)	(14)	(15)	(18)	(19)	(20)	(18)	(19)	(20)
1	70	50,551	10,238	0	1,000,000	39,469	19,079	1,000,000
2	71	50,551	17,850	0	1,000,000	79,085	60,961	1,000,000
3	72	50,551	23,459	7,600	1,000,000	119,775	103,917	1,000,000
4	73	50,551	26,786	13,193	1,000,000	161,512	147,919	1,000,000
5	74	50,551	27,673	16,346	1,000,000	204,552	193,225	1,000,000
6	75	50,551	11,373	2,311	1,000,000	249,807	240,745	1,000,000
7	76	50,551	0	0	0	296,874	290,078	1,000,000
8	77	50,551	0	0	0	346,150	341,619	1,000,000
9	78	50,551	0	0	0	397,945	395,679	1,000,000
10	79	50,551	0	0	0	452,427	452,427	1,000,000
11	80	0	0	0	0	466,776	466,776	1,000,000
12	81	0	0	0	0	480,726	480,726	1,000,000

13	82	0	0	0	0	494,112	494,112	1,000,000
14	83	0	0	0	0	506,739	506,739	1,000,000
15	84	0	0	0	0	518,369	518,369	1,000,000
16	85	0	0	0	0	529,217	529,217	1,000,000
17	86	0	0	0	0	539,337	539,337	1,000,000
18	87	0	0	0	0	548,561	548,561	1,000,000
19	88	0	0	0	0	556,684	556,684	1,000,000
20	89	0	0	0	0	563,458	563,458	1,000,000
21	90	0	0	0	0	569,049	569,049	1,000,000
22	91	0	0	0	0	571,898	571,898	1,000,000
23	92	0	0	0	0	574,036	574,036	1,000,000
24	93	0	0	0	0	575,810	575,810	1,000,000
25	94	0	0	0	0	577,820	577,820	1,000,000
26	95	0	0	0	0	580,098	580,098	1,000,000
27	96	0	0	0	0	582,680	582,680	1,000,000
28	97	0	0	0	0	585,604	585,604	1,000,000
29	98	0	0	0	0	588,918	588,918	1,000,000
30	99	0	0	0	0	592,673	592,673	1,000,000
31	100	0	0	0	0	596,928	596,928	1,000,000
32	101	0	0	0	0	601,749	601,749	1,000,000
33	102	0	0	0	0	607,211	607,211	1,000,000
34	103	0	0	0	0	613,400	613,400	1,000,000
35	104	0	0	0	0	620,413	620,413	1,000,000
36	105	0	0	0	0	628,359	628,359	1,000,000
37	106	0	0	0	0	637,363	637,363	1,000,000
38	107	0	0	0	0	647,564	647,564	1,000,000
39	108	0	0	0	0	659,123	659,123	1,000,000
40	109	0	0	0	0	672,221	672,221	1,000,000
41	110	0	0	0	0	687,061	687,061	1,000,000
42	111	0	0	0	0	703,877	703,877	1,000,000
43	112	0	0	0	0	722,930	722,930	1,000,000
44	113	0	0	0	0	744,518	744,518	1,000,000
45	114	0	0	0	0	768,980	768,980	1,000,000
46	115	0	0	0	0	796,697	796,697	1,000,000
47	116	0	0	0	0	828,102	828,102	1,000,000
48	117	0	0	0	0	863,686	863,686	1,000,000
49	118	0	0	0	0	904,006	904,006	1,000,000
50	119	0	0	0	0	949,691	949,691	1,000,000
51	120	0	0	0	0	1,001,402	1,001,402	1,011,416

(21) Insurance coverage will cease in year 7 based on guaranteed elements. Insurance coverage would remain in force through year 51 (age 120) based on illustrated assumptions.

(22) A zero in the Premium Outlay column does not mean the policy is paid up. Charges will continue to be deducted from the Account Value as long as the policy remains in force. The actual premium amounts and number of years of premium payments that are needed to maintain the illustrated non-guaranteed policy benefits will depend on the policy's non-guaranteed elements and on your actual use of the policy's options.

UL Tabular Detail Notes

1) Name of insurer
2) Product name
3) Product description
4) Policy form (as filed with the state insurance department) and state of issue (California). The issue state should correspond to the state where the policyowner resides or does business.

5) Insured name

6) Insured gender and issue age. The issue age is either age nearest birthday (ANB) or age last birthday (ALB) as of the policy issue date. Most insurers use ANB while others use ALB. ALB may be advantageous for insureds who qualify for a one year younger issue age as compared to ANB.

7) Insured underwriting class as identified by smoker status. There may be multiple nonsmoker and smoker underwriting categories that are designated by the insured's health.

8) Death benefit option A signifies a level death benefit. Other options may include an option B, which is equal to the total face amount plus the account value and option C, which is equal to the total face amount plus the cumulative premiums paid less any withdrawals.

9) The total initial face amount includes both basic and term coverage.

10) The premium frequency is annual, which assumes an annual premium being paid on the policy anniversary date (i.e., beginning of the policy year). Other premium frequency (mode) options may include semi-annual, quarterly, and monthly.

11) The producer's (agent's) name and address.

12) The date the illustration was prepared. Since products and rates can change regularly, the advisor should verify that the illustration is current as of the review date.

13) Policy year as defined by the policy anniversary date.

14) The insured's age as of the beginning of the policy year shown. Some illustrations provide the age as of the end of the policy year.

15) The planned premium paid during the specified policy year. With universal life, the amount and frequency of premium payments are flexible, within limits. If resulting premiums are insufficient, then coverage terminates when the account value goes to zero. For this example, ten annual premiums are targeted to provide an account value equal to the death benefit at end of age 120 based on current assumptions.

16) Illustrated policy values in this section are based on guaranteed policy elements for interest credited and charges deducted. Actual charges assessed may not exceed the guaranteed charges and actual interest credited may not be less than the guaranteed minimum credited interest rate. Values shown are as of the end of the policy year (EOY). The guaranteed minimum credited interest rate is 3.00 percent. For this example, coverage ceases in policy year 7 based on guaranteed elements.

17) Illustrated policy values in this section are based on non-guaranteed policy elements for interest credited and charges deducted. Non-guaranteed illustrated assumptions may not be more favorable than the current assumptions or less favorable than the guaranteed elements. Current assumptions are the actual charges and credits being applied to the policy as of the illustration preparation date and are subject to change (but may not be less favorable than the guaranteed elements). Values shown are as of the end of the policy year (EOY). The illustrated credited interest rate is 5.45 percent. While illustrated elements used in this example are the current assumptions, it is not specified. For this example, the account value equals the death benefit at end of age 120 with current assumptions.

18) Account Value: Equal to the sum of premiums paid less all charges and withdrawals plus credited or accrued interest since the policy effective date. The account value provides the base for interest credits. This is not the amount available to the policyowner upon surrender (see surrender value below). Account value may also be referred to as accumulated value.

19) Surrender Value: Equal to the account value minus any applicable surrender charge. The amount paid to the policyowner upon surrender is the surrender value less any outstanding policy debt. Some products have no surrender charges while other products may have surrender charges for twenty years or more. This product has surrender charges for nine years.

20) Death Benefit: The amount payable to the beneficiary upon the insured's death (but will be reduced by any outstanding policy debt). For this example, the death benefit is level due to a designated death benefit option A (see (8). The death benefit will remain level unless the cash value grows to an amount that forces the death benefit to increase according to the definition of life insurance test. The death benefit may never be less than the account value.

21) Footnote specifying the year coverage ceases based on guaranteed elements and coverage remaining in force for life based on illustrated assumptions.

22) The illustrated premium outlay does not guarantee coverage for life. Resulting coverage depends upon future non-guaranteed elements (which may change) and future actual premiums paid. Changes in policy options, such as withdrawals, will also impact coverage.

Narrative Summary

Non-variable life illustrations must also contain a narrative summary. A **narrative summary** contains valuable information about the illustrated policy including descriptions of its benefits and mechanics, available riders and policy options, and identification and descriptions of column headings and key terms used in the illustrations. In addition to gaining a better understanding of how a policy works and the options provided, a narrative summary should be reviewed to understand policy differences that go beyond the illustrated numbers. As examples, guarantees can be important distinguishing features, such as a short term no-lapse guarantee rider that is automatically included at no additional premium, a bonus interest rate that is guaranteed, or a higher guaranteed minimum crediting rate than that of another policy. Other distinguishing items may be a late payment provision that automatically backdates late premium payments or an unlimited catch-up provision for guarantee purposes in a no-lapse guarantee policy (see Chapter 9). If the narrative summary is not reviewed, the advisor may be unaware of non-numerical distinguishing features and could miss valuable policy options.

Narrative summaries typically are many pages in length. To provide more detail on the information found in narrative summaries, we provide abbreviated commentaries on examples as seen in UL illustrations. Narrative summaries vary in content and format depending on the insurer and the policy type.

- Information about the *insured*: issue age, gender and risk classification.
- Summary of *coverage*: total face amount, death benefit option selected, premium frequency and illustrated riders.
- Description of *how the policy works*: flexible premium and adjustable death benefit with charges and interest credit applied to the account value, death benefit paid to the beneficiary at the insured's death, surrender charge may be applied to the account value if the policy is surrendered, and distributions in the form of withdrawals and loans can be made.
- Assumptions about *non-guaranteed policy elements*: some policy elements may be changed by the insurer at any time and for any reason, but cannot be less favorable to the policyowner than the policy's guaranteed policy elements. Some non-guaranteed elements are illustrated consistently with the insurer's current scale and are labeled as "current." Values shown in this illustration are based on non-guaranteed policy charges and non-guaranteed crediting rates. Over time, the policy's actual non-guaranteed elements are likely to vary from the assumptions used in this illustration. For these reasons, actual policy values will either be more or less favorable than shown in this illustration.

- Description of *death benefit*: the death benefit paid is equal to the total death benefit, which is comprised of base and term coverages and is impacted by the death benefit option less the amount of outstanding policy debt. This section also explains the term coverages and death benefit options that are available and how they affect policy performance.
- Description of *premium*: timing and frequency of payment, an explanation that deviations to the planned premium schedule will impact policy values, and evidence of insurability may be required for any premium paid that causes the death benefit to increase.
- Description of *crediting rate*: the amount of the current crediting rate (X.XX%), the period for which it is guaranteed, rate may be changed after the guarantee period but subject to the guaranteed minimum crediting rate (Y.YY%), interest is credited monthly, and a description of when any non-guaranteed bonus interest rate (0.ZZ%) is applied.
- Description of the *account value*: equal to sum of premiums paid plus interest credited and charges deducted, current interest and charges are not guaranteed but may not be less favorable than the guaranteed elements, coverage will terminate if charges exceed the account value unless additional premium is paid, and a description of the guarantee period for the current COI rates.
- Description of the *surrender value*: equal to the account value less a surrender charge, the net surrender value is available upon surrender and is the surrender value net of any outstanding loan balance, and a description of how the surrender charge is applied.
- Description of *policy loans*: describes the mechanics of a loan, including the maximum loan amount available, net loan interest rate, and disclosure that the loan interest rate is subject to change.
- Description of *withdrawals*: withdrawals will reduce the account value and death benefit.
- Description of *available riders*: includes rider names only and commentary that the producer can provide additional information and illustrations with the riders illustrated.
- Description of *illustrated riders*: description of benefits and costs of riders reflected in the illustration.
- *Tax* information: description of tax liability on death and surrender proceeds, a description of the definition of life insurance (DOLI) test, a description of a modified endowment contract (MEC) test, and commentary that failure of either test will result in adverse tax consequences. See Chapter 7.
- Definitions of *key terms*: account value, surrender value, death benefit, guaranteed columns, illustrated columns, policy debt, premium outlay, etc.

Numeric Summary

A numeric summary is also required in non-variable illustrations. A **numeric summary** provides a condensed one-page summary of illustrated policy values using three required assumption bases: guaranteed, intermediate, and current. **Intermediate assumptions** are the average of the guaranteed and illustrated assumptions. Non-guaranteed illustrated assumptions may not be more favorable than the current assumptions or less favorable than the guaranteed elements. The numeric summary must be signed by the applicant and agent and included in the application package sent to the insurer. Table 13-3 provides a sample numeric summary for a UL contract of a prominent life insurance carrier. Notes that describe each lettered item in the tabular detail are provided.

TABLE 13-3
Example Universal Life—Numeric Summary

| | | | Guaranteed (EOY) 3.00% (a) | | | Non-Guaranteed (EOY) | | | | |
| | | | | | | Intermediate (b) | | Illustrated 5.45% (c) | | |
Yr (d)	Age (e)	Cumulative Premium Outlay (f)	Cash Surrender Value (g)	Death Benefit (h)		Cash Surrender Value (g)	Death Benefit (h)	Cash Surrender Value (g)	Death Benefit (h)	
5	54	106,565	22,591	1,000,000		56,200	1,000,000	91,558	1,000,000	
10	59	213,130	35,805	1,000,000		123,139	1,000,000	218,480	1,000,000	
20	69	213,130	0	1,000,000		0	1,000,000	324,437	1,000,000	
30	79	213,130	##	##		##	##	451,046	1,000,000	

(i) Insurance coverage will cease in year 21 based on guaranteed elements. Insurance coverage will cease in year 21 based on intermediate assumptions. Insurance coverage would remain in force at least through year 71 (Age 120) based on illustrated assumptions.

(j) I have received and read a copy of this illustration and understand that any non-guaranteed elements illustrated are subject to change and could be higher or lower. The producer has told me that they are not guaranteed. I understand this is an illustration and not a contract. For full policy details, I will refer to the contract.

APPLICANT'S SIGNATURE   DATE
I certify that this illustration has been presented to the applicant and that I have explained that any non-guaranteed elements are subject to change. I have made no statements that are inconsistent with this illustration.

PRODUCER'S SIGNATURE   DATE

Numeric Summary Notes

(a) Guaranteed Values: Illustrated policy values in this section are based on guaranteed elements for interest credited and charges deducted. Actual charges assessed may not exceed the guaranteed charges and actual interest credited may not be less than the guaranteed minimum credited interest rate. Values shown are as of the end of the policy year (EOY). The guaranteed minimum credited interest rate is 3.00 percent.

(b) Non-Guaranteed Intermediate Values: Illustrated policy values in this section are based on non-guaranteed assumptions for interest credited and charges deducted. The non-guaranteed intermediate assumption for the credited interest rate is the average of the illustrated crediting rate (5.45 percent) and the guaranteed minimum crediting rate (3.00 percent), which is approximately 4.23 percent. The non-guaranteed intermediate assumption for charges is the average of the illustrated charges and the guaranteed maximum charges. Values shown are as of the end of the policy year (EOY).

(c) Non-Guaranteed Illustrated Values: Illustrated policy values in this section are based on non-guaranteed illustrated assumptions for interest credited and charges deducted. Non-guaranteed illustrated assumptions may not be more favorable than the current assumptions or less favorable than the guaranteed elements. Current assumptions are the actual charges and credits being applied to the policy as of the illustration preparation date and are subject to change (but may not be less favorable than the guaranteed elements). Values shown are as of the end of the policy year (EOY). The illustrated credited interest rate is 5.45 percent. While illustrated assumptions used in this example are the current assumptions, it is not specified.

(d) Yr: The policy year as defined by the policy anniversary date.

(e) Age: The proposed insured's age as of the beginning of the policy year shown. Some illustrations provide the age as of the end of the policy year.

(f) Cumulative Premium Outlay: Equal to the sum of the planned premium payments from policy year 1 through the current policy year as shown.

(g) Cash Surrender Value: Equal to the account value minus any applicable surrender charge. The amount payable to the policyholder upon surrender will be equal to the cash surrender value less any outstanding policy debt.

(h) Death Benefit: The amount payable to the beneficiary upon the insured's death. The death benefit is always reduced by any outstanding policy debt and increased by any applicable rider benefits.

(i) Required disclosure statement on how long the policy stays in force based on the three different assumptions.

(j) Required signature statements.

Supplemental Illustrations

A supplemental illustration may be provided in an illustration so long as:

1. It is appended to a basic illustration;
2. The non-guaranteed values shown are not more favorable than the values provided by the current assumptions;
3. It contains the same statement required by a basic illustration that non-guaranteed elements are not guaranteed;
4. The premium outlay shall be identical to the premium outlay shown in the basic illustration; and
5. It includes a notice referring to the basic illustration for guaranteed elements and other important information.

Examples of supplemental illustrations include:

- **Internal Rate of Return Illustration**—a hypothetical illustration showing the internal rate of return on death benefit and cash value. As discussed more fully in Chapter 16, the **internal rate of return** (IRR) as applied to life insurance gives a measure of illustrated performance that is derived by solving for the interest rate that causes accumulated scheduled premiums (net of dividends, if appropriate) at selected policy durations to equal that duration's death benefit and its cash surrender. An example is provided in Table 13-4.

TABLE 13-4
Abbreviated Example IRR Illustration

Year	Age		Non-Guaranteed Values (EOY) @ 5.45%				
		Premium Outlay	Account Value	Surrender Value	Death Benefit	Surrender Value IRR	Death Benefit IRR
1	50	21,313	17,508	9,259	1,000,000	−56.55%	4591.97%
10	59	21,313	218,480	218,480	1,000,000	0.45%	27.10%
20	69	0	324,437	324,437	1,000,000	2.73%	10.21%
30	79	0	451,046	451,046	1,000,000	2.97%	6.19%
50	99	0	592,585	592,585	1,000,000	2.27%	3.45%
71	120	0	1,000,206	1,000,206	1,010,208	2.35%	2.36%

◆ **Breakout of Policy Charges**—a hypothetical UL illustration showing the breakout of annual charges and credits to the account value. This illustration is helpful for understanding the impact of the different policy charges and credits on policy values. Sometimes it is used in policy comparisons to help understand why one policy illustrates as performing better than another one. It can also be used for in-force policy performance reviews to better understand why product performance has changed. An example is provided Table 13-5.

The charges and interest credit add to the ending surrender value. As an example, for policy year 2, the surrender value is equal to the account value from the previous year (policy year 1) plus premium paid, less charges, plus interest credited:

$$\underset{17{,}508}{AV} + \underset{21{,}313}{Premium} - \underset{1{,}268}{Expense} - \underset{90}{Admin} - \underset{2{,}964}{Coverage} - \underset{612}{COI} + \underset{1{,}939}{Interest} - \underset{7{,}332}{Surrender} = \underset{28{,}494}{\overset{Surrender}{Value}}$$

◆ **Loan Details Report**—a hypothetical illustration showing the loan amount, loan interest, total debt, net surrender value, and net death benefit. This report is designed to facilitate an understanding of the mechanics behind loans.

TABLE 13-5
Abbreviated Example Breakout of Policy Charges Illustration

Policy Year	Premium Outlay	Non-Guaranteed							
		Expense Charge	Admin Charge	Coverage Charge	Cost of Insurance	Interest Credit	Account Value	Surrender Charge	Surrender Value
1	21,313	−1,268	−90	−2,964	−472	989	17,508	8,249	9,259
2	21,313	−1,268	−90	−2,964	−612	1,939	35,826	7,332	28,494
3	21,313	−1,268	−90	−2,964	−757	2,933	54,993	6,416	48,577
4	21,313	−1,268	−90	−2,964	−872	3,975	75,086	5,499	69,587
5	21,313	−1,268	−90	−2,964	−1,002	5,066	96,140	4,583	91,558

- **Concept Reports**—concept reports may also be included for specific insurance applications, including:
    - Cash Flow Assuming Death at Age XX—a hypothetical illustration showing the impact to corporate cash flow and earnings if death occurred at a specific age or based on a specific mortality table.
    - Mortality Adjusted Insurance Cash Flow—a hypothetical illustration showing premium outlays and death benefit proceeds based on a specific mortality table. This report is helpful for multi-life cases when assessing the impact of a specific mortality assumption on corporate cash flow.
    - Hypothetical illustrations for insurance applications: split dollar, key person, defective trust, business continuation, 162 bonus, etc. See Chapters 11 and 12.

Variable Life Insurance Illustrations

The NAIC illustration model regulation previously discussed in this chapter does not apply to variable life insurance. At the time this book was published, the NAIC was in the process of developing illustration regulations for variable life. However, variable life illustrations are subject to FINRA (*Financial Industry Regulatory Authority*) standards and guidelines. FINRA regulates securities firms and is dedicated to investor protection.

FINRA has the following guidelines regarding variable life insurance illustrations:

- Hypothetical illustrations using assumed rates of return may be used to demonstrate the mechanics of a variable life insurance policy. The illustrations show how the performance of the underlying investment accounts could affect the policy cash value and death benefit. These illustrations may not be used to project or predict investment results as such forecasts are strictly prohibited.
- An illustration may use any combination of assumed investment returns up to and including a gross rate of 12 percent, provided that one of the returns is a 0 percent gross rate. The purpose of the 0 percent rate of return is to demonstrate how a lack of growth in the underlying investment accounts may affect policy values and to reinforce the hypothetical nature of the illustration.
- The illustrations must reflect the maximum (guaranteed) mortality and expense charges associated with the policy for each assumed rate of return. Current charges also may be illustrated in addition to the maximum charges.
- Preceding any illustration there must be a prominent explanation that the purpose of the illustration is to show how the performance of the

underlying investment accounts could affect the policy cash value and death benefit. The explanation must also state that the illustration is hypothetical and may not be used to project or predict investment results.

Sample variable universal life (VUL) ledger and summary illustrations from a prominent life insurance carrier are shown in Tables 13-6 and 13-7 respectively, including notes for specified numbered items.

TABLE 13-6
Example Variable Universal Life—Ledger Illustration

(1) ABC Life Insurance Company	(2) Variable UL—Life Insurance Illustration
	(3) Variable Universal Life Policy
	(4) Form # EFG—For Presentation in CA
(5) Insured Name (8) Death Benefit Option = A	(11) Producer Name & Address
(6) Male, Age 70 (9) Total Face Amount = $1,000,000	
(7) Nonsmoker (10) Premium Frequency = Annual	(12) Run: 10/01/2010

Ledger Illustration Non-Guaranteed Detail

(13) The purpose of this illustration is to show how the performance of the investment options could affect the policy Account Value and Death Benefit. The information is hypothetical and may not be used to predict investment results. This illustration assumes non-guaranteed policy charges and non-guaranteed earnings rates.

			(17) Hypothetical Values (EOY) @ 6.73% (6.00% Net)			
Yr (14)	Age (15)	Premium Outlay (16)	Annual Increase in Account Value (18)	Account Value (19)	Surrender Value (20)	Death Benefit (21)
1	70	43,365	31,455	31,455	12,924	1,000,000
2	71	43,365	31,887	63,343	46,871	1,000,000
3	72	43,365	32,458	95,801	81,388	1,000,000
4	73	43,365	32,999	128,800	116,446	1,000,000
5	74	43,365	33,878	162,678	152,383	1,000,000
6	75	43,365	36,075	198,752	190,516	1,000,000
7	76	43,365	37,848	236,601	230,424	1,000,000
8	77	43,365	40,127	276,728	272,610	1,000,000
9	78	43,365	42,763	319,491	317,432	1,000,000
10	79	43,365	45,560	365,051	365,051	1,000,000
11	80	0	12,657	377,708	377,708	1,000,000
12	81	0	12,593	390,301	390,301	1,000,000
13	82	0	12,697	402,997	402,997	1,000,000
14	83	0	12,950	415,948	415,948	1,000,000
15	84	0	11,733	427,680	427,680	1,000,000
16	85	0	10,451	438,131	438,131	1,000,000
17	86	0	9,460	447,591	447,591	1,000,000
18	87	0	8,373	455,964	455,964	1,000,000
19	88	0	7,481	463,445	463,445	1,000,000
20	89	0	6,456	469,901	469,901	1,000,000
21	90	0	3,024	472,925	472,925	1,000,000
22	91	0	2,094	475,019	475,019	1,000,000

23	92	0	2,350	477,369	477,369	1,000,000
24	93	0	2,637	480,006	480,006	1,000,000
25	94	0	2,960	482,966	482,966	1,000,000
26	95	0	3,321	486,287	486,287	1,000,000
27	96	0	3,728	490,015	490,015	1,000,000
28	97	0	4,183	494,198	494,198	1,000,000
29	98	0	4,695	498,893	498,893	1,000,000
30	99	0	5,269	504,161	504,161	1,000,000
31	100	0	5,913	510,074	510,074	1,000,000
32	101	0	6,636	516,709	516,709	1,000,000
33	102	0	7,447	524,156	524,156	1,000,000
34	103	0	8,357	532,513	532,513	1,000,000
35	104	0	9,379	541,892	541,892	1,000,000
36	105	0	10,525	552,418	552,418	1,000,000
37	106	0	11,812	564,230	564,230	1,000,000
38	107	0	13,256	577,486	577,486	1,000,000
39	108	0	14,877	592,363	592,363	1,000,000
40	109	0	16,696	609,059	609,059	1,000,000
41	110	0	18,737	627,796	627,796	1,000,000
42	111	0	21,028	648,823	648,823	1,000,000
43	112	0	23,598	672,422	672,422	1,000,000
44	113	0	26,483	698,905	698,905	1,000,000
45	114	0	29,721	728,626	728,626	1,000,000
46	115	0	33,354	761,980	761,980	1,000,000
47	116	0	37,432	799,412	799,412	1,000,000
48	117	0	42,008	841,421	841,421	1,000,000
49	118	0	47,144	888,565	888,565	1,000,000
50	119	0	52,908	941,473	941,473	1,000,000
51	120	0	59,371	1,000,844	1,000,844	1,010,852

(22) All values except premiums, policy loans, loan interest, and withdrawals are values at the end of the policy year. The Surrender Value column is equal to the Account Value, less any surrender charges. The Death Benefit column is the policy Death Benefit less any Policy Debt.

VUL Ledger Illustration Notes

1) Name of insurer.
2) Product name.
3) Product description.
4) Policy form (as filed with the state insurance department) and state of issue (California). The issue state should correspond to the state where the policyowner resides or does business.
5) Insured name.
6) Insured gender and issue age. The issue age is either age nearest birthday (ANB) or age last birthday (ALB) as of the policy issue date. Most insurers use ANB while others use ALB. ALB may be advantageous for insureds who qualify for a one year younger issue age as compared to ANB.
7) Insured underwriting class as identified by smoker status. There may be multiple nonsmoker and smoker underwriting categories that are designated by the insured's health.
8) Death benefit option A signifies a level death benefit. Other options may include an option B, which is equal to the total face amount plus the account value and option C, which is equal to the total face amount plus the cumulative premiums paid less any withdrawals.
9) The total initial face amount includes both basic and term coverage.
10) The premium frequency is annual, which assumes an annual premium being paid on the policy anniversary date (i.e., beginning of the policy year). Other premium frequency (mode) options may include semi-annual, quarterly, and monthly.
11) The producer's (agent's) name and address.

12) The date the illustration was prepared. Since products and rates can change regularly, the advisor should verify that the illustration is current as of the review date.

13) Note concerning hypothetical investment earnings assumption and impact on policy values. This illustration assumes non-guaranteed assumptions for policy charges and a non-guaranteed hypothetical investment earnings rate assumption.

14) Policy year as defined by the policy anniversary date.

15) The insured's age as of the beginning of the policy year shown. Some illustrations provide the age as of the end of the policy year.

16) The planned premium paid during the specified policy year. With universal life, the amount and frequency of premium payments are flexible, within limits. If resulting premiums are insufficient, coverage terminates when the account value goes to zero. For this example, ten annual premiums are targeted to provide an account value equal to the death benefit at age 120 based on the non-guaranteed assumptions.

17) Illustrated policy values in this section are based on non-guaranteed assumptions for investment earnings and policy charges. Non-guaranteed illustrated charges may not be more favorable than the current assumption charges or exceed the guaranteed charges. Current assumptions are the actual charges being applied to the policy as of the illustration preparation date and are subject to change (but may not be less favorable than the guaranteed charges). While not stated, the illustrated policy charges are based on the current assumptions for policy charges, which are the actual charges as of the illustration preparation date.

   The non-guaranteed illustrated earnings rate for variable UL is a hypothetical input option. The investment earnings rate is stated at gross (6.73 percent) and net (6.00 percent). The gross rate is the hypothetical earnings rate before investment portfolio expenses. The net rate is the gross rate less investment portfolio expenses. Investment portfolio expenses are unique to each investment option. The investment portfolio expenses do not include policy charges. The hypothetical investment earnings rate for variable UL illustrations may not be higher than 12 percent gross as prescribed by illustration regulations. There is no guaranteed minimum crediting rate for variable UL, as 100 percent of the investment risk is transferred to the policyowner. Negative investment earnings may be illustrated. Values shown are as of the end of the policy year (EOY). For this example, the account value equals the death benefit at end of age 120 based on the non-guaranteed assumptions.

18) Annual Increase in Account Value: Equal to the current policy year account value less the previous year account value. The amount represents the premiums paid in, charges deducted, withdrawals made, and investment earnings credited for the specified policy year.

19) Account Value: Equal to the sum of premiums paid less all charges and withdrawals plus investment earnings since the policy effective date. The account value provides the base for investment earnings credits. This is not the amount available to the policyowner upon surrender (see surrender value below). Account value may also be referred to as accumulated value.

20) Surrender Value: Equal to the account value minus any applicable surrender charge. The amount paid to the policyowner upon surrender is the surrender value less any outstanding policy debt. Some products have no surrender charges while other products may have surrender charges for twenty years or more. This product has surrender charges for nine years.

21) Death Benefit: The amount payable to the beneficiary upon the insured's death (but will be reduced by any outstanding policy debt). For this example, the death benefit is level due to a designated death benefit option A (see (8). The death benefit will remain level unless the cash value grows to an amount that forces the death benefit to increase according to the definition of life insurance test. The death benefit may never be less than the account value.

22) Footnote specifying timing of policy values, application of surrender charges in the surrender value, and death benefit value being net of any outstanding loans.

Interest Adjusted Indices

Other items that may be found in a life insurance illustration are interest adjusted net cost indices (although not commonly used). These indices, covered in Chapter 16, are intended by regulators to assist buyers in selecting a comparatively low cost policy. A key aspect of the indices is that they reflect the time value of money ("a dollar is worth more today than 10 years from now").

TABLE 13-7
Example Variable Universal Life—Summary Page

(1) ABC Life Insurance Company

(2) Variable UL—Life Insurance Illustration
(3) Variable Universal Life Policy
(4) Form # EFG—For Presentation in CA
(5) Producer Name
(6) Run: 10/01/2010

(7a) Summary Page Current Policy Charges

| | | Assuming Hypothetical Earnings Rate of | | | | | | | | |
| | | 0.00% (–0.68% Net) (10) | | | 6.00% (5.28% Net) (11) | | | 6.73% (6.00% Net) (12) | | |
Yr (8)	Premium Outlay (9)	Account Value (13)	Surrender Value (14)	Death Benefit (15)	Account Value (13)	Surrender Value (14)	Death Benefit (15)	Account Value (13)	Surrender Value (14)	Death Benefit (15)
1	43,365	29,149	10,618	1,000,000	31,206	12,675	1,000,000	31,455	12,924	1,000,000
2	43,365	56,677	40,205	1,000,000	62,608	46,136	1,000,000	63,343	46,871	1,000,000
3	43,365	82,678	68,265	1,000,000	94,325	79,912	1,000,000	95,801	81,388	1,000,000
4	43,365	107,063	94,709	1,000,000	126,305	113,951	1,000,000	128,800	116,446	1,000,000
5	43,365	130,091	119,796	1,000,000	158,861	148,566	1,000,000	162,678	152,383	1,000,000
6	43,365	152,908	144,672	1,000,000	193,273	185,037	1,000,000	198,752	190,516	1,000,000
7	43,365	174,948	168,771	1,000,000	229,080	222,903	1,000,000	236,601	230,424	1,000,000
8	43,365	196,555	192,437	1,000,000	266,747	262,629	1,000,000	276,728	272,610	1,000,000
9	43,365	217,892	215,833	1,000,000	306,583	304,524	1,000,000	319,491	317,432	1,000,000
10	43,365	238,876	238,876	1,000,000	348,691	348,691	1,000,000	365,051	365,051	1,000,000
15	0	158,966	158,966	1,000,000	388,025	388,025	1,000,000	427,680	427,680	1,000,000
20	0	##	##	##	388,444	388,444	1,000,000	469,901	469,901	1,000,000
25	0				321,743	321,743	1,000,000	482,966	482,966	1,000,000
30	0				204,650	204,650	1,000,000	504,161	504,161	1,000,000
35	0				3,195	3,195	1,000,000	541,892	541,892	1,000,000
40	0				##	##	##	609,059	609,059	1,000,000
45	0							728,626	728,626	1,000,000
50	0							941,473	941,473	1,000,000

Additional premiums will be required to maintain the requested benefits.

(16) The policy values under the Current Policy Charges heading reflect current policy charges, current cost of insurance rates, current coverage charges and the hypothetical gross earnings rate assumption described in the Investment Options section. Current policy charges and cost of insurance rates are subject to change. Policy values will vary from those illustrated if actual rates differ from those assumed. Current cost of insurance rates are not dependent upon future improvements in underlying mortality.

(17) The hypothetical net earnings rate reflects the daily compounding of the underlying portfolio's expenses and does not reflect the impact of policy charges. See the Variable Investment Options section for more information.

(7b) Summary Page Guaranteed Policy Charges

| | | Assuming Hypothetical Earnings Rate of | | | | | | | | |
| | | 0.00% (–0.68% Net) (10) | | | 6.00% (5.28% Net) (11) | | | 6.73% (6.00% Net) (12) | | |
Yr (8)	Premium Outlay (9)	Account Value (13)	Surrender Value (14)	Death Benefit (15)	Account Value (13)	Surrender Value (14)	Death Benefit (15)	Account Value (13)	Surrender Value (14)	Death Benefit (15)
1	43,365	##	##	##	##	##	##	##	##	##

Additional premiums will be required to maintain the requested benefits.

(18) The policy values assume maximum cost of insurance rates.

(17) The hypothetical net earnings rate reflects the daily compounding of the underlying portfolio's expenses and does not reflect the impact of policy charges. Se the Variable Investment Options section for more information.

VUL Summary Page Notes

1) Name of insurer.

2) Product name.

3) Product description.

4) Policy form (as filed with the state insurance department) and state of issue (California). The issue state should correspond to the state where the policyowner resides or does business.

5) The producer's (agent's) name and address.

6) The date the illustration was prepared. Since products and rates can change regularly, the advisor should verify that the illustration is current as of the review date.

7a) Summary page for this illustration includes illustrated policy values for the first ten years and every five years thereafter. Three hypothetical gross earnings rates are provided: 0 percent, 6 percent, and as specified by the illustration preparer. The policy charges are current (non-guaranteed), which are the actual policy charges being applied to the policy as of the illustration run date. Current assumptions are subject to change but may not be less favorable than the guaranteed maximum charges. Funding for this illustration is ten annual premiums to provide an account value equal to the death benefit at end of age 120 based on current policy charges and a hypothetical net investment earnings rate of 6.00 percent.

7b) Summary page for this illustration includes illustrated policy values for the first ten years and every five years thereafter. Three hypothetical gross earnings rates are provided: 0 percent, 6 percent, and as specified by the illustration preparer. The policy charges applied to the policy values are the guaranteed maximum charges. Future actual policy charges may not exceed the guaranteed maximum charges. Based on the specified funding level, the contract will terminate in the first year if guaranteed maximum charges are applied.

8) Policy year as defined by the policy anniversary date.

9) The planned premium paid during the specified policy year. With variable universal life, the amount and frequency of premium payments are flexible, within limits. If resulting premiums are insufficient, coverage terminates when the account value goes to zero. For this example, ten annual premiums are targeted to provide an account value equal to the death benefit at end of age 120 based on the specified hypothetical earnings rate of 6.00 percent net and current policy charges.

10) The policy values in this section are based on a non-guaranteed hypothetical investment earnings rate of 0.00 percent gross and –0.68 percent net. The gross rate is the hypothetical earnings rate before investment portfolio expenses. The net rate is the gross rate less investment portfolio expenses. Investment portfolio expenses are unique to each investment option. The investment portfolio expenses do not include policy charges. The hypothetical investment earnings rate for variable UL illustrations may not be higher than 12 percent gross as prescribed by FINRA. There is no guaranteed minimum crediting rate for variable UL as 100 percent of the investment risk is transferred to the policyholder. Negative investment earnings may be illustrated. For this illustration, the 0 percent gross rate is automatically shown (not user defined).

11) The policy values in this section are based on a non-guaranteed hypothetical investment earnings rate of 6.00 percent gross and 5.28 percent net. See (10) above for a description of gross and net. For this illustration, the 6 percent gross rate is automatically shown (not user defined).

12) The policy values in this section are based on a non-guaranteed hypothetical investment earnings rate of 6.73 percent gross and 6.00 percent net. See (10) above for a description of gross and net. The 6.00 percent net rate is defined by the illustration preparer.

13) Account Value: Equal to the sum of premiums paid less all charges and withdrawals plus investment earnings since the policy effective date. The account value provides the base for investment earnings credits. This is not the amount available to the policyholder upon surrender (see surrender value below). Account value may also be referred to as accumulated value.

14) Surrender Value: Equal to the account value minus any applicable surrender charge. The amount paid to the policyowner upon surrender is the surrender value less any outstanding policy debt. For this example, surrender charges are assessed for the first nine policy years.

15) Death Benefit: The amount payable to the beneficiary upon the insured's death (but will be reduced by any outstanding policy debt).

16) Footnote explaining non-guaranteed nature of policy assumptions and values. Policy charges are "current" (i.e., actual charges being assessed to the policy when the illustration was prepared and subject to change). The investment earnings rate is a hypothetical assumption. The current cost of insurance rates are not dependent upon future improvements in underlying mortality, which is important from a policy value sustainability perspective (see Chapter 14).

17) As stated in (10) above, the net investment earnings rate is equal to the gross rate less portfolio expenses, but does not include policy charges. Additional information is found in the narrative illustration that includes a variable investment options section containing information on the investment options selected including portfolio expenses.

18) The policy values for this illustration are based on maximum cost of insurance charges (future actual charges may not exceed the maximum charges).

Most states require the inclusion of these indices on policy illustrations provided in the state. Two sets of indices are required. The first set, net payment cost indices, is intended to be useful for death planning purposes. The second set, surrender cost indices, is intended to be useful for purposes of possible policy surrender.

Conclusions

Life insurance policy illustrations are almost always used in the sale of life insurance. In most cases, illustrations must be signed by the policyowner and agent and included in the application package to the insurer. Life insurance illustrations are regulated by the states to make illustrations more understandable and ensure that they do not mislead purchasers of life insurance. Life insurance illustrations provide illustrated policy values, as well as other valuable information such as product descriptions, descriptions of available riders and options, and descriptions of key terms. Illustrated policy values for cash value insurance (whole life and universal life) must be shown with guaranteed elements and are also typically shown with non-guaranteed assumptions. The non-guaranteed assumptions are subject to change and may not be more favorable than the current assumptions or less favorable than the guaranteed elements. Illustrations are useful for comparing performance between competing policies and for showing how insurance will fit into the overall financial plan.

Assessing the Sustainability of Illustrated Policy Values*

14

THIS CHAPTER CONTINUES PART V of the *Guide*, which explores life insurance illustrations and their uses. Specifically, this chapter will review the pricing factors that impact life insurance performance and assess the sustainability of illustrated policy values. The chapter begins with a reminder of the non-guaranteed nature of illustrations, transitions to a brief overview of life insurance pricing factors and a review of the influences on those pricing factors, and concludes with a suggested process for assessing the sustainability of illustrated life insurance policy values.

Non-Guaranteed Assumptions Inherent in Life Insurance Illustrations

As discussed in Chapter 13, universal life (UL) insurance illustrations are typically based on non-guaranteed assumptions (i.e., policy charges and credits). The non-guaranteed assumptions are called non-guaranteed policy elements, non-guaranteed assumptions, or simply current assumptions (i.e., the charges and credits currently being applied to the policy), and are intended to be based on current insurer experience for investment earnings, mortality (i.e., death claims), expenses, and persistency. Current assumptions may be changed by the insurer but can be no less favorable than the guaranteed elements. Current assumptions

---

*Authored by Wayne Tonning.

are intended to track actual experience; therefore, as emerging experience diverges (for better or worse) from past experience the carrier may adjust the current assumption(s) to reflect the new experience.

Participating whole life (WL) illustrations are based on non-guaranteed dividends, which incorporate current experience for mortality, investment earnings, expenses, and persistency (same assumptions as UL). Dividends are credited to the policy to the extent actual experience is better than the assumptions backing the guaranteed values. The dividend scale currently being applied to a policy as of the date an illustration is prepared is called the current dividend scale.

An Overview of Life Insurance Pricing

As discussed in detail in Chapter 6, the pricing of all life insurance policies involves four basic factors: mortality, investment earnings, expenses and taxes, and persistency. Figure 14-1 summarizes the Chapter 6 discussion.

FIGURE 14-1: Life Insurance Pricing Factors

Insurer Perspective (Pricing Factors)			Policyholder Perspective (Assumptions)
Mortality Experience	+	Mortality Margin	⟶ Mortality Charge
Investment Earnings	-	Interest Spread	⟶ Interest Credit
Expenses & Taxes	+	Expense Margin	⟶ Loading Charges

Some products, such as UL, are unbundled where the loadings and charges are transparent. Other products, such as WL, are bundled where the loadings and charges are not transparent (but the pricing factors still apply). The insurer uses policyholder charges to cover death claims and expenses, and credits interest to the policy based on investment earnings. The margins and spreads are incorporated by the insurer to provide contingencies for deviations in experience and provide profit. In addition, the insurer's persistency experience is incorporated into all of the charges and credits (see Chapter 6 for further explanation). Also of importance is the typical cross subsidization of assumptions. As an example, margins may be added to the mortality charge to cover expenses. The entire package of loadings and credits determines insurer profitability and policy performance, not necessarily any one pricing factor.

Influences on Illustrated and Actual Performance

To gain a better understanding of current illustrated performance, its sustainability, and possible changes to future performance, we examine the factors that influence current assumptions (charges and credits).

Crediting and Dividend Interest Rates

Universal life provides a crediting interest rate and whole life provides a dividend interest rate. Both rates are subject to guaranteed minimums and are typically backed by portfolios of high quality fixed income instruments such as bonds and mortgages.

Variable contracts are different in that their credited investment earnings are based on asset allocations, including equities, chosen by the policyholder and are not subject to a guaranteed minimum (i.e., 100 percent of the investment risk is transferred to the policyholder). The remainder of this section focuses on the crediting/dividend interest rates for non-variable contracts.

Supported Primarily by Yields on Bonds and Mortgages

Historically, the policy element assumption most likely to change is the crediting/dividend interest rate, as it is dependent on investment earnings that fluctuate. Insurance companies typically invest in investment grade bonds and mortgages to best match the insurance liability profile and due to regulatory constraints (see Chapter 4). Table 14-1 shows that more than 80 percent of the top 30 insurers' invested assets were bonds and mortgages as of year-end 2009.

Historical Interest Experience

New money bond yields have been decreasing since the early 1980s. Consequently, portfolio earnings have been under downward pressure, resulting in decreased crediting/dividend interest rates (see Figure 14-2).

Most crediting/dividend interest rates are based on the investment earnings of a seasoned portfolio. Because it takes time for investments to mature (and ultimately roll off the portfolio), there is a lag between the change in new

TABLE 14-1
Distribution of Invested Assets of Top 30 Life Insurance Companies as of December 31, 2009*

Bonds	72.7%
Mortgages	11.5%
Policy Loans	4.5%
Cash & Short Term	4.4%
Preferred Stock	0.4%
Common Stock	2.2%
Real Estate	0.7%
Other	3.8%
Quality of Invested Assets	
% Investment Grade Bonds	91.8%
% Performing Mortgages	99.7%

*Top 30 issuers of high face amount life insurance policies, representing 65 percent of total permanent face amount issued in 2009.

FIGURE 14-2: Historical Bond Yields and Sample Crediting Rates

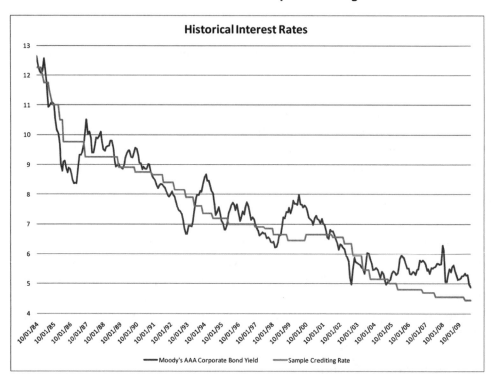

money rates and the resulting change to portfolio earnings and the crediting/dividend interest rate. However, some crediting/dividend interest rates are based on new money rates or a new portfolio and therefore the crediting rate will react more quickly to changes in new money rates.

Crediting and Dividend Interest Rate Considerations

Given that new money fixed income interest rates and resulting portfolio earnings change frequently, it should be anticipated that crediting/dividend interest rates will change frequently as well. If new money rates increase, then eventually portfolio earnings should increase, which should lead to an increase in the crediting/dividend interest rate (and vice versa). The extent to which portfolios have allocations to other investments, such as equities, will impact portfolio earnings and crediting/dividend interest rates, although the effect is minor as other asset allocations typically are small. Some insurers are known to have higher allocations of equities, which have impacted rates credited to policies. Later in this chapter, we provide analytical tools for assessing crediting/dividend interest rates.

Mortality Charges

For UL, the cost of insurance (COI) charge represents the mortality charge (this may also be called the insurance charge). For WL, the mortality charge is not explicitly revealed, but is included in the guaranteed values and dividends (i.e., bundled). Specifically for UL, the COI charge is a function of a COI rate multiplied by the net amount at risk (NAR). The NAR equals the total death benefit less the account or cash value. Consequently, mortality charges will be higher for lower premium funding due to the lower resulting account values (and higher NAR) and vice versa.

Supported by Mortality Experience

Mortality charges are intended to cover the death claims paid by life insurers. Mortality charges are primarily based on recent historical mortality experience. There are four primary sources of mortality experience, as discussed in Chapter 6:

- ◆ *Industry*: The Society of Actuaries (SOA) prepares mortality studies based on life insurance industry experience for specific observation periods. Recall from Chapter 6 that two kinds of life insurance mortality tables are developed from these studies: basic tables and valuation tables. Basic tables are based on actual industry mortality experience. Valuation tables are built from basic tables but loaded for conservatism (i.e., higher mortality rates) as they are used for calculating insurance reserves. The most recent tables are the *2001 Valuation Basic Table* and *2001 Commissioners Standard Ordinary Table*. Both tables are based on experience from 1990 to 1995 and have been adjusted with mortality improvements to reflect mortality as of 2001. Insurers typically review the *2001 Basic Table* when developing a mortality assumption for a life insurance policy, as this table is not loaded.
- ◆ *Reinsurance*: Reinsurers also conduct mortality studies based on the business they reinsure from multiple companies. These mortality studies typically are more refined by underwriting rating factors and classifications (including smoker and health status).
- ◆ *Company Specific*: Insurers conduct their own mortality studies. These studies reflect the insurer's actual underwriting/mortality results, which will differ from insurer to insurer, but results may be less credible due to smaller amounts of insurance in force.
- ◆ *Target Market*: For products marketed to well-defined target markets, segregating mortality experience can be an important competitive tool, as different target markets exhibit different mortality experience. As an example, high net worth insureds have exhibited much lower mortality experience than that generally found in the industry. Sources of credible segregated experience are often difficult to obtain. The SOA provides special studies, such as experience by face amount size (high net worth policyowners typically purchase larger face amounts); reinsurers and insurers themselves may also have segregated data.

Supported by Underwriting

While all insurers follow common underwriting principles, each company has its own underwriting practices. Because underwriting impacts mortality experience, pricing should reflect actual underwriting practices. Strict underwriting standards should result in better (i.e., lower) mortality experience and lower mortality charges (and vice versa). Very healthy individuals may benefit from strict underwriting that allows lower mortality charges. However, strict underwriting also entails higher expenses and reduces the volume of business as fewer individuals will qualify for coverage. This dynamic drives insurers' continual quest to find the right balance.

Historical Mortality Experience

Historically, mortality rates have fallen as quality of life factors and medical technologies improved. Over the last 50 years, mortality rates have decreased at an annual rate of 1 to 2 percent. More recently, mortality experience has continued to improve but at a lower pace. Table 14-2 provides recent annual mortality improvement rates based on mortality experience from 1985–90 to 1990–95. Observations on Table 14-2 include the following:

- ◆ Mortality improvement rates have tended to be higher for males than for females.
- ◆ Mortality improvement rates have tended to be lower at attained ages under 45 and attained ages above 85.
- ◆ Mortality improvement rates for males appear to be in the range of 1 percent for ages 55–80.
- ◆ Mortality improvement rates for females appear to be in the range of 0.5 percent for ages 55–80.
- ◆ Although not shown in Table 14-2, recent smoker experience has deteriorated.

Additionally, in 2010 the SOA released a mortality study based on the experience of 39 insurance companies from 2003 through 2007. The study showed an annual mortality improvement rate of approximately 3 percent over that time period (3 percent for males and 1 percent for females).

TABLE 14-2
Recent Annual Mortality Improvement Rates*

Attained Age	Male	Female
0–45	0.0%	0.0%
55–80	1.0%	0.5%
85	0.5%	0.5%
90+	0.0%	0.0%

*Society of Actuaries (2001 VBT report)

Mortality Charge Considerations

Continued mortality improvements are likely to have an impact on product pricing in the future. Most mortality experts believe that mortality rates will decline further in the future, albeit at slower rates. Reasons for this belief include the following:

- ◆ Medical advances, including:
  - ◆ Earlier disease detection and intervention;
  - ◆ Biologics—monoclonal antibodies;
  - ◆ Gene therapies;
  - ◆ Nanomedicine; and
  - ◆ Pharmaceutical development.
- ◆ Other research, including:
  - ◆ Anti-aging: antioxidants, resveratrol, sirtuins, caloric restriction; and
  - ◆ Blue Zones (common lifestyle characteristics that contribute to longevity).
- ◆ Motivation and enhanced resources.

Other researchers, however, are not as optimistic that future mortality gains will mirror those of the recent past, for the following reasons:

- ◆ Sedentary lifestyles
- ◆ Rise in obesity
- ◆ End of decrease in smoking
- ◆ High cost of health care
- ◆ Distracted driving

Insurance industry observers are generally optimistic about future improvements in insured mortality experience. They believe the insurance industry will develop an even better understanding of the risk factors affecting mortality and, in turn, will develop more refined underwriting tools and techniques. These observers also believe that future insurance applicants will be more affluent, on average, than in the past, leading to lower mortality experience. This is true because more affluent insureds live longer, on average, than less affluent insureds. Two factors drive this lower mortality: (1) access to better health care and more health care options and (2) greater awareness of risk factors that affect longevity.

Overall, based on the reasons above, mortality experts believe that general population mortality will continue to improve in the future, particularly for the insured population and even more so for the affluent. However, this view remains speculative and, of course, is no guarantee of superior future experience.

Impact on Future Mortality Charges

The impact of emerging mortality experience on future mortality charges depends on the product type. For UL, a distinction should be made between new policies and in-force policies. History tells us that insurers will reduce mortality charges for new policies to keep them competitive. However, most insurers have not passed on better mortality experience to in-force policies, instead retaining excess mortality margins for themselves. Other insurers have a track record and stated intention of passing on favorable gains to in-force policies. It is for this reason that an insurer's historical practice and future intent should be assessed when evaluating a policy for purchase. High net worth applicants may also want to consider purchasing a policy priced for that market, which may exhibit more favorable future mortality improvement than the industry in general.

For participating WL, the non-guaranteed dividend represents a credit for recent experience that is more favorable than the guaranteed pricing assumptions. Therefore, in theory, emerging mortality improvements (or worse mortality) should be reflected in the dividend. However, due to the bundled nature of traditional WL, it is not always possible to determine if the underlying mortality assumptions have been adjusted. For UL, the COI charge is obvious, and any mortality charge improvements can be verified.

Historical experience and practices are no guarantee of future performance. In addition, resulting mortality experience and mortality charges will certainly vary (for better or worse) by policy and insurer.

Loading Charges

For UL, all charges other than those for COI are loading charges. These can come in a variety of forms: a flat dollar amount assessed per month, a percentage of premium charge, a charge per $1,000 of face amount, and sometimes an asset-based fee (percentage of account value). For WL, the loading charges are bundled in the guaranteed values and dividends so usually they are not transparent, but they are certainly being applied.

Supported by Insurer Expenses

Loading charges are intended to cover insurer expenses, taxes, and contingencies. Expenses fall into two categories: direct and indirect. Direct expenses are those that are attributed to or incurred because of a particular policy form being sold. These are usually comprised of a combination of upfront development and distribution costs and ongoing maintenance costs.

Direct expense categories include:

◆ Product development: actuarial, regulatory, systems;
◆ Distribution: agent compensation and internal marketing and wholesaling;
◆ Underwriting: underwriter compensation and costs for medical exams and lab and specimen tests;

- ◆ Taxes: state premium tax, federal DAC (deferred acquisition cost) tax; and
- ◆ Administration: premium notices, annual statements, etc.

In addition to direct costs, and to continue as a viable entity, insurance companies must cover other costs that are not incurred directly because of the sale of a particular policy form. These indirect costs must be spread across all lines of business. Indirect expense categories include:

- ◆ Corporate: management, accounting, legal, advertising;
- ◆ Financial reporting: reserves, regulatory filings, rating agency filings;
- ◆ Investment operations: transactions costs, portfolio management fees;
- ◆ Distribution management: recruiting/licensing, training;
- ◆ General overhead: office space, office equipment, staff; and
- ◆ Corporate income taxes.

Historical Expense Experience

Historically, expenses incurred by insurers to issue and administer policies have consistently dropped due to emerging expense efficiencies, including technology enhancements.

Loading Charge Considerations

Expenses are typically predictable and manageable. Historically, it has been rare for a schedule of loading charges to be changed for in-force policies. It is anticipated that expense efficiencies will continue to be developed, specifically as can be seen today with rapid developing technology.

The comments regarding mortality and its impact by policy type (WL and UL) and policy status (new versus in-force) also apply here. For UL, insurers have historically reduced loading charges for new policies but not in-force policies. However, loading charges typically have less impact on policy performance than either mortality charges or the crediting/dividend interest rate. In addition, expense efficiencies have not been as material as mortality improvements. If historical trends continue, future expense efficiencies may be included in new policy pricing, but it is unlikely that in-force UL products will see loading reductions. However, as with mortality, some insurers have a track record of reducing loads on in-force policies. In theory, expense efficiencies should be included when calculating a current dividend scale for par WL; however, as stated earlier, it is usually not possible to verify an expense adjustment.

These are general observations and assessments that do not guarantee future pricing. Variations (for better or worse) will occur by policy and insurer.

The Sustainability of Illustrated Policy Values

Given that life insurance illustrations are not a guarantee of future policy performance, how can a buyer determine the sustainability of illustrated life insurance policy values? In general, current assumption illustrations should be based on current insurer experience that is determinable and credible. Basically, illustrated values should be sustainable if emerging insurer experience is not significantly different from current experience. However, some insurance policies are priced more aggressively than others and consequently may be at greater risk of negative policy adjustments.

Complexity in Assessing the Sustainability of Illustrated Policy Values

Due to the complexity of life insurance pricing, it is very difficult to assess whether illustrated policy values based on current assumptions are sustainable based on current experience. In addition to the basic pricing factors already discussed in this chapter (mortality, investment earnings, expenses, and persistency), insurance pricing typically deploys other tools to finance and manage the insurance risks: reserve methodologies, reserve financing, reinsurance, profit targets, and production quotas. As an example, an illustration with very low late duration insurance charges may be supportable due to reserves that are set aside from early duration profits to offset late duration negative mortality margins. If the carrier has lower profit targets than its competitors, this may be reflected in very competitive illustrated performance.

Assessing individual assumptions can be difficult due to cross subsidization within policy elements. For example, non-mortality policy charges may be loaded to cover some mortality costs and vice versa. Therefore, comparing specific assumptions may not be as revealing as one might hope.

With that said, however, a review of the current crediting rate for UL or the current dividend interest rate for WL can make sense. The interest crediting assumption and mortality charge assumption (i.e., COI charge for UL) have the greatest impact on policy performance. But while it has been uncommon for insurance charges to be adjusted on in-force policies, it has been quite common for interest crediting/dividend rates to be adjusted, primarily due to fluctuating investment returns (with decreasing interest returns over the last 25+ years).

A process for assessing the sustainability of illustrated policy values is provided below. Given the complexity of life insurance pricing and the audience of this *Guide*, the process will be general in nature. Advisors may wish to consult with experienced and knowledgeable insurance experts regarding questionable illustrations or large cases.

Illustration Assessment Process

Following is an overview of a suggested process for assessing the sustai
ity of illustrated policy values based on current assumptions: review the current crediting/dividend interest rate, review illustrated performance, perform
stress testing, review the insurer track record of policy management, and review the insurer intentions for managing future policy performance.

Review Crediting/Dividend Interest Rate

A number of tools/analytics can be used to assess a crediting/dividend interest rate.

Crediting and Dividend Interest Rate Benchmarks

The interest rate analytics provided below depend on following interest
rate benchmarks. As discussed previously in this chapter, invested assets backing life insurance products are typically investment grade bonds and mortgages. Historically, the crediting rate movements of seasoned UL portfolios
have tracked closely to movements in the five-year rolling average of Moody's
AAA Corporate Bond Yield (the crediting interest rate benchmark). The five-
year rolling average represents a portfolio of seasoned investments maturing
and rolling over with the purchase of new investments. See Figure 14-3.

FIGURE 14-3: Historical Five-Year Rolling Average of Moody's Bond Yields and Sample Crediting Rates

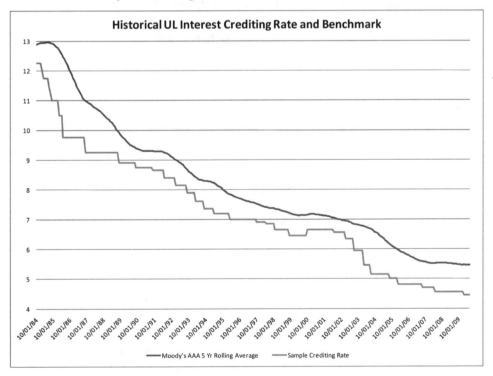

The seven-year rolling average of Moody's AAA Corporate Bond Yield has served as a better benchmark for WL dividend interest rates. The longer rolling average represents the slightly longer duration of investments that historically back a WL portfolio, which is most likely due to better policyholder persistency (which drives a longer duration liability profile). A complication with dividend interest rates is that many insurers incorporate mortality and expense experience as well as investment earnings. As an example, if investment earnings have declined, they may be offset with better mortality experience, resulting in less of a reduction to the dividend interest rate. Credits and charges are typically not transparent with bundled WL products.

Figure 14-4 shows the historical dividend interest rate for a sample WL policy and the WL benchmark (i.e., Moody's seven-year rolling average). The dividend interest rate generally tracks the benchmark. There are periods of time, 1997–2001 and 2006–2009, where the dividend interest rate was held constant even as the benchmark continued to decline. Perhaps the insurer's investments in equities, which provided substantial positive returns from 1995–1999 and again from 2003–2006, provided an offset to the lower interest rates and helped to maintain the dividend interest rate. It is also possible that good mortality experience helped to maintain the dividend scale. However, as expected, due to the continued drop in the interest rate benchmark, the dividend interest rate is eventually reduced.

FIGURE 14-4: Historical Whole Life Dividend Interest Rate and Benchmark

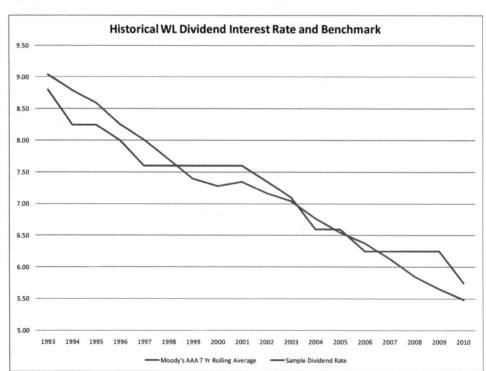

The example in Figure 14-4 shows the complexities involved with tracking both crediting and dividend interest rates. The benchmark does not account for meaningful portfolio exposures to other asset classes, such as equities, and will not account for other pricing elements (mortality and expenses), which may be found in dividend interest rates. However, as shown in Figure 14-4, the benchmark did provide an indication that the dividend interest rate was under downward pressure and eventually the dividend was reduced.

Crediting Rate Comparison

Now that interest rate benchmarks have been introduced, we can present our first interest crediting rate analytic. A crediting rate can be compared to the Moody's benchmark and other policy crediting rates. See the example in Table 14-3. The crediting rates for Policies B–D are lower than the benchmark, while Policy A has a crediting rate that significantly exceeds the benchmark. In addition, Policy A's crediting rate is 90 basis points (bps) higher than the next highest crediting rate. This should call into question the sustainability of Policy A's crediting rate. It is suggested that the advisor follow up with the insurer to gain a better understanding of the questionable crediting rate. See insurer policy questionnaire at the end of this chapter.

The declared dividend interest rate in a participating WL policy has a very different application than a UL crediting rate, and therefore dividend interest rates are not comparable on an absolute basis. To illustrate this point, in most participating WL policies one part of the dividend is based on a formula using the declared dividend interest rate. The formula can be generically described as taking the excess of the declared dividend interest rate over the policy guaranteed rate multiplied by the "policy value." While this formula is straightforward, its application varies widely by insurer and policy. For example, some insurers may make additional deductions from the declared dividend interest rate to cover expenses or mortality, some policies will have multiple guaranteed interest rates to pick from (e.g., one for policy cash surrender value and one for policy reserves), and there is wide variation in what is used in "policy value"—it may be a reserve, a cash surrender value, the greater of the two, a year-end value or a mid-year value, etc.

For these reasons, limited reliable conclusions can be drawn from comparing various policies absolute dividend interest rates. In fact, many insurers who issue participating WL policies have stopped publishing a dividend in-

TABLE 14-3
Current Crediting Rate Comparison

Moody's Benchmark*	Policy A	Policy B	Policy C	Policy D
5.50%	6.25%	5.05%	5.35%	5.25%

*5 year rolling average of Moody's AAA Corporate Bond Yield

terest rate because it has such different meanings, and reliance upon the absolute rate is misleading. However, this does not take away from the WL benchmark analysis, as changes in dividend interest rates over time have indeed tended to align with new money interest rate movements.

Crediting Interest Rate Change Indication

The difference between the current Moody's new money rate and the rolling average can provide an indication of future crediting rate changes. If the current new money rate is less than the rolling average, there is likely to be downward pressure on portfolio earnings and crediting/dividend interest rates. If the current new money rate is greater than the rolling average, there is likely to be upward pressure on portfolio earnings and crediting/dividend interest rates. See Table 14-4 for a comparison of new money rates versus the rolling average as of June 2010. This analysis indicates there may still be some pressure for a reduction in crediting rates post-June 2010, as the new money rate is 58 bps less than the rolling average. This suggests stress testing as described later in this section.

TABLE 14-4
June 2010 Crediting Interest Rate Change Indication

(A) Moody's New Money AAA Corporate Bond Yield	4.88%
(B) Moody's 5 Year Rolling Average	5.46%
Future Crediting Rate Indication (A)–(B)	–0.58% (–58 bps)

As of June 2010, and similar to UL crediting rates, there appeared to be continuing downward pressure for dividend interest rates as well. See Table 14-5.

TABLE 14-5
June 2010 Dividend Interest Rate Change Indication

(A) Moody's New Money AAA Corporate Bond Yield	4.88%
(B) Moody's 7 Year Rolling Average	5.48%
Future Dividend Rate Indication (A)–(B)	–0.60% (–60 bps)

Historical Crediting/Dividend Interest Rate Observation

Looking at historical crediting/dividend interest rates also can be beneficial. A crediting/dividend interest rate that remains unchanged as bond yields decline may suggest an impending reduction to the crediting/dividend interest rate. In Table 14-6, a particular UL policy held its crediting rate for two successive years as bond yields and the crediting rate benchmark dropped 35 and 18 bps, respectively. This suggested downward pressure on the UL crediting rate, which was realized two months later (March 2009) when the crediting rate was

TABLE 14-6
Historical Crediting Rate versus Benchmark Comparison

Month/Year	Crediting Interest Rate	Bond Yield*	Crediting Rate Benchmark**
January 2007	4.85%	5.40%	5.70%
January 2008	4.85%	5.33%	5.52%
January 2009	4.85%	5.05%	5.52%
Cumulative Drop	0.0%	–0.35%	–0.18%
March 2009	4.65%		

*Moody's AAA Corporate Bond Yield
**5 year rolling average of Moody's AAA Corporate Bond Yield

reduced by 20 bps. This rate movement type of analysis also applies for WL dividend interest rates, as dividend interest rate movements tend to align with movements in the Moody's WL benchmark (seven-year rolling average).

Historical New Money Interest Rate Observation

Another item to consider is historical and current bond yields. As of June 2010, they were lower than at any time over the previous four decades. See Figure 14-5. This suggested that bond yields and crediting/dividend interest rates may have been close to bottoming out.

FIGURE 14-5: Historical Moody's AAA Corporate Bond Yields

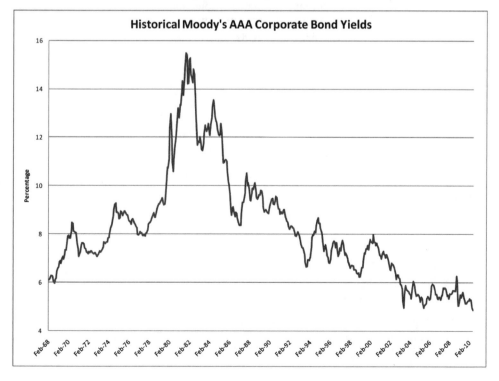

Hypothetical Benchmark Projections

A hypothetical projection of changes to future crediting rates can be prepared by using the appropriate crediting rate benchmark and assuming a hypothetical future new money bond yield assumption. Figure 14-6 provides a five-year hypothetical projection assuming future new money bond yields remain constant at the June 2010 level. The ultimate cumulative drop in the crediting rate benchmark is 58 basis points, as expected. But the drop occurs slowly over the five-year time period: 11 bps after one year, 24 bps by the end of year two, 38 bps after year three, 51 bps after year four, and 58 bps by the end of year five. The crediting rate benchmark projection can be prepared for any hypothetical bond yield assumption (i.e., increasing or decreasing yields). The projection is obviously not guaranteed, but provides an understanding of the effect on crediting rate movements.

Similar to the UL crediting rate benchmark, the WL dividend interest rate benchmark can also be used to project future movements in dividend interest rates. As the benchmark and new money spreads are similar between UL and WL (58 and 60 bps, respectively), the dividend interest rate benchmark has a similar projection as the crediting rate benchmark in Figure 14-6 (although the

FIGURE 14-6: Crediting Rate Benchmark Projection Assuming Hypothetical New Money Yields Remain Constant at June 2010 Level

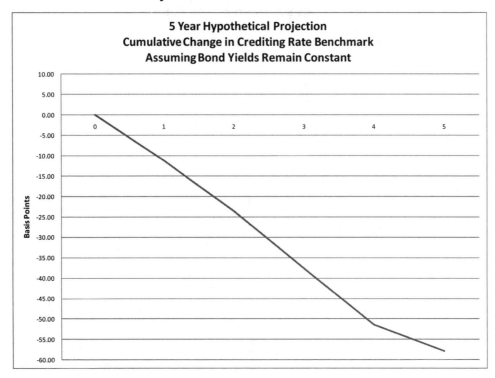

dividend benchmark drop will be slower over the seven-year time frame as compared to the five-year time frame for the UL benchmark). Current and historical Moody's AAA Bond Yields can be found on the Federal Reserve website. See http://federalreserve.gov/releases/H15/data/Monthly/H15_AAA_NA.txt.

Review Illustrated Performance

The next step in assessing an illustration is to perform an illustration performance comparison. Consider the example shown in Table 14-7. Policies B, C, and D have a premium solve that is at least 10 percent greater than that of Policy A. This substantial difference should raise a question as to the sustainability of Policy A's illustrated values. This question should be answered by the insurer (or an insurance expert), as addressed in the policy questionnaire provided later in this section. A **premium solve** is the premium calculated in the illustration system that will support the package of defined benefits (death benefit coverage and cash value target if applicable). See Chapter 16.

Note that, in reviewing illustrated performance, the entire package of costs and benefits should be observed. As an example, take a look at the surrender charges in Table 14-7. It is not uncommon for policies with very low premium solves also to have higher surrender charges. Table 14-7 shows that Policy A has 20 years of surrender charges, while the other policies have 10 years or less. From a pricing standpoint, a policy may be able to offer very low premium solves that are subsidized or offset with surrender charges. A potential policyowner would have to assess the tradeoff of low premiums versus low surrender values.

If there is a significant illustrated performance advantage, justification should be sought either from an insurance expert or the insurer. Examples of possible superior illustrated performance explanations could be: lower mortality charges as supported by a policy targeted for the high net worth market, an enhanced crediting rate supported by longer duration investments (taking advantage of a normal yield curve) with restrictions on fund transfers, or surrender charges that offset a low premium solve.

TABLE 14-7
Illustration Performance Review

	10-Pay Premium Solve (Current Assumptions)			
	Policy A	Policy B	Policy C	Policy D
Annual Premium	20,000	22,000	22,150	23,000
% Difference*		10.0%	10.8%	15.0%
Surrender Charge Duration	20 years	10 years	10 years	N/A

*Percentage difference in premium from policy A

Stress Testing

Irrespective of whether an illustration appears to be priced aggressively, all illustrations should be stress tested for negative assumption changes. **Stress testing** involves running illustrations with reduced crediting or dividend interest rates and at charges less favorable than those currently being applied to provide an idea of potential downside policy performance. It is useful for managing policyholder expectations. From the standpoint of the sustainability of illustrated policy values, an advisor should be wary of a policy that has a very competitive illustration based on current assumptions but experiences performance challenges under less favorable assumptions. Table 14-8 offers an example. Both policies are funded to achieve a cash value equal to the death benefit (CV=DB) of $1 million at age 121 based on current assumptions.

Policy B has a better premium solve but is slightly more susceptible to crediting rate reductions, particularly if the crediting rate is reduced to the guaranteed rate (most of which can be explained by a greater margin between the current and guaranteed rates for Policy B at 205 bps as compared to policy A at 175 bps). Sustaining the current crediting rate but increasing the policy charges to the guaranteed levels has an almost identical affect on both policies (lapse ages 77 and 75). Both policies also have similar performance based on guaranteed assumptions (lapse ages 75 and 73).

Depending upon the perception of future crediting rate movements, Policy A or B may be recommended. If the perception is that the current interest rate environment is at historical lows, suggesting a bottoming out of rates, and given that even with a 50 bps crediting rate reduction that Policy B stays in force to age 101, Policy B may be considered as providing the best overall price and risk package. However, if the perception is that crediting rates are at risk of future major reductions, Policy A may be recommended as it stays in force to age 97 even if the crediting rate is reduced to the guaranteed minimum.

TABLE 14-8
Stress Testing Comparison

Crediting Rate	Policy Charges	Lapse Age Policy A Premium = $27,173	Policy B Premium = $26,078
Current*	Current	CV=DB Age 121	CV=DB Age 121
−50 bps	Current	105	101
−100 bps	Current	101	95
Guaranteed**	Current	97	88
Current	Guaranteed	77	75
Guaranteed	Guaranteed	75	73

*4.75 percent for Policy A and 5.05 percent for Policy B
**3.00 percent for both Policy A and B

Other Illustration Assessment Considerations

In addition to the quantitative analyses provided above, a review of an insurer's track record for taking care of in-force policyholders should be undertaken. And that review could be accomplished by having a policy questionnaire completed, as provided below.

Life Insurer Intentions and Practices in Managing Policy Performance

Ultimately it is the track record, reputation, and intentions of the insurer that provide the most comfort regarding illustrated policy value sustainability. Does the insurer have a good track record for managing in-force policy performance? Does the insurer have a good reputation? Seasoned advisors and agents who service in-force policies that they have sold should have an understanding of which insurers treat their in-force policyholders the best. Some insurers have a questionable reputation regarding in-force policy performance and service, while others have quite positive reputations.

In addition, it is important to have a sense of the insurer's intentions for managing policy performance going forward. If emerging experience is similar to recent experience, will the insurer maintain the current assumptions used in the illustration or will unfavorable adjustments be needed because the insurer priced with expected experience improvements that were not realized? Even though the NAIC illustration regulation limits the use of experience improvements, it is still possible for insurers to deploy pricing practices that provide some level of experience improvements while still complying with the regulation.

Will the insurer pass on favorable experience to in-force policies through reduced policy charges or will the insurer retain the additional profits? Some insurers have a track record and stated intention of passing on better emerging experience to in-force policies. Such insurers have reduced COI charges on in-force policies due to better emerging mortality experience. This in-force management philosophy keeps in-force policies fresh and current, thereby reducing the pressure to replace the policy with a more competitive one, which would require new underwriting at a time when an insured's health may have deteriorated.

In addition, there are agent groups who, on behalf of their clients, monitor, provide feedback, and may even influence insurers regarding in-force performance and service.

Policy Pricing Questionnaire

The above analyses of the sustainability of illustrated policy values may lead to questions. Below is a list of questions that should either be answered by a knowledgeable insurance advisor or by the insurer.

Policy Questionnaire

Name of Insurer:

Name of Policy:

General Pricing
◆ What superior pricing factors drive this policy's competitive illustrated performance? (Example answer: policy is targeted and priced for the high net worth market that has exhibited superior mortality experience.)

Investment Earnings
◆ Is the current crediting or dividend interest rate sustainable if future new money bond yields remain at today's level? If not, please comment.

Mortality
◆ Will the current dividend scale or schedule of mortality charges need to be adjusted if emerging mortality experience remains consistent with current mortality experience? If yes, explain why.
◆ Do the underlying mortality charges for the current dividend scale or schedule of mortality charges cover the mortality pricing assumption in all durations? If not, how does the insurer cover the negative mortality margins?
◆ Has the insurer increased mortality charges or the mortality charge component of the current dividend scale on any in-force life insurance policy in the last 10 years? If so, provide examples and reasoning.
◆ Has the insurer decreased mortality charges or the mortality charge component of the current dividend scale on any in-force life insurance policy in the last 10 years? If so, provide examples and reasoning.
◆ If emerging mortality experience is better than the pricing mortality, will the insurer pass on the better experience to in-force policyholders through a reduction in the schedule of mortality charges or increases in the mortality component of the dividend scale?

Expense
◆ Do current policy charges or the policy charge component of the current dividend scale fully cover the insurer's actual expenses for issuing and administering this product? Explain.
◆ Has the insurer increased any policy loadings or policy charge component of the current dividend scale on any in-force life insurance policy in the last 10 years? If so, provide examples and reasoning.
◆ Has the insurer decreased any policy loadings or policy charge component of the current dividend scale on any in-force life insurance policy in the last 10 years? If so, provide examples and reasoning.
◆ If emerging expense experience is better than the pricing expenses, will the insurer pass on the better experience to in-force policies through reduced policy loads or increases in the expense component of the dividend scale?

Conclusions

Mortality, investment earnings, expenses, and persistency are the primary drivers of life insurance policy performance. Historically, mortality rates have improved and driven reduced insurance charges in life insurance products, particularly new policies. Expectations are that mortality rates will continue to fall in the future but at a slower pace. Investment earnings are driven by yields on bonds and mortgages. Those yields have decreased over the past 25+ years, resulting in lower crediting and dividend interest rates. Historically, expense efficiencies have been realized and passed on to policyholders through reduced policy loads, particularly on new policies. As technology continues to improve, it is expected that future expense efficiencies will be realized and priced into products.

Illustrations are based on non-guaranteed current assumptions: interest credits and policy charges. Policy charges reflect insurer death claims and expenses, while policy credits reflect insurer investment earnings. Current assumption illustrated values are considered sustainable if the assumptions are based on current insurer experience that is determinable and credible. Assessing the sustainability of illustrated policy values is difficult, and consultation with an insurance expert may be needed. However, three suggested analyses can be performed: (1) review the crediting/dividend interest rate for sustainability, (2) perform an illustration competitive comparison to determine if illustrated performance may be too good to be true, and (3) apply stress testing to gain an understanding of how future unfavorable assumption changes could affect policy performance. Positive consideration usually should be given to policies whose illustrated performance is less negatively affected when assumptions are changed for the worse. To complement this analysis, gaining an understanding of the insurer's track record, reputation, and policy management intentions is important. A sample policy questionnaire has been provided that addresses the insurer's policy pricing, track record, and future intentions.

Determining Appropriate Policy Funding Levels for Flexible Premium Life Insurance*

15

THIS CHAPTER CONTINUES PART V on assessing and using life insurance illustrations. Here we explore a methodology of using policy illustrations to determine an appropriate funding level for flexible premium policies, which includes stress testing. We begin this chapter with a short discussion of the importance of choosing an appropriate policy funding level, followed by a discussion of setting funding targets and using stress testing. We conclude by providing illustration examples to show the offsetting factors of cost versus risk protection to make the appropriate funding level decision. The following chapter completes this part of the *Guide* by reviewing methods and measures for competitive illustration comparisons.

The Importance of Choosing an Appropriate Funding Level

Flexible premium life insurance, including all forms of universal life (UL), gives the policyholder discretion with regard to the timing and amount of premium payments, so appropriate policy

---

*Authored by Wayne Tonning.

funding is critical. The policy funding decision for flexible premium policies includes the frequency of premium payments, the length of time that premiums will be paid, and the amount of premium to be paid.

At first blush, funding the policy at the lowest level may be considered to be desirable. However, lower premiums can translate into a greater risk of policy lapse. As an example, a policy could be funded to keep it in force to age 85. However, there could be significant risk that the insured could outlive coverage. Changes in policy credits and charges also could have an adverse effect and shorten the coverage period.

On the other hand, over funding can have a high cost, if the sole purpose for purchasing life insurance is death benefit protection. An experienced life insurance advisor helps buyers find an appropriate balance between cost and risk by using policy illustrations to show multiple funding scenarios. Illustrations serve as the basis for making informed policy funding decisions. Note that funding for flexible premium policies is a dynamic process that works best with policy monitoring over time (see Chapter 17).

For products like whole life (WL), which have fixed premium schedules, the insurance company makes the funding decision on behalf of the policyowner. While non-guaranteed dividends can be used to pay premiums, the amount of the ongoing premium does not change. As an example, assume that without dividends an annual $100,000 of premium to age 100 will guarantee coverage for life. With the current dividend scale, dividends can be used to reduce the number of out-of-pocket premium payments to ten. If dividends actually paid are increased or decreased, the number of payments will be adjusted accordingly; however, the premium amount of $100,000 does not change.

Using Policy Illustrations to Determine an Appropriate Funding Level

Policy illustrations provide information that can facilitate decisions about the appropriate funding level (i.e., the amount of premium to be paid). This can be done by solving for the premium needed to support a specified death benefit and achieve a target cash value. **Target cash value** or **cash value target** is the amount of cash or account value sought, commonly $1.00 or an amount equal to the death benefit, within a policy illustration at a specified age, such as age 121. A stress test is then performed for the premium needed to fund to the target cash value based on assumptions less favorable than those prevailing currently (e.g., a reduction of 100 basis points (bps) in the current crediting rate), then noting the reduced illustrated performance, such as policy lapse. Evaluating the cost and risk factors for different funding levels is critical to making an appropriate funding decision.

Setting Funding Targets

The specific insurance need typically drives the funding target. Life insurance is purchased for many reasons, as discussed in Chapter 10. For present purposes, we divide motivations into two broad categories: those that are driven primarily by the need for death protection and those driven by the need for cash value accumulation. For sales that are driven primarily by a need for death benefit protection, the death benefit is known and the premium funding level is to be determined. For sales that are primarily for cash value accumulation, the funding level typically is known and the death benefit level is to be determined.

Death Benefit Protection

When death benefit protection is the primary motivation, the funding target is typically specified as a function of the number of premium payments and a cash value target at a specified age. For example, we might solve for the annual premium that, if paid for the first ten policy years only, would result in a $1.00 cash value at age 121. The cash value target is critical, as coverage terminates when the cash value is zero. A higher cash value target provides more of a cushion. Examples are provided later in this chapter. In addition to providing policy risk protection, cash values provide flexibility for future life developments that may require: collateral for loans, emergency cash, retirement income, and value towards a policy replacement.

In circumstances for which there is a need for death protection, but with little or no corresponding interest in cash value accumulation, a no-lapse guarantee (NLG) policy commonly is suggested. As with all death benefit protection sales, the amount of coverage is known but, unlike other death benefit protection sales, the funding target need not incorporate a cash value target, as coverage is guaranteed regardless of the cash value. The funding target, therefore, is typically a function of the length of the guarantee coverage period and the number of premium payments.

Some buyers may be comfortable with less than lifetime coverage (such as to age 101). Some NLG policies provide generous premium discounts for lowering the length of coverage guarantee, and some NLG policies provide steep premium discounts for shorter pays (such as 10-pay or less funding). See the special considerations for NLG section at the end of this chapter for more detail.

Cash Value Accumulation

The other generic type of insurance sale is one driven primarily by the desire to use the policy as a vehicle for cash value accumulation, with less emphasis on death protection. Here, the funding level is known, and the amount of death protection is to be determined. The premium funding level is set to the amount of cash to be invested but is tailored to keep the contract from becoming a modified endowment contract (MEC) to avoid negative income tax consequences from potential policy distributions (see Chapter 7 for a discussion of the MEC test and tax consequences). Illustration systems will solve for a minimum non-MEC death benefit based on a defined premium level. Cash values accumulate more efficiently with a low death benefit due to lower mortality charges. A minimum non-MEC death benefit example is provided later in this chapter.

A variation of the desire for cash value accumulation is the desire to use a policy's cash value as a source of retirement income. Again, the funding level typically is known and cash needs to accumulate efficiently. Therefore, the death benefit is typically the minimum non-MEC death benefit and distributions that achieve a specified cash value target are calculated. The cash value target considerations in death benefit protection sales will also apply here.

Death Benefit Protection Funding Targets

As mentioned above, the funding target for death benefit protection sales is typically specified as a function of the number of premium payments and the amount of cash value to target at a specified attained age (assuming current assumptions for policy charges and credits).

Premium Length

The number of premium payments is a function of how much cash the policyowner has available in current and subsequent years to fund to a cash value target. Fewer premiums—no more than ten annual premiums (i.e., "short pays")—result in a higher annual outlay in the short term. Getting more cash into a policy early allows for more efficient accumulation of cash value due to interest compounding and reduced mortality charges from the reduced net amount at risk (NAR). Recall that NAR equals the death benefit less the account value. "Long pays"—more than ten annual premiums—permit a lower annual outlay but are less efficient in terms of accumulating cash value within the policy. Short pays typically provide a lower present value of premiums compared to long pays (when discounting at the cost of money). Examples are provided later in this chapter.

Target Cash Value

The target cash value involves setting both the desired amount of illustrated cash value and the age at which it will be realized. Two common goals are:

- ◆ Target $1.00 of cash value at age 121
- ◆ Target a cash value equal to the death benefit at age 121

Most contemporary cash value products are paid up at age 121 if there is at least $1.00 of cash value at age 121; then, no further charges are assessed and the policy will not lapse. Therefore, targeting at least $1 of cash value at age 121 is a logical funding choice.

However, one question remains: does one really need to fund to age 121? Most people do not believe that they will live past age 100, let alone to age 121. And life expectancy is well below age 121, typically in the late 70s to mid 80s (and higher for affluent insureds). But because approximately 50 percent of people live beyond life expectancy, funding to less than age 121, such as age 100, has the associated risk of the insured outliving the coverage. Further, funding to a lower age provides less cushion against unfavorable changes, such as reductions to the crediting rate, which is why stress testing is needed.

Illustration Stress Testing

Stress testing involves running illustrations with assumptions less favorable than the current assumptions (policy charges and credits) and provides a measure of the risk protection for a certain funding level used in death benefit protection sales. Stress testing will show that higher premium funding provides greater cushion for less favorable assumption changes, albeit at a greater outlay, as compared to lower funding. The tradeoff may then be evaluated. See Chapters 6 and 14 regarding insurance pricing and assumptions.

Reduce Crediting Rate

The most commonly tested assumption is the crediting rate for universal life (UL) or the earnings rate for variable universal life (VUL), because crediting rates and earned rates change over time due to changing investment yields on the assets supporting these liabilities. (Chapter 14 offers explanations of the impact of future crediting rate changes.) For VUL earnings rates, 100 percent of the market value risk is transferred to the policyowner; therefore, the earned rate can vary and is dependent on the policyholder's investment selections.

For UL, the illustrated crediting rate can be any rate between the current and guaranteed rate. For stress testing, the current crediting rate can be reduced by a selected number of basis points, such as 25 bps, all the way down to the guaranteed crediting rate. For the earned rate assumption in VUL, the maximum permitted illustrated rate is 12 percent gross—there is no minimum (guaranteed) rate.

Increase Policy Charges

Policy charges, including cost of insurance (COI) charges, are less likely to change, as expense levels and mortality rates are more predictable. Historically, mortality rates have continued to fall, and actuarial experts predict that this trend will continue. (Chapter 14 offers a more detailed discussion of mortality experience and mortality charges.) Regarding options to change policy charges, illustration systems typically lump all policy charges together, both COI charges and all policy loads. Therefore, one cannot, for example, increase the COI charges and keep the other charges at current levels. In addition, illustration systems typically allow policy charges to be run only at either current or guaranteed levels, although some systems allow charges to be increased by a specified percent (such as 110 percent). Stress testing should include charges at guaranteed levels and percentage increases if available.

Death Benefit Protection Stress Testing

With death benefit protection stress testing, reduced levels of cash value or policy lapse (where the cash value goes to zero and coverage is terminated) are noted. As an example, a policy that is funded to achieve $1.00 of cash value at age 121 based on current assumptions may lapse at age 99 when the current crediting rate is reduced 50 bps. Examples are provided later in this chapter.

Cash Value Accumulation Stress Testing

Stress testing for cash value accumulation sales typically focuses on reduced crediting or earned rates and the associated impact on the surrender value internal rate of return (SV IRR). The **SV IRR** is a measure of illustrated life insurance performance derived by solving for the interest rate that causes accumulated scheduled premiums (net of dividends, if appropriate) at selected policy durations to equal that duration's cash surrender (see Chapter 16). Typically, SV IRRs will be reduced by approximately the same amount as the crediting/earned rate reduction if the policy is max funded (i.e., minimum non-MEC death benefit). As an example, if the crediting rate is reduced by 10 bps, the SV IRR will typically also be reduced by approximately 10 bps. This is not the case for lower funding (death benefit protection) sales where the associated drop off in surrender value IRR would be much greater than the crediting/earned rate drop. This is because there is much greater mortality charge leverage with low funding versus high funding. With low funding, the cash values are lower, which results in a higher NAR. Recall that COI charges are applied to the NAR. See the minimum non-MEC example later in this chapter. With high funding, the risk is typically not policy lapse but reduced cash value performance.

Cost versus Risk Protection

It is important to weigh offsetting factors when determining an appropriate funding level in connection with death benefit protection purchases. Running illustrations with different cash value targets and stress testing will provide information regarding cost and risk, which can facilitate an appropriate policy funding decision.

As mentioned previously, age 121 is commonly used for identifying a target cash value, because charges terminate at that point and the policy is paid up if there is at least $1.00 of cash value (charges cease at age 100 for some policies). A target cash value equal to the death benefit (CV=DB) provides a cash value cushion for less favorable assumption changes. It is typically considered to be the maximum funding level target for death benefit protection purchases, as funding higher than CV=DB provides a death benefit in excess of what is needed. Targeting $1.00 of cash value, while providing a lower premium cost than the target of CV=DB, affords less cushion for less favorable assumption changes.

Life Expectancy and Probability of Survival

To assess funding targets and associated risk properly, it is helpful to understand levels of life expectancy or probability of survival. Many individuals believe that they will not live past age 90 and certainly not past age 100. But historical mortality experience tells us that many individuals will indeed live into their 90s and even 100s. Many individuals, therefore, may be underfunding their policies, because they are unaware of the true risk.

Table 15-1 provides life expectancy and survival rates for specified issue ages based on nonsmoker experience for high net worth male insureds who have been underwritten. There is at least a 40 percent and 10 percent probability of survival to ages 90 and 100, respectively.

Death Benefit Protection: 10-Pay Examples

Below we review some illustration examples for 10-pay funding with various common funding targets, followed by stress testing using different assumptions. Table 15-2 provides an example of 10-pay funding with a target of CV=DB at age 121. Two policies have been included for a male, age 55, nonsmoker, with a $1 million level death benefit.

TABLE 15-1
Male Nonsmoker Mortality
(High Net Worth Underwritten Insureds)

Issue Age	45	55	65	75
Life Expectancy	87	88	90	93
Probability of Survival				
Attained Age 75	84%	88%	94%	100%
Attained Age 80	74%	79%	85%	95%
Attained Age 85	60%	64%	70%	83%
Attained Age 90	43%	46%	50%	61%
Attained Age 95	26%	28%	30%	37%
Attained Age 100	12%	13%	14%	18%
Attained Age 110	0.6%	0.7%	0.7%	0.9%

TABLE 15-2
10-Pay CV=DB Age 121 Example

Policy	A	B
Current Crediting Rate	5.00%	5.05%
Guaranteed Crediting Rate	3.00%	2.40%
Annual Premium	$23,724	$23,404
Present Value Premium	192,350	189,755

Crediting Rate Decrease	Lapse Age	
10 bps	n/a	120
25 bps	n/a	108
50 bps	113	101
100 bps	100	95
150 bps	95	92
200 bps	91	90
Guaranteed	91	86
Guaranteed Charges and Crediting Rate	73	70

SV IRR—Current Assumptions		
Age 65 (Policy Yr 10)	–1.63%	–0.29%
Age 75 (Policy Yr 20)	1.36%	2.41%
Age 85 (Policy Yr 30)	1.71%	2.61%

Policy A illustrates as not lapsing if the current crediting rate is reduced by up to 25 bps and not until ages 113 and 100 with crediting rate reductions of 50 bps and 100 bps, respectively. To evaluate crediting rate declines properly, consideration should be given to the current economic environment and likely future changes in interest rates. (Chapter 14 covers the pricing factors that impact policy performance, including influences on those pricing factors.) As an example, if interest rates are at historical lows and one believes that crediting rates are unlikely to drop, a 100 bps crediting rate reduction could be viewed as a remote possibility. With those views and the knowledge that the probability of living past age 100 is approximately 10 percent, CV=DB at age 121 may be considered a safe funding level for Policy A.

Policy B provides a slightly lower premium solve (1 percent) and much better surrender value performance (SV IRR). However, it does not hold up quite as well as Policy A when the crediting rate is reduced. Policy B illustrates as lapsing at age 95 (five years earlier than Policy A) when the crediting rate is reduced by 100 bps, with an associated risk of approximately 25 percent that the insured will live past age 95 (i.e., outlive coverage). If the perception is that the current crediting rate is unlikely to drop 100 bps, Policy B may be considered to have the best combination of cost and risk protection.

Two key observations from Table 15-2 are:

◆ Funding to a cash value target of CV=DB at age 121 can provide significant risk protection from crediting rate reductions; and
◆ Different policies will react differently to assumption changes (i.e., some policies will hold up better than other policies over time).

Next we evaluate cost and risk between two policies based on the commonly used target cash value of $1.00 at age 121.

Table 15-3 shows the same policies from Table 15-2. By targeting $1.00 of cash value at age 121 versus CV=DB, the annual premium can be reduced. The 1.8 percent premium reduction for Policy B might be considered insignificant, while the 6.5 percent reduction for Policy A may be considered significant.

For a 50 bps crediting rate reduction, both policies illustrate as remaining in force at least to age 99 (with only an associated risk of approximately 10 percent of outliving coverage), and, even with a 100 bps crediting rate reduction, both policies illustrate as staying in force at least to age 94 (with approximately a 25 percent risk of outliving). If the perception or insight is that

TABLE 15-3
10-Pay Funding—CV=DB versus $1.00 Cash Value Age 121 Examples

	CV=DB Age 121		$1.00 CV Age 121	
Policy	**A**	**B**	**A**	**B**
Current Crediting Rate	5.00%	5.05%	5.00%	5.05%
Guaranteed Crediting Rate	3.00%	2.40%	3.00%	2.40%
Annual Premium	$23,724	$23,404	$22,192	$22,978
% Reduction From CV=DB			−6.5%	−1.8%
Present Value Premium	192,350	189,755	179,929	186,302
Crediting Rate Decrease		**Lapse Age**		
10 bps	n/a	120	114	111
25 bps	n/a	108	108	104
50 bps	113	101	102	99
100 bps	100	95	95	94
150 bps	95	92	92	92
200 bps	91	90	88	89
Guaranteed	91	86	88	86
Guaranteed Charges and Crediting Rate	73	70	72	70
SV IRR—Current Assumptions				
Age 65 (Policy Yr 10)	−1.63%	−0.29%	−2.10%	−0.39%
Age 75 (Policy Yr 20)	1.36%	2.41%	0.98%	2.33%
Age 85 (Policy Yr 30)	1.71%	2.61%	1.20%	2.49%

crediting rates are unlikely to drop more than 50 bps, then funding to $1.00 at age 121 may be considered an appropriate funding level.

Key observations from the example are:

◆ Policies provide different relative illustrated performance at different funding levels. In Table 15-3, Policy B provides a lower premium solve for CV=DB, but Policy A provides a lower premium solve when targeting $1.00 of cash value.

◆ The magnitude of premium reductions when lowering the funding target can be materially different by policy.

◆ As compared to CV=DB funding, some policyowners may find the increased risk acceptable (persist to age 95 with a 100 bps crediting rate reduction) given the lower premium solve (6.5 percent), particularly if the perception is that crediting rates have bottomed out.

◆ As compared to CV=DB funding, cash value accumulation suffers for the lower $1.00 funding level, with age 85 surrender value IRRs reduced by 12 to 51 bps.

What about individuals who feel that they could never live to age 100? Table 15-4 provides a less common funding level, target $1 of cash value at age 101 for the same two policies. The problem with funding at this level is that

TABLE 15-4
10-Pay Funding - CV=DB versus $1.00 Cash Value Age 121 & 101 Examples

	CV=DB Age 121		$1 CV Age 121		$1 CV Age 101	
Policy	A	B	A	B	A	B
Current Crediting Rate	5.00%	5.05%	5.00%	5.05%	5.00%	5.05%
Guaranteed Crediting Rate	3.00%	2.40%	3.00%	2.40%	3.00%	2.40%
Annual Premium	$23,724	$23,404	$22,192	$22,978	$20,273	$21,148
% Reduction From CV=DB			−6.5%	−1.8%	−14.5%	−9.6%
Present Value Premium	192,350	189,755	179,929	186,302	164,370	171,464
Crediting Rate Decrease			**Lapse Age**			
10 bps	n/a	120	114	111	99	99
25 bps	n/a	108	108	104	97	97
50 bps	113	101	102	99	94	95
100 bps	100	95	95	94	91	92
150 bps	95	92	92	92	87	90
200 bps	91	90	88	89	85	88
Guaranteed	91	86	88	86	85	85
Guaranteed Charges and Crediting Rate	73	70	72	70	71	69
SV IRR—Current Assumptions						
Age 65 (Policy Yr 10)	−1.63%	−0.29%	−2.10%	−0.39%	−2.81%	−0.74%
Age 75 (Policy Yr 20)	1.36%	2.41%	0.98%	2.33%	0.39%	2.02%
Age 85 (Policy Yr 30)	1.71%	2.61%	1.20%	2.49%	0.31%	1.96%

any less favorable assumption change will now cause the policy to lapse before age 101, and therefore there is no cushion against pre-age-101 lapses. However, these policies do hold up fairly well, with only a five year reduction in policy coverage (age 95) if the crediting rate is reduced by 50 bps.

Key observations from the example include:

♦ As compared to CV=DB funding, premium reductions are materially lower at 10 percent to 15 percent.

♦ Lapse risk may be considered unacceptable, with a 25 percent chance of outliving coverage if the crediting rate is reduced 50 bps.

♦ Cash value growth suffers dramatically (with age 85 surrender value IRRs 65 to 140 bps lower than CV=DB at age 121 IRRs).

Death Benefit Protection: Pay-to-Age 120 Example

Are the results significantly different for longer pays than short pays? Table 15-5 provides another example for the same two policies, but this time with premiums paid to age 120 (commonly referred to as a full-pay). The cash value target is $1.00 at age 121.

TABLE 15-5

$1.00 Cash Value Age 121 Funding—10-Pay versus Full-Pay Examples

	10-Pay $1.00		Full-Pay $1.00	
Policy	**A**	**B**	**A**	**B**
Current Crediting Rate	5.00%	5.05%	5.00%	5.05%
Guaranteed Crediting Rate	3.00%	2.40%	3.00%	2.40%
Annual Premium	$22,192	$22,978	$10,200	$11,001
% Reduction in Annual Premium			−54.0%	−52.1%
Present Value Premium	179,929	186,302	205,643	221,792
% Increase in PV Premium			14.3%	19.0%
Crediting Rate Decrease		**Lapse Age**		
10 bps	114	111	116	113
25 bps	108	104	111	107
50 bps	102	99	105	102
100 bps	95	94	99	97
150 bps	92	92	96	95
200 bps	88	89	93	93
Guaranteed	88	86	93	89
Guaranteed Charges and Crediting Rate	72	70	66	59
SV IRR—Current Assumptions				
Age 65 (Policy Yr 10)	−2.10%	−0.39%	14.26%	−7.52%
Age 75 (Policy Yr 20)	0.98%	2.33%	−5.26%	−1.04%
Age 85 (Policy Yr 30)	1.20%	2.49%	−3.80%	−0.19%

Key observations for this example, when comparing short-pay and full-pay funding with the same cash value target of $1 at age 121, include:

- As expected, the annual premiums for full-pay are dramatically lower than 10-pay (over 50 percent).
- However, on a present value basis using a 5 percent discount rate, the ten annual premiums are lower than the pay-to-age-120 annual premiums by at least 14 percent. This is due to interest compounding and lower COI charges facilitated by a lower NAR (which occurs when more cash is paid into the policy earlier in the life of the policy). An example is provided below to demonstrate the impact of funding on insurance charges. The higher funding example provides a resulting COI charge that is $100 less than the low funding COI charge. Due to the COI leverage pickup, there may be motivation for a policyowner to pay into a policy earlier or provide higher funding.

COI Example

Face amount = $1 million and the COI rate is $1.00 per thousand of NAR
High funding cash value is $500,000
Low funding cash value is $400,000
High funding NAR = ($1,000,000–$500,000) = $500,000
Low funding NAR = ($1,000,000–$400,000) = $600,000

High funding COI = NAR/1,000 X COI Rate = $500,000/$1,000 X 1.00 = $500
Low funding COI = NAR/1,000 X COI Rate = $600,000/$1,000 X 1.00 = $600

- The same concept of getting money into the policy early holds for surrender value growth. The 10-pay age 85 SV IRRs are 250 bps to 500 bps higher than the full-pay IRRs. The full-pay SV IRRs are still negative through policy year 30. As a result, the policyowner will not recover the sum of the premiums paid if the policy is surrendered during the first 30 years.
- When stress testing with a reduced crediting rate, full-pay funding holds up better than 10-pay funding by two to five years (i.e., stays in force longer). This is because less interest compounding is given up with full-pay funding as compared to shorter funding. In general, shorter pays will be more susceptible to crediting rate decreases than longer pays.
- With guaranteed charges and crediting rate, full-pay funding illustrates as lapsing 6 to 11 years sooner than 10-pay funding. This is because of the higher COI leverage associated with longer funding. In general, longer pays will be more susceptible to COI increases than shorter pays.

Cash Value Accumulation: Minimum Non-MEC Death Benefit Example

Table 15-6 shows a cash value accumulation policy designed to efficiently accumulate cash value. The example includes the two policies we have been reviewing but assumes that $50,000 of annual premium is to be paid into each contract for seven years, and solves for the lowest death benefit that will not trigger a MEC. The lower the death benefit for a given level of funding, the lower the insurance charges, and consequently the higher the SV IRR performance. Contracts with a death benefit below the MEC limit are subject to punitive taxes for distributions. Specifically there is a 10 percent penalty tax on distributions before age $59^1/_2$ and distributions are taxed on a LIFO basis (taxable portion is assumed to be withdrawn first).

The MEC test occurs during the first seven policy years, where the cumulative premium paid cannot exceed the sum of the seven-pay MEC premium. However, if a material change occurs, such as a change in the death benefit coverage or an addition of a rider post issue, then a new seven-pay test period begins. This high funding level is typical for corporate-owned policies where the corporation is purchasing insurance to fund deferred benefits for employees. In addition, some individuals fund at the maximum level to accumulate cash values on a tax deferred basis because the inside build up of cash value is not taxed until the policy is surrendered. Chapter 7 offers a discussion of MEC contracts.

TABLE 15-6
Cash Accumulation—Minimum Non-MEC Death Benefit Example

Policy	A	B
Current Crediting Rate	5.00%	5.05%
Guaranteed Crediting Rate	3.00%	2.40%
Annual Premium	$ 50,000	$ 50,000
Death Benefit	$763,544	$745,263
SV IRR—Current Assumptions		
Age 65 (Policy Yr 10)	2.24%	2.95%
Age 75 (Policy Yr 20)	3.69%	4.33%
Age 85 (Policy Yr 30)	4.04%	4.64%
Crediting Rate Decrease	**Age 85 SV IRR**	
10 bps	3.94%	4.54%
50 bps	3.54%	4.15%
100 bps	3.04%	3.65%
Guaranteed	1.76%	1.16%
	Lapse Age	
Guaranteed Charges and Crediting Rate	85	83

Some policies are priced to accumulate cash value more efficiently than other policies. In Table 15-6, Policy B provides an age 85 SV IRR of 60 bps higher than that of Policy A (4.64 percent compared to 4.04 percent). It can also be seen that cash values accumulate much more efficiently with maximum funding, as the age 85 SV IRRs in Table 15-6 are more than 200 bps higher than IRRs from the CV=DB funding examples in Table 15-2. For Policy B in particular, only 41 bps in charges have been assessed (5.05 percent crediting rate less the 4.64 percent SV IRR).

At this level of funding, even if the crediting rate is reduced to the guaranteed rate, the policies illustrate as remaining in force for life. Only with guaranteed charges and interest do the policies lapse (ages 85 and 83). For crediting rate decreases of 100 bps or less, the SV IRR drop is identical to the crediting rate drop. As an example, for Policy A when the crediting rate is reduced by 50 bps, the corresponding SV IRR also reduces by 50 bps (3.54 percent compared to 4.04 percent). This is because there is little COI leverage with maximum funding. However, at some point, if the crediting rate drop were large enough, it could provide some downside COI leverage. As an example, for Policy A when the crediting rate is reduced by 200 bps to the guaranteed rate, the SV IRR reduces by 228 bps (1.76 percent compared to 4.04 percent).

These examples are provided to demonstrate the process, including an assessment of tradeoffs, for determining an appropriate funding level. Different policies and funding targets can produce materially different results, and therefore the examples provided are not necessarily representative. Illustrations should always apply to specific cases.

Special Considerations for Specific Policies

Some life insurance policies require special considerations when examining funding options. Here we briefly explore those applicable to VUL, equity indexed UL, and NLG UL.

Variable Universal Life

The key funding question for VUL is the rate to use for the earned rate assumption. As discussed in Chapters 7 and 14, premiums are allocated to funds made available by the insurer (both fixed income and equity options), and 100 percent of the underlying market value risk is transferred to the policyowner—there is no guaranteed minimum earnings rate. Therefore, the resulting rate credited to the policy can be quite volatile as compared to a general account UL crediting rate.

Historical fund performance can provide some perspective but is no guarantee of future returns. In addition, the monthly volatility in market value returns can either help or hurt policy performance. For these reasons, it is recommended that a conservative earnings rate be used to determine funding levels. If actual investment earnings are better than illustrated, a decision can be made about suspending premium payments earlier than illustrated or even withdrawing cash. Otherwise, the conservative earned rate will provide a cushion in case actual market performance falls short of assumptions.

Equity Indexed Universal Life

As with VUL, the crediting rate assumption for equity indexed universal life (EIUL) is critical. EIUL is subject to return volatility, albeit not as dramatically as VUL. The crediting rate is based on the returns of a stock index but typically subject to a maximum rate (cap) and minimum rate (floor). Historical index returns can be used to provide some perspective but are no guarantee for future returns. Therefore, it is recommended that a conservative crediting rate is used when determining an appropriate funding level.

No-Lapse Guarantee Universal Life

Funding NLG UL could be considered straight forward: simply pay the required premium to guarantee coverage for life. However, with the flexible nature of NLG products, a less-than-lifetime guarantee can be dialed in. Examples include guaranteeing coverage to ages 90, 100, or 110. As one would expect, the required premium for guaranteeing coverage for less than the whole of life is lower, but now there is a risk of outliving coverage, which may require exorbitant catch-up premiums to keep the policy in force.

Relative guaranteed premium levels can be quite different depending upon the length of the guarantee from policy to policy. Table 15-7 shows an ex-

TABLE 15-7
NLG Premium Funding—Ages 101 and 121

Funding/Guarantee to Age	Policy A	Policy B
Full-Pay/Age 121	$18,546	$18,718#
Pay-to-Age 100/Age 101	16,978	18,718
Catch-Up Premium*	58,765	200
10-Pay/Age 121	33,964	35,993
10-Pay/Age 101	29,983	35,982
Catch-Up Premium*	59,037	200

#Premium to age 100, then only minimum annual premiums of $200 are required to guarantee coverage to age 121
*One time premium paid at age 101 to keep the policy in force to age 102

ample for a male, age 65, nonsmoker, with a level $1 million death benefit. Policy A provides a significant premium discount when reducing the length of guarantee from lifetime (age 121) to age 101, whereas Policy B does not. But Policy A has a significant one time catch-up premium if the insured lives past age 101, whereas Policy B does not. For Policy B, the shadow account policy charges virtually cease at age 101, with only a required minimum annual premium payment of $200 from ages 101 to 120 to maintain the shadow account (i.e., to secure guaranteed coverage to age 121). As recalled from Chapter 7, coverage remains in force for as long as either the cash value or the shadow account remains positive.

An idea of life expectancy and survival probabilities should also be considered when making a decision regarding the duration of the guarantee. As seen in Table 15-1, high net worth underwritten insureds (male nonsmoker) have approximately a 40 percent probability of living past age 90, a 25 percent probability of living past age 95, and a 10 percent probability of living past age 100. And the probabilities of survival increase with survivorship policies. See Table 15-8 below. The probability of at least one person living to age 100 is approximately 20 percent as compared to 10 percent for a single life.

Conclusions

Determining an appropriate funding level for flexible premium life insurance is critical but not an exact science. The trade offs of cost and risk protection must be weighed. All policyowners are different, with different risk/reward profiles, and each policy and policy type can perform quite differently under different scenarios. Illustrations can be used to gauge the cost/risk tradeoff.

TABLE 15-8
Survivorship Nonsmoker Mortality
(High Net Worth Underwritten Insureds)

Issue Ages (Male/Female)	45/42	55/52	65/62	75/72
Life Expectancy Years	52	42	33	25
Probability of Survival				
20 Years	99.8%	99.2%	95.1%	75.8%
30 Years	98.5%	92.6%	67.2%	23.3%
40 Years	91.1%	63.6%	19.7%	0.6%
50 Years	61.9%	18.4%	0.5%	0.0%
60 Years	17.9%	0.4%	0.0%	0.0%
70 Years	0.4%	0.0%	0.0%	0.0%

Premium levels can be calculated (solved for) to achieve a specified cash value at a given age or to guarantee policy coverage for a specified number of years.

A baseline illustration is prepared with current assumptions, solving for the premium that achieves the specified target. Stress testing is then performed by varying the elements of the illustration that could impact product performance such as crediting rate, earned rate, or funding over a different length of time. Both cost and the risk (lapse) of not achieving the desired objective are noted and used to determine an appropriate funding level. Results can vary significantly by policy and funding level, which make illustrations, the expertise of a life insurance advisor, and ongoing in-force policy management (Chapter 17) critical to successful outcomes over the life of the policy.

*Using Policy Illustrations for Competitive Comparison Purposes**

16

THIS CHAPTER CONCLUDES PART V on life insurance illustrations and the sustainability of policy values. Here we examine the use of policy illustrations for competitive comparison purposes as a factor in policy selection. We begin with a review of the factors to consider when making illustration comparisons and conclude with a review of illustration performance measures.

Why Compare Illustrated Policy Values

Illustrated policy values are compared between policies to determine illustrated policy performance (i.e., competitiveness), a key factor in policy selection. The market contains numerous life insurance policies that exhibit a wide range of illustrated performance. It is virtually impossible to estimate a policy's competitiveness without comparing it to other policies. Some policies may have comparatively low premiums but correspondingly low cash value accumulation, while other policies may have comparatively high premiums with correspondingly high cash value accumulation. Illustrated policy performance can vary greatly depending on insured characteristics (gender, age, and risk classification),

---

*Authored by Wayne Tonning.

premium funding (both amount and duration), and policy type. The only way to determine if a policy illustrates competitively is to conduct a comparison.

Illustration comparisons are also used to review the sustainability of illustrated policy values. If an illustration appears to be "too good to be true" (i.e., illustrated policy values are far superior to those of all other policies), perhaps the illustrated values are, indeed, "not true." However, it is also possible that the insurer has superior experience characteristics that support the illustrated policy values. In any event, further research would be needed. (Chapter 14 offers a review of illustrated policy value sustainability.)

Factors to Consider for Illustration Competitive Comparisons

Several factors warrant consideration when conducting a policy illustration comparison. These factors also provide perspective for making a policy selection.

Non-Guaranteed Nature of Policy Illustrations

Illustration comparisons should be put in context. It is worth emphasizing that illustrated policy values are no guarantee of future policy performance. Most are predicated on non-guaranteed policy elements or current assumptions, as we have emphasized throughout this *Guide*, especially in Chapters 6 and 14. Therefore it is recommended that policy selection should not be based purely on illustrated performance, especially when the illustrated performance differential is small, as even small changes in future current assumptions (such as adjusted crediting or dividend interest rates) may change the actual relative policy performance. Other policy selection factors should be considered, including: insurer financial strength (see Part II), underwriting, policy service, insurer historical treatment of in-force policyholders and insurer intentions of managing future in-force policy performance (see Chapter 14).

Illustrations, however, can also be prepared based on assumptions that are less favorable than those prevailing at the time the illustration is prepared. The least favorable illustration would be the one constructed using only guaranteed policy elements.

As an example, illustrations may be prepared with a reduced crediting or dividend interest rate assumption but no worse than the guaranteed rate in order to provide some perspective of downside risk. Recall that illustrations are not permitted to be run at assumptions better than presently prevailing, and that most commonly insurers and agents cannot run illustrations based on other than guaranteed and currently prevailing non-guaranteed charges. The non-guaranteed nature of illustrations leads logically to the need for assessment of the sustainability of illustrated policy values (see Chapter 14) and to periodic policy reviews (see Chapter 17).

Preparing Consistent Illustration Comparisons

For illustration comparisons to be meaningful, they should be based on as many identical policy characteristics and scenarios as possible. For example, one would ideally compare only policies of a similar product type (e.g., universal life, whole life, term); death benefit amount, duration, and pattern; premium amount and duration; and target cash value (if applicable).

This ideal world, however, is not always the one in which we live and make decisions. When searching for the policy that seems to offer the best value, WL policies often must be compared to UL policies and each of these is sometimes compared to term policies. We emphasize the word "seems" as we typically rely on non-guaranteed policy elements that will certainly change in the future from those shown today. There is no way to know, with certainty, which policy will offer the best value; we can only make our best estimate and, sometimes, only our best guess.

In this section, we explore those policy elements that we seek to hold constant across all comparisons. As we make clear later in this chapter, not *everything* can be held constant. If we assume the same premium payment amount and duration and the same death benefit amount, duration, and pattern between two policies, cash values obviously must be allowed to vary between the two policies. Similarly, if we assume the same target cash value and death benefit amount, duration, and pattern with each policy, different premium amounts must result to fund these otherwise similar packages of benefits. In other words, as will be shown, all policy comparisons "solve" for the policy element not held constant between the policies. We can call this the dependent policy element as its value *depends* on the values chosen for other policy elements. Thus, in any comparison, and other things being the same, we would prefer the policy whose dependent policy element is the highest if that policy element were the death benefit or cash value or distributions from the policy or the lowest if that dependent policy element were the premium.

Rating Categories and Risk Classification Factors

Obviously, all policies should assume the same gender and issue age for the insured. The same gender should pose no difficulties, but age can occasionally differ between carriers because of the way it is derived. Some insurers consider a proposed insured's age to be that of his or her last birthday, while most insurers consider age to be that which is closest to either the last birthday or the next birthday (e.g., age nearest birthday). Thus, an insured aged 55 years and 11 months would be 56, not 55. Rather than try to determine "age," it is always better to simply enter the insured's date of birth into the illustration software.

Some insurance companies allow backdating. **Backdating** is the practice of setting a policy issue date before the application or policy date, but no more than six months earlier, to secure a one-year-earlier issue age and lower insurance charges. As an example, backdating may be allowed by an insurer if the insured's issue age has increased by one year during the underwriting process. While the mortality rates will be lower due to the younger issue age, the cost reduction will be partially or completely offset by having to pay for coverage during the backdate period in which no coverage actually was in place. It is not always beneficial to backdate a policy.

Other rating factors include smoker status, further subdivided by health factors, as discussed in Chapter 6. As an example, there may be three non-smoker rating categories: super-preferred, preferred, and standard. Individuals that meet the strictest health requirements would receive a super-preferred rating, individuals that meet the next strictest requirements would receive a preferred rating, and all other nonsmokers would receive a standard rating. Then there are the various substandard classifications for individuals who have substantial health ailments. The number of rating factors and risk classes will vary from policy to policy. Also, companies may not rate health factors the same, thereby providing a different rating category for the same insured. If specific underwriting offers from each insurance company are known, these should be used to derive illustrations.

If underwriting results are not known or used for general comparison purposes (i.e., not for a specific case), then the rating factor categories and risk classification ordinarily should be the same for all policies in the comparison (e.g., best nonsmoker comparison or a standard nonsmoker comparison). Advisors are wise not to put much stock in the name each company gives to its various rating factor categories. For example, a preferred plus category for one company may be the same as a super preferred category for another company. Instead, consider using the rating factor category number system shown in Table 16-1.

Complications can arise when rating factors do not align, as seen in Table 16-1. One company may have four nonsmoker categories while another has three. One comparison may be to run best class to best class, but this is not

TABLE 16-1
Rating Factor Categories

Rating Factors	Four Categories	Three Categories	Two Categories
Best Nonsmoker	1/4	1/3	1/2
Second Best Nonsmoker	2/4	2/3	
Third Best Nonsmoker	3/4		
Standard Nonsmoker	4/4	3/3	2/2

perfect as some individuals may qualify for the best class in the three class policy but the second best class for the four class policy due to stricter criteria for the best class. In this case, it may also be helpful to review the second best class from the four class product to the best class of the three class product. In the end, careful consideration should be taken when determining appropriate risk classes for a comparison where underwriting is not known.

Premium Funding Levels, Death Benefits, and Cash Value Targets

Premium funding level and duration; death benefit amounts, duration, and pattern; and cash value targets (if applicable) should be consistent for all policies included in the comparison. Chapter 15 offers a discussion of determining appropriate funding levels. Note that the dependent policy element will vary based on the consistent independent policy elements.

For flexible premium death benefit protection sales where the funding level is known and specified, the death benefit amount is the dependent policy element for which we solve, assuming a cash value target. As an example, if one has $10,000 to pay into the policy annually over the next ten years, then how much level death benefit will that buy with a cash value target of $1 at age 121?

For death benefit protection sales where the death benefit coverage is known and specified, the dependent policy element for which we solve is the premium level, assuming a cash value target (if applicable). As an example, if one needs $1 million of level death benefit coverage, then how much premium is required to target a cash value equal to the death benefit (CV=DB) at age 121? Furthermore, is it better to pay one premium up front or spread out premium payments over the next number of specified years? Typically, it is optimal to have the same number of identical premiums with UL policies to achieve the greatest degree of comparability.

One of the decisions to make when preparing an illustrated performance comparison for death benefit protection applications for UL is the cash value target. Common targets are CV=DB or $1 of cash value at age 121. Age 121 is key for most cash value policies as coverage continues but charges are not applied after age 121 (i.e., the policy is paid up at age 121). Some products terminate policy charges earlier, such as age 101. Cash values provide cushion for the possibility of less favorable assumption changes (i.e., a crediting rate reduction or policy charge increase). For UL, coverage terminates (lapses) if the cash value goes to zero. The goal is to appropriately fund a policy to build cash value and limit exposure to a policy lapse. Downside scenario illustrations, such as a reduced crediting rate, should be prepared to determine funding for the risk profile of the policyowner. (See Chapter 15 for determining appropriate funding levels.)

For typical cash value accumulation sales, the amount of premium funding is known and the death benefit is set to the minimum non-MEC (modified endowment contract) death benefit to accumulate cash efficiently. A lower death benefit for a given funding level provides lower insurance charges. While a resulting death benefit that is lower than the minimum non-MEC death benefit provides slightly better cash value accumulation, it will trigger negative tax consequences if distributions are taken from the policy (see Chapter 7). Distributions from non-MEC policies do not carry negative income tax consequences.

Illustrated Assumptions

Illustrations can be run based on different assumptions for charges and credits for UL or dividend scales for participating WL. Comparisons should be run based on non-guaranteed elements or current assumptions prevailing presently with each company. Other illustrations often are run at each company's current assumptions with a reduction of the current crediting or dividend interest rate by a selected number of basis points (bps) to understand the impact of a rate reduction. Compliant illustrations must also show policy values based on guaranteed policy elements (see Chapter 13), which provide perspective as to the guaranteed least favorable policy performance.

Matching crediting rates for UL or dividend interest rates for WL (e.g., using a 5 percent crediting rate for all policies) does not provide a level playing field. Current crediting rates and dividend interest rates are based on current experience. If one policy has a higher crediting or dividend interest rate due to higher underlying investment earnings, that higher rate should be reflected; that is a legitimate competitive advantage for that policy. In addition, UL interest spreads (the difference between the earned rate on underlying investments and the current crediting rate) typically differ from policy to policy, resulting in different crediting rates (a higher interest spread will produce a lower crediting rate and vice versa). (See Chapter 6.) One policy may be priced with a low interest spread that is offset with higher policy charges and vice versa. In other words, overall product pricing determines a package of interest credits and loads charged.

Policy Options and Riders

Policy options and riders should be matched. For example, comparing a policy with an increasing death benefit to one with a level death benefit would not provide an accurate assessment as the former would have higher cost of insurance (COI) charges. Additionally, it is wise to have all policies comply with the same income tax definition of life insurance (DOLI) test (discussed in Chapter 7). Recall that policies must meet either the guideline premium test (GPT) or cash value accumulation test (CVAT). The selected DOLI test will have an impact on illustrated performance. Typically, the GPT will provide the lowest premium solves for death benefit protection sales. For cash value accumulation sales, CVAT with a level death benefit provides the highest early duration cash values, while GPT with a death benefit Option B (increasing) then switching to Option A (level) in an optimal year provides the highest long-term cash value accumulation.

If policy riders are included, the same or similar rider should be illustrated for all policies. Most riders provide some sort of an additional benefit for an additional cost. Examples of common riders include: overloan protection, waiver of premium, accidental death benefit, enhanced cash value, accelerated living benefits, children's term, and guaranteed insurability. (See Chapter 9 for a description of common policy features and riders.)

Riders are included automatically in some policies at no identifiable additional cost. Those should be noted. A common example of an automatic rider is a short-term no-lapse guarantee that provides guaranteed coverage for a specified number of years (typically 20 years or less) if the required premium is paid. Another example is the waiver of premium feature. If a policy does not offer the rider of interest, then that policy is typically not included in the comparison. However, a comparison without the rider of interest would also be recommended to gain an understanding of the relative cost of the rider.

Other Considerations for Specific Policies

Additional considerations apply when performing illustration comparisons for variable universal life (VUL), equity index universal life (EIUL), and no-lapse guarantee (NLG) universal life.

Variable Universal Life

The discussion above focused on general account products, which have a crediting rate or a dividend interest rate. However, VUL, which have funds allocated to separate accounts, do not have a crediting rate as such. Instead, with VUL illustrations, an assumed hypothetical earnings rate is used. The earnings rate is intended to represent the market value investment earnings assumption on the underlying asset allocation, as determined by the illustration preparer based on funds offered by the insurer, and is represented as an annual rate of return credited to the policy values. There is no "current" rate or "guaranteed" rate. One hundred percent of the investment risk is transferred to the policyowner.

What is the Appropriate Earnings Rate to Illustrate?

There is no "correct" rate to use when illustrating variable life. However, the earnings rate selected should be relevant to the asset allocation chosen. Historical rates of return for the specified funds can provide some perspective of risk and return, but historical performance is neither a guarantee nor a predictor of future performance. Some illustrations provide a historical fund performance summary for the specified asset allocation. Otherwise, the insurer should be able to provide a summary on request.

Depending on the asset allocation, we suggest a conservative earned rate assumption due to the potential underlying volatility of fund returns. However, an earned rate assumption typically would be higher than current crediting rates, as otherwise a general account selection would be the logical choice. Variable is usually selected because the policyowner believes the underlying separate account funds chosen will outperform general account investment grade fixed income returns

A complication to note with VUL is that the investment yield and product loads are applied monthly. The loads are applied based on the market value of the underlying assets on the monthly processing date. If the market value has dropped, then more units must be sold when the loads are applied and vice versa. In addition, COI charges are based on the underlying net amount at risk (NAR), which is a function of the underlying policy value. COI charges will vary based on the monthly investment yield as it impacts the policy value. This subjects VUL to interim yield performance volatility. As an example, the underlying fund(s) may return 10 percent for a policy year, but overall policy performance may differ from a projected level 10 percent annual yield due to the interim monthly yield volatility. The same concept applies in illustrations with a level earned rate assumption in all years. As an example, the policy's underlying funds may return 8 percent over the life of the policy, but actual policy performance will be quite different due to the volatility in the annual (and monthly) yields. Resulting policy performance may be better or worse than the 8 percent level yield. Illustrations typically allow the earned rate assumption to be changed on an annual basis, but not monthly. In addition, illustrations may not be run at an earned rate in excess of 12 percent gross, whereas historical annual market returns have exceeded 12 percent in some years.

Another complication with VUL is that the earned rate can be specified as either a gross rate or a net rate. A gross rate does not reflect investment management fees and expenses. The net rate is the gross rate net of the investment management fees and expenses. For some illustrations, the net rate is also reduced for the mortality and expense charge (M&E). See Figure 16-1.

When to Match the Gross Rate

If the comparison is for a specific case and/or the asset allocation is known, and each policy offers comparable funds, then applying an identical asset allocation and gross earnings rate assumption to all policies is appropriate. This method appropriately reflects the actual investment management

FIGURE 16-1: Variable Earnings Rate Detail

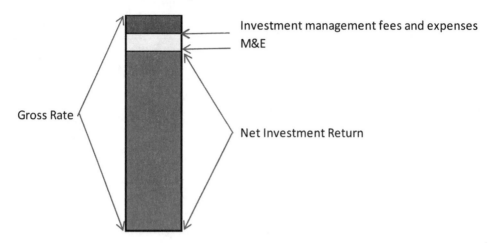

fees and expenses that can be different from policy to policy. A comparable fund that has lower investment management fees and expenses has a competitive advantage, which should be reflected in the comparison. If a policy does not offer a comparable fund, it may not be appropriate to include in the comparison.

When to Match the Net Rate

For comparisons where the asset allocation is unknown or comparable funds are not offered, an enlightening comparison can be made that focuses on the underlying policy charges (i.e., does not reflect differences in net investment earnings) by using the same net earned rate for all products included in the comparison. The net rate should be net of the investment management fees and expenses, but not net of M&E charges, as it is an insurance policy charge (whereas investment management fees and expenses are an investment charge). The M&E charge is not intended to cover routine death claims (mortality) but to provide mortality and expense margins akin to, and for the same reason as, those applicable to general account policies. See Chapter 6 for a discussion of policy loads.

The net rate for most illustrations does not include the M&E charge and, therefore, no adjustment need be made. When the M&E charge is included in the net rate, the illustration preparer should adjust the net rate downward by the amount of the M&E charge. (This is not exact due to compounding but is close enough.) Refer to Table 16-2 for an example. Without a net rate adjustment, Policy B has a 15 bps advantage over Policy A, which is not fair since both policies have identical investment management fees and M&E. With the net rate downward adjustment for Policy B, the ending net credit to the policy is matched for Policies A and B.

TABLE 16-2
Match Net Rate of 8.00 percent

	Policy A	Policy B	Policy B*
	Net Rate does not include M&E	Net Rate includes M&E	Net Rate includes M&E
Gross Rate	8.25%	8.40%	8.25%
Investment Management Fees	0.25%	0.25%	0.25%
M&E	n/a	0.15%	0.15%
Net Rate	8.00%	8.00%	7.85%*
M&E	0.15%	n/a	n/a
Net Credit to Policy	7.85%	8.00%	7.85%

*For this example, the illustration preparer would reduce the net rate to 7.85 percent for Policy B.

By matching net rates, we focus on the underlying insurance policy pricing differences that impact policy performance (i.e., product loads and COI charges but not investment management fees and expenses). This methodology is not exact; variable policies typically are priced with an insurance policy charge buried in the investment management fee to provide a lower explicitly disclosed M&E charge. The net rate comparison method will favor policies that have a comparatively high insurance policy charge included in the investment management fee, but it is difficult to adjust for this as the buried insurance policy charge is either not disclosed or difficult to ascertain. (Chapter 7 provides more information on VUL.)

Equity Index Universal Life

While EIUL has a crediting rate, it is different than the crediting rate for generic UL. The EIUL crediting rate is based on the return of a stock index, typically subject to a cap, floor, and participation rate. As an example, the index may be the S&P 500, a participation rate of 70 percent, a 12 percent cap, and a floor of 0 percent. This means that the crediting rate would return 70 percent of the growth in the S&P 500 index (not including dividends) and would never be higher than 12 percent or lower than 0 percent. (See Chapter 7 for a review of EIUL.) The index strategies are typically different from policy to policy (i.e., the index, participation rate, cap, and floor vary by policy). This makes it difficult to determine an appropriate crediting rate assumption for EIUL policies included in the comparison as the resulting crediting rates will be different.

What is the Appropriate Crediting Rate to Illustrate for EIUL?

As with the earnings rate in variable life, there is no definitive answer to this question. EIUL illustrations will contain a default crediting rate, but there is no consistency or regulatory standard as to what that rate should be. Some products appear to have a more aggressive crediting rate while others appear to be more conservative. Certainly a review of the growth rate history for the specified index strategy can be enlightening. Some insurers are now including a summary of historical growth rates for the index strategy in the illustration; otherwise, the growth rate history should be available from the insurer upon request. However, interpreting this information can be challenging as many indexes do not have a long historical track record.

Historical summaries may include hypothetical calculated growth rates for the time periods before the index strategy was implemented. The hypothetical calculated growth rates are based on current index strategy mechanics (participation rate, cap, and floor). An issue with calculating historical growth rates is that the current index mechanics are not guaranteed and may not have been applicable historically as they are based on current market pricing (interest rates and option prices). It is likely that the historical index strategy mechanics would have fluctuated with changing market conditions, and therefore it is not known what the actual historical growth rates would have been. It is helpful to delineate actual index growth rates versus hypothetical or calculated index growth rates when reviewing historical rates provided by insurers. In addition, historical index growth rates neither guarantee nor predict future growth rates.

A review of the history of changes to the index strategy mechanics can also be enlightening. Some policy's index strategies have had more changes than others and may appear to be more susceptible to future changes. As an example, noting that the cap rate has been reduced from 12 percent to 10 percent can provide some perspective on historical index returns and expectations for future returns (i.e., are the index mechanics more susceptible to change than other index strategies?). In particular, where an insurer has an index product with aggressive mechanics and a history of making index changes, the sustainability of the current index mechanics comes into question. Perhaps another company offers an index product with conservative index mechanics but has a good track record of maintaining the index mechanics. Guarantees on the cap, floor, and participation rate should also be noted.

As with the variable earnings rate for VUL, it is suggested that a conservative index crediting rate be used for illustration funding purposes and managing policyholder expectations. Historical returns suggest EIUL provides returns similar to UL with a bit of a "kicker," and therefore an index crediting rate that is 25 to 50 bps higher than current UL crediting rates might be appropriate. (See Chapter 7 for a review of EIUL.) Below are examples of some suggested EIUL comparisons that tackle the crediting rate issue.

- ◆ **Match Crediting Rate.** One comparison approach is to match the crediting rate. Much like the net rate comparison method previously discussed for variable life, this approach factors out the crediting rate differential and instead focuses on the underlying insurance policy loads (i.e., product loads and cost of insurance charges). See example in Table 16-3. This example shows that Policy A will have the better illustrated performance (i.e., requires lower premium funding) if the index crediting rates are identical.

TABLE 16-3
Premium Solve when Matching Crediting Rates

Policy	Crediting Rate	Premium Solve*
A	6.50%	$10,000
B	6.50%	10,500

*See the premium measures section of this chapter for a discussion regarding the premium solve performance measure.

◆ **Determine Crediting Rate that Matches Best Illustrated Performance.** A suggested next step would be to increase the crediting rate on those products with less favorably illustrated values until illustrated performance is matched. See example in Table 16-4. This example shows that the index crediting rate for Policy B will need to earn an additional 25 bps (6.75 percent less 6.50 percent) as compared to Policy A to match the premium solve of Policy A. The question then is whether the index crediting rate for Policy B will outperform the index crediting rate for Policy A by at least 25 bps.

TABLE 16-4
Increase Crediting Rate to Match Premium Solve

Policy	Crediting Rate	Premium Solve
A	6.50%	$10,000
B	6.50%	10,500
B	6.75%	10,000

No-Lapse Guarantee Universal Life

In many respects, comparing the illustrated performance of NLG policies can be less complicated than other policy types as the main focus is on the premium that guarantees coverage for life. There is no need to have a cash value target or vary assumptions as the premium and death benefit are guaranteed, provided the premium is paid on time as per the required premium schedule. However, a couple of issues make NLG comparisons more complicated. First, not all policyowners want guaranteed coverage for life (age 121). Second, some policyowners, particularly for insureds ages 65 and below, want to take cash values into consideration as they wish to preserve the policy flexibility. Recent cash value accumulation NLG policies have been developed that provide stronger cash values than traditional NLG policies.

Considerations for Less than Lifetime Guarantees

Many NLG policies are sold with funding for a guarantee that is less than lifetime (such as to age 95). Numerous individuals believe that they will not live to age 100, let alone to age 121. Thus, there is no need to pay the additional premiums needed to guarantee coverage to these advanced ages. Instead, premiums may be illustrated to guarantee coverage to age 90, 100, etc. Of course, such funding creates the risk of the insured outliving coverage, so catch-up premiums should be considered when funding for less than life. This issue can be particularly troublesome for survivorship and the high net worth market that exhibits lower mortality. As an example, a healthy couple may have a joint life expectancy into the attained age 90's.

Also consider that about one-half of insured's outlive their life expectancy, so funding past life expectancy often is considered wise. Life expectancy ideally would be estimated taking into consideration not only the insured's age and gender but also his or her health and financial situation. This life expectancy can be helpful in determining an appropriate period of time to guarantee coverage. Policies that are highly competitive for a lifetime guarantee may not be competitive when guaranteeing for less than life and vice versa. Table 16-5 provides an example where Policy A has a higher premium when guaranteeing coverage for life but the lower premium when guaranteeing coverage to age 100.

TABLE 16-5
Guarantee Coverage for Life versus Age 100

Policy	Guarantee for Life	Guarantee to Age 100
	Annual Premium	
A	$25,000	$23,000
B	24,500	24,000

Consideration for Catch-Up Premiums

If the illustration comparison is for funding less than the entirety of life, catch-up premiums for each product should be compared. Recall that a catch-up premium is the additional premium required after the initial guarantee period to restore guaranteed coverage for a specified number of additional years. The policyowner can thereby avoid losing coverage if the insured lives past the initial guarantee period. Catch-up premiums can be significantly different from policy to policy. Table 16-6 provides an example of a policy that has a lower annual premium to guarantee coverage to age 101 but a substantially higher catch-up premium to provide coverage for one more year. It could be more appealing to the prospect to choose Policy B, which has a slightly higher premium to age 100, but a significantly lower catch-up premium.

TABLE 16-6
Catch-Up Premium

Policy	Premium to Guarantee Coverage to Age 101	Age 101 Catch Up Premium*
A	$23,000	$150,000
B	24,000	27,500

*Premium paid at beginning of age 101 to guaranteed coverage for one more year

Consideration for Cash Values

As mentioned previously, it may be appropriate to review cash values as they provide flexibility for unexpected life events. This consideration can be especially relevant for younger insureds. Cash values can provide funding for retirement income needs, be put up as collateral for loans, and fund short-term cash needs, among other purposes, (see Chapter 18). In such instances, it may be worth paying a slightly higher guaranteed premium to secure substantially higher cash values.

Careful consideration should be applied when contemplating taking distributions from a NLG policy. Distributions, including both withdrawals and loans, will shorten the length of the guarantee period. Also, even cash value versions of NLG products typically do not provide the same level of cash values as provided in generic current assumption UL products.

Common Measures of Illustrated Policy Performance

As noted earlier, if we assume the same premium payment amount and duration and the same death benefit amount, duration, and pattern between two policies, cash values must be allowed to vary between the two policies and similarly, for matching other policy elements. All policy comparisons "solve" for the dependent policy element not held constant between the policies. Other things being the same, this element becomes critically important in distinguishing among the expected competitiveness among different policies.

No one performance measure provides a definitive answer for which policy will have the best illustrated performance. For this reason, it is common practice to examine several performance measurements. The purpose(s) for which the insurance is being purchased dictates which measures are most relevant. Below we provide an overview of common illustrated performance measures for life insurance.

Premium Measures

There is one basic premium measure, which can be expressed on two different bases: (1) premium solve and (2) premium per $1,000 of death benefit. The odd-sounding term **premium solve** refers to the practice within the life insurance industry of setting a death benefit amount, pattern, and duration and, if applicable, a target cash value by a certain policy year then *solving* for the premium necessary to support that package of benefits. It may be the most popular illustrated performance measurement. It is applicable to both flexible-premium policies, such as UL, and fixed-premium policies, such as WL, which are derived and offered with their premiums already determined or solved.

To solve for the premium, the number of annual payments must be specified. Typically, premiums are level. Common premium payment periods are one (single-pay), ten (10-pay), pay-to-age 65, and pay-to-age 100 (older cash value policies) or 120 (newer policies). These latter payment durations are variously referred to as **level-pay**, **full-pay**, and **life-pay**. Common cash value targets are CV=DB or $1.00 at ages 101 or 121. (Chapter 15 discusses how to determine appropriate funding levels.)

Table 16-7 provides an example of a premium solve comparison. The example assumes a male, age 55, best nonsmoker class, level death benefit of $1 million, and current assumptions. Policy A provides the lowest premium solve for the specified death benefit and cash value target, with the other three products requiring premiums that are 1 percent, 5 percent, and 10 percent greater.

Sometimes the premium is expressed on the basis of each $1,000 of death benefits. This is readily accomplished by dividing the premium by death benefit amount in thousands. For Policy A in Table 16-7, the premium per $1,000 is $20 [$20,000/($1 million/$1,000)]. However, caution must be exercised in allowing this figure to be interpreted as the premium per $1,000 always being $20 regardless of the death benefit. This will not always be true, particularly when charges vary by death benefit band.

TABLE 16-7
Premium Solve Example
10-Pay CV=DB Age 121

Policy	Premium Solve (Annual)	Percent Difference*
A	$20,000	
B	20,200	1.0%
C	21,000	5.0%
D	22,000	10.0%

*Percentage difference in premium from the lowest premium

Death Benefit Measures

Two common death benefit measures are (1) the internal rate of return on the death benefit (DB IRR) and (2) death benefit solve (DB solve).

Death Benefit Internal Rate of Return

Death benefit internal rate of return is perhaps the most common death benefit measure. DB IRR is derived by solving for the interest rate that causes accumulated scheduled premiums (net of dividends, if appropriate) at selected policy durations to equal that duration's death benefit. The DB IRR can be interpreted as the yield that the beneficiary would have realized if the insured dies at the set duration, assuming no changes in the policy or its elements. It is an intuitive measure, as DB IRRs can be compared to the returns of other financial instruments such as stocks and bonds.

Ideally, in comparing returns on other financial instruments with DB IRRs, both should be on a tax equivalent basis. Of course, life insurance death proceeds ordinarily are income tax free and premiums are not tax deductible, so the return on other instruments should be evaluated on the same basis. Table 16-8 provides an example of DB IRRs. The example assumes a male, age 55, best nonsmoker class, level death benefit of $1 million, and current assumptions (same as Table 16-7).

For this example, the policy with the lowest premium (Policy A) produces the highest DB IRR in all policy years as the death benefit for all policies is an identical level $1 million. The DB IRRs decrease over time reflecting a longer period until payment of the death benefit and more premium payments. A stronger focus or weighting may be placed on the DB IRR at life expectancy (around age 85 for this case). For this example, when comparing Policy A to Policy B, 1 percent higher annual premium translates into a DB IRR reduction of only 4 bps at age 85. For Policy C, 5 percent higher annual premium translates into a 20 bps reduction to the DB IRR at age 85 as compared to Policy A. For Policy D, 10 percent higher annual premium translates into a 39 bps reduction to the age 85 DB IRR as compared to Policy A. Note that differences in DB IRRs are reduced as the policy year increases (when comparing Policy A to Policy D, the DB IRR difference is 166 bps at end of policy year 10 but only 16 bps at end of policy year 66). Caution should be considered in making a policy selection based on small differences in performance measurements, particularly given the number of future years involved and the non-guaranteed nature

TABLE 16-8
DB IRR Example for a 10-Pay CV=DB Age 121

		Death Benefit Internal Rate of Return			
Policy Year	Age	Policy A Premium=$20,000	Policy B Premium=$20,200	Policy C Premium=$21,000	Policy D Premium=$22,000
10	66	28.21%	28.04%	27.36%	26.55%
20	75	10.64%	10.58%	10.31%	10.00%
30	85	6.45%	6.41%	6.25%	6.06%
45	100	4.04%	4.01%	3.91%	3.79%
66	121	2.69%	2.67%	2.61%	2.53%

of illustrated policy values. Future changes in current assumptions may flip flop relative performance results. As discussed in Chapter 14, obtaining information about an insurer's track record of providing value to in-force policyholders and intentions of managing future policy values is recommended.

Death Benefit Solve

Typically an amount of coverage is determined and known (see Chapter 1 and 10). Sometimes, however, funds available to pay premiums are limited, so the policyowner purchases as much insurance as those funds will buy. We call this approach of solving for the amount of death benefit that a specified funding level will purchase **death benefit solve**. Table 16-9 provides an example of death benefit solves. The example assumes a male, age 55, best nonsmoker class, and level death benefit for ten annual premiums of $20,000 and assuming a cash value target of $1 at age 121. Policy A provides the highest death benefit with the other policies solving for a death benefit that is 5 percent to 10 percent lower than Policy A.

TABLE 16-9
Death Benefit Solve

Policy	Death Benefit Solve	Percent Difference*
A	$1,000,000	
B	950,000	–5.0%
C	900,000	–10.0%

*Percentage decrease in death benefit from the highest death benefit

Surrender Value Measures

Recall that surrender values are the amounts that the insurer will pay to policyholders on voluntary policy termination and are equal to the account value less surrender charges, if applicable (and also net of policy loans and withdrawals). There are several common surrender value measures, with the most common being the internal rate of return on surrender value (SV IRR). The other surrender value measures are surrender value amount (SV$) and surrender value to premium ratio (SV to Premium Ratio).

Surrender Value Amount

The surrender value amount (SV$) is the actual dollar amount of the surrender value for the specified policy year. This measure is applicable when the premium funding level for a specified death benefit coverage is matched for all policies in the comparison. The surrender value is the dependent policy element. The SV$ measure is most commonly used for cash value accumulation sales where funding is identical. The SV$ measure is not appropriate when the premium funding level is not consistent across all policies, as it does not consider the amount or timing of premium payments that generates the surrender value. This is important, as higher premiums will usually generate higher surrender values. Therefore, if the funding level is not identical for all policies, then the SV to Premium Ratio and SV IRR measurements may be more relevant.

Surrender Value to Premium Ratio

The surrender value to premium ratio (SV to Premium Ratio) is equal to the ratio of surrender value to cumulative premiums paid for the specified policy year. The SV to Premium Ratio is a common measure for showing the relationship between a policy's surrender value and the sum of premiums paid over some period, such as the first 10 to 20 policy years. The **cross-over point** is the first policy year at which the surrender value exceeds the sum of the premiums paid (i.e., when the ratio first exceeds 100 percent). As an example, an application of the ratio is common for corporate owned policies, where the first year SV to Premium Ratio is compared and typically needs to be in excess of 100 percent (in order for the corporation not to take a first year loss on the purchase of the policy).

Surrender Value Internal Rate of Return

The SV IRR, the companion to the DB IRR, is derived by solving for the interest rate that causes accumulated scheduled premiums (net of dividends, if appropriate) at selected policy durations to equal that duration's cash surrender.

Table 16-10 provides an example of the three surrender value measurements. As with the previous tables, Table 16-10 assumes a male, age 55, best nonsmoker class, level death benefit of $1 million, and current assumptions.

For this example, Policy C provides the highest surrender values (SV$) through policy year 20. Policy C also has the highest premium. The SV to Premium Ratio and SV IRR adjust for these differences. In policy year 10, Policy C has the highest surrender value but provides the second best SV to Premium Ratio and SV IRR due to the higher premiums paid.

TABLE 16-10
Surrender Value Measurements Example for a 10-Pay CV=DB Age 121
(Shaded areas denotes top illustrated performance measure)

	SV$			SV to Premium Ratio			SV IRR		
	Pol A	Pol B	Pol C	Pol A	Pol B	Pol C	Pol A	Pol B	Pol C
Premium	$20,000	$20,200	$21,000	$20,000	$20,200	$21,000	$20,000	$20,200	$21,000
Yr/Age									
1/56	$0	$8,141	$16,451	0%	40%	78%	−100%	−60%	−22%
10/65	211,869	206,822	215,792	106%	102%	103%	1.05%	0.43%	0.49%
20/75	285,810	301,807	315,847	143%	149%	150%	2.32%	2.61%	2.65%
30/85	357,447	417,344	413,871	179%	207%	197%	2.29%	2.87%	2.68%
45/100	464,073	495,257	398,719	232%	245%	190%	2.10%	2.23%	1.59%
66/121	1 million	1 million	1 million	500%	495%	476%	2.69%	2.67%	2.61%

The SV IRR measure is typically negative in the early policy years due to upfront issue loads, including surrender charges, and then turns positive as the account value grows. The SV to Premium Ratio will have the same pattern as SV IRR, where typically it starts out below 100% (unless the policy is designed for corporate owned life insurance) during the early policy years and eventually exceeds 100% (which is when premiums have been paid back without interest).

The SV IRR will be less than the crediting rate (or earning rate for variable life) due to policy loads and COI charges. The difference between the crediting rate or earning rate and the SV IRR provides an idea of the amount of charges coming out of the product expressed as an annual asset based charge. As an example, if the crediting rate is 5 percent and the SV IRR is 2.5 percent, then the illustrated charges could be expressed as 250 basis points of annual asset charges.

Some advisors and policyowners may be uncomfortable with low or zero surrender values as seen with Policy A (red shading) in Table 16-10. A policyowner may be more comfortable paying a slightly higher premium to secure greater cash value accumulation from policy inception, as with Policy B. Also some policies include a rider that enhances the early year surrender values (although typically with a tradeoff of slightly lower long-term surrender values).

Distribution Measure

If life insurance is being purchased to provide income or distributions in addition to death benefit protection coverage, the annual amount of solved for distribution can be a common performance measure to consider. Typically the funding level, death benefit amount, distribution period, and cash value target (if applicable) are matched for all policies contained in the comparison, and a resulting distribution is solved for. A **distribution** is any amount taken from a cash value policy during life that is based on its cash value, including withdrawals and loans. Table 16-11 provides an example where Policy A provides the highest annual income (withdraw to basis and switch to loans) beginning at age 66 and terminating at age 85. Typically, policies that provide a combination of low premium cost (due to competitive COI charges) and strong cash value accumulation provide the most competitive distributions. The other critical factor that determines competitive loan distributions is the

TABLE 16-11
Distribution Solve

Policy	Annual Distribution	Percent Difference*
A	$25,000	
B	$24,000	−4.0%
C	$20,000	−20.0%

*Percentage decrease in distribution from the highest distribution

spread between the interest charged on the loan and the interest credited on the loaned amount. Obviously a policy with a 0 bps loan spread will provide higher loan distributions as compared to another policy that has a positive loan spread, all else being equal. Therefore it should not be assumed that a policy that provides the most efficient cash value growth may necessarily provide the highest distributions.

Interest Adjusted Net Cost Indices

While not commonly used by advisors, other illustrated performance measures commonly found in a life insurance illustration are interest adjusted net cost indices, which are intended by regulators to assist buyers in selecting a comparatively low cost policy. The indices are calculated to reflect the time value of money ("a dollar is worth more today than 10 years from now"). Most states require inclusion of these indices on policy illustrations provided in the state.

Two sets of indices are required: (1) net payment cost indices and (2) surrender cost indices. Net payment cost indices (NPCIs) are death benefit measures of illustrated policy performance. They inform the prospective buyer of the estimated average annual net payment or outlay per $1,000 of insurance over selected time periods (ordinarily 10 and 20 years) taking into consideration only the policy's premiums and illustrated (non-guaranteed) dividends, if any, and adjusting them for the time value of money. They answer the question, what would have been the average annual net *payment* per $1,000 of death benefit under the policy if the insured paid premiums as scheduled and died at the selected time period.

Actual 20 year net payment cost indices for two policies are shown in Table 16-12. Both policies have a level $1 million death benefit and are funded with ten annual premiums to provide CV=DB at age 121. For Policy A, if the policyowner purchases $1 million of coverage and the insured dies 20 years later (and the beneficiary receives the death benefit), the average annual net payment per $1,000 of insurance would be $16.16 assuming that the policyowner values money at 5 percent per year. On its own, the net payment cost of $16.16 is not an intuitive measure, but when we compare it to the $21.30 index for Policy B, it tells us that Policy A has the lower illustrated net payment cost (i.e., Policy A has superior death-based performance).

TABLE 16-12
Year 20 Net Payment Cost Indices

Policy	Death Benefit	Annual Premium	Net Payment Cost @5%
A	$1,000,000	$26,078	$16.16
B	1,000,000	34,384	21.30

Surrender cost indices (SCIs) are surrender based measures of illustrated policy performance. They are intended to inform the prospective buyer of the estimated average annual net cost per $1,000 of insurance over selective time periods (same as NPCIs) taking into consideration the policy's premiums, illustrated dividends or other non-guaranteed policy values, and surrender values and adjusting these values for the time value of money. The SCI calculations are identical to the NPCI calculation except that they include credit for the surrender value at the specified year. They answer the question, what would have been the average annual net *cost* per $1,000 of death benefit under the policy if the policyowner paid premiums as scheduled and surrendered the policy at the selected time period.

Table 16-13 shows the SCIs for the same two policies shown in Table 16-12. For Policy A, if the policyowner purchases $1 million of coverage and surrenders it 20 years later for its cash value, the average annual illustrated net cost per $1,000 of insurance would be $5.73, assuming that the policyowner values money at 5 percent per year. Again, as with the net payment cost, the surrender cost of $5.73 is not an intuitive measure by itself, but when compared to the $7.34 for Policy B, it tells us that Policy A has the lower surrender cost (i.e., Policy A has superior illustrated performance).

As seen in examining the indices in Tables 16-12 and 16-13, the indices are not useful standing alone. They are relevant only in relation to each other and, even then, many question their value to prospective purchasers, particularly for the high-end market segment. Regulations make clear that they are to be used for comparing similar policies only, which means, for example, they should not be used for comparing greatly different funding patterns or amounts of coverage for the same or competing policies. A further drawback is that they presume that everyone values money at 5 percent per year. This assumption might be reasonable for some buyers, but certainly not for others, especially businesses. It is for these reasons that other measures, such as internal rates of return on death and surrender, are more commonly used in many market segments.

Example Illustrated Performance Comparison Summary

Figure 16-2 provides an example of a suggested comparison summary that may prove helpful in evaluating and comparing illustrated performance be-

TABLE 16-13
Year 20 Surrender Cost Indices

Policy	Death Benefit	Annual Premium	Surrender Cost @5%
A	$1,000,000	$26,078	$5.73
B	1,000,000	34,384	7.34

Figure 16-2: Illustrated Performance Comparison Summary

Carrier Policy	AA A		BB B		CC C	
Underwriting Class	Best NS		Best NS		Best NS	
Crediting Rate	5.00%		5.05%		5.35%	
Date Illustrated	10/1/2010		10/1/2010		10/1/2010	
FACE AMOUNT Total	1,000,000		1,000,000		1,000,000	
PREMIUMS Annual Premium # of Premiums	23,724 10		23,404 10		25,423 10	
Surrender Value						
Year 1	4,800		17,858		15,686	
Year 10	216,947		230,363		273,504	
Year 20	292,796		339,465		391,203	
Year 30	365,913		453,248		519,122	
Year 40	428,704		512,239		582,410	
Year 50	538,274		567,155		625,250	
SV to Premium Ratio						
Year 1	3	20%	1	76%	2	62%
Year 2	3	51%	1	81%	2	78%
Year 3	3	63%	2	83%	1	84%
Year 4	3	69%	2	85%	1	89%
Year 5	3	74%	2	87%	1	93%
Year 10	3	91%	2	98%	1	108%
Year 20	3	123%	2	145%	1	154%
SV IRR						
Year 10	3	−1.63%	2	−0.29%	1	1.32%
Year 20	3	1.36%	2	2.41%	1	2.80%
Year 30	3	1.71%	2	2.61%	1	2.83%
Year 40	3	1.68%	2	2.23%	1	2.36%
Year 50	3	1.81%	2	1.96%	1	1.99%
Death Benefit						
Year 10	1,000,000		1,000,000		1,000,000	
Year 20	1,000,000		1,000,000		1,000,000	
Year 30	1,000,000		1,000,000		1,000,000	
Year 40	1,000,000		1,000,000		1,000,000	
Year 50	1,000,000		1,000,000		1,000,000	
DB IRR						
Year 10	2	25.24%	1	25.48%	3	24.04%
Year 20	2	9.49%	1	9.58%	3	9.02%
Year 30	2	5.75%	1	5.81%	3	5.47%
Year 40	2	4.12%	1	4.16%	3	3.92%
Year 50	2	3.20%	1	3.23%	3	3.05%

tween policies. It contains performance measures for premiums, surrender values, and death benefits. The comparison also contains numerical rankings for the different measures. As an example, Policy B has the lowest premium outlay and therefore is ranked number one on this basis. Policy C has the highest surrender value measures starting in policy year three and shows corresponding number one rankings. Based on this summary where the dependent policy element is the premium solve, Policy B may be considered to have the best overall illustrated performance with the lowest premium outlay to provide a cash value target of CV=DB and strong cash values.

Considerations for Comparing Illustrated Performance between Different Policy Types

As mentioned previously, in an ideal world one would compare only policies of a similar policy type in order to have a consistent comparison. However, the real world is more complex, as different policy types can provide similar types of policy benefits. Therefore comparisons of different policy types may be valid, as they help to show which policy type or policy provides the best overall value to the client as defined by that client's specific risk/reward characteristics. Following is a discussion of some common comparisons between policy types, including specific examples.

Comparing Whole Life to Universal Life

Even though UL and WL are fundamentally different regarding premium and death benefit flexibility, valid illustration comparisons can be made. Both products are general account cash value products and provide illustrated performance based on both non-guaranteed assumptions and guaranteed policy elements.

A complication that arises when comparing UL and WL is that dividends are commonly used to purchase paid up additions (PUA) for WL. PUAs may be considered as net single premiums that purchase amounts of death benefit and increase cash values based on guaranteed policy elements (see Chapter 7). A similar feature is not included with UL. UL typically has two death benefit options: (1) level or (2) increasing. The increasing option provides a death benefit equal to the total face amount plus the accumulated value. Neither UL death benefit option will provide the same increasing coverage amount as WL with PUAs. A theoretical solution is to apply scheduled face increases to the UL policy, where the face increase schedule matches the WL coverage with PUAs. This could be done with matching on a policy year by policy year basis. However, practically speaking this would be complicated and restrictions may apply. In addition, if the future WL dividend scale changes, the PUAs will change as well. Whereas the UL scheduled face increases would not automatically change if the future underlying current assumptions change. Indeed, this comparison is difficult to prepare and evaluate.

A level death benefit comparison is less complicated and more relevant as WL can be structured to have a level death benefit by applying dividends to purchase a combination of decreasing one year term insurance and PUAs. A level death benefit option would be selected for the UL policy.

The other complicating factor is that WL has a required premium funding level. That funding level will typically provide for a cash value equal to the death benefit at age 100 or later. UL has premium funding flexibility and can fund with lower cash value targets (such as $1 at age 101).

Assuming a death benefit protection sale where the death benefit coverage is known (and hopefully matched between policies), the following illustration comparison steps are suggested when comparing UL and WL policies:

1. Match UL premium funding to the fixed WL premium funding level; and
2. Match UL cash value target to the fixed WL cash value target.

In addition, consider looking at lower cash value targets and resulting lower premium funding for UL. To round out the comparison, a review of downside performance risk by altering the policy assumptions is recommended (such as reduced interest rate assumptions and guaranteed policy elements).

When UL premium funding is matched to the WL level (and assuming the death benefit coverage is consistent) the resulting cash values will vary between the policies. Table 16-14 provides an example comparison of WL and UL policy surrender values with identical funding and level death benefit coverage (male, nonsmoker, age 55, and $2 million level death benefit). For the WL policy; dividends are paying premiums, purchasing PUAs, and purchasing decreasing term insurance to achieve a level death benefit and suspended premiums. Based on the current dividend scale, the WL policy requires ten annual premiums of $49,513, which is also matched by the UL policy. The surrender values are similar between the two policies, although the UL surrender values are superior after age 95. These results are an example of two selected policies, but of course relative differences in policy performance will vary based on the specific policies being compared.

Staying with our example in Table 16-14, the required WL funding level provides a cash value equal to the death benefit at age 111 for the WL policy and before age 105 for the UL policy. This may be considered to be a very conservative funding level. UL provides the flexibility to fund at lower levels. Table 16-15 shows examples of lower premium funding options for the UL policy. The first option is to fund the UL policy that achieves the same cash value target as the WL policy (CV=DB at age 111). When the cash value target is matched, the UL policy solves for an annual premium that is approximately

TABLE 16-14
Whole Life versus Universal Life—Matched Premium Funding and Death Benefit Coverage

Policy Year	EOY Age	Whole Life	Universal Life
10 Annual Premiums		49,513	49,513
Surrender Values			
1	56	17,543	32,355
5	60	194,573	230,652
10	65	523,567	557,506
20	75	855,484	795,786
30	85	1,252,307	1,116,922
40	95	1,603,611	1,654,130
50	105	1,810,134	2,735,520
60	115	2,295,137	4,582,472

TABLE 16-15
Whole Life versus Universal Life—UL Premium Funding Flexibility

Product	Cash Value Target	Annual Premium	% Difference*
Whole Life	Required: CV=DB Age 111	49,513	
Universal Life	CV=DB Age 111	44,393	–10.3%
Universal Life	CV= $1 Age 121	40,454	–18.3%

*Percentage change in premium from WL premium

10% less than the WL premium. But UL can be funded at even lower levels, such as a cash value equal to $1 at age 121, with a corresponding annual premium that is approximately 18% lower than the WL premium.

It is recommended that testing with downside scenarios be performed in order to see how the illustrated policy values hold up for each policy type when assumptions are less favorable (e.g., stress testing). Table 16-16 contin-

TABLE 16-16
Whole Life versus Universal Life—Stress Testing

Product	Whole Life	Universal Life	Universal Life	Universal Life
Cash Value Target	Required CV=DB Age 111	Match WL Premium	Match WL CV Target CV=DB Age 111	$1 Age 121
10 Annual Premiums	49,513	49,513	44,393	40,454
# of Premium Payments*				
Current Interest	10	10	10	10
50 bps Interest Drop	12	11	12	12
100 bps Interest Drop	13	12	14	13
Guaranteed Interest	26	18	22	20

*Number of premium payments to obtain the original cash value target

ues our WL versus UL comparison by testing both policy types with reduced interest rates. Additional premiums will be required if the dividend interest rate is reduced for WL. Three additional (thirteen in total) premiums are required if the dividend interest rate is reduced by 100 bps for the WL policy. No matter the assumption change and resulting required premium funding, the WL policy will still illustrate a cash value equal to the death benefit at age 111, which is the required cash value target for this WL policy.

The additional premiums for the UL policy are solved for to achieve the original baseline cash value target. If the crediting rate is reduced by 100 bps and the cash value target is to remain at CV=DB age 111, the UL policy needs one additional premium payment (14 in total) as compared to the WL policy (or the same three additional premiums if the cash value target is CV=$1 age 121). If the dividend and crediting interest rate is reduced to the guaranteed rate, the WL policy requires 26 premiums (with CV=DB age 111) while the UL policy only needs 22 with CV=DB age 111 or 20 with CV=$1 age 121.

Of course with UL, the additional premiums are not required and the policy may lapse if the additional premiums are not paid. As an example, for the cash value target of $1 at age 121, the UL policy will lapse at age 97 with a 100 bps crediting rate drop and no additional premiums.

As noted earlier, this is an example for two specific policies, and results will vary for comparisons of other policies.

Comparing Equity Indexed Universal Life to Generic Universal Life

As EIUL is a general account product and is typically marketed as a UL product with the potential for an enhanced crediting rate, comparing EIUL to generic UL can be a valid comparison. Since EIUL does not have a *current* crediting rate, an enlightening comparison is to solve for the EIUL crediting rate that equals the UL illustrated performance at current assumptions. See example in Table 16-17. This example shows that the EIUL crediting rate needs to be at least 30 bps higher than the UL current crediting rate for the EIUL policy to provide superior illustrated performance. This raises the question whether the index strategy will provide an enhanced crediting rate of 30 bps as compared to the UL crediting rate. This is a simple comparison that does not take into consideration the additional volatility associated with index

TABLE 16-17
EIUL versus UL—Match Premiums by Solving for EIUL Crediting Rate

Policy	Crediting Rate	Premium Solve
UL	5.00%	$10,000
EIUL	5.30%	10,000

growth rates (albeit subject to the floor and cap) versus UL crediting rates. The volatility for EIUL can leverage policy performance either up or down compared to a level rate (see interim yield volatility discussion in the earlier VUL section). Many illustration systems allow the index growth rate (and crediting rate for UL) to vary annually.

Comparing No-Lapse Guarantee Universal Life to Generic Universal Life

Both NLG UL and generic UL are general account products, with each having performance trade-offs. While NLG UL may provide guaranteed coverage for life at a relatively low outlay, it typically comes with lower cash values. And while generic UL does not provide lifetime guaranteed coverage at a guaranteed low outlay, it does provide the potential for a lower premium outlay and with much stronger cash values, plus downside protection if funded appropriately.

An informative comparison between the two types of policies is to illustrate funding a generic UL policy at the same level as a NLG policy and then note the resulting illustrated performance differences. Follow-up downside assumption illustrations for UL can reveal how well it holds up. Table 16-18 offers an example. The NLG policy is funded for lifetime guaranteed coverage. If the UL policy is funded at the same premium level as the NLG policy, it provides significantly better cash values, including no surrender charges and a cash value that ultimately equals the death benefit. In contrast, the NLG policy has surrender charges for the first 20 policy years and an account value that ultimately decreases to zero at age 90. In addition, the UL product has good downside protection with a cash value equaling the death benefit at age 106 with a crediting rate reduction of 100 bps and not lapsing until age 110 (well beyond life expectancy) with a crediting rate reduction to the guaranteed rate.

TABLE 16-18
NLG for Life versus UL (Male Age 65—$1 Million Death Benefit)

Policy	Crediting Rate	Premium	Surrender Charge	Cash Value
NLG	Current	$28,400[1]	20 years	Zero age 90
UL	Current	28,400	None	CV=DB age 101
UL	−100 bps	28,400	None	CV=DB age 106
UL	Guaranteed	28,400	None	Lapse Age 110
UL	Current	25,000[2]	None	CV=DB age 121
UL	−100 bps	25,000	None	Lapse age 103
UL	Guaranteed	25,000	None	Lapse age 95

[1]Premium to guarantee coverage for life.
[2]Premium to provide CV=DB at age 121.

Continuing with the example, a lower level of funding can be chosen for UL that still may be considered as providing adequate downside protection. The UL funding level can be lowered to CV=DB at age 121, making for a 12 percent lower premium than that of the NLG policy ($25,000 versus $28,400), and also providing some downside protection with the policy not lapsing until age 103 (well beyond life expectancy) with a 100 bps crediting rate reduction or not lapsing until age 95 with the guaranteed crediting rate. UL policies that have a smaller spread between the current and guaranteed crediting rates may provide better downside risk protection when stress testing with the guaranteed rate. Some policyowners will want the absolute guaranteed coverage provided by NLG, while other policyowners may want the potentially lower cost and/or better cash values provided by UL, particularly when they are comfortable with the downside performance risk. This example is illustrative in nature as the relative competitive position of UL and NLG products have varied over time due to changes in market pricing, and therefore it is a comparison that advisors should keep up to date.

Conclusions

Illustrated policy performance is an important consideration when choosing a life insurance policy, recognizing the non-guaranteed nature of illustrated values. For this reason, small differences in illustrated policy performance over periods of many years should be put in perspective. Further, the longer the period illustrated values are shown, the less credibility the illustrations should have when making a buying decision. One should be cautious when illustrating policy values in a lower interest rate environment, which may magnify poor policy values over time as there may be potential for future increases in interest rates and crediting rates. Conversely, one should not magnify the impact of a high interest rate over a long period of time.

To determine a policy's illustrated competitiveness, it must be compared to other policies. When comparing the illustrated performance between policies, it is important to use consistent parameters across all policies, if feasible. Where complete consistency is not obtainable, differences should be acknowledged and carefully considered. Complications can arise in trying to level the playing field, particularly concerning the earned rate of return assumption for variable policies and the index crediting rate assumption for equity indexed UL. Special considerations apply when comparing illustrated performance with VUL, EIUL, and NLG products. Complications also exist when comparing policies of different policy types; however, valid comparisons may still be performed.

Several performance measures are available, the most common of which are included in this chapter, but others exist. These common measures should prove insightful in conducting a comprehensive illustrated performance review. In general, no one measure should be solely relied upon for policy selection. It is recommended that the package of benefits be reviewed and considered. Providing and reviewing a comparison that contains performance measures for premium, surrender value, and death benefit allows for an overall evaluation that can provide a better informed policy selection. In addition, as a reminder, final policy selection will be a global process that also includes a review of the financial strength of the carrier, the underwriting offer, and policy service.

Ongoing Policy Management

Using Policy Reviews to Sustain Policy Viability and Achieve Insurance Goals*

17

THIS CHAPTER BEGINS PART VI of the *Guide*, a two-chapter review of ongoing policy management. Here we first discuss why policy reviews are a critically important component of ongoing policy management. There follows a discussion of the nature of policy reviews, noting that both annual and detailed periodic reviews are important. The chapter closes with analyses of what can be done when emerging policy values seem either insufficient or greater than necessary to sustain a client's policy-related goals. The next chapter provides a review of alternatives for securing "living" values from life insurance.

The Importance of Policy Reviews

The actual performance of a policy containing non-guaranteed elements (assumptions) inevitably varies over time from that which was illustrated originally. Additionally, policyholder actions, such as not paying planned premiums or adjusting the death benefit under a universal life (UL) policy, can cause a policy to deviate from its original projection. It is for these reasons that the performance of such policies should be monitored regu-

*Authored by Harold D. Skipper and Wayne Tonning.

381

larly via policy reviews to determine whether actual and emerging policy values seem likely to enable the policy to accomplish the client's financial goals.

Policy reviews are also important audit devices. They can reveal administrative or other errors by the insurer or agency, although such errors are rare. Finally, policy reviews are important components of any reevaluation of a client's insurance-related goals. While this chapter's scope is limited to policy performance evaluation and does not encompass new or revised insurance planning per se, its material will be relevant to any such planning.

Policy reviews are intended to reveal whether some policyholder action is needed to keep or get a policy back on track and, if so, what action; and also whether the deviation from expectation was caused by changes in current assumptions by the insurer, or changes in funding or policy benefits by the policyholder. If current and/or likely future values are lower than expected, the policy may lapse or otherwise fail to provide the needed insurance. If current and/or likely future values are higher than expected, excess value may be accumulating within the insurance policy that could be put to better use elsewhere.

As we explore below, policyholder actions in response to both negative and positive deviations can include doing nothing, changing future payments, changing death benefits, and taking distributions or making one-time premium contributions. Replacement of an underperforming policy is another option.

The Nature of Policy Reviews

Policy reviews typically are of two types: annual and detailed. Annual reviews are typically simple. Detailed reviews are more in depth and usually occur less often than annual reviews. Annual reviews are precipitated by and rely upon the statements of policy activity that insurers provide to policyholders annually. Annual reviews most commonly are the triggers for detailed policy reviews. Detailed reviews rely on a current performance benchmark and comparing to up-to-date illustrations of a policy's possible future performance—called in-force illustrations—which are detailed renderings of future values for a policy already in effect assuming that premiums are paid as shown and that future non-guaranteed policy elements will be identical to those shown in the illustration. For many policies, in-force illustrations can be generated by the agent; otherwise, they must be obtained from the insurer.

Annual Reviews

Insurers provide policy statements to policyholders annually on the policy anniversary. An annual statement contains the beginning and ending policy year values, including the surrender value, account (cash) value, and death benefit. Transactions affecting any policy cash flows and values also will be shown, including withdrawals, partial surrenders, loans, and loan interest due and paid. For par whole life (WL) policies, they show dividends paid and how they were used during the year. For UL policies, they show actual policy cost of insurance (COI) and loading charges assessed and interest credited to account values during the policy year. The relevant interest crediting rates are also typically shown. For variable universal life (VUL) policies, the statement also shows policy value detail by fund or account.

General Considerations

Annual reviews consist of comparing the current policy values and elements against those illustrated in the most recent policy illustration. That illustration may be the one provided at the time the policy was sold—called as-sold illustrations in industry jargon—or in-force illustrations from some later period. The objective of the comparison is to determine whether the policy remains on track to meet the policyholder's insurance goals.

Table 17-1 provides two examples of such a comparison. Policy A has been in force for five years, and the most recent illustration was the one provided at time of sale. The previous four annual statement reviews reconciled to the as-sold illustration. The annual statement for the fifth policy year was just received and shows an account value of $59,300. The advisor pulls out the as-sold illustration that shows an illustrated account value of $58,800 for the policy at the end of the fifth policy year, based on the original non-guaranteed assumptions. As the table shows, the actual account value is 1 percent greater than that which was illustrated at policy inception. The advisor ordinarily would follow up to determine the source of the deviated value, such as a crediting rate change, policy load change, or a premium payment different from the illustrated schedule.

TABLE 17-1
Example of an Annual Account Value Comparison

	Policy A				Policy B		
	Account Value				Account Value		
Policy Year	As-Sold Illustration	Annual Statement	Percent Change	Policy Year	In-force Illustration	Annual Statement	Percent Change
1	$10,500	$10,500	—	21	$242,100	$242,100	—
2	21,500	21,500	—	22	253,800	253,800	—
3	33,200	33,200	—	23	265,800	265,800	—
4	45,600	45,600	—	24	278,300	278,300	—
5	58,800	59,300	1%	25	291,200	288,300	(1%)

Policy B has been in force for 25 years, and the most recent illustration is an in-force illustration from policy year 21 based on current assumptions prevailing at that time. The previous annual reviews for policy years 21 through 24 were reconciled to the most recent in-force illustration. In policy year 25, the advisor notes that the annual statement value is 1 percent lower than the old in-force illustration value for the end of policy year 25. Again the advisor ordinarily would determine the source of the change, which should be provided via an explicit notice in the annual statement. The NAIC Life Insurance Illustrations Model Regulation requires that the annual statement provide notice and explain the nature of any adverse changes in non-guaranteed elements made by the insurer during the previous policy year. This regulation also requires that the annual statement include a notice if the policy would lapse by the end of the next reporting period based on guaranteed policy elements.

For any policy change, whether positive or negative, a detailed review is recommended as even seemingly small changes can drive material differences in future illustrated policy values (including excess insurance value or a policy lapse). A detail review and examples of how to manage policy performance are discussed later in this chapter.

Considerations Applicable to Particular Policies

Annual policy reviews can differ by policy type. The following are considerations and sample annual reviews for WL, UL, VUL, and no-lapse guarantee (NLG) UL policies.

Considerations for Whole Life

WL premium schedules are determined by the insurer at policy issuance and, if paid, will keep the contract in force for life. A problem can arise with par WL policies if dividends actually paid are less than those illustrated, and accomplishment of the client's insurance goals were built around those illustrated dividends. For example, consider a WL policy for which dividends were illustrated originally as accumulating in such a way as to permit the policy to become self-sustaining after payment of ten annual premiums of $100,000 each. Adverse developments in the insurer's investment portfolio, for example, could result in reduced dividends and require out-of-pocket payments beyond ten years. The client then faces limited options, as we explore below, but at least annual policy reviews should have alerted the advisor and the client early of the impending problem.

Annual reviews of WL policies can be considered as being less technical than those for unbundled policies, because of the fixed relationship between policy values and premiums and the bundling of policy charges and credits (which makes it difficult to identify the reason for any performance deviation). Table 17-2 offers an abbreviated sample of a WL policy annual statement.

TABLE 17-2
Abbreviated Example of Whole Life Annual Statement

Policy Information

Plan:	Whole Life AA
Policy Date:	July 1, 20XX
Premium Payment:	$121,250
Billing Cycle:	Payable Annually

Benefit Summary

	Death Benefit as of July 1, 20XX	Cash Value as of July 1, 20XX	Cash Value as of July 1, 20XX-1
Guaranteed Values	$5,500,000	$720,000	$600,000
Dividend Additions	350,000	170,000	120,000
Total	$5,850,000	$890,000	$720,000

Additional Benefits

Dividend Options	Amount
Dividend additions	$35,000

Your current annual dividend of $35,000 was applied to purchase $72,000 of dividend additions.

Policy values should be audited by comparing each annual statement to the previous year's annual statement and to the most recent policy illustration. The beginning values for the current statement should match the ending values of the previous year's statement. If the dividend scale has not changed since the policy was issued or the last in-force illustration, current values should match those illustrated at that time. If they do not match, the reason for the deviation should be discovered. If the dividend scale has changed, the guaranteed values shown in the current statement still should match the guaranteed values from the most recent illustration. Of course, dividend changes will affect the value of dividend additions.

Considerations for Universal Life

With their flexibility in premium payment, UL policies have the potential exposure of being underfunded by the policyholder reducing premium payments below those originally anticipated to accomplish the client's goals. This very premium flexibility, however, affords the policyholder the convenient option of adjusting premiums to get the policy back on track. This discussion applies equally to general account UL, VUL, equity-index universal life (EIUL), and NLG UL, with additional considerations for VUL and NLG UL presented below.

Annual statements for UL policies are more detailed than those for WL policies due to the unbundling of policy charges and credits and premium flexibility. In addition to providing beginning and ending year policy values, UL annual statements typically include a summary of the year's policy activity. Table 17-3 shows an example of UL policy activity. In addition to the sum

TABLE 17-3
Example of a Universal Life Summary of Policy Activity

Account Value as of July 1, 20XX-1	$58,000
Premiums Received	+60,000
Premium Charges	− 3,600
Interest Credited	+ 5,600
Sum of Monthly COI and Expense Charges	−23,000
Account Value as of July 1, 20XX	= $97,000

of the annual activity, some annual statements also provide policy activity by month. A UL annual statement also includes the current and monthly crediting rates for the policy year.

As with WL, current UL policy values should be compared to the previous annual statement and to the most recent illustration. Beginning values from the current statement should match the ending values from the previous year's statement. Whether current policy values deviate from the point-in-scale values from the most recent illustration should be noted. The summary of policy activity can reveal which policy credits or charges caused any change in values. It may be advisable to conduct a detailed policy review via a current in-force illustration to gain an understanding of the illustrated impact of any change on future values. As noted earlier, we recommend that a current illustration be obtained whenever the interest crediting rate or a schedule of policy charges is changed.

Considerations for Variable Universal Life

VUL has the same product engine as UL and therefore the same flexibility and associated policyholder-related risks and opportunities as UL. However, VUL has additional risk/opportunities due to the ability of policyholders to invest in multiple equity and other funds, effectively retaining all investment risk, as VUL offers no minimum interest crediting rate guarantees as found with UL. Indeed, the funds' earned rates can be negative, thereby causing substantial changes in policy values. It is for this reason that ongoing policy reviews for VUL can be even more important than reviews of non-variable products.

In addition to the information already described for WL and UL, annual statements for VUL include policy value detail by fund allocation. Table 17-4 shows an example of a VUL summary by account during the recent recession. The fund value equals the number of shares times the share value. Shares are bought each time a premium is paid and sold to cover monthly charges, based on that day's share value.

The summary by account allows for an assessment of policy performance by account. As seen in Table 17-4, both funds had negative returns with

TABLE 17-4
Example of a Variable Universal Life Summary by Account

Fund Name	No. of Shares	Share Value	Fund Value
Beginning Balance as of July 1, 20XX-1			
Small Cap	150,000	$22.00	$3,300,000
International	150,000	18.00	2,700,000
Total	300,000		$6,000,000
Ending Balance as of July 1, 20XX			
Small Cap	145,000	$15.00	$2,175,000
International	145,000	10.00	1,450,000
Total	290,000		$3,625,000

the small cap share value decreasing by 32 percent (15 ÷ 22 – 1) and the international share value decreasing by 44 percent (10 ÷ 18 – 1). Of course, at other times, returns can be positive, with historical results for equity funds usually being positive over a period of many years.

A VUL annual statement should also include a one year projection based on planned premiums, guaranteed charges, and a 0 percent gross annual rate of return on the variable investment option (or the guaranteed crediting rate on the fixed account). Table 17-5 shows an example of the VUL history and projection of policy values. The projection provides an idea of the amount of cushion inherent in existing policy value to be able to weather an adverse scenario. Of course, the policy will lapse if the account value goes to zero.

Unacceptable fund performance can provide a basis for reallocating funds. An in-force illustration should be obtained when actual fund returns deviate meaningfully from the earned rate assumption used for determining the funding level.

Considerations for No-Lapse Guarantee Universal Life

On first blush, it might appear that policy reviews for NLG UL are not required as coverage is guaranteed. However, coverage is guaranteed only if premiums are paid on time as per the premium schedule. NLG UL has the same premium flexibility as does any UL policy. A missed premium payment

TABLE 17-5
Example of Variable Universal Life History and Projection of Policy Values

	Actual Value as of July 1, 20XX-1	Actual Value as of July 1, 20XX	Projected Value as of July 1, 20XX+1
Face Amount	$10,000,000	$10,000,000	$10,000,000
Account Value	$6,000,000	$3,625,000	$3,500,000
Surrender Value	$5,400,000	$3,443,750	$3,500,000

TABLE 17-6
Example of a No-Lapse Guarantee Universal Life Summary

No-Lapse Guarantee as of July 1, 20XX	
Net Account Value	$90,000
Net No-Lapse Guarantee Value	$100,000

or one paid four months late will reduce the term of the NLG. In addition, loans and withdrawals and other policy changes (such as changing the death benefit option) will also affect the guarantee period. Therefore, annual reviews for NLG UL are arguably even more critical.

A NLG UL annual statement is similar to any other UL annual statement but adds information about the guarantee. For most NLG products sold today, the guarantee is in effect as long as either the net (of loans) NLG shadow account value or the net policy account value is positive. The NLG shadow account value may not be surrendered for cash and is used only to determine whether the guarantee remains in effect. Table 17-6 offers an example of a NLG UL summary. Unfortunately, it is not possible to determine from this summary whether the NLG value is on schedule as it is shown for the current year only.

Detailed Reviews

Detailed periodic policy reviews are needed to assess the impact on illustrated future policy performance of actions by policyholders and of changes by insurers in current assumptions. As noted earlier, these reviews rely on up-to-date policy illustrations. The objective of the review is to determine whether illustrated future policy performance would fulfill the policyholder's life insurance goals and, if necessary, to make appropriate adjustments in policy funding or other policy options.

In general, the advisor should consider conducting a detailed review if an examination of an annual policy statement or any other material or notices received by the client reveals that any of the following has occurred:

- Premiums were not paid as scheduled or planned, either as to amount or timing.
- Distributions inconsistent with the original schedule were made.
- Changes were made in any aspect of the policy that could affect future performance or achievement of policyholder goals.
- The interest crediting rate or, for variable life, the actual earned rate deviated from that shown in the most recent annual statement or illustration. Due to the expected return volatility associated with VUL, particularly when premiums are allocated to equity funds, a one year

return that deviates from the funding return assumption may not require a detailed review. A detailed review is recommended for successive years of material return deviations.

◆ The premiums for indeterminate premium policies, the COI rates for unbundled policies, or mortality charges for par WL for which such charges are disclosed differ from those shown in the most recent annual statement or illustration.

◆ Expense loadings for unbundled policies or, if disclosed, for par WL policies differ from those shown in the most recent annual statement or illustration.

◆ Dividends actually paid deviated from those in the most recent illustration.

Additionally, detailed reviews should be conducted periodically, such as every five or so years, even if none of the above actions had occurred (which is unlikely). The reason for a periodic review of this type is not so much to ensure that the policy remains on track to accomplish the client's goals as to determine whether the existing policy continues to offer good value relative to other policies from high quality insurers. A life insurance policy that offers poor value can remain on track because, for example, general investment returns increased but the insurer chose to pass on little or none of that increase. The techniques discussed in Chapter 16 and below would be applied to the existing and one or more possible replacement policies.

Detailed reviews typically are built around newly acquired in-force illustrations. These illustrations will show the existing account values and will reflect a planned premium payment schedule. Future illustrated cash values and death benefits will be shown based on prevailing current assumptions. For example, an as-sold illustration may have been predicated on a then-current interest crediting rate of $5\frac{1}{2}$ percent. Five years later, the crediting rate may be 5 percent. An in-force illustration predicated on this lower rate would show lower future values than those shown in the as-sold illustration, all else being the same. Of course, an in-force illustration can also be run with less favorable assumptions (although no worse than the guarantees) for stress testing purposes.

Let's take a look at interest rate changes in an actual UL policy. Table 17-7 shows the 10-year crediting rate history for a well known company's UL policy issued in 2001. The general trend in this policy's crediting rate is downward, consistent with the downward trend over this period in both insurer investment earnings and crediting rates. The crediting rate was reduced by 190 basis points (bps) over the 10-year time frame (6.75 percent − 4.85 percent = 1.90 percent).

TABLE 17-7
Actual Universal Life
Policy Interest Crediting Rate History

Policy Year	Crediting Rate (%)	Policy Year	Crediting Rate (%)
1 (2001)	6.75	6 (2006)	6.10
2 (2002)	6.50	7 (2007)	5.85
3 (2003)	6.70	8 (2008)	5.40
4 (2004)	6.70	9 (2009)	5.10
5 (2005)	6.50	10 (2010)	4.85

Now let's assume the following:

◆ Male, issue age 55, nonsmoker, preferred.
◆ $1 million level (option A) death benefit.
◆ The payment of the planned premium of $18,634 for ten years was il-
  lustrated as being sufficient at the time of policy sale and based on
  non-guaranteed assumptions prevailing at that time, including the 6.75
  percent crediting rate, to cause the policy cash value to equal the
  death benefit at the end of age 120 or, stated equivalently, at age 121.
◆ The policy has been in force for 10 years and annual premiums of
  $18,634 have been paid each year.

We further assume that this review is being conducted at the very end of
policy year 10 and that no detailed policy review has ever been conducted in
the past, contrary to sound in-force policy management. Obviously, a detailed
policy review is past due as the crediting rate has dropped significantly and
because the (hoped-for) last premium has been paid in accordance with the
original premium payment plan.

Table 17-8 provides excerpts from the as-sold illustration and the just acquired in-force illustration as of the end of the tenth policy year. As known from
previous annual reviews, the reduction in crediting rate is the only change to
the policy's non-guaranteed elements. The as-sold illustration is based on the
original crediting rate of 6.75 percent, whereas the in-force illustration is based
on the current crediting rate of 4.85 percent. Typically, an in-force illustration
includes future illustrated values only, but Table 17-8 also shows actual historical values to provide context. Note that the policy was originally intended to
have the account value equal the death benefit at age 121, based on the as-sold
assumptions. The in-force illustration shows that, with no further premium
payments and assuming that current assumptions do not change, the policy
will lapse during age 91. This result typically would lead to an analysis of policyholder actions that could be taken to maintain the policy beyond that period,
as the likelihood that the insured could outlive policy coverage has increased.

This analysis shows why annual policy reviews can be misinterpreted.
Note that the actual tenth year policy value of $163,264 is only 6 percent less

TABLE 17-8
Actual As-Sold and In-force Universal Life Illustration Excerpts

			As-Sold Illustration				In-force Illustration			
Policy Year	Cal Year	BOY Age	Crediting Rate	Premium	EOY Account Value	EOY Death Benefit	Crediting Rate	Premium	EOY Account Value	EOY Death Benefit
1	2001	55	6.75%	$18,634	$13,437	$1,000,000	6.75%	$18,634	$13,437	$1,000,000
2	2002	56	6.75%	18,634	27,493	1,000,000	6.50%	18,634	27,423	1,000,000
3	2003	57	6.75%	18,634	42,342	1,000,000	6.70%	18,634	42,246	1,000,000
4	2004	58	6.75%	18,634	57,941	1,000,000	6.70%	18,634	57,810	1,000,000
5	2005	59	6.75%	18,634	74,404	1,000,000	6.50%	18,634	74,084	1,000,000
6	2006	60	6.75%	18,634	91,954	1,000,000	6.10%	18,634	91,036	1,000,000
7	2007	61	6.75%	18,634	110,499	1,000,000	5.85%	18,634	108,566	1,000,000
8	2008	62	6.75%	18,634	130,166	1,000,000	5.40%	18,634	126,435	1,000,000
9	2009	63	6.75%	18,634	151,013	1,000,000	5.10%	18,634	144,689	1,000,000
10	2010	64	6.75%	18,634	173,069	1,000,000	4.85%	18,634	163,264	1,000,000
20	2020	74	6.75%	0	270,377	1,000,000	4.85%	0	201,096	1,000,000
30	2030	84	6.75%	0	395,994	1,000,000	4.85%	0	174,319	1,000,000
40	2040	94	6.75%	0	453,477	1,000,000	4.85%	0	##	##
50	2050	104	6.75%	0	510,469	1,000,000	4.85%	0	##	##
60	2060	114	6.75%	0	704,232	1,000,000	4.85%	0	##	##
66	2066	120	6.75%	0	1,001,757	1,000,000	4.85%	0	##	##

Lapse age 91

than the baseline value of $173,069. This seemingly small difference could lead one to conclude that policy values are not much behind schedule, and therefore no policyholder actions are required. However, interest compounding coupled with the leverage of increasing COI charges creates a dramatic impact on future illustrated values. This effect cuts both ways: increased crediting rates would have led to decreasing COI charges relative to those illustrated at issuance and an even more rapid build-up of policy values. It is for this reason that an in-force illustration is needed to fully appreciate the potential impact of changes in the crediting rate (and of changes in the schedule of policy charges) on future policy values.

Options to Achieve Insurance Goals

Deviations of actual from illustrated policy values are all but certain under current assumption policies. Of course, policyholders are more concerned about negative than positive deviations, but both types can warrant action. We explore both situations below.

When Policy Values are Insufficient

When reasonable illustrations of current plus future policy values are insufficient to allow a policy to meet the policyholder's insurance goal, consideration should be given to needed desirable actions to be taken. These actions can include one or more of the following:

- Doing nothing;
- Making additional payments;
- Reducing the policy death benefit; or
- Replacing the policy.

We continue to reference the policy from Table 17-8 to illustrate points. Recall that the policy, based on current assumptions, is illustrated to lapse during age 91 as compared to the original goal of the account value equaling the death benefit at age 121.

Do Nothing

The policyholder always has the option of doing nothing about an illustrated negative deviation. This may be the wise course of action under the following circumstances:

- The insured's health has deteriorated and the expectation of his or her living past the projected date of policy lapse is remote; in our example, of living past age 91. For WL policies, consideration might be given to allowing the policy to go under the extended term nonforfeiture option, especially if the term period is long and the insured's life expectancy is short.
- The review is taking place early in the life of the policy, and sufficient time remains for future non-guaranteed policy elements to move in a favorable direction, allowing policy values to get back on track. This optimistic view might be reinforced if the policyholder believes economic factors are pointed to a positive upswing, such as if new money rates had been moving higher recently, and the policy's crediting rate had not yet been adjusted. As insurers and agents are not permitted to use rates higher than those presently credited, the advisor and policyholder are unlikely to know just how much higher rates must move to erase negative deviations. A policy rebound may be more realistic with a variable policy for which equity market return fluctuations can be significant, but near-term (i.e., less than 10 years) volatility can render this hope illusory. If this "do nothing" option seems feasible, downside in-force illustrations should be obtained to show the additional risk of further crediting rate reductions. Such illustrations can be especially important if interest rates have been decreasing and the crediting rate has held, implying downward pressure on the crediting rate.
- The policyholder is unable to pay additional premiums. If the policy being reviewed is par WL, paying additional premiums may not be a viable option anyway. If dividends were earmarked to allow a policy to become self-sustaining, and they are now illustrated to be inadequate

to accomplish that goal, the WL policyholder's problem is more or less the same as that of the UL policyholder in the same position. Both could consider reducing the policy death benefit but doing so could put near-term insurance goals at risk for uncertain long-term goals (see below). If this course is taken, it might be wise to purchase a separate term policy as a temporary augmentation of near-term coverage (which may not be feasible if the insured's health has deteriorated as underwriting will be required). The premium requirement for the term coverage should be less than the additional premiums for the existing cash value policy. In any event, in-force illustrations can show results under both scenarios.

Make Additional Payments

For UL, an in-force illustration can be run that solves for the additional premium needed to achieve the funding goal. Recall that, for the Table 17-8 illustration, the goal was having the account value equal to the death benefit at age 121. Table 17-9 shows in-force illustration premium solve options based on this goal. Recall that this review is occurring at the end of the tenth policy year.

The second set of columns shows that payment of a single premium of $93,850 in policy year 11 would get the policy back on track based on current assumptions. That a policyholder may not find this option desirable is understandable, especially as $93,850 is significantly higher than the original 10-pay premium of $18,634. Such a large single payment also may be undesirable because of tax gift implications for insurance owned outside the policyowner's estate.

A more realistic funding option from the policyholder's viewpoint may be to continue to pay the original annual premium of $18,634, as shown in the third set of columns. Our example shows that six additional premiums would be needed to get the policy back on track, based on current assumptions.

It may be appropriate to provide the policyholder with an in-force illustration showing the extra required outlay if payment of additional premiums were delayed. Delaying premiums causes reduced interest compounding and higher COI charges due to the leverage from the associated higher net amount at risk (NAR). Recall that the COI charge is applied to the NAR. As shown in the fourth set of columns, six additional premiums turns into somewhat more than eight additional premiums if the additional payments are delayed five years.

For par WL, the additional payment alternatives will vary depending on the dividend option elected. For the one-year term, accumulate at interest, and paid-up additions (PUAs) options, no additional payments ordinarily will be accepted unless special riders are attached—see Chapter 9. If the dividend

TABLE 17-9
Example of Universal Life In-force Illustrations with Additional Premiums

Policy Year	Cal Year	BOY Age	Credit Rate	Single Premium			10-Pay Premium			Delayed 10-Pay Premium		
				Premium	EOY Account Value	EOY Death Benefit	Premium	EOY Account Value	EOY Death Benefit	Premium	EOY Account Value	EOY Death Benefit
1	2001	55	6.75%	$18,634	$13,437	$1,000,000	$18,634	$13,437	$1,000,000	$18,634	$13,437	$1,000,000
2	2002	56	6.50%	18,634	27,423	1,000,000	18,634	27,423	1,000,000	18,634	27,423	1,000,000
3	2003	57	6.70%	18,634	42,246	1,000,000	18,634	42,246	1,000,000	18,634	42,246	1,000,000
4	2004	58	6.70%	18,634	57,810	1,000,000	18,634	57,810	1,000,000	18,634	57,810	1,000,000
5	2005	59	6.50%	18,634	74,084	1,000,000	18,634	74,084	1,000,000	18,634	74,084	1,000,000
6	2006	60	6.10%	18,634	91,036	1,000,000	18,634	91,036	1,000,000	18,634	91,036	1,000,000
7	2007	61	5.85%	18,634	108,566	1,000,000	18,634	108,566	1,000,000	18,634	108,566	1,000,000
8	2008	62	5.40%	18,634	126,435	1,000,000	18,634	126,435	1,000,000	18,634	126,435	1,000,000
9	2009	63	5.10%	18,634	144,689	1,000,000	18,634	144,689	1,000,000	18,634	144,689	1,000,000
10	2010	64	4.85%	18,634	163,264	1,000,000	18,634	163,264	1,000,000	18,634	163,264	1,000,000
11	2011	65	4.85%	93,850	259,915	1,000,000	18,634	186,086	1,000,000		167,795	1,000,000
12	2012	66	4.85%	0	269,497	1,000,000	18,634	209,887	1,000,000	0	172,289	1,000,000
13	2013	67	4.85%	0	279,307	1,000,000	18,634	234,683	1,000,000	0	176,689	1,000,000
14	2014	68	4.85%	0	289,393	1,000,000	18,634	260,578	1,000,000	0	181,024	1,000,000
15	2015	69	4.85%	0	299,739	1,000,000	18,634	287,616	1,000,000	0	185,248	1,000,000
16	2016	70	4.85%	0	310,371	1,000,000	13,029	310,371	1,000,000	18,634	207,474	1,000,000
17	2017	71	4.85%	0	321,190	1,000,000	0	321,189	1,000,000	18,634	230,514	1,000,000
18	2018	72	4.85%	0	332,192	1,000,000	0	332,191	1,000,000	18,634	254,417	1,000,000
19	2019	73	4.85%	0	343,366	1,000,000	0	343,365	1,000,000	18,634	279,227	1,000,000
20	2020	74	4.85%	0	354,717	1,000,000	0	354,717	1,000,000	18,634	305,012	1,000,000
21	2021	75	4.85%	0	366,804	1,000,000	0	366,803	1,000,000	18,634	332,352	1,000,000
22	2022	76	4.85%	0	379,099	1,000,000	0	379,098	1,000,000	18,634	360,867	1,000,000
23	2023	77	4.85%	0	391,581	1,000,000	0	391,580	1,000,000	18,634	390,629	1,000,000
24	2024	78	4.85%	0	404,236	1,000,000	0	404,235	1,000,000	1,023	404,236	1,000,000
25	2025	79	4.85%	0	417,103	1,000,000	0	417,102	1,000,000	0	417,102	1,000,000
66	2066	120	4.85%	0	1,000,048	1,010,048	0	1,000,008	1,010,008	0	1,000,041	1,010,042

option were to reduce premiums, the policyholder has but to change to another option, such as purchasing PUAs. This change enables the policy to pay the full premium out-of-pocket each year rather than an amount equal to the difference between the full premium and the dividend.

If the dividend option were to accumulate dividends to meet future premium payments, whether additional payments would be desirable turns on whether the premium payment status was "active"—meaning that the policyholder was paying premiums out-of-pocket—or if the premium payment status was "inactive"—meaning that premium payments were being met fully from deferred and current dividends. For an active premium status, the new payment schedule (as shown in an in-force illustration) would be a continuation of the current premium. For example, if an annual out-of-pocket premium payment of $100,000 was originally scheduled for ten years, and the dividend scale was reduced in the fifth policy year, the new schedule may involve out-of-pocket payments of the $100,000 premium for 12 years.

If the premium payment status was already "inactive" and a change in dividend scale were otherwise sufficiently grave to require the resumption of out-of-pocket payments, the insurer may provide several alternatives for getting the policy back on track to endow for the death benefit at age 100 (or 121). Table 17-10 shows two alternatives: single pay and partial deferred payments. The example assumes that the policy has been in force for 16 years

TABLE 17-10
Example of Whole Life In-force Illustrations with Premium Payment Options

Policy Year	BOY Age	Single-Pay Premium			Partial Premiums		
		Premium	EOY Surrender Value	EOY Death Benefit	Premium	EOY Surrender Value	EOY Death Benefit
16	78	$—	$1,524,374	$3,731,517	$—	$1,524,374	$3,731,517
17	79	170,421	1,755,464	3,884,847	—	1,577,094	3,625,584
18	80	—	1,810,529	3,790,767	—	1,624,013	3,526,527
19	81	—	1,863,159	3,703,015	—	1,668,311	3,433,572
20	82	—	1,913,495	3,620,934	—	1,710,135	3,346,061
21	83	—	1,967,412	3,544,163	—	1,755,363	3,263,617
22	84	—	2,026,139	3,480,127	6,998	1,812,506	3,203,100
23	85	—	2,093,777	3,433,741	39,542	1,912,539	3,203,100
24	86	—	2,169,604	3,405,049	25,993	2,008,119	3,203,100
25	87	—	2,253,404	3,392,084	13,693	2,099,792	3,203,100
26	88	—	2,334,014	3,393,731	2,098	2,176,667	3,203,100
27	89	—	2,411,443	3,395,430	2,098	2,250,338	3,203,100
28	90	—	2,492,117	3,397,158	2,098	2,327,212	3,203,100
29	91	—	2,572,875	3,398,904	2,098	2,404,087	3,203,100
30	92	—	2,653,782	3,400,661	2,098	2,480,961	3,203,100
37	99	—	3,587,291	3,587,291	2,098	3,371,423	3,371,423
Present Value Premium @ 5%							
		170,421			75,317		

and is in an "inactive" premium status; i.e., premiums are being met from present and accumulated dividends. The present and future illustrated dividends, however, are insufficient to meet all future premiums; i.e., to carry the policy to end-of-year age 100 without out-of-pocket payments.

In this example, the premium of $82,250 was paid by the policyholder through policy year 15 with the intention that accumulated and future dividends would pay all premiums thereafter. Dividends actually paid, however, were less than those originally illustrated. To get this policy back on track, the policyholder can either pay an out-of-pocket premium of $170,421 immediately (policy year 17) or delay making additional payments for five years and then make partial payments to age 99. The payment options are based on the current dividend scale and will change in the future as the dividend scale changes. The partial payment option is considerably less than the single-pay option on a present value basis, but the single pay option provides higher surrender values and death benefits.

Reduce Future Death Benefits

If the policyholder cannot or chooses not to make additional payments, reducing the face amount could be considered. For UL, an in-force illustration can be run that solves for a reduced face amount based on a specific cash value goal at a set age; for our example, at age 121.

Table 17-11 continues our UL example, showing two options for reducing death benefits. If the reduction occurs in policy year 11, a new face amount of $647,000 could be maintained to the end of age 120 with no further premium payments, based on current policy assumptions. Obviously, this option is more attractive if the policyholder's insurance need is lower. If the need for $1 million is expected to continue for life, the policyholder must weigh the risk of outliving coverage of the optimal amount against a significantly reduced risk of outliving coverage of a lower face amount but that will not completely fulfill the insurance need.

The second option shows a death benefit reduction to $564,000 when delayed to policy year 21. As with the additional cost of delaying premium payments, there will be a larger reduction by delaying the death benefit change. As the UL death benefit reduction is flexible, we could also solve for a death benefit that achieves $1 of account value at any advanced age, such as 110. This would show lower death benefit reductions while continuing coverage for a longer time.

The same concept applies to WL in electing the reduced paid-up nonforfeiture option. Premiums cease and the death benefit is reduced, but there is no flexibility regarding the amount of the reduction. The existing cash

TABLE 17-11

Example of an In-force Universal Life Illustration with Reduced Face Amount

				Face Reduction			Delayed Face Reduction		
					EOY	EOY		EOY	EOY
Policy	Cal	BOY	Crediting		Account	Death		Account	Death
Year	Year	Age	Rate	Premium	Value	Benefit	Premium	Value	Benefit
1	2001	55	6.75%	$18,634	$13,437	$1,000,000	$18,634	$13,437	$1,000,000
2	2002	56	6.50%	18,634	27,423	1,000,000	18,634	27,423	1,000,000
3	2003	57	6.70%	18,634	42,246	1,000,000	18,634	42,246	1,000,000
4	2004	58	6.70%	18,634	57,810	1,000,000	18,634	57,810	1,000,000
5	2005	59	6.50%	18,634	74,084	1,000,000	18,634	74,084	1,000,000
6	2006	60	6.10%	18,634	91,036	1,000,000	18,634	91,036	1,000,000
7	2007	61	5.85%	18,634	108,566	1,000,000	18,634	108,566	1,000,000
8	2008	62	5.40%	18,634	126,435	1,000,000	18,634	126,435	1,000,000
9	2009	63	5.10%	18,634	144,689	1,000,000	18,634	144,689	1,000,000
10	2010	64	4.85%	18,634	163,264	1,000,000	18,634	163,264	1,000,000
11	2011	65	4.85%	0	169,290	647,000	0	167,795	1,000,000
12	2012	66	4.85%	0	175,482	647,000	0	172,289	1,000,000
13	2013	67	4.85%	0	181,823	647,000	0	176,689	1,000,000
14	2014	68	4.85%	0	188,341	647,000	0	181,024	1,000,000
15	2015	69	4.85%	0	195,029	647,000	0	185,248	1,000,000
16	2016	70	4.85%	0	201,903	647,000	0	189,109	1,000,000
17	2017	71	4.85%	0	208,899	647,000	0	192,676	1,000,000
18	2018	72	4.85%	0	216,014	647,000	0	195,901	1,000,000
19	2019	73	4.85%	0	223,241	647,000	0	198,723	1,000,000
20	2020	74	4.85%	0	230,584	647,000	0	201,096	1,000,000
21	2021	75	4.85%	0	238,404	647,000	0	207,893	564,000
66	2066	120	4.85%	0	665,968	672,627	0	564,481	570,126

value is applied as a single premium at the insured's attained age and gender to purchase whatever amount of single premium WL insurance that it will buy. If dividends are paid in future years, the amount of the guaranteed death benefit is increased.

WL policies also offer extended term as a nonforfeiture option. Extended term continues the death benefit for a guaranteed number of years less than an entire lifespan. For example, the existing cash value may be applied as a single premium to purchase paid-up term insurance to remain in force until the insured's age 85, at which time it expires with no value and with no possibility of extending it. The coverage period is extended beyond age 85 if dividends are paid in future years.

Replace the Policy

If a policy's actual and/or illustrated future performance is disappointing relative to that of other policies in the market, consideration should be given to replacing it with a better performing policy. Several factors are critical in this decision, as examined in Chapter 18. In short, the insured must be willing and able to meet new insurability requirements. A sound basis should exist to believe that the new policy or policies will provide superior value in comparison to the existing policy. The new policy should be from a financially sound company. Ideally, the replacement qualifies as a 1035 exchange.

As discussed in Chapter 18, a 1035 exchange allows for the tax-free exchange of one insurance policy for another. Ordinarily, income tax is due on any gain realized on surrender of a policy (on the excess of receipts over the cost basis) but need not be realized in a qualified policy exchange. The cost basis in the original policy is carried over into the new policy.

Table 17-12 provides replacement options for the UL example policy referenced throughout this chapter, assuming the insured qualifies for the same risk classification as with the original policy. Recall that the policy review is occurring at the end of the tenth policy year.

The first replacement option illustrates a 1035 exchange into a new UL policy with no further premium payments. Note that the new UL policy is illustrated to lapse during the same age (91) as the current policy and that the surrender values are less, due to up-front issue charges. In some cases, carriers will waive some of the up-front charges. We could also consider exchanging into a policy that has no surrender charges. The net result is that the first replacement option seems unattractive.

The second replacement option illustrates a 1035 exchange into a new NLG UL policy with no further premiums, solving for a death benefit that can be guaranteed for life. Note that the guaranteed death benefit is only $574,660, a significant reduction from the current $1 million death benefit and less than the face reduction of $647,000 to carry the policy on a non-guaranteed basis as seen in Table 17-11. However, maybe the policyholder is frustrated with the non-guaranteed crediting rate drops and places high value on a guaranteed death benefit, even with such a dramatic reduction. Another consideration may be the significantly lower surrender values. NLG policies typically have much lower surrender values than generic UL policies, which should be considered in any exchange. This option also probably would be viewed as unappealing due to the significantly reduced death benefit.

Another replacement option is to execute a 1035 exchange into a NLG policy, funded with the same additional premiums needed to get the UL policy back on track (based on current assumptions). Table 17-13 illustrates this possibility. Identical funding levels provide for a guaranteed lifetime death benefit of $937,040 in the NLG policy as compared to the current UL death benefit of $1 million whose viability is dependent on future non-guaranteed policy values. A policyholder might consider taking a slight reduction in death benefit if guaranteed for life. But also note the significantly lower surrender values for the NLG policy.

Table 17-12
Example of Replacement Options with No Additional Premium

Policy Year	Cal Year	BOY Age	In-force Illustration			Option #1: 1035 to New UL			Option #2: 1035 to NLG		
			Premium	EOY Surrender Value	EOY Death Benefit	Premium	EOY Surrender Value	EOY Death Benefit	Premium	EOY Surrender Value	EOY Death Benefit
10	2010	64	$18,634	$163,264	$1,000,000	$163,264	$158,659	1,000,000	$163,264	$104,536	$574,660
11	2011	65	0	167,795	1,000,000	0	163,825	1,000,000	0	106,131	574,660
12	2012	66	0	172,289	1,000,000	0	168,367	1,000,000	0	106,970	574,660
13	2013	67	0	176,689	1,000,000	0	171,943	1,000,000	0	107,112	574,660
14	2014	68	0	181,024	1,000,000	0	176,648	1,000,000	0	106,793	574,660
15	2015	69	0	185,248	1,000,000	0	181,116	1,000,000	0	105,349	574,660
16	2016	70	0	189,109	1,000,000	0	185,945	1,000,000	0	103,039	574,660
17	2017	71	0	192,676	1,000,000	0	191,271	1,000,000	0	100,135	574,660
18	2018	72	0	195,901	1,000,000	0	196,449	1,000,000	0	95,958	574,660
19	2019	73	0	198,723	1,000,000	0	202,354	1,000,000	0	90,760	574,660
20	2020	74	0	201,096	1,000,000	0	186,512	1,000,000	0	0	574,660
30	2030	84	0	174,319	1,000,000	0	##	1,000,000	0	0	574,660
40	2040	94	0	##	##	0	##	##	0	0	574,660
50	2050	104	0	##	##	0	##	##	0	0	574,660
60	2060	114	0	##	##	0	##	##	0	0	574,660
66	2066	120	0	##	##	0	##	##	0	0	574,660

Lapse age 91

TABLE 17-13
Example of Replacement Option with Additional Premium

Policy Year	Cal Year	BOY Age	In-force Illustration			Option #3: 1035 to NLG		
			Premium	EOY Surrender Value	EOY Death Benefit	Premium	EOY Surrender Value	EOY Death Benefit
10	2010	64	$18,634	$163,264	$1,000,000			
11	2011	65	18,634	186,086	1,000,000	$181,898	$100,883	$937,040
12	2012	66	18,634	209,887	1,000,000	18,634	116,588	937,040
13	2013	67	18,634	234,683	1,000,000	18,634	131,435	937,040
14	2014	68	18,634	260,578	1,000,000	18,634	145,589	937,040
15	2015	69	18,634	287,616	1,000,000	18,634	159,493	937,040
16	2016	70	13,029	310,371	1,000,000	13,029	167,465	937,040
17	2017	71	0	321,189	1,000,000	0	163,589	937,040
18	2018	72	0	332,191	1,000,000	0	158,734	937,040
19	2019	73	0	343,365	1,000,000	0	151,790	937,040
20	2020	74	0	354,717	1,000,000	0	143,166	937,040
30	2030	84	0	478,344	1,000,000	0	0	937,040
40	2040	94	0	535,917	1,000,000	0	0	937,040
50	2050	104	0	596,473	1,000,000	0	0	937,040
60	2060	114	0	768,588	1,000,000	0	0	937,040
66	2066	120	0	1,000,008	1,010,008	0	0	937,040

When Policy Values are Greater than Necessary

Policy values can evolve to be greater than those shown in an as-sold illustration, either because the policy has performed very well relative to others, such as from strong equity market returns in a variable policy, or because the post-issue economic environment was better than the pre-issue environment. In the latter case, the non-guaranteed elements underpinning originally illustrated policy values would naturally have resulted in those values being less than actual emerging values. In other words, a policy may be "overfunded" because it has performed exceptionally well or because the original underlying policy assumptions proved conservative. Certainly, policyholders prefer over- to underfunded policies, but caution should be exercised in concluding that a policy must offer good value and must be performing at an acceptable level solely because of the fact of overfunding. Therefore, even with overfunding, it is recommended that periodic policy replacement reviews be performed, particularly if the insured's health has not deteriorated.

A policy can be considered as being overfunded if current and future illustrated values exceed those needed to allow the policy to accomplish the policyholder's insurance goals. The policyholder can consider these options in response to this condition:

♦ Doing nothing;
♦ Reducing future payments;
♦ Increasing future death benefits; and
♦ Taking policy distributions.

Do Nothing

At first blush, making no changes may appear to be the most logical response when current and future illustrated policy values exceed those necessary to accomplish client goals. The policy is ahead of schedule, so why try to fix what is not broken? This first impression may indeed represent a wise course of action, especially when inflation is taken into consideration. If the need is for life insurance whose purchasing power remains at $1 million now and in the future, provision ideally should be made for a steady increase in the policy death benefit to account for expected inflation. Doing nothing may provide that boost.

We will use a new example to explore this issue further. Table 17-14 shows a VUL policy whose as-sold illustration five years ago assumed an 8 percent annual return supporting 10-pay premiums that would cause the policy cash value to equal the death benefit at age 121. The actual earned rate over each of the first five policy years was 10 percent, as shown in the table. The in-force illustration as from the end of policy year five reverts to the as-sold illustration assumption of 8 percent for all future policy years. The earned rate assumption is always critical. The in-force illustration shows that, if the original 10-pay premium schedule were maintained, the account value would approximately equal the original policy death benefit of $1 million by age 105 and have an ultimate death benefit of $3.5 million. This may lead to a recommendation of no changes as excess insurance value (i.e., where the death benefit exceeds the original death benefit) is not illustrated to occur until age 105 and also to leave a cushion in the policy for future returns that

TABLE 17-14
Example of As-Sold and In-force Variable Universal Life Illustrations

Policy Year	BOY Age	As-Sold Illustration				In-force Illustration			
		Earned Rate	Premium	EOY Account Value	EOY Death Benefit	Earned Rate	Premium	EOY Account Value	EOY Death Benefit
1	55	8.00%	$15,481	$10,461	$1,000,000	10.00%	$15,481	$10,697	$1,000,000
2	56	8.00%	15,481	21,460	1,000,000	10.00%	15,481	22,161	1,000,000
3	57	8.00%	15,481	33,168	1,000,000	10.00%	15,481	34,602	1,000,000
4	58	8.00%	15,481	45,551	1,000,000	10.00%	15,481	48,024	1,000,000
5	59	8.00%	15,481	58,723	1,000,000	10.00%	15,481	62,589	1,000,000
6	60	8.00%	15,481	72,874	1,000,000	8.00%	15,481	77,067	1,000,000
7	61	8.00%	15,481	87,944	1,000,000	8.00%	15,481	92,493	1,000,000
8	62	8.00%	15,481	104,066	1,000,000	8.00%	15,481	109,003	1,000,000
9	63	8.00%	15,481	121,302	1,000,000	8.00%	15,481	126,661	1,000,000
10	64	8.00%	15,481	139,687	1,000,000	8.00%	15,481	145,505	1,000,000
20	74	8.00%	0	230,813	1,000,000	8.00%	0	244,568	1,000,000
30	84	8.00%	0	355,026	1,000,000	8.00%	0	391,598	1,000,000
40	94	8.00%	0	411,644	1,000,000	8.00%	0	539,350	1,000,000
50	104	8.00%	0	465,109	1,000,000	8.00%	0	952,749	1,000,000
60	114	8.00%	0	669,260	1,000,000	8.00%	0	2,144,542	2,165,988
66	120	8.00%	0	1,010,584	1,020,689	8.00%	0	3,492,070	3,526,991

may be less than 8 percent. As an example, the excess cushion provides that the policy would stay in force to age 95 even if the future earned rate is reduced 100 bps to 7.0 percent.

For WL, if dividends actually paid under a par WL policy purchase PUAs and the paid dividends were greater than those originally illustrated, the policy's total cash value and death benefits would be higher than originally illustrated. Having these higher values could permit a future change of dividend option to allow dividends to cover some or all of the premiums, freeing up funds in the future for other purposes, as might be desirable in retirement, for example.

We know from Chapter 7 that all cash value life insurance policies are required to have corridors (net amounts at risk) of certain minimum amounts, depending on the insured's age, if they are to meet the IRC definition of life insurance (DOLI) and thereby qualify for favorable income tax treatment. Were a policy's cash value to intrude into the corridor, the insurer would automatically increase the death benefit to maintain the required corridor and/or refuse to accept additional premiums. The corridor is larger at early ages, reducing to zero for ages 95 to 100. High performing policies with resulting large account values may bump into the corridor causing a face amount increase (as shown in Table 17-14). The policy maintains a very small corridor from age 100 forward, rather than a corridor of zero. The DOLI prescribes a minimum corridor, but insurers can choose to price a policy with a higher corridor.

Reduce Future Payments

For par WL policies whose dividends are earmarked to reduce present or future premium payments (to permit the policy to be self sustaining), having greater-than-illustrated dividends means that out-of-pocket payments automatically will be reduced below those anticipated formerly. Payments also can be reduced at some point in the future by a change then from the PUAs to reducing premium outlays, as discussed in the preceding section.

For UL policies for which planned premiums are being paid, the policyholder can simply reduce future planned premiums by solving for the lower premium that would allow the policyholder's insurance goal to be obtained. Continuing with our example from Table 17-14, we note that the policy is presently overfunded through payment of the first five of ten anticipated premiums and based on an 8 percent earned rate assumption going forward. We can solve for the level of the next five premium payments that would allow the policy to achieve its age 121 goal of having the account value equaling the death benefit (CV=DB).

Table 17-15 shows in the first in-force illustration that the annual premium may be reduced to $14,508 from $15,481, and achieve the target of CV=DB at age 121. The second in-force illustration shows another reduced

TABLE 17-15
Example of As-Sold and In-force VUL Illustrations with Reduced Premiums

Policy Year	BOY Age	As-Sold Illustration				In-force Illustration #1				In-force Illustration #2		
		Earned Rate	Premium	EOY Account Value	EOY Death Benefit	Earned Rate	Premium	EOY Account Value	EOY Death Benefit	Premium	EOY Account Value	EOY Death Benefit
1	55	8.00%	$15,481	$10,461	$1,000,000	10.00%	$15,481	$10,697	$1,000,000	$15,481	$10,697	$1,000,000
2	56	8.00%	15,481	21,460	1,000,000	10.00%	15,481	22,161	1,000,000	15,481	22,161	1,000,000
3	57	8.00%	15,481	33,168	1,000,000	10.00%	15,481	34,602	1,000,000	15,481	34,602	1,000,000
4	58	8.00%	15,481	45,551	1,000,000	10.00%	15,481	48,024	1,000,000	15,481	48,024	1,000,000
5	59	8.00%	15,481	58,723	1,000,000	10.00%	15,481	62,589	1,000,000	15,481	62,589	1,000,000
6	60	8.00%	15,481	72,874	1,000,000	8.00%	14,508	76,085	1,000,000	15,481	77,067	1,000,000
7	61	8.00%	15,481	87,944	1,000,000	8.00%	14,508	90,446	1,000,000	15,481	92,493	1,000,000
8	62	8.00%	15,481	104,066	1,000,000	8.00%	14,508	105,798	1,000,000	15,481	109,003	1,000,000
9	63	8.00%	15,481	121,302	1,000,000	8.00%	14,508	122,199	1,000,000	15,481	126,661	1,000,000
10	64	8.00%	15,481	139,687	1,000,000	8.00%	14,508	139,678	1,000,000	9,708	139,672	1,000,000
20	74	8.00%	0	230,813	1,000,000	8.00%	0	230,792	1,000,000	0	230,778	1,000,000
30	84	8.00%	0	355,026	1,000,000	8.00%	0	354,969	1,000,000	0	354,933	1,000,000
40	94	8.00%	0	411,644	1,000,000	8.00%	0	411,445	1,000,000	0	411,319	1,000,000
50	104	8.00%	0	465,109	1,000,000	8.00%	0	464,347	1,000,000	0	463,864	1,000,000
60	114	8.00%	0	669,260	1,000,000	8.00%	0	666,352	1,000,000	0	664,509	1,000,000
66	120	8.00%	0	1,010,584	1,020,689	8.00%	0	1,004,128	1,014,169	0	1,000,024	1,010,024

premium schedule for which the current premium of $15,481 is paid through policy year 9 and then the premium is reduced in policy year 10 to $9,708. This option also achieves our cash value target and has the advantage of continuing the original premium, which the policyholder is already accustomed to paying, and providing some extra account value cushion in case policy performance deteriorates during policy years 6–10.

Table 17-16 shows the more dramatic effect on account values and death benefits if we assume a future earned rate equal to that of the past five years; i.e., 10 percent. If the ten premiums were paid as planned and the account value earned 10 percent per year over the entire policy period, substantial excess insurance value would result, with an ultimate death benefit of $28.6 million. Under these circumstances, an even greater reduction in future premium payments would seem justified, provided one has faith that illustrated future values will materialize. The second set of columns shows that premiums can be reduced to $6,853 and achieve policy goals.

However, as variable policy values can be quite volatile, the advisor would be wise to insist on a stress test of the new premium (and other policy elements as appropriate). The third set of columns shows one such test. Here we assume that the reduced premium of $6,853 is paid but that the future earned rate is the original 8 percent. Under these assumptions, the policy lapses at age 87.

Increase Future Death Benefits

As explained above, "doing nothing" can be the equivalent of increasing future death benefits. This course of action may be appropriate for planning purposes, either because future death-related needs are expected to increase or to account for anticipated inflation.

Take Policy Distributions

Another means of getting an overfunded policy back on track is to take distributions (withdrawals and/or loans) from the policy. As seen in Table 17-16, continuing to pay the $15,481 premium for the next five years and assuming a 10 percent earned rate results in substantial extra illustrated value; value that may not be needed. Distributions can reduce this excess value, and so long as the sum of withdrawals does not exceed the policy's cost basis, they are received free of income taxation. Table 17-17 shows two examples of distributions. The distributions are a combination of first withdrawing to basis and then taking loans thereafter thus avoiding taxable income. The examples are derived from in-force illustrations that solve for appropriate distribution levels.

The first distribution example shows ten annual withdrawals of $34,735 each beginning in policy year 21 (attained age 75) that would achieve policy goals at age 121 based on a 10 percent earned rate assumption. The death

TABLE 17-16
Example of Reduced Premium Funding for Overfunded VUL Policy

Policy Year	BOY Age	Original Premium Schedule				Reduced Premiums				Reduced Premiums Stress Test			
		Earned Rate	Premium	EOY Account Value	EOY Death Benefit	Earned Rate	Premium	EOY Account Value	EOY Death Benefit	Earned Rate	Premium	EOY Account Value	EOY Death Benefit
1	55	10.0%	$15,481	$10,697	$1,000,000	10.0%	$15,481	$10,697	$1,000,000	10.0%	$15,481	$10,697	$1,000,000
2	56	10.0%	15,481	22,161	1,000,000	10.0%	15,481	22,161	1,000,000	10.0%	15,481	22,161	1,000,000
3	57	10.0%	15,481	34,602	1,000,000	10.0%	15,481	34,602	1,000,000	10.0%	15,481	34,602	1,000,000
4	58	10.0%	15,481	48,024	1,000,000	10.0%	15,481	48,024	1,000,000	10.0%	15,481	48,024	1,000,000
5	59	10.0%	15,481	62,589	1,000,000	10.0%	15,481	62,589	1,000,000	10.0%	15,481	62,589	1,000,000
6	60	10.0%	15,481	78,547	1,000,000	10.0%	6,853	69,678	1,000,000	8.0%	6,853	68,360	1,000,000
7	61	10.0%	15,481	95,896	1,000,000	10.0%	6,853	77,225	1,000,000	8.0%	6,853	74,337	1,000,000
8	62	10.0%	15,481	114,838	1,000,000	10.0%	6,853	85,330	1,000,000	8.0%	6,853	80,587	1,000,000
9	63	10.0%	15,481	135,517	1,000,000	10.0%	6,853	94,017	1,000,000	8.0%	6,853	87,102	1,000,000
10	64	10.0%	15,481	158,055	1,000,000	10.0%	6,853	103,280	1,000,000	8.0%	6,853	93,832	1,000,000
20	74	10.0%	0	339,716	1,000,000	10.0%	0	184,178	1,000,000	8.0%	0	122,407	1,000,000
30	84	10.0%	0	800,542	1,000,000	10.0%	0	303,941	1,000,000	8.0%	0	66,796	1,000,000
40	94	10.0%	0	2,128,607	2,149,893	10.0%	0	358,391	1,000,000	8.0%	0	##	##
50	104	10.0%	0	5,761,762	5,819,379	10.0%	0	403,738	1,000,000	8.0%	0	##	##
60	114	10.0%	0	15,601,650	15,757,667	10.0%	0	611,674	1,000,000	8.0%	0	##	##
66	120	10.0%	0	28,364,185	28,647,827	10.0%	0	1,008,845	1,018,934	8.0%	0	##	##

Lapse age 87.

TABLE 17-17

Example of Variable Universal Life In-force Illustrations with Distributions

Policy Year	BOY Age	Earned Rate	Distribution Example #1				Distribution Example #2			
			Premium	Distribution*	EOY Account Value	EOY Death Benefit	Premium	Distribution*	EOY Account Value	EOY Death Benefit
1	55	10.00%	$15,481	$0	$10,697	$1,000,000	$15,481	$0	$10,697	$1,000,000
2	56	10.00%	15,481	0	22,161	1,000,000	15,481	0	22,161	1,000,000
3	57	10.00%	15,481	0	34,602	1,000,000	15,481	0	34,602	1,000,000
4	58	10.00%	15,481	0	48,024	1,000,000	15,481	0	48,024	1,000,000
5	59	10.00%	15,481	0	62,589	1,000,000	15,481	0	62,589	1,000,000
6	60	10.00%	15,481	0	78,547	1,000,000	15,481	0	78,547	1,000,000
7	61	10.00%	15,481	0	95,896	1,000,000	15,481	0	95,896	1,000,000
8	62	10.00%	15,481	0	114,838	1,000,000	15,481	0	114,838	1,000,000
9	63	10.00%	15,481	0	135,517	1,000,000	15,481	0	135,517	1,000,000
10	64	10.00%	15,481	0	158,055	1,000,000	15,481	0	158,055	1,000,000
20	74	10.00%	0	0	339,716	1,000,000	0	0	339,716	1,000,000
21	75	10.00%	0	34,735	331,571	965,265	0	0	368,264	1,000,000
22	76	10.00%	0	34,735	322,274	930,530	0	0	399,563	1,000,000
23	77	10.00%	0	34,735	311,679	895,795	0	0	433,941	1,000,000
24	78	10.00%	0	34,735	299,632	861,060	0	0	471,783	1,000,000
25	79	10.00%	0	34,735	286,007	826,162	0	0	513,590	1,000,000
26	80	10.00%	0	34,735	270,499	790,386	0	0	559,782	1,000,000
27	81	10.00%	0	34,735	252,734	753,626	0	0	610,851	1,000,000
28	82	10.00%	0	34,735	232,233	715,856	0	0	667,383	1,000,000
29	83	10.00%	0	34,735	208,587	677,047	0	0	730,242	1,000,000
30	84	10.00%	0	34,735	181,382	637,171	0	0	800,542	1,000,000
31	85	10.00%	0	0	186,850	631,450	0	0	879,670	1,000,000
32	86	10.00%	0	0	191,652	625,572	0	0	969,316	1,017,782
33	87	10.00%	0	0	195,723	619,533	0	94,719	969,369	1,017,838
34	88	10.00%	0	0	199,236	613,327	0	94,719	969,262	1,019,468
35	89	10.00%	0	0	202,107	606,951	0	94,719	968,818	1,023,856
66	120	10.00%	0	0	1,000,938	1,016,471	0	94,719	1,000,175	1,059,331

*Withdrawals and loans are distributed in 12 equal monthly payments beginning with the policy anniversary

benefit is reduced significantly below the original death benefit of $1 million once distributions begin, because distributions reduce the death benefit dollar for dollar. Taking distributions before there is excess death benefit may be undesirable.

The second distribution example has the policyholder waiting to take distributions until the year after the death benefit first increases (i.e., policy year 33 or attained age 87). At this point, we solve for a level distribution that will achieve the insurance goal of having the account value equal the death benefit based on the 10 percent earned rate assumption. The resulting annual distribution is $94,719 through age 121. Note that the death benefit never falls below the original death benefit of $1 million. Even if the policyowner does not need income at this stage of his or her life, the distributions can be gifted to children or could provide funding for a charitable donation. One might curtail distributions if performance worsens.

Of course, distributions can be made from both WL and UL policies. Distributions under WL policies ordinarily would be taken first from PUAs and dividends on deposit. Further distributions likely would be via policy loans and, thereafter, via partial policy surrenders, but only if essential or if the surrendered insurance was no longer needed. Distributions under UL and VUL policies are more direct than with WL distributions but can result in cash values being so low as to risk policy lapse. See Chapter 18 for potential adverse tax consequences from lapses of policies with outstanding loans.

Conclusions

Life insurance policies containing non-guaranteed policy elements require on-going policy management. Their actual performance will almost certainly deviate from that illustrated at time of sale, and policyholder actions can further put policies at risk. Annual and detailed periodic policy reviews are the most effective on-going policy management tools. Annual reviews consist of comparing current with recently illustrated policy values to determine whether the policy is on track and, if applicable, also determining causes of any deviation.

When changes are made by the insurer in underlying policy elements, or actions are taken by the policyholder that can affect future policy values, a detailed policy review is recommended. Additionally, detailed reviews should be performed periodically independent of insurer changes or policyholder action to ensure that the policy remains competitive. Detailed reviews may reveal policy over- or underfunding in light of the client's goals. Resultant corrective actions may include doing nothing, changing funding, changing death benefits, taking distributions, or replacing the existing policy for a better performing one.

Securing Lifetime Values from Life Insurance

18

THIS CHAPTER CONCLUDES PART VI of the *Guide*, on securing lifetime values from life insurance.[1] Here we explore the various aspects of a life insurance policy that can provide values during the policyowner's lifetime as opposed to policy death proceeds. We begin by providing an overview of the income tax treatment of cash values and dividends. We then explore the procedures for, taxation of, and considerations with policy surrenders, withdrawals, loans, replacements, and accelerated death benefits. We close the chapter with a parallel discussion of selling life insurance policies in the secondary life insurance market.

Introduction

Life insurance is thought of customarily in terms of its vital role in assisting families and businesses to maintain their financial security in the face of an untimely death of a family member, business owner, or key employee, as we explored in Chapters 10–12. In addition, life insurance often plays an important role in

---

Authored by Harold D. Skipper.
[1]This chapter draws in part from *Advanced Designs Professional Guide: Life Insurance Taxation* (Pacific Life Insurance Company, October 2009) and Kenneth Black, Jr. and Harold D. Skipper, Jr., *Life and Health Insurance* (13th ed.; Upper Saddle River, NJ: Prentice-Hall, 2000), Chapters 12 and 13.

assisting families and businesses with financial issues during the life of the insured.

Cash values often supplement retirement income. Also, accessing cash values might be desirable because of a pressing need for cash, a reduction or elimination of the obligation or need for which the policy was purchased originally, a desire to terminate an underperforming policy, divorce, sale or insolvency of a business that owned the policy, death of the beneficiary for whom death proceeds were intended, possible estate tax repeal or reform, among other myriad reasons. Indeed, as emphasized throughout this *Guide*, many life insurance buyers are motivated to accumulate cash values and purchase policies that facilitate this goal. Life insurance cash values accumulate on a tax favored basis and typically earn a competitive rate of return.

Life insurance can be efficient and effective in playing these dual roles of providing death protection and accumulating values for lifetime purposes because of its flexibility as a financial instrument and its favorable tax treatment. We have already explored aspects of the flexibility inherent in many modern life insurance policies (see Chapters 6–9) and also introduced the favorable tax treatment accorded death benefits and, to a lesser extent, cash values (see Chapters 7 and 10–12). In this chapter, we extend this exploration by focusing exclusively on the uses and flexibility of life insurance in the context of securing lifetime values from policies, while offering more detail about the income tax consequences associated with each use. Our exploration is intended to highlight the benefits of flexibility, not to encompass the broad issues associated with whether each use is suitable to the client. We introduce some considerations that advisors often take into account to provide context.

An Overview of Income Taxation of Cash Values and Dividends

Lifetime values can be accessed under life insurance policies in several ways, including via dividends, partial or complete cash surrenders, matured endowments, withdrawals, policy loans, and accelerated death benefits. Policies also can be sold in the secondary life insurance market. We cover all of these means in this chapter, but first we introduce important information about certain IRC definitions that influence tax treatment of lifetime values and also about generic income taxation associated with cash values and dividends.

The Effect of Internal Revenue Code Definitions on Life Insurance Income Taxation

As discussed in Chapter 7, the favorable income tax treatment accorded life insurance death benefits and cash values applies only if the policy meets the IRC definition of a life insurance contract. Recall that this definition applies to all policies issued after December 31, 1984 and requires the policy to satisfy one of two **definition of life insurance** (DOLI) tests: (1) a cash value accumulation test or (2) a guideline premium and cash value corridor test. If at any time the contract fails to meet the test, the policy will lose its tax favored treatment.

Another important IRC definition that determines the income tax treatment of lifetime values under life insurance policies is that of a **modified endowment contract** (MEC), which is any policy entered into after June 20, 1988 that meets the IRC Section 7702 definition of life insurance as discussed in Chapter 7, but that fails to meet the so called seven-pay test. A life insurance policy fails to satisfy the **seven-pay test** if the cumulative amount paid under the contract at any time during the first seven contract years exceeds the cumulative amount that would have been paid had the policy's annual premium equaled the net level premium for a seven-pay whole life (WL) policy (provided material changes were not made in the contract—see Chapter 7).

Note that the test has nothing to do with the actual number of premium payments. It must be applied in three situations:

1. All policies entered into after June 20, 1988.
2. Policies entered into after June 20, 1988 for which the death benefit is reduced within the first seven contract years, in which case the policy is to be retested as if the policy had been issued at the reduced level of benefits.
3. Any policy (regardless of date entered into) that undergoes a material change in future benefits after June 20, 1988, in which case the policy is subjected to a new seven-pay period and limit. Material changes include increases in face amount, reductions in a substandard rating, change of non-smoker status, or substitution of an insured. Material changes cause a loss of the policy grandfathered status.

A MEC is subject to income tax rules during the insured's lifetime that differ from those applicable to non-MEC policies. The IRC was amended to include this differential tax treatment because of the practice of many insurers selling single premium WL policies more as tax preferred savings instruments than as policies providing protection against the financial consequences of premature death. The tax treatment of death benefits is unaffected by whether a policy is a MEC. Carriers' illustration software automatically puts limitations on premiums or death benefits to facilitate compliance with the DOLI and MEC tests.

Income Tax Treatment of Cash Values

The interest credited to a life insurance policy's cash value is not subject to current income taxation if the policy meets the IRC definition of life insurance. This favorable tax treatment applies also to MECs. If a policy fails to meet the IRC definition, a portion of the year's cash value increase will be subject to ordinary income taxation if the year's benefits under the policy exceed the premiums paid during that year. "Benefits" are the sum of (1) the year's cash value increase, (2) the value of pure life insurance protection, and (3) dividends received. The value of the pure insurance protection is determined by multiplying the net amount at risk by the lesser of (1) the applicable IRS uniform premium rate or (2) the cost of insurance (mortality) charge, if any, stated in the contract.

If a life insurance policy meets the IRC definition originally but later fails to do so, all prior years' tax deferred income will be included in the taxpayer's/policyowner's taxable income in the year that the policy first fails to meet the definition. The policyowner relies on the life insurance company to ensure that this does not occur.

Another exception to the general rule of tax-free inside interest buildup on cash value policies can occur with regard to a C-corporation's alternative minimum tax (AMT) calculation. As with death benefits payable to C-corporations (see Chapter 12), if the year's internal buildup of cash values on corporate owned life insurance exceeds the year's premiums paid, the difference can influence whether the corporation is subject to the AMT.

Income Tax Treatment of Dividends

Dividends payable under participating (par) life insurance policies normally are considered a nontaxable return of excess premiums. This result is unaffected by the dividend option selected. If dividends are left on deposit to accumulate at interest, the interest credited on the accumulation is, of course, taxable. Unless used to purchase paid-up additional insurance, (PUAs), dividends reduce a policy's cost basis.

Two exceptions exist to the general rule that dividends are not taxable. *First*, if the policy is a MEC or fails to meet the IRC definition of life insurance, dividends taken as distributions (i.e., received in cash, credited against the premium, or accumulated at interest) are taxable. Also, dividends payable under a MEC may be subject to an additional 10 percent penalty tax, as discussed below. *Second*, if the total of the dividends received as distributions (i.e., paid in cash or held on deposit) under a non-MEC policy exceeds the total of the premiums paid, all dividend amounts received in excess of the sum of premiums paid constitute taxable income.

Policy Surrenders and Maturities

One of the most common means of accessing life insurance policy values is by surrendering the policy for its cash surrender value. A far less common means is by waiting for a policy to mature as an endowment.

The procedure to affect a policy surrender is quite simple. The insurance company or agent first provides the appropriate form to the policyowner that directs the company to terminate the policy for its cash surrender value. The owner directs that this value be paid directly to the policyowner or applied under one of the settlement or nonforfeiture options (see Chapter 9).

The form is completed (including providing the owner's tax identification number), signed, and returned to the insurer. The insurer complies with the instructions shortly thereafter. Payment of the lifetime maturity value under a life insurance policy is equally simple and involves the same process, except that payment of a policy's maturity value typically is automatic, not elective with the policyowner.

While traditional endowment policies are no longer generally sold in the U.S. because they would not meet the IRC definition of life insurance, by maturing before age 95, some older WL and highly funded UL policies can endow if the insured lives to an advanced age. These older policies can endow at ages 95 or 100, typically when the cash value equals the face amount (although for UL the cash value may be less than the face amount). Structuring policies in this way usually was not advantageous to the policyholder as income taxes had to be paid on what often was a type of forced gain.

To remedy this problem, many companies provided that, at the end of the stated policy period (i.e., age 95 or 100), the face amount was reduced to equal the cash value—if it did not already equal it by contract, as with a WL policy—and the policy continued in force with no further premium payments or charges until the insured's death. This often was accomplished by extended maturity riders, which many insurers incorporate within newer policies as well. WL and UL policies issued under the *2001 CSO Mortality Table*—see Chapter 6—generally have no maturity dates; i.e., dates at which the policy's cash value must be paid.

Income Tax Treatment of Surrenders and Maturities

The general rule for taxation of lump sum cash surrender value payments and lifetime maturity payments under life insurance policies is the **cost recovery rule** under which the amount included in the policyowner's taxable income is the excess of the gross proceeds received over the cost basis. This difference is taxed as ordinary income, not capital gains. The **cost basis** of a life insurance contract, also called **investment in the contract**, normally is the sum of the premiums paid less any untaxed distributions. Untaxed distributions include any withdrawals and the sum of any dividends received as distributions. **Gross proceeds** are the amounts paid on surrender, including the cash value of any PUAs.

To illustrate: assume that Pauline owns a policy on which she has made 15 annual premium payments of $1,000 each. Assume further that she has received dividends in cash over this period totaling $6,000, that the policy's cash surrender value today is $12,000, and that she has made no withdrawals or partial surrenders. Her cost basis would be calculated as follows:

	Sum of premiums paid	**$15,000**
Less:	Dividends received	–6,000
Equals:	Cost basis	$9,000

If she surrendered the policy for its $12,000 cash surrender value, her gain, which would be taxed as ordinary income, would be calculated as follows:

	Gross proceeds (cash surrender value)	**$12,000**
Less:	Cost basis	–9,000
Equals:	Taxable gain	$3,000

Policy loans outstanding lower a policy's cost basis by the amount of the loans. On policy surrender, any policy loans can be thought of as having been an advance of cash surrender values in an amount equal to the loan, as the loan is netted against the policy cash surrender value to yield its net cash surrender value. Premiums paid for supplementary benefits such as the waiver of premium and accidental death benefit features and interest paid on policy loans have no affect on a policy's cost basis.

The cost basis of a life insurance policy includes the pure cost of insurance. Theoretically, yearly mortality charges, which exist with every life insurance policy with a positive net amount at risk, should be excluded from the basis as representing current expenditure and not an investment. Thus, taxable income to the policyowner technically is understated by the value of these mortality charges, another tax benefit of life insurance.

Losses on surrender of a life insurance policy normally cannot be recognized for income tax purposes. The rationale for disallowing a deductible loss is that the method for computing taxable gain (and loss) makes no allowance for mortality charges. Therefore, any loss is assumed to be composed, in whole or in part, of such mortality costs.

As alluded to above, the same tax treatment applies when a policy terminates as an endowment or maturity value at a date specified in the contract and the cash value is paid to the policyowner. Such an event may be undesirable as the insured likely is elderly and does not need the cash, and taxes due on the gain can be substantial. As noted above, to avoid this outcome, many policies include riders that extend the maturity date of the contract, an increasingly important option as insureds live longer, and most contracts issued under the *2001 CSO Mortality Table* contain no maturity provision.

Another alternative to taking the lump sum maturity amount would be to apply the cash value under one of the policy settlement options as an annuity. In this situation, the maturity proceeds are taxed under the IRC Section 72 annuity rules. This section spreads the taxable gain over the expected annuity payment period.

Considerations in Policy Surrenders and Maturities

Numerous factors can bear on whether to surrender a life insurance policy and/or to take lifetime maturity values. The first consideration in most situations is whether the insurance death proceeds continue to be needed. If they are not, and other factors suggest a surrender to be wise, then surrender may be the rational choice. Even if the death proceeds are still needed, but the owner can no longer afford to pay the premiums and the policy's cash values are desperately needed, surrender may again be the rational choice. Careful consideration, however, ideally would have been afforded to other options that would allow the owner to keep the policy in force. These other options include electing a nonforfeiture option that maintains some insurance, changes in the policy itself (e.g., reducing the face amount, policy loans, cash withdrawals, partial surrender, accelerated death benefits), or sale of the policy in the secondary market.

As is clear from the above discussion, the tax consequences of either type of policy termination can be substantial and will have been carefully considered. The section below on replacement explores options to taking any gain into taxable income in situations involving the purchase of another policy, but such a replacement purchase might not be desired or contemplated.

Policy Withdrawals, Partial Surrenders, and Loans

Policy withdrawals, partial surrenders, and policy loans are each means of using policy cash values as the basis for securing cash under a policy without having to terminate the policy and losing its death benefit coverage in the process. Policy withdrawals occur when the policyowner removes cash value from a life insurance policy with no effect on the policy's net amount at risk. Withdrawals are commonly associated with universal life (UL) and current assumption whole life policies (CAWL) and not with bundled WL policies. The withdrawal decreases the total death benefit and cash value by the amount of the withdrawal. Another form of withdrawal occurs with par WL policies when the policyowner, having elected the accumulate-at-interest dividend option, withdraws some of those dividends.

A partial surrender is associated with bundled life insurance policies. Not all bundled cash value contacts give the owner a right of partial surrenders, but most insurers allow them. Cash value withdrawals, as such, ordinarily are not permitted with bundled policies, except for withdrawals of dividends accumulating at interest. Rather, as discussed in Chapter 7, to obtain cash values the policyowner must surrender portions of the policy. For example, assume that Mildred owns a bundled policy having a $1.0 million face amount and a $400,000 cash surrender value. She wants to secure $200,000 or one-half of the policy's cash surrender value. To do so, she must execute a partial surrender of one-half of the policy, reducing not just the cash surrender value but the face amount, the net amount at risk, and the policy premium by one-half as well.

Another form of partial surrender occurs with par WL policies when the policyowner, having elected the PUA dividend option, surrender portions of those PUAs. For example, assume that Bradley elected the PUA option when he bought a par WL policy 20 years ago. These PUAs now provide an additional $60,000 of life insurance and have a cash surrender value of $30,000. Bradley wants $20,000 cash from the PUAs, so he executes a two-thirds surrender of them, reducing not just their cash surrender value by two-thirds but their death benefit and net amount at risk by two-thirds as well.

Finally, policyowners may exercise the contractual right to secure a loan under their cash value policies on the security of and in an amount up to the policy's net cash surrender value. Policy loans are discussed in Chapter 9. Interest is due on policy loans and is paid either in cash or by a further policy loan.

In each of the above instances, the policyowner completes and signs a form provided by the agent or insurer that authorizes the action. The process is simple and rarely time consuming.

Income Tax Treatment of Withdrawals, Partial Surrenders, and Loans

Other things being the same, withdrawals and partial surrenders are taxed in the same favorable way, with the exceptions noted below. Generally, distributions from a policy are excluded from taxable income until they equal the policy's cost basis. Such distributions are treated as coming first from the cost basis; i.e., the FIFO (first-in, first-out) method of taxation. Thereafter, withdrawals and partial surrenders are from the policy's gain so are taxed as ordinary income. The general rule is that the taking out of a policy loan is not in itself a taxable event.

Policy loans can lead to unpleasant tax surprises in connection with a policy surrender, lapse, or exchange. When a policy is terminated other than by the insured's death, any outstanding loans are taxable to the extent there is gain in the policy because the loan is repaid by being netted against the cash surrender value. (This forgiveness of debt is referred to as "boot" in IRC.) For example, assume that Susie Mae decides that she no longer needs her policy and surrenders it. Assume that she has paid premiums over the past 30 years totaling $250,000. The policy's cash surrender value is $550,000, on which she has loans outstanding of $450,000. After the insurer deducts the loan from the cash surrender value, she receives a check for the net surrender value of $100,000.

As we know, her taxable gain is the difference between her gross proceeds and her cost basis. Policy loans reduce a policy's cost basis. Her cost basis is, therefore, –$200,000 ($250,000 minus $450,000). Her gross proceeds on surrender are $100,000. Thus, her taxable income from the surrender is $300,000 ($100,000 minus –$200,000). In other words, she receives $100,000 and owes taxes on $300,000.

The same calculation applies to policy lapses—potentially an even more unpleasant surprise if the policy has no net cash surrender value. The policyowner receives no cash but could be facing a potentially high tax obligation. Taxation also can occur in a Section 1035 exchange (see below) in which a policy with an outstanding loan is exchanged for another policy, but the loan is not carried over to the new policy.

Withdrawals, partial surrenders, and policy loans do not receive the favorable FIFO tax treatment when the policy runs afoul of the IRC definition of life insurance or the policy is a MEC. Any distribution from a MEC, including withdrawals, partial surrenders, and policy loans, are treated as coming from income first and cost basis last (i.e., LIFO—last-in, first-out—tax treatment). Thus, any distribution, such as a withdrawal, is considered first ordinary income to the extent of any gain in the policy, opposite that which occurs with cash withdrawals under non-MEC policies.

Additionally, if within its first seven years a policy becomes a MEC by ceasing to meet the seven-pay test, all future distributions are subject to LIFO taxation. Further, distributions made within the two years prior to the policy becoming a MEC are treated as being made in anticipation of the policy becoming a MEC and are subject to LIFO taxation as well.

Finally, to add insult to injury, in addition to LIFO taxation of all policy distributions, a 10 percent premature distribution penalty tax may also apply, unless one of three exceptions is met. These exceptions include that the distribution was made (1) after the taxpayer attained age $59^{1}/_{2}$, (2) to a taxpayer because of a qualifying disability, or (3) as part of substantially equal periodic payments over the lifetime or based on life expectancy of the taxpayer. These adverse income tax consequences apply only to distributions under MECs and have no effect on the tax favored growth of undistributed cash values or to income tax-free death benefits.

Also, withdrawals and partial surrenders do not enjoy FIFO treatment in the following situations:

◆ The policy fails to meet the definition of life insurance, in which case the interest earned on the cash value is effectively taxed as ordinary income.

◆ If a cash "force out" occurs. A cash force out occurs if a withdrawal within the first 15 policy years is accompanied by a reduction in policy benefits which causes the policy to fail to continue to meet the definition of life insurance. In this instance, the distribution is subject to LIFO taxation.

Considerations in Withdrawals, Partial Surrenders, and Loans

Securing cash via withdrawals, partial surrenders, and loans is comparatively simple and easy. No institution's approval is needed. Withdrawals and loans are available as a contractual right and may be repaid at the convenience of the policyowner or the policy allowed to continue without repayment. Plus, the transaction is confidential; it is between the insurer and policyowner only.

For these very reasons, a little caution may be appropriate, depending on the need for the distribution. The effects of these distributions are to reduce death benefit protection and to make life insurance policies less secure. The policyowner, and perhaps the beneficiary, should be well aware of these consequences and make an informed decision to proceed. At the same time, reducing the death protection and making a policy less secure are not necessarily negative; indeed, the policy may be no longer needed or the time may have arrived to implement a previously planned strategy of periodic distributions.

For example, we know that non-MEC life insurance policies enjoy FIFO tax treatment on withdrawals and partial surrenders, meaning that they are not included in taxable income until the sum of such distributions equals the policy's cost basis. And we know that ordinarily loan transactions are not taxable. Combining these two types of distributions can yield a tax efficient strategy for securing income under a life insurance policy. Withdrawals are taken until they equal the policy's cost basis, whereupon they cease. These are not taxable. Thereafter, a series of policy loans are initiated that also are not taxable events. Ideally, the difference between the policy loan rate and the interest crediting rate on the cash value is not great, thereby allowing for many years of loans. When the insured dies, the loans are repaid from death proceeds, and no taxation should occur.

Policy Replacements

As its name suggests, a **replacement** occurs when a new life insurance policy is purchased and, in connection with that purchase, an existing policy is surrendered or otherwise terminated. State insurance regulations (see below) extend this definition to include discontinuing premium payments on an existing policy and other acts that have the effect of reducing the benefits otherwise provided under that policy.

We have included policy replacements in this chapter, even though they are not commonly considered to be a means of accessing cash from a policy in the same way as the other means analyzed in this chapter. Economically speaking, a replacement is or at least can be such a means, as the replaced policy may be surrendered for its cash surrender value. Alternatively, if done properly, the replaced policy's cash value may be rolled over into the new policy, enhancing its value while avoiding taking any gain on surrender into taxable income.

Many within the life insurance industry have strong views as to whether replacements in general are good or bad for consumers, with advocates on both sides of the debate. Many agents and executives, including many state insurance regulators, argue that replacements generally are not in the consumer's best interest. For reasons enumerated later in this section, they believe that a new policy is unlikely to be better for the policyholder than an existing policy. Many others contend that there are so many life insurance policies sold each year that are overly costly, perform poorly over time, and/or are ill-suited for customers that the presumption should be reversed: replacements generally *are* in the consumer's best interest. Still others take a neutral position that replacements are neither inherently good nor bad for the consumer and that each case should stand alone, being judged on its own merits.

Some readers may view this intra-industry debate with detached amusement and perhaps curiosity. "And why *wouldn't* one take a position of neutrality, allowing facts to speak for themselves?" In fact, most agents probably are reluctant to recommend replacement either because their views place them into "replacements are bad" category, they wish to avoid the hassle associated with replacement, they wish to avoid complicating a sale, or they prefer to avoid having to imply that an existing policy, perhaps sold to a client by his or her friend, does not offer good value or is not suitable. On the other hand, some agents probably "never met a policy that shouldn't be replaced." We mention this issue solely as an alert to readers and to encourage a careful review and analysis of clients' existing policies over a discussion singularly focused on the value of potential new policies.

Replacement Procedures

While individual life insurers and agents have their own procedures for replacements, these will have been dictated to a great extent by state insurance replacement regulations. These regulations set out the requirements that all agents and insurers doing business in the state must follow with respect to re-placements. They are patterned after the *Model Life Insurance and Annuities Replacement Regulation* or one of its predecessors as promulgated by the *National Association of Insurance Commissioners* (NAIC).

The regulations impose sales-related obligations on both insurers and agents. The obligations apply to almost all individually issued life insurance policies, including variable life. The obligations that affect customers directly and will be part of every agent's and insurer's procedures are summarized here.

First, agents are required to submit to their insurers, with or as part of the application, the applicant's signed statement whether the applicant owns existing policies. If the applicant does not have existing policies, the agent's duties regarding replacement are satisfied.

If the applicant has existing insurance, the regulations require the agent to present and read to the applicant, not later than at the time of taking the application, a "Notice Regarding Replacement." The reading requirement can be waived by the applicant. The notice cautions the policyowner that he or she should carefully consider whether a replacement is in his or her best interest, then offers some reasons why it might not be and sets out a series of statements and questions intended to cause the owner to consider all aspects of the prospective transaction. The notice also inquires whether a replacement is being considered.

If a replacement is being considered, as defined within the notice, information is to be provided about the policies to be replaced and the reason for the replacement. The replacing insurer must within five days notify the exiting insurer of the contemplated replacement and provide it with information and data about the proposed policy. The existing insurer is then required to contact its policyowner, reminding the owner of the right to receive information and data about the existing policy. If the existing insurer receives a request to surrender the policy or to take a policy loan or withdrawal under the policy, it is required to send a notice informing the owner that the action may adversely affect policy values!

Both the applicant and agent must sign the notice, irrespective of whether replacement is being considered, attesting to the accuracy of the responses. A copy of the notice is to be left with the applicant.

Income Tax Treatment of Replacements

Ordinarily, any gain realized on the surrender of a life insurance policy is taxable income to the policyowner, as discussed above, and any loss does not reduce taxable income. Section 1035 of the IRC, however, permits the carryover of the cost basis of a surrendered policy into a new one thereby avoiding recognition of the gain or loss, provided certain conditions are met. These transactions are called **Section 1035 exchanges** or simply **1035 exchanges**.

An exchange as defined under the IRC is narrower than a replacement as defined in the NAIC replacement regulation. The NAIC definition of replacement includes a cessation of premium payments under an existing policy or any reduction of benefits or value, not just the termination of one policy and the purchase of a replacement contract. Only the latter transaction can meet the definition of an exchange for purposes of satisfying Section 1035.

The following conditions must be met for a policy exchange to be a tax-free transaction:

1. There is an exchange of one qualifying insurance contract for another. Section 1035 applies only to exchanges of life insurance and annuity contracts, but they can be either general account or separate account products. One policy may be exchanged for multiple policies and vice versa.
2. The insured under both the new and old contract must be the same.
3. The owner under both the new and old contracts must be the same. Ownership transfers either before or after an exchange are not inconsistent with this requirement, although a transfer ideally should not take place too close in time to the exchange.
4. A life insurance policy can be exchanged only for another life insurance policy, an endowment contract, an annuity, or a qualified long-term care contract.

Procedurally, the existing policy is assigned and surrendered directly to the new company. Information about the policy's cost basis, gains, and losses is also given to the new company, as provided by the old company. The policyowner must not, directly or constructively, receive any surrender proceeds if the exchange is to pass IRS muster. The IRS imposes no reporting requirements on the old insurer provided the exchange does not result in a "designated distribution." A designated distribution is "any payment or distribution from or under an employer deferred compensation plan, an individual retirement plan or a commercial annuity."

Considerations in Replacements

Arguments as to whether replacements are generally good or bad provide the individual contemplating replacement little help. The question that he or she wants answered is whether his or her existing policy should be replaced. Many replacements are, no doubt, contrary to the policyowner's best interests. No less doubtful is that many other replacements are justified and that many policies should be replaced but are not.

The policyowner considering replacement should weigh several factors. The questions and statements included in the state-mandated "Notice Regarding Replacement" are a good place to begin an analysis of whether a suggested replacement is in a client's best interest. Box 18-1 shows these questions and statements as relates to life insurance replacements.

BOX 18-1: Life Insurance Questions from the NAIC "Notice Regarding Replacement"

"You should discuss the following with your insurance producer [agent] to determine whether replacement or financing your purchase makes sense:

PREMIUMS:

◆ Are they affordable?
◆ Could they change?
◆ You are older—are premiums higher for the proposed new life insurance policy?
◆ How long will you have to pay premiums on the new life insurance policy? On the old life insurance policy?

LIFE INSURANCE POLICY VALUES: New policies usually take longer to build cash values and to pay dividends.

◆ Acquisition costs for the old life insurance policy may have been paid, and you will incur new costs for the new one.
◆ What surrender charges do the policies have?
◆ What expense and sales charges do the policies have?
◆ Does the new life insurance policy provide more insurance coverage?

INSURABILITY: If your health has changed since you bought your old life insurance policy, the new one could cost you more, or you could be turned down.

◆ You may need a medical exam for a new life insurance policy.
◆ Claims on most new policies for up to the first 2 years can be denied based on inaccurate statements.
◆ Suicide limitations may begin anew on the new coverage.

IF YOU ARE KEEPING THE OLD LIFE INSURANCE POLICY AS WELL AS THE NEW LIFE INSURANCE POLICY:

◆ How are premiums for both policies being paid?
◆ How will the premium on your existing life insurance policy be affected?
◆ Will a loan be deducted from death benefits?
◆ What values from the old life insurance policy are being used to pay premiums?

. . . [questions dealing with annuities omitted]

OTHER ISSUES TO CONSIDER FOR ALL TRANSACTIONS:

◆ What are the tax consequences of buying the new life insurance policy?
◆ Is this a tax-free exchange? (See your tax advisor.)
◆ Will the existing insurer be willing to modify the old life insurance policy?
◆ How does the quality and financial stability of the new company compare with the exiting company?"

Source: NAIC Insurance and Annuities Replacement Model Regulation.

Unfortunately, one of the most critical elements in analyzing whether a replacement makes economic sense receives only generalized treatment in the notice. The notice urges the individual to make "a careful comparison of the costs and benefits of your existing life insurance policy . . . and the proposed life insurance policy. . . ." It further notes that one way of doing this is to ask the existing company or agent to provide information and data on current and illustrated future policy values, based on "certain assumptions." The client presumably is then somehow to divine how to conduct a comparison between the existing and proposed policy illustrations. More likely, the client seeks assistance from a knowledgeable advisor. Further, a comparison likely was already conducted by the agent proposing the replacement.

The questions and statements contained in the notice warrant careful attention, but many of them constitute explanations for why a detailed analysis might possibly reveal that a replacement is *not* in a client's best interest. In themselves, most offer no justification for failing to replace. For example, take the statements and questions under the heading LIFE INSURANCE POLICY VALUES. None of them would be a reason not to replace an old policy with a newer one *if* a reasonable cost/benefit analysis found a replacement to be justified. The chapters in Part V and this part of this *Guide* are intended to help facilitate such analyses.

As the notice advises, "new policies usually take longer to build cash values and to pay dividends" as most cash value life insurance policies have their initial costs charged against early policy cash values. An existing policy likely would have already amortized these high initial costs to varying degrees and surrender charges likely would have begun to decline, depending on the policy's age. For this reason, an existing policy may be less costly than a new one. On the other hand, a cost/benefit analysis of the existing versus the proposed policy will automatically take these factors into consideration. It will be concluded that either the proposed policy or the existing policy seems to offer better value. The analysis should also have taken numerous other factors listed in the notice into account including the magnitude, duration, and possible changes in the two policies' premiums and that the client is older; any substandard ratings (or the client is healthy and gets the new select period that reduces the ongoing COI); and the magnitude of death benefits and cash values.

The analysis should include consideration of the tax impact of any exchange and the meaningful differences, if any, in the terms of the two contracts. The notice further advises that the incontestable and suicide clauses begin anew under new policies. But for the non-suicidal, honest person, these two factors will be of little relevance. Moreover, some companies will waive these clauses on new policies to the extent that they had elapsed under the older policy.

If an older policy is perceived as not in the client's best interest, the existing insurer may be willing to make an internal exchange on more beneficial terms than those that a new insurer may be willing to offer. Also, older policies sometimes can be adjusted to meet new circumstances through changes in dividend options or through policy loans and other alterations. These options usually are worthy of exploration, other things being the same.

We suggest that a proposed policy replacement be approached with no prejudices either for or against replacement. Replacement is a neutral financial activity and a sound, fair analysis will help determine whether, in a given situation, it should be undertaken. As a general rule, if results of the analysis do not provide a reasonably clear decision in favor of replacement, the policyowner probably should not replace. A policyowner should never discontinue existing coverage before the new coverage is approved for issuance by the replacing company and is in effect.

Accelerated Death Benefits

With the HIV/AIDS crises of the 1980s, a secondary market for life insurance arose in the early 1990s that allowed infected insureds to sell their policies for amounts greater than the cash values that they would have received on policy surrender. As individuals infected with AIDS at that time had a life expectancy of about two years from diagnosis, the economic value of policies insuring infected persons was always well in excess of such policies' cash values.

Life insurers responded by supporting changes in tax and other relevant laws that allowed them to make their policies more responsive to terminally ill insureds. Perhaps the most important response was the introduction of **accelerated death benefits**, also called **terminal illness coverage**, under which insureds with shortened life expectances can now receive substantial advances on their policies' death benefits without incurring adverse income tax consequences.

This and other living benefit coverages are discussed in Chapter 9. Recall that, with accelerated death benefits, the insurer promises to pay a specified maximum percentage of from 25 to 100 percent of the policy's face amount if the insured is diagnosed as having a terminal illness, usually subject to a specified overall maximum payment, such as $250,000. Most provisions require that the insured have a maximum of one or two years to live, unless state law mandates otherwise.

The procedure for securing these benefits is that the policyowner first must request them, indicating the amount desired. Some insurers also want the beneficiary to sign the necessary forms, indicating his or her understanding that an acceleration of benefits will decrease the amount ultimately paid to him or her. The policyowner must provide satisfactory evidence that the insured suffers a terminal illness, including (1) certification by a physician, (2) hospital or nursing home records, and, possibly, (3) a medical examination (paid by the insurer). Some companies make no explicit charge for the coverage while others assess an administrative expense charge (e.g., $200) for processing the request and may reduce the amount payable to reflect lost interest.

Income Tax Treatment of Accelerated Death Benefits

Accelerated death benefits are fully excludable from income taxation if the insured is terminally ill. A terminally ill individual is one who has been certified by a physician as having an illness or physical condition that can reasonably be expected to result in death within 24 months from the date of the certification.

An exception to this excludability rule rules occurs if the policyowner is a business and the insured is a director, officer, or employee of that business or has some other financial interest in the business. In this situation, accelerated benefit payments will not be treated as tax-free death benefits.

Considerations in Taking Accelerated Death Benefits

Several factors may have a bearing on the amount and whether to accelerate a policy's death benefits. Assume first that the policy or insurer allows acceleration and that the insured's condition qualifies for acceleration. Here are some of the factors that warrant consideration:

- ◆ Whether the balance of the death benefit remaining after acceleration is sufficient to meet the needs of those for whom the insurance was purchased originally. If the balance is insufficient for the beneficiary's needs, the difficult decision of what to do will likely turn on the relative needs, emotions, and benefits derived by the involved people.
- ◆ A clear understanding of the means by which the insurer will provide these benefits, whether by advancing some of the policy's death benefit or via liens against it. Related to this is the effective cost to the beneficiary in terms of charges assessed by the insurer as fees or interest or discounts against the ultimate payout?
- ◆ Any affect these benefit payments might have on Medicaid or other government-sponsored benefits received by the insured.
- ◆ Whether acceleration will expose the payments to the claims of creditors which, but for the acceleration, death proceeds would not be exposed.

Sale of the Policy in the Secondary Life Insurance Market

The market for life insurance policies purchased from insurance companies is called the **primary life insurance market**. The market in which existing life insurance policies are bought and sold is called the **secondary life insurance**

market. The HIV/AIDS crises of the 1980s gave impetus to the secondary market for life insurance where infected insureds could sell their policies for amounts greater than the cash values. These sales were labeled **viatical settlements** or simply **viaticals.**

As the viatical market dried up with improvements in HIV/AIDS treatment, entrepreneurs then shifted from buying policies on terminally ill insureds to buying policies on those whose health had become merely impaired. Sales of such policies are commonly known as **life settlements** to distinguish them from viaticals. Except for tax and regulatory matters, the dividing line between viaticals and life settlements is arbitrary, and both terms today are understood to refer to sale of an existing life insurance policy in the secondary market.

Life settlements, like viaticals, have been associated with considerable fraud and incomplete disclosure. Concerns about fraud and inappropriate sales practices led the NAIC to amend its 1993 *Viatical Settlements Model Act* in 2007 and the National Conference of Insurance Legislators (NCOIL) to adopt its own model act, also in 2007, the *Life Settlements Model Act*. One of the chief concerns related to so-called stranger-owned life insurance as explained in Box 18-2.

The Process and Economics of Life Settlements

The secondary life insurance market, as with all markets, relies on willing buyers and sellers arriving at agreeable prices. The sales process usually involves a life insurance agent or broker (producer) locating owners willing to sell their policies and negotiating the sale on behalf of the owners with life settlement firms, often called **providers**. Producers are paid commissions by the firms that purchase the policies. Commissions can be quite high, with one long-time knowledgeable consumerist labeling them "obscene."[2] Policies sold in the secondary market are sometimes said to have been **settled**.

The typical target insured is age 65 and older whose health has deteriorated. The minimum eligible policy face amount is in the $250,000–$500,000 range or greater, and the insurance typically is no longer needed or wanted. The objective of the settlement firms (or the speculators to whom the policies are then sold) is to acquire portfolios of life insurance policies and, thereby, to earn profits from the death benefits that they receive under the policies being greater than that which they paid to acquire and maintain the policies. Settlement firms expect to make their profits in one or both of two ways: (1) what they believe is mispricing by some life insurers on some products and/or (2) a disparity that develops over time in life insurance policies between their cash values and their economic or actuarial values.

---

[2] See, Joseph M. Belth, "Obscene Commissions for Intermediaries in the Secondary Market for Life Insurance Policies," *The Insurance Forum* (January 2008), pp. 1–3.

BOX 18-2: "Stranger-Owned Life Insurance" (STOLI)

Individuals who acquire life insurance policies possessing a legitimate insurable interest at inception are free to dispose of them in whatever way they may wish, including selling them in the secondary market via a life settlement. These types of sales occur regularly and represent a valuable option when a policyowner's objectives and/or circumstances change over time. However, a policy procured with the intent—at inception—that it would be sold to someone with no insurable interest is inconsistent with insurable interest requirements and arguably void for lack of insurable interest. It is in this shady realm that we encounter "stranger-owned (or originated) life insurance" or STOLI.

A few years ago, family members and investor/promoters began convincing elderly parents and grandparents to apply for these large policies, not for true estate conservation purposes, but for the purpose of selling the policies to unknown investors ("strangers"). The intent was to treat the policies as financial commodities and sources of profit. This true purpose is never disclosed to the life insurance companies. The value of the proposed insured's net worth is commonly grossly overstated to convince the companies to issue much more insurance on the person's life than they would otherwise.

Life insurance companies will not knowingly issue STOLI-driven policies, as they present several problems. First and most importantly, as wagering transactions on human life, they arguably are not valid life insurance as they lack a bona fide insurable interest from inception, unlike generic life settlements. Second, from the life insurance industry's viewpoint, they impose great costs on the industry as the insurance companies' pricing assumptions do not match the reality of STOLI policies. Third, they represent a threat to the present tax-favored treatment of life insurance. Fourth, the insurance industry is concerned that they represent a threat to its long-term reputation. Fifth, STOLI is said to violate state laws prohibiting rebating if an inducement is provided to the insured. Finally, it has been argued that elderly consumers who participate in STOLI transactions do not fully comprehend the varied implications of doing so, so producers and providers are taking unfair advantage of them.

Mispricing can occur if an insurer underestimates the magnitude of future mortality rates or overestimates future lapse rates involving certain types of pricing. The prominent driver of life settlement profits is from purchasing policies on insureds whose health has deteriorated faster than anticipated in insurers' pricing; in other words, from those whose health has become impaired in some way. It is from within this group that we find the main market for life settlement firms. Such policies' economic values should be greater than their cash values.

Income Tax Treatment of Selling a Life Insurance Policy

The tax treatment to the owner of a policy sold in the secondary market is more complex than that found with most other lifetime transactions involving life insurance. If a policy is sold to an unrelated third party, the policyowner must take any gain into taxable income. Part of any taxable gain may be taxed as ordinary income and another part as capital gains.

The portion of the gain considered ordinary income is the difference between the cash surrender value and the aggregate premiums paid under the policy, which is the same as the taxable amount for a cash surrender. The portion of gain considered capital gains is the difference between the policy sale price and the adjusted basis *minus* any amounts subject to ordinary income tax. The adjusted basis equals the sum of premiums paid less the cost of insurance charges.

To illustrate: assume that Bettie sells her policy, which has a cash surrender value of $78,000, to an unrelated third party for $80,000 and that she had paid premiums totaling $64,000. Assume also that cost of insurance charges totaling $10,000 had been assessed against the policy, so the adjusted basis is $54,000 ($64,000 − $10,000). In this case, she must recognize $14,000 ($78,000 − $64,000) as ordinary income and $12,000 ($80,000 − $54,000 − $14,000) as capital gains.

A policy on a terminally ill or chronically ill insured that is sold to a life settlement company generally will receive the same tax treatment as that of an accelerated death benefit; i.e., the sale price will be treated as tax-free death benefits.

Considerations in Selling a Life Insurance Policy

In the past, a policyowner deciding to terminate his or her life insurance policy because insurance was no longer needed or affordable surrendered the policy to the insurance company for its cash surrender value or simply allowed it to lapse. Today, a wiser financial decision may be to sell the policy in the secondary market, if the policy qualifies.

Many factors enter the decision whether to sell a policy. Laws in many states require that persons considering life settlements be provided brochures by the broker outlining such considerations. A few considerations are:

- ◆ If the insurance is no longer affordable but still needed, are there alternatives to surrender or sale such as reducing the size or altering the policy in some way or taking policy loans?
- ◆ If the insured suffers from a terminal condition, might it be wiser to request an acceleration of the policy death benefit?
- ◆ Have proposals from several competing life settlement firms been obtained?
- ◆ What are the commission arrangements?
- ◆ Is the insured comfortable knowing that investors having no insurable interest in his or her life will benefit from his or her death? (Some safeguards are in place to limit disclosure of personally identifiable information.)

♦ Would receipt of settlement proceeds adversely affect eligibility for government benefits?

♦ Is the insured comfortable being contacted every three months or so about his or her health?

♦ Is it important that the sale of the policy could limit the amount of life insurance for which the insured qualifies in the future?

When contemplating the sale of a policy, it is important to assess the original reason for which the policy was purchased and to determine whether those reasons remain valid. Of course, if insurance continues to be needed, the possibility of selling an existing policy in the secondary market and replacing it with a new policy may make sense. At the same time, however, a Section 1035 policy exchange may make even more economic sense.

Conclusions

When structured properly, life insurance offers not only tax-favored benefits at the death of the insured, but also tax-favored benefits during the insured's lifetime. These lifetime benefits can be in the form of cash from a full or partial surrender, withdrawals, loans, tax-qualified replacements, or accelerated death benefits. In each instance, favorable tax treatment is assured if well understood conditions are met. Careful consideration will have been given to whether any such distribution is consistent with sound financial planning and family or other needs. Distributions from policies are rarely costless, with some measure of death protection and policy flexibility usually lost.

Appendices

Life Insurance
Agent Questionnaire

Agents are expected to conduct themselves with fairness, competence, integrity, and diligence. Please respond to the following questions that touch on each of these four areas.

I. Fairness

    A. What is the justification for your recommendation regarding the:

        i. Amount of insurance?

        ii. Type of policy?

        iii. Policy funding technique?

        iv. Beneficiary?

        v. Policy ownership arrangement?

        vi. Insurance company?

    B. Did you review multiple insurers and products, including policy performance comparisons? Which ones and why did you eliminate them?

    C. With what life insurance companies do you place most of your business and why?

    D. Are you free to place business with insurers not affiliated with your primary insurer? If not, explain why the client should be satisfied with your primary insurer.

II. Competence

    A. What is your educational and professional background, including professional designations?

433

    B. What do you consider your area of expertise?

    C. For how many years have you worked fulltime in the life insurance business, and for how many years have you devoted most of your time in your area of expertise?

    D. What are the qualifications and experience of your support staff?

    E. What continuing professional development activities have you undertaken in the past three years, including pursuit of any professional designations?

    F. To what professional organizations do you belong? What positions have you occupied within them?

III. Integrity

    A. Do you or your firm have a written and enforced confidentiality policy and accompanying guidelines?

    B. Do you or your firm have a written and enforced ethics policy and accompanying guidelines?

    C. Has any client ever sued you or registered any complaints against you with any professional society, government regulatory agency (including any state insurance department), or the Financial Industry Regulatory Authority (FINRA) and, if so, explain the circumstances?

IV. Diligence

    A. What is your understanding of the client's financial needs, goals, and circumstances?

    B. What is your policy regarding working with other professionals? With how many have you worked in the previous year and what is their expertise?

    C. What is the platform/administrative set up on which you provide ongoing policy service and how do you monitor policy and insurer performance, including treatment of in-force policies and insurer financial strength?

    D. Explain the source of any leverage that you have with insurers in connection policy negotiation and pricing and re-pricing.

    E. What have been the first-year lapse rates on the business that you have written in each of the preceding three years?

Descriptions of Four Rating Agencies' Rating Categories

A.M. Best Company

Secure Ratings

A++ A+	Superior. Assigned to companies that have, in our opinion, a superior ability to meet their ongoing obligations to policyholders.
A A-	Excellent. Assigned to companies that have, in our opinion, an excellent ability to meet their ongoing obligations to policyholders.
B++ B+	Good. Assigned to companies that have, in our opinion, a fair ability to meet their ongoing obligations to policyholders.

Vulnerable Ratings

B B–	Fair. Assigned to companies that have, in our opinion, a fair ability to meet their ongoing obligations to policyholders, but are financially vulnerable to adverse changes in underwriting and economic conditions.
C++ C+	Marginal. Assigned to companies that have, in our opinion, a marginal ability to meet their ongoing obligations to policyholders, but are financially vulnerable to adverse changes in underwriting and economic conditions.

C	Weak. Assigned to companies that have, in our opinion, a weak
C–	ability to meet their ongoing obligations to policyholders, but are financially very vulnerable to adverse changes in underwriting and economic conditions.
D	Poor. Assigned to companies that have, in our opinion, a poor ability to meet their ongoing obligations to policyholders and are financially extremely vulnerable to adverse changes in underwriting and economic conditions.
E	Under Regulatory Supervision
F	In Liquidation
S	Rating Suspended

Affiliation Codes

g	Group Rating
p	Pooled Rating
R	Reinsured Rating

Rating Modifiers

U	Under Review
Pd	Public Data Rating
S	Syndicate Rating

"Not Rated" Categories

NR-1	Insufficient Data
NR-2	Insufficient Size and/or Operating Experience
NR-3	Rating Procedure Inapplicable
NR-4	Company Request
NR-5	Not formally followed

Fitch Ratings

Secure Ratings

| AAA | Exceptionally Strong. Denotes the lowest expectation of ceased or interrupted payments. Assigned only in the case of exceptionally strong capacity to meet policyholder and contract obligations. This capacity is highly unlikely to be adversely affected by foreseeable events. |

AA+ AA AA−	Very Strong. Denotes a very low expectation of ceased or interrupted payments. Indicates very strong capacity to meet policyholder and contract obligations. This capacity is not significantly vulnerable to foreseeable events.
A+ A A−	Strong. Denotes a low expectation of ceased or interrupted payments. Indicates strong capacity to meet policyholder and contract obligations. This capacity may, nonetheless, be more vulnerable to changes in circumstances or in economic conditions than is the case for higher ratings.
BBB+ BBB BBB−	Good. Indicates that there is currently a low expectation of ceased or interrupted payments. The capacity to meet policyholders and contract obligations on a timely basis is considered adequate, but adverse changes in circumstances and economic conditions are more likely to impact this capacity. This is the lowest "secure" rating category.

Vulnerable Ratings

BB+ BB BB−	Moderately Weak. Indicates that there is an elevated vulnerability to ceased or interrupted payments, particularly as the result of adverse economic or market changes over time. However, business or financial alternatives may be available to allow for policyholder and contract obligations to be met in a timely manner.
B+ B B−	Weak. If obligations are still being met on a timely basis, there is significant risk that ceased or interrupted payments could occur in the future, but a limited margin of safety remains. Capacity for continued timely payments is contingent upon a sustained, favorable business and economic environment, and favorable market conditions. Alternatively, assigned to obligations that have experienced ceased or interrupted payments, but with the potential for extremely high recoveries.
CCC+ CCC CCC−	Very weak. If obligations are still being met on a timely basis, there is a real possibility that ceased or interrupted payments could occur in the future. Capacity for continued timely payments is solely reliant upon a sustained, favorable business and economic environment, and favorable market conditions. Alternatively, assigned to obligations that have experienced ceased or interrupted payments, and with the potential for average to superior recoveries.
CC	Extremely Weak. See Fitch web site for description.
C	Distressed. See Fitch web site for description.

Moody's Investors Service

Secure Ratings

Aaa	Exceptional. Insurance companies rated Aaa offer exceptional financial security. While the credit profile of these companies is likely to change, such changes as can be visualized are most unlikely to impair their fundamentally strong position.
Aa1 Aa2 Aa3	Excellent. Insurance companies rated Aa offer excellent financial security. Together with the Aaa group, they constitute what are generally known as high-grade companies. They are rated lower than Aaa companies because long-term risks appear somewhat larger.
A1 A2 A3	Good. Insurance companies rated A offer good financial security. However, elements may be present that suggest a susceptibility to impairment sometime in the future.
Baa1 Baa2 Baa3	Adequate. Insurance companies rated Baa offer adequate financial security. However, certain protective elements may be lacking or may be characteristically unreliable over any great length of time.

Vulnerable Ratings

Ba1 Ba2 Ba3	Questionable. Insurance companies rated Ba offer questionable financial security. Often the ability of these companies to meet policyholder obligations may be very moderate and thereby not well safeguarded in the future.
B1 B2 B3	Poor. Insurance companies rated B offer poor financial security. Assurance of punctual payment of policyholder obligations over any long period of time is small.
Caa1 Caa2 Caa3	Very poor. Insurance companies rated Caa offer extremely poor financial security. Such companies are often in default on their policyholder obligations or have other marked shortcomings.
Ca	Extremely Poor. Insurance companies rated Ca offer extremely poor financial security. Such companies are often in default on their policyholder obligations or have other marked shortcomings.
C	Lowest. Insurance companies rated C are the lowest-rated class of insurance company and can be regarded as having extremely poor prospects of ever offering financial security.

Standard & Poor's

Secure Ratings

AAA	Extremely Strong. An insurer rated AAA has extremely strong financial security characteristics. AAA is the highest insurer financial strength rating assigned by Standard & Poor's.
AA+ AA AA–	Very Strong. An insurer rated AA has very strong financial security characteristics, differing only slightly from those rated higher.
A+ A A–	Strong. An insurer rated A has strong financial security characteristics, but is somewhat more likely to be affected by adverse business conditions than are insurers with higher ratings.
BBB+ BBB BBB–	Good. An insurer rated BBB has good financial security characteristics, but is more likely to be affected by adverse business conditions than are higher rated insurers.

Vulnerable Ratings

BB+ BB BB–	Marginal. An insurer rated BB has marginal financial security characteristics. Positive attributes exist, but adverse business conditions could lead to insufficient ability to meet financial commitments.
B+ B B–	Weak. An insurer rated B has weak financial security characteristics. Adverse business conditions will likely impair its ability to meet financial commitments.
CCC+ CCC CCC–	Very weak. An insurer rated CCC has very weak financial security characteristics, and is dependent on favorable business conditions to meet financial commitments.
CC	Extremely Weak. An insurer rated CC has extremely weak financial security characteristics and is likely not to meet some of its financial commitments.
R	Regulatory Action. An insurer rated R has experienced a regulatory action regarding solvency. The rating does not apply to insurers subject only to nonfinancial actions such as market conduct violations.

Public Information Ratings

pi	Based on an analysis of an insurers published financial information, as well as additional information in the public domain.

Attributes of Term and Cash Value Life Insurance Policies

Attribute	Term Life Insurance	Cash Value Life Insurance							
		Whole Life Insurance			Universal Life Insurance				
		Nonpar Fixed	Nonpar Current Assumption	Par	Generic	No-Lapse Guarantee	Equity Indexed	Variable
Overview									
✓ Primary Policy Appeal?	Guaranteed coverage for specific period and low premium outlay	Guaranteed lifetime coverage with all policy elements fixed	Guaranteed lifetime coverage, transparency, backed by conservative investments	Guaranteed lifetime coverage, backed by conservative investments	Flexibility, transparency, backed by conservative investments	Guaranteed lifetime coverage at low premium outlay	Flexibility, transparency, with limited equity-like returns and a guaranteed floor	Flexibility, transparency, with mutual fund returns
✓ Bundled or unbundled?	Bundled	Bundled	Unbundled	Bundled	Unbundled	Unbundled	Unbundled	Unbundled
✓ Contains non-guaranteed policy elements?	No, typically	No	Yes, via current interest credits and charges	Yes, via dividends	Yes, via current interest credits and charges	Yes, via current interest credits and charges for cash values; no for guaranteed coverage	Yes, via equity index changes and current charges	Yes, via market value changes and current charges
Death Benefits									
✓ Guaranteed	Yes	Yes	Yes	Yes	Yes	Yes	Yes	No
✓ Duration?	Fixed term	Life	Life	Life	Flexible, including life	Flexible, including life	Flexible, including life	Flexible, including life
✓ Adjustability of duration?	No	Not easily	Not easily	Not easily	Yes	Yes	Yes	Yes
✓ Death benefit adjustable?	No	No	Yes	Not easily	Yes	Yes	Yes	Yes
✓ Choice of level or increasing?	No, typically	No	Yes	Yes, via riders or dividends	Yes	Yes	Yes	Yes

Attribute	Term Life Insurance	Cash Value Life Insurance						
		Whole Life Insurance			Universal Life Insurance			
		Nonpar Fixed	Nonpar Current Assumption	Par	Generic	No-Lapse Guarantee	Equity Indexed	Variable
Cash Values								
✓ Builds cash values?	No	Yes	Yes	Yes	Yes	Yes	Yes	Yes
✓ Guaranteed?	n.a.	Yes	Yes, if not relying on non-guaranteed premium	Yes, except for illustrated cash values attributable to dividends	Yes, if funded to guarantees	Yes, if funded to guarantees	Yes, if funded to guarantees	No
✓ Location and nature of underlying investments?	General account; bonds and mortgages	General account; bonds and mortgages	General account; bonds and mortgages	General account; bonds and mortgages	General account; bonds and mortgages	General account; bonds and mortgages	General account; bonds and mortgages and equity index call options	Separate account; fixed income and equity mutual funds
✓ Increased likelihood of lapse with adverse development in current assumptions?	No	No	No, unless relying on non-guaranteed premium	No, unless relying on dividends to fund	Yes, but can be managed with additional premiums	No	Yes, but can be managed with additional premiums	Yes, but can be managed with additional premiums
✓ Impact of changes in market value on cash value?	n.a.	None	Indirect and muted	Indirect and muted	Indirect and muted	Indirect and muted	Indirect and muted	Direct
✓ Policyholder control of fund allocations?	n.a.	None	None	None	None	None	Allocations to index account	Total
✓ Policy loans available?	No	Yes	Yes	Yes	Yes	Yes, but will impact NLG	Yes	Yes
✓ Withdrawals available?	No	No	No	Yes, indirectly via surrender of PUAs	Yes	Yes, but will impact NLG	Yes	Yes

Attribute	Term Life Insurance	Cash Value Life Insurance							
		Whole Life Insurance			Universal Life Insurance				
		Nonpar Fixed	Nonpar Current Assumption	Par	Generic	No-Lapse Guarantee	Equity Indexed	Variable
✓ Fixed relationship to death benefit?	n.a.	Yes	Yes	Yes	No	No	No	No
✓ High early cash values?	n.a.	No	Yes	No, typically	Yes, often	No	Yes, often	Yes, often
✓ Protected from claims of insolvent insurer's creditors?	n.a.	No	No	No	No	No	No	Yes
Premiums								
✓ Flexible?	No	No	No	No	Yes	Yes, but need to manage NLG	Yes	Yes
✓ Ability to mimic any other policy type?	No	No	No	No	Yes	Yes	Yes	Yes
✓ Skipping premium payment possible?	No	Not easily	Not easily	Not easily	Yes	Yes, but will reduce NLG duration	Yes	Yes
✓ Effect if premium not paid?	Lapse	Paid via policy loan if APL elected, o/w lapse to NFB*	Paid via policy loan if APL elected, o/w lapse to NFB*	Paid via policy loan if APL elected, o/w lapse to NFB*	Nothing, smaller policy value	Nothing, but will reduce NLG duration and policy value	Nothing, smaller policy value	Nothing, smaller policy value
✓ How to resume premium payments and full coverage after premium nonpayment?	Pay past due premiums and re-qualify for insurance	If under NFB, pay past due premiums and re-qualify for insurance	If under NFB, pay past due premiums and re-qualify for insurance	If under NFB, pay past due premiums and re-qualify for insurance	Payments optional; full coverage remains if sufficient value	Payments optional; full coverage remains if sufficient value	Payments optional; full coverage remains if sufficient value	Payments optional; full coverage remains if sufficient value
Mortality Charges								
✓ Guaranteed maximum mortality charges?	Yes	Yes	Yes	Yes, if mortality gains cannot be negative	Yes	Yes	Yes	Yes

Attribute	Term Life Insurance	Cash Value Life Insurance						
		Whole Life Insurance			Universal Life Insurance			
		Nonpar Fixed	Nonpar Current Assumption	Par	Generic	No-Lapse Guarantee	Equity Indexed	Variable
✓ Can actual charges differ from those at policy issuance?	No, typically	No	Yes	Yes	Yes	Yes for cash value; no for NLG	Yes	Yes
✓ Who determines mortality charges?	Insurer	Insurer	Insurer	Insurer	Insurer	Insurer	Insurer	Insurer
✓ Actual mortality charges disclosed to policyholder?	No, but premium may be near actual	No	Yes	No	Yes	Yes	Yes	Yes
✓ Volatility of mortality charges?	None, typically	None	Low	Low	Low	Low for cash value; none for NLG	Low	Low
Crediting Rates								
✓ Guaranteed minimum crediting rate?	n.a.	Yes	Yes	Yes, if investment gains cannot be negative	Yes	Yes	Yes	Yes
✓ Can actual crediting rates differ from those illustrated at issue?	n.a.	No	Yes	Yes	Yes	Yes for cash value; no for NLG	Yes	Yes
✓ Who determines crediting rate?	Insurer	Insurer	Insurer	Insurer	Insurer	Insurer	Insurer and index	Actual investment return
✓ Actual rate disclosed to policyholder?	n.a.	n.a.	Yes	No, except for some insurers	Yes	Yes	Yes	Yes

Attribute	Term Life Insurance	Cash Value Life Insurance							
		Whole Life Insurance			Universal Life Insurance				
		Nonpar Fixed	Nonpar Current Assumption	Par	Generic	No-Lapse Guarantee	Equity Indexed	Variable
✓ Volatility of crediting rate?	None	None	Low to moderate depending on allocation method	Low to moderate depending on allocation method	Low to moderate depending on allocation method	Low to moderate for cash value; none for NLG	Low to high depending on allocation	Low to very high depending on fund choice
✓ Crediting rate includes dividend income?	n.a.	n.a.	Yes, but modest	Yes, but modest	Yes, but modest	Yes, but modest	No	Yes
Policy Loading Charges								
✓ Guaranteed maximum loading charges?	Yes	Yes	Yes	Yes, if expense gains cannot be negative	Yes	Yes	Yes	Yes
✓ Can actual charges differ from those illustrated at issue?	No	No	Yes	Yes	Yes	Yes for cash value; no for NLG	Yes	Yes
✓ Who determines loading charges?	Insurer	Insurer	Insurer	Insurer	Insurer	Insurer	Yes Insurer	Insurer
✓ Actual loading charges disclosed to policyholder?	No	No	Yes	No	Yes	Yes	Yes	Yes
✓ Volatility of loading charges?	None	None	Low	Low	Low	Low for cash value; none for NLG	Low	Low

*APL = **automatic premium loan**, an option offered by insurers whereby premium not paid within the grace period (typically 30-61 days following its due date) is paid automatically via a loan established against the policy cash value. NFB = **nonforfeiture benefits**, triggered when a premium is not paid within the grace period whereby the cash value is used to purchase either (1) **extended term insurance**, which is single premium term insurance in an amount equal to the policy face amount for whatever duration the cash value will fund or (2) **reduced paid up insurance**, which is single premium whole life insurance for whatever amount the cash value will fund. The automatic NFB ordinarily is extended term insurance. Reduced paid up can be elected.

Example Term Life Insurance Tabular Detail

(1) ABC Life Insurance Company
(2) A Level Premium Term Life Insurance Quote   (5) Form # EFG
(3) Company ABC Term   (6) Producer Name & Address
(4) Guaranteed Contract Premiums   (7) Run: 10/01/2010

Assumptions

(8) Sample   (11) Initial Death Benefit $1,000,000
(9) Male—Nonsmoker   (12) Billing Mode: Annual
(10) Age: 50   (13) State: CA

Policy Year (14)	EOY Age (15)	Death Benefit (16)	Contract Level Premium		
			10-Year (17)	15-Year (18)	20-Year (19)
1	51	1,000,000	1,130	1,680	2,210
2	52	1,000,000	1,130	1,680	2,210
3	53	1,000,000	1,130	1,680	2,210
4	54	1,000,000	1,130	1,680	2,210
5	55	1,000,000	1,130	1,680	2,210
6	56	1,000,000	1,130	1,680	2,210
7	57	1,000,000	1,130	1,680	2,210
8	58	1,000,000	1,130	1,680	2,210
9	59	1,000,000	1,130	1,680	2,210
10	60	1,000,000	1,130	1,680	2,210
Totals:			11,300	16,800	22,100
11	61	1,000,000	23,620	1,680	2,210
12	62	1,000,000	26,140	1,680	2,210
13	63	1,000,000	29,220	1,680	2,210
14	64	1,000,000	32,650	1,680	2,210
15	65	1,000,000	36,240	1,680	2,210
16	66	1,000,000	40,010	40,010	2,210
17	67	1,000,000	43,780	43,780	2,210
18	68	1,000,000	47,580	47,580	2,210
19	69	1,000,000	51,650	51,650	2,210
20	70	1,000,000	55,820	55,820	2,210
Totals:			398,010	264,040	44,200
21	71	1,000,000	60,900	60,900	60,900
22	72	1,000,000	66,550	66,550	66,550
23	73	1,000,000	74,000	74,000	74,000
24	74	1,000,000	81,800	81,800	81,800
25	75	1,000,000	89,950	89,950	89,950
26	76	1,000,000	98,810	98,810	98,810
27	77	1,000,000	108,420	108,420	108,420
28	78	1,000,000	119,550	119,550	119,550
29	79	1,000,000	132,510	132,510	132,510
30	80	1,000,000	147,430	147,430	147,430
Totals:			1,377,930	1,243,960	1,024,120

31	81	1,000,000	163,610	163,610	163,610
32	82	1,000,000	181,940	181,940	181,940
33	83	1,000,000	200,890	200,890	200,890
34	84	1,000,000	221,190	221,190	221,190
35	85	1,000,000	243,550	243,550	243,550
36	86	1,000,000	268,420	268,420	268,420
37	87	1,000,000	295,850	295,850	295,850
38	88	1,000,000	325,630	325,630	325,630
39	89	1,000,000	357,330	357,330	357,330
40	90	1,000,000	390,530	390,530	390,530
Totals:			4,026,870	3,892,900	3,673,060
41	91	1,000,000	424,900	424,900	424,900
42	92	1,000,000	456,760	456,760	456,760
43	93	1,000,000	489,710	489,710	489,710
44	94	1,000,000	524,240	524,240	524,240
45	95	1,000,000	560,460	560,460	560,460
Totals:			6,482,940	6,348,970	6,129,130

Initial Modal Premium

Please note if you elect either the semi-annual, quarterly, or monthly frequency, an additional charge will apply, resulting in annualized premiums that are higher than if you elected the annual frequency.

(20) Annual	$1,130.00	$1,680.00	$2,210.00
(21) Semiannual/Annualized	$580.50/$1,161.00	$863.70/$1,727.40	$1,136.70/$2,273.40
(22) Quarterly/Annualized	$300.00/$1,200.00	$445.70/$1,782.80	$586.20/$2,344.80
(23) Monthly/Annualized	$102.10/$1,225.20	$150.30/$1,803.60	$196.60/$2,359.20

Term premiums are based on a current scale guaranteed for the selected number of years (i.e., 10, 15, 20 years); subsequent current premiums are based on non-guaranteed elements that are subject to change by the insurer. Actual non-guaranteed premiums may be less than shown but can never exceed the maximum guaranteed premium.

Term Tabular Detail Notes

1) Name of insurer
2) Level premium term life insurance quote
3) Product name
4) The guaranteed contract premiums are for the selected number of years (10, 15, 20). Renewal premiums after the guaranteed period are non-guaranteed and subject to change (but can never exceed the contractual maximum guaranteed premium).
5) Policy form (as filed with the state insurance department)
6) The producer's (agent's) name and address.
7) The date the illustration was prepared. Since products and rates can change regularly, the advisor should verify that the illustration is current as of the review date.
8) Sample quote for specified insured.
9) Insured's gender and underwriting class as identified by smoker status. There may be multiple nonsmoker and smoker underwriting categories that are designated by the insured's health.

10) Insured's issue age. The issue age is either age nearest birthday (ANB) or age last birthday (ALB) as of the policy issue date. Most insurers use ANB while others use ALB. ALB may be advantageous for insureds who qualify for a one year younger issue age as compared to ANB.

11) Amount of the initial death benefit.

12) The premium frequency is annual, which assumes an annual premium being paid on the policy anniversary date (i.e., the beginning of the policy year). Other premium frequency (mode) options may include semi-annual, quarterly, and monthly. Refer to modal premium section at the bottom of the ledger illustration for details on premium mode options.

13) The policy issue state (California), which should correspond to the state where the policyowner resides or does business.

14) Policy year as defined by the policy anniversary date.

15) The insured's age as of the end of the policy year shown. Some illustrations provide the age as of the beginning of the policy year.

16) Death Benefit: The amount available to the beneficiary upon the insured's death for the specified policy year.

17) The premium paid during the specified policy year. The level premiums for policy years 1–10 are guaranteed. Subsequent premiums are not guaranteed, and are subject to change, but may not exceed the contractual maximum guaranteed premium.

18) The premium paid during the specified policy year. The level premiums for policy years 1–15 are guaranteed. Subsequent premiums are not guaranteed, and are subject to change, but may not exceed the contractual maximum guaranteed premium.

19) The premium paid during the specified policy year. The level premiums for policy years 1–20 are guaranteed. Subsequent premiums are not guaranteed, and are subject to change, but may not exceed the contractual maximum guaranteed premium.

20) The annual premium based on an annual premium mode (one premium is paid at the beginning of the policy year).

21) The semiannual premium based on a semiannual premium mode (two premiums are paid, one at the beginning of the policy year and the other at the beginning of the seventh month of the policy year). The annualized premium amount is the sum of the two semiannual premiums. The annualized premium amount is greater than the annual premium (20), reflecting an additional charge to support the delayed payments to the insurer.

22) The quarterly premium based on a quarterly premium mode (four premiums are paid at the beginning of each quarter within the policy year). The annualized premium amount is the sum of the four quarterly premiums. The annualized quarterly premium amount is greater than the annual premium (20) and the annualized semiannual premium (21), reflecting an additional charge to support the delayed payments to the insurer.

23) The monthly premium based on a monthly premium mode (twelve premiums are paid at the beginning of each month within the policy year). The annualized premium amount is the sum of the twelve monthly premiums. The annualized monthly premium amount is greater than the annual premium (20), the annualized semiannual premium (21), and the annualized quarterly premium (22), reflecting an additional charge to support the delayed payments to the insurer.

Example Par Whole Life Insurance Tabular Detail

(1) ABC Life Insurance Company

(2) Whole Life 123

(3) Insured Name   (6) Benefit $1,000,000

(4) Male, Age 70, Nonsmoker

                                   (7) Total First Year Premium $ 70,630.00

(5) Dividend Option: Paid Up Additions

Basic Illustration Tabular Detail   (8) Run: 10/01/2010

		Guaranteed (11)			Current (15)		
Policy Year (9)	Age at Start of Year (10)	Annual Premium (BOY) (12)	Cash Value (EOY) (13)	Death Benefit (EOY) (14)	Net Premium (BOY)* (16)	Cash Value (EOY)* (17)	Death Benefit (EOY)* (18)
1	70	70,630	0	1,000,000	70,630	0	1,000,000
2	71	70,630	21,350	1,000,000	70,630	38,900	1,017,550
3	72	70,630	61,760	1,000,000	70,630	99,702	1,047,164
4	73	70,630	101,890	1,000,000	70,630	163,120	1,079,893
5	74	70,630	141,850	1,000,000	70,630	229,338	1,115,653
6	75	70,630	181,700	1,000,000	70,630	298,606	1,154,489
7	76	70,630	221,320	1,000,000	70,630	373,700	1,199,212
8	77	70,630	260,490	1,000,000	70,630	454,808	1,251,162
9	78	70,630	298,910	1,000,000	70,630	542,060	1,310,587
10	79	70,630	336,320	1,000,000	70,630	635,592	1,377,724
11	80	70,630	372,690	1,000,000	70,630	732,924	1,449,960
12	81	70,630	407,760	1,000,000	70,630	834,050	1,526,635
13	82	70,630	441,770	1,000,000	70,630	939,243	1,607,752
14	83	70,630	474,790	1,000,000	70,630	1,048,707	1,693,348
15	84	70,630	506,750	1,000,000	70,630	1,162,531	1,783,570
16	85	70,630	537,460	1,000,000	70,630	1,280,748	1,878,709
17	86	70,630	566,800	1,000,000	70,630	1,402,410	1,978,035
18	87	70,630	594,720	1,000,000	70,630	1,527,399	2,081,429
19	88	70,630	621,300	1,000,000	70,630	1,655,702	2,188,894
20	89	70,630	646,750	1,000,000	70,630	1,787,355	2,300,385
21	90	70,630	668,920	1,000,000	70,630	1,920,008	2,415,809
22	91	70,630	690,690	1,000,000	70,630	2,055,722	2,534,114
23	92	70,630	712,500	1,000,000	70,630	2,194,639	2,654,870
24	93	70,630	734,870	1,000,000	70,630	2,336,867	2,777,752
25	94	70,630	758,670	1,000,000	70,630	2,482,766	2,902,372
26	95	70,630	785,240	1,000,000	70,630	2,632,941	3,028,183
27	96	70,630	817,740	1,000,000	70,630	2,790,272	3,154,458
28	97	70,630	860,290	1,000,000	70,630	2,957,366	3,279,728
29	98	70,630	920,210	1,000,000	70,630	3,138,972	3,401,499
30	99	0	924,370	1,000,000	0	3,258,089	3,516,074
31	100	0	927,970	1,000,000	0	3,378,879	3,632,760
32	101	0	931,500	1,000,000	0	3,501,549	3,750,968
33	102	0	934,950	1,000,000	0	3,625,974	3,870,500
34	103	0	938,340	1,000,000	0	3,752,133	3,991,266
35	104	0	941,640	1,000,000	0	3,879,851	4,113,216

36	105	0	944,860	1,000,000	0	4,009,106	4,236,300
37	106	0	948,000	1,000,000	0	4,139,792	4,360,431
38	107	0	951,050	1,000,000	0	4,271,803	4,485,561
39	108	0	954,020	1,000,000	0	4,405,070	4,611,598
40	109	0	956,890	1,000,000	0	4,539,436	4,738,491
41	110	0	959,680	1,000,000	0	4,674,923	4,866,200
42	111	0	962,370	1,000,000	0	4,811,369	4,994,677
43	112	0	964,980	1,000,000	0	4,948,806	5,123,889
44	113	0	967,490	1,000,000	0	5,087,119	5,253,843
45	114	0	969,920	1,000,000	0	5,226,405	5,384,567
46	115	0	972,250	1,000,000	0	5,366,505	5,516,036
47	116	0	974,500	1,000,000	0	5,507,533	5,648,284
48	117	0	976,650	1,000,000	0	5,649,389	5,781,355
49	118	0	978,820	1,000,000	0	5,792,786	5,915,301
50	119	0	980,630	1,000,000	0	5,935,650	6,050,284
51	120	0	1,000,000	1,000,000	0	6,186,421	6,186,421

(19) The values illustrated are based on the assumption that the non-guaranteed elements, including dividends will continue unchanged for all years shown. This is not likely to occur and the actual results may be more or less favorable than those shown.

*Values are non-guaranteed and may be affected by dividends.

Par Whole Life Tabular Detail Notes
1) Name of insurer
2) Product name
3) Insured name
4) Insured's gender, issue age and underwriting class. The issue age is either age nearest birthday (ANB) or age last birthday (ALB) as of the policy issue date. Most insurers use ANB while others use ALB. ALB may be advantageous for insureds who qualify for a one year younger issue age as compared to ANB. The underwriting class is identified by smoker status, and there may be multiple nonsmoker and smoker underwriting categories that are designated by the insured's health.
5) Defines the dividend option applied to the illustrated values. Paid up additions provide additional death benefit and cash values by the dividend being used to purchase chunks of single-premium whole life insurance. Dividends are not guaranteed and are subject to change.
6) The initial death benefit is $1 million but may grow if dividends purchase additional death benefit. The death benefit is the value paid to the beneficiary upon the insured's death. The death benefit would be reduced by any outstanding loan balance.
7) The amount of total premium paid in the first policy year.
8) The date the illustration was prepared. Since products and rates can change regularly, the advisor should verify that the illustration is current as of the review date.
9) Policy year as defined by the policy anniversary date.
10) The insured's age as of the beginning of the policy year shown. Some illustrations provide the age as of the end of the policy year.
11) Illustrated values in this section are guaranteed if the contract premium is paid as shown.
12) The guaranteed maximum annual premium for the base policy and any riders at the beginning of the year. With whole life, premiums are not flexible. The level premium must be paid to age 98 to guarantee the specified coverage for life.

13) The guaranteed cash value of the base policy and any riders at the end of the year. The cash value is the amount payable to the policyowner upon surrender. The cash value would be reduced by any outstanding loan balance.

14) The guaranteed death benefit of the base policy and any riders at the end of the year. The death benefit is the amount payable to the beneficiary upon the insured's death (but will be reduced by any outstanding policy debt). With no paid up additions, the death benefit remains level in all years.

15) Illustrated values in this section are based on the current dividend scale as of the illustration run date and are not guaranteed. The current dividend scale reflects current company experience (mortality, investment earnings, expenses, and persistency) and may change if emerging experience changes, including no dividends paid (see guaranteed columns).

16) The annual contract premium paid at the beginning of the policy year to support the illustrated policy values. For this illustration, dividends are not used to reduce premiums but are applied to purchase paid up additions.

17) The total cash value at the end of the year based on the non-guaranteed current dividend scale and is equal to the sum of the basic (guaranteed) and dividend cash values. The cash value is the amount payable to the policyowner upon surrender. The cash value would be reduced by any outstanding loan balance.

18) The death benefit at the end of the year based on the non-guaranteed current dividend scale and is equal to the sum of the basic (guaranteed) and paid up addition death benefits. The death benefit is the amount payable to the beneficiary upon the insured's death (but will be reduced by any outstanding policy debt).

19) Non-guarantee disclosure statement.

Example No-Lapse Guarantee Universal Life Insurance Tabular Detail

(1) ABC Life Insurance Company

(2) UL NLG—Life Insurance Illustration
(3) Flexible Premium Adjustable Life Insurance Policy
(4) Form # EFG—For Presentation in CA

(5) Insured Name   (8) Death Benefit Option = A   (11) Producer Name & Address
(6) Male, Age 70   (9) Total Face Amount = $1,000,000
(7) Nonsmoker   (10) Premium Frequency = Annual   (12) Run: 10/01/2010

Basic Illustration Tabular Detail

			Guaranteed Values (EOY) @ 3.00% (16)			Non-Guaranteed Values (EOY) @ 5.50% (17)		
	BOY	Premium	Account	Surrender	Death	Account	Surrender	Death
Yr	Age	Outlay	Value	Value	Benefit	Value	Value	Benefit
(13)	(14)	(15)	(18)	(19)	(20)	(18)	(19)	(20)
1	70	54,403	33,096	0	1,000,000	34,814	0	1,000,000
2	71	54,403	63,692	27,444	1,000,000	69,248	33,000	1,000,000
3	72	54,403	93,710	61,993	1,000,000	104,183	72,466	1,000,000
4	73	54,403	122,989	95,803	1,000,000	139,532	112,346	1,000,000
5	74	54,403	151,669	129,014	1,000,000	175,486	152,831	1,000,000
6	75	54,403	156,734	138,610	1,000,000	214,615	196,491	1,000,000
7	76	54,403	157,502	143,909	1,000,000	254,198	240,605	1,000,000
8	77	54,403	154,051	144,989	1,000,000	295,495	286,433	1,000,000
9	78	54,403	145,240	140,709	1,000,000	338,765	334,234	1,000,000
10	79	54,403	129,642	129,642	1,000,000	384,100	384,100	1,000,000
11	80	0	56,312	56,312	1,000,000	392,813	392,813	1,000,000
12	81	0	0	0	1,000,000	400,510	400,510	1,000,000
13	82	0	0	0	1,000,000	406,908	406,908	1,000,000
14	83	0	0	0	1,000,000	411,661	411,661	1,000,000
15	84	0	0	0	1,000,000	414,341	414,341	1,000,000
16	85	0	0	0	1,000,000	415,035	415,035	1,000,000
17	86	0	0	0	1,000,000	413,616	413,616	1,000,000
18	87	0	0	0	1,000,000	409,643	409,643	1,000,000
19	88	0	0	0	1,000,000	402,566	402,566	1,000,000
20	89	0	0	0	1,000,000	391,706	391,706	1,000,000
21	90	0	0	0	1,000,000	376,038	376,038	1,000,000
22	91	0	0	0	1,000,000	353,405	353,405	1,000,000
23	92	0	0	0	1,000,000	326,147	326,147	1,000,000
24	93	0	0	0	1,000,000	294,208	294,208	1,000,000
25	94	0	0	0	1,000,000	257,959	257,959	1,000,000
26	95	0	0	0	1,000,000	216,818	216,818	1,000,000
27	96	0	0	0	1,000,000	170,123	170,123	1,000,000
28	97	0	0	0	1,000,000	117,126	117,126	1,000,000
29	98	0	0	0	1,000,000	56,976	56,976	1,000,000
30	99	0	0	0	1,000,000	0	0	1,000,000
31	100	0	0	0	1,000,000	0	0	1,000,000
32	101	0	0	0	1,000,000	0	0	1,000,000

33	102	0	0	0	1,000,000	0	0	1,000,000
34	103	0	0	0	1,000,000	0	0	1,000,000
35	104	0	0	0	1,000,000	0	0	1,000,000
36	105	0	0	0	1,000,000	0	0	1,000,000
37	106	0	0	0	1,000,000	0	0	1,000,000
38	107	0	0	0	1,000,000	0	0	1,000,000
39	108	0	0	0	1,000,000	0	0	1,000,000
40	109	0	0	0	1,000,000	0	0	1,000,000
41	110	0	0	0	1,000,000	0	0	1,000,000
42	111	0	0	0	1,000,000	0	0	1,000,000
43	112	0	0	0	1,000,000	0	0	1,000,000
44	113	0	0	0	1,000,000	0	0	1,000,000
45	114	0	0	0	1,000,000	0	0	1,000,000
46	115	0	0	0	1,000,000	0	0	1,000,000
47	116	0	0	0	1,000,000	0	0	1,000,000
48	117	0	0	0	1,000,000	0	0	1,000,000
49	118	0	0	0	1,000,000	0	0	1,000,000
50	119	0	0	0	1,000,000	0	0	1,000,000
51	120	0	0	0	1,000,000	0	0	1,000,000

(21) Insurance coverage would remain in force at least through year 51 (age 120) based on guaranteed and illustrated assumptions.

(22) The Flexible Duration No-Lapse Guarantee will be in effect through the insured's lifetime provided that premiums are paid as illustrated and other assumptions are realized. See the Illustrated Riders section for more information.

(23) A zero in the Premium Outlay column does not mean the policy is paid up. Charges will continue to be deducted from the Account Value as long as the policy remains in force. The actual premium amounts and number of years of premium payments that are needed to maintain the illustrated non-guaranteed policy benefits will depend on the policy's non-guaranteed elements and on your actual use of the policy's options.

No-Lapse Guarantee Universal Life Tabular Detail Notes

1) Name of insurer
2) Product name
3) Product description
4) Policy form (as filed with the state insurance department) and state of issue (California). The issue state should correspond to the state where the policyowner resides or does business.
5) Insured name
6) Insured gender and issue age. The issue age is either age nearest birthday (ANB) or age last birthday (ALB) as of the policy issue date. Most insurers use ANB while others use ALB. ALB may be advantageous for insureds who qualify for a one year younger issue age as compared to ANB.
7) Insured underwriting class as identified by smoker status. There may be multiple nonsmoker and smoker underwriting categories that are designated by the insured's health.
8) Death benefit option A signifies a level death benefit. Other options may include an option B, which is equal to the total face amount plus the account value and option C, which is equal to the total face amount plus the cumulative premiums paid less any withdrawals.
9) The total initial face amount includes both basic and term coverage.

10) The premium frequency is annual, which assumes an annual premium being paid on the policy anniversary date (i.e., beginning of the policy year). Other premium frequency (mode) options may include semi-annual, quarterly, and monthly.

11) The producer's (agent's) name and address.

12) The date the illustration was prepared. Since products and rates can change regularly, the advisor should verify that the illustration is current as of the review date.

13) Policy year as defined by the policy anniversary date.

14) The insured's age as of the beginning of the policy year shown. Some illustrations provide the age as of the end of the policy year.

15) The planned premium paid during the specified policy year. With no-lapse guarantee universal life, the amount and frequency of premium payments are flexible, within limits. Deviations from the illustrated premium schedule will impact the guaranteed coverage. For this example, ten annual premiums are targeted to provide lifetime guaranteed coverage.

16) Illustrated policy values in this section are based on guaranteed policy elements for interest credited and charges deducted. Actual charges assessed may not exceed the guaranteed charges and actual interest credited may not be less than the guaranteed minimum credited interest rate. Values shown are as of the end of the policy year (EOY). The guaranteed minimum credited interest rate is 3.00 percent. For this example, even though the account value goes to zero in policy year 12, coverage is maintained for life due to the no-lapse guarantee being in effect.

17) Illustrated policy values in this section are based on non-guaranteed illustrated assumptions for interest credited and charges deducted. Non-guaranteed illustrated assumptions may not be more favorable than the current assumptions or less favorable than the guaranteed elements. Current assumptions are the actual charges and credits being applied to the policy as of the illustration preparation date and are subject to change (but may not be less favorable than the guaranteed elements). Values shown are as of the end of the policy year (EOY). The illustrated credited interest rate is 5.50 percent. While illustrated assumptions used in this example are the current assumptions, it is not specified. For this example, even though the account value goes to zero in policy year 30, coverage is maintained for life due to the no-lapse guarantee being in effect. Changes in current assumptions will not impact the no-lapse guarantee coverage.

18) Account Value: Equal to the sum of premiums paid less all charges and withdrawals plus credited or accrued interest since the policy effective date. The account value provides the base for interest credits. This is not the amount available to the policyowner upon surrender (see surrender value below). Account value may also be referred to as accumulated value.

19) Surrender Value: Equal to the account value minus any applicable surrender charge. The amount paid to the policyowner upon surrender is the surrender value less any outstanding policy debt. Most no-lapse guarantee products have surrender charges and very low surrender values, typically with surrender values going to zero before age 120 when funded at the guaranteed level. For this example, surrender charges are assessed for nine years.

20) Death Benefit: The amount payable to the beneficiary upon the insured's death (but will be reduced by any outstanding policy debt). For this example, the death benefit is level due to a designated death benefit option A (see (8)). The death benefit will remain level until the account value grows to an amount that forces the death benefit to increase according to the definition of life insurance test. The death benefit may never be less than the account value.

21) Footnote specifying coverage remaining in force for life based on both guaranteed elements and current assumptions.

22) Important note that coverage is guaranteed only if premiums are paid on time as illustrated. Distributions or benefit changes will also impact the no-lapse guarantee. Changes in current assumptions will not impact the guaranteed coverage. In addition, the riders section should be reviewed to gain an understanding of the no-lapse guarantee rider.

23) The illustrated premium outlay does not guarantee coverage for life. Changes in policy options and benefits, such as withdrawals/loans, will impact the guaranteed coverage. Changes in non-guaranteed assumptions will not impact the guaranteed coverage.

Example Equity Index Universal Life Insurance Tabular Detail

(1) ABC Life Insurance Company

(2) Equity Index UL—Life Insurance Illustration

(3) Indexed Universal Life Policy

(4) Form # EFG—For Presentation in CA

(5) Insured Name

(6) Male, Age 70

(7) Nonsmoker

(8) Death Benefit Option = A

(9) Total Face Amount = $1,000,000

(10) Premium Frequency = Annual

(11) Producer Name & Address

(12) Run: 10/01/2010

Basic Illustration Tabular Detail

			Guaranteed Values (EOY) @ 0.00% (16)			Non-Guaranteed Values (EOY) @ 6.00% (17)		
Yr (13)	BOY Age (14)	Premium Outlay (15)	Account Value (18)	Surrender Value (19)	Death Benefit (20)	Account Value (18)	Surrender Value (19)	Death Benefit (20)
1	70	46,848	5,180	0	1,000,000	36,027	17,902	1,000,000
2	71	46,848	8,039	0	1,000,000	72,200	54,075	1,000,000
3	72	46,848	8,609	0	1,000,000	109,450	91,325	1,000,000
4	73	46,848	6,658	0	1,000,000	147,764	129,639	1,000,000
5	74	46,848	2,056	0	1,000,000	187,378	169,253	1,000,000
6	75	46,848	0	0	1,000,000	229,252	214,752	1,000,000
7	76	46,848	0	0	1,000,000	273,029	262,154	1,000,000
8	77	46,848	0	0	1,000,000	319,083	311,833	1,000,000
9	78	46,848	0	0	1,000,000	367,708	364,083	1,000,000
10	79	46,848	0	0	1,000,000	419,067	419,067	1,000,000
11	80	0	0	0	1,000,000	433,686	433,686	1,000,000
12	81	0	0	0	1,000,000	448,056	448,056	1,000,000
13	82	0	0	0	1,000,000	462,023	462,023	1,000,000
14	83	0	0	0	1,000,000	475,404	475,404	1,000,000
15	84	0	0	0	1,000,000	487,981	487,981	1,000,000
16	85	0	0	0	1,000,000	500,026	500,026	1,000,000
17	86	0	0	0	1,000,000	511,626	511,626	1,000,000
18	87	0	0	0	1,000,000	522,642	522,642	1,000,000
19	88	0	0	0	1,000,000	532,908	532,908	1,000,000
20	89	0	0	0	1,000,000	542,230	542,230	1,000,000
21	90	0	0	0	0	549,561	549,561	1,000,000
22	91	0	0	0	0	554,086	554,086	1,000,000
23	92	0	0	0	0	557,989	557,989	1,000,000
24	93	0	0	0	0	561,610	561,610	1,000,000
25	94	0	0	0	0	565,530	565,530	1,000,000
26	95	0	0	0	0	569,682	569,682	1,000,000
27	96	0	0	0	0	573,970	573,970	1,000,000
28	97	0	0	0	0	578,259	578,259	1,000,000
29	98	0	0	0	0	582,385	582,385	1,000,000
30	99	0	0	0	0	586,114	586,114	1,000,000
31	100	0	0	0	0	590,345	590,345	1,000,000
32	101	0	0	0	0	595,146	595,146	1,000,000

33	102	0	0	0	0	600,595	600,595	1,000,000
34	103	0	0	0	0	606,778	606,778	1,000,000
35	104	0	0	0	0	613,795	613,795	1,000,000
36	105	0	0	0	0	621,758	621,758	1,000,000
37	106	0	0	0	0	630,794	630,794	1,000,000
38	107	0	0	0	0	641,048	641,048	1,000,000
39	108	0	0	0	0	652,685	652,685	1,000,000
40	109	0	0	0	0	665,891	665,891	1,000,000
41	110	0	0	0	0	680,877	680,877	1,000,000
42	111	0	0	0	0	697,883	697,883	1,000,000
43	112	0	0	0	0	717,181	717,181	1,000,000
44	113	0	0	0	0	739,082	739,082	1,000,000
45	114	0	0	0	0	763,935	763,935	1,000,000
46	115	0	0	0	0	792,138	792,138	1,000,000
47	116	0	0	0	0	824,143	824,143	1,000,000
48	117	0	0	0	0	860,463	860,463	1,000,000
49	118	0	0	0	0	901,680	901,680	1,000,000
50	119	0	0	0	0	948,452	948,452	1,000,000
51	120	0	0	0	0	1,001,531	1,001,531	1,011,546

(21) Insurance coverage will cease in year 21 based on guaranteed elements. Insurance coverage would remain in force at least through year 51 (age 120) based on illustrated assumptions.

(22) The Medium Duration No-Lapse Guarantee will be in effect through year 20 provided that premiums are paid as illustrated and other assumptions are realized. See the Illustrated Riders section for more information.

(23) A zero in the Premium Outlay column does not mean the policy is paid up. Charges will continue to be deducted from the Account Value as long as the policy remains in force. The actual premium amounts and number of years of premium payments that are needed to maintain the illustrated non-guaranteed policy benefits will depend on the policy's non-guaranteed elements and on your actual use of the policy's options.

Equity Index Universal Life Tabular Detail Notes
1) Name of insurer
2) Product name
3) Product description
4) Policy form (as filed with the state insurance department) and state of issue (California). The issue state should correspond to the state where the policyowner resides or does business.
5) Insured name
6) Insured gender and issue age. The issue age is either age nearest birthday (ANB) or age last birthday (ALB) as of the policy issue date. Most insurers use ANB while others use ALB. ALB may be advantageous for insureds who qualify for a one year younger issue age as compared to ANB.
7) Insured underwriting class as identified by smoker status. There may be multiple nonsmoker and smoker underwriting categories that are designated by the insured's health.
8) Death benefit option A signifies a level death benefit. Other options may include an option B, which is equal to the total face amount plus the account value and option C, which is equal to the total face amount plus the cumulative premiums paid less any withdrawals.

9) The total initial face amount includes both basic and term coverage.

10) The premium frequency is annual, which assumes an annual premium being paid on the policy anniversary date (i.e., beginning of the policy year). Other premium frequency (mode) options may include semi-annual, quarterly, and monthly.

11) The producer's (agent's) name and address.

12) The date the illustration was prepared. Since products and rates can change regularly, the advisor should verify that the illustration is current as of the review date.

13) Policy year as defined by the policy anniversary date.

14) The insured's age as of the beginning of the policy year shown. Some illustrations provide the age as of the end of the policy year.

15) The planned premium paid during the specified policy year. With universal life, the amount and frequency of premium payments are flexible, within limits. If resulting premiums are insufficient, then coverage terminates when the account value goes to zero. For this example, ten annual premiums are targeted to provide an account value equal to the death benefit at end of age 120 based on the non-guaranteed assumptions.

16) Illustrated policy values in this section are based on guaranteed policy elements for interest credited and charges deducted. Actual charges assessed may not exceed the guaranteed charges and actual interest credited may not be less than the guaranteed minimum credited interest rate. Values shown are as of the end of the policy year (EOY). The guaranteed minimum credited interest rate is 0.00 percent. For this example, even though the account value goes to zero in policy year 6, coverage is maintained for 20 years due to the medium duration no-lapse guarantee being in effect. See (22).

17) Illustrated policy values in this section are based on non-guaranteed policy elements for interest credited and charges deducted. Non-guaranteed illustrated assumptions may not be more favorable than the current assumptions or less favorable than the guaranteed elements. Current assumptions are the actual charges being applied to the policy as of the illustration preparation date and are subject to change (but may not be less favorable than the guaranteed elements). For this example, the non-guaranteed values are based on current policy charges (although "current" is not stated on the page), which are the actual charges as of the illustration preparation date. The hypothetical credited interest rate for index UL illustrations can range from the guaranteed rate to a specified maximum rate. There is no "current" crediting rate for index UL. The non-guaranteed illustrated crediting rate for index UL is simply a hypothetical input option. The mechanics of the index crediting rate should be reviewed to gain an understanding of potential returns. The index strategy for this example has a 0 percent guaranteed minimum crediting rate. Values shown are as of the end of the policy year (EOY). The non-guaranteed hypothetical credited interest rate assumption is 6.00 percent. For this example, the account value equals the death benefit at end of age 120 based on the non-guaranteed assumptions and illustrated premium schedule.

18) Account Value: Equal to the sum of premiums paid less all charges and withdrawals plus credited or accrued interest since the policy effective date. The account value provides the base for interest credits. This is not the amount available to the policyowner upon surrender (see surrender value below). Account value may also be referred to as accumulated value.

19) Surrender Value: Equal to the account value minus any applicable surrender charge. The amount paid to the policyowner upon surrender is the surrender value less any outstanding policy debt. Some products have no surrender charges while other products may have surrender charges for twenty years or more. This product has surrender charges for nine years.

20) Death Benefit: The amount payable to the beneficiary upon the insured's death (but will be reduced by any outstanding policy debt). For this example, the death benefit is level due to a designated death benefit option A (see (8)). The death benefit will remain level unless the account value grows to an amount that forces the death benefit to increase according to the definition of life insurance test. The death benefit may never be less than the account value.

21) Footnote specifying the year coverage ceases based on guaranteed elements and coverage remaining in force for life based on current assumptions.

22) Footnote explaining that the medium duration no-lapse guarantee is in effect for 20 years. The no-lapse guarantee is impacted by changes in premiums, withdrawals/loans, and policy options, but not changes in current assumptions. The rider section should be reviewed to gain a better understanding of the medium duration no-lapse guarantee.

23) The illustrated premium outlay does not guarantee coverage for life. Resulting coverage depends upon future non-guaranteed assumptions (which may change) and future actual premiums paid. Changes in policy options, such as withdrawals/loans, will also impact coverage.

Glossary

Absolute assignment—transfer by a policyowner of all rights in a life insurance policy to another person or entity; a change of ownership.

Accelerated death benefit—promise under a life insurance policy to pay some or all of its face amount and/or other benefit prior to the insured's death if the insured suffers specified adverse health conditions. Also called **living benefit rider** and **accelerated benefit rider** (or **provision**).

Accidental death benefit—rider that provides that double (or other multiple) of the face amount is payable if the insured dies as a result of an accident. Sometimes called **double indemnity**.

Account value—internal savings element within cash value life insurance, especially under universal life policies. Often called the **cash value**, **policy value**, or **accumulated value**.

Account value provision—provision within nonparticipating life insurance contracts that contain non-guaranteed policy elements, which explains the nature of the non-guaranteed elements and how they are determined and applied within the policy. Also called **policy value provision**.

Accredited investor—a wealthy investor who meets SEC requirements as to minimum net worth (in excess of $1.0 million) or annual income (in excess of $200,000).

Accumulation universal life—specialized universal life products that emphasize cash value accumulation but require higher premiums per $1,000 of face amount. Contrast with **death protection universal life**.

Add to cash value—option allowing dividends paid under participating policies to accumulate as additional cash value; adds no net amount at risk, generating a unit of additional death benefit for each unit of additional cash value.

Adjusted taxable gifts—gifts made after 1976 for which a gift tax return was required to be filed.

Administrative charge—assessment of a flat annual (or monthly) amount or percentage of the account value under unbundled policies to cover policy administration expenses.

Admitted assets—assets permitted to be included in determining an insurer's solvency under statutory accounting principles.

Agent—state-licensed salesperson under contract to sell an insurer's products, typically for a commission and on a face-to-face basis. Also called a **producer**.

Allowable deductions—for purposes of calculating federal estate taxes owed, amounts that may be deducted from the gross estate, including funeral and administration expenses, debts of the decedent, as well as bequests to charities and the surviving spouse. See **taxable estate**.

Annual gift tax exclusion—that value of a gift of a present interest on which no gift tax is owed; $13,000 per donee for 2010.

Annual renewable term—term life insurance whose premiums increase yearly. Also called **yearly renewable term**.

Annuitant—person to whom annuity payments are made or, more technically, the person whose life determines the duration of life annuity payments.

Annuity—stream of periodic payments.

Anxiety—collection of fears resulting in unpleasant uneasiness, stress, generalized pessimism, and risk averse attitudes.

Applicant—person who applies for a life insurance policy and usually will be the owner of the policy.

As-sold policy illustration—policy illustration provided at the time of policy sale.

Asset share—allocation of the accumulated assets arising from a group of policies proportionately among those policies.

Assignment provision—states that the policyowner may assign his or her life insurance policy to another person but that the insurance company need not recognize the assignment unless it is filed with the company.

Authorized control level risk-based capital—formula intended to show an insurer's required capital and surplus based on the risks inherent in its assets, insurance, interest exposure, and business.

Automatic premium loan—usually an optional life insurance policy provision under which a premium not paid within the grace period (typically 31 to 61 days following its due date) will be paid automatically via a loan established against the policy cash value.

Aviation exclusion—rarely used optional clause that excludes coverage under a life insurance contract if the insured dies in an aviation accident.

Back-end load—penalty assessed against a policy's cash value for early termination. Also called a **surrender charge** and **back-end loading**.

Backdating—practice allowed by some insurers of setting a policy issue date before the application or policy date, but no more than six months earlier, to secure a one-year earlier issue age and lower mortality charges.

Basic mortality table—mortality table that reflects the actual experience of the insured population from which the data were drawn.

Beneficiary—within a life insurance policy, the person or entity designated by the applicant or policyowner to receive the policy face amount on the insured's death. Within a trust, person or persons for whose benefit the property is held.

Beneficiary clause—provision within a life insurance contract that typically states that the policyowner may have policy death proceeds paid to whomever and in whatever form desired, subject to contract terms.

Bond—publicly traded debt security under which the borrower (seller of the bond) agrees to pay a fixed amount of interest periodically and repay a fixed principal at bond maturity. Also called **fixed income security**.

Branch manager—within the life insurance business, the person responsible for the management of a field office and for increasing sales and recruiting and developing career agents.

Break-even—with respect to life insurance policy pricing, the year in which accumulated profits under a life insurance policy cover prior years' losses, with the lower the break-even year the better for the insurer.

Broker—within the life insurance business, a commissioned salesperson who works independently of the insurer with whom insurance is placed and who has no minimum production requirements with that insurer.

Bundled policy—life insurance policy under which under the portions of premiums allocated to pay cost of insurance changes; to build cash values; to cover an insurer's operational expenses, taxes, and contingencies; and to support a scale of dividends are not disclosed to policyowners. Contrast with **unbundled policy**.

Buy/sell agreement—arrangement under which owners of a business agree to sell their interests on their deaths and an entity or the surviving owners or others agree to purchase that interest. Also called **business continuation agreements**.

Capital liquidation approach—in life insurance needs analysis, assumption that both principal (capital) and interest are liquidated over a relevant time period to provide a desired income.

Capital retention approach—in life insurance needs analysis, assumption that desired income is provided from investment earnings on the principal (capital) only.

Capital and surplus—excess of assets over liabilities. Also called **net worth** and sometimes **surplus** or **capital**.

Captive agents—life insurance agents who represent a single insurance company or group of affiliated companies. Also called **exclusive agents**.

Career agency system—life insurance sales system under which life insurance companies recruit, train, finance, house, and supervise their agents. Also called **agency-building distribution channel** and **captive distribution channel**. Contrast with **independent distribution channel**.

Career agents—commissioned life insurance agents who usually represent a single insurance company or group of affiliated companies.

Cash refund annuity—immediate life annuity and also nonforfeiture option under which annuity payments begin immediately and continue for the greater of the lifetime of the annuitant or when payments equal to the original annuity principal have been made. If death occurs before payments equal to the principal have been made, the life insurance company must pay to the beneficiary as a single sum the difference between the two amounts. Contrast with **installment refund annuity**.

Cash surrender value—amount available to be paid to the policyowner on surrender of the policy after subtracting any surrender charge but before repaying any policy loans. Also defined to include repayment of policy loans. Also called simply **surrender value** and, with universal life policies, sometimes called **cash value**.

Cash value—internal savings element within cash value life insurance. Also called the **account value**, **policy value**, or **accumulated value**, especially with universal life policies.

Cash value accumulation test—under the IRC definition of life insurance, requires that a policy's cash value may not at any time exceed the net single premium that would be required to fund future insurance benefits (defined to be mainly death and maturity benefits) provided under the contract, net of loadings, at the insured's attained age and based on certain required assumptions.

Cash value corridor test—test under the IRC for determining whether a life insurance contract complies with the IRC definition of life insurance, being met if the policy's benefits at all times are at least equal to certain percentage multiples of its cash value, these percentages ranging from 250 percent for insureds of attained ages up to 40, grading to 100 percent for attained age 95.

Cash value life insurance—type of life insurance that combines term insurance and internal savings within the same contract. Also called **permanent life insurance**.

Cash value target—amount of cash or account value sought, commonly $1.00 or an amount equal to the death benefit, within a policy illustration at a specified age, such as age 121. Also called **target cash value.**

Catastrophic illness coverage—provides benefit payments if the insured has been diagnosed as having one of several listed catastrophic illnesses. Also called **dread disease coverage**.

Catch-up provision—if the required minimum premium was not paid under a no-lapse guarantee life insurance policy, permits payment of additional premiums to restore the no-lapse guarantee.

Charitable remainder trust—living, irrevocable, tax-exempt trust in which the donor contributes property to the trust, reserving to him- or herself (or someone else) an income stream from the trust, with the remainder interest ultimately passing to a charity.

Closely held business—one whose ownership interests have no ready market.

Closely held corporation—one that is typically owned and managed by a small number of investors, often family members, with shares of stock not listed on any organized exchange. Also called a **close corporation** and **closed corporation**.

Collateral assignment—temporary transfer of partial life insurance policy ownership rights to another, such as a bank to cover a loan.

Collateral assignment approach—split dollar life insurance under which the insured employee applies for and owns the policy and is primarily responsible for premium payments and designates his or her own personal beneficiary.

Combination plans—life insurance or annuity contracts combined with long term care insurance riders.

Comdex—composite index of rating agency ratings, expressed as the average percentile of a life insurance company's ratings; i.e., the proportion of rated insurers that are rated lower.

Commingling—wrongful combining of monies belonging to policyowners with those belonging to an agent.

Conservation order—court order directing the state insurance regulator to act as receiver for the conservation of assets of an insurance company within his or her jurisdiction.

Contingency risks—classes of risks as labeled by the actuarial profession to which insurers are exposed. They are:

- asset default risk—C-1 risks
- insurance (mortality) risk—C-2 risks
- interest rate risk (asset/liability interest disintermediation)—C-3 risks
- general business risk—C-4 risks

Contingent beneficiary—person or persons named to receive death proceeds payable under a life insurance policy if no primary beneficiary is alive at the time of the insured's death. Also called **secondary beneficiary**.

Continuation rider—provision under a combination plan that, upon exhaustion of long term care payments originating from a policy's death benefit, payment will be continued for a period of years selected at policy issuance. Also called **extension of benefits rider**.

Contribution principle—with participating life insurance, precept that divisible surplus should be distributed to policies in the same proportions as the policies are considered to have contributed to the surplus.

Conversion feature—grants the policyowner the right to exchange a term policy for a cash value policy without having to prove insurability, for an amount up to that of the face amount of the term policy.

Corporation—business legally separate and distinct from its owners and possessing these characteristics:

- Owners' liability for corporate obligations is limited to their investment in the corporation;
- Easy transfer of owners' interests in the corporation by sale of their shares of stock; and
- Owners' deaths have no effect legally on the corporation's continued existence.

Corrective order—formal insurance regulatory action in the form of written directive requiring an insurer to (1) obtain state approval before undertaking certain transactions, (2) limit or cease its new business writings, (3) infuse capital, or (4) cease certain business practices.

Cost basis—for a qualified life insurance contract, normally the sum of the premiums paid less any untaxed distributions. Also called **investment in the contract**.

Cost of insurance (COI) rates—within unbundled life insurance policies, explicit mortality charges assessed against cash values per $1,000 of net amount at risk.

Cost recovery rule—general rule for the income tax treatment of lump sum cash surrender value payments and maturity payments under life insurance policies by which the amount included in the policyowner's taxable income is the excess of the gross proceeds received over the policy's cost basis.

Credit default swaps—financial instruments bought by investors to insure against defaults on bonds.

Credit shelter trust—trust created to receive property equal in value to the federal estate exemption amount on the death of the first spouse. Also called **bypass trust**, **B trust**, **non-marital trust**, and **residuary trust**.

Cross-over point—first policy year at which a policy's surrender value exceeds the sum of the premiums paid.

Cross purchase buy/sell agreement—one in which each owner binds his or her estate to sell his or her business interest to the surviving owners, and each surviving owner binds himself or herself to buy the interest of the deceased owner.

Crummey trust (or **provision**)—irrevocable trust, the gifts to which qualify as present interest gifts and so for the annual gift tax exclusion, provided trust beneficiaries have a reasonable opportunity to demand distribution of amounts contributed to the trust.

Current assumption whole life insurance—unbundled whole life policy that operates as a universal life policy except that premiums set by the insurer are required to be paid to maintain the policy in effect. Also called **interest sensitive whole life** and **fixed-premium universal life**.

Current assumptions—those non-guaranteed pricing components being applied within a life insurance policy as of an illustration date that can be changed unilaterally by the insurer, subject to any guaranteed policy elements.

Death benefit—amount of money stated in a life insurance contract to be paid on the death of the insured. Also called **face amount** and **insurance amount**.

Death benefit internal rate of return—a measure of illustrated life insurance performance derived by solving for the interest rate that causes accumulated scheduled premiums (net of dividends, if appropriate) at selected policy durations to equal that duration's death benefit. See **surrender value internal rate of return**.

Death benefit only plan—nonqualified deferred compensation plan under which the employer promises to pay an income benefit to the employee's survivor on the employee's death.

Death benefit provision—clause within universal life type contracts that sets out the various death benefit options available to the policyowner and explains the method of determining the policy death benefit.

Death benefit solve—in the context of a life insurance illustration, determining the death benefit that can be purchased for a specified premium.

Death benefit universal life—specialized universal life products that emphasize death benefits and allow competitive premiums per $1,000 of face amount but typically also offer low cash value accumulation and/or have heavy surrender charges. Also called **protection universal life**. Contrast with **accumulation universal life**.

Definition of life insurance—contract of life insurance that meets either a cash value accumulation test or a guideline premium and cash value corridor test specified in Internal Revenue Code section 7702 and thus does not lose its favorable income tax treatment.

Delay clause—provision required within life insurance contracts that grants the insurance company the right to defer cash surrender value payments, withdrawals, and the making of a policy loan (except for purposes of paying premiums) for up to six months after its request.

Direct expenses—those directly attributable to a specific life insurance product (e.g., agent's commission).

Direct recognition—linkage of a policy's cash value interest crediting rate or dividend interest rate to the policy loan rate.

Direct response distribution channel—life insurance sales system in which the customer deals directly with the insurer, without an intervening intermediary or firm.

Discretionary income—individual or family income remaining after paying taxes and for family necessities and financial commitments.

Distribution—any amount taken from a cash value policy during life that is based on its cash value, including withdrawals and loans.

Distribution channels—means by which life insurance companies sell their products to customers. Also called **distribution systems** and **marketing channels**.

Dividend—share of surplus distributed under participating policies to their owners.

Dividends actually paid—schedule of amounts actually paid as dividends. Also called a **dividend history**.

Dividend illustration—listing of the dividends that would be paid under a policy in the future if the mortality, expense, and interest experience implicit in the current scale of illustrated dividends remained unchanged in the future.

Divisible surplus—that amount of surplus earned from each year's operations that the insurer's board of directors decides to pass on to participating policies in the form of dividends.

Due care—process by which an advisor comes to his or her recommendations to clients regarding life insurance after acquiring a thorough understanding of the client's financial needs, goals, and circumstances, followed by appropriate research and documentation. Due care requires the advisor to conduct his or her business affairs with diligence, prudence, and competence, including investigation of the quality, value, and suitability of recommended insurance.

Due diligence—legal requirement that a broker/dealer ensures that a securities investment, including variable life insurance, is as represented.

Emotions—learned reactions to a set of experiences or perceptions that have been either very favorable or very distressing.

Employer owned life insurance—under the IRC, life insurance owned by and payable to an employer on the life of a present or former employee or director. Death proceeds payable under such policies are subject to income taxes to the extent that the benefits exceed the employer's tax basis in the policy, unless certain conditions are met.

Endorsement approach—split dollar life insurance under which the insurance on an employee's life is applied for and owned by the employer that is primarily responsible for premium payments.

Endow—occurs when a policy terminates by its terms during the insured's lifetime by payment of a maturity amount equal to its cash value; cash value equals face amount with most endowment policies. Also called **maturity**.

Endowment insurance—generic type of life insurance that makes two mutually exclusive promises: to pay a specified benefit if the insured dies during the policy term or if the insured survives the stated policy term.

Enhanced cash value rider—eliminates or reduces surrender charges applicable to qualified life insurance policies during the first few policy years.

Entire contract clause—required provision within a life insurance contract, provides that the policy itself and the application, if a copy is attached to the policy, constitute the entire contract between the parties.

Entity buy/sell agreement—one in which the business entity itself is obligated to buy the ownership interest of any deceased owner, with each owner having bound his or her estate to sell if he or she were to be the first to die.

Equity indexed universal life—universal life policy whose interest crediting rate can be based on an equity index or the life insurance company's regular crediting rate. Also called **indexed universal life**.

Estate conservation—use of life insurance death proceeds to cover some or all of the estate taxes due on the decedent/insured's death. Also referred to as providing **estate liquidity**.

Executive bonus plan—nonqualified executive benefit under which an employer pays for premiums for individually issued life insurance for selected executives who own the policies. Also called a **Section 162 plan**.

Exemption amount—value of a taxable estate exempted from estate taxation by virtue of the unified credit.

Expense margin—amount included in policy loading intended to provide for contingencies, for profits or surplus accumulation, and/or to cover losses from early policy lapses. Also called **safety margin**.

Experience factors—actuarial and regulatory term for an insurer's actual results as to mortality, investment returns, expenses and taxes, and persistency.

Expires—termination of a term policy without value after its term has run its course.

Extended term insurance—nonforfeiture option under which single premium term life insurance is purchased with a life insurance policy's net cash surrender value in an amount equal to the policy death benefit less policy loans and based on the insured's sex and attained age, for whatever duration that value will sustain the coverage.

Face amount—amount of money stated in a life insurance contract that is to be paid on the insured's death. Also called **death benefit** and **insurance amount**.

Family rider—optional benefit under life insurance policies for an additional premium that provides insurance on the lives of one or more members of the family of a person who is the insured under the base policy to which the rider is attached. Also called **spouse rider**, **children's rider**, and **additional insured rider**.

Families and households—living arrangements that can be categorized as follows:

Blended family—family or household created when one or both members of the couple have children by a previous marriage. Also called **reconstituted family** and **step family**.

Extended family—one or more nuclear families living together along with other relatives, such as aunts, uncles, and/or grandparents.

Husband-wife family—married couple living in one household with no children under the age of 18 present.

Dual income, no kids (DINKs)—husband-wife family in which both are in the labor force.

Multigenerational family—three or more generations of individuals related by blood or marriage living together. Extended families can be multigenerational but need not be.

Nuclear family—married couple and their children under age 18 sharing living facilities together.

Traditional family—nuclear family in which the father is the sole bread-winner.

One-person household—individual who lives alone.

Opposite-sex unmarried couple—unmarried male and female living together.

Same-sex couple (or **partner**)—individuals of the same sex sharing living quarters and having a close personal relationship.

Single-parent family—single parent plus dependent children living together.

Federal estate taxes owed—amount owed to the federal government after applying all applicable credits against the tentative federal estate tax.

Field force—insurance company's agents.

Field offices—geographically dispersed offices housing an insurance company's agents or field force.

Financially impaired insurer—one for which its ability to conduct normal operations is impaired, capital and surplus have been determined to be insufficient to meet legal requirements, and/or financial condition has triggered regulatory concern.

First-to-die life insurance—generic life insurance policy that promises to pay the face amount of the policy on the first death of one of two (or more) insureds. Also called **joint life insurance**.

Fixed amount option—settlement option under which the policyowner or beneficiary can direct a life insurance company to liquidate a set amount of a policy's death or surrender proceeds over whatever time period the original principal plus earned interest will support. Contrast with **fixed period option**.

Fixed period option—settlement option under which the policyowner or beneficiary can direct a life insurance company to liquidate death or surrender proceeds and interest earned thereon systematically over a defined period of months or years, usually not longer than 25 or 30 years. Contrast with **fixed amount option**.

Fixed premium universal life—unbundled whole life policy that operates as a universal life policy except that premiums set by the insurer are required to be paid to maintain the policy in effect. Also called **interest sensitive whole life** and **current assumption whole life**.

Flat extra—substandard rating method under which a level additional charge unrelated to the insured's age is added to the standard premium.

Form 10-K—annual performance report that public companies, including stock life insurers, in excess of a certain minimum size must file annually with the *Securities and Exchange Commission* (SEC); includes detailed information related to the company's history, nature of its business, organizational structure, risk factors, equity, subsidiaries, and audited financial statements, among other information.

Front-end load—amounts assessed against premiums paid to cover a life insurance company's cost of doing business.

Full costing—allocation of an insurance company's direct and indirect expenses to each product on some standard unit such as policies, face amount, or premium.

Full-pay—under universal life policies, the illustration of premiums being paid throughout a policy's entire potential duration such that the account value equals at least $1.00 at the end of that duration (commonly age 121). Also called **level-pay** and **life-pay**.

Future interest—any ownership interest in property that does not pass into the donee's possession or enjoyment until some future date. Contrast with **present interest**.

General account—location of assets that back the liabilities associated with a life insurance company's guaranteed, fixed benefit contracts.

General agent—person responsible for creating and managing an agency or field office and is primarily responsible for increasing sales and recruiting and developing career agents.

General partnership—one in which partners are actively involved in the management of the firm and fully liable for partnership obligations.

Generally accepted accounting principles—accounting conventions required by the accounting profession of all corporations and predicated on the concept of a business being a going concern.

Generation skipping transfer tax—levied on the value of a property interest transferred to persons two or more generations younger than the transferor, with some exceptions.

Gift—transfer of property ownership for less than adequate consideration.

Gift tax marital deduction—provision under the IRC whereby gifts to one's spouse are free of gift taxes.

Grace period provision—required provision within a life insurance contract that requires the insurer to accept premium payments for a certain period after the premium due date (typically 31 or 61 days) or if the policy has insufficient account value to permit it to continue in force.

Grantor—person who establishes a trust. Also called the **settlor** and **creator**.

Gross estate—value of all property or interests in property owned or controlled by a deceased person.

Gross proceeds—amount received by a policyowner on surrender and used to calculate taxable gain under a life insurance policy; includes the net cash surrender value of any paid up additions and dividends retained by the insurer at interest.

Group term carve out—allowing older, higher-paid employees to be "carved out" of a group term life insurance plan and provided with cash value life insurance.

Growth cap—within the index account of equity indexed universal life, the maximum interest crediting rate.

Growth floor—within the index account of equity indexed universal life, the minimum interest crediting rate.

Growth rate—within the index account of equity indexed universal life, the tentative rate to be applied to the index account value before consideration of the growth cap and growth floor. Derived by multiplying the participation rate by the index performance rate.

Guaranteed assumptions—those pricing components within a life insurance policy that cannot be changed unilaterally by the insurer. Also called **guaranteed policy elements** and **guaranteed elements.**

Guaranteed insurability option—rider granting a policyowner the right to purchase additional life insurance on the insured's life without having to provide evidence of insurability. Also called **additional** or **guaranteed purchase option**.

Guaranteed policy elements—those pricing components within a life insurance policy that cannot be changed unilaterally by the insurer. Also called **guaranteed assumptions** and **guaranteed elements**.

Guideline level premium—under the IRC, the level annual amount payable over a period ending not before the insured's age 95 for a life insurance contract's benefits at the insured's attained age and based on certain required assumptions.

Guideline premium and corridor test—two-part test under the IRC for determining whether unbundled life insurance policies comply with the IRC definition of life insurance, which is met at all times if the total of the gross premiums paid under a contract do not exceed the guideline premium limitation and meets a cash value corridor requirement.

Guideline premium limitation—test under the IRC for determining whether a life insurance policy complies with the IRC definition of life insurance, the test being met if the gross premiums paid do not exceed the greater of a guideline single premium or a guideline level premium.

Guideline single premium—under the IRC, the gross single premium that would be required to fund future insurance benefits (defined to be mainly death and maturity benefits) provided under a life insurance contract at the insured's attained age and based on certain required assumptions.

Illiquid assets—those not available to meet income or other monetary needs because they cannot or will not be liquidated on death.

In-force policy illustration—detailed rendering of future values for a life insurance policy already in effect, assuming that premiums are paid as shown and that future non-guaranteed policy elements will be identical to those shown in the illustration.

Incontestable clause—required provision within a life insurance contract providing that the validity of the contract cannot be contested after it has been in force for two years.

Independent distribution channel—life insurance sales system under which life insurance companies do not seek to build their own sales forces, instead relying on established agents for their sales. Also called **non-agency-building distribution channel**. Contrast with **captive distribution channel**.

Independent property/casualty agents—independent, commissioned agents whose primary business is the sale of property/casualty insurance for several insurers.

Index account—that portion of the cash value of an equity indexed universal life policy for which the interest crediting rate is determined by changes in an equity index, subject to a growth floor and a growth cap.

Index crediting rate—within the index account of equity index universal life, rate applied to the index account determined by applying the growth floor and growth cap to the growth rate for the segment term.

Index performance rate—within the index account of equity indexed universal life, change in the relevant index's market value, ordinarily excluding dividend income, as measured over a segment term.

Indirect expenses—those which cannot be attributed to one specific product line only.

Inside interest buildup—interest credited each year on life insurance policies' cash values and not included in a policyowner's taxable income for that year.

Installment refund annuity—immediate life annuity and also nonforfeiture option under which annuity payments begin immediately and continue for the greater of the lifetime of the annuitant or when payments equal to the original annuity principal have been made. If death occurs before payments equal to the principal have been made, the life insurance company continues to make payments to a beneficiary until the sum of all payments equals the principal. Contrast with **cash refund annuity**.

Insurance agent—state-licensed salesperson under contract to sell an insurer's products, typically for a commission and on a face-to-face basis. Also called a **producer**.

Insurance amount—amount of money stated in a life insurance contract to be paid on the death of the insured. Also called **face amount** and **death benefit**.

Insurance commissioner—executive officer of a state charged with enforcing its insurance laws and regulations. In some states, the officer is called **insurance superintendent** or **insurance director**.

Insurance company—corporation authorized under state insurance law to sell insurance. Also called **insurer** and **carrier**.

Insured—with regard to life insurance, the individual whose death triggers payment of the face amount under a life insurance policy.

Insurer—insurance company.

Intentionally defective irrevocable trust—deferred sale arrangement between a grantor and an irrevocable trust that allows the grantor to make transfers of appreciated income producing property to junior generations free of gift tax. Also called an **intentionally defective grantor trust**.

Interest adjusted net cost indices—death benefit and surrender value measures of illustrated policy performance that take into account the time value of money. See **net payment cost index** and **surrender cost index**.

Interest crediting rate—interest rate credited by the life insurance company or separate account to a policy's cash value.

Interest margin—difference between an insurer's actual investment return and its interest crediting rate. Also called **investment margin** and **spread**.

Interest option—settlement option under which the policyowner or beneficiary can direct a life insurance company to retain death or surrender proceeds and receive interest on those proceeds.

Interest sensitive whole life insurance—unbundled whole life policy that operates as a universal life policy except that premiums set by the insurer are required to be paid to maintain the policy in effect. Also called **fixed premium universal life** and **current assumption whole life**.

Intermediate assumptions—under the *Life Insurance Model Illustrations Regulation* promulgated by the National Association of Insurance Commissioners, that portion that requires use of the numerical average of the illustrated guaranteed and current assumptions to develop policy values.

Internal rate of return—a measure of illustrated life insurance performance derived by solving for the interest rate that causes accumulated scheduled premiums (net of dividends, if appropriate) at selected policy durations to equal that duration's death benefit and its surrender value. See **death benefit internal rate of return** and **surrender value internal rate of return**.

Investment expenses—costs incurred by a life insurance company in making, processing, and protecting its investments.

Investment generation method—determination of the current interest crediting rate from the average investment return on assets acquired over some period (*generation*), more or less approximating the lifetime of one or more blocks of policies.

Investment margin—difference between an insurer's actual investment return and its interest crediting rate. Also called **interest margin** and **spread**.

Irrevocable beneficiary designation—one that can be changed only with the beneficiary's express consent.

Irrevocable life insurance trusts—irrevocable trust that owns and is beneficiary under a life insurance policy, usually on the life of the grantor.

Irrevocable trust—trust that the grantor cannot terminate or alter. Contrast with **revocable trust**.

Joint and survivorship (or **survivor**) **life income option**—nonforfeiture option under which policy death or surrender proceeds are payable in installments for as long as at least one of two beneficiaries (annuitants) is alive.

Joint life insurance—generic life insurance policy that promises to pay the face amount of the policy on the first death of one of two (or more) insureds. Also called **first-to-die life insurance**.

Key person insurance—life insurance purchased to indemnify a business for an expected decrease in earnings brought about by the death of one or more individuals whose efforts are important to the business's success. Also called **key employee** (and **key man**) **insurance**.

Lapse—termination of a life insurance policy for nonpayment of premiums or, in the case of variable life and universal life policies, the depletion of the account value below that required to maintain the policy in force.

Lapse-supported pricing—practice by some life insurers of pricing some products such that later gains from lapses are used to subsidize early policy cash flows.

Life expectancy—average number of years of life remaining for individuals of a given age and gender and sometimes other characteristics as derived from mortality tables.

Life income option with period certain—nonforfeiture option under which policy death or surrender proceeds are paid in installments for as long as the primary beneficiary lives, but should this beneficiary die before a predetermined number of years, installments continue to a second beneficiary until the end of the predetermined number of years, such as 10 years.

Life insurance—contract under which an insurance company agrees to pay a stated sum of money if the insured dies while the policy is in effect; contract meeting the definition of life insurance under Internal Revenue Code section 7702 by meeting either a cash value accumulation test or a guideline premium and cash value corridor test and thus does not lose its favorable income tax treatment.

Life insurance company—corporation authorized under state insurance law to sell products that involve life contingencies; i.e., those that insure against dying or living.

Life insurance needs analysis—process whereby it is determined whether life insurance is needed and the amount needed by *identification* of the client's financial objectives if he or she were to die prematurely, *assembling and analyzing* relevant information, and *development and implementation* of a plan to accomplish the client's post-mortem life insurance objectives. Also called **life insurance programming**, **personal financial planning**, and **personal risk management**, among others.

Life insurance policy illustration—detailed rendering of future values for a policy assuming that premiums are paid as shown and that future non-guaranteed policy elements will be identical to those shown in the illustration.

Life settlement—sale in the secondary life insurance market of an existing life insurance policy. Compare with **viatical**.

Life settlement firms—businesses that purchase existing life insurance policies in the secondary life insurance market. Also called **providers**.

Limited partnership—one having at least one general partner and one or more limited partners who are not actively engaged in partnership management and who are liable for partnership obligations only to the extent of their investment in the partnership.

Limited payment whole life insurance—whole life insurance that provides for premiums to be paid over a period shorter than an insured's possible entire life, such as to age 65.

Liquid assets—those available to be liquidated on the client's death with reasonable price certainty. Contrast with **illiquid assets**.

Liquidation—with regard to insurance regulation, the winding up of an insurance company's entire business operations, with the state insurance commissioner being given title to all assets of the insurer in his or her capacity as the receiver to make final settlement of the insurer's affairs.

Living benefit rider (or **provision**)—promise under a life insurance policy to pay some or all of its face amount and/or other benefit prior to the insured's death if the insured suffers specified adverse health conditions. Also called **accelerated death benefit** and **accelerated benefit riders** (or **provisions**).

Living trust—trust created during life. Also called an **inter vivos trust**.

Loadings—amounts assessed under life insurance policies to cover some of an insurer's operational expenses, taxes, and provision for profits and contingencies. Also called **loading charges, loading, expense charges, fees,** and **policy loads**.

Loaned cash (or **account) value**—in life insurance industry jargon, that portion of the cash value backing a policy loan.

Long term care insurance rider—provides for the payment of monthly benefits under a life insurance policy if the insured suffers a qualifying chronic health condition.

Marginal costing—with regard to life insurance, the allocation of only the insurer's direct expenses for a specific product on some standard unit such as policies, face amount, or premium.

Marital deduction—provision under the IRC whereby bequests made to a deceased person's spouse are free of estate taxes.

Marital trust—trust created to receive property that qualifies for the marital deduction on the death of the first spouse.

Material misrepresentation—inaccurate statement by a proposed insured or applicant that causes an insurer to issue a policy on terms or at a price more favorable than it would have had the statement been accurate. The basis for rescinding a policy during its period of contestability.

Maturity—occurs when a policy's cash value equals its face amount. Also called **endow**.

Misappropriation—wrongful use by an agent of funds entrusted to him or her.

Misstatement of age provision—required provision within a life insurance contract stipulating that if, on the insured's death, his or her age is found to have been inaccurate, the insurance amount will be adjusted to be that which would have been purchased had the correct age been used at policy issue.

Modified endowment contract (MEC)—any life insurance policy entered into after June 20, 1988 that meets the IRC Section 7702 definition of life insurance, but that fails to meet the seven-pay test.

Modified whole life—whole life insurance under which premiums are redistributed so as to be lower than an otherwise identical policy during the first three to five years and higher thereafter.

Mortality margins—additions to underlying mortality rates to develop the actual mortality charges to be assessed within a policy.

Mortality tables—displays of yearly probabilities of death by age and sex and sometimes other characteristics.

Mortgage backed securities—bonds backed by residential or commercial mortgages.

Mortgages—debt instruments by which the borrower gives the lender a lien on property as security for the repayment of a loan.

Multiple-line exclusive agents—commissioned captive agents who sell the life and health and property and liability insurance products of a single group of affiliated insurers.

Multiple table extra—method of assessing a substandard rating within a life insurance policy that varies by age and expected additional mortality. Also called **table rating**.

Mutual life insurance company—policyowner owned and controlled corporation authorized to sell life insurance products with net profits inuring to the benefit of policyholders.

Narrative summary—required to be provided to a prospective policyholder if a life insurance illustration is used in connection with a policy sale, contains information about the illustrated policy including descriptions of its benefits and mechanics, available riders and policy options, and identification and descriptions of column headings and key terms used in the illustrations.

National Association of Insurance Commissioners—trade organization composed exclusively of state insurance regulators.

Net amount at risk—difference between a policy's face amount and cash value.

Net cash surrender value—residual after deducting policy loans from a policy's cash surrender value. Also sometimes called **net cash value, surrender value**, and **cash surrender value**.

Net payment cost index—death-benefit-based measures of illustrated policy performance that inform the prospective buyer of the estimated average annual net payment or outlay per $1,000 of insurance over selected time periods (ordinarily 10 and 20 years) taking into consideration only the policy's premiums and illustrated (non-guaranteed) dividends, if any, and adjusting them for the time value of money. See **surrender cost index**.

Net worth—excess of assets over liabilities. Also called **capital and surplus** and sometimes called **surplus** or **capital**, neither of which is technically accurate.

No-lapse guarantee rider—provides that, if a specified minimum premium is paid regularly, a life insurance policy will not lapse for a specified period or for life, even if the account value goes to zero. Such riders that guarantee coverage for less than the whole of life are sometimes called **guaranteed minimum death benefit riders**.

No-lapse guarantee universal life—policy guaranteeing that, if a specified minimum premium is paid regularly, a life insurance policy will not lapse for a specified period or for life, even if the account value goes to zero.

Non-admitted assets—with regard to life insurance statutory accounting principles, those deemed less reliable in being converted into cash and that may not be counted in determining compliance with state solvency requirements, such as amounts owed the insurer by agents, furniture, certain equipment, and some other items.

Non-guaranteed policy elements—those pricing components within a life insurance policy that can be changed unilaterally by the insurer, subject to any guaranteed policy elements. Also called **non-guaranteed assumptions** and **current assumptions**.

Nonforfeiture options—different means stated in a life insurance contract by which policyowners may use a policy's cash surrender value.

Nonforfeiture provision—provision required within life insurance contracts that states the mortality table, rate of interest, and method used in calculating a policy's nonforfeiture values and the options available if the policy is terminated or lapses.

Nonparticipating (nonpar) life insurance—policies for which the policyowner has no right to share in any distribution of surplus funds by the insurer. Most nonpar cash value policies contain non-guaranteed elements other than dividends that ensure that such policyholders can share in the favorable (and unfavorable) actual or reasonably anticipated operational experience of the insurer.

Nonparticipating provision—provision required within nonparticipating life insurance contracts that states that the policy does not share in an insurer's surplus or does not pay dividends.

Nonqualified deferred compensation plan—nonqualified executive benefit arrangement under which compensation for services rendered is postponed, usually until retirement.

Nonqualified executive benefit arrangement—benefit provided by an employer to an employee, which does not meet the requirements for preferential tax treatment and nondiscrimination among employees as set out under the Employee Retirement Income Security Act and the IRC.

Numeric summary—under the *Life Insurance Model Illustrations Regulation* promulgated by the National Association of Insurance Commissioners, that portion of an illustration that requires delivery of a condensed one-page summary of illustrated policy values using three required assumption bases: guaranteed, intermediate, and current.

One-way buy/sell agreement—one in which the estate of a sole owner of a business is obligated to sell and another party is obligated to purchase that owner's interest.

Operating expenses—costs incurred by life insurance companies in normal business operations. Insurers usually record such expenses as falling into one of four categories:

Acquisition expenses, sometimes called **first-year expenses**—costs relating to the procurement and issuing of new business, including underwriting.

Development expenses—costs incurred in developing a new product line.

Maintenance expenses, also called **renewal expenses**—costs incurred to maintain and service policies after they are in force.

Overhead expenses, also called **administrative expenses**—those costs incurred not directly related to a specific product, such as executive salaries, rent, utilities, etc.

Option (or **optional**) **buy/sell agreement**—one in which a party is afforded the option of buying a business interest but is not required to buy it.

Overloan protection rider—life insurance contract provision that guarantees that a policy will not lapse if policy loans equal or exceed the policy account value.

Override commissions—sales compensation based on an agent's production that is paid to the agent's supervisor.

Ownership provision—within life insurance contracts, states that the policyowner may exercise all rights under the policy without the consent of anyone else, unless a beneficiary is named irrevocably.

Paid up—condition under which a life insurance policy is guaranteed to remain in effect for a specified period including for life with no further premiums due.

Paid-up additions—option allowing dividends paid under participating policies to purchase single premium whole life insurance.

Participating (par) life insurance—policies for which the policyowner has a contractual right to share or participate in an insurer's favorable (and unfavorable) operational experience via dividends.

Participation provision—provision required within participating life insurance contracts that states that the policy will participate in any surplus that the insurer's board of directors decides to distribute to policyowners. Also called **distributable surplus provision**.

Participation rate—with equity indexed universal life, proportion of the index performance rate used to derive the actual crediting rate, to yield the growth rate. A participation rate of 100 percent means that the entire growth rate is considered and a rate of 80 percent means that 80 percent of the growth rate is considered.

Partnership—voluntary association of two or more individuals for the purpose of conducting a business for profit as co-owners.

Permanent life insurance—type of life insurance that combines term insurance and internal savings within the same contract. Also called **cash value life insurance**.

Persistency—percentage of life insurance policies not terminated by lapse within one year. A lapse occurs whenever a premium necessary to maintain the policy in full effect is not paid.

Personal financial planning—process whereby an individual's or a family's overall financial objectives are used to develop and implement an integrated plan to accomplish the objectives.

Personal-producing general agent—experienced, independent, commissioned agent who focuses on personal production but who is paid both direct and override commissions plus some type of expense allowance.

Policy illustration—detailed rendering of future values for a life insurance policy, assuming that premiums are paid as shown and that future non-guaranteed policy elements will be identical to those shown in the illustration.

Policy loan provision—required provision within cash value life insurance contracts that grants the policyowner the right to secure a loan from the life insurance company on the security of the policy's net cash surrender value at an interest rate stated in or determined by the policy.

Policy reserves—regarding life insurance companies, liabilities appearing on their balance sheets to account for actual and potential future claims outstanding.

Policy value—see **cash value**.

Policy value provision—provision within nonparticipating life insurance contracts that contain non-guaranteed policy elements that explains the nature of the non-guaranteed elements and how they are determined and applied within the policy. Also called **account value provision.**

Policyholder—owner of a life insurance policy who exercises all contractual rights and with whom the insurer deals. See also **policyowner**.

Policyowner—owner of a life insurance policy who exercises all contractual rights and with whom the insurer deals. See also **policyholder**.

Portfolio average method—determination of the current interest crediting rate from the average investment return of a life insurance company's entire general account investment portfolio.

Premium—payment made to an insurance company to place and usually to maintain an insurance contract in effect.

Premium provision—required provision within a life insurance contract that explains the nature of premiums due or otherwise payable under the policy.

Premium solve—in the context of a life insurance illustration, determining the annual premium payment needed over a specified premium payment period to support a specified death benefit amount, pattern, and duration and, if applicable, to develop a target cash value at some specified future time; e.g., solving for the annual premium payable over ten years to cause the cash value to equal the death benefit at age 121.

Present interest—ownership interest in property that passes immediately and fully into a donee's possession and enjoyment. Contrast with **future interest**.

Primary beneficiary—person or persons named as the first to receive death proceeds payable under a life insurance policy.

Primary life insurance market—market for life insurance policies purchased from insurance companies. Contrast with **secondary life insurance market**.

Private placement—corporate bond purchased by a financial institution that has negotiated directly with the issuing corporation over its terms.

Private placement life insurance—individually tailored variable life insurance policies not subject to SEC regulation, which are designed specifically for and available only to accredited investors or qualified purchasers.

Producer—salesperson licensed by the state and under contract to sell an insurer's products, typically for a commission and on a face-to-face basis. See also **insurance agent**.

Producer group—marketing organization operating independently of life insurance companies and whose member agents specialize in the high-end market.

Product margin—sum of a life insurance policy's expense, morality, and interest margins designed to help ensure that the insurer will be able to meet its contractual obligations even under adverse circumstances.

Proprietary life insurance—life insurance policy that is targeted and priced for a specific market and available to be sold exclusively by a cohesive group of agents.

Providers—businesses that purchase existing life insurance policies in the secondary life insurance market. Also called **life settlement firms**.

Pure life income option—settlement option under which the policyowner or beneficiary can direct the life insurance company to pay death or surrender proceeds systematically in installments for as long as the recipient lives, but no longer.

Qualified purchaser—under requirement laid down by the SEC, individual or family organization with net investments of $5.0 million or more.

Rating agencies—businesses that provide information and opinions about the ability of firms to meet their obligations.

Rebate—act of giving something of value to an applicant in return for purchasing life insurance, most commonly in the form of the agent giving the applicant a portion of his or her commission.

Reduce premium—option under which dividends paid under a participating policy are used as a credit against the premium due.

Reduced paid up insurance—nonforfeiture option under which single premium whole life insurance is purchased with the policy's net cash surrender value for whatever amount that value will purchase at the insured's attained age and sex.

Reentry provision—option within some term life insurance policies that grants their owners the right to pay a lower premium than otherwise if the insured can demonstrate periodically that he or she meets continuing insurability criteria.

Rehabilitation—order granting to the state insurance commissioner title to a domestic insurance company's assets and the authority to carry on its business until the insurer is either returned to private management after the grounds for issuing the order have been removed or liquidated.

Reinstatement clause—required provision within a life insurance contract that gives the policyowner the right to reinstate a lapsed policy if he or she can furnish satisfactory evidence of insurability and pays past due premiums or charges.

Remainder interest—residual corpus of a charitable remainder trust that ultimately passes to a charity after the trust has completed payments due to the donor.

Renewable—continuation of a term policy for another period by paying an increased premium.

Replacement—occurs when a new life insurance policy is purchased and, in connection with that purchase, an existing policy is surrendered or otherwise terminated.

Reset feature—permits the guaranteed duration or the amount of guaranteed coverage under a no-lapse guarantee policy to be reset based on adjusted future specified premiums.

Results clause—war exclusion clause that provides that a life insurance company is excused from paying the face amount if the insured's death is a direct *result* of war. Contrast with **status clause**.

Retained asset account—option offered by insurers to have death proceeds held in an interest bearing account, with the beneficiary free to leave proceeds in this account or to write drafts or checks to withdraw any portion or all of the proceeds.

Retained interest—value of a trust, often in the form of income, that is reserved for use by the beneficiary.

Return of premium term policy—term life insurance under which the policy promises to return the premiums paid if the insured survives the policy term, which may be from 10 to 30 years, depending on the insured's age and insurer's requirements.

Revocable beneficiary designation—one that may be changed by the policyowner without the beneficiary's consent.

Revocable trust—trust that the grantor can terminate or alter. Contrast with **irrevocable trust**.

Rider—supplemental benefit or option available under some life insurance policies, usually for an additional premium.

Right of return policy provision—provision required within life insurance contracts that grants policyowners an unconditional right to return a policy to the insurer within 10 (or sometimes a greater number of) days of its receipt. Sometimes called a **free look provision**.

Risk-based capital plan—required of life insurers whose risk-based capital ratio falls below certain stated limits, which describes the causes of the threat to the insurer's solvency, offers proposals to correct the situation, estimates five years of financial projections, and includes other relevant information.

Risk-based capital (RBC) ratio—ratio of an insurer's total adjusted capital to its authorized control level RBC.

Risk classification factors—information used by underwriters to determine whether the proposed insured's health and other characteristics dictate the assessment of charges beyond those dictated by the rating factors (age, sex, smoker, etc.).

Second-to-die life insurance—generic life insurance policy that insures two (or sometimes more) lives and pays the face amount only on the death of the second (or last) insured to die. Also called **survivor life insurance** and **last-to-die life insurance**.

Secondary beneficiary—person or persons named to receive death proceeds payable under a life insurance policy if no primary beneficiary is alive at the time of the insured's death. Also called **contingent beneficiary**.

Secondary life insurance market—market in which existing life insurance policies are bought and sold. Contrast with **primary life insurance market**.

Section 1035 exchanges—exchange authorized under the IRC of an existing life insurance policy for a new one which, if certain conditions are met, permits the carryover of the cost basis of the surrendered policy into the new one thereby avoiding recognition of any gain or loss. Also called **1035 exchanges**.

Section 303 stock redemption—stock redemption authorized under the IRC through which an income tax free redemption is permitted qualifying estates in an amount to cover federal and state death taxes, funeral expenses, and estate administration expenses.

Segment—with equity indexed universal life, the characterization of funds transferred at a specific time into the index account.

Segment term—with equity indexed universal life, specified duration of each segment.

Separate accounts—location of investments that support liabilities arising from pass-through products for which all investment risk is borne by the policyholder, as with variable life insurance.

Settled—sale of an existing life insurance policy in the secondary life insurance market.

Settlement options—provisions within life insurance contracts that grant policyowners and beneficiaries options as to how death proceeds and often net cash surrender proceeds can be paid.

Seven-pay test—test to determine whether a life insurance policy is a modified endowment contract and so receives less favorable income tax treatment. A policy fails to satisfy the test if the cumulative amount paid under the contract at any time during the first seven contract years exceeds the cumulative amount that would have been paid had the policy's annual premium equaled the net level premium for a seven-pay whole life policy.

Shadow account—within no-lapse guarantee policies, the values derived from the application of a set of guaranteed policy charges and credits differing from those applicable to the regular account value to determine whether the guarantee remains in effect. The policy lapses if neither the regular account nor the shadow account value is positive.

Skip person—heir who is beyond those of the immediately following generation.

Sole proprietorship—unincorporated business owned by an individual who usually also manages it.

Specified premium test—original no-lapse mechanism that provides that coverage remains guaranteed as long as a certain minimum premium is paid.

Split dollar life insurance—nonqualified executive benefit whereby one party (often an employer) assists another (often an employee) in purchasing life insurance by sharing (splitting) the premium payments and policy benefits between the two parties.

Split option—under a survivorship policy, grants the owner the right to exchange the policy for two individual policies, one on each insured's life.

Spread—difference between an insurer's actual investment return and its interest crediting rate. Also called **investment margin** and **interest margin**.

Standard Nonforfeiture Laws—part of the insurance codes of each state that establishes minimum nonforfeiture values, thereby prohibiting forfeitures of policyowner contributions in excess of those necessary to cover current and past mortality charges and expenses under non-variable policies.

Status clause—war exclusion clause that provides that the life insurance company need not pay the policy face amount if death results while the insured is in the military service, regardless of the cause of death. Contrast with **results clause**.

Statutory accounting principles—accounting conventions required to be followed by life insurance companies as promulgated by state insurance regulators, predicated in part on the liquidation value of the business.

Stock—financial instrument signifying ownership in a corporation represented by shares that are a claim on its assets and earnings.

Stock life insurance company—shareholder owned corporation that is authorized to sell life insurance products.

Stock redemption agreement—entity buy/sell agreement under which a corporation is obligated to purchase the shares of stock from a deceased shareholder and the deceased shareholder's estate is obligated to sell those shares to the corporation.

Stress test—use in life insurance illustrations of non-guaranteed policy elements, such as reduced interest crediting rates and/or higher mortality and other charges, that are less favorable than those currently being applied to estimate the adverse affect on future policy values of less favorable current assumptions.

Substandard rating—additional charge levied for a life insurance policy to account for higher than average expected mortality.

Suicide clause—optional provision routinely included in life insurance contracts that excludes payment of the death benefit if the cause of death is suicide occurring within the first two policy years.

Supplemental executive retirement plan (SERP)—nonqualified executive benefit plan that provides retirement benefits to selected employees only. Two popular SERPs are:

Excess SERP—which provides a benefit amount equal to the difference between (1) the full amount under the employer's qualified retirement benefit formula that would be paid to the executive but ignoring any ERISA-imposed limits and (2) the actual retirement benefits payable to the executive under the qualified retirement plan and Social Security and

Target SERP—which is intended to replace retirement benefits lost by ERISA-imposed limits *and* counteract the bias in Social Security retirement benefits in favor of low income workers.

Surplus strain—drain on an insurer's surplus that results from having negative cash flows during policies' first few years.

Surrender—voluntary termination of a policy by its owner for its net cash surrender value.

Surrender charge—penalty assessed against a policy's cash value if the policy is terminated early.

Surrender cost index—surrender-based measures of illustrated policy performance that inform the prospective buyer of the estimated average annual net cost per $1,000 of insurance over selective time periods taking into consideration the policy's premiums, illustrated dividends or other non-guaranteed policy values, and surrender values and adjusting these values for the time value of money. See **net payment cost index.**

Surrender value—difference between a life insurance policy's cash value and its surrender charge. Also called **cash surrender value** and sometimes **cash value** with universal life policies.

Surrender value internal rate of return—a measure of illustrated life insurance performance derived by solving for the interest rate that causes accumulated scheduled premiums (net of dividends, if appropriate) at selected policy durations to equal that duration's cash surrender. See **death benefit internal rate of return.**

Survivorship clause—provision within a life insurance contract providing that the beneficiary must survive the insured by a fixed period of time after the insured's death to be entitled to the death proceeds. Also called a **time clause**.

Survivorship life insurance—generic life insurance policy that insures two (or sometimes more) lives and pays the death proceeds only on the death of the second (or last) insured to die. Also called **second-to-die life insurance** and **last-to-die life insurance**.

Table shaving program—special programs offered by some life insurance companies under which proposed insureds who ordinarily would require a table rating can be offered life insurance at standard rates.

Tabular detail—under the *Life Insurance Model Illustrations Regulation* promulgated by the National Association of Insurance Commissioners, that portion of an illustration that is required to show the planned premiums in the case of universal life policies or contracts premium in the case of fixed premium policies along with the guaranteed death benefits and surrender values for at least each policy year from one to ten and every fifth policy year thereafter for the possible policy duration. Policy values based on current assumptions may also be included (and they almost always are so included).

Target cash value—amount of cash or account value sought, commonly $1.00 or an amount equal to the death benefit, within a policy illustration at a specified age, such as age 121. Also called **cash value target.**

Target market—segmented group of individuals or businesses having similar needs on which an insurer or agent has chosen to focus its marketing efforts.

Taxable estate—difference between the gross estate and allowable deductions.

Ten-pay—under universal life policies, the illustration of sufficient premiums being paid during the first ten policy years to support, with illustrated future interest credited to the account value, all future illustrated policy charges and to cause the policy account value to equal a specified amount, such as the death benefit or $1.00, at a specified age, such as 121.

Tentative federal estate tax—result from applying the appropriate estate tax rate to the tentative tax base.

Tentative tax base—result from adding adjusted taxable gifts to the taxable estate.

Term life insurance—generic type of life insurance that pays a death benefit if the insured dies within a set time period, such as 20 years, and pays nothing if the insured survives the period at which time the policy expires.

Terminal illness coverage—provides that a specified maximum percentage of from 25 to 100 percent of the policy's face amount can be paid if the insured is diagnosed as having a terminal illness, usually subject to a specified overall maximum payment, such as $250,000. Also called **accelerated death benefits**.

Tertiary beneficiary—person or persons designated to receive life insurance policy death benefits if neither primary nor contingent beneficiaries are alive at the death of the insured.

Testamentary trust—trust created at death through a person's will.

Total adjusted capital—insurer's statutory capital and surplus increased by liabilities intended to smooth balance sheet fluctuations.

Total disability—commonly defined within life insurance contracts for purposes of waiver of premium provisions as inability of the insured, because of illness or injury, to perform either (1) the duties of his or her own occupation or (2) the duties of any occupation for which he or she is reasonably suited by reason of education, training, or experience.

Transfer for value rule—exception within the IRC to the rule that life insurance death benefit payments ordinarily are received income-tax free, if policy ownership is transferred for a valuable consideration. In such instances, the excess of (1) the gross death proceeds over (2) the consideration paid for the policy plus premiums paid are taxable to the beneficiary, with some stated exceptions.

Transferor—person making a transfer of property; the decedent for federal estate taxation and the donor for federal gift taxation.

Transparent—characteristic of unbundled life insurance policies, such as universal life, wherein their internal operation, interest rates, and cost of insurance and loading charges are disclosed each year to the policyowner.

Trust—legal arrangement whereby one party transfers property to another which holds the legal title and manages the property for the benefit of beneficiaries.

Trustee—person who receives the legal title and manages property held in a trust.

Twisting—practice by an agent of inducing a policyowner through misrepresentation to replace an existing life insurance policy with the purchase of a new one.

Unbundled policy—life insurance policy under which the portions of premiums allocated to pay cost of insurance charges; to build cash values; and to cover an insurer's expenses, taxes, and contingencies are disclosed to the policyowner. Contrast with **bundled policy**.

Underwriting—process by which an insurer decides whether to issue requested insurance and, if so, on what terms and price.

Unified credit—transfer tax credit available to offset estate taxes otherwise due.

Unit costs—for life insurance pricing purposes, allocation of insurer operating expenses in such a way as to result in cost per dollar of premium, per $1,000 of insurance, and/or per policy.

Universal life insurance—generic type of unbundled life insurance characterized by flexible-premiums, adjustable death benefits, whose cash values and durations depend on the premiums paid into them.

Valuation mortality table—mortality table with margins added and used as the basis for calculating minimum reserves and cash values.

Variable life insurance—generic form of life insurance under which the policyowner allocates whatever proportion of premiums wished to separate accounts whose investment results are passed directly through to the policy's cash value, with the policyowner bearing the investment risk.

Variable universal life insurance—variable life insurance with a universal life chassis.

Variable whole life insurance—variable life insurance with a whole life chassis.

Viatical settlement—commonly thought of as the sale in the secondary life insurance market of an existing life insurance policy under which the insured has less than two years to live. Also called **viaticals**. Compare with **life settlements**.

Wait-and-see buy/sell agreement—one in which shareholders and the business may postpone the decision between a cross purchase and stock redemption agreement until the death of a stockholder.

Waiver of monthly charges—provision or rider within unbundled life insurance contracts that provides that monthly policy loadings and cost of insurance charges will be "waived" if the insured becomes disabled. Compare with **waiver of a specified premium**.

Waiver of a specified premium—provision or rider within unbundled life insurance contracts that provides that an agreed upon premium amount will be "waived" if the insured become disabled. Compare with **waiver of monthly charges**.

Waiver of premium—provision or rider within fixed-premium life insurance contracts that provides premiums otherwise due will be "waived" if the insured becomes disabled. Also called **premium waiver**.

War exclusion clause—provides that the insurer need not pay a claim if the insured's death occurs under certain military conditions. See **status clause** and **results clause**.

Wash rate—having a life insurance policy's interest crediting rate and policy loan rate equal.

Wealth replacement trust—irrevocable life insurance trust that owns and is beneficiary of life insurance roughly equal to the value of property transferred to a charitable remainder trust or otherwise gifted.

Whole life insurance—generic type of bundled life insurance that pays the policy face amount whenever the insured dies and, therefore, provide life insurance intended to remain in effect for the insured's entire lifetime.

Yearly renewable term—term life insurance whose premiums increase yearly. Also called **annual renewable term**.

Index

Absolute assignment, 215
Accelerated death benefits, 218, 424–25
Accidental death benefit riders, 217
Accountants, 32–33
Accounting standards, 71–72. *See also* Generally accepted accounting principles (GAAP)
Account value, 109, 203
Accredited investors for PPLI, 168
Accumulated earnings, 276
Accumulated value, 109
Accumulation UL, 149
ACL (Authorized Control Level), 74
Acquisition expenses, 127
Additional insured riders, 216
Additional purchase option riders, 217
Add-to-cash-value option, 179, 214
Adjusted taxable gifts, 243
Administrative expenses and fees, 128, 130, 146
Admitted assets, 60
Advisors, 29–33
Age, misstatement of, 203–4
Agency building distribution, 33
Agents. *See* Insurance agents
AIG, 51, 75
Alcohol and drug usage for underwriting, 119
Allowable deductions, 243

Allstate Insurance, 35
Alternative minimum tax (AMT), 279–80, 412
A.M. Best, 50, 86–87, 93, 95
American Accounting Association, 33
American Bar Association, 33
American College (Bryn Mawr, PA), 30, 31
Annual gift tax exclusion, 245–46
Annual renewable term, 108, 143. *See also* Yearly renewable term (YRT)
Anxiety over death and planning, 4–5
APLs (Automatic premium loans), 185–86, 213
Applicant, defined, 10
Appropriate amount of life insurance, 12–13
Assets
  accounting standards, 71
  types of, 231–32
Assignment/ownership provision, 214–15
  estate tax and, 244
Assumptions. *See also* Current assumptions
  earned rate assumption, 335
  non-guaranteed assumptions, 309–10
Attorneys, 32–33
Attribution rules, 277
Authorized Control Level (ACL), 74

Automatic premium loans (APLs), 185–86, 213
Aviation
 exclusion clause, 204–5
 underwriting consideration, 119

Backdating, 352
Back-end loads, 149
Basic mortality table, 114
Belth, Joseph M., 100
Beneficiary
 changing, 207
 defined, 10, 248
 simultaneous death of insured and beneficiary, 207–8
Beneficiary clause, 206–8
Best. *See* A.M. Best
Best's Review, 103
Blended families, 229, 233
Bonds, 55–56
 non-investment grade, 61
 yields supporting dividend interest rates, 311
Bonus plans, 8, 280–81
Branch managers, 34
Brokerage, 35–36
"BrokerCheck Reports," 43
Brokers, 35
Bundled policies, 111, 113, 130
Business continuation arrangements, 271–80
 tax aspects of life insurance, 278–80
Business planning, 10–22, 226, 263–86, 409
 business applications of life insurance, 268–86
 business continuation arrangements, 271–80
 key person indemnification, 269–71
 forms of business organizations, 264–67
 tax considerations, 267–68
Business profile, 90
Buy/sell agreements
 cross purchase, 273, 283
 factors influencing choice of, 276–77
 one-way, 272
 partnership, 274–75
 wait-and-see, 275
Bypass trusts, 248

Capital and surplus, 52
 adequacy, 59–60
 ongoing capital requirements, 73–74
 solvency surveillance methods, 73–74
 state minimum requirements, 67
Capital liquidation approach, 234
Capital retention approach, 234
Captive agents, 34, 168
Captive distribution, 33, 34–35
Career agency system, 34
Career agents, 34–35
Cash
 as dividend option, 214
 investments, 57
 objectives in life insurance planning, 231, 260–61
 as settlement option, 208–9, 211
Cash flow, 277
Cash flow testing, 75
Cash refund annuity, 210
Cash surrender value, 160, 222
Cash value
 attributes of policies, 179, 410
 income tax treatment, 411–12
Cash value accumulation test (CVAT), 140
 comparison of policies and, 354–55
 funding target, 333–34
 minimum non-MEC death benefit example, 343–44
 stress testing, 336
Cash value corridor test, 141
Cash value life insurance, 14, 108–11
 cash value attributes, 180
 crediting rate attributes, 192
 death benefit attributes, 177
 loading charge attributes, 195
 mortality charge attributes, 189
 overview of, 175
 premium attributes, 196
Cash value targets, 332, 334–35
 policy illustrations, 353–54
Casualty agents, 37
Catastrophic illness coverage, 218
Catch-up provision, 159
CAWL. *See* Current assumption whole life
Certified Financial Planner (CFP), 31, 39
Charges. *See* Pricing

Charitable remainder trusts (CRTs), 251–53
Chartered Financial Consultant (ChFC), 31, 39
Chartered Life Underwriter (CLU), 30, 39
Children's riders, 216
Closely held corporations, 265
  business continuation arrangements, 271–72
  death of majority shareholder in, 266–67
  loan limitations on, 276
Code of Professional Responsibility of the Society of Financial Service Professionals (SFSP Code), 37
COI. *See* Cost of insurance (COI) rates
Collateral assignment, 215, 281–82
Colonial Penn Life Insurance Company, 18
Combination plans, 219
Comdex, 94
Commingling of funds, 69
Commissions, 63–64
  charge-backs, 134
Companies. *See* Life insurance companies
Company Action Level, 74
Competence, 39–40
Complaint data, 99–100
Concept reports, 301
Conservation order, 78
Contingency risks, 73
Contingent beneficiary, 206
Continuing education of agents, 68–69
Contribution principle, 163
Conversion, 144
Corporate governance rules, 76
Corporations, 265–67, 275–80
  life insurance, use of, 277–78
  nonqualified executive benefit arrangements, 280–85
  split dollar life insurance, 281–83
Corrective orders, 77
Corridor test, 141
Cost basis, 140, 413
Cost of doing business, 127–29
Cost of insurance (COI) rates, 117, 118, 120–23, 146, 342, 354
Cost recovery, 413
Credit default swaps, 51

Crediting rates, 191–94, 311–12
  actual vs. those at policy insurance, 191–92
  determination of, 193
  disclosure of, 193
  dividend income included in, 194
  equity indexed universal life (EIUL), 359–60
  guaranteed minimum, 191
  stress testing, 335
  sustainability of illustrated policy values, 319–25
  volatility of, 193–94
Credit shelter trusts, 248
Cross-over points, 366
Cross purchase buy/sell agreements, 273
  split dollar life insurance and, 283
CRTs (Charitable remainder trusts), 251–53
Crummey trusts, 249
Current assumptions
  inherent in life insurance illustrations, 309–10
  likelihood of lapse with adverse development of, 182
  non-guaranteed policy elements, 110
  UL type policies, 80
Current assumption whole life (CAWL), 146, 166, 173, 176, 237
CVAT. *See* Cash value accumulation test

Death
  of majority shareholder in closely held corporation, 266–67
  of minority and 50/50 shareholder, 267
Death benefit
  accelerated, 218, 424–25
  adjustability of benefit amount, 178
  adjustability of policy duration, 176–78
  attributes, 176–79
  choice of level or increasing amount, 178–79
  comparison of policies, 363–65
  defined, 10
  funding targets, 333, 334–35
  generic universal life patterns, 147–48
  guaranteed minimum riders, 222

increase of future benefit, 404
minimum non-MEC example, 343–44
nature and duration of guarantee, 176
pay-to-age 120, 341–42
policy illustrations, 353–54
provisions, 205–6
reduction of future benefit, 396–97
stress testing, 336
10-pay funding, 337–41
Death benefit only plans, 285
Death benefit solve, 365
Death benefit UL, 149
Delay clause, 204
Development expenses, 128
DINKs, 228
Direct expenses, 128
Direct recognition, 183
Direct response distribution channel, 33
Discretionary income, 236
Distribution, 367–68, 404–7
Distribution channels, 33–35
    captive distribution, 34–35
    independent distribution, 35–37
Distribution solve, 367
Diversification of assets, 60–61
Dividends
    actually paid, 164
    crediting rates included income
        from, 194
    definition and purpose of, 80
    equity indexed universal life, 152
    history, 164
    illustration, 164
    income tax treatment, 412
    interest rates, 311–12
        sustainability of illustrated policy
            values, 319–25
    options, 213–14
    participating policies, 163
    restrictions, 68, 75
Double indemnity, 217
Dread disease coverage, 218
Dual income, no kids (DINKs), 228
Due care, 85–104
    defined, 41
    other sources of information, 96–104
        complaint data, 99–100
        financial statement information,
            97–99
        insurance agents, 102–3

insurance companies, 102
NAIC and state insurance depart-
    ments, 96–101
publications, 103
risk based capital ratios, 100–101
Securities and Exchange Commis-
    sion (SEC), 101–2
stock analysts' reports, 103
rating agencies, role of, 85–96. *See
    also* Rating agencies
Due diligence, 41

Earned rate assumption, 335
Economic Growth and Tax Relief
    Reconciliation Act of 2001
    (EGTRRA), 242
EIUL. *See* Equity indexed universal life
Emotions related to death and plan-
    ning, 5–6
Employees. *See also* Executives
    group term carve outs, 285–86
    nonqualified retirement plans, 283,
        284–85
    split dollar life insurance, 282–83
Employer-owned life insurance (EOLI),
    267–68
Employer-provided death benefits, 8–9
Endorsement approach, 281
Endowment insurance, 14, 110. *See
    also* Modified endowment
    contract (MEC)
Enhanced cash value riders, 222
Entire contract clause, 199–200
Entity buy/sell agreements, 273
Equity indexed universal life (EIUL),
    151–53
    attributes of, 174
    comparison of policies, 358–60
        with generic universal life, 374–75
    considerations, 152–53
    funding levels, 345
    operational details, 151–52
    risk tolerance and, 237
Estate conservation, 255
Estate liquidity, 255, 260
Estate planning, 10–22, 241–61
    life insurance analysis for, 254–61
        development and implementation
            of plan, 257–61
        information analysis, 257

information collection, 256–57
nature of insurance need, 258
objectives identification, 255–56
policy options for, 260–61
trusts, 247–54. *See also* Trusts
Estate Planning Councils, 33
Estate tax, 169, 242–44
calculation, 243
generation skipping transfer (GST)
tax, 247, 254
of life insurance, 244
marital deduction, 243, 258–59
rates, 242–43
ETI (Extended term insurance), 187,
212
Evidence of insurability, 201
Excess capital, incentives to avoid
holding, 52–53
Excessive policy value, 400–407
Excess SERPs, 285
Exclusive agents, 34
Executive Life, 50, 86
Executives
bonus plans, 8, 280–81
nonqualified executive benefit
arrangements, 280–85
nonqualified retirement plans, 283,
284–85
split dollar life insurance, 282–83
supplemental executive retirement
plans, 285
Expense margin, 129
Expenses, 63–64, 68, 146
loading charges, 127
Experience factors, 112
Expiration of policy, 142
Extended families, 229, 233
Extended term insurance (ETI), 187,
212

Face amount
defined, 10, 109
restrictions, 80
Fairness, 37–39
Family history for underwriting, 119
Family riders, 216–17
Family security, 225–40, 409
family structures and, 227–30
financial characteristics of client,
236–38

life insurance needs analysis, 230–40
development and implementation
of plan, 235–40
information analysis, 233–35
information collection, 231–33
nature of insurance need, 239–40
objectives identification, 230–31
planning, 10–22, 226
Family split dollar, 283
Family structures, 227–30
Farmers Insurance, 35
Federal Deposit Insurance Corporation
(FDIC), 82
Federal estate taxes owed, 243. *See
also* Estate tax
Federal Home Loan Banks, 56
Federal National Mortgage Associa-
tion, 56
Fees, 127, 129, 146. *See also* Expenses
Field force, 34
Field offices, 34
Financial Analysis Solvency Tools
(FAST) system (NAIC), 74–75
Financial characteristics of client,
236–38
Financial consequences of death, 6–10
additional savings/investments, 7–8
employer-provided death benefits,
8–9
individual life insurance, 9–10
for relatives, 7
Financial discipline of clients, 238
Financial Industry Regulatory Authority
(FINRA), 30, 32, 43, 301
Financial institution employees, 31–32
Financially impaired insurers
described, 49–50
regulation, 76–79
formal actions, 77
guaranty associations, role of, 78–
79
implications to policyholders, 79–
82
informal actions, 77
liquidation, 78
rehabilitation, 77–78
Financial profile, 91–92
Financial statement
filings, 72–73
information, 97–99

Financial status for underwriting, 119
Financial strength of life insurance
    companies, 47–64
  assessing, 58–64
    capital and surplus adequacy, 59–
      60
    leverage, 60
    liquidity, 62
    operational performance, 62–64
    quality and diversification of
      assets, 60–61
  due care. *See* Due care
  importance of, 47–48
  incentives to avoid holding excess
    capital, 52–53
  incentives to have strong financials,
    51–52
  insurer management of, 51–53
  investments of life insurers, 53–58,
    71, 124
    bonds, 55–56
    cash and miscellaneous, 57
    mortgages and real estate, 56–57
    policy loans, 57
    stocks, 57
  lessons from the past, 49–51
FINRA. *See* Financial Industry Regula-
    tory Authority
First Financial Resources, 37
First-to-die life insurance, 170
First-year expenses, 127
Fitch Ratings, 87–88, 93, 95
Five-year renewable term, 143
Fixed amount option, 209–10
Fixed income securities, 55
Fixed period option, 209
Fixed-premium universal life policies,
    166
Flat extra method, 122
Form 10-K (SEC), 101
Form 10-Q (SEC), 102
Form 712 (IRS), 246
Fraternals, 17
Fraud, 200
Front-end loads, 130
Full costing, 128
Full-pay premiums, 363
Funding levels, 331–47
  cash value accumulation, 333–34
  choosing appropriate level, 331–32

cost vs. risk protection, 336–44
death benefit protection, 333, 334–35
equity indexed universal life (EIUL),
    345
minimum non-MEC death benefit
    example, 343–44
NLG universal life (UL) policies,
    345–46
pay-to-age 120, 341–42
policy illustrations for, 332–44,
    353–54
reduced funding for overfunded VUL
    policy, 405
setting funding targets, 333–34
10-pay funding, 337–41
variable universal life, 344–45
whole life vs. universal life, 373
Future interest in gifts, 245

GAAP. *See* Generally accepted account-
    ing principles
Gender, misstatement of, 203–4
Gender differences, 117
General account, 53
General agents, 34
Generally accepted accounting princi-
    ples (GAAP), 58, 60, 72, 101
General partnerships, 264
Generation skipping transfer (GST)
    tax, 247, 254
Gift tax, 243, 244–47
  annual exclusion, 245–46
  calculation of, 244–45
  generation skipping transfer (GST)
    tax, 247, 254
  of life insurance, 246–47
  marital deduction, 245
GLP (Guideline level premium), 141
Government bonds, 55–56
Grace period provision, 201
Grantor, defined, 248
Gross estate, 243
Gross proceeds, 140, 413
Gross rate of variable universal life
    policies, 356–57
Group term carve outs, 285–86
Growth cap, 151
Growth floor, 151
Growth rate, 151
GSP (Guideline single premium), 141

GST (Generation skipping transfer) tax, 247, 254

Guaranteed insurability option, 217

Guaranteed maximum mortality charges, 188–90

Guaranteed minimum crediting rates, 191

Guaranteed minimum death benefit riders, 222

Guaranteed policy elements, 80
mortality rates and, 115

Guarantees, 179–96. *See also* No-lapse guarantee
availability of policy loans, 183–84
availability of policy withdrawals, 184
high early cash values, 185
impact of cash values of changes in investments' market values, 182–83
likelihood of lapse with adverse development of current assumptions, 182
location and nature of investments backing policy reserves, 181
policyholder control over fund allocations, 183
protection against claims of insolvent insurer's creditors, 185
relationship between cash values and death benefits, 184

Guaranty associations, role of, 78–79

Guideline level premium (GLP), 141

Guideline premium and corridor test, 141, 354–55

Guideline single premium (GSP), 141

Health information for underwriting, 118–19

Husband-wife families, 227–28, 233, 258–59

IDITs (Intentionally defective irrevocable trusts), 253–54

ILITs. *See* Irrevocable life insurance trusts

Illiquid assets, 232

Illustrations. *See* Policy illustrations

Income objectives in life insurance planning, 231, 232–33

Income tax treatment, 139–42, 410–12
accelerated death benefits, 425
cash values, 411–12
dividends, 412
IRC definition of endowment contract, 141–42, 411
IRC definition of life insurance, 140–41, 410–11
maturities, 413–15
replacements, 420–21
sale of policy, 427–28
tax-favored status of life insurance, 140
withdrawals, partial surrenders, and loans, 416–18

Incontestable clause, 200

Increasing premium term, 143. *See also* Yearly renewable term (YRT)

Indemnification, 269–71

Independent distribution, 33, 35–37

Independent property/casualty agents, 37

Index account, 151

Index crediting rate, 151

Indexed UL, 151

Index performance rate, 151

Indirect expenses, 128

Individual life insurance, 9–10

Inside interest buildup, 172

Insolvency risk, 161

Installment refund annuity, 210

Institute of Business Appraisers, 275

Insufficient policy value, 391–400

Insurance agents, 29–31
competence, 39–40
diligence, 41–43
evaluating, 37–43
fairness, 37–39
financial information on companies from, 102–3
integrity, 40–41
licensing, 68–69
professionalism, 37–41
sources of information on, 43

Insurance amount, defined, 10

Insurance commissioners, 66, 72

Insurance companies. *See* Life insurance companies

The Insurance Forum (Belth), 100, 103

Insurance regulation. *See* Regulation

Insurance Regulatory Information System (IRIS), 75
Insured, defined, 10
Integrity, 40–41
Intentionally defective irrevocable trusts (IDITs), 253–54
Interest adjusted indices, 304–7
Interest adjusted net cost indices, 368–69
Interest crediting rate, 123–27, 311–12
  determining, 125–26
  effect on policy values, 126–27
  investment returns, 124–25
Interest margin, 125
Interest option, 209
Interest sensitive whole life policies, 166
Internal rate of return (IRR), 299–300
  death benefit, 364–65
  surrender value internal rate of return (SV IRR), 336, 338, 366–67
Inter vivos trusts, 248
Investment expenses, 127
Investment generation method, 193
Investment in the contract (cost basis), 140, 413
Investment management fees, 130
Investment margin, 125
Investments. *See* Financial strength of life insurance companies
IRR. *See* Internal rate of return
Irrevocable designation, 207
Irrevocable life insurance trusts (ILITs), 249–54, 259, 260
Irrevocable trusts, 248

Joint and survivorship life income option, 210
Joint life insurance, 170

Key person insurance, 269–71

Lapse, 131
  rates, 42, 134
  rider protection against, 220–22
Largest life insurance companies, 16
Last-to-die life insurance, 169
Ledger illustration, variable life insurance, 302–4
Level-pay premiums, 363

Level-premium whole life. *See* Whole life (WL) insurance
Leverage, 60
Liabilities
  accounting standards, 71
  life insurance planning, 232
  valuation, 70
Licensing of insurers, 67
  revocation of, 77
Life expectancy, 11, 337
Life-expectancy term, 143
Life income option with period certain, 210
Life insurance
  advantages of, 22–23
  amount appropriate, 12–13
  basics, 107–37
  defined, 10
  disadvantages of, 23–24
  distribution channels, 33–35
  as financial instrument, 22–24
  IRC definition of, 140, 410–11
  on multiple lives, 168–70
  need for, 11–12, 226, 239–40
  options to achieve goals for, 391–407
  policies. *See* Policies
  pricing, 111–35. *See also* Pricing
  programming, 226
  regulation. *See* Regulation
  special nature of, 48
Life insurance advisors, 29–33
Life insurance companies
  agents. *See* Insurance agents
  determining from whom to purchase policy, 15–18
  financial strength, 47–64. *See also* Financial strength of life insurance companies
  issuing at least 1,000 cash value policies of $200,000, 20–21
  largest, 16
  licensing, 67
  organizational structures of, 15–18
  organizing new companies, 67
  policy protections, 204–5
  profitability of, 135–36
  regulation of. *See* Regulation
  as source of financial information, 102
  target market, importance of, 18–22

Life Insurance Illustrations Model Regulation (NAIC), 292
Life-pay premiums, 363
Life settlements, 426
Limited partnerships, 264–65
Limited-payment whole life insurance, 165
Liquid assets, 231–32
Liquidation of financially impaired insurers, 78
Liquidity, 62, 255, 260
Living benefit riders, 218–20
Living trusts, 248
Loading charges, 127–31, 194–96, 316–17
   actual vs. those at policy insurance, 196
   considerations, 317
   determination of, 196
   disclosure of, 196
   guaranteed minimum, 194–96
   historical expense experience, 317
   volatility of, 196
Loaned cash (account) value, 183
Loans, 415–18
"Long pays," 334
Long term care (LTC) insurance riders, 219–20
Lump sum of cash as settlement, 208

Maintenance expenses, 128
Management's Discussion and Analysis, 72, 99
Mandatory Control Level, 74
Marginal costing, 128, 136
Marital deduction
   estate tax, 243, 258–59
   gift tax, 245
   trusts and, 248–49
Marital trusts, 248
Marketing channels, 33
Marketing practices, regulation of, 68–70
Material misrepresentation, 200
Maturities, tax treatment of, 413–15
MBSs (Mortgage backed securities), 56, 57
MEC. *See* Modified endowment contract
M Financial Group, 37
Military service for underwriting, 119

Minority and 50/50 shareholder's death, 267
Misappropriation, 69
Misstatement of age or gender provision, 203–4
Modified endowment contract (MEC), 141–42, 334, 411
   minimum non-MEC death benefit example, 343–44
Modified whole life policies, 166
Moody's Investor's Service, 87, 88, 89, 95, 319–20, 323, 325
Mortality and expense (M&E) charges, 130
Mortality charges, 113–23, 188–91, 312–16
   actual vs. those at policy issuance, 190
   considerations, 315–16
   determination of, 190
   developing for proposed insured, 118–22
   disclosure of, 190
   effect on policy values, 122–23
   future mortality charges, 315–16
   guaranteed maximum, 188–90
   historical mortality experience, 314
   influences on mortality experience, 115–16
   mortality experience and tables, 113–15
   standardized, 116–18
   types of, 116–22
   volatility of, 190–91
Mortality margins, 116
Mortality tables, 11, 113–15
   population vs. insured mortality, 114
   smoker vs. nonsmoker tables, 114–15, 346
   valuation vs. basic tables, 114
Mortgage backed securities (MBSs), 56, 57
Mortgages, 56–57
   in default, 61
   yields supporting dividend interest rates, 311
Multigenerational families, 229–30, 233
Multiple-line exclusive agencies, 35
Multiple-line exclusive agents, 35
Multiple lives, life insurance on, 168–70

Multiple table extra, 120
Mutual Benefit Life, 50, 86
Mutual life insurance companies, 17, 80, 113, 166

Narrative summary, policy illustrations, 296–97
National Association of Certified Valuation Analysts, 275
National Association of Insurance Commissioners (NAIC), 66
  Accelerated Benefits Guideline for Life Insurance, 218
  automated solvency monitoring, 74–75
  complaint data, 99–100
  Financial Analysis Solvency Tools (FAST) system, 74–75
  financial information on insurers, 96–97, 99
  forms, standards for, 67
  Life Insurance Illustrations Model Regulation, 292
  Model Policy Loan Interest Rate Bill, 213
  Model Replacement Regulation, 69, 420
  "Notice Regarding Replacement," 422
  risk-based capital (RBC) model law, 73
  Securities Valuation Office, 71
National Association of Securities Dealers. *See* Financial Industry Regulatory Authority (FINRA)
Nationally Recognized Statistical Rating Organizations (NRSROs), 86
National Organization of Life and Health Insurance Guaranty Associations (NOLHGA), 79
The National Underwriter, 103
Need for life insurance, 11–12
  for estate planning, 258
  for family security, 225–40. *See also* Family security
  nature of, 239–40
Net amount at risk (NAR), 109, 121–23, 146, 313
Net cash surrender value, 183, 211

Net rate of variable universal life policies, 357–58
Net worth, 52
No-lapse guarantee, 81, 156
No-lapse guarantee (NLG) riders, 222
No-lapse guarantee (NLG) universal life (UL) policies, 158–62
  attributes of, 174
  comparison of policies, 360–62
    with generic UL policies, 162, 375–76
  considerations, 159–62
  death benefit protection, 333
  fair market value, 246
  financial discipline of clients and, 238
  funding levels, 345–46
  operational details, 158–59
  partnerships, 274
  policy reviews, 387–88
  risk tolerance and, 237
Non-admitted assets, 60–61, 71
Nonagency building distribution, 33
Nonforfeiture provision, 202, 211
Non-guaranteed nature of policy illustrations, 290–92, 350–51
Non-guaranteed policy elements, 80, 81, 110
Non-investment grade bonds, 61
Non-marital trusts, 248
Nonparticipating (nonpar) policies, 113, 165
  attributes of, 173, 202–3
  risk tolerance and, 237
Nonqualified deferred compensation plans, 284–85
Nonqualified executive benefit arrangements, 8, 280–85
Nonqualified retirement plans, 283, 284–85
Nonsmoker mortality. *See* Smoker vs. nonsmoker mortality tables
Nuclear families, 227, 232–33, 258–59
Numerical ratings, 120
Numeric summary, policy illustrations, 298–99

Occupation for underwriting, 119
One-person households, 228–29, 233
One-way buy/sell agreements, 272

On-site financial examinations, 76
Operating expenses, 127
Operational performance, 62–64
Opposite-sex unmarried couples, 229,
    233
Option buy/sell agreements, 273
Ordinary life insurance. *See* Whole life
    (WL) insurance
Overhead expenses, 128
Overloan protection riders, 221
Override commissions, 36
Ownership provisions, 214–15

Paid-up-at-65 whole life, 165
Paid-up policies, 165
PAM (Portfolio average method), 126,
    193
Partial surrenders, 415–18
Participating (par) policies
    attributes of, 173, 202–3
    corporations, use of, 278
    defined, 80
    dividends and, 163
    executive bonus plans, 280
    non-guaranteed assumptions, 310
Participation rate, 151
Partners Group, 37
Partnerships, 264–65, 273–375
Payment of premiums. *See* Premiums
Pay-to-age 120, 341–42
Permanent life insurance, 14
Persistency, 131–35
    determining rate for, 135
    effect on current assumptions, 135
    importance of, 132–33
    influences on, 133–35
Personal financial planners, 29–31
Personal financial planning, 226
Personal-producing general agents, 36
"Pigeonhole" investment guidelines, 71
Policies, 107–37
    assignment/ownership provision,
        214–15
    attributes, 171–96
        generic, 171–73
        specific, 173–79
    beneficiary clause, 206–7
    cash value attributes, 178–79
    companies issuing at least 1,000 cash
        value policies of $200,000, 20–21

content and format, 197–99
death benefit provisions, 205–6
delay clause, 204
entire contract clause, 199–200
exclusion clauses, 204–5
expiration of, 142
fixed amount option, 209–10
fixed period option, 209
grace period provision, 201
guarantees. *See* Guarantees
illustrations. *See* Policy illustrations
incontestable clause, 200
insurance companies protected by,
    204–5
interest option, 209
loans allowed by, 57, 212–13
misstatement of age or gender
    provision, 203–4
nonforfeiture provision, 202, 211
options, 354–55. *See also* Riders
paid-up, 165
participation/policy value provision,
    202–3
persistency, 131–35
policyholder flexibility allowed,
    205–15
premiums. *See* Premiums
pricing, 111–35. *See also* Pricing
provisions and features, 199–215
purchase of, 27–29
    determining from whom to
        purchase, 15–18
reinstatement clause, 201–2
replacement of, 69, 397–400, 418–24
reviews, 381–91
    annual reviews, 382–88
    considerations, 383–88
    detailed reviews, 388–91
    nature of, 382–91
    no-lapse guarantee universal life,
        387–88
    universal life, 385–86
    variable universal life, 386–87
    whole life, 384–85
riders, 215–22. *See also* Riders
right to return policy, 205
settlement options, 208–11
suicide clause, 204
suitable. *See* Suitability of policies
surrender of, 131, 412–15

survivorship clause, 208
sustainability of illustrated policy
    values, 309–29
time clause, 208
types of, 107–11, 139–70
    cash value life insurance. *See*
      Cash value life insurance
    term life. *See* Term life insurance
    universal life. *See* Universal life
      (UL) insurance policies
    variable life. *See* Variable life
      insurance
    variable universal life. *See* Variable
      universal life (VUL) policies
    whole life. *See* Whole life (WL)
      insurance
war exclusion clause, 205
Policyholders
    defined, 10
    flexibility allowed in policies, 205–15
    protections, 66–72, 199–204
Policy illustrations, 289–307
    comparison of policies, 349–77
      assumptions, 354
      cash value targets, 353–54
      common measures, 362–71
      consistent illustration compar-
        isons, 351–55
      death benefit measures, 363–65
      death benefits, 353–54
      distribution measures, 367–68
      equity indexed universal life
        (EIUL), 358–60
      equity indexed universal life with
        generic universal life, 374–75
      interest adjusted net cost indices,
        368–69
      no-lapse guarantee universal life
        policies, 360–62
      no-lapse guarantee with generic
        UL policies, 162
      no-lapse guarantee with generic
        universal life, 375–76
      non-guaranteed nature of policy
        illustrations, 350–51
      performance comparison sum-
        mary, 369–71
      policy options, 354–55

premium funding levels, 353–54
premium measures, 362–63
rating categories and risk classifi-
    cation factors, 351–53
riders, 354–55
surrender value measures, 365–67
variable universal life, 355–58
whole life with universal life,
    371–74
content of, 292–307
defined, 289
funding levels for flexible premium
    life insurance, use of, 332–44
interest adjusted indices, 304–7
internal rate of return (IRR), 299
ledger illustration, 302–4
narrative summary, 296–97
non-guaranteed nature of, 290–92,
    350–51
non-variable life insurance, 292–301
numeric summary, 298–99
overview, 289–90
summary page, variable life insur-
    ance, 305–7
supplemental illustrations, 299–301
sustainability of values, 319–25. *See
    also* Sustainability of illustrated
    policy values
tabular detail, 289–90, 292–95
use of, 290
variable life insurance, 301–4
Policy loads, 127
Policy loans, 57, 212–13
Policy reserves, 70
Policy value, 109, 203. *See also* Values
Population vs. insured mortality ta-
    bles, 114
Portfolio average method (PAM), 126,
    193
Premiums, 185–88
    ability to mimic other type of policy,
      187
    ability to pay, 236–37
    additional payments, 393–95
    automatic premium loans (APLs),
      213
    calculation. *See* Pricing
    comparison of policies, 362–63

defined, 10
flexibility, 185–87
full-pay, 363
future payments, reduction of, 402–4
grace period, 201
level-pay, 363
life-pay, 363
minimizing outlay for, 258
nonpayment, effect of, 187–88
number of, 334, 363
policy provision, 200–201
replacement option, 399–400
resuming payments and full coverage
    after nonpayment, 188
skipping payments, 187
by types of policies. *See specific*
    types of policies
waiver of premium/charges riders,
    220–21
Premium solve, 325, 363
Present interest in gifts, 245
Pricing, 111–35, 310
    interest crediting rate, 123–27
        determining, 125–26
        effect on policy values, 126–27
        investment returns, 124–25
    loading charges, 127–31
        costs of doing business, 127–29
        determining, 129–30
        effect on policy values, 130–31
    mortality charges, 113–23. *See also*
        Mortality charges
    questionnaire, 327–28
    stress testing, 335–36
    waiver of premium/charges riders,
        220–21
Primary beneficiary, 206
Primary life insurance market, 425
Private placement, 55, 168
Probabilities of death, 11
Producer groups, 36–37
Producers, 29
Product margins, 136–37
Professionalism, 37–41
Professional oversight, 76
Profitability, 135–36
Proprietary life insurance, 167–68
Protection UL, 149

Providers, 426
Psychological aspects of death and
    planning, 4–6
    anxiety, 4–5
    emotions, 5–6
Publications providing financial infor-
    mation, 103
Pure life income option, 210

Qualified purchasers for PPLI, 168
Quality and diversification of assets,
    60–61

Rating agencies, 85–96
    defined, 86
    importance of, 86
    major rating agencies, 86–89
    methodology example, 89–92
        business profile, 90
        financial profile, 91–92
    rating categories. *See* Rating
        categories
    reports, 92–93
    using reports and ratings, 94–96
Rating categories, 93–94
    policy illustrations for, 351–53
RBC. *See* Risk-based capital (RBC)
    requirements
Rebating, 69
Reconstituted families, 229
Reduced paid up insurance, 187, 211
Reentry provision, 144
Regulation, 65–84
    accounting standards, 71–72
    agent licensing, 68–69
    asset limitations and valuation, 71
    financially impaired insurers, 76–79
        formal actions, 77
        guaranty associations, role of,
            78–79
        implications to policyholders,
            79–82
        informal actions, 77
        liquidation, 78
        rehabilitation, 77–78
    liability valuation, 70
    licensing of insurers, 67
    marketing practices, 68–70

nature and purpose of, 66
policy forms and rates, 67–68
policyholder protections, 66–72
solvency, 70–72
solvency intervention, implications
    for policyholders, 82–83
solvency surveillance methods,
    72–76
  capital requirements, 73–74
  cash flow testing, 75
  dividend restrictions, 75
  financial statement filings, 72–73
  NAIC automated solvency moni-
    toring, 74–75
  on-site financial examinations, 76
  professional oversight, 76
  risk-based capital (RBC) require-
    ments, 73–74
unfair trade practices, 69
Regulatory Action Level, 74
Rehabilitation of financially impaired
    insurers, 77–78
Reinstatement clause, 201–2
Reinsurance, 313
Relatives. *See also* Family structures
  financial consequences of death for,
    7
Remainder interest, 251
Renewable policies, 143
Renewal expenses, 128
Replacement of policy, 69, 397–400,
    418–24
Reports
  "BrokerCheck Reports," 43
  concept reports, 301
  rating agencies, 92–96
  stock analysts' reports, 103
Reserves, 70
Reset provision, 159
Residuary trusts, 248
Results clause of war exclusion clause,
    205
Retained asset accounts, 208
Retained interest, 251
Retirement plans
  cash value accumulation and, 334
  nonqualified retirement plans, 283,
    284–85
  supplemental executive retirement
    plans, 285

Return of premium term policy, 144
Revocable designation, 207
Revocable trusts, 248
Riders, 215–22, 354–55
  accidental death benefit riders, 217
  catastrophic illness coverage, 218
  continuation riders, 219
  enhanced cash value riders, 222
  extension of benefits riders, 219
  family riders, 216–17
  guaranteed insurability option
    (GIO), 217
  lapse, protection against, 220–22
  living benefit riders, 218–20
  long term care (LTC) insurance
    riders, 219–20
  no-lapse guarantee riders, 222
  overloan protection riders, 221
  terminal illness coverage, 218,
    424–25
  term riders, 216
  waiver of premium/charges riders,
    220–21
Right to return policy, 205
Risk-based capital (RBC) requirements,
    73–74, 75, 100–101
Risk classification factors, 118
  policy illustrations for, 351–53
Risk tolerance, 237–38

Safety margin, 129
Sale of policy, income tax treatment,
    427–28
Same-sex couples (partners), 229, 233
S&P. *See* Standard & Poor's
SAP. *See* Statutory accounting principles
Savings/investments, 7–8
Secondary beneficiary, 206
Secondary life insurance market, 425–29
Second-to-die life insurance, 169
Section 162 plans, 8, 280–81
Section 303 stock redemption, 277, 279
Section 1035 exchanges, 420–21
Securities and Exchange Commission
    (SEC), 101–2, 154–55
Segment term, 151
Separate accounts, 54
Series 6 license, 30
SERPs (Supplemental executive retire-
    ment plans), 285

Settlement options, 208–11
  cash, 208–9
  cash refund annuity, 210
  fixed amount option, 209–10
  fixed period option, 209
  installment refund annuity, 210
  interest option, 209
  joint and survivorship life income
    option, 210
  life income option with period
    certain, 210
  life settlements, 426
  other arrangements, 211
  pure life income option, 210
  single life income option, 210
Seven-pay test, 142, 411
SFSP (Society of Financial Service
    Professionals), 30, 33
Shadow account, 159, 160, 161
"Short pays," 334
Simplified issue life insurance, 115
Simultaneous death of insured and
    beneficiary, 207–8
Single life income option, 210
Single-parent families, 228, 233
Single-premium whole life insurance,
    165
Skipping payments, 187
Smoker vs. nonsmoker mortality tables,
    114–15, 346
Society of Actuaries (SOA), 313
Society of Financial Service Profes-
    sionals (SFSP), 30, 33
Sole proprietorships, 264, 272–73
  split dollar life insurance, 283
Solvency
  intervention, implications for policy-
    holders, 82–83
  regulation, 70–72
Solvency surveillance methods, 72–76
  capital requirements, 73–74
  cash flow testing, 75
  dividend restrictions, 75
  financial statement filings, 72–73
  NAIC automated solvency monitor-
    ing, 74–75
  on-site financial examinations, 76
  professional oversight, 76
  risk-based capital (RBC) require-
    ments, 74

Specified premium test, 158
Split dollar life insurance, 9, 281–83
Split option, 169
Sports and avocations for under-
    writing, 119
Spousal lifetime access trusts, 260
Spouse riders, 216
Spreads, 125
Standard & Poor's (S&P), 87, 88–89, 93,
    95
State Farm Insurance, 35
State insurance regulators, 51, 96–97.
    See also Regulation
  list of contact information, 98
Status clause of war exclusion clause,
    205
Statutory accounting principles (SAP),
    58, 59, 60, 71–72, 101
Step families, 229
Stock analysts' reports, 103
Stock companies, 17, 101
Stock redemption, 275, 276
  Section 303 stock redemption, 277,
    279
Stocks, 57
Stranger-owned life insurance (STOLI),
    427
Stress testing, 326, 335–36, 373
Substandard ratings, 120, 121
Suicide clause, 204
Suitability of policies, 13–15
  persistency and, 134
Supplemental executive retirement
    plans (SERPs), 285
Surplus, 52
  divisible surplus, 163
Surrender, 131, 412–15
  partial, 415–18
Surrender charges, 134, 149
Surrender value, 365–67
Surrender value internal rate of return
    (SV IRR), 336, 338, 343–44,
    366–67
Survival rates, 337
Survivorship clause, 208
Survivorship life insurance, 169
Sustainability of illustrated policy
    values, 309–29
  assessment considerations, 327
  complexity of, 318–19

crediting and dividend interest rates, 311–12, 319–25
influences on illustrated and actual performance, 310–17
loading charges, 316–17
mortality charges, 312–16
non-guaranteed assumptions, 309–10
performance review, 325
policy pricing questionnaire, 327–28
stress testing, 326

Table rating, 120–21
Table shaving programs, 121
Tabular detail, policy illustrations, 289–90, 292–95
Target cash value. *See* Cash value targets
Targeted exams conducted by insurance regulators, 76
Target markets, 18–22
persistency and, 133–34
Target SERPs, 285
Taxable estate, 243
Taxes, 129. *See also* Estate tax; Gift tax; Income tax treatment
business planning, 267–68
corporate business continuation agreements, 278–80
partnership buy/sell agreements, 274–75
split dollar life insurance, 282–83
10-pay funding, 337–41
1035 exchanges, 160, 420–21
Ten-paid whole life insurance, 165
Tentative federal estate tax, 243
Tentative tax base, 243
Ten-year renewable term, 143
Term blending, 216
Terminal illness coverage, 218, 424–25
Term life insurance, 14, 107–8, 142–45
cash value attributes, 180
considerations, 144–45
crediting rate attributes, 192
death benefit attributes, 177
group term carve outs, 285–86
loading charge attributes, 195
mortality charge attributes, 189
mortality charges, 111

overview of, 175
premium attributes, 196
types of policies, 142–44
unique features of, 144
Term riders, 216
Term-to-age 65, 143
Tertiary beneficiary, 206
Testamentary trusts, 248
Three-year renewable term, 143
Time clause, 208
Total adjusted capital, 74
Total disability, 220
Total operating income, 63
Traditional families, 227
Training and examination of agents, 68
Transfer for value, 172
Trusts, 247–54
charitable remainder trusts (CRTs), 251–53
Crummey trusts, 249
definitions, 247–48
intentionally defective irrevocable trusts (IDITs), 253–54
irrevocable life insurance trusts (ILITs), 249–54
marital deduction and credit shelter trusts, 248–49
wealth replacement trusts, 253
Twisting, 69
2001 Commissioners Standard Ordinary (2001 CSO) Table, 114, 313
2001 CSO Mortality Table, 148, 414
2001 Valuation Basic Table (2001 VBT), 114, 313

Unaffiliated investments, 62
Unbundled policies, 112, 113, 127, 130, 166
"Under review" rating, 95
Underwriting
considerations, 115–20
defined, 118
strict, 314
Unfair trade practices, 69
Unified credit, 243, 258–59
Unified transfer tax law, 243
Uniform Simultaneous Death Act, 207
Unit costs, 128

Universal life (UL) insurance policies, 14, 80–81, 110, 145–50. *See also* Variable universal life (VUL) policies
 additional premium payments, 394
 attributes of, 174
 comparison of major types, 157
  with equity indexed universal life, 374–75
  with no-lapse guarantee, 375–76
  with whole life, 371–74
 considerations, 149–50
 corporations, use of, 278
 crediting rates, 191–94, 311–12, 335
 death benefit attributes, 176–79
 equity indexed universal life, 151–53
 executive bonus plans, 280
 guarantees, 179–96
 illustration, tabular detail, 289–90, 293–95
 interest crediting rate, 124, 126
 key person indemnification, 271
 loading charges, 194–96
 mortality charges, 188–91
 no-lapse guarantee universal life, 158–62
 nonforfeiture options, 212
 non-guaranteed assumptions, 309–10
 nonpar policies, 113
 numeric summary, policy illustrations, 298–99
 operational details, 145–49
 partnerships, 274
 policy reviews, 385–86
 premiums, 185–88
 reduced face amount, 397
 risk tolerance and, 237
 sole proprietorships, 273
 unbundled, 112

Valuation mortality table, 114
Values
 cash value. *See headings starting with "Cash value"*
 excessive policy value, 400–407
 insufficient policy value, 391–400
 interest crediting rate's effect on, 126–27

 mortality charges' effect on, 122–23
 nonpar policies, 203
 sustainability of, 309–29. *See also* Sustainability of illustrated policy values
 target cash value. *See* Cash value targets
Variable life insurance, 14, 110–11, 154–57
 considerations, 156–57
 illustrations, 301–4
 investments of insurers and, 54
 ledger illustration, 302–4
 loading charges, 130
 operational details, 155–56
 summary page, 305–7
Variable universal life (VUL) policies
 as-sold vs. in-force, 401, 403
 attributes of, 174
 comparison of policies, 355–58
 earned rate assumption, 335
 executive bonus plans, 280
 funding levels, 344–45
 gross rate, 356–57
 nature and duration of guarantee, 176
 net rate, 357–58
 operational details, 155
 policy reviews, 386–87
 reduced funding for overfunded VUL policy, 405
 risk tolerance and, 237
Viatical settlements, 426

Wait-and-see buy/sell agreements, 275
Waiver of premium/charges riders, 220–21
War exclusion clause, 205
Wash rate, 183
Wealth replacement trusts, 253
Whole life (WL) insurance, 14, 110, 162–67
 additional premium payments, 395
 attributes of, 173
 comparison with universal life, 371–74
 considerations, 166–67
 crediting rates, 191–94

death benefit attributes, 176–79
dividend interest rates, 311–12
guarantees, 179–96
investment returns, 124
key person indemnification, 271
loading charges, 194–96
mortality charges, 111, 188–91
non-guaranteed assumptions, 310
nonpar policies, 113
participating and nonparticipating
    life insurance, 163–65
partnerships, 274
policy reviews, 384–85
premiums, 185–88
risk tolerance and, 237
sole proprietorships, 273
types of, 165–66
unbundled, 112
variable, 156
Winding up of business, 78
Withdrawals, 415–18

Yearly renewable term (YRT), 108, 113,
    117, 143, 150